A Student-Centered Language Arts Curriculum, Grades K-13:
A Handbook for Teachers
1973 Impression

_____

_____

_____

James Moffett

Houghton Mifflin Company · Boston

ATLANTA   DALLAS   GENEVA, ILL.   HOPEWELL, N.J.   PALO ALTO

FOR SCHOOLCHILDREN

INCLUDING MY OWN

LISA AND JUDY

*The preparation of this book was principally
supported by a two-year grant from Carnegie
Corporation of New York. The statements made
and views expressed are solely the responsibility of
the author.*

PRINTED IN THE U.S.A.

ISBN: 0–395–14758–1

Sequence for Interaction

Kindergarten through Third Grade

Decoding	74–76
Spelling	92
Punctuation	94
Reading	99–115
Writing Out	117–125
Writing Down	127–136
Writing Up	139–147

Grades Four through Six

Acting Out	165–171
Writing Down	173–182
Sensory Writing	183–198
Memory Writing	213–220
Writing Fiction	231–242
Idea Writing	245–254

Grades Seven through Nine

Acting and Speaking	283–292
Dialogue	295–324
Monologue	325–340
Narrative	343–359
Poetry of Observation	361–370
Journals and Diaries	371–381

Grades Ten through Thirteen

Autobiography and Memoir	387–406
Reportage and Research	409–434
Reflection	437–446
Generalization and Theory	449–473
Invention	477–497

Games of Language and Logic

Kindergarten through Three	149–156
Four through Six	257–263

Foreword

The last several years have seen vigorous professional attempts to redefine the teaching of English from the preschool through the college, to establish the limits and possibilities of the subject, to assess priorities anew, and to relate to modern programs the findings of scholarship in language and language development which have become recently available. Few trends promise more for teaching than the distinction being drawn today between competence in language and performance in language. Competence is concerned with basic understandings, be they innate or acquired; performance, with the individual's actual use of language as social communication. It is with language *performance* that the model for a new English curriculum presented by James Moffett essentially deals, particularly the productive language of children and adults, their writing and speaking, and the social and psychological forces which affect their growing command of the native tongue. For too long our schools have neglected the importance of oral language and failed to recognize that ability in written language relates in no small measure to facility and command of oral forms. For too long school programs designed to teach our children to read have been separated from those designed to teach them to write and speak. Yet students in child development and psycholinguistics are demonstrating repeatedly the interrelationship of linguistic and cognitive growth, and classroom experimentation is suggesting that for many pupils power in reading is closely associated with power in writing and speech. As Constance M. McCullough asserted at the 1968 national convention of the International Reading Association, "The great dichotomy (between programs in reading and the language arts) must be as one."

In advancing a new model for a K-13 curriculum in English, James Moffett sees oral and written language, indeed all expressive experiences, as central in the educative process. These are the experiences which lead young people to intellectual, emotional, and social engagement. For example, he questions attempts to confine skill development in comprehension to the province of reading alone, feeling that perception, understanding, and evaluation are part of the total language experience. Some readers may question his personal evaluation of different approaches and materials for teaching beginning reading, as they may wonder about the priorities he sets for later educational levels, but they will find the assessment compatible with his view that the crucial element in language learning is the child's active involvement in using his native tongue. It is what the student does with what

iii

he reads that is critical in this curriculum; it is the ways in which he employs and uses language.

Thus, mime, improvisation, drama, and small group discussion take on a new significance. Writing, an active language experience, becomes the key to literary appreciation; discussion in large and small groups, the way to effectiveness in expression. With C.C. Fries, Mr. Moffett would agree that "There is no language apart from the speaker active in expression," and in the classrooms he envisions young people are continuously engaged in expressing their own ideas and feelings.

But more than activity for its own sake is suggested in this curricular model. It is not enough to involve young people in just any experience with language. The experiences themselves must be thoughtfully structured and be cumulative in effect, so that through them children may ultimately be introduced to the entire range of discourse. Behind the specific language experiences advanced in this curricular model, one finds a carefully conceived rationale to guide exploration of an entire range of language experiences appropriate at each instructional level.

Not the least concern of English specialists during recent years has been the lack of clearcut developmental programs for the elementary and secondary years. In advancing his own model for reform of school teaching, James Moffett suggests that sequence may be found not through the allocation of subject matter or through emphasis on discrete skills, but rather through ordering the language experiences in which young people become engaged with reference to both the social and psychological characteristics of the learners and the nature of discourse itself. Both for the potential power of its theoretical basis and for the incisive and practical application presented in this volume, his thesis commends itself to serious professional attention.

James R. Squire

Preface

During the four years that have elapsed since this book was published, I have thought further, others have reacted to the book, and the educational world has continued changing. How well do its ideas hold up now? Both the favorable response from educators and my own experience in the interim allow me still to believe strongly in what I wrote, not because all the suggestions work without problems but because whatever problems occur are the best to have, and not because the ideas are all perfectly true but because thinking about them helps teach better. What I see now as a shortcoming of the book is that it does not go far enough in a couple of its thrusts. I think, however, that readers will be able to extend them in their minds much as I have in my own. The following remarks may help.

I said originally that the conventional curriculum has been very much determined by irrelevant factors that keep us fighting false problems and trying to do things that shouldn't be done at all. That statement was not strong enough. After several years of consulting nationally for school systems and teacher training colleges, I am convinced that all the important problems of learning to read and write are not *learning* problems but *institutional* problems. Learning to speak is inherently much more difficult than learning to read and write but it turns out to be easier because at home the learner enjoys precisely those conditions of spontaneity, individualization, support, and motivation under which learning occurs best. In short, the real problem of reading and writing is trying to learn them *in school,* that is, under negative conditions not only of large student numbers but of political and economic struggles aimed at other goals entirely.

A second thrust toward individualization also did not go far enough. Before, I assumed, for the most part, that even though a class would be working in small groups, classmates would be working with the same assignment at the same time. Now I feel it is essential for the different working parties to be doing different things at the same time. Some may never do what others have done, or they may simply do it another week or year. Daily lesson-planning is a major stumbling block, I have found, to improvement. It is one of those nonfunctional habits that institutions fall into when they do not yet know how to deal with the very real and legitimate problem of numbers. A class should do the same thing at the same time only when an activity can be better done by a group that large (as choral reading can). Otherwise small groups and individuals should make their ways separately among the array of activities and materials offered. This does not conflict with what I say in the book, but I think readers will get more out of my suggestions for assignments if they assume that the assignments are being chosen by the students, under the combined influence of inner urges, peers, and teacher, and that they are being differently sequenced by different students. When in the book I forget this, remember for me.

Programmed learning, has made a show of beating institutionalism by trying to individualize, and sometimes it looks good, compared to bad teaching, by at least leaving kids alone. But its solution is also its problem: programmed learning is isolated rather than individualized learning and hence lacks utterly the *interaction* so vital to learning language. The whole point of individualization is to allow for differences among individuals in how and when they need to learn things. A system that puts everybody off in a corner with a machine or workbook, that sends everybody through the same sequence allowing only minor variations in things such as pace, hardly comes to grips with the real issue. Programmed learning, in fact, usually delivers the learner into the hands of the enemy, partly because it fits only too well some of the political and commercial interests that hamstring public institutions, and partly because the learner is so pleased at the paltry but new control he is allowed in manipulating materials that he mistakes it for real power and real decision-making and thus seriously mis-learns what choosing is all about.

Numbers are not all negative. What is a dismal disadvantage when translated as mere standardization can actually supply the one big thing missing from home learning — more people and resources to interact with. Although the political problems have to be solved in a larger arena, I think the basic problem of numbers can be solved by a student-centered curriculum such as the one proposed here, because it takes advantage of numbers instead of being done in by them.

In the original introduction to this book, I said that I hoped to offer a way of teaching not incarnated in textbooks, "an alternative to the installation of a prepackaged curriculum." I still feel strongly that organic English is killed by special books for writing, speaking, spelling, skill-building, etc., and that it is far too basic ever to be embodied in textbooks, especially those committed to this or that concept of literature or rhetoric. But I have directed a new program of school materials called *Interaction: A Student-Centered Language Arts and Reading Program.* To readers who have not seen the program this may appear to contradict the stand in this book. Actually, *Interaction* came about as an effort to offset some limitations of this book.

As I acknowledged within, this book cannot deal well enough with actual reading selections; so *Interaction* contains 176 paperback anthologies covering all the types of literary and nonliterary discourse discussed in this book and found in our culture. The book's fundamental approach to beginning reading and writing assumed a literacy kit independent of age or reading matter, aimed equally at decoding and encoding, and built on translating between voice and print; so *Interaction* contains a multimedia independent literacy kit made up of films and games and allows for all approaches that work, not just one. In this book, I proposed letting some children learn to read by listening to recordings as they follow the text, teaching punctuation by vocal intonation, encouraging students to perform virtually any text as a rehearsed reading, and making the classroom a rich mixture of styles and dialects; so *Interaction* contains eighty hours of recordings of the anthology's selections performed by professionals. For games of language and logic I originally advocated card games that did not exist, so these were created for *Interaction*.

Most of all, as I talked and worked with people trying to implement this book, I felt over and over that some way ought to be found to help both teacher and school reorganize themselves so that innovation would have a better chance. Since so many of the difficulties boiled down to managing numbers, *Interaction* contains hundreds of unsequenced activity cards written to students and directing them how to do the assignments proposed in this book (plus more). The main points are to let students do different things at the same time and to get the teacher out from under lesson-planning and direction-giving so that he or she can afford to do all the things that really make education work — the individualized coaching and counseling, the small-group arranging, and so on. Eighteen classroom films showing other students doing the less familiar dramatic and small-group activities were made to illustrate for both teacher and student what these look like and how they may be done, since a book cannot convey everything about them.

The ideas set forth in this book can serve additionally those people who would like more background and detail for *Interaction* as well as the more general audience in the profession for whom it was originally written.

James Moffett

Acknowledgments

In an era when institutions are more apt to deaden than invigorate individual endeavor, it is with particular pleasure that I acknowledge the liberal and sensitive support I have received from three institutions. During the early stages of developing the curriculum ideas presented in this book, the Phillips Exeter Academy provided me a year's sabbatical leave to devote to this study. Later, the administration there released me for further curriculum research by halving my teaching load for the better part of a year, and printed at its expense the experimental book upon which were based the trials reported in this book, even though these ventures went well beyond the needs of the Academy's own English Department, being in fact chiefly concerned with public school education.

At this point Carnegie Corporation of New York awarded a grant, through the Harvard Graduate School of Education, that enabled me to work full time on the project for two years. Besides an office and some services funded by its Center for Research and Development in Educational Differences, the Harvard School of Education provided valuable association with schools and with its own personnel. Since it is not routine for administrators of schools of education and private foundations to risk their resources on the projects of unknown and undoctorated individuals not affiliated with a university, my expression of gratitude to these people is not merely routine either.

The debt I owe the many teachers who tried out assignments for me, and often discussed results after hours without compensation, is too great to discharge here; I will mention them individually in footnotes.

To scores of students I owe nothing less than that portion of this book—rather considerable—which they wrote.

Of the many colleagues whose conversation has helped me to understand my own thoughts about teaching I would like to mention especially Kenneth McElheny, Thomas Hinkle, William Schwarz, the late George Bennett, Joel Weinberg, Davenport Plumer, John Mellon, and Wayne O'Neil. S. I. Hayakawa and his San Francisco associates helped me understand better the processes of symbolization.

Readers who criticized the manuscript prompted me to make important and, in some areas, extensive revisions. They were, for Grades K-6, Jeanne Chall, Blanche Serwer, Bernice Christensen, and William Durr. For the whole manuscript they were John Maxwell, Janet Emig, Robert A. Bennett, William A. Jenkins, and Richard Hodges.

ix

I have already thanked in person my wife Janet for reading and helping prepare the manuscript, not to mention tolerating the author while he wrote it.

James Moffett

Contents

Foreword   iii

Preface   v

Acknowledgments   ix

INTRODUCTION

Chapter 1. General Orientation   3

A K–13 Curriculum in One Presentation   3
Present or Future?   4

Local Curriculum Building   5
Heterogeneous Classes   5

Concessions to Current Realities   6
Material Problems   7

Group Process   7
Making up Marks   7
Setting up an Experiment   8

Use by the Individual Teacher   8

Chapter 2. Principles and Purposes   11

Summary of Principles   11
The First Misconception   13

Historical Determinants of Curriculum   13
The False Rationale for Teaching the Science of Language   14
The British View   15

The Second Misconception   16

The Fallacy of "Reading Skills"   16
Negative Effects   17

Mis-diagnosis   17
Misguided assignments   17
Curriculum imbalance   18

Causes of Reading Incomprehension   *18*

Poor motivation   19

Environmental deprivation   19

Egocentricity   19

How the Program Develops Reading Faculties   *20*

Attention   20

Recollection   20

Conception   21

Inference   21

Interpretation   23

Critical assessment   24

Organization and Proportions of this Curriculum   *24*

What Is Excluded   *25*

What Is Included in the Bias Toward Production   *26*

The Chapter Divisions of the Book   *26*

Purposes of Sample Student Writing   *27*

Other Aspects of the Presentation   *29*

Sequence   *29*

Disclaimer of Scientific Evidence   *29*

Personal Quality of this Book   *31*

Claims for this Curriculum   *31*

PART ONE   KINDERGARTEN
THROUGH THIRD GRADE

Chapter 3. Acting Out   **35**

Play with Objects   *36*

Movement to Sound   *37*

Materials   *37*

Providing the Stimuli   *38*

Pantomime   *39*

Early Procedures   *39*

Later Procedures   *40*

Relation of Physical Movement to Language   *41*

Combining Movement and Speech   *41*

Enacting Ready-made Stories *41*
Free Improvisation *42*

   The "minimal situation" *42*
   Conclusions from some trials *43*

Chapter 4. Speaking Up   45

Rationale *45*

   The Need for School Talk *45*
   "Class Discussion" and Small-Group Discussion *46*
   Relation of Drama to Discussion *46*
   Status of Discussion in the Curriculum *47*

Unstructured Discussion *47*

   Account of Some Trials *47*
   Conclusions from the Trials *50*

Structured Discussion — "Grouptalk" *51*

   Definition and Procedure *51*
   Conditions for Similar Small-Group Discussion *52*

Small-Group Discussion Led by a Teacher *54*

   Conditions for Concentration *54*
   Size and Membership of Groups *55*
   Ground Rules *56*
   General Role of the Teacher *56*

      Establishing the meaning of the topic *57*
      Encouraging participation *57*
      Keeping the focus *57*
      Focusing attention *58*
      Handling the impulsive interrupter *58*
      Leading the summary *59*
      Helping with hang-ups *59*

   Questioning *60*
   Framing Topics *61*

      Topics inviting enumeration *62*
      Topics inviting comparison *62*
      Topics inviting chronology *63*

   Scribes *63*
   Panels *64*

Holding Forth   *64*

Show-and-Tell   *65*

The value   65

Procedures   65

Chapter 5. Becoming Literate   67

Research Indications   *69*

Two Basic Approaches to Reading   *69*

How New Materials Meet Objections to Decoding   *74*

The Objections   *74*

Avoiding Confusion and Distortion of Letter-Sounds   *75*

Avoiding Word-Calling   *75*

Contextual Clues and Whole-Word Learning   *76*

Irregularity of English Spelling   *76*

Criteria Other than Research   *77*

Reading Readiness   *78*

Brief Survey of Literacy Materials   *79*

Recommendations   *89*

Preferred Materials   *89*

Versatility of Approach   *90*

Language experience   91

Listening while reading   91

An Open Mind   *92*

Spelling   *92*

Punctuation   *94*

Defining the Learning Problem   *94*

Procedures   *96*

Chapter 6. Reading   99

Classroom Procedures   *99*

The Teacher Reading Aloud   *99*

Children Reading Aloud   *100*

The problem of the "reading circle"   100

Individual coaching   100

Choral reading   101
Individual reading aloud to a small group   102

Dramatization and Discussion   *103*
Individual Silent Reading   *104*
Special Measures to Increase Efficiency   *105*

Visual processing of words   105
Differences between visual and auditory processing   106
Eye movements   106
Breaking early reading habits   107
The bugaboo of comprehension   107
Methods for increasing speed   108
Recommendations   110

Remedial Reading   *110*
Selecting Reading Material   *112*

Material to Accompany the Literacy Program   *113*

Phonetically controlled reading   113
Material for the teacher to read aloud   113

Printed Material after the Literacy Program   *114*

Publishing sources   114
Principles of selection   115

The Children's Own Material   *115*

Chapter 7. Writing Out   **117**

Rationale   *117*

What Stories Mean to Children   *117*
The Need for Stimulants   *118*

Recommendations   *119*

Younger Children Dictating Stories to Older Children   *119*
Writing Captions   *120*
Literature and Writing   *121*

Imitating forms   121
Borrowing the content   122
Oral reading as springboard   122

Song Writing   *123*
Writing about Pictures   *124*
Riddles, Puns, and Jokes   *124*

General Remarks on Writing   *124*

Creating Their Own Books   *124*
The Writing Workshop   *125*
The Teacher's Role   *125*

Chapter 8. Writing Down   **127**

Sensory Recording   *127*

Motives for Observing and for Writing Observations   *128*
The Recording of Sound   *129*

Pre-writing practice   *129*
Differences between sounds and sights   *130*
Writing down sounds   *130*
Discussing the order of recorded sounds   *131*
Discussing the form of notation   *131*
Correcting spelling   *132*
Recording on paper in groups   *132*

Recording the Sense of Touch   *134*

General procedure   *134*
Purposes   *134*

Taking Dictation   *135*

Teacher Dictation of Short Passages   *135*

Function of teacher dictation   *136*

Calendars and Letters   *136*

Procedures   *137*
Purposes   *137*
Writing Calendar Entries as Letters   *138*

Chapter 9. Writing Up   **139**

Burning Issues   *139*
Nature Study   *142*

Account of Trials   *142*
Recommended Nature Project   *146*

Focusing on single senses   *146*

Specific Procedures   *147*

Making books   *147*

Chapter 10. Playing Games of Language and Logic   149

Writing Telegrams   *149*
Expanding Baby Talk   *150*

   Procedure   *151*
   Purposes   *151*

Scrabble-type Games   *152*

   Anagrams   *152*
   Unscrambling Words   *153*
   Unscrambling Sentences   *153*
   Sentence Building   *153*
   Purposes   *154*

Checkers   *154*
Card Games   *155*

   Purposes   *155*
   Categorical Games   *155*
   Serial Games   *156*

PART TWO
GRADES FOUR THROUGH SIX

Chapter 11. Acting Out   165

Body English   *165*

   Guessing Games   *165*
   Charades   *167*
   Enacting Stories and Music   *167*

Verbal Drama   *169*

   Enacting without Scripts   *169*
   Improvisation   *169*

     Practices   *169*
     Values   *171*

Chapter 12. Writing Down   173

Principles of Teaching Transcription   *173*
Taking Dictation from the Teacher   *174*
Punctuating Unpunctuated Texts   *175*
Principles of Punctuating by Voice   *175*

What Can Be Heard   *176*
What Is Difficult to Hear   *176*
Meanings of the Symbols   *176*
Punctuation of Single Words   *177*

Taking Dictation from Classmates   *177*
Taking Dictation from Younger Children   *178*
Dialogue Recording   *179*
The Use of Tape Recorders   *182*

Chapter 13. *Sensory Writing* 183

Account of Trials   *183*

Around the School   *183*
Away from School   *185*
Formulating the Problems and the Assignments   *186*
Results and Conclusions   *190*

Difficulties of note taking   *191*

Improvements to be Made over the Trials   *192*

Engagement with the material   *192*
Purpose of the writing   *193*
Revising   *193*

Recommendations   *194*

Procedures   *194*
The Writing Workshop   *195*

Cross-teaching   *197*

Sequence   *198*

Discussion of Some Samples   *198*
Advantages for the Slower Pupil   *208*
Recapitulating Pantomimes and Improvisations   *209*

Pantomimes   *209*
Improvisations   *210*

Chapter 14. *Memory Writing* 213

Account of Trials   *213*

Directions   *214*
Results and Problems   *217*

Making the assignment clear   217
Timing and grouping   218
Phasing the writing process   218

Improvements to be Made over the Trials   *219*

Creating books of memories   220
Fuller use of workshop   220
Freer rewriting   220

Samples   *221*
Summary   *228*

Chapter 15. *Writing Fictions*   **231**

Writing About Pictures   232
Writing Memories of Literature   232
Points of Departure for Inventing   235

An Unfinished Sentence   236
Loaded Words   237
Song and Verse Forms   238
Fables   240
General Ways of Stimulating Creativity   242

Chapter 16. *Idea Writing*   **245**

Verbal Stimulus   245
Diaries and Letters   247
Writing up Show-and-Tell   248
Writing Directions   249

Oral Directions with Puzzles   249
Oral Directions with Other Materials   250
Writing Directions for How to Make and Do Things   251
Writing Traveling Directions   251

Unrecommended Writing   252

Criteria for Judging a Writing Assignment   253
Book Reports   253
Reference Papers   254
Literary Analysis   254

Chapter 17. Playing Games of Language and Logic   **257**

Chess   *257*

Card Games   *257*

   Example of Classification Card Games   *257*
    Form of the first decks   258
    How to play with the first decks   259
    Later decks   260
   Games that Combine Classification with Serial Ordering   *260*
   Games Fostering Original Concept Formation   *261*
   Games for Deductive Reasoning   *262*

    Wiff 'n Proof   262
    Conjunctive categories   263
    Disjunctive categories   263

Chapter 18. Review and Preview   **265**

Establishment of Learning Process   *265*
Thinking   *265*
Speaking and Listening   *267*
Writing   *269*
Reading   *273*

PART THREE
GRADES SEVEN THROUGH NINE

Chapter 19. Acting and Speaking   **283**

The Drama period   *283*
The Workshop   *284*
Enacting Scripts   *285*

   Values of Rehearsal   *285*
   Procedures   *286*

    Student scripts   286
    Published scripts   287

Improvisation   *288*

   Procedures   *288*
   Kinds of Minimal Situations   *289*

Panel Discussions   *291*

   Setting up Panels   *291*
   Audience Feedback   *292*

Chapter 20. Dramatic Dialogue   295

Writing Short Scripts   *295*

   Procedures   *295*
   Samples from Trials   *296*

      Duologue   297
      Three-way dialogue   298
      Complete short play   299
      Dialogue by maturer students   302

Writing Plays of More Than One Scene   *305*

      Learning about technique during the cycle of play creation   308
      Learning to describe   309
      Dramatizing speech behavior   309

Writing Scripts Based on Reading Selections   *314*

Chapter 21. Socratic Dialogue   317

Samples from Trials   *317*
Procedures   *322*
Relation to Discussion   *323*
Values   *323*
Collateral Reading Texts and Other Materials   *324*

Chapter 22. Monologue   325

Dramatic Monologue   *325*

   Procedures   *325*

      The oral assignment   325
      The written assignment   326

   Samples   *326*

      Playing with style   327
      Grasping literary technique   327

   Variations of the Written Assignment   *330*
   Collateral Work with Literature   *331*

Interior Monologue   *332*

   Procedures   *332*
   Samples   *333*

Movement of language, movement of mind 333
A kind of personal essay 334
Simulating another's mind 336
Issues for workshop commentary 338

Inventing Soliloquies for Literary Characters 339

Monologues and the Understanding of Literature 340

Chapter 23. *Narrative* 343

Memory Writing 343
Autobiographical Incident 348

Workshop Issues 349
Related Reading 350

Memoir — Human Incident 350
Memoir — Nature Incident 352
Reportage 354

Compositional Differences Between Memoir and Reportage 354
Setting up a Newspaper Operation 354
How Workshop Issues Are Raised Before the Whole Class 355
Other Workshop Issues 358
Related Reading 359

Chapter 24. *Poetry of Observation* 361

Haiku 361

Presenting Haiku in Class 362
Writing Haiku 364

The problem of over-abstracting 365
When generality is not over-abstraction 366
The philosophic epigram 366

Further Reading of Haiku 368

Drawing the image 368
Comparing translations 368

Other Short Poems 368

Pairing Haiku with Other Poems 368

The difference that length makes 369

Reading   369
Writing   369

Metaphor   370

Chapter 25. *Journals and Diaries*   371

Account of Trials   371

The Assignment Directions   371
Purposes   372
Results   372

The matter of privacy   372
How to abstract   373
Social interest   373

Samples   374

The Snapshot Technique   374
The Categories-of-Experience Organization   376
Thematic Abstraction   377

Recommendations   379

The Public Journal   379

Specializing journals   379

The Private Diary   380

Entries   380
Compositions   380

Summary of Sequence   380
Inventing and Reading Diaries and Journals   381

PART FOUR
GRADES TEN THROUGH THIRTEEN

Chapter 26. *Autobiography and Memoir*   387

Memory Writing   387
Portion of Autobiography   390

The Notion of a Phase   390
Sample   391
Issues for the Writing Workshop   394

      Organization   394
      Vantage point   395

   The Threat of Autobiography   *396*
   Parallel Reading   *397*

  Portion of Memoir   *398*

   Firsthand Biography   *398*
   Sample   *399*

      Double organization   402

   Issues for the Writing Workshop   *402*
   Parallel Reading   *403*

  Firsthand Chronicle   *404*

   Sample   *404*
   Parallel Reading   *406*

Chapter 27. Reportage and Research   409

Poems of Observation   *409*

   Imitation and Originality   *409*
   Techniques   *411*
   Other Descriptive Poetry   *413*

The Observational Visit   *414*

   Samples of Twelfth-Grade Sensory Recording   *414*
   Sample of Sought-Out Human-Interest Story   *416*

The Interview   *417*

   Procedures   *418*

      Interviewing peers   418
      Issues for discussion   419
      Other developments of the assignment   419

   Sample   *419*
   Parallel Reading   *422*

The "Reporter-at-Large"   *422*

   Procedures   *423*
   Sample   *423*
   Issues for the Writing Workshop   *428*
   The Value as Research   *429*

The Case   429

   Purposes   430
   Procedures   430
   Parallel Reading   432

The Profile   432
Research with Documents   434

Chapter 28. *Reflection*   437

Stream of Consciousness   437

   Account of Trials   437

      Purposes   438
      Assignment directions   438
      Results as registered in notes   439
      Conclusions   441

   Sample   441

Spontaneous Reflections   442

   Assignment Directions and Results   442
   Samples   443

Recommendations for Combining the Two Assignments   445

   Procedures   445
   Reading and Writing Poetry   446

Chapter 29. *Generalization and Theory*   449

Discussion   449

   Techniques for Training Discussants   450
   Topics   451
   Relation of Talking and Writing   452

Writing Socratic Dialogue   452

   The Shift from Dialogical to Monological Continuity of Ideas   452

      Sample of socratic dialogue   453
      Sample of socratic dialogue converted to essay   454

   Recommendation   455

Thematic Collection of Incidents   458

   Sample   458
   Issues for the Writing Workshop   460

Purposes   *460*

Writing about Reading Selections   *461*

   Sample   461

   Comparison of the samples   462

Drawing Writing Material from Previous Writing   *463*

Single-Sentence Generalization   *463*

Parallel Reading   *464*

Generalization Supported by Instances   *466*

Issues for the Writing Workshop   *467*

   Illustration and generalization as levels of abstraction   467

   Technical problems   467

   Common faults   468

Sample   *468*

General   *470*

Combining Generalizations into a Theory   *471*

Procedures   *471*

Issues for the Writing Workshop   *472*

Sample   *473*

Chapter 30. Invention   477

Improvisation   *477*

Treating Certain Literature as Scripts   *478*

Dialogue Poems and Stories   *479*

   Determining the voicing   480

   Joining socratic and dramatic dialogue   480

   Short stories   481

Dramatic Monologue Poems and Stories   *481*

   Memorization   481

   Example of "My Last Duchess"   482

   Reacting   482

   Casting by sex   482

   Kinds of literary monologuists   483

   Short stories   483

   Comedy monologues   483

Interior Monologue Poems and Stories   *483*

Procedures for Plays *484*

  The Components of Plays *484*
  Whole Plays *485*
  A Sequence of Plays *485*

Fiction *488*

  A Reading Sequence from *Points of View* *488*

Chamber Theatre *490*

  Definition *490*
  Procedure *491*

Writing Inventions *492*

  Free Assignments *492*
  Invented Correspondence *493*
  Subjective Narrator *497*

Chapter 31. Summary   **501**

A Student-Centered
Language Arts Curriculum,
Grades K-13:
A Handbook for Teachers

INTRODUCTION

This book is for teachers on the job, student teachers, and all others concerned with teaching the language arts and reading. I have tried to describe and illustrate particular language activities that students and teachers would engage in from kindergarten into college. The program thus outlined is meant to be integrated both in the sense that continuity is sustained from one general stage of growth to another and in the sense that reading, speech, literature, drama, composition, and language are learned by means of each other and interrelated to the point of effacing some conventional categories of the field.

I would like to propose a way of teaching the native language that features the learner's own production of language and that adjusts automatically to the students at hand. It is therefore meant for use in any kind of school, public or private, and with any kind of student population, advantaged or disadvantaged, of low or high ability. But what I am presenting is not a definitive, thoroughly tried-and-proven "method"; it is, rather, a chart for further exploration and a kind of rallying call.

Chapter 1

General Orientation

The base of this curriculum is trials, begun a number of years ago in my own classes, picked up and modified by colleagues, proposed as an experiment to a wider and wider circle of teachers, expanded farther and farther into other grades as the need for developmental continuity became critically apparent, and spreading across more and more language activities as the implications of the trials were borne in on me. The ideas in this book have benefited considerably not only from these trials but from reactions by teachers in schools where I have consulted, other teachers who have tried parts of the program on their own, Master of Arts in Teaching candidates I taught in a curriculum and methods course, and my fellow participants at the Anglo-American Conference on the Teaching of English (a one-month convocation at Dartmouth in 1966 of around fifty leaders in English education from the United States and the United Kingdom). So what I have to say is partly a narrative report of trials, partly an extrapolation from experience into possibility, partly a relaying of other people's experience and ideas, and partly a statement of principles.

A K–13 Curriculum in One Presentation

The reason for putting a K–6 or K–13 program in a single book stems from my conviction that, without descending to formulas and mechanical syllabuses, English teaching should build in some sensibly cumulative way. I do not think that important improvements can come about until teachers up and down the line know what their colleagues in other grades are doing and are enabled by their administration to meet and collaborate. The main thing I have learned from experimenting in schools is this: how well a student fares with a certain assignment in, say, tenth or eleventh grade depends enormously on what he was asked to do in the lower grades; sometimes this past education seems even more critical than age and ability. The same assignment can produce extremely different results among students of the same grade and achievement level, these results being relative to what assignments they have or have not done in the past. This relativity partly explains why this book could not have been written merely as a reference book in which the teacher could look up the grade he teaches and not bother with the rest.

For elementary teachers the K–6 sections of this book have been made available in a separate edition. Although it is certainly desirable for these teachers to know how their work is followed up in the later years, it seemed best to acknowledge that many might not want to read more than is actually necessary. To provide some tie, the K–6 edition ends with a summary of what is to come. But every elementary teacher will have to read the whole of the K–6 sequence, not only to find out just where his own classes actually fall on it, but also to know where his work with them fits into the total program. He will have to proceed differently with pupils who have not previously followed the program than with those who have. By understanding how he is carrying forward his pupils' previous experience, and how later teachers will pick up where he left off, he will have more confidence and purpose and gain a greater sense of satisfaction. (By the same token, a teacher working all alone with this program will have a more difficult time.)

Teachers of grades 7–13 will need to read the sections on K–6 for the simple reason that those sections contain indispensible material for *all* years. Not only the second half of the book, but the whole book, is relevant to the secondary and college years, for the presentation is cumulative. Activities and assignments are dealt with in the first half that are only alluded to in the second half but continue in force. Some new assignments grow out of earlier ones that teachers in grades 7–13 must have knowledge of. Also, if students are new to the program, their teachers will often have to dip down into the earlier years to catch them up. In the sections covering 7–13, I have discussed only new work or new developments of old work. Otherwise the book would have become unmanageable. The problem inheres in any effort to present a whole curriculum in a single work.

Present or Future?

In putting this program together I have had constantly to decide whether I was to write it up for the present or the future. In some ways it is directed toward more ideal conditions toward which one would hope some present trends are leading, and yet I have made several concessions to current conditions that are not likely to disappear overnight. Two of the hopeful trends I am banking on are the gradually rising quality of teachers and the increasing local experimentation within school systems. The teaching profession is drawing more intelligent, independent, and dedicated people than it used to. Schools of education may soon begin to give them a better training that includes dramatic work and practical experience with the dynamics of small groups and the realities of writing. School systems are more inclined now to give teachers time off to think about what they are doing, look for ideas, and get in-service training, and many are hiring more specialists, coordinators, and supervisors.

LOCAL CURRICULUM BUILDING

All of this means that more questions are being asked about curriculum than just which publisher's series to order for next year. The dependence of teachers and school systems on prepackaged programs that can be served from books in daily doles may begin to lessen if these trends continue, although some seductive new materials offered by the education industry will perhaps create new temptations. Underlying the teaching of English is this noneducational drama of who is to determine what happens in the classroom from day to day. Will local strength build up fast enough to prevent a very unfortunate meshing of big business interests with the teacher's fears of inadequacy? My point here is that the program described in this book depends on a fair measure of knowledge and self-assurance on the part of the teacher and good collaboration and support within a school system bent on forging its own curriculum. This would, of course, be true of any serious effort at innovation in English teaching. But local educators have a right to expect help from the outside and a mission to look for it. With this book I wish to offer some such help.

HETEROGENEOUS CLASSES

Another prophesy whose fulfillment would ratify this program is that the language classes of the future will be heterogeneously grouped. More learning takes place when students of different ability, achievement, socio-economic class, dialect, sex, and race are mixed together. An English classroom should be as richly varied a speech community as can be mustered. Today opposition to the sorting of students by ability is growing rapidly. The stand taken at the Anglo-American Conference on English was that tracking, streaming, and grouping, within schools and among schools, should be abolished[1]

[1] Recently reported in two books: John Dixon, *Growth Through English,* published in England in 1967 by the Modern Language Association, The National Association of Teachers of English, and The National Council of Teachers of English, and written for the profession; and Herbert J. Muller, *The Uses of English* (New York: Holt, Rinehart, & Winston, 1967), written for the public. This unanimous stand in favor of heterogeneous classes is all the more remarkable if one considers how heterogeneous a group the participants in the conference were themselves, and how little agreement they were able to reach on some other matters.

and a flexible kind of sub-grouping should be instituted within each class. The ideal of the diversified in-class speech community can, of course, no more be attained in an insulated, well-to-do suburban school system than in an urban ghetto. The possibilities of cutting across municipal lines and of eventually redistricting a whole metropolitan area for school purposes are being explored in a number of cities, some of which have experimented with the bussing of students from one part of the city to another. Metropolitan planning may soon make mixed classes a reality. Though the program I am submitting here does not depend on such mixing, it would be most fully realized by it.

Concessions to Current Realities

The concessions I have made to the present facts of school organization concern *the division of the book into blocks of grades,* and *the treatment of English as a separate subject.* To have crept through the grades one at a time would have been absurd. Part of my criticism of some prepackaged curricula is precisely that the work for each grade cannot be specified by someone who knows nothing of the school population and of the past training of each class. Whenever specifying either a grade or a grade-block, I have tried to make it clear that these are relative indications. Pending the supremacy of the un-graded school (and, I hope, also encouraging it) I compromised by emphasiz-ing stages while referring to grades. It is of course, only the stages of de-velopment that count.

Sharing the view of some other educators that, ultimately, there should be a total program in discourse running laterally across subject fields as well as longitudinally over the years, I have felt severely constrained at times in trying to keep this program contained within a separate learning area called English. (It is in secondary school, of course, that the problem becomes acute.) The reader will undoubtedly feel this strain at those points where I have advocated writing assignments that might well be done in science and social studies classes. Having to assume a discontinuity between English and other subjects was my most costly compromise, but I have pushed the fron-tiers as hard as possible, by recommending assignments that place students in the role of natural and social scientists and by recommending some non-literature in the reading program. I hope future reorganization of the total school curriculum will make such pushing unnecessary. If others who try this program feel the same discomfort in this regard that I have felt in assembling it, then perhaps a stronger force will be exerted to break down the compartmentalization of subjects and to ascribe to team-teaching a larger meaning than is generally found in it. (The "Core" program is cer-tainly no answer.)

Material Problems

There are some practical matters to consider in connection with this program. These include the division of classes into smaller groups, arriving at marks, and setting up an experimental program.

GROUP PROCESS

This program calls for the deployment of a class into five or six smaller groups for the purposes of dramatizing, discussing, reading aloud, and commenting on each other's writing. This creates a problem that can be solved in terms of either time or space. That is, either the small groups can operate one at a time while the rest of the class is doing something else, which allows the teacher to lead each group, or else the groups can operate simultaneously in spatially separated areas, which permits the teacher either to pass among the groups or to stay with one group. I am assuming the worst conditions — one teacher, one normal-sized classroom, and 25 to 40 students. Imaginative building, scheduling, and organization of staff could produce better solutions, but I know that teachers have succeeded in running the small-group process even under the least favorable conditions. To picture this process in action, one has to imagine it as a staple school activity in which students would be taught to participate from the earliest years. Serious, effective work in autonomous groups is definitely feasible. The first efforts with uninitiated students give no just indication of this feasibility.

MAKING UP MARKS

Since my focus in this book has been entirely on learning and not on testing — deliberately so, for the two are often in conflict — I suggest a particular way of arriving at marks. A folder of each student's papers is kept and passed on yearly from teacher to teacher. Instead of deciding upon marks by making up tests, putting grades on papers, and doing a lot of bookkeeping, the teacher looks over the folder at the end of the marking period, makes a general assessment of the student's papers, adds in his observations of the student's oral and dramatic work, and either translates this into a letter grade, if the administration insists, or, preferably, writes a two- or three-sentence assessment. Being qualitative, the latter assessment is actually more valuable for most purposes. This procedure, furthermore, has several other advantages: the teacher gets a better picture of trends; the time he spends on marks is less but more meaningful; and the student becomes oriented toward intrinsic learning issues instead of toward grades. Though it is often criticized, the administrative need for tests and marks has tampered with educational processes, especially in English, even more than most of its critics have ever asserted.

SETTING UP AN EXPERIMENT

For school systems wishing to set up a large, longitudinal experiment I suggest the following general plan, assuming some additional funds, perhaps government or foundation support. A wave of students is launched into the program in kindergarten or first grade; at the same time, older students begin it in the later grades in some form that allows for their previous learning background. As the "wave" group rolls through, the teachers who have them for a given year and the teachers who are to take them over the following year are given some time off to meet once a week, review results, make adjustments, and collaborate on the articulation of the two adjacent years. Teachers of all years use this book as a guide and are given some in-service training by specialists in drama, writing, and small-group discussion. A liaison is created with a local school of education, where some faculty member undertakes to give a special course for training student teachers who will enter that system and replace those who leave. An essential part of such a course, which is geared to this program, is to have student teachers themselves do the sorts of assignments recommended in this book, including improvisations and small-group discussion, and to discuss results in workshop fashion. Additional liaisons with psychologists and other researchers would be valuable for both parties: psycholinguists, linguists, and learning psychologists, for example, might find it very useful to follow the wave, and, by some exchange arrangement, might agree to discuss their insights with the teachers.

As for evaluating such an experiment, I will say here only that a learning program should be assessed on its own terms, not shrunk to the narrow limits of conventional, easily quantifiable tests. Fairness would require both long-term evaluation and some way of judging a cross-section of authentic student discourse. I suggested that outside judges be asked to assess samples taken from student writing folders and from tapes of their speech, and perhaps to compare these with samples from a control group. Interpreting of some individual cases should be done, tracing the development of selected students over a span of several years. Broad measures of cumulative effects would be most appropriate, but for the sake of perhaps valuable correlations, I see no reason, secondarily, not to do some standard measuring as well.

Use by the Individual Teacher

I do not mean to imply that only the mounting of a large project would be worthwhile. Many individual teachers have requested copies of the unpublished experimental book from which this book grew, drawn sequences of assignments from it, and used them in their own classes. Often their colleagues became interested in what they were doing, and started an enclave in their department that influenced the curriculum. Many of these individuals were department heads who proposed to their staffs an experiment with some version of the program. In fact, a large amount of unsolicited interest in the program, from individuals who had heard about it, is something that I can offer as some sort of testimonial and is one of the things that encouraged me to write this book. Some of this interest has resulted in the adoption or adaptation of the program by a number of schools and school systems in different localities. But if the book does no more than serve as a practical source of assignments and teaching concepts for the individual teacher, its existence will be justified.

Chapter 2

Principles and Purposes

Summary of Principles

I would like to set down here the main assumptions and beliefs that underlie the program. More of this philosophy will emerge gradually in the course
of delineating the program. A fuller argument of rationale can be found in
Teaching the Universe of Discourse,[1] which is a theoretical companion to
this book and may answer many questions unanswered here about the thinking that underlies the curriculum.

1. Most profoundly considered, a course of language learning is a course
in thinking. A writing assignment, for example, is a thinking assignment.
Conceiving and verbalizing must be taken together.

2. But the stuff to be conceived and verbalized is primarily the raw stuff
of life, not language matters themselves. Rendering experience into words is
the real business of school, not linguistic analysis, or literary analysis, or
rhetorical analysis, which are proper subjects only for college. It takes all
of 13 years just to get off to a good start the lifelong learning of how to produce and receive language well. There is no justification for teaching concepts of literary criticism or theories of grammar and rhetoric as an aid to
speaking, reading, and writing. And there is neither time nor sufficient
reason to teach them for their own sake, except perhaps in separate, elective
courses.

3. What a student needs most of all is to perceive how he *is* using language and how he *might* use it. What this requires is awareness, not information. The student will be aided by practical perceptions about what he
and others are doing when they speak and write, not generalizations about

[1] James Moffett (Boston: Houghton Mifflin Company, 1968).

11

what people regularly do with language or formulated advice about what they ought to do with it.

4. The role of teachers is to help students expand their cognitive and verbal repertory as far as possible, starting with their initial limits. The goal is for the student to become capable of producing and receiving an increasingly broad range of kinds of discourse, compositional forms, points of view, ways of thinking, styles, vocabulary, and sentence structures.

5. The sequential pathway to this goal is a growth scale going from the personal to the impersonal, from low to high abstraction, from undifferentiated to finely discriminated modes of discourse.

6. The most effective and best motivated learning process for approaching this goal is trial and error, if the trials are roughly sequenced to provide a cumulative experience, and if, through full feedback, the errors are turned to maximum advantage. This means that, in a general way, the teacher selects the trials — the speaking, reading, and writing assignments — and that he sets in motion classroom processes that allow each student (1) to act verbally and (2) to receive an enlightening reaction to what he has done. This is an action-response model of learning; the student speaks, writes, or reads and others respond to his statement, composition, or interpretation.

7. The only way, short of tutorial, to provide individual students enough language experience and feedback is to develop small-group interaction into a sensitive learning method. The teacher's role must be to teach students to teach each other. Thus he frequently breaks the class into small groups for conversing, acting, reading, and writing, setting the structure of these groups by training them, consulting with them, and relating their activities to whole-class presentations.

8. Using language is essentially a social action, which, however, becomes internalized as a private behavior. The quality of individual utterance depends much on the kinds of dialogues that have been previously absorbed. Thus a good group process provides the external model for the inner processes it will foster.

9. Producing language is more difficult than receiving it. That is, the *composing* act involved in speaking and writing — choosing and patterning words — poses more intricate learning problems than the act of *following* sequences of words as in listening and reading. A student can read some kinds of discourse before he can write them. Also, the problems of writing different kinds of discourse vary much more from one kind to another than do the problems of reading different kinds of discourse. The difference warrants greater attention to the learning problems of producing than to those of receiving, though not necessarily a disproportion in the amount of student time spent on each.

In summary, the approach of this program could be called "naturalistic," and the curriculum, "student-centered." Emphasis is on active output by the learners, on their speech production and their response to others' productions. The goals here are not substantially different from conventional ones; the main departure is in the means. My conviction is that reading comprehension, literary appreciation, compositional skill, and understanding of language all come about most effectively and humanely when these principles are followed.

The main thesis of this book, then, is that learners should *use* language far more than they customarily do in most schools today. Two main misconceptions of the language arts keep the student in a receiving posture and prevent him from practicing language in authentic ways. In discussing these misconceptions I can elaborate some of the principles above.

The First Misconception

The first is that the learner must be given facts about our language system, concepts of literature, and advice about composition. For the sake of this knowledge he must study some textbooks that present him, through exposition and exercises, the history and science of language or the history and science of literature, and that undoubtedly would, if they could, present the history and science of composition. Since rote learning is considered in poor taste today, these presentations fly the banner of "discovery" or "self-instruction." What the student is learning, of course, is still history and science, on the false analogy that one's native language is an informational subject with a content of its own, like empirical subjects. But he is neither using language nor experiencing literature nearly as much as he might.

HISTORICAL DETERMINANTS OF CURRICULUM

There is no evidence to support the belief that presenting generalizations about language, literature, and composition — by whatever *method* — will influence favorably the development of thinking, speaking, listening, reading, and writing, which are presumably the goals of a language arts curriculum. It is certainly not the *success* of such an approach that warrants it, for it has been tried for generations and found severely wanting. That is one reason why English teaching is ripe for reform today. But reform too often consists of replacing old content with new. What a shame, we feel, to waste the brilliant new theories of modern linguistics and of literary criticisms. Let's turn right around and teach them in the schools! But it is precisely my point that curriculum has been determined far too much by university disciplines and not nearly enough by perceptions about language learning.

The awful truth is that English teaching in America is what it is today mainly because of local historical accidents. The first is that a chronological-critical teaching of literature happens to be the tradition of university English departments and has produced English majors who know virtually nothing about the vast field of language and discourse besides literary periods and influences or how So-and-So achieves his effects.

The second accident is that just as educational research was discrediting grammar teaching there came along some stunning achievements in linguistics that English educators felt must somehow be the godsend they needed to launch a New English like the New Math or New Physics, and to placate the critics who were claiming that after 12 years of studying English students had precious little to show for it.

THE FALSE RATIONALE FOR TEACHING THE SCIENCE OF LANGUAGE

Linguistics filled the bill to dispel the last wisps of progressivism and to establish the post-Sputnik age of "intellectual rigor." By a deft switch of rationale we could now go on teaching grammar, not as an aid to speaking and writing — for massive evidence forbade that — but as a "humanity" for its own sake, or as an intellectual discipline (like Latin) to develop the mind. A student who is told to learn the different kinds of "determiners" or to transform one arbitrary sentence into another arbitrary sentence might well ask, "If it's a humanity, why is it so inhumane?" It can only be a symptom of hysteria in the profession to swallow the argument that any modern grammar is a humanity or that the study of it has some special virtue for developing thinking. A study of the uniquely human ability to produce language and organize life symbolically is indeed a humanity, but that study is conducted by paying attention to everyday verbal behavior, and, in later years, by becoming acquainted with psychology, sociology, and anthropology, subjects which are hardly even touched on in the overall pre-college curriculum. Yes, language is central to human life, but grammar is a drastically small and specialized subject, limited essentially to nothing broader than syntax, that is, the relations and patterns of words in a sentence.

As for developing thought and intellectual rigor, that comes about in a host of ways as the learner actually tries to symbolize his experience and to understand the symbolizations of other people. Indeed, verbal thinking is the main concern of the program offered in this book. But it does not follow that the student who learns the terms, concepts, and formulations of a rigorous discipline like linguistics is himself learning to think; or if he is, that linguistics is the cause. Study of *any* subject will develop thinking. The only advantage I see in studying the rule-governed system of a grammar is the same advantage one finds in mathematics and symbolic logic, which offer better opportunities for the development of deduction because they are purer logical systems having none of the aberrations of everyday language. Transformational grammar, in fact, represents an attempt to bring order out of everyday language by applying mathematical and symbolic logic to it. Whatever deductive learning would take place in grammar would take place better in a course of mathematics, especially as it is taught today.

This is not a criticism of linguistics itself but a criticism of its inclusion in the language arts curriculum. I return to the point that in our uncertainties about how to teach our extremely difficult subject we too readily drag down university disciplines into elementary and secondary school. (In the case of grammar, this tendency is reinforced by the irrational hold that grammar has on the curriculum because of a long-standing tradition revered by the public perhaps more than by the profession. In the mystique it is equated with "a good basic education," and educators are often exposed to heavy criticism if they drop it.) Besides Noam Chomsky's transformational grammar, we want to teach Francis Christensen's rhetorical analysis of the sentence and the paragraph, or Northrop Frye's mythic theory of literature. For the teacher these are all important things to learn about. They may increase enormously his understanding of what he is trying to teach and help him see how best to go about teaching it. But to teach them directly to his students, or to base exercises on them in the "discovery" manner, is misguided, for this effort to transmit, in one way or another, the generalities of scholarship almost always ends by forcing on students an arbitrary and therefore unwelcome knowledge, and by forcing out of the curriculum much more powerful learning activities such as this book attempts to present. Thus we have students learning what morphemes are, for no reason they can discern, but speaking little and writing less; or answering questions designed to get them to see how "The Millionairess" is an example of satire ("Satire must be something I don't know anything about yet or they wouldn't be defining it for me.") instead of relating the play to their own satiric impulses by acting out scenes from it.[2]

THE BRITISH VIEW

British educators do not at all share our American penchant for scientizing the teaching of English. They are appalled by the mechanized materials that pour forth from curriculum centers and educational publishers here — the programming in minute steps re-enforced by right answers, the highly structured literature presentations, the technical grammar programs for all ages, the inhibited composition assignments loaded fore and aft with solemn rhetorical analyses. In British schools today the strongest trend is away from teaching grammar, marking papers, and using textbooks, and toward creative writing, dramatics (even in secondary school), and a generally more spontaneous curriculum. There is, of course, no reason to think that the British are more right than we are, and this revulsion to our materials is no doubt a reaction against the tyranny of their own external examination and certain rigidities of their recent past. But the point is that until teachers can perceive

[2] A fuller discussion, "The Case Against Teaching Grammar," occurs in Chapter Five of *Teaching the Universe of Discourse*.

the ways in which their teaching methods are merely drifting with historical currents it is impossible to think through learning problems and put methods on a relevant footing.

The Second Misconception

The second major misconception of the language arts concerns reading. Or, rather, it does not especially concern reading but — precisely — appears to. A long list of mental activities that any psychologist would consider general properties of thinking that occur in many different areas of human experience have somehow or other all been tucked under the skirts of reading. "Recalling," "comprehending," "relating facts," "making inferences," "drawing conclusions," "interpreting," and "predicting outcomes" are all mental operations that go on in the head of a non-literate aborigine navigating his outrigger according to cues from weather, sea life, currents, and the positions of heavenly bodies. Not only do these kinds of thinking have no necessary connection with reading, but they have no necessary connection with language whatever.

The Fallacy of "Reading Skills"

It is understandable, in a way, that these skills have wound up as "reading skills," because in reading, as in anything else, one is confronted with a set or string of phenomena that one has to make sense of, put together, comprehend. And it is true too that a reader has two simultaneous levels of phenomena to cope with — the letter symbols and the things or concepts referred to. But if he has learned to decode letters into voice, then he has no more to cope with than if someone were speaking to him. A child who fails to understand a text either cannot decode letters, or else cannot understand the text for reasons having nothing to do with printed words; he would not understand even if the text were read aloud to him. In other words, reading comprehension is merely comprehension.

The prevailing assumption in education, however, is that failing to comprehend a text is something more than just a literacy problem and yet still a *reading* problem. This is impossible. If a reader can translate print into speech — read it aloud as sentences with normal intonation patterns — and still fails to grasp the idea or relate facts or infer or draw conclusions, then he has no *reading* problem; he has a *thinking* problem, traceable to many possible sources, none of them concerning printed words. A reading specialist would probably reply that of course these mental operations occur elsewhere than in reading but that he is concerned with them only as they crop up in his specialty; when they operate in reading they are called reading skills. But this has caused enormous confusion in the field and had negative effects throughout the curriculum.

My heart goes out to the reading specialist. Reading has been so broadly construed that his job is in some ways an impossible one. He is made responsible for general mental activities like recalling, inferring, and concluding that belong no more to reading than to any other intellectual activity. Vocabulary building and concept formation are placed in his domain, even though neither of these has any necessary connection with reading. Subject-matter reading, as in science and social studies, is supposed to require additional "skills" that also fall under his charge, when in fact what is difficult for the young reader are the vocabulary, the concepts, and the knowledge context, all of which can be learned without ever opening a book. There are educators who would have us recognize dozens of different reading skills; some even count a couple of hundred.

NEGATIVE EFFECTS

Mis-diagnosis. First, many so-called "comprehension problems" are literacy problems incorrectly diagnosed. Many children have in fact not learned very early to decode letters into voice, and have limped along in reading, understanding some things but missing the individual meanings of some words and the total meaning of some word sequences because they were still having to devote too much attention to unlocking the letters. It is easy to confuse this case with the case of a child who decodes perfectly well but does not have some of the words in his vocabulary or has not grasped certain concepts yet, however they are worded, or has a general cognitive problem in putting facts together, or simply is not motivated to stick with the text. The first child has a problem for which the only *good* solution is the efficient literacy instruction that he failed to receive before. For the other child, the solutions lie in many activities besides reading — conversing, playing games of logic, doing dramatic work, writing, and simply getting more life experience. In brief, I question the whole concept of "reading skills," beyond the level of word recognition.

Misguided assignments. Another result of this misconception is that many children spend a large amount of school time plowing through "reading labs," "skill builders," "power builders," or "practice readers" — that is, reading snippets of this and that and answering comprehension questions afterwards. Then, finally, a considerable amount — in most schools, the majority — of the writing that the students are asked to do is really a check on the reading: it is assigned either to make sure that the reading was done or to monitor the comprehension of it or to "get students to think about it more." (I want to know why students would *not* read the text, or comprehend it, or think about it more. Isn't all this just a poor substitute for other things like motivation before and group discussion afterwards?) This practice drives students away from both reading and writing, because each comes into negative association with the other. An integrated program does not consist of writing about reading — or of reading about writing.

Curriculum imbalance. It is understandable that reading should have become the main preoccupation of a language arts curriculum. It is the pathway to most other school learning and the main measure of successful teaching. But in some ways it has swelled out of reasonable proportion, to its own detriment as well as to the detriment of other activities. Too much is included in it that can be learned better elsewhere. It crowds out those very activities that it desperately needs. It dominates the curriculum at the expense of itself and of speech, drama, and writing — the expressive language arts — which are shunted aside as peripheral "enrichment" because the main business of the day, reading, is not coming along well enough to permit such extravagances. And that is why reading is not coming along well enough.

Let me make it clear that I would not for one moment deemphasize reading, if by that one means reducing the amount of reading or neglecting comprehension. On the contrary, if we dispense with the notion of reading skills and with the practices based on it, it will be possible to let children do more reading of an authentic sort and at the same time to help them develop the faculties necessary to read for meaning.

CAUSES OF READING INCOMPREHENSION

It must also be clear that decoding skills are real indeed. Unlike problems of comprehension, the problems of recognizing vocal speech in print do not involve only universal mental operations but also involve the specific learning of spelling and punctuation conventions, which involves auditory discrimination among speech sounds and intonations, visual discrimination among printed symbols, and the associative pairing of one set with the other so that correspondence is achieved between sights and sounds. When incomprehension results from decoding problems, the case is truly remedial, for inadequate learning of the speech-print correspondences must be remedied by returning to them. The test of literacy is to be able to read a text aloud with normal intonation. This does not mean that the reader understands the text. All literate adults frequently read texts they do not comprehend — even when they know all the words — because of inadequate knowledge of the subject matter, failure to grasp certain concepts, cognitive difficulty in relating statements, or failure of the *writer* to make himself clear. (Writers for children have to take some responsibility for incomprehension). The best way to head off reading inefficiency at the literacy level is an early, intensive, and direct teaching of sound-spelling relations, which is indicated by research and provided for in all the new, and some old, beginning reading materials. (In the chapter, "Becoming Literate," certain materials are recommended.)

Poor motivation. Given a sound literacy instruction, what causes reading problems? A major cause may simply be lack of motive. Some children have not yet become interested in language generally and in books in particular and do not see what they have to gain personally from either. This problem is clearly not going to be solved by practice reading and comprehension questions, but rather by receiving and producing language in social activities — being read to, singing, discussing with peers, expressing oneself in writing, playing word games, and doing dramatic play. Only widespread involvement in language can solve the problem of poor motivation, and that involvement, as most teachers realize, must occur first outside the realm of silent reading; later, self-chosen books, as in individual reading programs, insure against loss of interest.

Environmental deprivation. Another major cause is experiential and, by definition, cannot be removed except in other activities. A book may refer to things with which the reader has no acquaintance. These things may be physical objects, concepts, ideas, or a whole knowledge framework. Because the problem never ceases to exist, it goes far beyond "reading readiness." A layman reading about quasars in a journal of astronomy will probably have trouble comprehending. I once heard Aldous Huxley say that our education is far too verbal, and that much of the literature presented to young people is meaningless to them because they have not yet had the emotional experiences that are prerequisite for understanding it. (Huxley was advocating more nonverbal education to the Friends of the San Francisco Public Library!)

Films and television can help enlarge experience and supply vocabulary. Playing games with picture cards, as described on page 157, will also extend visual acquaintance with objects and living creatures. The practice of taking classes on field trips is well justified in this respect. Emotional experience and point of view can be enlarged somewhat by playing roles in dramatic work. The small-group process advocated in this book provides considerable social experience. Thus schools can, to some extent, acquaint children with the things that words and sentences refer to, but reading comprehension will always stand in some ratio to what an individual has done, heard, seen, and felt in his personal life.

Egocentricity. Suppose a student is missing the point of the text because of subjectivity. Certain words or phrases have special power or private meaning for him; they trigger strong feelings or irrelevant associations that act as static to interfere with clear reception. These words or phrases arrest too much of his attention, causing him to ignore or slight other portions of the text, so that he gives a distorted reading, misconstruing statements or the relationships among statements. Once beyond the early stages, any reader tends to fill in words and phrases subjectively, according to expectancy cues provided by salient letters, syntax, and the drift of the sense. But the problem reader may fail to see how his filling in does not square with meaning cues elsewhere in the text. Or he may be too undeveloped intellectually to infer unstated connections the author is implying. Comprehension questions reveal such failures to understand, but do nothing to help the reader know why he misinterpreted; they test but do not teach. The learner is wrong but does not know why, and will continue to misread. Since egocentricity consists of being unaware that any other interpretation is possible, the learner needs other points of view on the text, which is exactly what he will get in a small-group discussion with peers. When he finds out that others his age read the same text differently, his egocentricity is broken, and he may even be helped to perceive just how his subjective responses derailed him or made him obscure the significant with the insignificant. Such learning is much more powerful than being told by the teacher or the answer sheet that one was wrong, for in the latter case children tend to care only about being right, squaring with the authority, and often take a luck-of-the-draw attitude — "Oh well, next time I'll guess better." In drama work, on the other hand, students enacting a story or poem have to deal specifically with problems of egocentricity because differences in understanding crop up in the enactment and have to be straightened out

How the Program Develops Reading Faculties

I would not expect teachers and other educators who believe in reading skills to embrace very eagerly the idea that speaking, acting, writing, and playing card games can develop reading for meaning (what other kind is there?) better than "practice reading" itself as found in the skill-building programs. So let me try to illustrate this claim.

It would be hard to find an activity recommended in this book that does not rather directly help to develop the faculties necessary for reading comprehension, for though the program features the language output of the learner, the combining of that emphasis with small-group process actually places the individual constantly in the position of receiver as well. Let's take some of these faculties one by one.

Attention. The ability to attend closely the words of others and to follow their meaning sequences is developed through concentrated, interactive discussions among five or six peers and through dramatic enactments and improvisations. The point here is that what each participant says himself depends on what his partners have just said. Unless he learns to attend he has no basis for his own actions. This habit of interacting makes for active, responsive receivers and generates that attention to the words of others that is the indispensable basis of reading.

Recollection. Recalling depends on attention in the moment and on later efforts to retrieve the information acquired by attending. The writing process set forth in this book frequently consists of taking notes on ongoing events and basing later composition on these notes. The notes may be on the speech of others, when taking a turn as discussion scribe or when recording overheard conversation, or they may even be on reading text themselves, as entailed in some advanced composition assignments. But most often, the notes are on other sounds and sights that the learner is registering. The general habit of deliberately storing and retrieving information — selectively noted — is thus established early and made integral to whatever experience is being registered.

As for recalling texts themselves, this occurs when enacting a piece of literature or when discussing, say, an expository selection. *In order to* act out a story or converse about a topic drawn from the reading, the groups have to recall together the actions or facts. And, of course, performing short scripts requires actually memorizing the text (in which case the actor must try to comprehend it *in order to* perform it). Finally, a regular feature of topic-centered discussion is recalling what the group has said. Since recall is almost always selective, it inevitably leads to the additional skill of summarizing.

Conception. Concept formation is directly fostered, outside the area of reading, by card playing and topic-centered small-group discussion, but the very important impact of those two activities is hard to convey in a book. The card decks remain to be created; and only experience with small-group discussion is really convincing. Whereas card games with special decks present the learner with standard concepts, which he learns by classifying instances of the concept, the framing and pursuing of topics in discussion crystallizes, through group definition, some of the more slippery and ambiguous concepts that underlie words and that cause ambiguity in reading. Since, incidentally, the card games are based on super-classes and sub-classes, they also help the learner to recognize *subordination,* which is also a constant issue in composition and comprehension.

Inference. Let's turn now to the general and major faculty of putting two and two together, reading between the lines — otherwise known as *drawing inferences and conclusions.* From what an author says is true one is supposed to assume that certain other things not said are also true. Inference supplies everything from implied conjunctions of time and causality to the syllogistic reasoning that if statements A and B are true, then a reasonable conclusion would be C. In other words, anything that teaches relating and reasoning will foster this aspect of comprehension. There are many children who do not *expect* things to be related because they are not used to connectedness in their personal or family life and seldom try to tie the facts of real-life experience together, much less statements in a text. They are not *looking* for relations. Until they begin generally to relate facts, they are not going to do so in reading.

Many aspects of the program offered in this book will develop inference. Dramatization is helpful because it elaborates the text and thus brings out what is merely implied. Anything serving as a script — a story or poem or play — is bound to be incomplete. Even stage directions themselves do not by any means spell out everything. The actors must infer many of their positions, movements, expressions, and lines of dialogue, not to mention personality, feelings, and character relationships. Consider also the value of witnessing charades, pantomimes, and performed dramas, all of which require that the spectator put two and two together for himself. An important trait of drama, in fact, is that no guiding narrator or informant takes the spectator by the hand. And for the actor, the enacting of the text is one way of making explicit many of its implications.

A major purpose of small-group discussion of the reading is to allow students to compare the inferences that they have drawn from the text and cite evidence that would justify some inferences and not others. In a more explicitly logical way, students learn to make deductions in earlier years by playing checkers and special card games and in the later years by working directly with verbal syllogisms. But any good discussion, regardless of topic, furthers inference. Since a listener has to infer the implications of what any oral speaker says as much as he does those of what a writer puts in a book — perhaps even more because speech statements are less carefully worded and organized — all discussion teaches this aspect of comprehension. The effect of discussion on reading has never been measured, however, because continuous, regular, and well trained discussion by peers in small groups has seldom if ever played a large role in the language arts curriculum. My claim is that reading comprehension will benefit far more from discussion than from a program of practice reading with comprehension questions. This is so because discussion must deal continually with the speakers' understanding of each other's utterances. The *reasons* for misunderstanding come out. Comprehension can be explored at its very roots. In the case of inference, for example, no matter what the subject is, the *process* of building and cancelling statements inevitably calls attention to the implications in statements and the relationships among them. In fact, a large part of discussion consists, in effect, of testing the implications of statements. If the discussion, furthermore, is about a text the group has read, any disagreement not resolvable by pointing to a certain sentence is almost certainly to be about inference. As the group collectively makes clear the implications, each member not only can see what he missed but also can perhaps see exactly what he failed to relate. Generally, by participating in the group action of putting two and two together, the individual learns how to do it by himself.

The small-group cross-commentary in the writing workshop permits writer and reader to approach inference-making from both points of view at once and thus to see how it is a factor of rhetoric — that is, of compositional decisions that determine what the reader deduces and to which the reader must become attuned. Thus the student-reader says what he understood the student-writer to mean so that when one makes the wrong inferences they can pinpoint together exactly what makes and breaks reading comprehension.

It is interesting that when textbook writers want to make sure that students understand what they are saying they add connectives and state their points explicitly, employing bold type, color, and italics if necessary, leaving nothing to chance, but when they want to test students, they understate. The central issue of all writing concerns how explicitly the writer should convey his ideas and how much he can assume that the reader will fill in. Judging this is no easy matter, for the writer has his own problems of egocentricity. My point is that the learner should, from the outset, be let in on this issue as both receiver and producer. How much the writer has to lead his reader by relating and drawing inferences and how much the reader should be expected to do these things on his own are central to an English curriculum. Comprehension must be approached simultaneously from both reader's and writer's viewpoints, in order to understand how misreading occurs and to realize that reader and writer share responsibility for preventing it. Thus writing is one of the main keys to reading comprehension, especially if it includes commentary by the learners on each other's papers.

A pupil undergoing a reading skills program would be justified in feeling that the writer is always right, for whenever the pupil misunderstands, it is always *his* fault. By implication, when it is the pupil's turn to be writer, the reader can jolly well watch out for himself; any failure of communication is due to poor reading comprehension. The right-or-wrong multiple choice answers unintentionally teach the pupil that only a certain predictable set of implications and conclusions can be drawn from a reading text. Throwing in what-do-*you*-think questions at the end of the exercise does not offset this. (Notoriously, on standardized comprehension tests, brighter students often make mistakes because they see inferences other than the conventional ones the egocentric test-maker had in mind.)

If the learner is given plenty of opportunity, very early, to render his ideas on paper and to have them reacted to by his fellows, he can exercise his ability to relate things in words (composition) and at the same time have the experience of being both understood and misunderstood in print. What did *he* leave out? What made *his* reader take a different direction from the one he was supposed to? The principle I am getting at here is that when *reader and writer can talk together* they can reach a much profounder understanding, than when dealing with printed texts, of what both composition and comprehension hinge on — the incompleteness of a text and how the writer must set cues and the reader look for them. When you become aware yourself of what you are putting in and leaving out, playing up and playing down, you understand that you must, when reading, fill out the text by relating items in it according to cues, the same cues that your own readers indicate you should put in your writing — such as main statements, paragraphing, transitions, emphasis, and subordination.

Interpretation. Here we are into the complex mental operation of putting together inferences and structural cues, and of noting tone, focus, and emphasis. It involves sensitivity to word choice, patterns, symmetry, and form. In dramatic activities, students become attuned to tone and style by imitating characters and playing roles. The structural cues and patterns of word sequences encountered in silent reading can often be translated into visual, auditory and spatial equivalents. An enormous amount of what students miss or misinterpret when reading can be attributed to a kind of childish passivity whereby printed words impose themselves with an authority that makes them seem either inevitable or arbitrary; the learner has no sense of the choices that have been made, whether these concern diction or sentence structure or overall organization. Through writing and discussion of writing he can become aware of how texts are created and therefore of the choices that have been made. In order to interpret well, he must confront choice himself. The inadequacy of trying to teach interpretation through practice reading lies in the fact that a finished text provides no sense of alternatives. Without a background of alternatives there is no way to discriminate what the author did from what he might have done. This is why texts remain featureless to some students and hence difficult to interpret. The writing program presented here is based on compositional choices that range from selection and shaping of the raw subject matter to alternative ways of phrasing part of a sentence. As the learner works constantly on focus and emphasis in his own composing process, he becomes an alert and perceptive interpreter of others' compositions.

Critical assessment. As regards literary form and whole modes of discourse such as poetry, fiction, drama, essay, autobiography, reportage, research, and argumentation, this principle of learning to read by writing is pursued right to the very foundations of this program. Students produce all the modes of discourse that they receive. By learning these modes from the inside, so to speak, as practitioners, they know how to read them. The writing assignments make possible a truly informed evaluation of reading texts, because particular composition-comprehension issues peculiar to each kind of discourse are examined closely under the dual writer-reader aspect of the writing workshop, where criteria for judging are generated.

Organization and Proportions of this Curriculum

This discussion of misconceptions in the language arts has been necessary to make clear what this book is about and what needs it is intended to fulfill. Because the presentation omits some things that readers may be looking for, and reclassifies certain other things, the opportunities for misinterpreting are rife. The emphasis on student language production would seem to cover only half of a total English curriculum, or — which is a more likely misinterpretation — to cover only some secondary activities that can be indulged in if there is time left over from building reading skills, doing analyses of grammar, rhetoric, and literature, and writing artificial papers about the reading. I have been arguing, of course, that the goals underlying these conventional activities can be more effectively and humanely furthered if some aspects of the total curriculum are reconceived and some proportions altered. In short, I know perfectly well that the recommendations in this book about speech, drama, writing, and some other activities will not be taken seriously so long as the misconceptions remain, for there will simply not be sufficient room for them in the total program. One purpose of this book, then, is to right an imbalance. But it is better to think of the curriculum unfolded herein as *replacing* than as *fitting into* the conventional curriculum.

What Is Excluded

While some omissions are founded on educational principles, others are founded on personal limitations. These need to be distinguished. That is, grammar study, pre-arranged literary analysis, rhetorical analysis of models, composition precepts, and reading comprehension exercises are omitted as either inappropriate for the basic, required English course or as misguided methods for arriving at worthwhile goals. During the K–6 years, attempts to "structure" the reading of literature by anything more than general growth seem pointless. The main thing is to give children a rich mixture of whatever literature they are able and eager to read, without schematizing it or thematizing it. A design for sequencing literature in the elementary years is therefore omitted on principle.

The omission, however, of reading lists for all years stems from my own lack of knowledge. I do not feel that I know enough about what reading materials are available and appropriate for different ages to delineate a continuous reading program as specifically as I have detailed other activities. As regards developmental reading suggestions, then, this book needs to be supplemented.

Because the interplay of reading and writing is very important, it is with regret, and not on principle, that I have dealt less with the content of reading, and offered titles only in a suggestive and illustrative way. I would certainly not have students read less than they customarily do; in fact, if relieved of the activities I have deliberately omitted, and if allowed to produce more language themselves, I feel sure that they will have more time and motivation to read. For the sake of righting a balance, I have stressed learning to read by talking and writing, but it is equally true that one learns to talk and write by reading. Without rich input, good production of language is impossible. Similarly, far from being underplayed, literature holds a central place in this program, though teachers should not expect to find the forms of it classified in familiar ways, or to encounter a "literature program" separate from other discourse and from the writing program. (My own background is chiefly in literature.)

What is Included in the Bias Toward Production

Given these reservations and the principles mentioned before, this book is intended to offer a far more nearly complete curriculum than the emphasis on language production might initially suggest. First, its bias is deemed proper because production is more difficult than reception. Second, when students act as audience for each other, they are receiving while they are producing. Third, examining their own productions and their responses to the reading will help them to understand language, rhetoric, semantics, and literary technique more effectively than will programmed presentations of these matters, the critical difference being in whether the matters come up in timely psychological connections or merely under prearranged logical headings. Fourth, many problems that *reveal themselves* in reading are less treatable there than in other activities, mainly of the productive sort. Fifth, the readings in both literature and nonliterature are distributed under categories that make it possible to integrate reading and writing but that also may give to teachers expecting these to be presented as separate programs a false impression that they are being slighted.

The Chapter Divisions of the Book

The last point concerning the organization of this book requires more explanation. The chapters in the Kindergarten to grade six portion are named for *activities,* which are established in elementary school and continue for the most part into secondary school. These activities are acting, conversing, playing language games, reading, and writing. The chapters are about procedures for teaching each activity. The order of chapters is not a learning order, since the activities are concurrent, but an order of exposition. The chapters on writing predominate, but *every writing assignment is a reading assignment,* because children read each other's writing. Laid over against the program of reading in published works, then, is a very full program of reading in pupil productions.

In the second half of the curriculum the reading of published works and the reading of student productions coincide more in time, because published selections are assigned when students are doing a corresponding kind of writing. The chapters covering grades seven to thirteen, consequently, are mostly named for the various sorts of dramatic, narrative, poetic, and expository discourse, to be both read and written. This manner of organizing was essential for showing the integration of activities and the interrelations of the accumulating orders of discourse, in accordance with the theories in *Teaching the Universe of Discourse.* But in cutting across some conventional categories of both teaching and literature, these units based on types of discourse may mislead some readers, especially since the illustrations of the types of discourse are all drawn from student writing.

PURPOSES OF SAMPLE STUDENT WRITING

These numerous student papers fulfill several functions at once. First, since student productions are the textbooks in this course, it seemed wise to give a generous sampling of what one is to teach from. I have exploited this sampling for occasions to talk to the teacher about an assortment of things, from spelling to poetic technique, that come up for learning in student productions. This is to demonstrate suggestively an important part of a student-centered approach to teaching aspects of English usually arranged and presented topically.

Second, at the same time that the student papers illustrate the writing assignments, they illustrate the kinds of discourse students will also be reading, because the writing assignments all correspond to authentic discourses produced outside of school. Had I chosen to exemplify kinds of discourse by drawing selections from professional writers, some readers might then even regard this curriculum as literature-centered, and its equal orientation toward reading would have been more evident. But the multiple purpose of the samples would then be lost. Instead, I have referred the reader to titles of works that are professional equivalents and can be assigned for reading. These works can be looked up elsewhere; student papers cannot be.

Again, I have not attempted to supply reading lists for all grades or to structure a strict sequence of reading. *But each kind of discourse is a reading unit despite the fact that it is illustrated with student writing.* A lot of the commentary with which I have surrounded the samples can illuminate, I hope, student problems of comprehension as well as composition, if the teacher will maintain a dual orientation toward reading and writing. This manner of integrating the two activities, however, is *not* to be confused with model writing, whereby a text is subjected to rhetorical analysis and students are then told to compose the way the old pro did. The approach in this program is indeed the opposite of model writing; though reading is meant to influence writing, students are never asked to follow precepts and prescriptions when comparing. Analyzing finished texts is generally unprofitable.

Third, the writing samples also show that young people can create, at their own level of maturity, the same sorts of discourse that they are asked to read, both literary and non-literary. My hope is to interest teachers in what students produce and to make a case that their own working life will be more interesting when they base their teaching on these productions. They will stay in close touch with the minds of learners and discover more clearly what teaching is really about than they ever can when textbooks come between them and their students. Perhaps these samples will give teachers a feeling of familiarity with the kinds of responses they will get from these assignments. My own commentaries about the samples by no means exhaust what is to be said about them. The reader's own responses may often be more helpful to him. It is only after he is steeped in his students' speech and writing that the teacher really begins to understand what he can do to facilitate their learning of language.

Fourth, emphasizing student writing more than reading, with each kind of discourse, is based on the conviction, already expressed, that creating these kinds of discourse is much harder than reading them and that, consequently, it raises more problems and more opportunities for learning. The main difference is in the myriad choices one makes in composing. The *process* of reading does not differ greatly from one kind of discourse to another. Shifting, for example, from first to third person discourse, or third to first, affects very little what the reader *does,* though it may affect very much how he feels. But for the writer this shift changes enormously what he does. As students attempt to create each new kind of discourse, they encounter new learning trials. In arraying the varieties of discourse across a curriculum, I have found it necessary to detail much more what is involved in producing these discourses than what is involved in reading them. I think one of the reasons writing is so often neglected or reduced to sterile exercises is that the problems of teaching the authentic forms of it as actually practiced in the world beyond the school have intimidated teachers. I hope very much that this emphasis on composition will give needed help to the teacher with these problems, and that the small-group cross-commentary recommended here will show teachers that it is possible to handle a very large volume of writing in effective ways.

Fifth, the samples are meant to unfold gradually the panorama of mental growth in language and the building of whole knowledge structures. Writing assignments are thinking tasks, the ones in fiction, poetry, and drama as well as the ones in reportage, research, and generalization. At bottom, both reading and writing are conceptual and cognitive more than they are linguistic, at least when one considers the learning problems they entail. Writing is the embodiment of mind in language. Far too long and far too much, we have thought of reading and writing as technical language matters, when the fact is that composing and comprehending are deep operations of mind and spirit having no necessary connection with the world of letters, or even with oral speech. To solve language learning problems in more than a shallow fashion, the basic approach, paradoxically, has to be extra-linguistic. This program is based on ways in which people process information from the ground up. Though ultimately verbal, the "writing assignments" are really external equivalents for processes of conceptualizing that go on inside us all the time, whether we verbalize or not. Above everything else, a course in one's native language should be about symbolizing experience at various abstraction levels and in various verbal modes. Thus the samples of writing done in response to the assignments of the program depict, however imperfectly, the transformation of sensory data, memories, and vicarious experience into generalizations and fictions, the building of higher abstractions on lower ones, the growth of thought.

Other Aspects of the Presentation

SEQUENCE

This conceptual growth is the developmental basis for sequence in this program. There is much more to say about the abstractive theory of growth underlying this program. Again, I refer the reader to *Teaching the Universe of Discourse*. But as regards the organization of the present book, it is necessary to point out that chapters are not placed in chronological order. Generally, the book traces a progression of activities spanning from kindergarten into college. And I have suggested many sub-sequences along the way. But except where indicated otherwise, the activities described in each chapter run concurrently with those of other chapters in the same grade block. In other words, though framed within a general progression, the chapters themselves are expository and do not follow consecutively as regards learning sequence, but wherever sequences seem indicated by experience or specific trials, I have said so within the chapters. To specify sequences more definitely than is warranted by current knowledge strikes me as poor policy. Thus a fair amount of room is left for local experimentation in the specific timing of recommended activities.

DISCLAIMER OF SCIENTIFIC EVIDENCE

And this is my cue to talk about ignorance, both my ignorance and that of the whole profession. Any book attempting what this book attempts is bound to be incomplete and tentative in some ways. No one knows very much yet about how children can best learn to produce and receive language or what the exact stages of an optimal learning sequence would be. Why, then, attempt to delineate a K–13 program of the language arts, student-centered or not? And what proof backs up the many assumptions and assertions made in this chapter and in those to follow.

The fact is that language instruction goes on and will go on, evidence or no evidence. On what proof rests the teaching that is taking place at this very moment? Precious little. Though many teaching materials claim to be backed by scientific evidence, in actuality there are very few classroom practices that have such backing. Educational research itself is notorious for both inadequate methodology and the verdict of "no significant difference" in its findings. The cry is for better methodology, but truly scientific experiments in a classroom may simply be impossible; controlling variable factors, without converting the school into an unreal laboratory, presents a virtually insoluble problem. And when university research in child development and learning theory is conducted rigorously enough to be reliable, the findings are usually trivial for education; when the findings result in a broad, suggestive and stimulating theory, it seldom gains acceptance beyond one "school of thought" in the discipline. Thus educators can choose B. F. Skinner's "reinforcement" theory of learning as embodied in programmed materials or the very different "discovery" theory as promulgated by Jerome Bruner and others. The theories of the leading figure in child development, Jean Piaget, are disputed; even when scholars and researchers embrace them, they acknowledge that the theories have not been empirically proven in accordance with rigorous research standards and may in fact not be susceptible to scientific verification at all. Though scientific research sometimes helps make decisions when all other things are equal, it has not so far furnished big answers and may never to able to do so.

In any case, of course, education cannot simply wait on research. Pending more knowledge, if it is to come, teachers have to go on making decisions about what to do and not to do, how to do, and when to do. We make the decisions on several bases — practical experience, intuition, definitions of goals, and theories about language, literature, and composition that do not purport to be pedagogical but are attractive for one reason or another. *Very few if any of the practices recommended in this book, or currently reigning in schools, have been scientifically proven superior to others.* By skillfully citing various studies and authorities, one could back up not only the program of this book but virtually any other as well. Research findings and scholarly theories exist to support a host of opposing practices. Therefore I have not attempted to justify the curriculum herein on those grounds. Though these citations might have had scholarly interest for some readers, the effort to document the assertions and practices contained in this book would obstruct considerably its practical purposes and yet prove nothing, though it would give the book a fashionable gloss. Two exceptions are the considerably negative findings about teaching grammar, which all linguists I know of seem to accept, and a general research indication that beginning reading fares best when launched by an early, systematic, and intensive instruction in sound-spelling correspondences, an indication reflected in all new reading programs I have seen that appeared for the first time in the 1960's, as well as in recent revisions of older programs.[3] As I stated earlier, what is determining teaching practices in English is not scientific evidence but historical accident, unproven conventions, abstractly logical conceptions of the field, and intellectually attractive theories about it that were not originally conceived for teaching purposes at all (like Aristotle's categories of language and literature, which were definitions for people who already know, not *pedagogical* concepts). Very little of current teaching is based on research evidence or scientific proof.

---

[3] Useful books for reading about these two research findings are, respectively: H. C. Meckel, "Research on Teaching Composition and Literature," in N. L. Gage (ed.), *Handbook of Research on Teaching* (Chicago: Rand-McNally, 1963), and Jeanne Chall, *Learning to Read: The Great Debate* (New York: McGraw-Hill, 1967).

PERSONAL QUALITY OF THIS BOOK

In line with the disclaimer of scientific evidence is the decision to write this book in the first person. Though I have drawn widely from sources other than my own teaching and experimental trials — from books, meetings, consultations with specialists, countless conversations with teachers, and classroom observation — the main presentation in this book is the work of one person, a fact that I feel the reader should be periodically reminded of, along with whatever hazards and advantages the fact implies. Impersonal, third-person style would undoubtedly have invested the curriculum with a more "professional" and authoritative aura, but would have profited no one. By speaking more personally, I have been able to indicate varying degrees of conjecture and conviction, or at least to help the reader retain a tentative spirit even when I myself may have begun to sound dogmatic. It is difficult to take a flexible stand constantly and at the same time offer definite recommendations. However definite I may sound later, let me say once and for all that *no one* knows the best way to teach English and that my recommendations are made in the belief that this kind of a curriculum offers the most likely way to find out.

I should also head off here the impression possibly created later that I do not realize how much many of the assignments included in this book are in common use today. Just as tedious as repeating "some teachers might like to try . . . ," is the constant sorting of what is standard practice from what is rare or unorthodox. Being more teacher than scholar, I have relied a lot on first-hand trials, in making recommendations, rather than relaying reports of trials third-hand to my readers. To those teachers who have conducted similar trials and who may have employed for some time practices and assignments recommended here, this book may very well be in some way indebted, and to those teachers it is meant in turn to lend support.

If the personal quailty of this book seems arrogant in view of the scope of the subject and the limited knowledge available to us about language learning, I can only repeat that this curriculum is a chart for exploration, not a panacea, and say further that in a time when some educators have declared the teaching of our native language a "national disaster area,"[4] when the drop-out rate is rising and correlates with reading failure, when college students cannot read and write acceptably after 12 or 13 years of language teaching, I would rather risk arrogance than indolence.

Claims for this Curriculum

If this curriculum is no more founded on research evidence than other programs, how does it recommend itself? First, a direct or naturalistic approach, whereby students learn essentially by doing and getting feedback on

[4] Manifesto of the Huntting Conference of Writers and Teachers, June, 1966.

what they have done, embodies the safest assumption about learning. Much general experience supports this assumption in other areas of life. If the goals of the curriculum are to help learners think, speak, listen, read, and write to the limit of their capacities, then the most reasonable premise is that they should do exactly those things. *Whoever assumes anything else bears the burden of proof.* Indirect methods need more justification. To assume that generalities about language aid speaking and writing, that concepts and categories of literature improve literary comprehension and appreciation, that rhetorical analysis and precepts teach composition is to assume also the burden of proof. (Although "practice reading" designed to build "reading skills" seems to fit the principle of learning by doing, this is an illusion caused by a misnomer. As I have tried to show, the skills that need practicing are general thinking skills that have no necessary connection with reading.) Learning by doing is not simple, however; practice of the target activities can be a sterile perseveration in old habits from which little is learned. This is why the small-group process of interacting and feeding back is essential. Also, the teacher must propose a variety of tasks that allow the learner gradually to expand his verbal and cognitive capacities across the whole spectrum of discourse.[5]

Second, since it is student-centered, this curriculum offers the best opportunity for teachers to learn what they need to know to teach well. We would know a lot more than we do now if textbooks had not been allowed to bypass the teacher and present over-structured materials to students. Learners have been transmitted to so much, and attended to so little, that after generations of teaching we are still very ignorant of what makes for good language learning. Fancily rationalized indirect approaches falsely centered on a "subject" have been given a long and humanly expensive trial that is merely perpetuated by most of the new materials for English. Virtually the whole national school system has been the lab for this bit of research. A student-centered curriculum, on the other hand, is a teacher-teaching curriculum.

[5] See also "Learning to Write by Writing," in *Teaching the Universe of Discourse.*

_____

_____

_____

Part One

KINDERGARTEN THROUGH

THIRD GRADE

As stated in the last chapter, the order of the ensuing chapters is not chronological. Each, rather, centers on a language activity that, throughout these years, weaves in and out of other, concurrent activities. Most chapters, however, contain suggestions for sequencing the work they treat. And certainly the introduction of dramatic activity, speech, and literacy instruction before reading and writing makes a certain rough developmental sense, if only as a reminder of what the latter are founded on. I begin with drama, which, taken in an everyday sense, is the wellspring of language activities. It is that preverbal way of understanding, expressing, and representing that underpins not only literacy but oral speech as well.

Chapter 3

Acting Out[1]

"Acting out" is meant to have a double sense — both "expressing oneself" and "filling out" a ready-made story. Thus dramatic activity breaks down into two main kinds — inventing one's own dramas and enacting the stories of others. Both are improvisational; the difference is in whether the pupil makes up the main situations and actions or merely makes up the details of word and movement that flesh out the borrowed story. In both cases there are "givens" — some concrete points of departure or stimulants that both suggest and limit the dramatic idea. Putting on a crown, for example, invests the pupil with kingship and thus provides a source of ideas at the same time it restricts the range of possibilities.

What we will be concerned with here is drama, not theater. Drama is the acting out of feeling and takes the point of view of the participant, for whom it exists; spectatorship is an irrelevance and, until a certain stage of development, a hindrance. Theater concerns performance before an audience, whose point of view is included and for whose benefit effects are calculated. Theater is a secondary effect of drama, an outgrowth appropriate only much later, after elementary school. ("Children's theater" — the performing of plays for children by adults — is a different matter; I am speaking here of what the *child* does.)

The purposes of acting out at this age are: (1) to promote *expression* of all kinds, movement and speech harmonizing and reinforcing each other; (2) to limber body, mind, and tongue; (3) to *begin* to single out the verbal mode from the others and thus to activate speech in particular; (4) to forge drama

[1] The suggestions for dramatic activities in this curriculum have been amalgamated from many sources, including some reading in the area, but mostly from talk with teachers, first-hand trials, observation of special classes, and personal participation in dramatic activities. I am particularly indebted to Douglas Barnes and Anthony Adams of England for discussions that helped sharpen some ideas in this and later chapters on drama.

into a learning instrument for continued use throughout all grades; (5) to make the first school experience with language fun and meaningful in children's terms; (6) to habituate pupils to working autonomously in small groups; (7) to further peer socialization of a learning sort not usually possible outside of school; (8) to gain intuitive understanding of style as voice, role, and stance, and of rhetoric as achieving effects on others; (9) to develop in the more familiar mode of dramatic play those characteristics necessary for the less familiar process of discussing, such as attending, responding, interacting, and turn taking; (10) to exercise and channel emotions.

Younger children seem to invent more freely and feel more comfortable when dressed in borrowed robes and otherwise stimulated from outside. Therefore I suggest that dramatic work begin within a framework of conventions of the sort children like — familiar props and settings, stock characters, and symbolic pieces of costume. They want to "be" an ogre, or a fox, or a fireman. They seem to have to be themselves by being something else. In primitive fashion, they wish to take on — to invest themselves with — the qualities and powers of some object, animal, or fantasy figure. Or they wish to test out adult roles symbolizing powers they wish to have. They work out realities through fantasies and thus prefer the symbolic and ritualistic to the actual and original. This does not mean, however, that play-acting conventional roles in borrowed situations is learning to be unoriginal and stereotyped. It is simply that small children require masking and stereotyping as conditions for being creative. They are less interested in what they are — weak, fearful, dependent — than in what they want to be — powerful, fearless, and self-providing. Sometimes they act out both roles at once by assigning to a toy or a puppet the weaker role and assuming the more powerful role themselves. Realistic role-playing, imitating various kinds of adults, may be both an assumption of power roles and also an effort to understand adults.

The various activities described in this chapter represent different ways in which children can be stimulated to act out. They take place concurrently in the curriculum but should be introduced, I suggest, in staggered fashion, following the order of their presentation in this section.

Play with Objects

The first dramatic activity is solitary play. At first, toys are the stuff of drama. For the small child, they automatically imply some words and deeds; he has a point of departure. Grasping a stuffed animal, a Dorothy of Oz puppet, a wand, a sword, a stethoscope; donning a feather, a cap, a belt, or a kerchief; standing before a moon or gate or counter — all these tell a child what to do, by evoking a host of associations in which the item is embedded in his mind. (Of course these associations vary somewhat among cultures; a southern Negro or a Harlem Puerto Rican may find meaning in different objects than a middle-class white.) The classroom of the early school years should contain many dolls, puppets, toys, bits of costume, props, and sets, some of which the children themselves could certainly make or bring from home. For all grades, rostrum blocks (small, portable platforms) can be important equipment, since they permit children to work with vertical space. All the teacher need do at first is to provide a time and climate — a period every day — for this activity, and to help the child come together with the right objects. The teacher's only role is to foster and facilitate, to sponsor a play process that takes care of itself if there are plenty of fantasy objects and playmates.

Experience suggests that a natural sequence is from playing alone to playing in pairs to playing in larger groups. Children will vary, of course, in their social growth. An advantage of acting out at school rather than at home is that individual play soon becomes group play as children become interested in and influenced by what others are doing. A child may begin by monologuing his fantasy as he plays, or by making up a conversation between two puppets, and end by playing doctor to several patients. Certain props, such as a pair of telephones or a cash register and money, naturally call for social play and promote interaction. Furthermore, chatting over a phone or buying and selling over a cash register promotes the specific social play of talking.

Movement to Sound

The second point of departure for dramatic activity is sound, including rhythm and music. As a stimulant, sound has some advantages over toys: it leaves more to the imagination, and it prompts the child to use his body more. Since the teacher makes the sounds while the children react, a controlled activity of the whole class becomes possible.

MATERIALS

As for most drama work, a large floor area is needed, preferably a special room set aside and equipped with piano, record player, and other sound instruments, but a classroom will do if the desks can be moved. Cafeterias and gymnasiums will also serve well but may not be available for enough hours of the day. For strong rhythms and tattoos, percussive instruments — drum, tambour, and tambourine — are needed; for arresting interjections, cymbals and gongs and whistles; for tones and note sequences, a pipe, flutaphone, or other simple wind instrument; for rhythm and melody combined, a piano or record player, if not both. Such equipment allows you to create a wide variety of stimuli which the children can translate into a correspondingly wide variety of body movements. Many sound-makers, of course, can be improvised from common materials like cans and sticks.

PROVIDING THE STIMULI

Diversifying the sound is important for perceptual discrimination, emotional range, and bodily articulation. Play with all the possibilities: shift the stress in rhythms, speed up and slow down tempo, raise and lower or shorten and lengthen the notes, widen and narrow the intervals between notes, make the sound skip or trip or drag or slide, alternate quiet and turbulence. Isolate one at a time the various dynamics of music — staccato, glissando, crescendo, accelerando, ritardando — then join them later into little sequences that create reaction sequences for the children. The ability to act with the body — to pretend to be a rabbit, or an old man climbing a snowy mountain — depends a lot on the repertory of body movements a child can bring into play. As in all other matters, access to a broad spectrum of possibilities directly increases one's creative invention. Enlarging the repertory, in this case, need not be done through systematic exercises; if frequent enough, diverse stimulation will eventually lead children to discover the repertory. Learning to discriminate various auditory dynamics will sensitize them to pattern and structure in other media, including literature. And running the sound spectrum is running the emotional gamut — exercising feeling in a controlled, communal fashion.

These movement-to-sound sessions, which I recommend two or three times a week for younger children, can progress from movement of the whole class in concert (not in unison) to individualized movement and thence to interaction of individuals. I suggest this because personal invention comes slowly, and because many children are shy of bodily exposure, which is minimized when everyone is doing the same sort of thing together. In so many areas, the individual develops by shedding his dependence on the group. But once he is able to express himself somewhat in his own way, the child can learn to interact with other individuals in a more truly social way than when he was merely a herd member. The following procedural suggestions reflect this progression. The three stages are for convenience, and I will not attempt to say how long a period of time they span.

1. *Herd movement.* Beat a strong, simple rhythm that children will take as a cue to either skip or run or tiptoe or slide-step, directing them only to "move the way the sound tells you to." They almost always fall into a circular movement, often following one or two leaders. Both this ritual and your control of the sound production impose order on this mass energy. Try out many of the variations mentioned above, gradually complicating the sound sequences by producing different dynamics in succession.

2. *Individual invention.* Begin to alternate these locomotions with movements-in-place by directing them sometimes to move each in a small area of his own, and occasionally even telling them not to move their feet. But first make the sound while they are resting and ask for ideas about how to move

to it. Let the class then try out these ideas one at a time in concert. The
question would be: What is happening? Who are you? Where are you? This
so that they can verbalize or demonstrate the movement idea in dramatic
terms. Then dispense with the practice of asking for ideas and just tell the
children to move in place as the sound tells them to. Those who still have
to imitate will do so, and those who are ready will invent. Occasionally
repeat a sound sequence and tell them to do a different movement to it than
they did the first time. Continue the sound variations. Encourage the children to imagine a setting, an action there, and a personage. Have them be
that person or thing doing that action in that place. Introduce more extended
pieces of music, especially music suggestive of mood and action. Let them
know that they may speak as they move. Let them move about, each in his
own area.

3. *Small-group interaction.* Place the class in pairs, trios, and quartets
(gradually increasing the number in each group) and direct them to share
space with their partners. The point is not to make children act or dance
together but simply to clump them for spontaneous interaction, to let them
influence each other in a group-defined space. They may move in place or
move about, but in either case they should remain in their areas. Recompose
the groups on each occasion. Continue sound variations.

These stages are cumulative; to enter a new stage is not to abandon previous ones but to add to them.

Pantomime

After movement to sound has become a regular activity and has reached
the stage of individual invention, those sessions may be combined with
pantomime. Instead of toys or sounds, the stimulant now is an *idea* of an
action.

EARLY PROCEDURES

Ask the children to pretend to be all sorts of things, at first selecting simple
acts: a giant striding, a hobbled prisoner, someone hauling on a rope or
pulling a sled, someone opening a door or window or umbrella or difficult
bottle, someone drinking something unpleasant or pleasant. Select actions
that will continue to enlarge the repertory of movements — bending, twisting, contracting, stretching — with all parts of the body, and in all directions. Tell them, for example, to imagine that they are standing close to a
building, facing it, and straining to look up at someone in a very high window; then the person at the window throws something out that curves slowly
over their head and falls behind them; they follow it with their eyes, bending
back until, as it nears the ground behind them, they finally have to twist

around. Or station them all along the walls and tell them to try to push the wall over in as many different ways as they can think of without *striking* the wall.

Once the children are familiar with the game, ask them for suggestions, and from then on merely relay individual ideas to the group, which can try them out one at a time in concert. Continue to select the ideas, however, both for muscular and dramatic variety. Then give them an action made up of a series of acts, such as entering a window, taking something from a chest, hiding it on one's person, and leaving. Narrate or read aloud a story step by step, and expressively, allowing the children time to pantomime each new act and to "be" each new character that comes up. All children play all roles, including objects. Next, help them make up together a verbal story that they can proceed to act out in the same step-by-step manner as you tell it over.

LATER PROCEDURES

As with movement to sound, progression at this point is two-fold — toward individuals doing different things at the same time and toward individuals forming small groups that also do different things at the same time. For the former, direct them each to think out and execute alone an action of his own, and then pass among them and try to guess what some of them are doing. You may provide very helpful feedback just by saying what you think you see. If this is different from what the child has in mind, you can then say also what he did or did not do that gave you your impression. That is enough for the child to learn from; there is no point in either gushing praise or correction of technique. In fact, if commenting seems to spoil the children's involvement or to create self-consciousness, it would be better to defer it to a later age.

As for the small-group work, this can begin after the pupils are well experienced with solo pantomimes and after they have achieved some social maturity. The class is divided into groups of three or four and directed to make up a short scene or to enact one from a story they know. Tell the groups to start thinking of an action that has parts for everyone and say that you will pass among them to help them organize. This planning talk itself is important as task-centered conversation, and, although you should help the groups to settle on an action and on the casting if they cannot resolve these matters, the ideal is self-organization as soon as they are able. (Many later assignments call for small-group projects, and the children should become habituated early to running their own groups.)

Remind the class that the game of pantomime is played without words and without props; their bodies alone tell the story. Objects are suggested by movement in feigned relation to them or can be played by other children (rock, tree, revolving door, etc.). When they have been through their pantomime once, they are directed to discuss making changes, to rotate roles, and to do it again. Both the revisions and the role reversals are important. Doing different versions of the same basic action is a form of composition and also draws some attention to technique (the commentary coming from the participants, not from the teacher or any other audience). Recasting roles establishes early the principle of flexibility and point of view in role playing and breaks the type-casting based on traits of personality and physical build that children by themselves are apt to institute. Again, the main value is in the acting itself and in the pupil discussion entailed by it; the teacher does not even hint that one group should perform while the others watch. When children think of this, it is usually because they got the idea from adults.

Relation of Physical Movement to Language

Though movement to sound and pantomime do not seem at first glance to relate directly to the development of speech, they in fact lay an important base for it. For small children, speech is only one physical activity among others (as indeed it really is), and not a preferred one. As a specialized mode of communication and expression, speech only gradually singles itself out from movement and gesture until, in print, it becomes totally separate. For children generally — and boys especially — speech *accompanies* other action and justifies itself only when it can do what other actions cannot. Movement to sound and pantomime permit the child both to develop his powers of nonverbal modes of expression and to run up against their limitations. Too often schools attempt to make speech abruptly supplant these modes, forcing the child off native ground onto strange territory. The fact is that the two realms blend without a seam, and the nonverbal expression can provide the best pathway to speech development. The sheer socialization of school helps to promote speech — or can, if the activities permit socializing. The teacher can insure that speech grows out of physical play and bodily movement by extending nonverbal expression into the verbal. More concretely, the teacher orchestrates play with objects, movement to sound, and pantomime into full-blown improvisation, which in this curriculum will be a major method of learning to use language.

Combining Movement and Speech

ENACTING READY-MADE STORIES

When a teacher feels that his pupils are ready, he may combine the three foregoing activities by breaking the class into groups and directing the groups to act out a short familiar story with speech and movement. The assignment is broached before the whole class, and the children are asked to nominate stories. They are to understand that they will take the main action of the story and do it in their own way, filling it in, making up the details and dialogue, or using details and dialogue that they remember. It should be clear that they will improvise, not learn their parts. They should feel free to change and add things. The story could be one they have read together, one the teacher has read, one a pupil has written or dictated, or one that all the children know anyway. The teacher moderates the selecting of a story or scene and leads preparatory discussion in which the story is recalled if necessary and decisions are made about: the number of parts, which props if any are needed, whether some inanimate things should be played by people, which roles need to be played by boys and which by girls, whether musical or rhythmic accompaniment is wanted, and whether individual or choral singing seems called for (as in enacting some story songs).

Another possibility is to enact a story just after reading it. This strengthens two of the aims of drama — to tie the printed word to the physical world of behavior, and to sharpen reading comprehension by translating the subject into another medium. For example, during the preparatory discussion, the teacher would have the children refer to the book when making decisions about how to do the story.

The reason for holding all groups at first to the same story is that preparatory discussion is then class-wide and led by the teacher. This discussion can become the model for small-group procedure when several groups are going to act out different stories and hence must organize themselves more on their own. After a certain amount of experience with enacting, the groups might indeed select different stories. If, in the whole-class nominating session, several factions feel strongly about different choices, they can become the nuclei of groups to act out those choices. The class would then break up, and some time would be allowed for small-group planning with the help of the teacher when he comes around. Whether doing the same or different stories, the groups proceed as they did with pantomime: they act out the story with one cast, discuss that version, rotate roles, and do further versions.

FREE IMPROVISATION

The "minimal situation." A free improvisation is based on a story idea, the least elaborated, most summarized statement of character and event that will give the players the feeling of having enough to go on. This idea may be called the "minimal situation." The difference between enactment and improvisation is necessarily a matter of degree only, since there are always some "givens," suggestive ideas that are the starting point for acting out. In improvising, one makes up more of the story as he goes along; when enacting, one has more details specified in advance. Since small children's inventions are drawn so much from familiar stories anyway, the distinction breaks down even more at this age. Nevertheless, launching the children from a minimal situation rather than from a known story does place them farther along the way toward individual creativity.

Minimal situations might come from a number of sources — the children's own captioned drawings, ideas suggested in class, local events, and common real-life circumstances. In regard to the last, a first-grade teacher[2] and I tried such situations as: two teachers chatting during a coffee break; a parent and teacher having a conference about a pupil; two brothers arguing; and several other family scenes. Despite a number of mistakes I made due to my ignorance at the time, these trials were successful enough to suggest that under the right circumstances children can work well with realistic minimal situations. The procedure would be to select a situation in preliminary class discussion, then to break into groups and improvise it with the usual rotation of roles. The teacher passes among the groups to offer an occasional suggestion when a group seems to need more priming.

Conclusions from some trials. I will pass along a little more of the experience of the trials just referred to, pointing out at the same time that what I learned the hard way is well corroborated in books by drama specialists.[3] I will let my trials stand as typical of what would probably happen to any well intentioned but not well informed teacher who should blunder into improvisations too soon (for himself and for the pupils). (Often in this book, my advice will be not to do what I did.)

When the children were asked who wanted to be so and so, hands waved furiously, but once they were front and center many children became blanks (which never seems to happen when playing unwitnessed). They wanted to "be" but did not know what to do. Masking themselves behind puppets and costumes helped, but even then the boys resorted to an embarrassed kind of physical banging, and both boys and girls uncreatively repeated action or became "silly." If the group was as large as four or five, the participants left the initiative to others, or in effect dropped out and stared or smiled at the audience. Good movements came only when an unusually poised child — almost always a girl — could stay in role and invent ways to stimulate fellow actors. The teacher was held in tension between wanting to maintain a free climate and feeling that the unnatural silliness and physical violence was a perversion of the whole activity. The children asked for time to work out the main story idea or situation before improvising, but such planning did not usually reassure them or help them to maintain involvement with the action rather than with the audience.

My conclusion was that the spontaneous play process should not be tampered with by having it witnessed. Most children of this age are not really

[2] My thanks to Miss Mena Topjian of the Franklin Elementary School in Lexington, Massachusetts.

[3] For such a book, by perhaps the most important pioneer in this area, see Peter Slade, *An Introduction to Child Drama* (London: University of London Press) a book I read only in the course of revising this book, but which accords rather well with most recommendations made here. To find more detail on method and rationale, teachers should become familiar with Slade's work.

interested in performing before others, do not do it well, and become considerably inhibited when asked to do so. The name of the game changes. *They transfer their involvement with the original objects or people to the audience, and yet they do not allow for that audience.* That is, they become self-conscious and tongue-tied, and at the same time they speak too low, unwittingly hide some of their action, and do mysterious things that only their partners understand.

If a puppet theater is available, as it should be, one or two pupils may ask for an audience; the teacher could then watch and let other children join her as they want. This is an easy kind of first audience because the puppets are the focus, and the puppeteers, feeling hidden, can act through them. They will use their voices more boldly because they think of them as issuing from the puppets. (The child's feeling of identity with the puppets is especially strong when he has made them himself.) Despite the common belief that small children are born show-offs and have unfettered imaginations, I think the fact is that premature performing can spoil the very important evolution of play into other dramatic activities. Furthermore, first grade is too early for free improvisation, which should be gently and thoroughly led up to. A slow growth through the activities I have described, fostered by a watchful but patient teacher, will promote the most effective learning in drama.

Chapter 4

Speaking Up

Rationale

THE NEED FOR SCHOOL TALK

To develop their language powers the simple fact is that children must talk a lot. They must *use* language and use it an enormous amount. Learning to read and write will depend in large measure on the growth of oral speech. Like dramatic play, conversing is something the child does before he comes to school, a fact that implies two things. First, it is something that the school can build on from the outset, a familiar medium to extend and use as a substratum for reading, writing, and thinking. Second, since children learn to talk out of school, their talk within school should provide additional learning not easily acquired anywhere else.

School should be a place where children talk at least as much as outside, for fostering speech is the business of the language classroom. Too often there is the hidden inscription above the door that says, "Abandon all speech ye who enter here." The kids get the message. "Speech is not wanted (that is for another time and place). Here you sit quietly and don't socialize; paper work is what they care about in school except when they want you to read aloud or answer a question. Talking to other children is bad behavior." So long as talking is excluded from the curriculum and not utilized within it, peer conversation can only appear as a disciplinary problem. As the last section was concerned with harnessing play for learning purposes, this section is concerned with formalizing peer talk sufficiently to provide learning of a sort that seldom occurs in casual out-of-school conversation.

45

"Class Discussion" and Small-Group Discussion

What I will recommend here has little to do with what is generally called "class discussion," which is rarely a real discussion. Although class-wide talk is often helpful or necessary, it cannot *teach* discussion; it can only *benefit* from discussion's having been learned some other way. So far as I can tell, the only way is pupil-to-pupil talk in small groups of no more than six. The sheer size of "class discussion" precludes a high enough degree of attention, participation, and interaction — essential qualities of discussion. The teacher has to talk too much to maintain continuity, and invariably does talk too much. He resorts to prompting by questions, and except for occasional solos by a loquacious few, the children play the very restricted role of answering these questions. As vocal exchange, such a process is severely limited. The heart of discussing is *expatiation*, picking up ideas and developing them; corroborating, qualifying, and challenging; building on and varying each other's sentences, statements, and images. Questioning is a very important part, but only a part, and should arise out of exchanges among students themselves, so that they learn to pose as well as answer questions. For his part, the teacher should be relieved from the exhausting, semi-hysterical business of emceeing.

Serial exchanges between teacher and pupil A, pupil B, etc. may serve some other purposes such as checking information or soliciting scattered opinions, but children should never be allowed to think that this is discussion. Discussion is a process of amending, appending, diverging, converging, elaborating, summarizing, and many other things. Most of all, it is an external social process that each member gradually internalizes as a personal thought process: he begins to think in the ways his group talks. Not only does he take unto himself the vocabulary, usage, and syntax of others and synthesize new creations out of their various styles, points of view, and attitudes; he also structures his thinking into mental operations resembling the operations of the group interactions. If the group amends, challenges, elaborates, and qualifies together, each member begins to do so alone in his inner speech. This is not a proven point, but I believe that general experience bears it out. The teacher's job is to establish the forms of discussion that, when internalized by individuals, will most enhance the growth of thought and speech.[1]

Relation of Drama to Discussion

Dramatic interaction will further the goal of developing thought and speech considerably because it promotes the diverse forms of expatiation. Indeed, therein lies much of the ultimate value of improvisation. Using the words of others as cues for one's own response is the heart of both improvisation and discussion. But discussion differs from drama in valuable ways

[1] The full theory of internalization of speech is set forth in "Drama: What Is Happening," in *Teaching the Universe of Discourse.*

that enable it to carry on where drama leaves off. It is more abstract and more verbal. Relatively, it immobilizes the body and detaches itself from things. The vocal mode is singled out. Emphasis is more on the content of speech than on speech as a behavior. Appeal is more to reason than to emotion. But none of these differences represents a clean break; in fact, discussion retains a dramatic underpinning that provides continuity from one to the other and should never be lost. Any experienced discussant acknowledges the big part that "group dynamics" plays in discussion, however intellectual the subject. What the teacher should keep in mind is this whole relation of drama to discussion and its importance for an articulated curriculum.

STATUS OF DISCUSSION IN THE CURRICULUM

Peer discussions in small groups should be a staple learning activity for all grades, alloted a large amount of time in the curriculum, and conducted with the same regularity and sense of method that, for example, the traditional reading groups are accorded during these early years. I am aware that a number of teachers do from time to time permit children to talk about something in separate groups. But discussions need to be carried out with frequency, regularity, and method. Usually teachers feel that they are indulging the children in a side activity, and do not bring to it nearly the conviction and professional confidence that they do to reading and other activities. The lack of conviction and professional confidence derives directly from lack of experience and method. Too few teachers feel that they know how to manage small-group discussion, and indeed there has not been much precedent or support for it.

What I would like to do here is to make small-group discussion respectable and show that it can have method. This will not be easy because it has been explored very little as a serious, staple activity. And it does not, like writing, break down into a variety of specific assignments; it is a basic process that grows gradually over the years in ways not easy to define, at least not yet. Given these difficulties, I will approach the matter by describing some trials that I know about, and by extrapolating this experience into guidelines for further experimentation.

Unstructured Discussion

ACCOUNT OF SOME TRIALS

I asked the teachers of two classes combining second- and third-graders (called the Beta team)[2] to break their two classes into heterogeneous groups

---

[2] At the Franklin Elementary School in Lexington, Massachusetts. I am indebted to the teachers, Mayrae Means and Charles Mitsakos, who were assisted by a student teacher, Tina Feldman.

of three and four and direct them to discuss some magazine photographs for five to ten minutes in different parts of the same room at the same time. We provided no adult leadership after the general directions were given to the whole class. No pupil leader was appointed, but one often emerged. After two rounds of small-group discussions of the photographs, which were deemed provocative for children, the teachers felt that the subject was too open and the children did not have enough to go on. So they directed them first to jot down notes about the photographs first, as demonstrated on the chalkboard, and then to use these as a basis for talk. Still there was too little interaction. Often the children made a few remarks on the photo, then talked of other things or gazed away. Some children would not talk to certain others, presumably for personal reasons. Next, the groups were asked to make up a story about the picture. One teacher described the results as "awful," another as "the best yet" (contradictions spice life for the researcher), but the one had hoped for single, unified narrative and the other had settled for description. Results were indeed mixed: often the stories were good, often they were flatly descriptive of the photo; some children inferred motives and circumstances, some elaborated a single idea, some gave several interpretations.

We considered what might precede and follow the group discussion. Whereas our question initially was, "What do children really want to talk about?" it later became, "Why do they talk when they do? In what circumstances?" For children to discuss photographs and live animals (another subject we used) seemed somehow arbitrary and unmotivated, even though we knew they were in some sense interested by these subjects. The assignment came from nowhere and went nowhere. We began to feel that the children needed the talk to produce something, to be a means toward some other end. Thus we considered talk centered on a task, like making a magnet — planning talk, problem-solving talk. The idea was for some of their action to engender the task and for the talk, in turn, to make possible other action. We replaced isolated talk for its own sake with purposeful talk continuous with other tasks.

This change led to two major procedures — setting a larger goal that would *require* talk along with a series of other activities, and having a scribe take notes of the talk to use in panel discussions. The following example will illustrate both procedures. The process evolved in a groping fashion from the imaginative efforts of the participating teachers to solve the problems raised above. I offer the process here as a teaching method that can be used many times with the same children but with different subjects. I would, however, expect other teachers to want to ring variations on it.

The participating teachers first learned from the children what would be for them a "burning issue" to deal with practically. The petty stealing of pencils, rulers, and erasers turned out to be such an issue. Feelings ran very high — higher than most adults would ever have foreseen — about this ubiquitous daily problem that involved every child in the classes. The children were told that they could try to solve the problem of stealing and each class was broken into eight or nine groups of three members each (four being considered a bad number because of the tendency to pair off). The function of the talk was to produce some ideas about how stealing occurs and what might be done about it that could then be relayed to the whole class. The groups were given five to ten minutes. In each group a scribe was appointed to record whatever ideas occurred. The groups were told in advance that the scribes would later form a panel so that ideas from all the groups could be pooled. Armed with their notes (brief, to be sure) the eight or nine scribes met as panelists before the rest of the class. Actually, these meetings were not so much true panels as series of reports, but the remarks of the scribes could be compared for similarities and differences, and some interaction did take place among panelists. Afterwards, the teacher asked the rest of the class to comment on the panel. Some disagreement came out as well as an occasional new idea.

At this point each of the two classes decided on a second phase of action: one was to make posters about stealing, and the other to prepare a publication about it. The class doing the publication brainstormed in the small groups for five minutes about items that might go in it, then looked these ideas over. After scribes reported these ideas at the panel, the whole class refined and pared them down to eight items: a report of a survey about sentiments on stealing, ads, lost-and-founds, tall-tales about what happens to stealers, "wanted" pictures of those who steal, what-to-do-when-you-find-something, what-to-do-if-you-don't-want-something-stolen, and an invitation to form a club. Some children were to explain the campaign to other classes to whom the publication was to be distributed. Two children wrote the survey questionnaire and two others compiled it with the teacher. Participation in the brainstorming was total, and every child wrote an article, even those who were hitherto "non-writers." The articles were read in the small groups, the good but not necessarily best ideas were singled out in discussion, and the papers were revised. Thus, through rewriting and proofreading in the groups, final copy was produced. Then each group discussed these and selected one for the publication, which was called *Beta-Gram* and is reproduced on page 140. After distributing the posters and *Beta-Grams* to other classrooms, the participating children went in pairs to garner reactions to their ways of dealing with stealing. The small groups discussed these reactions, and their scribes compared notes at a panel that stimulated a final class discussion about actually implementing a campaign in the school.

Probably no adult of sound mind would have thought up in advance such an intricate rigamarole. Being of sound mind myself, I certainly did not offer it as an experimental idea to the participating teachers. They had the courage to pursue my bare notion of small-group discussion wherever it needed to go, the wit to improvise and orchestrate activities, and the sensitivity to play by ear with the children. The process just described, which spread over two or three weeks, did not go off without a hitch, but the problems were those of a first trial, when teachers did not know what the next phase was to be. Certainly this air of adventure and freedom accounted for a lot of excitement and involvement, but, as the teachers felt, some things such as the assemblage of *Beta-Gram* and the visiting of other classes was hasty and sloppy. One visiting educator was concerned about how a scribe should be chosen and his role explained, and also whether he imposes a list format on his group discussion. To answer the last question first, I think he does impose a list format in some measure, but enumeration is a primary form taken by any young children's discussion anyway, one which they need in the earliest stages of learning to converse. Other forms of discussion, of course, should grow from it, as I shall try to sketch later. In the experiments the scribe was chosen first by the teacher but later ones were volunteers. The first time the process is run through, the teacher should probably choose a more verbally able child, but on other occasions the role should be rotated automatically.

Conclusions from the Trials

As one of the teachers said, the project may not prevent stealing, but it works well for language development. For motivating pupils to speak and write, and to do so in real and meaningful ways, it seems indeed very successful. The teachers felt that the pupils came alive and became involved in language as they never had before. Four features of the process account for this, I believe, and would be desirable traits of other speaking and writing assignments for this age. (1) Though paramount to the teachers, speech was, in the pupils' eyes, incidental to the goal of social action; it was a means to a real-life end, solving the problem of stealing. (2) The various speaking and writing tasks formed a long-range continuity that imparted practical sense to each task and accumulated momentum as one led into the next. (3) Pupils were allowed to socialize, make decisions with peers, and exercise some independence as groups. (4) The high motivation cut out distraction and impelled the children to interact within their groups. Obviously, other teachers using the process should keep the spirit of it and never formularize it. For the hardships of playing somewhat by ear they will be rewarded by keen response and a sense of progress.

These trials, especially the picture discussions, undoubtedly resemble some that other teachers have conducted. They may stand as generally representative of what happens when second- and third-graders are asked to talk in small groups about a preselected topic without adult leadership and without special training in the art of discussing. Assuming a goal of autonomous peer discussion, my approach was to start with the most open situation and then to note where structure was needed. I drew these conclusions: (1) Unstructured, leaderless discussion needs to be embedded within a larger project that entails the discussion, thereby giving it a practical function and an end beyond itself; (2) even such task-oriented discussion would benefit considerably from prior training under adult leadership. In other words, the key issues are the motive to talk and the learning of good talking habits. These habits concern qualities mentioned earlier — participation, attention, and interaction — none of which are very easy for children who are still learning to socialize and to focus. To some extent, high motivation itself reduces these problems, but the natural egocentricity of their age may still cause children to listen only to themselves and to make irrelevantly subjective remarks. Although the stealing project showed that children can talk effectively on their own, and want to, I felt convinced that specific training in small-group discussion should provide a model and basic experience that pupils could transfer to other discussions and that would enable them to participate most advantageously in groups not led by the teacher.

Drawing on the experience of these trials, of leading small-group discussions in my own secondary classes, and of participating in adult "awareness" groups, I settled on a notion of training whereby the teacher would lead one group at a time — directing the group process, not joining in the discussion of the subject — and would establish at the outset a few common-sense principles about listening, responding, and sticking to the subject.

Structured Discussion — "Grouptalk"

At this point I came upon the work of Dr. Babette Whipple, who had been doing research among fifth-graders with just such a training, which she called, as a kind of trademark, Grouptalk. This research, more extensive and systematic than my own, was first conducted under the auspices of the Elementary Social Studies Project of Educational Services Inc., at a Newton (Massachusetts) public school, and is being continued at the same school under the Newton school system. She reports a very enthusiastic response from children and a high degree of success. She and teachers under her guidance are currently trying Grouptalk with children of lower grades, including second, the method being adaptable to all ages. Since her Grouptalk illustrates essentially the kind of training method I have in mind, and has undergone a substantial trial, I will give an account of it here.

DEFINITION AND PROCEDURE

In a monograph entitled *The Grouptalk*, Dr. Whipple has defined Grouptalk as

> A formal discussion of a question by a small group and a leader following the specific rules that all members of the group contribute relevantly to the discussion and that all help in the effort to summarize it.[3]

[3] Occasional Paper Number Ten, Educational Development Center, Cambridge, Mass., 1967, obtainable by writing to EDC, 44a Brattle St., Cambridge, Mass. Undoubtedly, she will produce further reports as she continues to explore Grouptalk.

"Formal" refers to the governing influence of the rules, not to the atmosphere, which is relaxed and lively. "Small" means three to six. The group is heterogenously composed. "Implicit in the definition are three primary functions of a leader: (1) to direct strategy, (2) to keep the group relevant, (3) to see that summary is achieved." The group shares with the leader the responsibility for calling attention to departures from the rules, and, by this means, "the teacher prepares for a gradual transfer of leadership to a student." Dr. Whipple stresses the point that the teacher concerns himself with group process, not with content or information. He is teaching children *"how* to think, not *what* to think."[4] The topic, always worded as a question, may be chosen by the teacher or suggested by the children. It is written on a chalkboard so that it can be read aloud and referred to. Ideally, the group meets in a separate room, for 30 to 45 minutes, and has the use of a tape recorder.

The rules are printed on cards, and are read and paraphrased by individuals during the first few sessions. As most recently formulated by Dr. Whipple, they are:

Rule 1: Understand. Everyone thinks about the meaning of the question before the group tries to answer it.

Rule 2: Contribute. Everyone tries to answer the question.

Rule 3: Listen. Everyone tries to understand what is said so that he can respond.

Rule 4: Be Relevant. Everyone keeps to the point.

Rule 5: Sum up. Everyone tries to state the main point of the discussion.[5]

As I see it, Rules 2, 3, and 4 merely crystalize, as concepts for the child, certain common-sense principles. Perhaps the same is true for Rules 1 and 5, but Rule 1 is also a more specific bit of method for getting children to define key words and for insuring that discussants are assuming the same meanings in common. (Do they agree to include birds and fish in the meaning of "animals"?) And the summary (Rule 5), which is usually initiated by the teacher after a certain time has elapsed, is also designed to elicit a special activity, selective recall.

Conditions for Similar Small-Group Discussion

Dr. Whipple has developed Grouptalk under research conditions that do not characterize the normal teaching situation. The group has been taken

---

[4] These quotations are from pages 8 and 9 of *The Grouptalk.*
[5] I am indebted to Dr. Whipple for this provisional reformulation and for criticizing this portion of the manuscript dealing with small-group discussion.

aside to a separate room while the regular teacher remains in charge of the rest of the class. Regular teachers who have led Grouptalk have been trained to do so by participating themselves in Grouptalk led by Dr. Whipple. And the children's sessions have been taped and played back to them immediately afterwards so that they can become more aware of the way they interact. Children love to hear themselves, and through playback they become aware of how they converse and of how to improve. Experimenting teachers, moreover, can gain skills by analyzing the tapes later. In short, the rather ideal conditions included a separate room facilitating concentration and recording, a separate teacher, in-service training, and a generous time allowance of 30 to 45 minutes per group. Can the school approximate these conditions?

First of all, the essentials of Grouptalk or of any other small-group discussion do not require all of these conditions. Though valuable, playback is not necessary.[6] Eliminating it would cut the duration of sessions in half and reduce the importance of a separate room and separate teacher. A teacher can take one group at a time into the corner of the classroom while the rest of the pupils are doing something else, as is the practice now for reading groups. The presence of a student aide or a student teacher would of course solve the problem more gracefully. As for in-service training, virtually any important innovation in the curriculum calls for some new knowledge or skill on the part of the teacher, as was certainly the case in revisions of the teaching of mathematics and the physical sciences. Until schools of education provide direct experience with small-group process, the experience will have to be gained in-service. Two able teachers who, at my suggestion, tried Grouptalk without special training[7] certainly achieved worthwhile results from the beginning and quickly learned a lot about the technique from criticizing the first few sessions, which were taped, but I am sure that Dr. Whipple is right to insist on special teacher training for the best results.

And this is my second point about achieving ideal conditions: the effort should be made. Makeshift is always possible but not always efficient. Dispensing with playback, for example, may save time but may equally well protract the learning period by rendering the whole process less effective, so that the moment when pupils can take over leadership of the group is deferred longer then if playback were allowed. The problems of small-group discussion can be solved in better ways than by making shift — by reconceiving uses of time, space, and staff. When educators become convinced that a certain kind of instruction is vital, they find the means. The power of verbal interaction to develop thought and speech is so important that I would go so far as to say that it obliges every school to make room for it, whatever the effort requires. Educational needs should dictate routines and facilities, not merely conform to them.

---

[6] In recent correspondence, she has informed me that "the current definition of Grouptalk incorporates the tape recorder, which is no longer considered optional." Thus discussion of playback becomes a key feature.

[7] Frank Lyman and Kayda Cushman.

Grouptalk is only illustrative. For developing verbal interaction in a way not necessarily practiced by children outside of school, it offers the best method I have heard of to date, but it may not be the only method or the best. I endorse it heartily, but I have given an account of it here mainly because it helps to fasten down my main concept of training in small-group discussion and exemplifies the problems entailed. Henceforth "small-group discussion" will refer broadly to any peer discussion with six members or less, whether led by the teacher or not. The following pages represent my own thinking on the matter, but I gratefully acknowledge the influence of Dr. Whipple's research.

Small-Group Discussion Led by a Teacher

Since not enough experimentation has been done to differentiate methods for K–3 from methods for 4–6, these recommendations will stand generally for all of elementary school, and even for later years, although I will try to sketch, roughly, some lines of sequence. The more detailed the suggestions, the more tentative they must be. But I can advance the general idea rather confidently.

Two kinds of small-group discussion are set in motion. One is of the problem-centered or task-oriented sort, embedded in a project, not led by the teacher. Probably, but not necessarily, these groups discuss at the same time in different parts of the room, and their membership will vary with the occasion. The other kind of discussion, led by the teacher for the purpose of teaching discussion itself, often has a nonfunctional topic but one that is of great interest to the children. Of necessity, only one group discusses at a time, and membership will remain constant over long periods of time. The two sorts of discussion take place concurrently, the first being employed on many occasions in connection with acting, writing, and reading, and the second being scheduled regularly, at least once a week for each group. The assumption is that what is learned in discussions structured by the teacher will transfer to the autonomous, temporary groups. Since the operation of these self-governing groups depends on what pupils bring to them, and since a lot of what they bring will depend in turn on the operation of teacher-led groups, I will concentrate on the latter. Because of its spontaneous nature, the talk of working parties cannot be separately dealt with here. What happens in these groups will be determined by the kind of task, as well as by the habits acquired from training.

CONDITIONS FOR CONCENTRATION

For children of the K–3 age the two new and difficult things to learn will be: concentrating on a single subject, which is a matter of focal attention, and adapting their talk to interlocutors, which means abandoning egocentric chatter and allowing for a listener. Attunement to the group is, in short, the main quality. And the main problem is distraction, whether it comes from outside the group, from private associations of ideas, or from entanglements of personalities. So at first, the teacher exerts an influence against distraction and for concentration.

This need not and should not be done in a disciplinary way. Physical distraction from outside the group should be minimized by taking the group aside to a quiet corner of the room (carpets help), preferably partitioned off, or ideally, to another room, while the rest of the class is doing something else. Like the reading group, the talking group is seated in a circle, perhaps around a table. A specific visual focus may help: write the subject on a placard or chalkboard close by, or place the picture or object within easy view. I have noticed, however, that first-graders cannot look at an object and talk about it at the same time; they seem to need to alternate. This needs more experimentation. I am not sure at just what stage of maturation children can do both at once and when they may have to look first and talk later, away from the object. In any case, placing the written topic before them does help them to focus and to stay on the subject. But, most of all, it is motivation that overcomes distraction. Interacting and sticking to the subject depend enormously on the interest of the topic.

SIZE AND MEMBERSHIP OF GROUPS

The size of the group should probably not exceed six, simply because participation and interaction drop below a desirable level in groups of larger numbers. Research in group process, mostly with adult subjects indicates that five is an ideal number. If the group is smaller, the cross-stimulation is likely to be insufficient for nonfunctional discussion. Small, even-numbered groups tend to split in two, and trios tend to produce a situation of two against one. The number may quite possibly need to change with maturation, discussion experience, and the degree of teacher direction or non-direction. The children should stay in the same groups for weeks or months so that trust, understanding, and a sense of group identity can build up. Shifting individuals from group to group sets off a lot of emotional static, and the new group regards the individual as an intruder. If changes are to be made, it is better to recompose all the groups completely. For the sake of an enriching variety and the development of communication skill, groups should comprise *differences* — of dialect, sex, socioeconomic status, verbal ability, intelligence, and so on. Speech develops best when one has to talk to people *unlike* oneself, because overcoming differences requires more clarifying and explaining. This principle is important enough to warrant heterogeneous composition of classes themselves (from which homogeneous sub-groupings can be formed for other purposes). I think that the teacher should compose the groups, but an argument can be made for sometimes letting pupils choose whom they are to be with. This matter needs trial and would depend perhaps on age and the makeup of the whole class.

GROUND RULES

I do not think that discussion rules are the same for all ages or that they are always necessary. Their purpose is to induce certain speaking habits, such as listening and responding, and certain conceptual habits, such as defining and summarizing. Once the habits have been formed, the rules can be dropped. Rules about participating, listening, and sticking to the subject are appropriate for beginners only and would be discontinued once children learned to do these things (well before fifth grade if they began in first). On the other hand, a rule about summarizing may not have much interest or meaning for children before third grade. Small children like rules and rituals, but I think this aspect should be emphasized no more than is necessary to induce the habits.

The initial presentation of rules on cards is probably a good idea; Dr. Whipple may well be right in maintaining that reading aloud and talking about rules help children to *conceptualize* the behavior expected of them, which in turn helps them to achieve the behavior. But I think the main thing that shapes small-group process is adult direction and the children's imitation of it. Children's departures from the rules will have more to do with distraction, impulsivity, poor motivation, and egocentricity than with ignorance of common-sense discussion principles, and the teacher would do better to gain insight into these causes, as he will through experience, than to harp on the rules.

One rule that I suggest for beginners concerns taking turns. The understanding should be that a discussant who wants to talk does not raise his hand; his cue to speak is someone else's stopping. One of the main problems of teacher-led discussion is that children tend to talk to the teacher instead of to each other. If the teacher calls on children who raise their hands, he inevitably becomes the focus of the group, which is difficult to avoid in any case, since he is being directive in other ways. A rule about hearing out the last speaker and then starting to speak without signalling will help children to focus on each other and reinforce the rule about listening.

Finally, it may well be true that a very experienced teacher need not set up rules at all but can let the children generate their own as they criticize the playback of their discussions during early sessions.

GENERAL ROLE OF THE TEACHER

The most basic thing is to create the proper climate for talk — relaxed but concentrated. The tone is warm and friendly but not saccarine. The teacher does not have to revere children's words; but everything he does should show that he truly values what they say. The art of conversing is a profound cognitive activity, not an application of etiquette like practicing table manners. It must be understood that this is the time for children to talk, and to talk to each other; the teacher is there to facilitate this by setting up and maintaining certain conditions. He does not participate as a discussant of the subject matter; his participation is at the level of process and not of content. The measure of his success is how well the discussion goes without him, how soon the children can take over his role and function autonomously. If he enables them to exchange with their peers in learning ways he has given them a great educational gift for the rest of their lives. After all, the ultimate goal of a teacher is to eliminate himself. But a teacher who needs too much to feel needed unconsciously keeps the students dependent on him.

Establishing the meaning of the topic. Specifically, the teacher does several things, *all of which should eventually be done by the pupils themselves.* First, make sure that they all understand the topic in the same way, by asking someone to say what it means to him and asking the others if they agree. It may be necessary to ask how they define certain key words. If they define "animals" so as to exclude birds and fish, that definition stands, though it is incorrect. Correction can take place at other times. Actually, as Dr. Whipple points out, these sessions give the teacher insight into children's concepts and knowledge so that he can better fit his other teaching to their needs. Discussing key words is also a way for children to acquire vocabulary and sharpen concepts. This agreement on the meaning of the topic is the touchstone for relevance throughout the discussion when teacher or pupil remarks that some utterance is off the subject. After settling on the sense of the topic, the children start where they will.

Encouraging participation. If someone does not participate for a long time, say, "Bobby, we haven't heard from you yet," or "What comes to your mind about this, Bobby?" Sometimes just looking at a child will draw him out. Children who habitually withdraw may need a skillful alternation of encouraging and letting alone.

Keeping the focus. Usually all that an off-subject utterance requires is a neutral reminder. But try to be aware of why children digress. If too many children wander frequently from the topic, you had better ask if the topic really interests them, or determine what else the matter might be. They might discuss what would be a better topic. Digressing is, after all, mostly a matter of involvement. Think of how difficult it is to divert a child from something he wants to do very badly. But digression may also arise because of involvement. Something just said may remind a child that "Daddy locked himself out of the house yesterday" or set him to wondering "What would happen if a locomotive got too hot and started to turn red all over."

Though irrelevant to the group's present focus, these are legitimate private associations and should not appear as enemies to the teacher or as mistakes to the child. The teacher simply says, "That might be a good incident to act out next time" or "You can suggest that for a later topic." No remark is ultimately inappropriate, only immediately inappropriate. All ideas will get their time; another idea has the floor now.

Focusing attention. If a child is not listening well, this will probably show up in a high percentage of non sequiturs and repetitions. In the latter case, simply say, "Joan has already mentioned that," or "Did you hear Joan say that before?" This lets the repeater know that he may have missed something, and also shows that you are setting an example of listening.

A major reason children do not listen to each other is that they do not value what peers have to say. Their first inclination is, in school at any rate, to assume that they can learn only from adults, who are all-powerful and all-knowing, not from other small critters like themselves. If the teacher attends and values their peer talk, they will also. As in many other matters, real attention establishes value. If you praise and blame, or otherwise make yourself the motive center of the group, children will talk to and for you, not to and for peers, and consequently will listen only to you and use the time while another child is talking to prepare their next bright remark for you to praise. Listening to peers, then, is directly related to honoring peer ideas, and the problem of inattention decreases as the peer-to-peer nature of the group becomes real to children (they may not believe it at first).

Some non sequiturs, however, are not born of inattention; a child may be breaking new ground in another aspect of the topic. When you feel that the abrupt switch shows that the speaker did not hear his predecessor, you might ask him if he heard, then ask that previous speaker to repeat what he said, then let the present speaker continue. Occasionally, when you feel that a certain remark is especially fruitful or difficult or deserving of thought, ask someone to paraphrase what was said. Such feeding back can help the speaker to know how well he was understood as well as sharpen listening among peers. Part of the teacher's role is to influence pace so that ideas are given their due and the discussion thickens and thins at appropriate places.

Handling the impulsive interrupter. If someone seriously interrupts another's sentence, say, "Ellen hasn't finished yet," in a factual rather than accusing tone of voice, or "Remember about waiting your turn," or make a simple gesture that says, "Hold off a moment." In extreme cases, when a chronically impulsive child habitually interrupts, you may as well focus the group momentarily on this problem and discuss it before proceeding, if the group seems mature enough. Ask what they all might do to help Plunger listen more and wait for his turn. The lesson is that when an individual problem impairs group functioning it is then a group problem also, and time should be taken to restore functioning. Turning in annoyance on the individual as culprit makes him defensive and makes matters worse; he needs rational help. If the group can think of no solution, ask Plunger to act as recorder for several minutes, listening only, and perhaps taking notes, and then, when the time is up, to tell in his own words the gist of what the group said, and to voice what he thinks of what they said. If this is done to help the individual and not to punish him, I think it will bring him around. At the same time, as it causes him to delay his responses and to become involved in listening during this delay, it also assures him that he in turn will have a definite and full hearing. Plunger's difficulty in waiting usually stems from one or more of these three things — impulsive inability to delay responses, egocentric disregard for what others say, or overanxiety about having a chance to get attention.

Leading the summary. Since the teacher controls the duration of sessions, it is up to him at first to initiate summary, but pupils should take over this function too as soon as they are able to follow time and to sense when discussion is ready for a summary. Ask the group to try to recall the main ideas that have occurred to them. Summarizing is important for developing thought because it is abstracting. Younger children will content themselves with selective recollection, but as they grow, their manner of summarizing will also grow; it will approach the drawing of conclusions. Sometimes new ideas occur as previous ideas are reassembled, thrown in a different order, paraphrased, and checked for omissions. Once all the returns are in, perspective is sometimes different. At this point the teacher can call for suggestions about the next topic, or air his own suggestions. Tying the summary of one session to the choosing of a topic for the next increases the likelihood of good continuity and momentum.

Helping with hang-ups. Besides insuring adherance to ground rules, the teacher looks for blockages and hang-ups. His job is not just to get the children over a difficulty but to help them understand what the difficulty was and how it can be overcome. He makes them aware of what makes and breaks communication so that they can eventually solve these problems themselves. Disagreement is not in itself necessarily a blockage, but it *may* be. Dr. Whipple has neatly classified disagreement into three categories —disagreements of definition, information, and value. Certainly the teacher needs to be adept at spotting mere definitional hang-ups, where different children are attaching different meanings to the same word or concept. The initial agreement about what the topic means should head off some definitional misunderstandings, but of course as new words and concepts are introduced into discussion the problem may crop up again. Say, "Mary, I think when you say 'transportation' you are including a lot of things Stephen isn't thinking about." Or ask another member if he thinks those two children mean the same thing by the word. Either another pupil or the teacher should try to say what Mary means and what Stephen means. Stephen and Mary can be asked if that is in fact what they mean. In other words, hang-ups should come under discussion until, again, the group process continues unimpaired.

Definitional disagreements should make way for more important ones. If the teacher believes a disagreement stems from different information — Alice has seen so and so and Elmer has heard or read something different — he may ask, "How do you know?" or "Where did you learn that?" or "What do you think proves what you say?" Partly, this questioning is intended to establish the habit of asking for, and giving, evidence. Identifying and documenting *factual* statements is something that small-group discussion should pursue later in many ways. Mainly, for now, the teacher helps them to see how some disputes may be resolved by getting more or better information, or at least to see that different information is the source of dispute. This could lead to research that could be brought into the next session. For disagreements founded on different values, you can only remark that "Beauregard and Abigail seem to be arguing over a difference in what they like. He considers machines very important and she doesn't because she cares a lot more about live things." This does not, of course, resolve the disagreement — which is not the point — but it serves to clarify the basis of the disagreement.

Often blockages reflect personal relations among the children. If doing so does not embarrass them too much, the teacher may remark that "Ed and Rick always seem to disagree, no matter what the subject is," or ask, "Do you always agree with Julia?" Another child may say, "Sure, they like each other" (giggles). "Do you think you can like each other and still disagree sometimes?" It is true that an adult cannot meddle much with children's interrelationships without creating fear of exposure. He can say, however, that when feelings they have about each other interfere with the activities of the group, the group may need to talk about them. Ganging up, jeering, or chronic arguing for the sheer sake of contest certainly play havoc with discussion. Since the whole purpose of the group is to learn how best to talk together, no malfunction can be ignored, whatever the reason for it. If members do not seem aware that discussion is being determined by personal feelings, the teacher should at least say that he thinks that it is. How far he should go beyond that is too difficult to say here; playing by ear is wisest in such sensitive matters.

QUESTIONING

The teacher's role in discussion will shift as the children become adept and begin to follow the rules for themselves. He does not need to try to do all things all the time. The less he has to concern himself with the fundamentals of the process, the more he can concentrate on making discussion more sophisticated.

The first way the teacher makes discussion more sophisticated is by sparely interjecting questions calling for elaboration, clarification, or qualification. These questions are not mere conversation prompters; they should express the teacher's real feeling that what a child has said is incomplete, unclear, exaggerated, or overgeneralized. Whereas a declarative statement to that effect sounds critical and omniscient, a question or request makes the speaker think a little more and sets an example of questioning for the listeners, who may well have found the statement incomplete or unclear too but were not aware that they did, or, with childish acceptance, did not realize that questioning might relieve their uncertainty. The teacher might say: "Will you explain that a little more?" (clarification); "*All* animals?" or "Is there a time when that is *not* true?" (qualification); "Tell us some more about what they do because I'm not sure yet how that fits in" (elaboration). Since the teacher is in the same role of listener as the other children, each question suggests what they too might have asked, or could ask in the future. At the same time the speaker is given feedback to help him come more on his true course by adding to or adjusting his first statement. This elaborating and adjusting under the influence of feedback will become an increasingly important learning process in later years. Though children are less interactive in these early years, if the teacher sets the example of questioning, small-group discussion can begin to become already a model of good thinking for the child to internalize.

FRAMING TOPICS

Topics may be of all sorts, but in the early grades they should be specifically stated in some predicated form, not just named with a noun or phrase. This would usually mean a question like "What are the different ways animals get food?" not "Animals" or "How Animals Get Food." The topics should be of the greatest possible interest to children, whether they come from the children or from the teacher. This means *emotional involvement*. For very young children, try topics into which a lot of feeling can be projected: "What would you do if the animals got loose in the zoo?"

Common information will provide a good basis for discussion among second- and third-graders, though teachers have to remember that it is not the purpose of these discussions to *convey* information; that should be done elsewhere. Films might serve well, but other experiences can furnish common information to all children — trips, reading, classroom pets, and, of course, universal life experiences outside school. To choose topics for their moralistic value to the teacher would be to pervert the whole intent. Subjects such as safety rules, good and bad manners, or the behavior in the auditorium yesterday would be dead give-aways that the teacher is merely converting small-group discussion into an agency of indoctrination and law enforcement.

Interest is considerably increased if subjects can in some way be carried over from one session to the next. Continuity and momentum are created by dove-tailing related topics and by framing a series of sessions within an overall goal or project.

One means of increasing the sophistication of discussion is to frame the topics in ways that progressively call for more difficult thinking tasks. *Why* questions, for example, are relatively difficult, entailing as they do not only a grasp of continuity of events and a concept of cause and effect but also a certain analytic ability to distinguish and classify events. Causation in familiar physical phenomena is easier, moreover, than causation in abstracter realms.

Topics inviting enumeration. The kind of topic most appropriate for beginning conversationalists calls for listing or enumeration: "How many different ways does an animal get food?" First, listing is a simple kind of thinking but an important one, and we know that small children can do it and learn from it. Cognitively, the process is one of furnishing positive instances of a category, Animal Ways of Food-Getting or Uses of the Magnet. This relates to concept formation. Disagreement occurs when an instance is offered — say, birds flying south to get food — and another child objects, in effect, that the instance is negative, not positive. (Birds fly south, he says, for reasons other than to get food.) If the category is "vehicles," "sled" may be disputed as an example. These disputes lead to precision of concepts and finer discrimination, to more analytic thinking.

Second, listing requires the least interaction among pupils. Essentially it is a piling of ideas, or "brainstorming." One pupil influences another mainly by thought association: a suggestion by one makes another think of something along the same line. Disagreement over instances, however, does represent greater interaction and a step upward from mere influence by association.

Enumerative topics may be of different sorts that can be roughly scaled to form a progression. One scale can run according to the abstractness, complexity or novelty of the category — its difficulty: "How many things can be done with a bottle?" "How do people get other people to do what they want?" "How can you tell what things will cost a dollar and what things a dime?" (Isolated, such topics are arbitrary, but they could be very pertinent in a context.)

Topics inviting comparison. Enumeration can lead to comparison topics by making the category one of similarities or differences, but taking only one or the other at a time. "In what ways are cars and airplanes alike?" "What are the differences between dogs and cats?" Dealing simultaneously with both similarities and differences — full comparison — is rather advanced and should probably be deferred to grades four through six. Researchers in the development of children's thought disagree about whether the perception of similarity or of difference comes first. This indicates, perhaps, that the order does not make much difference and that both kinds of topics could be dealt with alternately.

Topics inviting chronology. Another kind of topic for beginners calls for chronological ordering — making up a group story, planning an action, or telling how something is made. Such topics could be interspersed with the enumerative kinds. Most often they will relate to other activities such as drama, writing, and making things. The purpose of discussion is to work out an order of events that is going to be carried out in some way. The process is one of building, act by act or step by step, which is relatively simple in itself but usually entails reasons for choosing one suggestion over another. Thus, the main form is easy but invites some more complex kinds of thinking. Undoubtedly children will leap ahead and then later think of things that should have gone before. This backtracking and readjusting is something a summary could help put to rights.

The fixed groups led by the teacher should be used sometimes for planning, so that when children are placed in temporary groups for certain projects, they can exploit the experience. The topic might be a story problem to be enacted afterwards: "How does John get his bicycle back?" or a planning problem such as working out the stages of a campaign: "What steps should we take to prevent stealing?" or a planning problem about how to make something: "How should we go about making a bird feeder?" The enumerative and chronological may dovetail. For example, a listing of things that birds will be attracted to and will peck at might have to precede a session on construction , in order to settle on the type of feeder. The groups that selected the kinds of writing to be included in the *Beta-Gram* on stealing resorted to enumerating (ads, lost-and-founds, etc.) in the midst of carrying out one of the chronologically planned phases of the campaign.

SCRIBES

One of the many aspects of discussion that needs much more exploration is the use of a scribe, some pupil designated to take notes during a session and, after the group has summarized at the end, to read his notes as a summary to be compared with theirs. This would provide individual as well as group practice in summarizing, and would also act as a check on memory and perspective. Another procedure is for the scribe to participate in discussion until the summary and then take notes on the summary alone. Either way, children have opportunities for well motivated writing and the group has a record of their talk for the next session or for carrying out a plan. (The record may be helpful to the teacher also, in lieu of or in addition to a tape recording.) Of course many children are not able to write well enough or fast enough to act as scribe before the second grade, but even a few key words would be a good beginning.

PANELS

A further use for notes, as in the *Beta* experiment, is to form a panel when the class wants to pool ideas or to know what other groups have thought on the same subject. The scribes meet in a semicircle in front of the class, and each reports what his group has said. These panelists are invited to comment on each other's reports, and then the class is invited to comment.

Many of these recommendations not only apply to grades four through six but would be inappropriate before then. But not enough is known about small-group discussion among children, and especially its evolution over the years, for me to be able to distinguish two main stages of it, as I have for most other activities in elementary school. The ways in which topics, rules, grouping, and the role of the teacher should shift as pupils mature are critical matters for experimentation. Especially moot issues are: (1) the point at which groups can become self-governing for discussion of designated topics (so that, for one thing, simultaneous discussions can take place); (2) the uses of pupil leaders; (3) the likelihood that the teacher should periodically resume leadership of the groups to train pupils in new skills of thinking and discussing made possible by their increasing experience and maturity. These new skills might entail some changes in procedure and in the leader role (examples being a more abstract way of summarizing, or the citing of evidence to support statements). With a sense of method, such as these recommendations are intended to instill, the teacher should be able to cope with the problems of further experimentation and to enjoy the excitement of it.

Holding Forth

Solo talk, monologuing, is a special case of "speaking up" that I shall call "holding forth." The utterances of children in the lower grades tend to be short. The purpose of encouraging monologues is to let children practice extending their utterances. Whereas the continuity of dialogue is provided by the give and take of social exchange, the continuity of a monologue must come from within the speaker, from his perception of how to string his utterances together to develop a subject. He does this spontaneously, of course, without thinking ahead, but practice in holding forth can improve what he does spontaneously. Since developing a subject is what composition is generally about, holding forth is, in a real sense, learning to write without paper. After all, writing is a more sophisticated form of monologue.

Although I do not believe that monologuing can be carried very far in the K–3 years, because extended utterances must wait on several kinds of maturation, a definite beginning is possible. Monologue is born of dialogue, when a single voice takes over momentarily, like an aria in an opera. Holding forth means elaborating, which is not a small child's first tendency. He is at home with the reciprocal prompting of dialogue, where his thought can develop in bits and pieces under the influence of others, and where the problem of linking sentence to sentence, idea to idea, does not come up in a serious way. He should not be pushed to monologue, but he can be helped at this age to start stringing his bits and pieces into some kind of continuity.

Show-and-Tell

The basic idea of talking while showing is very sound because it is transitional between play prattle and addressing an audience, between talking to toys and talking about them. Though monologue in the sense of sustaining a subject to a group comes slowly, nothing comes easier to a child than prattle, talking to himself and to his toys as he manipulates the toys. This kind of soliloquizing is fluent and may make for some very long continuities indeed. What provides continuity is the ongoing play to which the prattle is an accompaniment. What he does with the toys supplies a steady stream of cues for speech.

The value. Show-and-tell allows the child to take off from prattle but requires him to modify his speech for the sake of an audience. His subject is a familiar or loved object that he knows a lot about, but he must allow for outsiders who do not share his familiarity with the object. As he talks he can look at the object and do things with it, which will suggest things to say, but his speech continuity can no longer merely follow the blow-by blow continuity of his play. What he does is tell stories about how he got the object or what he has done with it, or give information about what it is and how it works. The difference is essentially that speech diverges somewhat from the ongoing action, becomes more independent, and necessarily becomes more abstract. While pointing, he inevitably talks of some things that cannot be pointed to — the past, feelings, purpose and function, and certain general information. But to be an important kind of learning, show-and-tell must be taken seriously and shaped into a distinct process.

Procedures. First, since nearly all small children are shyer in large groups, they are likely to talk more freely in a small group. Thus, holding forth could occur in the same teacher-led groups used for discussion, either before discussion begins or, if that makes too long a session, on another occasion. Once experienced, children can be placed in groups around the room and directed to take turns.

Second, the other children should question. Let the shower-teller begin as he will. When he has said all that initially occurs to him, encourage the audience by solicitation and example to ask natural questions. "When did they give it to you?" "What happened to the wing there?" "What's the red button for?" "What do you do if you want to get the money out again?" "Where do you keep it?" "Do you let your brother use it?" These are model questions calling for anecdote, explanation, and information. They are asked at first by the teacher and then by the children as they grasp the possibilities. Questions act as cues or prompts that replace play as a source of ideas. They cause the speaker to sustain his subject, to elaborate — fitfully, it is true; but I assume that, with experience, the speaker will anticipate questions and supply more information and background without waiting for questions to prompt him. Thus the monologue element will grow. A lot of practice in oral explaining can even influence the *order* of information — the mentioning of certain items first so that later items will be clearer. Questioning, then, is fixed as a part of the procedure.

Third, specialize the talk by asking the children to bring, on different occasions, something that (1) has a good story behind it, (2) they made or grew, (3) especially means a lot to them, or (4) moves or works in a funny or interesting way. This is how show-and-tell can become somewhat like a composition assignment. Narrative, exposition, and explanation are emphasized in turn by calling for objects associated with memories or having certain characteristics. Some objects were acquired in an interesting way or have had curious things happen to them; thereby hangs a tale (narrative). Drawings and paintings that the child has done also contain stories — fantasies or real events — that the artist can relate as he explains his picture. If the object was made or grown, the child tells how he made or grew it (description of a process). If it has special meaning for him, he tells how he feels about it (personal essay). Gadgets, machines, and other apparatus elicit explanation of purpose and operation.

Show-and-tell will grow as children grow, for their meaningful objects will reflect their maturing amusements, crafts, thoughts, and feelings. It is another staple activity that will continue beyond elementary school, and it is an important element in the later development of composition.

_____

_____

_____

Chapter 5

Becoming Literate

Two main ideas underlie the following remarks and recommendations. The first is that *literacy is a two-way street*. When we go from speech to print, we call that writing; when we go from print to speech, we call that reading. The teaching of literacy must do equal justice to both, whatever that may require. It is necessary to say this because literacy instruction is traditionally biased toward reading, to which writing is attached as an adjunct.

The second idea is that *reading is mere decoding of print into speech, and writing is mere transcription of speech into print*. Speech is the given, the base, which children acquire before school and out of school. With speech goes a stock of meanings that has no necessary connection with reading and writing, that is independent of both, as indeed it must be for illiterate people. At the outset, then, I would distinguish, in reading, between decoding and comprehension, and, in writing, between transcription and composition. This distinction between literal and conceptual levels is obvious but easy to lose sight of.

The real issue of learning to read is not "getting meaning from the page"; we get meaning from the speech sounds that the letters represent. The real issue of learning to read is decoding the letters into words we already know and to which meanings are already attached. Reading comprehension is merely comprehension. Difficulties in comprehending are difficulties with concepts, ideas, and their relationships, not with printed words. A text that presents a problem of understanding to a child when he reads it will present the same problem of understanding when he hears it. Does he hear a voice behind the words when he reads them? *That* is the real problem of learning to read — decoding letters and punctuation into speech.

The same argument holds for writing. Just as comprehension is independent of reading, composition is independent of writing. We acknowledge this when we speak of oral composition and oral literature. The problems of composition are problems of selecting and ordering speech units — words, phrases, sentences, and whole monologues — and are essentially the same for the speaker as for the writer. Rendering a meaningful sequence of images and ideas into graphic symbols, on the other hand, is mere transcription, taking dictation from oneself. Spelling and punctuation belong to transcription, not to composition. It is understandable that transcribing and composing should become confused, since a person writing does both at once. And, of course, the fact of writing does influence composition and cause written speech to differ from vocal speech: writing down thoughts permits revision and relieves the memory load. (In an oral culture, one revises by memorizing and retelling.) But transcribing and composing are quite distinct activities and entail very different learning problems.

In this view, then, reading and writing are matters of getting between one symbol system and another, between some sounds and some sights that one learns to pair off — letters with vocal sounds, and punctuation and other typographical signals with intonation. Comprehension and composition, on the other hand, are deep operations of mind and spirit, concerning the relations between symbols and those complexes of perception and conception that we call meanings. There is no way simply to pair off meanings with symbols by rules of regularity. So the two-way street between speech and print is a symbol-symbol relation involving an essentially perceptual learning that for most children seems no longer developmental beyond the age of about first grade. I cannot imagine what the future maturation of a student can contribute to the problems of decoding and transcribing if he has not already learned by then to do those things. The rest is remedial.

This is not to minimize, however, the obvious difficulties that many children have learning to decode and transcribe. My point is that these difficulties can be greatly reduced by treating the two activities as nothing more than what they are — the matching of an auditory symbol system with a visual symbol system — and by treating meaning as nothing less than what it is — the matching of thought with speech. In short, literacy, I am convinced, can be better learned if it is not confused with the much broader issue of meaning. But this separation does not argue for a split in the learner's experience, only for a conception of literacy that helps to bring out which problems of reading and writing are *unique* to reading and writing and which are general problems of thought and language encountered in oral speech as well.

Since some recommendations in this chapter will consist of referrals to particular published materials for literacy instruction, I would like to propose criteria for choosing some materials over others. These criteria are based on the indications of research and on certain principles. Let me take the research first.

Research Indications

In a recent book, *Learning to Read: The Great Debate*,[1] Jeanne Chall presents an interpretive synopsis of what is known so far about beginning reading. This three-year study for Carnegie Corporation consisted of reviewing the old and new research on reading, analyzing textbooks, interviewing proponents of different methods, and observing literacy teaching in classrooms. It is because Dr. Chall has tried to characterize the present state of our knowledge about the subject, rather than merely to report certain research, that I would like to relay some of her points. She calls the central controversy one of *emphasis* as between a decoding approach and a meaning approach. The decoding approach would teach the phonographemic relations sooner and more systematically, as the key to unlocking new words, whereas the meaning approach would preteach whole words before they are read and feed in phonics gradually over several years as a supplementary way to recognize words. For new teachers especially, a somewhat fuller definition of these approaches may be helpful.

Two Basic Approaches to Reading

The *meaning approach*, incarnated in the conventional basal reader series[2] and enjoying almost unquestioned supremacy until recently, is based on these tenets, according to Dr. Chall:

1. Comprehension and interpretation should be a part of reading instruction right from the start.

2. Early reading should consist of recognizing words already pretaught by the look-say method.

3. Children should begin with whole words and sentences.

4. Silent reading should be stressed to avoid oral difficulties and "word calling."

5. After sight recognition of 50 words, instruction should begin in sound-letter relations.

6. The attack on new words should be through picture cues and contextual clues and through visual analysis and substitution.

7. Phonics and word analysis should be spread over six years of school, phonics gaining momentum in grades two and three.

8. Separate, systematic teaching of phonics is bad because it is boring and difficult; separate sounds should not be blended into words, but rather words broken down by phonic analysis.

[1] New York: McGraw-Hill Book Co., Inc., 1967.
[2] Typified by the Scott, Foresman and Co. Series of 1956 (now revised) and the Ginn and Company Series of 1961, which Dr. Chall analyzed in detail.

9. In grades one to three, the words in readers should be repeated often on a meaning frequency principle, the number of new words being very low in ratio to old words (necessarily, since new words are pretaught by sight).

10. Beginners should move slowly after a readiness or prereading period.

The *decoding approach* has been variously represented in the past and is even more variously represented in the present, now that the swing is back toward phonics. The only thing that all the different decoding methods have in common is an early and systematic teaching of sound-letter relations as an analytical tool to enable children to attack new words. Some people are opposed to certain tenets of the meaning approach, some to others. The variations among them concern principally whether phonic regularities are to be taught explicitly or inferred from controlled spelling of the reading matter, whether components are to be synthesized into words or words analyzed into components, whether words are to be spelled out or sounded out, whether devices such as machines and artificial alphabets are to be used, whether the alphabet is to be learned first by naming letters, whether pictures are to accompany stories, whether the method is to be used independently or in conjunction with conventional basals, and whether oral speech, writing, dictation, and activities other than reading are to be a part of the method.

What verdict does research evidence render on these two general approaches? In interpreting the evidence, Dr. Chall insists on one point that has often been a source of conflict in the past: one approach or method seems more effective at the end of the first grade but not at the end of second or third grades. (In any case, the evidence at present does not go beyond the beginning of fourth grade.) Given this, her general conclusion is that after two or three years, children read with better understanding, and recognize and spell words better, when they have learned by a decoding-emphasis method.

> Most schoolchildren in the United States are taught to read by what I have termed a meaning-emphasis method. Yet the research from 1912 to 1925 indicates that a code-emphasis method — i.e., one that views beginning reading as essentially different from mature reading and emphasizes learning of the printed code for the spoken language — produces better results, at least up to the point where sufficient evidence seems to be available, the end of the third grade.

Here are other conclusions from the findings:

1. Early decoding may result in lower comprehension and rate at the end of grade one but surpasses whole-word learning by the end of grade two. Decoding may achieve an early superiority in word recognition that does not show up on standardized silent reading tests (comprehension and vocabulary) in first grade, but by second and third grades the greater facility in word

[3] Chall, p. 307.

attack increases the ability to read for meaning, as measured by these same tests.

2. Children of lower intelligence and background seem to do better with an early code emphasis. (Children of higher intelligence and better background also gain from it, but the effect is not so great.)

3. Correlational studies support the experimental findings that an initial code emphasis produces better readers and spellers.

4. Learning the names of letters and their sound values before beginning to read helps early reading. In primary grades, a knowledge of letters and sound values appears to have a greater relation to reading achievement than intelligence.

5. There is some evidence that inferring phonic relations from texts that are controlled for spelling regularities is insufficient, that explicitly taught sound-letter knowledge is required in addition. The best results will probably come from controlling vocabulary for spelling *and* from direct teaching of phonic relations.

6. Clinical evidence shows failures in both camps, but the meaning approach seems to produce more serious failures than the decoding approach.

7. Children with a specific language disability all share a great difficulty with decoding, not with comprehension, and can be helped by phonic instruction combined with special kinesthetic and perceptual experience.

Although the findings clearly call for a reversal of the conventional emphasis — already apparent, as we shall see, in all the new materials — they do not give the nod to any one method of teaching the sound-letter relations, unless one is to give weight to the indications about teaching the names and sound values of letters before introducing reading texts, and about teaching the sound-letter relations explicitly rather than by inference or "discovery." These indications would distinguish some materials from others, since some withold the alphabet and some refuse to single out sounds and letters from whole words. The indication about explicit instruction, for example, would presumably give an edge to sounding-and-blending methods (synthesis), since they do present phonemes and graphemes in isolation from words, whereas the "linguistic" methods present them only in whole words grouped for minimal difference (analysis). But both aim for a phonic understanding that will enable children to decode new words for themselves.

Since Dr. Chall's synoptic research was conducted, a fresh set of research projects have been undertaken, under the auspices of the U.S. Office of Education, that constitute an essentially separate source of information from those that she synthesized. (In *Learning to Read: The Great Debate* she was able only to mention briefly the first reports.) The Cooperative Research Program in First Grade Instruction comprised 27 reading studies whose results were correlated at the University of Minnesota Coordinating Center. These studies compared several different beginning reading methods with "the" conventional Basal method. Ten of the studies have been continued through second grade.[4] Those methods for which results are available through second grade were designated Linguistic, I/T/A, Language Experience, and Phonic/Linguistic (the Lippincott *Basic Reading Series*). The 27 research projects compared one or more of these four methods with the Basal method *but not with each other.* There were other very important goals besides these comparisons, however, as the following findings indicate.

At the end of first grade it was found that whatever the method used, phonics-supplemented programs produced greater reading achievement. At the end of both grades, little significant difference was found between Basal and Language Experience or between Basal and Linguistic, though the latter tended to show a slight edge in word recognition and spelling. I/T/A did not differ significantly from Basal in reading comprehension but was superior in word recognition and spelling. The transition from I/T/A to traditional orthography appears to be a relatively simple task. Phonic/Linguistic (Lippincott) produced superior achievement over Basal in reading, spelling, and general language ability (but only two projects comparing these two, and hence much fewer subjects, remained at the end of grade two).

Several general results of these coordinated studies corroborate Dr. Chall's findings: (1) An early code emphasis appears to be highly related to word recognition and spelling achievement at the end of second grade (certainly as compared with basals). (2) Phonetic control of vocabulary helps the child recognize more words at an earlier stage. (3) Writing symbols in connection with phonic instruction aids the learning of both sound-symbol correspondences and irregular words; writing is an effective component of beginning reading. (4) Children can learn new words at a faster rate than has been commonly assumed in reading programs; expectations of pupil reading achievement can be raised.

The Cooperative Research report differs with Dr. Chall's in at least one important respect. Whereas Dr. Chall asserts that a decoding emphasis produces not only superior word recognition but also superior comprehension, thereby suggesting a strong relation between the two, the authors of the coordinated studies say:

> The superiority in word recognition of pupils in various phonics emphasis programs is not, as a general rule, demonstrated in the area of reading comprehension. . . . This finding does not support the contention that the pupils' only task in learning to read is to develop the ability to translate graphemic symbols into sounds on the assumption that once he has decoded the words he will understand their meaning. Direct instruction in comprehension is apparently essential.[5]

[4] The results for first grade alone are reported in *Reading Research Quarterly,* Vol. II, No. 4 (Summer, 1967) (Newark, Delaware: International Reading Association). The results for both grades are reported in *Continuation of the Coordinating Center for First-Grade Reading Instruction Program,* by Robert Dykstra, September 1967, Final Report of Project Number 6–1651, Minneapolis, Minnesota: Bureau of Research, U.S. Office of Education, University of Minnesota.

[5] *Ibid.,* p. 162.

First of all, Dr. Chall's evidence runs to the end of *third* grade. One of her points about such comparative research is that comprehension gains of the decoding approach show up late rather than early. Second, it is obvious that whether decoding will lead to comprehension or not depends on factors of attention, cognition, experience, motivation, environment, and so on that were not dealt with in these studies. It is indeed true that word recognition does not guarantee comprehension. A main contention of this book, in fact, is that comprehension involves so much more than letters that it should not be classified as a "reading problem." Finally, even if "direct instruction in comprehension" were possible, which I doubt, the purely logical assumption the authors make about its being essential should be regarded as a dangerous inference in a comparative study not purporting to analyze the learning process itself.

Fortunately, the coordinators of the USOE project have themselves stressed very hard the limitations of these studies. Thus, what may well be the most significant evidence they offer concerns the validity of most reading research itself. A striking finding was that reading achievement varied more within one method than it did between one method and another. And some differences in achievement seemed unrelated not only to method but even to pupil readiness or teacher qualifications, or to the particular class, school, and community the pupil was in. Variation, then, must be ascribed to factors not measured, about which one can only speculate.

> In general, projects appeared to have a greater influence on the reading ability of pupils than did the particular instructional method or materials utilized. Specific programs were relatively effective in one project, relatively ineffective in other projects. On the other hand, all programs used in the same project were found to be quite similar in effectiveness. This would indicate that the entire instructional setting is involved in the effectiveness of an instructional program in reading. Differences in method or materials alone do not alter, to any great extent, the reading growth of pupils. The section of the analysis again points out the importance in future research of focusing on teacher and learning situation characteristics rather than methodology and materials.[6]

Although in our ignorance we have no choice but to give some credence to reading research, the fact is that it is tremendously inadequate and should play only a limited role in determining curriculum. What it has produced so far simply must not be taken too seriously, for several critical reasons. Many severe limitations that are scrupulously acknowledged in these USOE studies characterize in fact practically all other classroom research as well, when it has not been downright amateurish and biased. Sophisticated computering and modern methodology are still not equal to the task of controlling all the variables that are operating in a classroom situation.

But to the sheer difficulty of establishing convincing controls, one must add the staggering problem of properly conceptualizing beforehand the nature

[6] *Ibid.*, p. 164.

of reading and the nature of learning to read. The USOE studies have performed the great service of showing that *we don't know what some of the more significant variables are.* The net catches a few fish, but suppose the secret is in the makeup of the sea itself? The power of research can be no greater than the power of the concepts by which it is designed. It is this poverty of conception, perhaps more than anything else, that accounts for the inconclusiveness, contradiction, and irrelevance of most reading research. Caleb Gattegno has put his finger on one telling weakness of this research:

> Reading research to date has "measured" not absolute learning, but the relative advantages of one method of teaching reading over another method. However, research in reading has not attempted to discover under what conditions a learner can acquire the skills of reading and writing as readily as he acquires the skill of speaking.[7]

For a good initial effort in the direction of better conceptualization I refer the reader to "Reading and Reading Difficulty," by Morton Wiener and Ward Cromer.[8]

"Action research" in classrooms has a practical look about it but has not in fact got us very far and may have done as much harm as good. Patient observation of particular children, as exemplified by John Holt[9] and by some clinical workers, plus basic investigation into the reading process of proficient readers, may help us much more to understand how children can best acquire literacy. The recommendations made farther on in this chapter attempt to allow for both the few safe generalizations and the many limitations of research as it stands today.

How New Materials Meet Objections to Decoding

THE OBJECTIONS

The materials now available for direct and early teaching of phonographemic relations show a very strong awareness of the long-standing objections to the decoding emphasis. Besides the general objection that phonics is dull and difficult, the principal ones mounted in the past and frequently still reiterated today are:

1. The building up of words from letters causes *confusion,* since alphabetic names usually differ from the pronunciation of the letters in a word, and *distortion,* since the combination of separately sounded phonemes results, for example, in *kuh-a-tuh* instead of *cat.*

2. Analytical word attack produces mere "word-calling," instead of mean-

---

[7] *Words in Color, Teacher's Guide* (Chicago: Encyclopedia Britannica Press), p. 3.
[8] *Harvard Educational Review,* Vol. XXXVII, No. 4 (Fall, 1967).
[9] *How Children Fail,* 1963, and *How Children Learn,* 1967 (New York: Pitman Publishing Corp.).

ingful reading. The term is a pejorative one denoting a mechanical sounding of one word after another as if words were not related in sequences of sense.

3. In basing word recognition on phonic clues, the approach deprives children of a very important reading aid, the meaning cues of context.

4. Many words in English — some of the most common, in fact — are irregular and hence not learnable through phonic instruction.

5. Memorization of whole words is a natural, humane, and meaningful way to become literate that the decoding approach discourages as being a bad habit.

AVOIDING CONFUSION AND DISTORTION OF LETTER-SOUNDS

Those of my readers who nodded in agreement with the criticisms above should look closely, if they have not already, at how current materials meet these objections. They do so in several ways. Some programs do not teach the alphabetic names of letters at all, or do not ask children to spell words aloud in connection with reading. If naming of letters and spelling are advocated (as in the linguistics-based programs), sounding and blending are dispensed with, the sounds being presented not in isolation but in whole words grouped for spelling regularity. When names of letters are taught in a sounding-and-blending program, care is taken to divorce the learning of one from that of the other. Some programs simply avoid sounding and blending phonemes, and among those programs that advocate it only one that I have looked at allows consonants to be pronounced artificially as in *kuh-a-tuh*. This is usually avoided by presenting them only in combination with vowels, frequently in whole words. On this matter one feels, in virtually all of these programs, the strong and beneficial influence of modern linguistics, which will not tolerate phonetic distortion and which, moreover, through its emphasis on structural patterns, has facilitated the use of whole words grouped for spelling regularities, whether these regularities are to be "discovered" or taught directly.

AVOIDING WORD-CALLING

Likewise, "word-calling" does not inhere in a decoding approach. The authors of one supplementary phonics method declare, "No mechanical word-calling in Phonovisual; we must have comprehension."[10] But how is word-calling to be avoided if, one way or another, sounds are isolated as phonetic components and words have to be "figured out" accordingly? A child who reads smoothly and meaningfully because he has memorized all words in advance is not confronting the issue. The test of "word-calling" is whether he can read *new* words in such a way that the sentences containing them come out as meaningful wholes uttered with a natural intonational

[10] A picture caption in the *Phonovisual Method* of Lucille Schoolfield and Josephine Timberlake. Washington, D.C.: Phonovisual Products Inc., revised edition, 1961.

contour. A child who has to puzzle out each word so laboriously that he loses the continuity of sense and intonation simply has not learned to decode well enough. As all proponents of a phonic approach emphasize, the point of the teaching is to make decoding second-nature, fast and automatic. It is the child who lacks inadequate tools for decoding who must drop sense and intonation to devote all his attention to puzzling out new words. Today's materials for early, intensive phonics are speech-based, having as their chief goal the unlocking of spellings into familiar vocal sounds to which meaning is already attached. In the *Lippincott Basic Reading Series,* the authors say frankly that reading *is* word-calling, giving the term a positive sense, because a child who has learned to decode efficiently is thereby permitted to call out words in the continuous and comprehending manner with which he would *speak* the word sequences.

The influence of modern linguistics is again felt in its reinforcement of the oral approach to reading and in its insistence on the importance of the *patterning* of words into syntactic and intonational sequences. In short, the assumption that focusing on components of words will exclude meaning and vocal continuity is unfounded. More likely, what produces word-calling, in the bad sense of haltering gibberish, is the child's having to focus on individual words because he does not know how to translate them into sounds and sense.

CONTEXTUAL CLUES AND WHOLE-WORD LEARNING

What I have said so far implies how the remaining three objections are met. "The whole phonic pattern and the whole meaning-pattern are joined in a single unit of perception.[11] As regards both contextual clues and whole-word learning, all of the current decoding programs that I have looked at recognize, as indeed they must, that these are natural and valuable aids in reading so long as they do not prevent the child from learning to crack the code itself. Although some new programs eschew *picture* cues, they do assume that children in their later reading will always use the verbal context of a word as an aid in recognizing it, their point being simply that children should not depend on context as the main means of word attack, for it is inadequate by itself. And every program includes some whole-word learning of frequently occurring words like *come* and *as* that need to be presented early to initiate reading but that are phonetically irregular.

IRREGULARITY OF ENGLISH SPELLING

Finally, to deal a bit more with the objection about irregularities, critics of phonics sometimes forget that even when part of a word is irregular the

[11] Glenn McCracken and Charles C. Walcutt, *Basic Reading Series* (Lippincott), p. vii, teacher's edition of all readers.

rest is often perfectly phonetic. Furthermore, far more English words are phonetic than not (about 80%). In reading, this means that knowledge of sound-letter correspondances provides powerful cues for beginnings, middles, and endings of irregular words so that contextual and other cues can operate more effectively in recognizing the whole word. In writing, it means that even when a child misspells a word, he will misspell within a relatively small range of phonetic possibilities (e.g., *ir, ur, er*) so that his task of memorizing which spelling is actually correct is greatly reduced.

All this is to say that the critics of the approach have been closely listened to, and that the practical experience of the last 30 years or so has been thoroughly incorporated in today's materials. But this is not to say that all of the materials are alike. Far from it, for when one comes to the point of committing himself to choices among them, differences loom large. Some of these differences have little to do with the matters just discussed, which I have turned over mainly in order to assure those of my readers who think of themselves as belonging to the meaning camp that the recommendations to follow will not be so much at odds with their experience and beliefs as they might have thought.

Criteria Other than Research

Since research indicates mainly just a general criterion, without providing *strong* reasons for choosing some decoding-emphasis materials over others, the teacher must invoke other criteria for making decisions — goals, convictions about learning, and other considerations such as how long the materials have been tried and how much of other things besides literacy instruction they include. In addition to what research indicates and what the individual teacher may want to judge by, I propose the following criteria:

1. The presentation of sound-letter correspondences should launch equally well and equally early both reading and writing.

2. This presentation should begin before or at the same time as reading and last only a few months, leaving most reinforcement and rehearsal of phonographemic knowledge to actual reading and writing instead of to continued drills and workbook exercises.

3. When a literacy program includes readers, these readers should comprise, by at least the end of the sound-letter presentation, real children's literature of the highest quality. Material written by the producers of the program should be limited to the earliest texts controlled for spelling regularities and presented only during the period when sound-letter correspondences are being learned.

4. An independent literacy program that limits itself to word attack, handwriting, and basic spelling is preferable to a large package that includes grammar, reading comprehension practice, discussion, or composition and

dramatization, some of which should not be taught and some of which should be taught more extensively, not as an adjunct to reading. Materials should permit flexible combination with other approaches. The integration of the language arts, moreover, takes place in the head of a learner, not in a package.

5. The more a program takes phonics out of a book and puts it on the chalkboard or in the air or in card games the more it is to be preferred, all other things being more or less equal. For general pedagogical reasons, this principle is directed against isolated bookishness in favor of a livelier, social learning medium that will also make use of cross-teaching among pupils.

6. Materials should enable teachers to become sensitive to childrens' learning problems in reading by enhancing, rather than obstructing, opportunities for insight.

7. Given an equal effectiveness for word recognition, synthetic phonics should be preferred over analytic phonics because it offers an extra benefit in the form of creative word building whereby the pupil may combine components into words of his own choice, according to all of the English possibilities, instead of merely breaking down words according to some internal similarity (as with *sh*all and wi*sh*).

The gist of these criteria is that an ideal literacy program gives the key to the code at the outset, fast and intensively, so that children can begin to read and write authentically and independently very early in the game. The teacher is free to make separate decisions about how to teach comprehension and composition, instead of having to "buy one, buy all." He is also free to combine the phonics instruction, for which materials are truly needed, with other methods of teaching literacy, to be mentioned later, for which materials are not always necessary.

Reading Readiness

It is important that the concept of "early" instruction in sound-letter correspondences not be misunderstood. It means that the literacy program begins before or simultaneously with reading and lasts for a relatively short while. It does not mean that children are pushed into the world of books and letters before they are ready. In other words, "early" refers to what comes after, not to what comes before. I fully accept the principle that children's readiness for literacy depends on their attaining a certain development in perceptual and motor skills and a certain amount of emotional and experiential maturity. Most literacy programs include materials and practices intended to enable children to discriminate letter shapes, make the writing movements, and acquire the top-bottom, left-right spatial orientation. But children who have not been talked with, not been read to, never even been shown a book, and seldom been given the opportunity to experience the things books talk about will see no meaning in literacy and have no motive to undertake it. These deprivations simply have to be overcome first, as the Head-start Program acknowledges so well.

It is terribly hard for one teacher alone to give a roomful of deprived children what they need. He can read to them, try to get them to talk, give them objects to play with, let them look through picture books, and take them on visits. But, I would like to submit, he can go much farther if well developed children are mixed with the underdeveloped, so that the one can help the other, and if dramatic play and peer talk are included in the activities. Those children who have not been talked with should talk with children who are used to conversing. They should have a chance to play with more emotionally mature children of their own age, and to pick up from the latter some of their knowledge of the world. The teacher alone cannot possibly provide enough of these experiences for each child. He can, however, set up social games among small groups and lead the class in some activities described in Chapters 3, 4, 7 and 10. What has not been sufficiently exploited in reading readiness is peer interaction, the teaching of some children by others. In a heterogeneous class, advantaged or abler children can begin the literacy program before disadvantaged or slow children and help bring along the latter. Besides talking with them, they can read to them, interest them in books, and even impart some of their knowledge about letter formation and spatial orientation. According to both Dr. Chall and the USOE reports mentioned earlier, the second most effective predictor of reading achievement — outranking intelligence — is auditory discrimination, which can be developed only by hearing many meaningfully discriminated sounds, mainly human speech. In short, since the timing of literacy instruction depends on individual development, and since some children will consequently be starting it before others, an additional and powerful force — pupil cross-teaching — can be brought to bear on the critical problem of reading readiness.

Brief Survey of Literacy Materials

Let me roughly classify for convenience the materials that teachers have to select from. I have examined most current materials, but I am sure I have missed some, and new ones are appearing all the time. The purpose of this survey is to narrow down the field in accordance with the criteria just discussed.

The first group comprises those basal reader series of the conventional sort that stress meaning and comprehension but do not begin with an intensive sound-letter program. I will not name them. Although some have appeared in revised editions that afford a greater decoding emphasis, they are still far inferior to the new materials in this respect. A quick repair job is just not enough. In addition, almost without exception, the basal texts are very poor, being mostly editor-written material based on a small vocabulary and on the

Dick-and-Jane principle that children want to read about familiar family life. Unfortunately, this group includes reader series especially created for racial minorities. In contrast to the saga of the neighborhood, a collection of folk and fairy tales, fables and legends, poems and songs has the advantage that, by not specifying familiar environments, it fits any school population, whatever the race or class. Besides being convinced that any small child would rather read about the remote or fantastic, I think it is impossible to make a reader series truly realistic, especially when children come from a subculture filled with crime, obscenity, and despair. A couple of ashcans do not depict a ghetto. The co-basal, or supplementary, reader series, however, sometimes contain very good children's literature and might be used with a literacy program taken from somewhere else. But both the teaching of sound-letter relations and, to a lesser degree the reading material of the basal programs are faulted by the criteria.

The second group of programs is based on spelling patterns derived from modern linguistics and on the inductive or "discovery" theory of learning. Thus sounds and spellings are focused on by presenting groups of words that are alike in spelling pattern but differ minimally with respect to one sound or letter (*mat, map*), with the intention that children should infer the patterns (consonant-short vowel-consonant) and discriminate the contrasts (*t* and *p*) themselves. This is a structural kind of whole-word learning that teaches phonographemic regularities without isolating phonemes and without sounding and blending. The early reading has a phonetically controlled vocabulary plus some irregular sight words of high frequency. All have some readers but vary in the number of them. Since all were put out for the first time in the 1960's, none has had a long trial in its present form. This group comprises *The Merrill Linguistic Readers,* by Fries, Wilson, and Rudolph (Columbus, Ohio: Charles E. Merrill Books, Inc.); *Let's Read,* by Bloomfield and Barnhart (Bronxville, N.Y.: Clarence L. Barnhart, Inc.); *The Linguistic Science Reader,* by Stratemeyer and Smith (New York: Harper & Row, Publishers); *The Basic Reading Series,* by Rasmussen and Goldberg (Chicago: Science Research Associates, Inc.); and *Sounds and Letters,* by Hall (Ithaca, N.Y.: Linguistics).

One effect of the inductive, word-grouping approach is to lengthen the time it takes to teach literacy. The presentation of the phonographemic relations in these materials takes a year or more. It seems to me that both the effort to cover all or most of the spelling patterns and the effort to do so by means of copious word groups make these programs unnecessarily heavy and academic. Another effect is to provide a perhaps less "direct" decoding approach than the research in reading seems to indicate is needed. As I said in discussing Dr. Chall's work, there is some evidence that many children need more explicit learning of sound-letter relations than inference affords, though the explicitness need not necessarily include statements of phonic rules. In fairness, this evidence may not be strong enough to warrant great consideration, and most of these linguistics-based programs have not had enough trial to be given a good chance to prove themselves or to be included in research.

The content of the readers is not the best obtainable for first grade. Though some delaying of literature may be caused by the slow presentation of the sound-spelling system and the prolongation of phonetically controlled vocabulary, the problem is partly that the reading material is often editor-written even when it might be drawn from children's literature. In general, the content of the readers in these programs is disappointing, not only for first grade but often for later grades as well.

In addition to the general objections to these programs, there are others applying to them individually that prevent me from recommending them. Some do not lead well into writing, either because they explicitly exclude it or because they provide insufficient writing of sounds and words, and little or no dictation. Some include comprehension practice, or otherwise overburden and overstructure the package.

The materials of the third group could actually be classed as linguistics-based programs but differ in that they are programmed for self-instruction. The first two try to cover considerably more than literacy. They are *Reading in High Gear,* The Accelerated Progressive Choice Program, by Woolman (Chicago: Science Research Associates) and *Programmed Reading,* by Buchanan and Sullivan (New York: McGraw-Hill Book Co., Inc.). Both teach whole words grouped according to spelling patterns. Both teach spelling and writing. The programs consist entirely of booklets that pupils fill in by themselves under some monitoring by the teacher. The booklets contain blanks to fill, questions to answer, reading passages, and (very poor) composition assignments. Though self-pacing may be an advantage, these programs suffer the same drawbacks as the linguistic programs and are even longer and heavier. Paperwork is the order of the day; speech and social interaction are virtually lost. And not only is the package far too big, with great emphasis on comprehension practice, but the whole idea of embodying self-instruction in a long series of workbooks based essentially on the reinforcement of right answers seems very dull and uncreative to me. Except for the far overstructured composition assignments, the whole learning sequence is specifically predictable.

In contrast to these two programs, and to American self-instruction in general, is *The Programmed Reading Kit,* by Stott (Glasgow, Scotland: W. & R. Holmes, Ltd.), which consists of nothing but a teacher's manual and 30 teaching aids — all sorts of matching and interlocking cards for playing a wide variety of games, frequently in pairs and groups. These materials do not attempt — mercifully — to cover nearly as much as the preceding ones, but word grouping is used and the children progress at different rates, playing each game as long as they need to. What the children do is predictable only within the broad limits of the game rules; they create and transform words and sentences. Writing is not included, but the program is easy to supplement because it is open. *The Programmed Reading Kit* has been tried a number of years. *Reading in High Gear* and *Programmed Reading* are in the development stage.

The fourth group comprises some admittedly rather varied materials that do have in common, however, the presentation of sound-letter relations through whole words grouped in patterns, some of these patterns deriving from linguistics and some not. In all but one, sounding and blending is avoided, as in all the other programs mentioned so far. Three of these, all of which appeared in the 1950's, are *Phonetic Keys to Reading,* by Sloop, Garrison and Creekmore (Oklahoma City: Economy Co.), *The Royal Road Readers,* by Daniels and Diack (London, England: Chatto and Windus); and *The Structural Reading Series,* by Stern (Syracuse: The L. W. Singer Company, Inc.). All three programs spend a year presenting the phonographemic relations and include reviews that go beyond the first year. All avoid isolating sounds from whole words. The reading material is almost entirely editor-written. In *Phonetic Keys to Reading,* which contains readers for grades 1–3 but no workbooks, the material is thin Dot-and-Jim stuff. This program seems to do little with spelling and writing. *The Royal Road Readers,* a full softcover and hardcover series for the elementary years, with accompanying workbooks, has more interesting texts but is still not an anthology of children's literature, as I think such a series should be. Children write words and letters in the workbooks but apparently do not take dictation. *The Structural Reading Series* runs from grades K–2, consisting of workbooks, reading booklets, and cards. Word grouping is employed in a particular way — to teach sound-letter correspondences principally through initial and final sounds. Spelling and writing are given their due. Professing to be half allied to the meaning approach, this program does stretch out phonic instruction and would presumably be used as a supplement to a basal series.

From Sounds to Words, the Silver Burdett Spelling Readiness Program (Morristown, N.J.: Silver Burdett Company, 1966), a single workbook for pupils with a teacher's edition, focuses on hearing and saying speech sounds, on seeing and writing the letters that spell these sounds, and on the building of words. Letters are learned from initial and final positions, and the presentation of sound-spelling relations is based on patterns from linguistics. The program is to begin at the time when pupils are reading at "the first-reader level," can already write the letters of the alphabet, and have a desire to write. I wonder, however, if it could begin sooner, its utility being to supplement a reading-biased literacy program such as *The Programmed Reading Kit,* with which it might be combined.

Read Along with Me, by Allen and Allen (New York: Bureau of Publications, Teachers College, Columbia University) also has a very special limitation: since the learner reads part of the text along with the teacher, only one to four pupils are accommodated. It is essentially a tutorial method for parents or for teachers who can work with very small numbers. It is partly based on spelling patterns from linguistics, but also presents phonenes in isolation. The sounding-and-blending does produce artificial syllables (*kuh* and *tuh*). This program contains a picture alphabet chart, a book of "rhyming words" and simple sentences, a manual, and a book of stories with the sentences to be read by the teacher in small print and those to be read by the child in large print.

The fifth group consists of three older supplementary phonic programs, employing sounding-and-blending, that have been tried for 20 or 25 years and revised somewhat in recent years. They all present the sounds and spellings of English in isolation from whole words, or single them out from whole words, but the sounding-and-blending process avoids distortion by sounding consonants in combination with vowels, and word grouping is used to bring out sound-spelling regularities. In fact, hardly any program available today does *not* exploit word grouping in teaching children to grasp spelling patterns and discriminate component sounds and letters. But some programs, like this group and a few in the preceding group, may base the groups and the sequence of groups on practical teaching experience rather than on the descriptions drawn from structural linguistics. Often linguistic grouping and pedagogical grouping coincide, and there is certainly reciprocal influence, but grouping is central to Group One and Two programs and only secondary in the third, fourth, and fifth groups and some of the other programs. The chief divergence, however, between the present group and those described up to here is between the whole-word methods of focusing on sound-spelling components, which work by inference and "discovery," and the more "direct" methods of presenting the components separately as well as in words, which work by sounding and blending. As noted before, research so far seems to give an edge to the latter methods, but it is difficult to know how heavily this indication should weigh.

The members of this group are *Reading with Phonics,* by Hay and Wingo (Philadelphia: J. B. Lippincott Co.); *The Phonovisual Method,* by Schoolfield and Timberlake (Washington, D.C.: Phonovisual Products, Inc.); and *The Writing Road to Reading,* by Spalding and Spalding (New York: Whiteside, Inc.). Appearing first in the 1940's, these three programs were designed to supplement conventional basal reader series emphasizing sight reading. They present the sound-letter correspondences gradually during the first year and review them in the second. They state some phonic rules. They offer readiness instruction that can begin in kindergarten. They can be used remedially for older children who have not had such a program before. All three programs have the children hear, speak, read, and write each phonene as it is presented. Dictation and written spelling get strong attention, though *The Writing Road to Reading* stresses them the most.

The *Phonovisual* materials are slim, relying mainly on charts, cards, games, the chalkboard, and oral work. Emphasis is on recognizing initial and final consonants, then on "tucking in the vowels."[12] There are a consonant work-book and a vowel workbook but no readers. *Reading with Phonics* is a hard-cover textbook containing mostly word groups and accompanied by several softcover reader-workbooks, the texts being phonetically controlled. It is the most detailed and thoroughgoing of the three — too much so, I believe. It covers more of the uncommon spelling patterns, gives many more phonic rules, and takes the strongest bent toward reading. The program includes "Talking and Writing Stories" (in a phonetically controlled vocabulary). *The Writing Road to Reading* centers around 70 "phonogram" charts repre-senting 45 sounds and has no readers or workbooks. It teaches handwriting before reading, and in addition to giving frequent dictation from Ayres lists, lets the children write new words in sentences.

Phonovisual and *The Writing Road* are generally recommendable if modi-fied. Though the latter emphasizes writing more, both lead well into it. In both cases, I would suggest dropping the second year, which in the Spaldings' program includes not only a review but the keeping of a spelling notebook. I would prefer these two over *Reading with Phonics* because the latter is overloaded and also because it prepares less well for writing. The fact that these programs are supposed to spend a year presenting the sound-spellings need not disqualify them, since, so far as I can see, there is no serious reason, except in the case of *Reading with Phonics,* why they could not be worked through in a half year or less. The original pace seems to have been set more by their association with conventional basal readers than by necessity[13]

The sixth category combines a sounding-and-blending method, as in the materials above, with a grades 1–6 series of hardcover readers and contains only one very recent program, *The Open Court Basic Readers,* edited by Arther Tracy (La Salle, Ill.: Open Court Publishing Co.). This program represents the classic package of a literacy course embedded in a reading series. But it differs from conventional basal series, and the revisions of them thus far, in several important respects. The literacy program, called the Foundation Program, is over by the middle of first grade. During this period the children complete two workbooks, which are sensibly limited and full of poems, and read six editor-written stories with a phonetically controlled vocabulary. The

[12] In experiments reported by Crovitz and Schiffman in "Visual Field and the Letter Span," *Journal of Experimental Psychology,* Vol. 70, No. 2 (1965), it was established that adults given very brief tachistoscopic glimpses of eight-letter words remembered better the initial and final letters, even though their eyes were fixed on the middle of the words, where vision should be best. The finding presumably reflects reading habits. Common experience also supports the notion that proficient readers identify words first by these salient letters and fill in the interiors of words according to meaning cues, subject to verification. Thus *The Phonovisual Method* and *The Structural Reading Series* may be well founded as regards the scanning-and-processing movements of eye and mind.

[13] *Breaking the Sound Barrier, A Phonics Handbook,* by Sister Mary Caroline (New York: The Macmillan Company) is aimed completely at reading. It is a reference book of practical rules and procedures for attacking new words.

first hardcover reader, for the second half of first grade, is a fine anthology of children's literature. The teacher asks a few comprehension questions, mostly open-ended ones, but the emphasis is on children's responses.

The Foundation Program presents sounds in isolation but also in poems and in word groups. Alternate spellings for the same sound are presented together. Children see, hear, speak, and write the sounds. A readiness program makes use of many sorts of cards, tracing paper, and games. The sounding and blending avoids false syllables. For every reading lesson there is a writing lesson. Though sounds and spellings are presented before the whole class, those children who need more practice are screened down and given additional sessions, so that some individual pacing is possible.

The creators of the series have clearly set out to make the large package still viable by removing or revamping those things for which the old basals have been so heavily criticized. This is especially reflected in the readers, which, with some unfortunate exceptions, continue in the later grades to be anthologies of poems, fables, legends, folk and fairy tales, and myths. (Grades 5 and 6 have not been published yet.) The high literary quality begins in the pre-reading stage, when the teacher reads poems to the pupils from his manual. The exceptions occur in sections of the second- and third-grade readers that are devoted to science and stereotyped social studies content.

Other aspects of the large package are less desirable but could be omitted. In aiming for an "integration of the language arts," the producers have again made composition an adjunct of reading. Though the composition assignments that ask children to write from literature are like those recommended later in this book, others are poor, and in general this "integration" merely gives the illusion that composition is seriously dealt with when actually it is considerably underplayed. In addition, the series has a curious and unnecessary moralistic vein running through it. Finally, the teacher's manuals for each of the readers make rather heavy going, partly because the inevitable review sets in after first grade, but partly also because the reading selections are overworked for word study (including diacritical marks) and suggestions for discussion and composition.

For grade 1 alone — for the Foundation Program and beginning reading — the Open Court materials look very good. For succeeding grades I would suggest that the readers be used only for content as any other anthologies. Except for some suggestions and information about the literature itself, the teacher's manuals could be ignored. Dramatization, discussion, and composition should not be handled in this limited fashion, though of course the selections themselves will often provide good stimuli for these activities. With these reservations I recommend this program as one of the better possibilities available today.

The seventh class of materials features the use of a special alphabet and is represented by the recent Early-to-Read i/t/a Program, *by Mazurkiewicz and Tanyzer* (New York: Initial Teaching Alphabet Publications, Inc.)

The Initial Teaching Alphabet (i/t/a) puts the 44 sounds that it recognizes into one-to-one correspondence with just 44 written symbols, thus reducing drastically the number of spellings the beginner has to deal with. The program is designed to last 15 months, beginning in the sixth month of kindergarten, or one year if begun in first grade. The most rapid learners, we are told, can be introduced to all 44 sounds in three or four weeks, but a slower rate is desirable. The transfer to the regular alphabet is normally accomplished by degrees toward the end of grade 1. Fears that the i/t/a would create learning problems during and after the transfer — that it would have to be unlearned — do not seem to be borne out by several years of trials, for which a high degree of success is reported in comparison with conventional beginning reading. But research does not show that the alphabet itself is responsible for the results; as Dr Chall suggests, it may be that teachers who use it tend naturally to emphasize decoding. At any rate, though the i/t/a is not itself a method, it has become associated in America, and in these materials, with an early, intensive teaching of word components.

The materials consist of an i/t/a alphabet book, a number book, a readiness workbook, symbols-sound cards, and six serial readers with workbooks. Except for some excerpts, the texts are editor-written up to Books 4–6, and these are made up of selections from *Humpty Dumpty Magazine*, which puts out fairly good reading material but not superior literature. By a joint publishing arrangement, some of the selections of Scholastic Book Services are made available in i/t/a, but in general, teachers do not have a wide choice of reading texts since they are limited to what is printed in the special alphabet. This problem, of course, might be eventually overcome, as it should, because an important claim of the program is that children can read early and are not limited by a highly controlled vocabulary.

Unfortunately, this program attempts to teach Comprehension, Concepts, and How to Think. I doubt that this lingering alliance with the meaning approach constitutes a strong enough reason to reject the i/t/a. There is no program I could recommend that does not contain some things better ignored, though admittedly the conjunction of this defect with the drawback in available reading material does make it harder to weigh the great advantage that i/t/a has in permitting children to read and write sooner and less restrictedly. All the other programs mentioned so far are working under the hardship of teaching the correspondences between 40-odd sounds and some 280 spellings. Any method that can make English phonetic deserves special consideration, because one-to-one matching can shortcut learning problems. Certainly teachers should follow the development of these materials and whatever reports issue from research in which the results of this program are compared with those of other *decoding* approaches. (And one should not forget that i/t/a itself is just an alphabet and may be used independently of any particular materials.)

The eighth class contains again a single member. Caleb Gattegno's Words in Color (*Chicago: Encyclopedia Britannica Press*) *also reduces sound-symbol relations to a one-to-one correspondence but without altering traditional orthography.* That is, each of the forty-seven English sounds he recognizes is represented by a color that stands for it in the spellings. The program is organized around sounds, for the sound-color relations remain constant whereas spellings change color according to their sound in a given word. Children read and write earlier than in any other program except perhaps the *Early-to-Read i/t/a.* From the outset they read and write in black and white. The program has been tried since 1961, and a series of books on classroom experiences with it has been begun,[14] but no research summaries so far include comparison of it with other methods.

The color symbolism is not Gattegno's most important innovation in literacy instruction. A profound part of his method concerns playing with letters and words in ways that strike me as capable not only of teaching very thoroughly the phonetic components of words but also of exploiting this for truly creative intellectual development. In what he calls "games of transformation," for example, children change one word into another word by reversing, substituting, inserting, and adding letters. The same game is played with words in sentences. (These activities are similar to some recommended later in Chapter 10, though the latter were not derived from Gattegno. Indeed, I do not mean to imply that no other materials contain interesting games with letters and words, but his games go farther because they are such a critical part of the method itself. In the beginning, children make up real and nonsense words from the sounds they know, however few. The set of sounds and letters they know at any given moment constitutes a "restricted language" with which they do everything possible. By pointing rapidly from one symbol to another as children sound them, the teacher gives "visual dictation" whereby the combining of sounds and symbols in any order becomes habitual. I should think that children who had run Gattegno's course would know words inside and out, having developed both a very strong attention to sound-letter relations and a playfully intellectual involvement in language. Furthermore, the word building and "visual dictation" should prove very effective for children having a specific language disability, whatever labels (dyslexia, cross-dominance, etc.) or causes are assigned to it.

The quickest way to become acquainted with Gattegno's method is to read the teacher's manual or *Background and Principles.* A demonstration would be better. The materials themselves are: colored chalk, 21 colored charts, a phonic code chart, a pack of word cards, 14 worksheets, three "basic" books that introduce sound-signs, a word building book that unfolds the entire set of sounds, and a book of stories, editor-written and phonetically controlled.

[14] The first book is *Creative Writing*, by Sister Mary Leonore Murphy (Berkshire, England: Educational Explorers Limited, 1966), a log book of a trial in Australia.

These materials may be used in different ways and orders. Gattegno, in fact, shows great respect for the independence and creativity of both teacher and pupils, though he has said that forthcoming revisions of *Words in Color,* by the Zerox Company, New York, will contain more detailed instructions to the teacher. Emphasis is always on the building of words from sounds, the building of words into sentences, and the building of sentences into stories — all of this predictable only within the limits of the "restricted language" of the moment. After Book One a pupil can work through the paper material on his own, but a considerable amount of the work is oral. The program, it is claimed, can be completed in a few weeks or months, depending on age and intensity.

The ninth and final category comprises a single and unusual reader series that flies in the face of research and yet is not of the basal type — The Sounds of Language, edited by Bill Martin (New York: Holt, Rinehart & Winston, Inc., 1967.) The series consists of nothing but five readers for the first three grades — not even manuals or literacy materials of the sort surveyed so far. Though it is possible to look on this series as a pure anthology — and a very good one, the selections being drawn almost entirely from the Little Owl books — such a view would not do justice to the astute and attractive ways in which Martin exploits the "melody of language" and the "sound of sense" to teach beginning reading. ("The sound of the sentence is the fundamental sound in language.")[15]

Each selection is marginally annotated, in the teacher's edition, with imaginative and useful suggestions about how the selection should be orally read and about how to help children relate the sounds of language to the structure of words and sentences. The pupil edition contains nothing but the selections themselves, but varied and arresting typography singles out words and patterns and calls attention to the visual aspects of language. Vocabulary is uncontrolled, and the very first selections are from authentic children's literature. Many suggestions for writing are derived from the selections, which are considered a storehouse of words, sentence structures, and ideas, and the suggestions incorporate Sylvia Ashton-Warner's idea of giving out the children's favorite words on cards to be accumulated and learned through use.

Martin's method partakes of the whole-phrase, whole-sentence approach (not to mention the pure-love approach). Although he rejects any systematic phonics, and emphasizes sight learning, his method is different enough from that of basals or of look-say to justify claiming that it has not been covered by research. Whole words are not pretaught or taught in isolation. Children learn the visual equivalents of speech sounds, initially at least, by hearing the teacher read selections as they follow in the book. They are invited to soak up and savor the sounds of sentences in poems and stories, then they memorize

[15] P. 13 of supplement to teacher's edition of each reader.

the text, say it aloud together, and, as they begin associating strings of sounds with strings of letters, read back to the teacher chorally and in voice parts. Each selection is handled somewhat differently, depending on the accumulating word knowledge of the children and on particular verbal features of each selection that may be exploited to further this knowledge. Similarities, differences, and patterns in the sounds and spellings of words are brought out constantly but informally so that the child's global perception of whole sentences becomes refined into perceptions of component words and word-particles. Essentially, the method relies on the incantative power of literary language and on the child's desire to possess this language by eye as well as by ear and tongue.

The combination of pure love and shrewdness has a lot going for it that experienced teachers will recognize. Many bright, alert, clearheaded children would undoubtedly learn to read well by this method alone. But the general evidence suggests that the risk for many, if not most, other children might be great (though we can hardly claim that the pure-love approach has been satisfactorily researched out!). My thought in including *The Sounds of Language* is that it ought to be seriously considered as a program to use *in conjunction with* one of the independent phonics programs described above. Furthermore, whatever materials teachers select, they should look at this series for its superior presentation of the sight-meaning approach and thus for its value in maintaining an open mind.

Recommendations

PREFERRED MATERIALS

My first choice among current literacy materials would be a combination of *Words in Color* with *The Sounds of Language,* closely followed in preference by either The Open Court program through first grade, for teachers who want an accompanying reader, or by *The Phonovisual Method* or *The Writing Road to Reading,* the latter two in conjunction also with *The Sounds of Language. Words in Color* probably requires the most learning and effort on the part of the teacher. Teachers who are to use it should see demonstrations of it or, better still, attend a workshop given by one of Gattegno's associates. (Arrangements may be made by writing Dr. Caleb Gattegno, Schools for the Future, P.O. Box 349, Cooper Station, New York, New York.) *Words in Color* seems best to me because it meets the criteria and, all other things being equal in the eyes of research at the moment, has some additional merits as described above. The spirit of Gattegno's materials, moreover, is close to that of the curriculum in this book, and his method, as he says, lends itself well to creative writing and to the "language experience" approach, which is also a part of this curriculum.

VERSATILITY OF APPROACH

This is the place to emphasize that opting for *Words in Color* or any one of the other methods recommended above does not settle the whole problem of beginning reading and writing. For one thing, methods and materials are not everything. As we have seen, they may be less important than the relationship of teacher to pupils, the general learning atmosphere, and many other things as yet unknown. But at least there is no necessity for using inferior materials simply by default, by not knowing what *else* is available and by not assessing their worth in the light of reasoned criteria.

Second, if there is any consensus among researchers and reading specialists it is that no one emphasis is adequate for all learners. However much statistics indicate that *most* children learn better with explicit sound-letter instruction, we know from common experience that many children have learned to read and write very well with absolutely no phonics, and that some children have learned with no instruction at all. A case was reported recently of a five-year-old Negro boy of illiterate parents who learned to read alone at home with no printed matter at all — apparently from watching television, that old archfoe of literacy![16]

The second sort of recommendation, then, concerns versatility. In becoming literate, a child should be able to avail himself of several learning modes, since it is either true that one mode in particular is best for him, in which case he needs to try them all out, or that all modes help him through reciprocal reinforcement. This means in turn that either the teacher can conduct testing and screening to determine which mode fits which child, or he can use multiple approaches on all children on the assumption that even if one is best for a given child any child will benefit enough from all to make them worthwhile. Though it may seem that individual tailoring would be ideal if feasible, there are two arguments against it. First, the amount of perceptual, cognitive, and emotional testing it takes to match child to method is so great that the disruption and loss of time may not be worth it, especially if the tests are fallible. Second, chances are that other modes of learning will be worthwhile for a child, even if one is dominant for him, either because the others indeed reinforce the one or because they further his general growth in other ways. Thus a child who does not "need" *Words in Color* in order to become literate will most likely learn to read and write better and faster if he has it, and will at the same time develop his logical and creative powers (through discriminating, combining, and reversing at will the components of words).

But in a versatile classroom, where children participate in all the literacy practices offered but are free to partake more of some than of others, or to shift emphasis as they feel the need, it may be possible to enjoy the benefits of

[16] Reported in a talk at the Harvard Graduate School of Education on November 14, 1967, by Jane Torrey, Connecticut College.

both individual learning and multiple approaches for all. This versatility seems the most appropriate strategy to recommend.

Language experience. One of the other modes of learning I have in mind is embodied in the so-called language experience approach, whereby children discuss experiences or make up stories, dictate them, see how their own words *look* when transcribed, then read them from memory. This and many related practices are described elsewhere in this book, being distributed over the chapters on speaking and writing. Indeed, it is a major article of this whole curriculum that literacy and later reading should not be conceived as specialties but as aspects of total verbal growth. Certainly, however much a child may need phonics, he also must be able to integrate this small-focus work with the true function and value of written language — to share experience. The language experience approach teaches literacy through the whole word and the whole sentence. Children memorize and look at letter strings that mean something to them because they have uttered them for their own expressive purposes. High motivation brings a powerful psychological force to bear on visual memory.

Listening while reading. Another approach recommended also exploits the perception of the whole word and the whole sentence. It consists of the pupils' listening to a text as they follow the words visually. So far as I know this has been done little, though, as we have seen, *The Sounds of Language* includes it. Apparently it is not considered a method, for the practice is rarely if ever compared, in research, with other approaches. The virtue of this practice is that the child sees and hears words *simultaneously* and has the opportunity also to associate intonational contours with sentence endings. As an extension of merely being read to, the method is simple, and there is no question that it is pleasurable for children. They learn unconsciously as those children do who climb on their parents' laps during story time and follow along in the book.

The obvious drawback is that a child may be looking at one word while the teacher is sounding another. But once they have acquired a certain reading vocabulary, children can follow known words well enough to be sure of encountering the unknown words at the same moment the teacher sounds them. Also, new words that are repeated, as in rhymes and jingles, can be identified by the fact that the new shape recurs at the same time its sound is heard again. The old bouncing ball that was used in community-sing film projections to synchronize the singing of the audience could solve this problem if the text is projected. A flashlight arrow-indicator may be used so that children can chant or sing along following the movements of the indicator. Machines such as the Controlled Reader may also be of help. In any case, by one means or another, perhaps by language laboratory equipment, I am sure that the problem of synchronization can be solved if the listening-while-looking method is taken seriously, as common experience certainly warrants, however inadequate research is on this score.

Some publishers of readers have put out tapes of their texts so that pupils can listen as they read. By using either these or locally recorded tapes of other books, this method may be used with an individual reading program, if enough tape recorders are available.

A number of reading specialists I have talked with agree that reading while listening has great potential, and have difficulty explaining its neglect. Apparently such a homely practice has been deemed too unsophisticated to warrant thoroughgoing experimentation! I see no inherent reason why it should not be placed on a par with other kinds of literacy instruction.[17]

AN OPEN MIND

The last recommendation is to keep an open mind about the various possibilities of teaching literacy. Not only has it been an area of heated controversy in the past, but future developments will undoubtedly generate more dispute. For one thing, I am thinking of electronic machines with which children can interplay, not just O.K. Moore's automated typewriters but other machines only now being pondered. Since literacy learning consists basically of perceptual pairing, electronics may conceivably offer some very real help. "Computer-Assisted Instruction in Initial Reading," by Richard Atkinson and Duncan Hansen, will give some notion of the possibilities in this direction.[18] But aside from electronic machines, other yet unthought of ways to teach literacy may be developed. I can only reiterate that the research today may merely reflect the current limits of pedagogical imagination and the failure to do enough basic investigation of reading processes that might in fact suggest new approaches to literacy.

Spelling

Instead of making spelling instruction a separate strand of the curriculum, I suggest that it be treated first under the two-way literacy program and continued later in several ways to be mentioned below. An early, intensive instruction in sound-letter correspondences should establish a strong spelling base. Rehearsing of spelling knowledge should come through dictation and the constant effort to write original sentences. I agree with the Spaldings

---

[17] "An Exploratory Study in Reading on the First Grade Level Using a Combination of Trade Books and their Corresponding Phonograph Recordings," Wilma Jean Pyle, 1964, unpublished dissertation, Wayne State University, Detroit, reports an experiment in which children who read while listening scored a year higher in reading over children who only listened.

[18] *Reading Research Quarterly*, Volume 2, No. 1 (Fall, 1966).

(*The Writing Road to Reading*) that practice spelling books are a waste of time because pupils either memorize individual words, when rules of regularity could apply, or simply copy. I would not, however, advocate the Spaldings' practice of having pupils keep notebooks of spelling rules.

The main issue is that, aside from knowledge of prefixes and suffixes, which are included in many literacy programs, there is very little that can be taught that should not already have been taught in the initial presentation of the sound-letter relations. Most *irregular* spellings have to be memorized one by one. What new knowledge will help students *figure out* how to spell a word? As I see it, the problem is either in loss of attention or in loss of memory. That is, either the learner misspells a word he knows how to spell, which is frequently the case and can be corrected by proofreading, or else he has forgotten some phonic principle for regular words or the "look" of some irregular words. How students continue to learn to spell once the literacy program is over thus resolves itself *mainly* into the question of reinforcing attention and memory. To this we should add, however, the fact that some minor spelling patterns, concerning small groups of words, are omitted from some literacy programs and may need to be pointed out by the teacher to individuals who have trouble with them.

My recommendations aim to develop self-correction and self-diagnosis. Students take responsibility for spelling, but the teacher sets up processes that make this possible:

1. The teacher occasionally classifies for a pupil the *kinds* of errors he is making and thus teaches him how to diagnose for himself. Some errors can be corrected by referring to the phonic regularities of the literacy program or by mentioning some rarer spelling pattern not covered in the program. Some errors stem from faulty pronunciation, and some can be corrected only by memorizing the word. The main point is that students do not all make the same sorts of errors; each wants to improve *his* spelling. The group process for handling the writing leaves the teacher free to circulate and make such individual diagnoses (see page 207 for an example). This is far preferable to special spelling programs, which not only are tedious and time-consuming, but do not deal in a specific and timely way with just what each pupil needs. Such a shotgun approach necessarily teaches much that a given individual already knows and fails to single out what he does not know. From teacher diagnosis that becomes self-diagnosis, the learner can reduce a host of errors to a manageable number of corrective actions.

2. From the very beginning, pupils point out errors to each other in the writing groups when they exchange papers. Proofreading in groups teaches each individual to proofread alone.

3. Pupils should use dictionaries. The value of the dictionary is slight if pupils are seldom asked to write original sentences. If a program calls for abundant original writing, however, the dictionary becomes a major help

in learning to spell, because the pupil is constantly trying to spell out what he has to say, to grope actively from speech to letters.

4. The visual memory of words seen repeatedly in reading helps to standardize pupil spelling perhaps more than anything else after literacy training. Many adults are not sure of a spelling until they *see* it. Copious reading, then, is an important key. Three factors are critical here: If a very *small* vocabulary is incessantly repeated, as in the conventional basal readers, pupils simply do not become visually acquainted with enough words. And if sight learning of whole words is preferred over early, synthetic phonics, visual memory is apt to be less precise about the letters within words, that is, the exact spelling. An early focusing on the spellings of individual sounds should make the visual memory of even irregular words more acute and thus increase the benefit to spelling of reading. Finally, if skill builders, spellers, workbooks, and lockstep readers are thrown out, children will have more time simply to read a lot individually — with, I wager, remarkable results for spelling.

5. On occasions when a whole class is writing about something that will elicit a vocabulary in common, as in recording sensations at the same locale, mutual problems of spelling can be worked out in class discussion. The pupils are told to spell phonetically those words that they are not sure how to spell. Then afterwards the teacher asks for words that many had trouble with. Correct spellings are furnished by other pupils or by the teacher if necessary, and the teacher remarks briefly on why the phonetic spellings were incorrect: the word is totally irregular, or it is assigned one regular spelling rather than an alternative one (*reins,* not *rains* or *ranes*).

6. The teacher can dictate words or sentences for spelling practice, and go over them afterwards to point out reasons for misspellings. But this should be a last resort. During the literacy program, and for a while following it, pupils can stay fairly involved in dictation, but the older they get, the leaner their interest and motivation become. For spelling practice, composition may be less systematic but is probably more valuable and efficient in the long run. (See also the sections on taking dictation, starting on pages 137 and 176, and the remarks on page 134.)

Punctuation

DEFINING THE LEARNING PROBLEM

Punctuation is like spelling in that it translates speech to print. Learning punctuation also involves perceptual pairing and applies equally to reading and writing. As with sound-letter relations, the task is to match some graphic symbols with some voice qualities — in this case, some things like commas and periods with some other things like pitch and pause. It helps to think of two kinds of punctuation, oral and written. Pre-school children and illiterate adults can talk all day and have no punctuation problems, because the voice indicates the segments of speech in meaningful ways. The issue of writing punctuation is how to transcribe certain significant voice qualities such as stress, pitch, and juncture (the interaction of which I will call somewhat inaccurately but conveniently "intonation"). The issue of reading punctuation is how to translate commas and periods back into voice qualities.

Punctuation is not part of grammar. It may reflect grammar (syntax), but only because intonation does. Above all, good punctuation is a set of signals showing the reader how to read the flow of words as the speaker would say them. It should be presented to pupils in this way, not as rules. The auditory principles that underlie the rules are simpler to understand, more profound, and more accurate. All the rules do is overgeneralize the relations among sense, syntax, and sound. "Separate clauses by commas" merely echoes the fact that a partial drop in intonation, together perhaps with a pause, *usually* separates them. But you have to understand "clause" to understand the rule. Moreover, the rule is inaccurate because it is rigid. Educated writers often do not separate clauses with a comma if the clauses are short and if no ambiguity results. What the rule describes is not always true of what we do, and what the rule prescribes is not always indicative of what we should do. What we should do is punctuate with pencil as we do with voice. And that is a simpler principle to follow.

In these early years, children will seldom need to do more than use:

1. A period for a full stop (indicated by final fall of intonation).

2. A question mark for an interrogative intonation.

3. An exclamation mark for emphatic stress.

4. Commas for series (indicated by a special suspended intonation).

5. Commas separating clauses and setting off words, when the sustained intonation is interrupted by a partial drop.

The main problem by far is breaking the flow of words into sentences. Defining a sentence as a complete thought is futile; not only children but linguists and philosophers as well do not understand what a complete thought is. It could be a word, a phrase, a sentence, a paragraph, or an entire book. I believe the only way a sentence can be defined is by vocal segmentation, the sense of closure conveyed by a complete intonation contour (which of course expresses the intuition of syntactic completion). Children know a sentence when they hear one, and this operational definition is what teachers should utilize. Often a pupil mistakenly puts a period and capital in the middle of a sentence even though he would read the sentence correctly. This results, I believe, from being confused by directions about how to punctuate. But the more common mistake is the failure to segment the word flow at all, a failure that frequently persists — needlessly — into junior and senior high school, causing dreary hours of proofreading by a long chain of teachers. The problem is not that difficult. That it persists is testimony to the inadequacy of the rules approach and the complete-thought definition.

The chief hurdle to punctuating well is not being aware of what one hears. Children hear and produce intonation with ease — in fact, with such ease that they are almost totally unconscious of what they are hearing and producing. The features of intonation — stress, pitch, and pause — are especially important cues to meaning when one's vocabulary is limited. Even when he does not understand the words, the child can tell from vocal cues much of an adult's meaning and intention. It is fair to say that children are at least as responsive to intonation as adults, probably more so. But in order to punctuate with periods and commas as they punctuate orally, the pupils will have to raise their intuition to the level of awareness. A combination of several techniques will do this.

PROCEDURES

In the first place, explain that when we talk, our voices rise and fall, pause and go on, lean hard on some words and lightly on others. Illustrate: "He likes candy," and "He likes candy?" Which is the question? How can they tell? Ask the difference between "I live in the white house," and "I live in the White House." How can they tell? Then say, " 'At night I sleep.' That is a sentence. My voice rounds it off and you can tell it is finished. This is a sentence too: 'Get your clothes.' And so is this: 'What did you eat?' Now, suppose I say, 'At night I sleep —' Is that finished? Why not? The whole sentence is 'At night I sleep with my teddy bear.' " Go on to pair off "Get your clothes —" with "Get your clothes off the bed," and "When did you eat —?" with "When did you eat the pie?" Make up other finished and unfinished sentences and ask them which is which. Then they can make up some pairs. In other words, through comparison, attention is focused on the vocal distinctions we make when we talk and listen.

Relate oral speech to print by saying, "But there is no voice in a book. How are we going to know how to read the words the way the person would say them? When we write, how can we let our reader know where our sentences begin and end?" This is the place to illustrate the use of periods, capitals, and question marks. Later, commas are introduced the same way.

Occasionally, when reading aloud as the children follow the text, tell them to notice how your voice follows the punctuation. Make a point of emphasizing pauses and intonation. When they read aloud remind them to "read the way the periods tell you to." Punctuation is constantly depicted as signals to guide the reader, to help him recreate the silent voice behind the words.

When they are writing in groups, tell the scribes to read aloud to their groups what they have written and the others to say where the periods and capitals go. Before passing on a group composition, the pupils test sentences in this way. Individuals writing alone should pair off, read their papers to each other, and check the segmenting. The writer understands that he is to read so that his listener can follow most easily; the listener says where he thinks the periods go. Of course, children just learning to read often read aloud haltingly, without being able to create the same intonation contours they would if speaking the same words in conversation. But a pupil reading his own writing does not have to decode the words one by one.

Sometimes a passage from a book or from pupil writing can be projected without punctuation, read aloud by the teacher or a pupil, and punctuated by the listening audience on their dittoed copies of the text. This is frankly a quiz with right answers, but it can be pleasant enough and will help beginners a great deal. For humor, project ambiguous strings of words that will inevitably be misread. One of my daughters, a five-year-old cracking her first primer, was reading to me one evening the sentence "Call the dog, Janet" but ignored the comma and read instead, "Call the dog Janet." She sensed the contradiction between her reading and what the meaning should have been, but could not put her finger on what was wrong. She merely paused and looked quizzical. I pointed out the comma and said that it meant the sentence should be read like *this,* and read it properly. She burst out laughing. When she had subsided a little, she explained the difference in meaning to me, read the sentence both ways several times, recalled the joke two or three more times, and broke up again each time.

Chapter 6

Reading

Though treated here as a separate topic, for convenience, reading is not, in this curriculum, deemed a specialty, to be isolated in scheduling or taught by a specialist, except perhaps for remedial decoding.

Since I do not undertake in this book to recommend titles of reading selections for the different grades, my remarks about reading will be necessarily general. In Chapter 2 I described an approach to reading that excludes some practices that one might ordinarily expect to find under the heading above. Here I would like to recommend some classroom procedures for handling the reading and some principles for selecting material. In most cases, the remarks are meant to apply throughout elementary school and even, where obviously relevant, to the years beyond.

Classroom Procedures

THE TEACHER READING ALOUD

The teacher should read large quantities of stories and poems to children. Before pupils can read much themselves, this practice is of course a necessity if their appetite for literature is to be both nourished and satisfied. It also makes reading a common part of everyday life and shows many children of non-reading parents what books are all about and what pleasure can be associated with them. And it puts the teacher in a giving position. While receiving this gift, the children become possessed of the urge to do themselves what the teacher does. In this respect he becomes a model to emulate. His continuing to read to children who have themselves learned how to read serves to show what good oral reading is like — how it recreates a storyteller's voice, how it brings out moods and feelings and meanings, how it follows cues of punctuation and typography. A very important part of reading to readers is having them follow the text with their eyes as they hear the teacher translate it into voice. The pupil can hear all aspects of the print brought to life — letters, typography, and paragraphing. Even in the upper elementary grades the teacher should periodically read, especially when the text contains a number of new irregular words, but also to maintain a good oral model.

Children Reading Aloud

The problem of the "reading circle." Children should read aloud so that they can hear the writer's voice in their heads when they read silently. The classic problem, however, concerns how each individual can have an ample opportunity to do this without boring his classmates, who, in the conventional reading circle, have to wait for him to figure out words haltingly but have no motive to do so because they have in their hands the same text he has. The halting can be somewhat resolved by asking the pupil to read a sentence silently before reading it aloud. And the motive to listen can be strengthened by asking the listeners to close their books while the reader carries the story forward. But these dodges do not resolve the real dilemma, which is that serial tutorial is being carried on in a group; the group cannot justify itself, and exists only because the teacher lacks time to coach each child individually. This managerial problem has arisen partly from a condition of the old basal readers, namely, that the slow introduction of words pretaught by sight entailed such a tight control of vocabulary that all children in a group had to be reading the same text together. A class was dependent on a single, graduated reader series through which all children marched step by step but at different rates according to the groups they were in. There is nothing inherent in learning to read that requires such a procedure.

When one child reads aloud to a group of classmates, he should do so because he alone has the text and they are not familiar with what they will hear. In other words, they constitute a real audience that he is entertaining, and they listen to hear what the book says, as when the teacher reads. But doesn't this already presuppose good oral reading? In a certain measure, yes. That is, the reader should have had some previous individual coaching, and, more immediately, he should have rehearsed his reading of the particular text for the day. My recommendations aim to make just these things possible.

Individual coaching. During the phase of beginning reading, children come up to the teacher and read aloud to him one at a time while the rest of the pupils are reading silently or doing other work. This practice stands in lieu of the conventional reading circle and is rendered feasible by other practices to be mentioned shortly. By taking a certain number each day, the teacher can hear all pupils once or twice a week. The procedure is that the pupil comes up and reads aloud some poem, short tale, or perhaps only a passage, that he has already read silently. The session is presented in the spirit of "now *you* read to *me*," a spirit that is easier to sustain if the children are reading from different books, and if time permits each to read a whole short selection. The coaching part consists of letting the pupil know if he is reading too softly or indistinctly, failing to follow punctuation, or misunderstanding the sound value of certain spellings. If the reading is very halting, the teacher should diagnose the problem: Is the child's decoding ability still poor in some respects, so that he has to puzzle out painstakingly? Is the text too difficult for him as regards either the amount of irregular spellings or the sophistication of the content? Sometimes the teacher may want the child to read a fresh text on sight, to determine how well he can do without a prior silent reading. Suppose a child reads inexpressively. Merely saying that he does and adding a directive to "put more expression into it" is not very helpful, and may even lead to contrived vocalizing. It is better to ask the reader what he thinks is the feeling under the lines, or the mood of the story situation, then to ask him to "make me feel that" or to "bring it to life the way you do when you're dramatizing a story." Convey the idea that you want to be read to in the same way he likes to be read to. Of course, this "read-to-me" spirit can be easily destroyed if the coaching is delivered in a severe fashion. The diagnostic remarks and suggestions should be perceived by the child as truly helpful for his own purposes, some of which relate to his role, discussed farther on, as reader to other children.

Choral reading. A social activity that children like very much is reading aloud in unison, as a chorus. Supported, and sometimes corrected, by the voices of the group, each individual can hide in the herd and let himself go. Better readers can carry along the less able ones, though it is also true that the latter can mumble uncertainly through, and that is why the individual coaching is necessary. Nevertheless, shaky readers can be bold, make guesses when they are not sure, without becoming personally exposed, and hear whether their guesses are right or not. Choral reading is, of course, one occasion when having a common reader is useful, but the teacher can also project texts overhead. These texts should have strong rhythms and cadences and varied and interesting "phrasing" (in the musical sense). Poetry is excellent, and songs especially will help teach phrasing and rhythm, since the melody usually parcels out word phrases according to musical phrases. Some of the books mentioned later in this chapter not only afford many good selections for choral reading but make particular suggestions to the teacher about how each one might be read, indicating which lend themselves to reading in "parts" or sub-choruses. Breaking the class into groups that alternate reading voice parts is, in fact, an especially pleasurable and instructive variation of choral reading. (What are the textual cues for each group?) It prepares for reading play scripts and remains popular among older children too. Generally, choral reading supplements the individual sessions by providing additional practice in sounding texts aloud. Both will undergird the following practice.

Individual reading aloud to a small group. Children take turns reading poems and stories to four or five other children to whom the text is either unknown or ever welcome. The main point in any case is that one pupil shall entertain others who shall constitute a real and expectant audience. This practice presupposes that children are reading from different books, and that a large variety of single copies are indeed on hand. Since the kinds of literacy programs I have recommended make individual reading possible in the first grade, there is no reason why pupils should all have to read the same texts. By reading to each other, they can all become familiar with a wide range of children's literature and begin the exchange of reading experience that is to continue in all the later years. The audience has a motive to listen because it does not know the text or, at any rate, does not have it before them. The reader has a motive to read fluently and expressively because his group is dependent on him for entertainment.

The procedure is to divide the class into groups of four to six as for other small-group activities and to direct each child to bring to the group a book from which he is going to read *something he has already read silently.* During silent reading periods, they are told to choose and, in effect, rehearse one selection for the group meeting. Then they take turns reading their selections, not necessarily all in one session. Explain that, without interrupting the reading too much, the listeners may let the reader know if they are having trouble hearing well, and may let him know if he has made an obvious mistake. After each finishes, the listeners may ask the group about things they did not understand or talk about the content of what was read. These sessions, in other words, may provide some feedback to the reader and also launch discussion of texts. Whether the groups should or should not comprise children of mixed reading abilities is something that trial must determine. My suggestion is to try mixing them first, so that abler readers can help the less able. As group process whereby pupils teach each other, the practice merely establishes in reading the same learning method employed in speech, drama, and writing.

But the success of this practice depends on a reinforcing coordination of all the reading activities, silent and oral. Choral practice and individual coaching by the teacher take place concurrently with reading to the group, in a long-range sense, and silent reading of different texts precedes, more or less immediately, each group session. This means a silent and an oral reading period virtually every day (for which time is freed by doing away with phonic drills and rehearsals and "skill-building" or "comprehension practice"). The teacher might schedule each day the meeting of all but two of the reading groups, always leaving free eight to twelve children (the members of the two "fallow" groups) who will come up and read individually to him. Or he may prefer to have individuals read to him during the silent period so that he can sit in on groups during the oral period. Choral reading can be more sporadic and presents no scheduling problems, since the whole class is involved.

So far as I know, this particular set of activities for dealing with reading has not been tried on a regular and thoroughgoing basis, but I think it may solve some important problems. In some such manner children must be allowed to receive individual help and at the same time to practice reading aloud in an authentic group without inflicting boredom on listeners and without inflicting on themselves, if they are slower readers, the painful embarrassment that often makes them want to avoid reading altogether and for good.

DRAMATIZATION AND DISCUSSION

To these practices we should add dramatic work and small-group discussion, which, although treated elsewhere in this book, play a considerable part in learning to read. Their essential relationship to reading is that through them reading texts are elaborated and further explored for implications. It is from reading that dramatization and discussion draw a large part of their content. And they furnish a major answer to the question of what to do with a text after reading it silently.

The frustrating issue for the teacher is that silent reading is not directly teachable. The child is alone, and what goes on in his head at that moment depends greatly on what learning has *already* taken place, though we shouldn't forget that self-teaching goes on during sheer practice. But what he does with his silent reading — afterwards — becomes part of the learning that will precede, and transfer to, his next session of silent reading.

The traditional practice is to pose questions to the pupil about what he read, comprehension questions designed to find out how well he understood (test) and to make him think more about it (teach). The latter is what is important, of course — to invite him to relate facts and draw inferences he may not have while reading silently, and therefore to help him do so the next time he reads a new text alone. But it would be hard to find a child who does not resent the inevitable quizzing, by the teacher or the printed questionnaire, on what he has just read. He has enjoyed the story and now he must face the music, endure the commercial, pay the piper. Has anyone attempted to estimate the damaging effect of this on children's will to read? In rat-and-pigeon psychology, this administering of a pain after a certain act would be called "negative reinforcement," when it is intended to discourage the act. Indeed, how many *adults* would read if they had to face a battery of questions afterwards?

In order to dramatize or discuss a text, pupils have to think about the meaning of it and follow out implications. Enacting a story or poem is translating a text into voice, movement, and space. Characterization, sequence of actions, mood, setting, build-up, and climax have to be grasped in order to be rendered by the children. Disagreements in interpretation have to be discussed. Inventing details of action and dialogue and extending stories are based on implications and potentialities of the text. They help pupils render future texts in their own minds.

Small-group discussion of texts should take off from children's own questions and spontaneous comments, as allowed for in the reading groups, or take off, in the trained, topic-centered groups, from subjects the pupils have drawn from common reading. Asking the group for help in understanding some point in the text should become a natural habit. There are some things a pupil *knows* he did not grasp; he should have plenty of opportunity to find out what he missed, and perhaps even why he missed it. Comparing reactions and interpretations is also of vast importance, for it allows the reader to discover other things he has misunderstood *without* knowing it. It also shows that his reaction or interpretation may not be the only one justified by the text. Comparison itself often starts good discussion, because each child can refer to the text to support his reading of it. It is in this way that textual examination should occur. The teacher may suggest sometimes that members of the reading groups take turns reading aloud a single poem or story and talk about the varying renditions. This discussion, too, may cause them to look back closely at the text.

A possible procedure for the small groups trained especially for topical discussion is to bring to the meeting their copies of something read in common, agree on one or two things in the selection they want to talk about, and then start discussion. Or, during the conclusion of one session, when the group is settling on a topic for next time, they may propose something in their current reading.

INDIVIDUAL SILENT READING

A final kind of talk about reading matter can occur in groups assembled expressly for the purpose of exchanging experiences in the individual reading program. So far I have assumed such a program but not described it. It consists essentially just of providing books and time for children to read a lot on their own, making their own selections from a diverse array in the classroom or library, and signing them out to take home voluntarily. After the literacy program, children ought to read considerably more alone than in common. But instead of awarding a gold star for the meritorious service of having read a book, or rewarding the pupil for his efforts by making him write a report on it, the children should meet once a week or so in small groups to show and tell about what they have read. The function of this, they are told, is to let them familiarize each other with the books available and to give others an idea of whether they also would want to read them. (Some books may be brought from home and exchanged on loan.) Each takes a turn showing and telling about his book. The others are to ask whatever questions they want. Some of these may be factual questions about the content, and some may be evaluative questions calling for a judgment. In either case, the reader may be prompted to think more about the book without feeling quizzed by an authority figure.

Finally, children do not always have to do something with what they have read. They should be allowed to read just for pleasure and the pursuit of interests. Sharing is important, but so is solitary rumination.

SPECIAL MEASURES TO INCREASE EFFICIENCY

At the beginning of the preceding chapter, I defined reading in a deliberately narrow way — as decoding or word recognition — in order to exclude from the definition whatever is not *unique* to reading. The purpose of this strategy was to clarify the problems of learning to read. Now I would like to qualify that definition so as to broach the problem of increasing reading efficiency once word recognition has been mastered.

Visual processing of words. What the definition needs is something about the visual assimilation and mental strategies that go on during reading. The proficient reader does not give equal attention to all words or to all parts of words. He does not need to. There are many cues of word structure, syntax, and sense that make it unnecessary to process every letter, word and phrase in the same way. In a very real sense, we do not see everything in a text even when we "read" every word of it. For example, proofreading for typographical errors is very difficult because we unconsciously "fill in" the obvious — the letters we know are there because of how the rest of the word is spelled, articles and prepositions we know are there because nothing else could occupy certain slots in the sentence. This means that if errors exist in these obvious positions, we will miss them. Familiarity with the text makes proofreading even more difficult, because we fill in even more. For another example, the cloze procedure of deleting some letters and words from a text does not prevent readers from getting all the meaning of the text — provided that deletions are of *redundant* items, that is, of items that are dispensable because their information is conveyed equally well by other cues. If more important items are deleted, however, the text will become ambiguous or cryptic. Compare:

_ole_ant
tol_ra_t

Surely the letters deleted in the first were more essential, while those in the second were more redundant. Compare also:

I would _____ found it difficult _____ believe.
I _____ have found it _____ to believe.

But redundance is relative to the knowledge and experience of the reader:

Give _____ this _____ our _____ bread.
Marx's theory of historical _____ derives from _____'s
concept of thesis and _____.

Scanning and guessing, in short, are integral to proficient reading. Swiftly, automatically, we attend to critical cues and infer what is in between. As we are reading along we constantly corroborate inferences by matching them against our ongoing interpretation. Occasionally, when something doesn't seem to fit, we "regress"; we flick our eyes back to a word or phrase and discover, for example, that what we took to be *importing* was actually the less common word *imparting*. It is useless to object that this is mere skimming or sloppy reading; it is what every proficient reader does, including those whose comprehension is best.

Differences between visual and auditory processing. Actually, not all of this perceptual scanning and mental processing is unique to reading. When we listen to someone speak we attend in the same selective fashion and have no more need to "hear" every syllable, in order to understand everything said, than we need to "see" every syllable when reading. Both seeing and hearing partake of the same general data-processing system. But there are differences too. One is that reading involves eye movements. Another is that reading concerns arrangement in space, whereas speech concerns movement in time. We can assimilate spatial information faster than temporal information — read faster than listen. These two differences are related: *how* fast we can assimilate visual information depends on how we have learned or not learned to move our eyes during reading.

Eye movements. A number of oculomotor studies have determined that reading consists of a series of fixations that last about a quarter of a second each, regardless of the reader's speed. About 94 percent of reading time passes in fixation. The rest is spent moving the eye from one fixation to the next. Time is lost, of course, in sweeping back to the left margin and in regressing. Since nothing can be seen during movement, only during fixations does true reading occur. Comparison of the eye movements of fast and normal readers shows that the fast reader fixates less often and regresses less often. The number of fixations, however, depends on how much area the eye takes in at each fixation and on what spatial pattern they create in moving over the page. It seems that the very fast reader moves his eyes in irregular fashion, which, I interpret, means that he fixates on critical textual points that he has learned to scan for, wherever these may occur on the page. Since we are told that four words represent the maximum area spanned in one fixation, very fast readers who comprehend well could not possibly be catching every word. By good scanning, they must be getting the maximum benefit of redundance. To this add the fact that the most rapid readers move their eyes vertically down the page, swinging to left and right in a smaller arc than do normal readers. They do not waste time sweeping from right margin back to left, like a typewriter, then moving all the way out to the right again. The vertical movement undoubtedly also enlarges the span of each fixation into a circle so that they catch words above and below the line of type fixated on.

Breaking early reading habits. How do habits of eye movement come about, and should they be changed? This is where the second difference between reading and speech must be considered — the difference between visual and auditory processing, spatial arrangement and temporal order. When first learning to read, children have to relate print to speech in order to recognize letter combinations in a book as familiar vocal words. Moving at first from one word to the next, they sound out words in succession just as one utters them in speech. Thus they learn the horizontal, left-to-right convention of reading and thereby learn at the same time the habits of eye movement that characterize the normal adult reader. This initial learning intensifies the habit of vocalizing while reading, and this habit, too, persists into adulthood, in the form of subvocalization. Thus the reading speed of normally proficient readers remains bound to the slow temporal order in which words are successively spoken. The advantage afforded by visual processing — the more rapid assimilation made possible by spatially presented information — is mostly wasted.

Both practical experience with fast readers and such considerations as I have just surveyed have led some reading experts to conclude that normally proficient adults read much more slowly than necessary, and that good school education should include the breaking of habits learned in beginning reading — namely, subvocalization and regular, horizontal eye movement. If they are right, as I believe they are, then a valuable kind of instruction has been much neglected. Educators have been justifiably wary, however, about believing the claims of speed-reading methods. The issue is whether one trades a gain in speed for a loss in comprehension.

The bugaboo of comprehension. Up to a point, the argument that fast reading increases comprehension makes good sense, for the accumulation of actions, images, or ideas that occurs as one reads has more effect and meaning for the reader if continuity is strongly sustained. Undoubtedly, some children read too slowly to comprehend well. On the other hand, when speed-reading proponents claim to increase rate without impairing comprehension, they run afoul the same problem that bedevils standard reading tests: Is there any really satisfactory way to measure comprehension?

Most teachers and school administrators have a much greater faith in standard reading tests than do either reading experts or testing experts, who are aware that the measuring of rate and comprehension is tremendously relative to the type of reading material and to the reader's purpose. The reader's purpose in turn determines how he reads — for detail, for main argument or story, or selectively for certain facts or points. A tester, however, must *assume* a certain reading motive and prepare questions that test the kind of comprehension matching the motive he has assumed. If the test is complex enough to allow for all possible reading purposes, then what is one to make of the scores, the meaning of which would vary according to each individual's motive in reading the texts about which he was questioned? Comprehension questions are of course designed to discover whether a reader has understood certain facts, points, or implications. A reader may miss some of these but catch others he was not asked about, because his purpose, emphasis, or interpretation lay in a different direction from that of the test maker. But let us suppose that any student taking a reading test has for motive the desire to score high, so that he assumes responsibility for total comprehension of small facts, main continuity, and all sorts of possible inferences. Then wouldn't a comprehension test covering all these matters give a valid index of his reading efficiency when combined with a test of reading rate? Or is it testmanship that is being tested? One junior high school student told me that during her elementary years she learned to take SRA comprehension tests, and score high, without even reading the passages — by looking first at the questions, which follow a pattern, and then by picking answers out of the texts! In sum, reading speed is dependent for significance on reading comprehension, and reading comprehension is dependent for significance on a host of factors that have not been accommodated and may never be satisfactorily accommodated in testing procedures.

Methods for increasing speed. Partly because the measurement of comprehension is fraught with unreliability, research on speed-reading methods is controversial and inconclusive. Also, some experiments indicate a loss of comprehension for students given a speed-reading course and some indicate that rate is substantially increased without loss of comprehension. These experiments usually involve college students and compare a speed-reading group with a control group when both groups are taking a common reading course. One experiment compared the four main speed-reading methods with each other. These methods were Tachistoscope, Controlled Reader, Controlled Pacer, and Paperback Scanning. All four were reported to produce higher rates and greater flexibility than normal without loss of comprehension, but the book-scanning method excelled over all three others,[1] which scaled down in this order — Controlled Pacer, Controlled Reader, and

[1] Leonard Braam and Allen Berger, "Effectiveness of Four Methods of Increasing Rate, Comprehension, and Flexibility," *Journal of Reading*, Vol. 11, No. 5 (Newark, Delaware: International Reading Association, 1968). This volume also contains a compact bibliography, "Ten Important Sources of Information on Speed Reading," by Allen Berger.

Tachistoscope. But the reading expert asks immediately, "What kind of comprehension test was used?" As the authors point out, the test covered only details.

The book-scanning method bears resemblance to the Wood Reading Dynamics Method, a well known commercial course that has increasingly gained the serious attention of reading experts, most notably of Russell Stauffer and his staff at the Reading-Study Center of the University of Delaware, which is certainly the best source of information and advice for teachers interested in reading speed and efficiency. The Wood Method teaches readers to move the eyes rapidly down the page while pacing with the hand. In order to break the habit of subvocalizing and of making numerous fixations, the students scan and turn the page at a rate far too fast for comprehension, then they slow down and practice scanning at a rate still higher than their usual speed, until the new habits of visual processing make good comprehension possible. There is more to the method than this, but these are the main ways it breaks the habits of beginning reading and allows eye and mind, not oral speech, to determine the speed of assimilation.

At the University of Delaware School of Education, the Wood Method has been much explored. Some of the staff have learned the method, taught it to students, and given outside teachers an in-service course on it. Various pieces of experimental research have been conducted, there and elsewhere, to determine if the Wood claims of greatly increased speed with no loss of comprehension are true. William Liddle conducted the most authoritative such experiment, with University of Delaware students, and found that reading rates were tripled and quadrupled in the experimental group but that this group scored lower on comprehension of fiction than the control group and lower also on comprehension of non-fiction in two of the three sub-tests (lower on "facts" and "Inferences" and the same on "Critical Reflection.")[2]

It would be very unfortunate if this finding confirmed the common prejudice that any effort to increase reading efficiency, including the Wood Method, is necessarily shallow and will produce mere skimming. Besides the uncertainties of measuring efficiency, I would point out here that the students in this experiment may simply have been pushed too far in order to achieve rates that tripled and quadrupled their initial speed. The fact remains that the overwhelming majority of adults are held to the speed at which they learned to read, even though their early reading habits are no longer functional for them. This is an absurd state of affairs, especially in an era of information explosion that requires adults to assimilate huge amounts of print. And it is this state of affairs that has prompted so many professional people and university students to seek out commercial courses that will do for them what schools never did. The problem of reading efficiency is one that schools must deal with. This does not mean that people *should* read fast

[2] "An Initial Investigation of the Wood Reading Dynamics Method," unpublished dissertation, University of Delaware, 1965, summarized in *Dissertation Abstracts*, Vol. 27 (September, 1966), p. 605-A.

but rather that they should be *able* to read fast when they want. The principle of flexibility — reading different texts in different ways for different purposes — is a principle now well established among many reading experts, but it will remain a hollow conviction if schoolchildren are stuck with their original habits and thus have no real options.

Recommendations. In view of the unsettled problems described above, it is difficult to make recommendations as definite as one would like about reading efficiency. But despite inconclusiveness, I strongly urge teachers to become acquainted with the Wood Reading Dynamics Method, which seems to be the best contender so far, and to try it with pupils whose mastery of word recognition makes subvocalization and short eye movements no longer necessary for them. (Russell Stauffer has suggested starting the Wood technique with able sixth-graders.) It would be very helpful for teachers to look at *Speed Reading: Practices and Procedures,*[3] especially "Uses and Limitations of Speed of Reading Programs" by Miles Tinker, who affirms, among other things, that book-scanning is equal to or better than methods employing machines. Tinker also points out that ineffectual eye movements do not cause reading problems; oculomotor behavior is flexible and adjusts to whatever perceptual and mental way of assimilating one chances to learn. My recommendation is that the way of assimilating print represented by the Wood Method be made available from the later elementary grades on, without pushing for immoderate speeds and pending further research and development in reading efficiency.

Practically, it seems necessary either for teachers to take a course at one of the Wood schools or for in-service training to be arranged for groups of teachers. Either the Wood Institute or the Reading-Study Center might help make such arrangements. At any rate, I know of no manual that enables the teacher to read about the method and then apply it. The basic technique, however, of scanning down the page at exaggerated speed, using the hand as a pacer, then slowing the speed and practicing regularly at one's maximum rate of understanding is a technique one might with discipline master well enough to teach to others.

Remedial Reading

The general view taken in this book on "non-readers" or "poor readers" of the later grades is that these children's problem results either from an inadequate decoding instruction or from personal characteristics such as low intelligence, faulty perception, poor motivation, or emotional disturbance that are *general* learning problems not confined to reading only and therefore not treatable as only reading problems.

[3] Volume X, March, 1962 (Newark, Delaware: Reading-Study Center, University of Delaware.)

As to the first, *Words in Color, Phonovisual,* and *The Writing Road to Reading,* like most independent phonics materials, are intended to be used, and have been used, to teach remedial reading or beginning reading to illiterate adults. (In fact, before creating materials for primary school, Gattegno developed his method while teaching older illiterates of different languages how to read.) A key feature of remedial work seems to be a decoding emphasis, usually explicit phonics instruction, even in schools where the initial literacy program does not show such emphasis. Chall's survey of clinical studies indicated that special focus on sound-letter pairing is a considerable help to children with a specific language disability. Such spokesmen for the Orton Society as Anna Gillingham have long asserted (along with the disputed theory of brain-lobal cross-dominance) that the synthesizing of separately presented letters and sounds affords the most effective help for those children tending to reversal and having subnormal auditory and visual discrimination. It is difficult to escape the implication that pupils who get this early will not wind up in a remedial program a few years later. If they do, the best remedy seems to be one of the literacy programs cited above, a proposal that is all the more feasible as they are virtually independent of graded reading material. Thus for remedying both poor initial instruction and some personal characteristics referred to as a specific language disability, a synthetic phonics course seems in order.

But, as I hope I have stressed enough, phonics itself is no panacea, because a mastery of decoding does not guarantee that a child will want to read, will pay attention to a text, or will get meaning from the ideas in it. Here we are into general learning problems of motivation, conceptual development, and emotional health that must be remedied by a variety of means that are treated in this book in other chapters — the opportunity for plentiful oral speech and dramatic expression, involvement in *making* books, the playing of logical games, and the general emphasis on meaningful reception and production of language. Moreover, the classroom procedures for handling reading proposed earlier in this chapter would be most helpful to problem readers of later grades. Far from being a luxury for the elite, for example, individual reading selections may be most important for the poorly motivated or less successful reader. Freedom from fear, individual coaching, help from classmates are all remedial aspects of the practices recommended. Being read to while following a text and participating in choral reading are easy, pleasantly social activities, appropriate for any age, that will ease problem readers into the more difficult solitary act. For especially arranged help under a remedial teacher, individual reading while listening to a tape of the text may well turn out to be the most effective single method.[4]

[4] Arthur Blumenthal and others, *Decoding for Reading* (New York: The Macmillan Co., 1968), is a remedial program consisting of 16 long-playing records designed to accompany some read-along books, but these recordings contain considerably more than just the text of books. In "Reaching the Culturally Deprived," *Saturday Review of*

Conventionally, however, poor readers whose problems go beyond decoding difficulties — if indeed the distinction is drawn — are made to undergo the sort of dull, mechanical course that actually requires the *most* motivation, confidence, and maturity to get through. They submit to "practice readers," "word study" workbooks, "skill builders," spellers, and so on. Remediation that consists of relentless drills and comprehension questions is based on a false assumption that the underlying problems are reading problems, whereas the problems are ones that *manifest* themselves in reading as elsewhere. For these children reading should be more, not less, fun than for others. Remedial reading specialists I have talked with in good school systems admit that they do not believe much in their own programs and are relieved to hear someone say what I have been saying here. But they do not feel free to admit this publicly, nor do they feel sure of offering alternatives.

As much as possible, poor readers should not be segregated. Part of the snowballing effect of reading failure stems from this segregation and its consequent effect on self-esteem. Abler children, moreover, should be tapped to help the less able. But special attention can be given within a heterogeneous class by taking poor readers aside for phonics work at the board and by coaching individually while the class is engaged in silent reading or in reading to each other in groups. Most of all, perhaps, poorer readers should be allowed to choose what they want to read, whatever the level and whatever the taste. When testing is absolutely necessary, it should be done as indirectly and humanely as possible, and other pressures should be removed.

If these recommendations for remedial reading essentially do not seem to differ enough from those for the regular reading program, it is because the latter has been designed to prevent reading problems. As in any other matter, the best remedy is prevention. But lest this seem too cavalier to those teachers into whose hands fall children with serious reading problems, let me say that the low-level technical approach has been tried for a long time and found wanting. A broader, more humane approach that eliminates fear and excites interest will be of most help. Where the technical avails is in solving a technical problem, namely the arbitrary conventions of letter symbols. The best advice can only be to filter out the true decoding problems, by listening to a child read aloud alone, and to remedy them as early as possible before they compound into despair the general learning problems that must be handled in broader ways. For the latter the whole human being must be considered.

Selecting Reading Material

From what has been said so far, it is clear that a classroom needs to contain books chosen for three purposes — for the teacher to read aloud, for

---

Literature (February 19, 1966), Terry Borton has described a successful way that he had disadvantaged students read literary texts while listening to homemade tapes of those texts.

children to read individually, and for children to read in common. The only necessity for buying class sets of the same book is to facilitate choral reading, group discussion, and dramatic work. On the other hand, some reading series, mainly of the supplementary sort, can be purchased simply as anthologies from which selections can be read either individually or in common. One principle here is that when sets are bought, it should be for their content, not for their method, unless a series contains the desired literacy program, for after that is over, the "method" is not something that can be embodied in textbooks. It follows that after the first few months of school, textbooks and trade books are in even competition, since the content is what counts, though some books aimed at schools, which I will mention, do have helpful suggestions to the teacher for oral reading.

MATERIAL TO ACCOMPANY THE LITERACY PROGRAM

Reading material is of two sorts — phonetically controlled texts that the children can read by themselves on the basis of the sound-spellings and sight words presented to them so far, and uncontrolled texts that the teacher reads to them, which are limited only by what the children can understand and take pleasure in.

Phonetically controlled reading. Words in Color contains some reading matter of the first sort, and the Foundation Program of the Open Court series contains some of both sorts. But *The Phonovisual Method* and *The Writing Road to Reading* do not include early readers, and teachers may in any case want to supplement whatever program they have chosen. Two good, phonetically controlled series for these first few months are the Dr. Seuss *Read by Yourself Books* (Boston: Houghton Mifflin Company) and the *Follett Beginning-to-Read Books* by Henry Lee Smith, Jr., and others, (New York: Harper & Row, Publishers). Both of these begin with the short vowel sounds, which is a point to remember (the Open Court series begins with long vowels, and *Words in Color* with short). The problem with phonetically controlled texts is that their order of presentation is meant to match a particular literacy program. On the other hand, they all feature *regularity* of spelling, and the farther along the child is, the less difference the order makes.

Material for the teacher to read aloud. The teacher needs to have on his desk one or two large, varied anthologies from which he can pluck any kind of poetry or prose that seems right for the class and the moment. The bible of this sort is *The Arbuthnot Anthology of Children's Literature,* edited by Mary Hill Arbuthnot (Chicago: Scott, Foresman & Company, 1961), a revised edition combining three of the author's previous anthologies. It is an omnibus for all ages. *Anthology of Children's Literature,* edited by Johnson, Sickels, and Sayers (Boston: Houghton Mifflin Company, rev. ed. 1960), and *a Golden Treasury of Poetry,* edited by Louis Untermeyer (Boston: Beacon Press, 1959), are also excellent omnibuses. The other books that I will mention below could also be purchased for children to read alone after the period of phonetically controlled texts is over. If ordered in sets, they would be good for choral reading and for reading aloud in parts.

Along with Northrop Frye, I feel strongly that much of the first reading matter should be poetry. The three *R*'s of poetry — rhyme, rhythm, and repetition — teach children a lot about individual words and patterns of words, and they do so in delightful and memorable ways. This very frank bias is reflected in the following recommendations. A very popular book of songs and poems is *A Rocket in My Pocket,* edited by Carl Withers (New York: Holt, Rinehart & Winston, Inc., 1948). A more recent and very lively collection of poems is Stephen Dunning's compilation, *On the Gift of a Watermelon Pickle . . . and Other Modern Verse* (Glenview, Ill.: Scott, Foresman, 1966). *Voices of Verse,* edited by Flynn, MacLean and Lund (Chicago: Lyons & Carnahan, 1933, 1944) is a series of poetry anthologies graduated for different ages. So is *Let's Enjoy Poetry,* compiled by Rosalind Hughes, (Houghton Mifflin, divided into Grades K–3, 1958, and 4–6, 1961). This series stresses oral reading, the poems being grouped according to how they can be read (chorally, singly, a-line-a-child, two-part, three-part, with emphasis on rhythm, with refrain lines) and accompanied also by helpful suggestions to the teacher for handling each. Both of these series have good selections but do not include much modern poetry. An excellent volume for both selection and helpful presentation is *The Sound of Poetry,* by Austin and Mills (Boston: Allyn and Bacon, Inc., 1964) (which is followed by a volume for the intermediate years, *The Reading of Poetry,* by Sheldon, Lyons, and Rouault, 1963). This pair of books is more up to date and also contains very good suggestions for oral reading. The *Sounds of Language* readers I have already mentioned. They contain prose and poetry and many very good asides to the teacher about the oral possibilities of each selection.

I do not mean that these are the only good books for the teacher to read aloud from, but among them a teacher could find about any kind of selection he might want to read. Also, several of them, as indicated, will teach the teacher himself a great deal about oral reading; instead of discussing the art myself, I refer teachers to the books indicated, which can demonstrate it with illustrative poems. These books, moreover, are good candidates to consider when ordering singles and sets for the general reading program.

Printed Material after the Literacy Program

Publishing sources. Three main sources of general reading material are open — trade books such as any parent might buy for his children to read at home; hardcover, graduated textbook series; and paperback books sold to children through school by such distributors as Scholastic Book Services.

The textbook series in literature may contain some editor-written material and some unsignalled abridgements and alterations of original works. Some of these amount to good anthologies but should be examined closely. Two especially good series are *The Umbrella Books,* selected by the Association for Childhood Education (New York: The Macmillan Co.) and the *Wonder-Story Books,* by Huber, Huber, and Salisbury (New York: Harper & Row, rev. ed.). The first contains much folk literature and the second contains many selections by first-rate creative writers. As noted before, *The Open Court Basic Readers* are excellent except for some editor-written sections. The book services rarely publish material for the first time but rather reprint trade books in school editions or anthologize already printed selections. These services are very useful for individual reading because they distribute trade books through schools at low prices.

Principles of selection. It would be foolish to attempt to survey either text or trade books. But some principles of selection may serve as a guide through the welter of choices. The first is that *content should be more important than anything else.* In literature, this means the highest quality creative writing, old or new, that children like. In social studies or other subject areas, it means the most up-to-date and best written books doing justice to the subject as defined by leaders in the area. The second principle reinforces the first: *do not adopt a package series just for the sake of the pedagogical paraphernalia it contains, or for the sake of some particular continuity.* The paraphernalia attempts to work over the content in ways better left to group processes, and the continuity can only concern some schematic or thematic irrelevance. (A sequence based only on generally increasing maturity and proficiency is a different matter.) The third is that *children's reactions must play an important part in selection.* Individual reading, of course, implies pupil-selected books, but for choice to be real the classroom must contain a large number of single copies of works that have passed the test of previous children. When large investments are to be made in hardcover sets, samples should be tried out first under conditions such as are outlined in this chapter. What do children say about books that have to stand or fall on sheer content — when children can talk spontaneously about them and thus reveal what they really got from them? In sum, teachers can apply Principles One and Two when screening down, but they can apply Principle Three only after observing their pupils' reactions. And all three principles do indeed throw text and trade books into a healthy competition.

THE CHILDREN'S OWN MATERIAL

Children following the curriculum in this book will pour forth an abundance of writing. They will be reading each other's productions constantly. Sometimes these productions will be in unfinished form as groups collaborate on a writing project or as workshop members exchange papers for reactions and commentary. Sometimes they will be printed and distributed for voluntary reading, or projected before the class. This reading matter will in a general way be automatically controlled for maturity of content and expression and for vocabulary and sentence structure. Expressing children's feelings, perceptions, and imaginings, it will interest children. It is home-produced for home consumption. What it lacks is what the best adult talents of the ages have wrought and what only greater resources of language and experience can bring to writing. It is only for this reason that published materials are needed at all. Otherwise, a reading program could be mounted with nary a book in the classroom, with nothing more than what pupils created themselves. This statement will not seem plausible until after the writing program has been unfolded in the following chapters.

What will the children write for each other? Picture captions, cartoon strips, songs, poems, stories, journal entries, jokes, riddles, telegrams, directions to follow, eyewitness accounts, personal recollections, personal essays, fables, editorials, and original nature booklets. Surely this constitutes a formidable reading program. Children will read generously in each mode of writing because doing so is entailed in group process. This material does not replace the vitally needed, rich input from the maturer culture, but it virtually doubles each pupil's reading practice, and it builds a bridge from his local world to that cultural legacy he meets in published books. As my reader continues through the remainder of this book, most of which appears to be devoted to composition, he will not forget, I hope, that every writing assignment is a reading assignment.

Chapter 7

Writing Out

Rationale

The kinds of writing treated later — writing down and writing up — are reality-oriented. Writing out, on the other hand, gives full play to the inventions of imagination and expresses inner psychic material.

WHAT STORIES MEAN TO CHILDREN

Children, of course, love to hear and tell stories, but we seldom think about why they do. My own theory is that storying is a child's way of thinking about nameless inner things, and that his thinking differs from ours mainly in the categories he establishes and in the symbolic ways he names them, not in the basic processes of logic. He is unable to acknowledge and designate his subjective categories of experience, and he does not yet possess either the vocabulary or the linguistic structures to classify and postulate *explicitly*. Nevertheless, through stories, he manipulates classes and formulates propositions.

To illustrate, let me translate into adult thought and language a very popular children's story, "The Three Billy Goats Gruff." An ogre tries to eat up anyone who crosses his bridge to graze on the pleasant slopes beyond. Between us and the attainment of our desires lie frightful dangers that we cannot go around. The smallest billy goat encounters the ogre at the bridge and persuades him to spare his life in favor of eating the larger goat to come. The second billy goat gets by the same way, and the third tears the ogre apart (into a satisfying number of small pieces). The three goats reach and enjoy the pasture. If you're weak and helpless, a child, you can refer the danger to Mother, who, if she cannot cope with it, can refer it to Daddy. *Some* "big person" will come along who is capable of overcoming the forces

117

of evil and ensuring that you get what you have to have without being destroyed in the process. The small are backed up by the mighty, but you may have to make shift with a stratagem of your own. And you have to play on your size, not deny it. (This sagacious advice is perhaps the main statement.)[1]

I believe it is the important meaning that underrides the story that makes "The Three Billy Goats Gruff" so popular. Children's fascination with stories cannot be entirely explained by the love of excitement and adventure, for these exist independently of stories. A favorite tale, such as an animal allegory, satisfies the desire for novelty and excitement but at the same time organizes experience in reassuring and resolving ways. Characters, objects, and events are types, classes, and categories of experience in disguise; a sequence of events postulates something about these categories. The fact that the meaning is unconscious, the categories veiled, the propositions implicit in the action does not make storying any less an act of thinking than adult cogitation. I make this point not to put children's fun in a solemn light but to remind teachers that children do all of their serious business in a play form. That is to say, it is a great mistake to regard their addiction to stories as mere childish pleasure-seeking to be catered to until they have sobered up enough to reflect on life. They are already reflecting an enormous amount; we can't *stop* them from doing it. All adults have to do is recognize the function of their fun, and honor stories as a genuine mode of thought. Adult fiction too embodies ideas; it too presents types and symbolizes inner experience that we cannot name and think about explicitly. Novels have a "logic of the events," and the ambiguous word "conclusion" applies to the climax of both stories and syllogisms.

The Need for Stimulants

Inventing, however, is actually difficult for children if they are merely told to "make up a story." They need definite stimulants and frameworks that prompt the imagination. Their original stories are recombinings of familiar stories in more or less new ways. My impression is that their originality is much greater in painting and modeling than in creating fiction, perhaps because language is more public and standard than art media, and also because their language stock is more limited anyway. The second issue is that *writing* a story, rather than merely telling it, calls for additional motivation. Third, writing restricts the children to a shorter length than telling, because they can talk longer than they can sustain a written story. The following recommendations attempt to provide easy starting points, tie writing into honest motivation, and allow for the necessary brevity.

[1] To this interpretation my wife adds this very just observation: "But the child doesn't just identify with the little goat; he can successively identify with all three in turn and 'grow' to handle the situation directly rather than passing the buck."

Recommendations

Younger Children Dictating Stories to Older Children

A general suggestion for getting story writing under way: have older children, from the fifth or sixth grade, take down the stories of kindergartners and first-graders as they dictate them. Exchange halves of classes with the other teacher and pair off the mixed pupils. (See page 180.) The point of this is to enable the younger children to spin out a story fluently without having to worry about the mechanical problems of writing and without having to limit themselves in length. Seeing their words rendered on paper helps establish a tie between vocal speech and writing. For the older children this gives practice in transcribing speech. The procedure permits a lot more dictation than a teacher could handle alone.

Here are two pieces dictated by less mature first graders during their first months of school:

Catherine's Story

When I sleep with my brother, he wets his bed. He's only three. When he wets his bed, I go up with my brother Ronald and he wets his bed and he's nine years old. When I sleep with my sister, she doesn't wet her bed. She's twelve years old. When I sleep with my sister, she's seven years old, she doesn't wet her bed. When my brother, Charles, sleeps with my mother and daddy, he wets his bed again. When I get up in the morning, I eat all my breakfast but I can't have oatmeal. When I have a stomach ache, I don't eat my breakfast.

Chase

One time me and my sister in the dark and then she ran ahead of me and I ran home because I was afraid. Then my mother said, "Why did you run home?" I said to her, "She ran ahead of me towards the store." Then when she ran ahead of me, I had to go back down after her. When she was at the store, I was at the store before her. Then she didn't know what to say to me but "go home." She wondered what I was doing down there at the store. She said, "Who sent you down here?" And I said, "My mother did." Then we walked home together through the dark.[2]

Though these two "stories" are not made up, they illustrate how dictation can catch the child's spontaneous composition of high-interest material, expressed with a fluency and maturity of language that he could not yet maintain in writing.

After he has been helped by the older child to read his own dictated story, the younger child pairs off with a partner of his own class and each

[2] I am indebted to Eleanor Grubb of the Cochituate Elementary School, Wayland, Massachusetts, for these two dictations.

reads his story to the other as the other follows along with his eyes. This fosters cross-teaching of reading.

WRITING CAPTIONS

A simple point of departure for writing stories is to make up phrases and sentences to print beneath one's own drawing or painting. Children's pictures usually encapsulate a story or have the makings of one. Probably the best practice is to keep on hand a stock of homemade caption strips of the right size to be scotch-taped to the bottom of the art paper. After a painting or drawing session, tell the pupils to get a strip and write on it what their picture is about. The children then assemble in small circles to look at each other's pictures and to read the captions. Members of the circle take turns holding up their pictures, and each picture is talked about.

As the children break into groups the teacher directs them, when each picture is exhibited, to look at it, read the caption, ask questions, and talk with the artist about it. Many captions will need further explaining because not everything is in the picture, and because things the caption refers to may not be evident to the other children. The point of this discussion is to let the children elaborate orally what the caption summarizes in writing. Give them time at the end of discussion to expand their caption in writing, to include more explanation of what action precedes and follows the picture, and to answer in writing the questions they were asked.

A variant of captioning is to write below the picture what the figures in it are saying. Demonstrate first on the board how the speech follows the character's name and a colon. A variant of the whole process is for the pupils to hold up their uncaptioned pictures before the group, one at a time, and let the other members write on a slip of paper a caption for what they see in the picture. The artist concerned gathers the slips and reads them aloud; the fitness of each caption is discussed. Afterwards, the artist reads his own caption, and his colleagues compare what he intended with what they saw. This also brings out different story possibilities suggested by the same picture.

A further step is to draw a series of pictures (on a roll of paper) that tell a story. This might be introduced, on the occasion of a single drawing, simply by asking the children to draw a succeeding picture, something that "comes after" the first one. At a subsequent time, direct them at the outset to draw a series of pictures like a cartoon strip. In fact, if the teacher selects and projects a few cartoon strips containing dialogue that the children can understand, the children can follow these as a model and create talking pictures by encircling the words of dialogue and connecting this "balloon" to the speaker. Captions are also added. This combines dialogue with narrative and joins both to visual sequence. Gradually the word-picture ratio is reversed until the text is primary and the drawing secondary (without, of course, appropriating all their art work for this purpose). After the children are used to writing on and under their pictures, tell them to write a story sentence first — a caption for an action — to illustrate that, and so on. Children who have a hard time getting an initial idea can be put together briefly in a group to stimulate each other first, following some prompts by the teacher: "Imagine a place, a bridge, a dark woods, or a broken down house; then imagine somebody in that place. Is it an animal or a person? What is it doing?"

Both single pictures and series can serve as ideas for dramatic enactments. While discussing pictures in groups, the pupils can select one that they would like to act out. Besides providing material for drama, this practice exploits drama as a means of further elaborating stories. Elaborating is a major issue in children's story-making because the length they can write seldom does justice to a story and forces them to oversummarize. The difference between dead and alive stories depends partly on the ratio of summary to elaboration. Whereas the length of children's writing cannot be forced, their written stories can be spun out by discussing and enacting them.

Reversing the relationship now, acting can serve as a point of departure for story writing. I recommended in Chapter 3 that group story-making be followed by enactment. Rotating roles and acting out the story several times creates varying renditions and encourages departure from the original idea. Each child can then render his personal version in writing. The directions are simply to "write down the story the way you like it best." Of course the writing should follow hard on the heels of the acting, while the story is still hot. A very particular and practical reason for this writing — which should be announced in advance — is to pass the stories on to other groups for them to enact. This also feeds new story ideas into each group.

LITERATURE AND WRITING

Imitating forms. Children need impersonal forms into which they can project feeling without knowing that they are doing so. The material of folk literature furnishes one kind of public medium. The technical forms of poetry and song offer another. David Holbrook has put the point well in giving an account of his work with children's writing.

> . . . I felt the only way to achieve this expression of feeling was by using as stimulants poems, passages, and themes which the child already recognized as means to the depersonalizing of his individual emotion — a way to that third ground which is a meeting-place between the "mind" of a community and his own. Such a depersonalized world, I have tried to suggest, exists in the sea-chanty, the folksong and the game-rhyme. It also exists in such poetry as the Chinese poems translated by Arthur Waley. The fairy tale provides it, and so too, I think, do certain other conventional types of chil-

dren's story — the story of exploration, for instance. And, it seems to me, even the wild western may provide a "half-serious, half irresponsible world" where self-identification may be indulged in, and painful feelings tolerated in an unfamiliar setting.[3]

In his work with children's writing, Holbrook has presented them certain poems, songs, and chanties that have a strong and simple pattern of metrical beat, refrain, or incremental repetition. The children read these in parts, dramatize them, and talk about them. Having absorbed the forms, they fill in the forms with their own words. They are asked to write a poem, song, or chanty like the one they have heard. The popularity of limerick writing attests to the feasibility and attraction of the idea.

I would like to recommend Holbrook's practice and at the same time take the opportunity to say that any program calling for pupils to produce must also give them a lot. Imaginative writing wells up from a source constantly enriched by an inflow. A teacher who would like his children to write should let them take in an enormous amount of folk literature from books and records. Not only do they absorb images and ideas that they can recombine in their own expression, but as they internalize the rhymes, rhythms, and other formal patterns, they are absorbing in a peculiarly effective way the vocabulary, locutions, and language structures bound to those patterns by association. Rhyme in particular is helpful for reinforcing phonics instruction; when the child sees and writes words of the same sound, occupying the same final position and receiving the same rhythmic stress, he has a particularly vivid opportunity to notice the different ways a certain sound is spelled and the different ways a certain spelling is sounded.

Borrowing the content. The content of literature is a less direct sort of stimulant. That is, instead of being directed to write a poem or story about such and such a character they have just read about, the children simply soak up from literature many characters and settings and story ideas that they can recombine when stimulated more specifically by some literary form. Through improvisation, however, they can extend some favorite stories in groups by borrowing characters and settings for which they invent new actions.

Oral reading as springboard. In connection with this intake of folk literature, two practices seem to me to be of great potential value in teaching reading along with writing. First, write out a poem, for example, on a transparency and project it before the class. Moving an opaque sheet of paper

---

[3] David Holbrook, *English for Maturity* (New York: Cambridge University Press, 1965), p. 112. Consulting this book would be valuable for teachers of all grades. Besides making the case that creative writing educates emotion and develops the whole child, he has compiled helpful lists of records and books containing folk songs, chanties, and poems for children of a wide age range.

down the transparency, line by line, either read the piece expressively and rhythmically, perhaps a couple of times, or play a recording of the piece and pace it by revealing the lines one at a time as they are sung. (Rhyme patterns, the refrains of chanties, and the incremental repetition of ballads ensure the recurrence of words in a manner certainly more interesting than vocabulary drills.) After reading or playing the piece a couple of times, ask the class to read it or sing it in chorus from the projection. This transfers reading from teacher to children. Now, when rhythms and repetitions are still pounding in their ears, and images swirling through their heads, send the children to paper to write their own nursery rhyme or ballad or limerick. They can brainstorm at first in groups, composing together as a scribe records. Then, when older, they can compose alone. A transition from collective to individual writing may occur naturally as group members think up variations on a common theme, using each other's ideas as stimulants.

Song Writing

Music can suggest words by means of technical cues having little to do directly with the mood or meaning. A sequence of stressed and unstressed notes in a musical phrase, for example, can evoke a parallel sequence of stressed and unstressed syllables in a verbal phrase. I was awakened one morning by hearing my five-year-old daughter singing, to the tune of "Happy Birthday," "Tapioca to you. Tapioca to you." With only slight distortion, she had fitted into the stress pattern of the notes for "happy birthday" the two troches of "tapioca." While concentrating on form, the child lets slip a content. Pauses, staccatos, the steep intervals between notes, lengths of phrasing — all elicit words and word clusters as well, perhaps, as images and ideas of actions. Such cues set up free thought associations, which determine the chain of ideas.

Inaugurate song writing by having the children sing a familiar short song together, then asking them to make up new words for the tune. Perhaps for a while they could collaborate on the lyrics in small groups, one offering a line and another adding to it or suggesting an alternative. A scribe could write down on a transparency the lines they decide on. Transparencies are projected one at a time, a member of the group that composed the song reads or sings it as others follow the written words, then the whole class sings the new lyrics.

Later, individuals write their lyrics alone, and the teacher introduces melodies that the class does not necessarily know. Seated at their desks, the pupils listen as the teacher plays phrases of the tune on a piano or flutaphone, or plays a tape of a previously recorded tune. Play a phrase at a time, and, while they are writing, repeat phrases and sections a number of times. When they have finished, tell them to entitle their song. Some of these lyrics too are projected, read, and sung by the class. Copied off the transparencies onto paper, entitled, and signed, the title of the original tune written below, these lyrics are compiled into individual or class songbooks. Thus, the purposes of writing are both immediate and long-range.

WRITING ABOUT PICTURES

Assemble a large collection of provocative photographs cut from magazines. Let each pupil choose one that he would like to write about. "Say what you think is happening in your picture. Make up a story from (or about) what you see." Role playing may be invoked: "Pretend you are that person (animal or thing) and tell what you are doing or what is happening to you."

RIDDLES, PUNS, AND JOKES

There is an oral folk culture among children embodied in such things as riddles, puns, and jokes that they take pleasure in passing on and thus would enjoy writing out in their own words. Inspired by these, the pupils can then make up their own.

Since jokes and riddles can perfectly well be shared orally in class, the purpose of putting them on paper or transparencies would be to circulate them more widely than can be done by word of mouth. The class compiles a book of them or puts them onto two or three transparencies, and these are exchanged with other classes. Whereas a book can only be read aloud to the class or put on a table for individual reading, transparencies carry this additional advantage: the teacher can use them as high-interest texts for a reading practice he can oversee, either reading aloud as the class follows visually or silently revealing a line at a time by slowly uncovering the transparency, to keep punch in the punch line. For riddles, pause before the answer and ask for guesses; then let the children read whether they were right or wrong. Since some jokes are based on a homonymous pun, the pupil writing the joke has to choose which of the homonyms to write down; you can ask the class what the other one is. (This game is called Sneaky Phonics.)

General Remarks on Writing

CREATING THEIR OWN BOOKS

Compiling books seems to have a very deep and widespread appeal for children. Exhibiting and reviewing their products gives them great satisfaction. Whatever they write beyond notes should be pinned up, projected, enacted, and compiled. As much use as possible should always be made of pupil writing. Papers should not end up on the teacher's desk. The child needs to feel strong reasons for bothering to put what he has to say on paper.

Pinning papers up for display, printing them for distribution, discussing them in groups — all provide motivation. All such broadcasting and preserving makes the abstraction of writing gratifyingly physical and social.

The principle underlying many of these learning activities is that children should in large measure write their own literature. Too many children think of themselves only as "consumers" and not as users of language. As creator one is more appreciative and discerning about others' creations. Moreover, when children write, they read more, they become more involved in language, they get caught up in cycles of giving and taking words that gather momentum and accelerate progress in both reading and writing.

THE WRITING WORKSHOP

Much of the writing at this age is composed by groups, as explained in succeeding chapters. In this case, members of each group revise sentences as they are proposed, and proofread them after the scribe has written them down. Out of collective composition develops the writing workshop, of which much will be made in this curriculum. Instituted to handle individual composition, it works like this: the class is broken into groups of three to six and directed to pass around papers they have just written, to read them, and to talk about them. The purposes are to provide each paper with peer reactions and to prepare it for printing. Pupils respond spontaneously to each other's writing and also make suggestions for changes, including but not dwelling on corrections of spelling and punctuation. Marginal notations of a proofreading sort are made, but at this age most other comments and suggestions are exchanged orally. These groups have dictionaries available to help them resolve uncertainties about spellings, and the teacher is available to help generally. For now, the responding to content and manner is left to the children themselves. Many other activities however, will influence their responses to and suggestions about each other's writing. What comes out in these group sessions will be the spontaneous reflection of much other learning experience, such as reading in literature, dramatic work, and punctuation practice, to name only a few. Although I will have occasion later to say more about the workshop, the reader may note for himself, as he reads on, a number of practices occurring outside the workshop that will sharpen the responses and suggestions that children will make within it.

THE TEACHER'S ROLE

In my view, there is no need for the teacher to write comments on pupil compositions or to grade them. For one thing, some of the writing at this age is composed by groups. For another, punctuation and spelling are not taught by marking papers. The teacher should give some help *during* the writing, by consulting, and, in a general way, *before* the writing, by means of other activities. As for grades, I suggest making general assessments of pupils' work by observing it closely — a procedure that the role of the teacher in this program makes more feasible, since he is free to pass among the groups, where he can both observe and respond to the work of his pupils. The printing of papers allows him to review conveniently the writing of different children. Of course, any teacher should have the right to remark on pupil writing, if only to encourage or appreciate, but I feel strongly that children should begin their careers thinking of the class as more the audience than the teacher, who should avoid making himself the source of evaluation. His paramount mission is to make group process so effective that children can teach each other.

Writing Down

Writing down is the recording of ongoing events. It refers to note taking and transcribing. The child writes down what he perceives as he is perceiving it. What may be written down divides into two main categories — perceptions of outer things like sights and sounds, and perceptions of inner things like thoughts and feelings. A specialized kind of sensory data, moreover, is human speech. Thus vocal sounds make up a special subdivision of external perception. Three kinds of writing ensue from these categories — sensory recording, dictation, and calendar keeping. All three go on concurrently, but I will take up sensory recording first.

Sensory Recording

My experiments with the following assignments were done in classes combining fourth- and fifth-graders, but the teachers there concluded that the activities should be moved down to the first three grades. They felt not only that younger children could do them but that they should, so that teachers in grades four to six could count on this background and thus launch their pupils into the fuller kind of sensory recording treated in Chapter 13. Sensory recording in grades one to three is distinguished from that in grades four to six by three differences: (1) the younger pupils record stimuli in school instead of outside; (2) they begin by recording one sense at a time instead of all at once; (3) they make fewer decisions about what to record. This principle of progressing from the more structured to the freer framework accords with other sequences recommended in this program and with the consensus among elementary teachers that smaller children need stronger guidelines for unfamiliar activities. Isolating the senses creates a small focus, to train observational attention and to eliminate choices between senses.

127

MOTIVES FOR OBSERVING AND FOR WRITING OBSERVATIONS

Even more than adults, children look *for* and listen *for*. Looking and listening for their own sake are rare and sophisticated. Though an infant's attention is diffuse, we all begin very early to tune in and out, to select according to our desires and fears. To say that children have a great curiosity and live in close touch with things in nature is not to say that their observation is pure and even. By school age their behavior is seldom random; it appears so to us only because we do not understand their selectors, the psychic focal points around which they are organizing the world. What I am getting at is a motivational issue: adults' efforts to train children to observe objectively are somewhat at odds with the child's reasons for looking and listening, which relate to private concerns. We should honor his more primal motivation by selecting stimuli likely to engage his attention, while at the same time directing him to focus where he might not have of his own accord, so that he may achieve some autonomy from his drives and observe more objectively what lies around him.

In other words, when we focus pupils on something, what motivation other than sheer obedience can we count on that will keep their attention where we have directed it? Excitation is one. It is true, however, that sensory excitation is to some extent a pleasure for them in itself, and that the range of attention is relative to the amount of anxiety a child feels about his desires and fears as he goes seeking and avoiding. The pleasure in games is another motivation, but too often we teachers rationalize ill-motivated exercises by calling them games even though the children do not perceive them as such. When we add to observing the *writing down* of observations, the plot thickens.

A general problem of writing at this age is: why write it when you can say it? To whom would the child be writing? And for what reason? Why do adults ever write? And why record? Why not just observe? Let us grant that elementary schoolers in general have a competence motive — to learn to do and become good at all sorts of crafts and skills valued by their social world and practiced by adolescents and adults. The competence motive is based on every individual's need to think well of himself, enjoy success, achieve things, and strengthen ego and identity. But, like game motivation, it can easily be abused, and when children discover that they have worked hard at something that is not "real" after all but just a teacher's invention for his own purposes, they feel cheated and resentful. This is a great source of cynicism among students of all ages. The younger the children are, the more willing they are to do something just because some adult asks them to. Although this compliance seems to simplify the problem of motivation, when looked at another way it means there is less check from the pupil against teacher irresponsibility. Truly absurd teaching practices could go off without a hitch, and the wish to comply could be relied on entirely even when more mature motives should be emerging and getting exercise. Unconsciously, moreover, pupils can defeat assignments even when they wish to comply, and attention in particular is notoriously hard for the conscious will to control.

These considerations, which may seem over-subtle at first, were prompted by experiments and by ensuing discussions with the teachers. That is, the pupils' response to my first version of the sensory recording assignments indicated that, even when the writing came out well, the teachers had to rely far too much on compliance. There was not enough pleasure and purpose. I could too easily envision these children in junior and senior high school still doing writing chores out of obedience, perfunctorily and not very profitably. So, while conditionally accepting the game, compliance, and competence motivations, I decided that sensory recording posed a special difficulty that could be solved only by embedding it in another activity for which motivation was assured.

To observe objectively and to write down observations for their own sake asked too much of the children, even in fourth and fifth grades, when the assignment was thus baldly presented. Second- and third-graders soon lost interest when asked on unrelated occasions to observe animals and merely say what they saw. But when they kept animals in the class for several weeks, cared for them, lived with them, and experimented with them, they not only observed them closely but they talked constantly about them, and wrote more about them than the teacher could have hoped for.

The lesson I learned — and this is why I have dwelled so long on this whole issue — is that a familiar, pleasurable, and well motivated activity can provide the context that will in turn motivate a new, different, and more advanced activity. With good gearing, motor power can drive an action that at first glance seems too remote. If objective regarding and recording are entailed in fulfilling a more basic and subjective intent, then children become engaged in it and learning occurs. These considerations of learning motivation, and the principle of engagement, will apply to other and future assignments, especially in the least natural domain of discourse — writing.

Posting these remarks as an introduction to sensory writing, I will turn now to two activities based on game and competence motives only but not, I believe, abusing them. These activities will prepare for much more extensive sensory recording, which henceforth will be assimilated into long-range projects, described in Chapter 9, Writing Up.

THE RECORDING OF SOUND

Pre-writing practice. Focusing on sound can begin in simple relaxation periods. "Rest, close your eyes, and listen. Relax completely and hear as many sounds as you can." After several minutes: "How many *far away* sounds do you hear?" Afterwards ask the children to list orally and compare the sounds they heard. Such a five-minute session should occur outdoors and in other places about the school as well as in the classroom.

With this background of listening and of saying what they have heard, the class can proceed to writing down the sounds. The stimuli may be either natural sounds around the school or ones taped by teachers elsewhere. Since school sounds will be limited, tapes would increase the range considerably. Also, when the children do not know the sources of the sound, an interesting game can be made of identifying the site where the tape was made and the actions producing the sounds.

Differences between sounds and sights. The isolated sense of hearing differs from sight in two ways that are obvious and yet not often considered. The experiments made me think seriously about these differences. One is that sound *must* issue from actions whereas sights *may* be and often are of still things. For a sound to be produced, something must happen, whereas what one sees may be action but it may equally well be static, a still-life. Hence sound falls into a sequence of happenings, and a record of them automatically becomes a story of sorts. (This movement in time makes part of the difference between music and painting.) Second, since hearing alone gives us very limited information, we are forced to *infer* more than we do when looking. Usually, of course, we synthesize hearing and seeing to get the facts, but even by itself seeing informs us more fully than hearing and therefore requires less inference.

These two differences help to define the recording of sound: it is action-centered, and it involves some guessing. Both are qualities children like. But, further, it can teach chronology and interpretation. For the latter, tapes are obviously better, since children taken on location to record receive a lot of information about the setting and possible actions even though their eyes may be on their papers during the listening period. Another advantage of taping is that setting and actions can be chosen for their particular interest to children. It is important, however, not to jam the tapes with sounds but rather to capture a series of distinct sounds that enables the children to distinguish them and that gives them time to write.

Writing down sounds. After the stage of listening without writing, place the class in the sound locale or play a tape to them. A home-made tape might present a short and simple sequence such as someone going out a door, whistling for a dog, placing a bowl down, and patting the dog while he eats. Distribute overhead projector transparencies and grease pencils to the children. Tell them that this time they are going to try to capture on paper what they hear, by writing it down in a short form. "Short form" means that they do not have to use whole sentences and keep repeating "I hear . . ." They are going to "take notes," an expression that will be used a lot and that relates to their work as scribes. To save time, they may write single words and short phrases. Tell them not to worry about getting down everything but to capture as much as they can; tell them also not to worry about spelling but to make good guesses. The latter is especially important, since one purpose of the assignment is to activate their knowledge of sound-letter relations through the effort to spell words they can pronounce. Recording should probably have an upper limit of ten minutes.

Discussing the order of recorded sounds. Immediately afterwards, or upon returning to the classroom, lead a discussion with the whole class of what they wrote. (After about the first two sessions, once a model has been established, this discussion is relegated to small groups.) Project one of the transparencies and say that they are going to put together a sound story from their notes. "Probably no one person could note all the sounds by himself, and some of you may have heard things that others didn't hear. So we will fill out the recording together." Read aloud the sounds on the transparency, then ask, "What other sounds did *you* hear?" As these additions are enumerated, write them on the transparency. But *where* do they go — before and after which other sounds? This leads not only to establishing chronological order but also to distinguishing it from simultaneity (sounds occurring together), and from repetition (recurring sounds). Discussing these temporal matters naturally entails using corresponding verb tenses and aspects — perfect, progressive, and repetitive ("keep"). Help the class set the record straight, writing on the transparency the sound events in order of occurrence, placing simultaneous sounds side by side, and inserting repeated sounds at points where the children agree that they occurred.

Discussing the form of notation. A second issue for discussion concerns the form of notation. Whether this should be brought up on another occasion is perhaps something for the teacher to decide in the light of his pupils' maturity and readiness. At any rate, looking at the transparency being projected, remark that some words tell the thing making the sound (*bell, airplane*), other words tell the action (*scraping*), and other words describe the sound (*click*). Sometimes a phrase may combine these (*bells ring, foot scraping, click of metal*). Point to the words that exemplify these different ways of recording, and remark that this pupil used all of one kind, or mixed them, or used more of one than the other. Put on another transparency and ask them which ways of noting *that* pupil used. Then direct them to look at their own recording and notice what they did. Finally, ask them which kinds of words do which things best. What do you want to know — the object involved, the action causing the sound, or what the sound is like?

The point, of course, is that recording, or note-taking, forces us to sacrifice some information for other information; things have to be left out. Also, the basic parts of speech are focused on in this way without being formalized —

nouns, verb forms, and sometimes adjectives (*loud banging*). *Foot scraping* comes closest to a sentence, having subject and predicate elements; it is the kernel of a kernel sentence. These two points are related as the practical matter of which kinds of words have which advantages for recording which kinds of information. This they discuss by means of particular items projected before them. I am not sure how far discussion at this age can pursue the matter — certainly not far at one sitting — but the teacher should set it before the class so that small groups will carry it on as far as they can. Later recording, for a specific purpose, will require choosing among alternative ways of noting that will yield different kinds of information.

A fine opportunity exists here to increase and refine vocabulary. While comparing variant wordings, children can discuss whether *bell* or *buzzer* is the best word for the sound source, whether the bell *rang* or *tinkled*. Sometimes only one child may know the correct name for something heard (*air conditioner*), but that name is then made available to the whole class. And the teacher can supply vocabulary.

Correcting spelling. The third issue the teacher deals with before the class is spelling. I place it at the end of discussion so that the children will, in their minds, place content before mechanics, but it will be a natural concern of pupils acquiring the competence of matching their oral vocabulary to written symbols. During the earliest sessions, make it clear that you expect misspelling and that they are going to help each other learn to spell by trading knowledge. Children do not, of course, misspell the same words or have trouble with the same phonic problems. Since they are recording the same sounds, however, they will be trying to spell a number of words in common. Ask them which words on the transparency are misspelled and what the correct spellings are. Since pupils will be generally expected to get spellings from each other or the dictionary, instead of relying on the teacher, supply only the spellings no pupil knows and only for words common to many of the recordings. Instead of writing these on the board, spell them orally so that the children will write them from the spelling, not merely copy them on their recording. Your spelling out gives them the sound particles and their own writing gives them the visual whole. (The literacy program is assumed to be over at this point.)

Recording on paper in groups. After two or three sessions, paper replaces transparencies, the class breaks into about five groups, and tapes become the only sound source. The groups are directed to do essentially what the whole class has done before except that now they have the general mission of guessing where the tape was made and what was going on there. Whereas the school sound recording drew only on compliance and competence motives, now game motivation is added. One child in each group is appointed as leader.

He is to read his list of sounds, ask his colleagues what else they heard, and write additions onto his paper. Again they discuss when the sounds occurred in relation to each other. Since they did not see the objects and actions producing the sounds, which in most cases could have been made in different ways, the effort to determine which items in a record are the same or different sounds will naturally cause the pupils to discuss differences in how they named them. They may discuss which names are best and which assume more than they know (words for sounds are safest, words for actions less so, and words for objects least). If one child challenges another's item *wheel turning*, he is questioning not just the other's wording but the amount of inference he made. But all he says is "How do you know it was a wheel?" Is that the same sound as someone else's item *clicking*? To answer that, they have to check where the two items came in the sound sequence.

In other words, merely comparing their recordings carefully ensures discussion of several important relations of words to things. This is basically their task, but of course the teacher cannot put it in that way. He has to recall to them the earlier discussion he led and state distinctly what they did then — collect everybody's sounds, put them in order, and find out what different words they used for the same sounds.

The second mission, the children are told, is to help each other get spellings right. They are to ask each other for spellings and then to pass around papers to check quickly for misspellings of words that the authors thought were correct and therefore did not ask about. If they are sure of how to spell a word that they see is written wrong, they are to change it and tell the author. Words that none know how to spell are looked up in a dictionary or saved for the teacher, who circulates among the groups helping with discussion problems and also with spelling, to the extent of answering questions about whether a spelling is right or not, referring to their sound-letter training when appropriate. While offering this kind of consultation about spelling, the teacher makes it ultimately the pupils' responsibility.

When the class is reunited, the leaders are asked to report what their groups decided was the locale and action of the tape. The climax of the game element in these sessions comes when the teacher tells them what is happening on the tape. (Clearly, some skill is needed to tape a sound sequence that is neither too easy nor too difficult to guess.)

As with all assignments in this program, the purpose is multiple. Though focused on rendering the sense of hearing into words, these sessions give practice also in reading, talking, reasoning, and writing. Seen simply, all note taking at this age merely provides one sort of occasion for children to write informally and fragmentarily before they are ready to write connected pieces comprised of whole sentences. It is a realistic kind of discourse for which isolated words and phrases are quite appropriate. The audience is the author himself and the members of his working party. This kind of writing can be contrasted for pupils with other kinds of writing, perhaps having other kinds of audiences, for which full and connected sentences are appropriate.

RECORDING THE SENSE OF TOUCH

General procedure. Recording tactile sensations also operates on essentially a game motivation. Place a lot of tactually interesting objects, recognizable when *seen* by these children, in five bags and give a bag to each group. One child reaches in and feels one of the objects, without seeing or revealing it, and says aloud what he feels — the shape, texture, consistency, and so on — but without *naming* it even if he thinks he can identify it. The others of the group write down what he says as well as they can keep up with him. (For examples of this kind of writing, done by fourth- and fifth-graders, see page 180.) It should be explained that each person may miss some things the "feeler" says, but that the group as a whole will probably be able to piece his words together later. "Just write down key words." These monologues are usually brief.

Afterwards, the group drafts a composite account of what he said, that is, a tactile description of the object, and this will be read before the class later so that the other groups can try to guess what it is. There will probably be time for only two people to be "feelers," but the others can get their turns on another day. Before the groups break up, they are allowed to see the objects they described from their bags but keep the secret within the groups. Their pleasure then is in seeing if the rest of the class can identify the object when one of them reads the description of it. In addition, these descriptions will be put together as a kind of riddle book and exchanged with those in other classes. These purposes are of course explained in advance.

To compose the description, one pupil reads to the group what he wrote down on his paper; the others make additions and, with the help of the speaker, settle on a rendering. Besides help with spellings, the teacher makes one specific suggestion: if the description so far composed repeats "It is . . ." and "It has . . . ," explain that these sentences can be combined by using series (a series of adjectives for "It is . . ." and a series of nouns for "It has . . .") and that commas are used to separate items in the series. Say that this shortening will make it possible to read a lot of riddle descriptions before the class and will save space in the books. This is the first step toward the economy of predication that results from combining several short sentences into one elaborated sentence ("embedding," in terms of transformational grammar).

Purposes. Children can learn several things from this activity besides verbalizing their sense of touch, which of course is learning one way to describe. As stenographers, they are taking dictation. As drafters of something to be read to the class and to be passed to other classes, they are composing and editing. As guessers themselves of what each object is, they can learn, by their absence, how names simplify identification and, conversely, how much can be said about a thing that does not appear in the name. Difficulty in guessing an object relates to the low sensory level of tactile information; ease in guessing relates to how *telling* the particular details are, whether the details mentioned are characteristic of many objects or of only a few, and whether these details combine to evoke the whole of the object. These matters could become a discussion topic either in the "feeling" groups or in small discussion groups given a set of riddle descriptions from another class and asked, of each piece read, "What makes this easy (or hard) to guess?" By way of summarizing that discussion, the question can be asked in a general way: "What makes some touch descriptions easy and some others hard?"

By third grade, pupils can probably be paired, one partner feeling and the other taking down what he says. Then they draft the description together and reverse roles.

Taking Dictation

Much more will be made of speech transcription in grades four to six than now. But besides the two forms of it already mentioned — taking down letter sounds and words dictated by the teacher during the literacy program, and taking down tactile descriptions by classmates — another sort can be undertaken during these years. The children transcribe whole short sentences dictated by the teacher.

TEACHER DICTATION OF SHORT PASSAGES

Choose interesting sentences that tell a story or have some other continuity. Use suspense to make dictation fun. The slow unfolding of a text makes the punch line of jokes more effective. A riddle contrasts question and statement intonations. Poems too are excellent for dictation if the ends of poetic lines correspond to the ends of sentences; otherwise, the two kinds of termination are at odds. Texts may be selected from booklets of pupil writing as well as from books. Before dictating the text, announce that you are going to read a sentence at a time. Choose sentences at first that have no internal punctuation. This means that every segment dictated will implicitly define what a sentence is. All they have to do with punctuation is put in capitals, periods, question marks, and exclamation marks. Although this sort of dictation is an important way of teaching the sentence, the emphasis is on spelling, the activation of word memory and phonic knowledge.

Whenever the children are ready for it, the next step is to dictate sentences having internal punctuation — half-drops and slight pauses for commas. Choose passages containing constructions the pupils themselves are starting to use in their own writing — series, offset phrases, perhaps some subordinate clauses. Since each sentence must be read off as a whole intonational contour, some children may have difficulty retaining the entire sentence in their minds until they can write it. Allow for these limitations of retention and writing speed by choosing rather short sentences and by repeating them.

Function of teacher dictation. I confess to some mixed feelings about dictation. Though confident that it will help a great deal to reduce the purely transcriptive problems of their own writing, I think it holds a limited interest for children. Compliance and competence motives, and some measure of game motive, may keep it interesting for a while, but the older the child, the weaker the motivation. Also, I hate to see children spending very much time copying when they could be composing. So I suggest that teachers play up the other ways by which the speech-print equivalence may be taught — reading aloud, listening and following the text as the teacher reads, choral reading, and perhaps most of all, doing genuine writing in collaborative groups. To the extent that these activities fail to clear up transcriptive problems, however, dictation may be in order. If spelling is coming along well but you feel that internal punctuation needs strengthening, ditto an interesting passage without its punctuation, read it aloud, and have the pupils write in the commas and periods on their copies. (For more about this procedure, see page 177.)

It is important to make clear that the whole point of teaching spelling and punctuation through dictation is to separate transcription from composition, in accordance with the principle stated earlier. When really *writing*, children should feel uninhibited by concern for spelling and punctuation, drawing spontaneously on what they have learned about these things in other contexts. (One such context is group proofreading, which *follows* composing.) Children should be encouraged to write any words, use any sentence structures, that come into their heads. The teacher does not write corrections of mechanics on their papers. Composition should *reflect* skill in spelling and punctuating; it is not the place to *teach* that skill. And we have to remember that, if children read and write a lot, spelling and punctuation gradually become more correct anyway, even without specific teaching. Children writing freely whatever they are capable of saying will make many more errors than those writing only what they know they can transcribe correctly. It is far preferable to give dictation than to spoil the writing flow by inducing fear of error.

Calendars and Letters

Noting down inner perceptions takes the form of brief entries in a homemade, personal calendar.

Procedures

The children cut up sheets of light-colored paper into squares about seven by nine inches, punch two holes along the nine-inch edge, and place enough of these leaves onto two notebook rings to equal the days of the oncoming month. With crayons or colored felt markers, they write at the top of each leaf the month, day of week, and date. This repeated writing of the names for the days and months should ensure their learning to spell them.

The children are told before they make the calendars what they will do with them. A few minutes each day will be set aside especially for them to make entries. These can be of two kinds — reminders for the immediate future and remembrances of the immediate past. The children turn to the leaf for today, look to see what they have written on it before, then write down on future leaves what they or their family are going to do. (Looking back prompts memories.) Then, on the leaf for today or yesterday, they note things that they did then, or that happened then that they would like to remember later. Explain that many adults write notes to themselves on a calendar so that they will remember things they have planned to do; the notes usually say what, when, where, who, and perhaps other things. Show them how to write times and distinguish the halves of the day — 6:00 A.M., 5:00 P.M. Then say that some people keep a diary of what they do and what happens around them so that they can look back later and recall what went on. This is like writing a real day-to-day story in pieces.

The children should understand that the calendars are theirs, that they will keep them at the end of the year, and that the teacher will not look at them unless asked to. They write for themselves, in whatever way the words come, not being held to complete sentences or to dressing things up for the teacher. They may draw decorations and illustrations on the calendar. Remind them, however, that if they do not write clearly, they may not be able to read their entries later.

Purposes

Keeping calendars helps to develop an objective sense of time, which in turn facilitates kinds of thinking based on it. Planning, tying events together, continuity, cause and effect, cyclic regularity, and the consistency of the self all relate to the public concept of time. Chronologic is, after all, a form of logic. This is not to say that it should replace the child's subjective sense of living in a timeless moment, to which he has a right and which has an existential reality not to be supplanted. Being practical and official, calendars are an appropriate learning to associate with the *public* concept of time. (Children's spontaneous stories, on the other hand, should not be brought into this association by imposing chronology on them.) We know that a serious difficulty among severely underpriviledged children is that life seems chaotic; there is no continuity, order, progression, or relation among events. This is true both of how they live and of how they talk about life. The result is both an emotional and a cognitive deficit; security and sense of self are weak, and temporal and causal ways of thinking are limited. Such children especially would benefit from calendar keeping.

But mainly, for all pupils, keeping calendars is writing practice of a real and well motivated sort, a variant of recording that can serve in turn as base for other writing. Differences are the future-oriented aspect, the more personal subject matter, and the necessarily more summary nature of the notes, which capsulize rather than actually record. In a sense, however, calendar keeping *is* an ongoing record — of what is passing through the child's mind during the five or so minutes. (Recording of thought streams will be pursued later.) Also, calendar keeping accompanies nature journals during the same years and lays a foundation for personal diaries recommended for later.

Writing Calendar Entries as Letters

Periodically, the pupils are told that they may write a letter to someone telling what they have been doing recently, using their calendars as reference. I am uncertain how long the period should be — a whole month or less — and the teacher may want to let different children write at different times, perhaps awaiting individual urges. At any rate, they decide first whom they want to write to, then read through their calendars and pick out events that they want to tell that person about and think he would like to hear. Then they write a newsy letter covering many things or dwelling on only a few. The teacher demonstrates on the board the form of dating, greeting, and closing, and the address positions on the envelope. They bring to school a stamped envelope and the address of their party. After reminding them that the postman cannot send their letter unless he can read the name, street, and city, the teacher tells them to address their envelope and ask a neighbor if he can read it. They post their letters in a mailbox replica made for the classroom and understand that the teacher will put them in a real mailbox; or if possible, they walk with the teacher to a mailbox near the school.

Besides motivating the writing, the letters provide an outside audience, and one at whom the content is especially directed. Of course, once introduced, writing letters need not depend on calendar keeping; the children may be asked occasionally if they would like to write a letter and then given time for it and help with it.

Chapter 9

Writing Up

"Writing up" refers to final writing that takes off from talk or notes and results in something complete for an audience or an overall purpose. As such, it digests other work and takes on a more public form requiring whole sentences and connectedness. It occurs in long-range projects such as I have only alluded to so far but will now treat in more detail. I can see two main kinds of projects, both lasting several weeks.

Burning Issues

The first kind of project is like the campaign against stealing and must necessarily be stated in an open and general way, since the subject comes from the pupils and the exact stages of the procedure will vary according to their intention. In Chapter 4, "Speaking Up," I described the process that two classes of second- and third-graders went through in order to determine the reasons for stealing and to propose remedies. It remains only to dwell a little on the part of the project involving writing up. The publication called *Beta-Gram* that the one class produced consisted of eight kinds of items or articles arrived at by small- and large-group discussion from which notes were made. Each child drafted an article, which the members of his group, acting as an editorial board, read and criticized for content and mechanics. These were rewritten and one or two from each group were chosen for printing. The audience and purpose of *Beta-Gram* were clear in the children's minds. A less desirable aspect, perhaps, was that not all articles were used.

What distinguishes this project is the writing up from discussions rather than from observations. The only facts involved were common experience and the questionnaire. This sort of project stems from feelings about moral or social matters and aims to treat these concerns in a tangible form. Such a campaign might germinate in one of the small-group discussions if the topic hits on some "burning issue" that the children want to pursue by other means than talk. "Other means" will not always entail writing but often will. (One class in the stealing project did posters.) The *Beta-Gram* that resulted from the experimental project is reprinted below. Since the contributions were screened, these generally were the best.

BETA SURVEY

As you remember Beta had a worksheet. It asked if you lost a pen or pencil this week. Then it asked how you felt about it. Some boys and girls said:

1. I feel badly because I don't have anymore.
2. I feel badly because I don't have anything to write with.
3. I don't feel badly because I have plenty left.
4. I feel good about it because I didn't lose any.

It also asked if you ever stole a pencil or pen. This is what some people replied:

1. People steal mine.
2. I found it, no one was around so I kept it.
3. It's not fair to the owner.
4. I wouldn't like it if somebody took mine.
5. I know it is wrong.

The worksheet also asked if you know a way to stop the stealing. There were lots of ideas. Here are some:

1. Put a mark on the pencils or put your name on it.
2. Have the children bring their pencils in a pencilcase.
3. Make them go to Mrs. Bears if they steal.
4. Keep them after school if they steal.

WHAT TO DO WITH LOST PROPERTY

If you find a pencil, troll, doll or anything of that sort give it to the teacher. When you lose something tell the teacher what you lost. If you find something put it in the lost and found box.

TALL TALE!

Bonnie Smith had lots of pencils stolen so she decided to find a way so people would not steal her pencils. She was talking about it in class. One of the boys had an idea. She decided to do it. She went to the store and got mouse traps. If someone tries to steal her pencils her fingers will get pinched.

The End

A TALL TALE

One day when I was in my room at school I herd the teacher yelling at Gurtrude Mcfuss for stealing a pencil. He "said" Gurtrude *why did* you steal that pencil?" But she would not say he did it. But finally she did. The teacher made her stay after for stealing and for lying "But when she got home she got in worst trouble. She went to bed with out any dinner That didn't help She just lying and stealing. She kepted going to bed with out any dinner and staying after school. Finally she learned she lesson. And thats how Gurturde Mcfuss learned her lesson. Never Steal!

If you don't want your toys or pencil's taken follow these simple rules:

1. Don't bring toy's to school unless necessary.
2. Keep your things in a box.
3. Give valuable things to your teacher.

PUNISHMENT FOR ROBBERS

This just might happen to you! If you steal pencils you will get into trouble. You may not get allowance for three weeks. You may get a spanking so WATCH OUT! Don't steal!

WANTED POSTERS

If you find this girl you will be rewarded 20¢

[Picture of one Pamela Cookie]

Beware she is a pencil thief. If you find the five pencils that she took you also will rewarded with 10¢. Bring her to 9–A They are all red pencils.

ADVERTISEMENT

Beware! If you steal pencils, you better stop it now! But keep this in mind if you might start, don't steal anything! If you don't steal, keep pencils in safe places. And If you steal — at least tell the truth. If you find a pencil — don't keep it but give it to the teacher.

A TALL TALE

Michael Byrne had to stay after school for stealing four pencils and he had to stay after one and a half hours. He had to tell his mother and father on the telephone what he did. When he got home he had to do work. He got a beating. He had to go to bed at six-thirty.

JOIN THE GOOD CITIZENS CLUB

To join the Good Citizens Club you have to have an application. It has to have your name, date that you joined, age, and homeroom. When you join the club you should do things that are good. You help people if they can't to it. You also do things for other people. Good Citizens never take things that belong to others, Bring the application to room 9–A

NAME _____

DATE _____

AGE _____

HOMEROOM _____

Your Application, Good Citizen Club

LOST AND FOUND PAGE

A leather comb case.
It is brown.
If found return to 6–A Eva Arsenau.

Orange pen that writes red. If found
return to Tommy Harvey. Room 1.

Nature Study

The second kind of project stems from observation of living things selected by either teacher or pupil. External reality, not inner concern, is the point of departure. You may say, "We are going to observe how a tadpole grows into a frog, and keep a record of its growth," or a pupil may bring in a pet that the class wants to keep a journal on. One thing leads to another. I will describe more fully an animal project devised in one of the classes participating in the campaign against stealing.

ACCOUNT OF TRIALS

I mentioned before that the group of second- and third-grade children did not become very interested in the animals until they began to live with them and care for them. Then they were so involved that a project not only crystallized but proliferated in many sub-projects. There were rabbits, gerbils, guinea pigs, and rats. The children observed and wrote descriptions of the animals (without, I should add, having had the sort of literacy training in punctuation and sound-letter relations advocated in this book):

APPEARANCE

She has a long tail. She has little pinkish eyes. Her ears are curled a little. She has long teeth. She has long whiskers.

APPEARANCE

Puddles is brown with a little white line on her head. She is small with little pointed ears. Her eyes are brown.

APPEARANCE

Cleo is brown, black and white. She is fat and she has big feet. She has four toes and she runs around in her cage all the time.

Ogden is brownish. He has sharp teeth. He is nice. His Eyes are black. His tail has hair on it.

How he Looks

Ginger is a rabbit. Ginger is black and white. Gingers eyes are blue. Ginger has four toes. Ginger is cute. Gingers toes are white. The bottom of her back front paws are brownish gray.

SNOWBALL

Snowball is white with red magic mark on her head so we can tell her from Whitey. She has long teeth. They are yellow. We have given her wood and meat t make her teeth shorter.

They made comparisons:

SNOWBALL COMPARED TO PUDDLES

They are different in color. Puddles has longer ears than Snowball. Snowball has a longer tail. Puddles has to be fed by Danny with an eye dropper.

COMPARING RABBITS

I am comparing Puddles to the other rabbit but puddles is smaller and than Ginger who is older, But both of them are cute. Ginger is the other name of the rabbit. Ginger is black and white. Puddles drinks from from an eye dropper But Ginger eats lettuce.

SNOWBALL

I compared Snowball the rat with Danny's baby rabbit. Snowball is bigger than the baby rabbit. Snowballs teeth are bigger than Dannys baby rabbit's. The rats eat a lot of food a day. Danny's babby rabbit gets fed by an eye-dropper.

They told where the animals came from:

WHERE CLEO CAME FROM

Cleo is a ginney pig. Cleo was born in a house. Cleo is 2 years old. Richard Parrish brought Cleo into school. The End

Where aminal came from.

Ginger and Sniffles came from West Acton. Ginger and sniffles are 4 months old. Ginger and Sniffles a my pet rabbits Ginger and Sniffles live in a very big   cage.

Where Whitey came from.

Whitey came from a lab in Wilmington Mass. Mrs Glassmen got her. We've had Whitey 5 weeks. When we first got Whitey. She weighs four oz and now she weigh's eight oz.

Snowball

Snowball came from a Labratory and Mrs. Glassman gave Snowball to our class. We feed her meat and lettuce and carrots and all most any, thing. She needs a Clean cage.

Where Puddles came from.

She came from a side of a garden. Everyone was touching about a half a dozen rabbits. You know that if you touch a rabbits, the mother will go away.

Ogden

Gerbils are from a desert climate. Ogden came from a gerbil farm. Then Miss Hoffman   was nice enough to bring it to Franklin School.

They told how the animals behave and how they have to be cared for:

The Desert animals

The gerbils name is Ogden. A gerbils cage is not cleaned often. About once a mounth. They are so clean. They eat sun flower seeds.

Caring for Cleo.

You have to hold her firmly. She eats celery, carrots and lettuce. She doesn't eat meat. We have to let her out of her cage so she can get exercise. She is fun to play with.

Ginger drinks water and eat rabbits pellets. She is cleaned once a week. She has exercise every day of the week and she chases other rabbit too. She plays games like tag and house with the other rabbit.

You clean whitey's cage every day. You feed whitey two time's a day. You let whitey ran through the maze. We are teaching the rat's to ran through the maze   whitey sometimes forgets the way to ran.

PUDDLES

She has to be fed often. Danny feeds her with an eye dropper.

TEACHING SNOWBALL

We have a maze. a rat starts am one side and is suppose to turn the corner. snoball is learning. But over the wekend she forgets

After the teacher wrote the first entry of the journal on a lined sheet and pinned it to the bulletin board, they took turns writing entries:

March 30, 1966
Cleo was to stuborn to come out of his cage. All she did was crawaled under newspapers. And messed up the cage.

whitey pedoon my hand and pam put white in a pisc of popor and snowbal did number to on debby hand The ene

April 4, 1966
Cleo was near the back black board. Cleo has no exercise. He was curious about his surroundings. He was eatting the papper I put on the floor.

April 5, 1966
Cleo would'nt come of. But at take us two miutes to get cleo out.

April 12, 1966
10:7 Snowball and Witey was resing. Cleo was on the pice of wood Then he was in the right hand eating the rabbit pelits.

Tue. 29
We got are rats. and we wher quiet. And our sturburn guine pig cleo would not come out of his cage. and when we got him out of his cage he wen't all over the room. and his cage was as messy as could be

One interesting report from the teachers was that the project stimulated many children to write who had been "non-writers" before, that is, pupils who had, because of difficulty and poor motivation, already begun to feel that writing was not for them.

Later, each child kept his own journal. In addition, they took the animals home on weekends and wrote an account of the animals' activities so that the rest of the class would not miss anything. They looked up related information. They visited the science museum. They ended by teaching rats to run a maze and keeping a journal on this experiment. Some of these ideas originated with the teacher, most with the children. The "project" was really a complex of activities thought up along the way. Teachers experienced in improvising this way can start with only an inspiration and not plan very much. This is ideal and undoubtedly the best "teaching method" in veteran hands. But many teachers will need at least a base plan from which to depart until they gain assurance.

RECOMMENDED NATURE PROJECT

A simple structure for an observation project is the physical development of some growing animal or plant. Bring in a bird or reptile egg, a newborn mammal, larvae, or tadpoles. Explain that the class is going to care for the creature and watch it grow up, but do not describe the course of growth in advance; their discovery will make it more fun. Tell them the food, temperature, and other requirements, and arrange a caretaking routine. Since waiting for an egg to hatch[1] or an animal to reach a new stage may leave little to observe at times, it is best to have a couple of things growing at once. Observation need not be daily if little is happening. With planning — and luck — the teacher can have the children record special events like births, moltings, and metamorphoses. And they can observe at times when particular events are taking place, such as the feeding of ladybugs to leopard frogs. Nature study should not be just cute — it can include preying and mating. The cycles and relationships in nature will teach the most and provide the most interesting material for recording. The child is rare, if he exists, who is not entranced by watching a caterpillar become a butterfly.

An alternative to growth as a project structure is the complex workings of social insects. It is possible to buy "ant farms" that have a transparent wall for observing. Or teaching animals to run a maze, by a reinforcement schedule of feeding, would provide an excellent structure.

It is in this way that sensory recording becomes integrated into projects. The stimuli are living things that interest children and that can be brought into class — animals and plants of all sorts. For this age the more the subject moves the better, although once involved in a project children do become motivated to observe small changes from day to day, if, say, they are growing certain plants, culture molds, or crystals. Since the foundation of science is observation, noting down sensations places pupils in the basic role of the scientist or naturalist. In fact, the children are told that they are going to "be" scientists and do one of the things scientists do.

Focusing on single senses. In order to focus on one sense at a time, choose a subject that naturally features one sense. For example, all one can do with underwater creatures in a tank is *watch* them; fish or seahorses would be good subjects. Or have the children watch the subject on one occasion and feel it on another. Observation of animals is mostly visual except for occasional sounds and smells. But of course mixing senses in a recording is ulti-

---

[1] A hatcher costs about $5. *A Sourcebook for Elementary Science* by Joseph and Victor Hone (New York: Harcourt, Brace & World, Inc., 1962) contains helpful information about caring for animals as well as suggestions for science projects.

mately desirable; the only reason for taking them one at a time is to increase acuity by focus and to simplify the task for beginners. We know from the experience of blind people that blocking out some senses increases the keenness of the others. We also know that asking younger children to write down all of their sensations is too vague and bewildering. Although silent movies and still photographs isolate vision, they are not practical. Children cannot write while they watch a film. And photographs are not only static, they present *simultaneously* an infinite amount of detail and therefore too many arbitrary choices of what to note down.

After working with isolated senses, tell the children to observe everything they can about their subject — to feel it, smell it, and (when safe) taste it as well as look and listen. While visiting one third-grade class that was recording what happened to candle flames when various things were done to them, I noticed that several group papers contained sentences beginning with *if-* and *when-* clauses, which appear rather rarely in the writing of children this age. Then I realized that it was their physical manipulations of the candles that were causing these sentence constructions: "If I put a jar over the candle, the flame goes out," or "When we throw alum on the flame, it turns blue." This is typical, I believe, of the organic way in which experiencing and thinking should lead to increased language complexity.

SPECIFIC PROCEDURES

Whatever the subject or the sense being focused on, the procedure is to let the children observe and record for five or ten minutes, in small groups or as a class body, depending on which is more practical for the subject, then to discuss their notes in groups of four or five. The function of the notes is, first, to remind each pupil of what he observed so he can "compare notes" with his colleagues and, second, to provide specific words, phrases, and observations for a group write-up of a collective recording. A scribe writes down on his paper what the others dictate to him from their notes. They discuss which items overlap, which wording of an observation is better, what the order of actions was, and which spellings are incorrect. Presumably, disagreements will arise about what was seen, interpretations of what was seen, and accuracy of color, shape, movement, and so on. Then, as the scribe writes on a fresh sheet of paper, they compose the account by suggesting and agreeing on sentences, an operation that involves discussing where sentences should begin and end, which words are capitalized, and perhaps other problems of mechanics. As the teacher passes among the groups, they call on him for help. The goal of this collaboration is to produce a full record of their observations, written in continuous prose.

Making books. The children are told at the outset that they will keep a journal and make a book. In effect, they will be writing their own science texts. The book will be on an individual animal or plant, or on a group of them. It will include the journal, a summary of the journal, drawings, and perhaps other pupil-created material. The first few times such a project is done, the journal and the book are group-written. By third grade, say, each individual can do his own.

A suggested program for the book collaboration goes like this: After observing and taking notes, the pupils collate their individual notes in small-group discussion, then write together their journal entry for that day (including the date). Weighing growing animals can provide additional data. Since a lot of the same words are used over and over, these can be gradually added to a long-standing list on the board, which pupils can consult for vocabulary and spelling. The entries are accumulated in a previously prepared booklet cover. Some observing sessions can be devoted to drawing pictures of the subject while watching it. These drawings can be dated and captioned to explain, for example, what the animal was doing at the time, and added to the booklet. At the end of the growth period or at some other appropriate time, each group meets to read over its whole journal and write a summary of it. Members of the group take turns reading entries and showing the drawings.

The process at this point becomes one of topic-centered discussion, the topic being something like "What are the changes Spot has gone through since he was born?" They discuss changes in appearance, behavior, feeding habits, weight, etc., referring to the journal for evidence. If the journal is about an ant farm, one would not expect the topic to get at development but at generalities in behavior: the routine operations and labor divisions of the colony. One would expect such a journal to record similar behavior on different occasions, so that gradually a general picture builds up. Thus the topic might be "What different kinds of ants are there and what does each kind do?" The journal might be summarized by asking several such questions and by writing up each separately. Discussion can serve to catch the gist of the journal. A scribe notes the ideas as the summary is going on, and the group rewrites these notes into the summary to appear at the end of the book. They check spellings and discuss where sentences should end.

Either teacher or pupils may have other ideas for writing to go into the book, perhaps arising out of some projects inspired along the way. Making the book not only motivates the writing part of the project but also fixes what they are learning and develops abstractive abilities. To avoid repetition of projects, teachers of kindergarten through grade six should work out a sequence designed to cover important kinds of knowledge.

Chapter 10

Playing Games of
Language and Logic

Writing Telegrams[1]

The children are asked to write a message limited to 15, 20, or 25 words, depending perhaps both on the children's ability and on the complexity of the story situation surrounding the message. "You want a friend of yours to stay overnight with you. You send him a telegram inviting him and telling him what he should bring with him. You have to tell him all the information he will need, but you also want to keep down the cost of the telegram. Each word costs a nickel." Besides bringing arithmetic into the game, weighing the cost against the adequacy of the information sets up a requirement that a minimum of words should convey a maximum of meaning. Another situation concerns a message to Grandma cancelling an invitation to visit because a sister is sick.

When these two situations were tried out in the second and third grades at a private school with classes of 15,[2] the children were eager to write the messages and spontaneously began a discussion about the kinds of personal articles a friend would or would not need for overnight, and about whether the sister's sickness was contagious or posed some other obstacle to Grandma's visit. When tried out in the second and fourth grades of an urban Boston school serving very disadvantaged Negro children, the researcher, who was not a teacher and did not know the class, ran into several difficulties, most of

[1] I am indebted to Anita Rui for the essential idea of this and the following game, and for the account of trials with both. Under the auspices of the Teacher-Researcher Project of the Harvard Research and Development Center in Educational Differences, she tried the telegram game in urban Boston classes.

[2] Lesley-Ellis in Cambridge, Massachusetts.

them resulting, as she reported, from her not having prepared the pupils sufficiently. These children needed to learn first what telegrams are, and to have the whole session paced more slowly — two problems the regular teacher could predict and solve. Also, they had been so thoroughly enjoined in their earlier career to write whole sentences that they could not adjust easily to the idea of telegraphic writing. Children used to sensory note-taking, however, will not be surprised. Indeed, one value of the telegram game is to present another but different writing situation in which word economy is an issue. The situation is different because telegrams are addressed to another person, not just to oneself, and therefore must communicate. (Teachers who may be concerned, understandably, that the game will encourage the writing of non-sentences should see the following assignment.)

The telegrams are read aloud and compared, or projected if written on transparencies, the latter being preferable since it affords reading practice and several telegrams can be viewed at once, for comparison, by overlapping the transparencies on each other in staggered fashion. The children should have a chance to see how a number of their fellows dealt with the problem of information versus economy and to discuss loss of intelligibility, adequacy of information, and unnecessary words. In so doing, they can learn the risks as well as the advantages of stripping down language. As the Boston trials showed, children who are forbidden to write anything less than whole sentences may become *unable* to adapt writing to other needs.

Expanding Baby Talk

This unusual and very successful game was inspired by the research of the Harvard psycholinguists Roger Brown and Ursula Bellugi, who have been tracing from its early stages the language acquisition of a boy and girl by transcribing their conversations with their mothers. A critical feature of such conversations, they have found, is the mothers' expansions of their children's utterances. Here are some samples from Brown and Bellugi.

Child	Mother
Baby highchair	Baby is in the highchair.
Mommy eggnog	Mommy had her eggnog.
Eve lunch	Eve is having lunch.
Mommy sandwich	Mommy'll have a sandwich.
Sat wall	He sat on the wall.
Throw Daddy	Throw it to Daddy.
Pick glove	Pick the glove up.[3]

[3] "Three Processes in the Child's Acquisition of Syntax," in *Language and Learning*, edited by Janet Emig, James Fleming, and Helen Popps (New York: Harcourt, Brace, & World, Inc., 1966), p. 12.

PROCEDURE

Copies of some of Brown's and Bellugi's transcripts were used as scripts and acted out by children at the two schools where the telegrams were tried (the second and third grades at the private school, third and fourth grades at the urban school). They read the mother's and child's parts, adding some gesture and movement. Then they were given some of the child's utterances similar to those in the sample above and told to fill them out on paper in the manner the mothers had done in the dialogue. They read aloud their various expansions and compared them in discussions. The ambiguity of a child's utterances, which a mother can expand rather accurately from context, can lead, of course, to very different sentences when pupils expand them without knowing the context. As Brown and Bellugi point out in regard to the samples above, what the child omits are mostly functor words — auxiliaries, prepositions, verb forms, articles, and pronouns. In other samples, inflected endings indicating number, possession, and person are also omitted (*He go out. Daddy brief case.*). The pupils, of course, do not all assume the same subjects of the action, times of the action, relations among objects, and so on.

PURPOSES

In expanding these utterances and comparing expansions, the children may learn, generally, the risks of telegraphic speech and therefore the value of whole sentences and, specifically, the importance of functors and inflections and the ambiguity their omission creates. Moreover, they can grasp intuitively the relations between full and incomplete utterances and how these relations depend on certain "parts of speech," although these parts should not be named. Finally, lower-class Negroes who characteristically omit many of these functors and inflections may become aware of their own speech traits and of the resulting ambiguity (ambiguity at least for speakers of standard dialect). The game could then be a tactful way of helping them to expand their home-learned speech. Alternating this game with telegrams opens up a two-way street between expansion and abridgement so that the pupils can move *deliberately and awarely* between potential sentences and actual sentences, being limited to neither and able to choose either, according to their purpose. "Sentence fragments," we note, have nothing to do with this two-way process, since these are almost always lopped-off phrases or clauses (*Into the town. As soon as they left.*) that result either from poor punctuation or from reading too many Volkswagen advertisements.

This game went very well with both the private school and urban school children. Why it had such appeal is interesting. They seemed to enjoy very much feeling superior to the smaller children, being able to do more with speech than this "younger generation" can. Perhaps they liked being a baby again and at the same time being more than a baby. And of course the mother-child relationship is intrinsically interesting to them. The dramatic and story element is fortunate also; in fact, the game can inspire playlets and stories if the children are asked to write their own mother-child dialogues, or to take their expanded sentence and make a story around it.

A practical difficulty with the whole idea is in obtaining authentic transcripts to use. Since publishers are not loath to supply more material for schools, a strong enough demand would undoubtedly inspire them to print such dialogues. Pending this possibility, someone in the school system might tape a few conversations between a mother and her 18-month- to three-year-old child, or a mother in the community might make some up out of her experience. Incidently, this game, like some that follow, illustrates how similar some language research activities and some school learning practices can be. If more ventures were launched similar to the Teacher-Researcher Project at Harvard, under whose auspices the telegram and baby talk games were tried, each party would probably find the other a source of helpful ideas for his profession.

Scrabble-type Games

A regular scrabble board might be used, after the teacher has explained the rules of the game. The children play in groups of three or four, but if the waits between turns prove too long for some children, pairing might be better. Among other things, the game affords practice in using the dictionary, since the players must frequently consult an authority to find out if they are spelling a familiar word correctly or if a certain combination of letters creates some actual word or merely a phonetically possible word. A regular dictionary could go with each game board (special children's dictionaries might not contain enough unknown words). The game is, of course, one way of learning spelling and vocabulary. A less obvious feature is that trying out various letter combinations can reinforce phonic understanding and flexibility in assigning possible sound values to letters. For example, given the letters T–H–A, one child might add an N to form THAN, whereupon another might think of further adding K to form THANK, a move that would change the sound values of all four preceding letters.

ANAGRAMS

Children who do not seem ready for scrabble (the crossing constellations of letters sometimes restrict rather severely the possibilities for further words) might begin with the simpler anagram type of game. The children are paired off and given a deck of homemade cards each of which bears one letter on one side, the more common letters occurring on more than one card. One child makes a word by picking up cards and forming a "hand" out of them. Then he shuffles that hand and gives it to his partner to unscramble into the original word. If the partner forms with the hand a real word other than the one intended, he must recombine the letters until he gets the intended word. Then partners turn about. Or the children might play the game as straight anagrams in the first place by trying to make up words that can become other words merely by transposing letters (re-ordering cards).

UNSCRAMBLING WORDS

Anagrams is based on combinational possibilities that can be extended to whole words or even sentences. One child writes a sentence on a strip of paper, cuts the strip between words, shuffles the words, and passes them to his partner to unscramble. Amusing possibilities can occur, of course, that the writer did not intend, and the scrambling has the appeal of secret codes. Children would, in effect, be playing with the syntactic possibilities of the language and with the syntactic ambiguity of many words that might be either nouns, verbs, or adjectives. The point of the game might be to get as many additional sentences as possible out of the set of words that forms an original sentence.

UNSCRAMBLING SENTENCES

Starting with a whole paragraph and unscrambling a mixed set of sentences leads to logical issues concerning which sequences of sentences can "make sense" and which cannot. The original sequence might sometimes be a story, sometimes a set of directions, sometimes something else, thus creating different logical problems. Although the point is to reconstruct the original sequence, the learning occurs in the trying out of different sequences and deciding which ones make sense. In watching his partner try out combinations, the writer can see alternatives to his original sequence that are equally logical.

SENTENCE BUILDING

Again playing in pairs, one child makes up a sentence by placing word cards in a sequence, then his partner attempts to add to that sentence with other cards, then the first child tries to build further, and so on, the object being to make as long a sentence as they can. Thus:

Bobby plays ball.
After school Bobby plays ball.
Every day after school Bobby plays ball with his friends.
Every day after school Bobby plays football with his new friends.
Every day after school Bobby plays football with his new friends until his mother calls him.
Every day after school Bobby plays football with his new friends until his mother calls him to come eat supper.

This is at once an intriguing game and a very important practice in sentence expansion.

The word cards may be manufactured ones or ones that children have made or asked the teacher to write out for them. Since their private stock of word cards may contain only nouns, verbs, adjectives, and adverbs, they will encounter the need for other sorts of words — prepositions, determiners, and conjunctions. If provided with plenty of blank cards or slips, they can write new words on them as they play the game, and these additions can be added to their stocks for use on other occasions.

PURPOSES

The fact is that all such combinational games are at bottom logical. The differences among playing with letters, words, and sentences are in the hidden premises involved — whether these premises are spelling rules, syntactic rules, or the rules of common sense. Essentially, trying out the possibilities allowed for by the various rules develops meaningful choice, which in the case of whole words and sentences opens stylistic and rhetorical possibilities as well.

For similar creative games of word- and sentence-building, see Gattegno's *Words in Color* (page 89).

Checkers

Checkers, too, is basically a game of logical possibility. Deciding which moves to make on the board is a concrete way of syllogizing: "If I move here, then he may move there, and then I jump this man." Move A and move B are premises, and move C is the conclusion. In playing these games one learns to predict, to extrapolate from the actual to the potential. Furthermore, one has to displace himself to the opponent's point of view, to play the role of the opposition (a feature of nearly all adversary games, including baseball): "What would I do if he made the move I am considering making?"

I believe that children's powers of thought — to turn over alternatives permitted by the rules, and to go beyond an egocentric point of view — can be considerably advanced by allotting them time to play checkers. While it can be argued that such games can be played at home and not in school, the fact is that in many homes parents would never think of introducing such a game to their children, and even if they did, the likelihood of a child's finding an equal partner in the home is very slight. Pitting oneself against a parent or an older sibling is not ideal, whereas school can provide matches with peers. Since the games could be purchased with some of the money now spent on unnecessary textbooks, the only other objection I can imagine is that the children would be having fun in school when they should be working.

Card Games

PURPOSES

I am concerned, first of all, with the logical ability to group different instances of a thing in order to form a category. Most conventional card games, and most children's card games, are based on categorizing. One makes "books," for example, by putting kings, threes, or hearts together, or, in small children's games, by putting lions or tightrope walkers together. It is interesting that researchers in psychology frequently use cards — mostly of their own devising — to study thought processes, especially concept formation and concept attainment.[4] Whereas concept attainment is the inferring of a previously established category from instances of it, concept formation is creating one's own categories by grouping instances according to one's choice of which attributes are to be the criteria. Teachers would presumably be concerned with both, with the child's grasping of conventional concepts and with his forging of his own categories of experience. And we may assume that experience in attaining conventional concepts will help him make explicit the concepts he forms on his own.

The second purpose of card games is to develop the ability to range concepts in some relationship to each other. One way of ranging is to place them over or above each other in the manner of classes and their subclasses. Another way is to place them in a successive order, or series, such that each "adds something" to the one before.

Hand in hand with the growth of concepts goes the growth of vocabulary. Although most expansion and refinement of vocabulary occurs in discussion, reading, and writing, this is the place where it may be presented systematically.

For these purposes I propose that children learn to play card games with decks especially created for schools. Since the possibilities of card games for classroom use could itself take up a book, I will merely sketch some of these possibilities and hope that enterprising teams of teachers will pick up the suggestions and work out particular decks and game rules through experimentation, making the decks in class at first, and then, when satisfied with results, proposing the more difficult decks to publishers (good illustrations are especially necessary).

CATEGORICAL GAMES

The earliest type of deck could consist simply of picture cards for children to group according to identical pictures, the object being to complete the

---

[4] See, for example, a *Study of Thinking,* by Jerome Bruner, Jacqueline Goodnow, and George Austin (New York: Science Editions, 1962).

most "books" or to go out of the game first by completing books. This kind of game could precede reading. Its main function would be to teach card playing itself, for the following purposes, and to associate it with classifying.

The next stage would be a deck of labeled cards bearing *non*identical pictures of animals, plants, vehicles, and other things in such a way that each picture card would be an instance of one such category. Each book would be a set of instances. Prior labeling of the pictures would not be necessary to the game but would merely be a form of sight learning of words. But the relation of subclass to superclass could be explicitly taught by placing the word *bus* beneath the picture of a bus and placing the word *vehicle* above it. Thus, all vehicle cards — airplane, bus, car, cart, etc. — would be individually named according to subclass and yet all would bear the name of the class concept that subsumes the subclasses. Such labeling might not be necessary to play the game, but it would help the child to range his concepts explicitly in a hierarchy. For new concepts, more abstract categories, and more finely discriminated subclasses, this double labeling would most likely be really necessary to play the game. Making books according to categories that are new to the children would probably be far enough to go with categorizing at this age. Many different decks would be rotated among pupils, each deck introducing new concepts and vocabulary.

SERIAL GAMES

Another cognitive feature of conventional card games is serial ordering. A very simple game like *War,* where players match single cards to see who has the highest card, presupposes knowing how to count serially. In fact, such games could be used to teach the higher numbers if special decks were made covering the tens, hundreds, and thousands. A further step along this line is to represent numbers arithmetically, as seven-minus-five or eight-plus-four instead of two and twelve; when players match cards to determine which is higher, they must first figure out the number of their respective cards. I am not merely digressing here into the teaching of mathematics, for there is continuity between mathematics and English, the bridge being logic. "Set theory" in math, for example, concerns the formation of classes, the grouping of items that are in some sense similar; the attributes criterial for a category can be quantitative or qualitative. Though most easily exemplified by numbers, serial relations do not have to be numerical; all that is required is a notion of "higher than" or "more than." Consider jack, queen, king, and ace. Social, royal, governmental, and military rank could be represented in a deck of cards, or series of figures or geometric shapes in which each item adds a "new wrinkle" to its predecessor, or chronological series, or series by size.

The earliest form of serial card games would be one-to-one matching of card after card until one player has acquired a whole deck. Then the game is changed to a higher level of sophistication: five cards are dealt each player, discarding is required after each draw, and the point becomes to get a "straight" — five successive cards — before the other players do.

The subject matter of both categorical and serial card games can embrace mathematics and social studies as well as commonalities. It is the processes of categorizing and ordering that we are after. The virtue of teaching different subjects through the same medium is that the method itself correctly implies to the child that these subjects are related and that what relates them are these thought processes.

Part Two

GRADES FOUR
THROUGH SIX

It is assumed that teachers of grades four through six will have read the preceding chapters on kindergarten through third grade. Many of the language activities to be proposed here are merely continuations of earlier ones in more mature form. For these continued activities I will suggest developmental modifications appropriate to this age. Teachers whose classes are new to the curriculum would need to give their pupils an adapted version of some previous assignments before proceeding with later assignments that evolve from them.

The classification of activities does not remain exactly the same as before, for several reasons. As writing becomes more differentiated, the three basic categories of composition in Part One — writing out, writing down, and writing up — now ramify into a larger variety of types. Since what I have to say about literacy has been said in Chapter 5, there is no separate chapter for it in Part Two. Pupils who have never had a course in sound-letter correspondences, or who read and write as if they had not, should be screened out and given one.

Since much of Chapter 6, "Reading," was meant to apply to all of the elementary years, it has no counterpart in Part Two. Teachers of grades four through six should refer back to it.

"Speaking Up" (Chapter 4) is discontinued for a different reason, which has been stated before: the account of small-group discussion for kindergarten through grade three applies equally to grades four to six, there being as yet insufficient knowledge

*to distinguish two stages of small-group method. By no means,
however, does this omission signify a diminution of its importance or practice. In lieu of further discussion of method, I
would like at least to give a sample of discussion by some sixth-
grade children and to refer to the research during which the
discussion occurred.*

*John Mellon and I set out to learn more about some of the
factors at play in small-group discussion among children — the
differences that age, group size, group composition, socio-economic background, topic, and leader role make in the thoughts
and language of children.[1] For one of our brief feasibility trials,
preliminary to future, controlled experiments, we taped trios
of children discussing four topics for several minutes each.
These were single sessions conducted in school with children to
whom we were strangers. Our purpose was to observe the close
interaction that we believed the minimally sized groups would
afford. There was no leader, and we experimenters did not
participate in discussion except at rare moments to spur the
talk from the sidelines. We used topics derived from earlier
trials, which seemed to show that brief "cases" posing a problem
worked better than other topics we tried. We made up a number
of cases, one of which appears below. I based it on an old
Chinese dilemma and aimed it at Negro ghetto children.*

*Ellen was a young mother alone in the world with a small baby.
Her husband had disappeared and she could not find a job. Besides,
who would take care of the baby while she worked? She felt so bad
about being alone and having no money that she left the baby on
the doorstep of a nice-looking house and went to another town to
look for work.*

*In that house lived a woman named Betsy whose children had
grown up and left home. She and her husband took in the baby
and cared for it as if it were their own. Betsy was pleased to have
a child again and loved it very much. They named the boy Jeff.*

*After five years Ellen came back to town. She had got a job and
then had married again. She went to the house where she had left
the baby and said the child was hers and she wanted him back.
But Betsy said, "You went off and left him, and now he's mine."
Ellen said, "I didn't want to but I had to. He's my child." Jeff
did not know his mother and clung to Betsy, not wanting to go off
with a stranger.*

How do you think the dispute should be solved?

[1] This research was supported by the Harvard Research and Development Center in Educational Differences and by the National Council

*Three sixth-grade girls discussed it, as reproduced below.
To appreciate the interaction process illustrated by this sample,
one should note the stand that each girl takes at first toward the
conflict, and then observe how these stands are modified as the
three influence each other.*

A: Well, in a way, I think that, um, Betsy should'a kept the chile',
     because, um, because — well, my cousin — well, you know,
     she um, she had to go to 'dis school for bein' bad, an' she had
     this little son, so my aunt's keeping him — so, ah — she's
     back now, though — so, um, I guess she wanted her chile'
     back too, but my aunt still has 'im an' she's gonna keep him,
     but da' boy — he knows his mother — but, um, ah' don't
     think she should get him back, though, becus' she — she
     wouldn't know, you know, how to handle him an' be married
     an', you know, so I think that she, um shouldn't give 'im back.
     So I think Betsy should keep him.

C: I think that Betsy should keep him because she had raised 'im,
     an' she had — went off and left him there! She probably
     really didn't care about 'im until she found the job, or any-
     thing like that.

B: But — um, Ellen — but she had no other choice! The baby
     would'a starved! She didn't have no money, an' she went to, um,
     work to get the money to support the baby. And she remarried.

C: Yeah, but couldn't — she hadda' — lef' a note in the backa'
     da' — whatever she lef' him in — ta' tell the lady 'dat — just
     ta' keep him until she finds a job n' gets married, but she
     wasn't thinkin' right then. See, she just took an' lef' the baby
     right on the steps an' let da' lady take 'im in — she didn't
     know who it was at all!

B: Now I think that, um, the baby should take his choice —
     which one he wants to stay with.

C: Yeah — that would be —

A: Yeh. Better. But — But he already did. He was clingin' ta',
     um, Betsy, so Betsy might as well just keep 'im.

     (Pause)

of Teachers of English. A preliminary report on this first phase of research is forthcoming and will be obtainable from the Publications
Office, Longfellow Hall, Appian Way, Cambridge, Mass. 02138.

A: *'Cause I think 'dat, um, if — 'cus the lady — she shouldn't have left him with no one while he was so young. She should'a — you know . . . .*

C: *And she really didn't know why she lef' 'im — de' only thing, now, she wants to keep 'im —*

A: *Uh huh. So — an' Betsy supported him an' everything, so I think dere' —*

B: *Well, I don't know —*

Adult: *Suppose you were a judge and the case was brought to you and you had to decide.*

A: *Well —*

B: *Well —*

A: *I'd give it — I'll give it to Ellen, n' tell her that if she ever does it again, then, um, you know, so — we'll just have ta' send the baby to an orphan an', if she supports him well an', you know, doesn't just keep remarryin' an', um, sendin' him to different houses an' stuff — that, then, I — then I would let her keep him. But if she does, you know, just does what she did again, and then expects to have the baby back — then I wouldn't give it to her.*

B: *Well, I think Ellen should have the baby — but if he would get used to her, an' den' I would let her — let him see Betsy, or visit Betsy — the one he was raised with. 'An let both of them really have the baby — like, spend some time with Betsy an' spend some time with Ellen.*

A: *But — but wouldn't it be harder —*

B: *I think —*

A: *— but then he'll think that Betsy was his mother, but once he get's used to Ellen, then you could do it that way, you know.*[2]

   A and C begin by stating that Betsy should have the child because Ellen is unfit, whereas B defends Ellen, remaining uncommitted about the choice, which she proposes that the child

[2] For their cooperation I would like to thank principal Forrest Lewis and teacher James Sullivan at the William Bacon Elementary School in the Roxbury district of Boston.

should make. This solution, which bypasses A's and C's assumption that they should decide in favor of one woman or the other, prompts second thoughts. But it occurs to A that the child has already *decided — a very neat objection. Then A and C return to their initial positions, having assimilated B's disagreement, and B returns to her indecision. At this point, feeling that they needed a new stimulus, I made my suggestion. I might have done better, but the effect of such an adult interjection is precisely what teachers should discuss together in reviewing tapes. A now reverses herself in favor of Ellen, conditionally. B is now inspired to offer a definite solution, one that allows for both women's claims. Though A objects that the compromise will confuse the child, she overrules her own objection by emphasizing the condition that the child should get used to Ellen before they both share him.*

What this discussion illustrates, I think, is that the pupils have influenced each other toward greater complexity of thought. The initial simplicity, based on condemnation or defense of Ellen's character, gives way to the multiple-viewpoint approach to the problem, in which implications are brought out and ideas are amended. Peer interaction without significant adult leadership has wrought this change, though adult sponsorship of the discussion was no doubt an important influence. This exchange may be taken as a miniature model of how group language behavior can improve individual utterances. I see A's last remark — with its two but's *— as symbolizing the increased complexity of thought that group process induces in each of the members.*

Chapter 11

_____

_____

_____

Acting Out

"Acting out" includes verbal drama and also pantomime, charades, "dance drama," and any other use of the body to imitate action and symbolize feeling.

Body English

Nonverbal expression remains important as a supplement to speech, a base for speech, and an alternative to speech. What should be explored are the advantages and limitations of both. One way to understand what speech can do is to withhold it: in pantomimes and charades, one sometimes fairly bursts to speak those things difficult to convey by movement and gesture alone. Conversely, body English can say some things with greater brevity and power. Some of the intention of the following is to relate words and deeds and, when possible, to translate from one to the other. In addition, physical action gives pupils a respite from paper work while at the same time enhancing it. Finally, some children issue from a relatively wordless world, which causes them to persist in uttering most meaning and intent through the body, whereas other children of this age are rapidly becoming verbalizers at the expense of physical expression. Both need a counteractive influence.

GUESSING GAMES

After they have acquired some confidence and ease from earlier pantomime, pupils can put on their actions individually before classmates in small groups and let the others guess what these actions represent. The ideas for these actions might come at first from suggestions by others: each member writes in advance on a slip of paper something that one person could act out alone — such as "a woman trying to hang out wash on a windy day" — and these are shuffled and passed around. Writing the directions has a value, too: the author of a slip sees his words translated into action and gets a sure-fire indication of whether his written speech is understandable or not. Pupils are reminded of the possibility of getting their own directions to act out. In fact, this possibility prepares for making up one's own act impromptu, a practice to follow this one in due time. After the pantomime and the guessing have ended, the actor reads aloud the directions he received.

At some point determined by the teacher, one group plans and silently acts out a situation or scene before another group, which attempts to guess, when the skit is over, what happened. (For now, this is as far as spectatorship will go.) Planning consists of either collaboratively making up an action or selecting one from material already known. If the material is from a poem or story that the class is familiar with, the guessing involves the recognition of it in nonverbal form, and the acting is translating. If the material is original, the spectators' guesses translate acting into words.

In the case both of individuals pantomiming before a small group and of groups pantomiming before other groups, guessing should be held off until the skit is over, and disagreements over interpretation parlayed into discussion, after which the situation or scene is revealed, verbalized, by the actor or actors. Spectators are asked to say specifically which gestures and movements made them construe the action as they did.

Comparing interpretations can be a valuable way to treat inference — how we assemble cues into inferences and how it is that, witnessing the same action, we can infer different things. This uncovers the sort of hidden assumptions and subjective reactions that operate in our interpretation of real life. After comparing is played out, they turn to the actor's statement of what he was trying to do. Further discussion can then center on discrepancies between what was intended and what was inferred. (It is assumed that actors try to communicate, not mislead.) From the remarks of the spectators, the actor knows which gestures and movements communicated and which did not. This feedback can now become a joint effort to think about how the discrepancies could be overcome, the deeds better matched to the intentions.

Learning to act, learning to write, and nearly all other kinds of learning depend on ascertaining the effects of one's efforts. For the best functioning of such discussion, the teacher relies on the pupils' prior experience with small-group discussion, but establishes in advance the two phases as just described and sits in for a while with each group. For more intensive work with inferences, in fifth and sixth grades, check out the planning of the groups to insure ambiguity in the skits so that, for example, some spectators will say that a pantomime is about a hunter stalking game and others will say it is about a detective tracking a criminal. This work with interpretation relates, of course, to sensory recording, which necessarily entails mixing inferences with observations (hence the double sense of "observation"), and to the comprehension of literature, where too the best interpretation is the one that allows for all the cues, not just a selected few. In short, a guessing game is an inference task, and the art of the teacher is to help children to learn one while enjoying the other.

Written recording of pantomime, which extends the whole activity, is described on page 211.

CHARADES

The guessing game can also, within small groups, be extended into the more adult form of charades, the acting out of verbal phrases, titles, and quotations. That is, what the audience tries to guess are not the actions themselves but certain words that the actions merely evoke. This feature, of course, makes the game more sophisticated and more abstract, since actions must be linked with particular words for them, not with just any words for them ("steed," not "horse"), and often, via purely verbal associations such as puns, the right word is arrived at secondarily ("aunt" by brushing off an ant). Also, instead of holding off the answer until the end of a whole presentation, the actor makes the audience guess at each act, each word. This makes for audience participation and fast feedback.

Thus, the actor learns very soon if he is communicating. In fact, before he can continue he must adjust his body English until he does communicate. When he fails, he tries another action. At the same time, his audience must keep offering words until *his* feedback lets them know that they have hit on the one wording that will do. Both are learning communicative precision, one by trying out gestures and the other by trying out words. The audience develops flexibility in interpreting and in wording because they must offer alternatives — a wholly different "reading" of the action, a one-word synonym, or a variant phrasing. The essential skill required of the actor is to play on associations he and the audience share, associations between things and words and between some words and other words. A fundamental part of writing is knowing which associations are in fact shared and can therefore be counted on for communicating. The art is to evoke one thing by means of another. Private associations will not work. The best way to sort private from public, to put oneself in the place of the audience, to discover a common coinage, is by playing precisely this sort of game, verbally and nonverbally.

ENACTING STORIES AND MUSIC

Wordlessly acting out fables, fairy tales, poems, stories, and music can be coordinated with verbal dramas so that the very process of deciding which material should be pantomimed and which dialogued receives major attention. The teacher breaks the class into small groups, not necessarily of the same size, and directs each to choose some piece they have heard or read in class or written themselves. They make their choice by nominating several pieces and discussing whether these would go better with or without words. The pieces rejected as needing dialogue can be saved for verbal enactment on another occasion. Such discussion also leads into planning of the action, which is in effect an editing and adapting job. The advisability of having a director for each group needs experimentation. In any case, roles are rotated and different versions enacted and compared in brief intervening discussions. An adjunct to this activity can be the showing of several kinds of silent films — some pantomime, some not, some fictive, and some actual. The absence of dialogue makes these especially good for discussion.

The writing assignments will also provide considerable material for both pantomime and verbal dramas. These possibilities will be pointed out in passages treating sensory and memory writing and original stories and poems. Conversely, writing based on pantomimes will also be described.

The use of music with pantomime creates two differences. One is that the necessity of playing music for the whole class at once means that all children will be acting from the same stimulant at the same time. But the possibilities are still open to simultaneous individual pantomimes, simultaneous group pantomimes, or even a single full-class pantomime. Individual acting can proceed from the movement-to-music sessions described on page 39, which permit each child to give a bodily rendition of the feeling or idea the music elicits from him. Group pantomimes can be planned, just after listening to the music once or twice; or, if known story-music such as "Peter and the Wolf" is used, roles can be simply assigned; or, furthering the suggestion on page 41, grouped individuals can invent movements in relation to, say, three partners, the directions being to move as one feels but to stay aware of the others, share the group space, and let oneself be influenced (reciprocal influence adds a social stimulant to the musical one). This last, which was a culmination in kindergarten through grade three, could become a regular activity at this age.

The second difference between dance drama and pantomime is that the feelings stirred by music act as a more vague, more subjective stimulant than words, while at the same time the ongoing rhythm and melody create a series of quite specific stimuli that are readily translateable to movement. The actions of pantomime tend to mimic recognizable things, whereas dance drama tends to express less explicit inner things given form by the music. The same movements might appear in both, but whereas they would be patterned by music into regularities and continuities, under verbal stimulus they would be determined by situational or story ideas. There is no reason to distinguish the two kinds of body English, however, except to clarify for the teacher the differences to the pupil between musical and verbal stimulants. Although story-music bridges the two somewhat, movement to music offers more opportunity for personal spontaneity and therefore comes closer to free improvisation.

Verbal Drama

Although I have separated body English from verbal drama, because I believe they should be alternating activities done on different occasions, the point, of course, is to integrate them while distinguishing them. The relation of the two corresponds to their relation in scripted plays, where stage directions indicate nonverbal behavior, and dialogue indicates verbal behavior, both fusing into a total action.

ENACTING WITHOUT SCRIPTS

Dialogue enlarges considerably the range of material that can be acted out. This can include the majority of selections children read, not only folk and children's literature, but excerpts from geography and social studies. A lot of their own writing can be dramatized, and the recording of live conversations (page 181) will, in fact, supply actual play scripts. The procedure is the same as for pantomime and for enactment in the lower grades: the groups choose the material (separately or as a class), discuss adaptation and roughly plan the action, act out with no spectators, rotate roles, and discuss and change successive versions.

IMPROVISATION

Practices. Henceforth the term "improvisation" will designate only impromptu acting with dialogue. Crowd scenes involving the whole class are one kind of improvisation that would be especially appropriate to begin with. The teacher describes the scene — the midway of a fair, a street corner in town at a certain time — and lets students make up roles for themselves, suggesting some himself if necessary. Talk is encouraged. After a few minutes the teacher creates an incident, perhaps by capitalizing on some bit of action going on in one part of the scene. He might suggest, for example, that a "child" wandering on the midway begin to bawl because he is lost. How do the others react? By this means he can extend actions and sustain the scene, taking the students through a sequence suggested by their spontaneous behavior. Later, the students supply ideas from the outset.

For small-group improvisation the teacher proposes a minimal situation — a child has brought home a pet and tries to persuade his parents to let him keep it — or asks the class for one. Once they get the idea, the children will readily supply good situations for a scene. The class breaks into groups containing enough members for all the roles — no more than three or four —

and all groups improvise at the same time, rotating and doing different versions.

Teachers who, at my request, tried out improvisations in their classes[1] reported that their pupils did them easily and eagerly, as they had pantomime before. There seems to be no doubt that children love to act, and jump at the chance. At the time, moreover, the improvising was introduced abruptly and done right off before the class — not a good practice, since improvisation should be prepared for and should remain unwitnessed throughout elementary school except for the assignment described on page 46. One of the situations used in the experiments was "report card night at the supper table." To give an idea of how such improvisations go, I offer here a recapitulation of one written shortly after the performance by a no doubt untypically able girl who watched it.

An Interview with the Smith Family

The Smith family was seated at the supper table, because today report cards had been brought home by everyone in the family. Father said to Jill "What did you get on your report card, dear?" "Well – a, let Susan tell what she got first." And Susan replied back "Well father asked you so you tell him." Jill was not pleased with what her sister had said, but she said in a sweet voice, "Well – a, I got a pretty good mark in math, well it was (amiably) it was, a "d". Father couldn't believe his ears so he said "Say that again." And so this time Jill trembled a little as she said once again a "d". Then mother asked Susan what she got on her report card, and Susan sighed, and said "I too got a good mark in math, a "d" also." This made their parents very angry as they asked Jimmy what he got on his report card. He said "Well I got and a in math, in chemistry I um, I um burnt a hole in the floor." And father said in a stern voice "You may pay for that with your own money." The father asked John what he got on his report card. And John replied, "I got "a" in every subject." This pleased father very much as he collected the report cards. First he looked at Johns and he had 5 f's. And father said "I thought you got all "A's". Then he looked at Jills report card and said "funny you got a "B, c and 5 d's", father was very displeased. Then father looked at Jimmy's report card and said "Well I see you did get a bad mark in chemistry." And at last he looked at Susan's report card which read [Here there was a drawing of the card.] First father ripped all the report cards, and told John to pick them up and put them in the wastebasket, as his punishment. Next he told Jimmy to go to school and repair

[1] Some members of the Omega team (fourth- and fifth-graders combined) at Franklin Elementary School in Lexington, Massachusetts. I wish to thank the whole team for their invaluable experimentation with many of the assignments in this section of the book, and for their willingness to meet frequently after school for a whole year to discuss the trials. They have supplied most of the pupil writing printed in this part. Team members were: Margaret Clark, team leader, Barbara Palermo, JoAnne Setzer, Judie Daly, Abby Dratz, Mary O'Connell, and Carole Scharfe. Other researchers than myself have benefited from the excellent experimental climate created in the school by the principal, Ethel Bears.

the floor. Then he told Susan to make the beds every week. And at last he said to Jill in a mysterious voice "Hmmm what *shall* I do for your punishment." And finally he said "You shall take the rubbish out every night"! The End!

Not all situations have to be drawn from real life, but many of those proposed by the students of this age are.

Values. It is best to think of improvisation as a learning instrument, like small-group discussion, that can be used for many purposes. The point is not just to teach drama but to teach other things *through* drama. To take on the role of a parent or shop girl or manager is to extend oneself into another life-experience, perspective, and style of speaking. And, as in the skit above, noncommunicative uses of language are put on display — dominating, evading, etc. Improvisation puts a great emphasis on verbal interaction and on rhetorical ploys, on getting effects with words.

Improvisation is especially valuable in elaborating over-condensed stories. Most myths, legends, and folk tales that come to us second-hand are in summarized form, lacking much dialogue or specific movement. The dullness of such summaries is a big stumbling block to presenting these fine stories to children of an age to be especially appreciative of them but not yet able to read the elaborations of them in the plays and epics of great authors. But they provide good "minimal situations"[2] which children can expand and bring alive through improvisation. The teacher reads the summary, and the groups take as their situation the few sentences that recount a scene. Take scenes, not plots; groups can do successive scenes on successive occasions.

Since their own writing is limited in length, children's narratives tend also toward digests that need elaboration. Although the writing assignments recommended for this age try to head this off by keeping the length of time covered by their narratives commensurate with the length of their writing, pupils will frequently over-condense. Expanding these digested actions through improvisation will help them to see the values and the possibilities of greater detailing. Generally, an important relation in writing and literature is that drama elaborates narrative and narrative summarizes drama. Novelists work within constantly varying degrees of résumé, and cover a lot of story ground, whereas playwrights present the total action of only a few carefully selected scenes. The principle of abstracting is that one always trades a gain in coverage for a loss of detail, and vice versa. By improvising dramas from narrative sketches, and, conversely, by writing narrative summaries of improvisations, pupils can grasp this abstractive relation between these two orders of discourse.

The report-card skit had a theme: children's failure to comply with parental demands. I find that children's skits always do. Such themes are natural topics for small-group discussion when preshaped by preliminary dis-

[2] See page 44 for definition.

cussing of the skits themselves. If small-group discussion and improvisation are coordinated, a very powerful learning, I feel sure, will result, because ideas can be dealt with — again — in two modes, at two levels of abstraction. A topic is a distillation, in question or statement form, of particular instances of some theme, any one of which can be improvised. And discussion of improvisations distills themes into topics. In other words, by improvising the instances that come up in small-group discussion the pupils can go from generality to example, and by discussing the material of improvisations in small groups they can go from example to generality. (Material can come from literature, everyday life, and social studies.) This movement between abstraction levels is not only a vital issue in writing but a major educational goal.

Chapter 12

Writing Down

Grades four through six are the time, I believe, when transcription should be learned once and for all. Of course this cannot mean a definitive mastery of spelling, simply because children will always be learning some new words for which the spellings have to be memorized. But certainly the segmenting of speech flow need not linger for years as a problem to exasperate both teacher and students; nor for that matter should the bulk of spelling remain a problem, for, after all, the growth of vocabulary beyond elementary school introduces only new words, not new phonic relations.

Principles of Teaching Transcription

A child leaving elementary school should be able to render graphically, with only a few misspellings, anything he can speak or understand orally. There is no aspect of transcription that his future development will make it possible to learn if it has not already been learned. Actually, a person's sensitivity to speech sounds and intonations is probably better in grades four to six than later, proponents of foreign language teaching at this age claim. This stage not only combines the good ear of the small child with the motor skill and phonic understanding of the older one, but it is the period of strong competence motivation, when children are still willing to master an ability somewhat for its own sake. By contrast, junior and senior high school students insist much more — and rightly, for their age — on meaning and content, and resent what they feel to be the nit-picking of fuddy-duddy clerics who are interested only in a hollow formalism, not in what you have to say. This attitude represents, in fact, greater maturity. A top priority goal of elementary school, then, should be to eliminate transcription as a problem so that the work of later years can be free to satisfy this riper motivation and can avoid alienating older students from writing as composition.

173

To teach transcribing is *not* to ride herd on mechanics. This is precisely why I suggest separating transcription from composition. Meaningful writing should be treated as such; the teacher helps with spelling and punctuation *before* composition takes place, and pupils can proofread each other's writing afterwards. Frequent printing of pupils' writing motivates proofreading and helps the teacher to associate spelling and punctuation with typography rather than with moral values. When either the teacher or other pupils misunderstand a paper because of transcriptive errors, however, this should be brought out in commentary or discussion as a matter of helpful feedback to the author of the composition.

A teacher who marks a paper up for mechanics almost inevitably establishes a value scale for pupils upon which transcriptive errors rank higher than content and composition. Only the future will tell us how much student writing has been made inferior by penalizing spelling and punctuation mistakes. Like the child who said she used the word "bar" instead of "trapeze" in a story because she was unsure how to spell the latter and didn't want to be marked down for it, most pupils adopt the error-avoiding strategy of using only words they are sure they can spell and sentence constructions they know they can punctuate. In the long run, avoiding risks can't possibly reduce error. Pupil strategy should consist of making educated guesses and of checking guesses later with the teacher, other pupils, or the dictionary. The teacher can, however, give personal diagnosis: "You have trouble knowing when to double consonants," or "You need to listen more for punctuation in the middle of a sentence."

With this as general procedure, we turn now to the transcriptive assignments themselves.

Taking Dictation from the Teacher

The goal is self-dictation, reproducing one's silent composing voice on paper, but it is very difficult to do this straight away. One takes his own intonation for granted, and becomes aware of it only gradually, from having to pay attention to someone else's in order to transcribe it. Also, taking dictation from another person gives a practice in spelling that is utterly unrelated to composition, and that at the same time ties punctuation to vocal cues.

In order to control the transcriptive difficulties and to focus on particular issues of spelling and punctuation, the teacher may need to give some dictation himself. (See page 138 for my reservation about the use of dictation and for suggestions on how to go about it.) The only justification for asking pupils to transcribe a passage verbatim is the felt need for work on spelling, for punctuation practice can be afforded much more efficiently in the manner described farther on. A language lab would be very valuable for transcribing prepared passages verbatim. A live voice or prerecorded tape dictates. A visual loop attached to the machine would enable each pupil to compare his transcription immediately with the printed text. Only those pupils who need the practice need go to the lab; the pupil can operate the machine himself and replay the parts of the passage he needs to hear again.

Punctuating Unpunctuated Texts

For segmenting the speech flow alone, the pupils can punctuate dittoed copies of an unpunctuated text as the teacher reads it aloud. This goes fast and is really only a variation of being read to; the pupils follow along on the dittoed sheet instead of on a projection, inserting periods and commas as they go by following the teacher's vocal punctuation. Afterwards, ask pupils what they put down and allow them to compare their transcriptions. High consensus helps to establish the more objective universals of punctuation, and allows individual pupils to note deviations of their own that may indicate areas of unawareness in hearing. Low consensus, or mixed response in places, can show the teacher which sorts of punctuation are difficult for his class. Let the disagreeing pupils justify their responses and then reread the sentences involved. If this brings no resolution, try to discover whether the problem is one of pause and intonation alone, or a subtler one involving logical options as well. As a humorous way to make a point, occasionally project a text that you have mispunctuated and read it according to the mispunctuation. For older students, I used to write on the board, "what is this thing called love," and ask them to read it aloud in as many different ways as they could and to tell me how each version should be punctuated. They thought of readings that had not occurred to me. Try it yourself.

As soon as it seems wise, ask the pupils to read pieces of their own writing aloud as the rest of the class punctuates dittoed copies of it from which punctuation is removed, first announcing that the pieces are not selected as either good or bad. These must not be picked as bad examples but on a rotation basis, so that every pupil's punctuation gets the benefit of class consensus and teacher attention. Pupils asked to read their writing for the class to punctuate are told to read without haste and in exactly the way they think their paper should be spoken. If members of the class have trouble punctuating the text, or disagree considerably, this provides a chance to bring the author's reading or writing more in line with his intentions, and to correct obvious intonational faults. His original punctuation can then be revealed and discussed.

Principles of Punctuating by Voice

Dissociating punctuation from rules and textbooks takes a lot of the mystery out of it. Replacing the foreign text with their own writing, and teacher reading with pupil reading, should thoroughly score the point that the authority for punctuation resides in shared speech habits and therefore in each person.

What Can Be Heard

Let's put it all this way. Except for questions and exclamations, which are obvious, a drop of the intonation contour almost unfailingly calls for a punctuation mark. The issue is which one — comma, dash, semicolon, colon, or period? Even if he chooses unwisely, a child who puts *some* mark of punctuation there has fulfilled the first principle of punctuation — to segment the flow of speech. Whether a comma or a period is called for depends on the length of pause and on whether the intonation drops merely to a lower point, somewhat suspended, or all the way to the bottom for a distinct closure. (Read this last sentence aloud.) A true comma splice would occur only when a full drop was mistaken for a half drop; a period after a sentence fragment would occur when a half drop was mistaken for a full.

What Is Difficult to Hear

And yet punctuation is not completely objective. There is a margin of personal option, and it is true that some of the more sophisticated usages governed by logic are not necessarily audible. One cannot always hear, for example, when two sentences are joined by a semicolon or colon and when they are separated by a period. And one would be hard put sometimes to distinguish by ear alone a colon from a semicolon or a comma from a dash, or a series of commas from a series of semicolons. But these are the only four cases involving option and logic where voice may be an inadequate guide, and they can be explained, through illustrations, when they come up in dictated passages to which the class gives mixed or uncertain responses. For example, unless read together in careful contrast, the punctuation of the following sequences might be rather difficult to detect:

(1) *He sprang up, he looked over his shoulder, he sprinted off.*
(2) *He sprang up; he looked over his shoulder; he sprinted off.*
(3) *He sprang up. He looked over his shoulder. He sprinted off.*

Meanings of the Symbols

The teacher can, however, compare the different punctuation marks to "rest" symbols in music, and describe them as a progression of increasingly larger breaks — comma, dash, semicolon, colon, and period — while remarking that the length of pause alone may not be enough of a clue to which of any two is called for, and that, furthermore, emphasis and meaning make a difference too. A dash is a kind of comma — but more emphatic. Like an arithmetical plus sign, a semicolon merely adds one sentence to another; this summing indicates closeness between their actions or meanings. A colon is like an equal mark: the sentences on either side of it restate each other. If illustrated, the practical purpose of using semicolons for a large series and commas for subseries contained within it is easy to grasp and remember. In fact, presenting sets of instances of each of these kinds of punctuation will do more good than lengthy explanations.

PUNCTUATION OF SINGLE WORDS

Another kind of logical punctuation that may or may not be audible is internal punctuation of individual words — apostrophes and hyphens. There is no way to hear the apostrophe of possession and contraction. It must be explained through instances. Hyphenation, however, can almost always be heard, because pitch is sustained through a compound word. Compare *He entered the second grade* and *He entered the second-grade classroom.* Write on the board some unpunctuated sentences that will be misread and cause a double-take: *He counted three toed sloths.* Ask the children what the problem is and how they think it can be solved. (Compare *three, toed* and *three-toed.*) Write an ambiguous sentence — *They saw many colored butterflies* — and ask someone to read it aloud. Can it be read another way? How would you show the difference to a reader? Ask them for examples of other compound words, remarking that two words that are compounded in one sentence may not be in another. After they are sensitized to the audible difference, make a statement to the effect that just as our voice joins the two words in speech, so the hyphen joins them in print.

Some capitalized words can also be distinguished by ear: *white house* and *White House.* Some remaining typographical equivalents of speech will be mentioned in connection with transcribing conversation.

I believe that such an account of written punctuation will cover all but the most abstruse of possibilities and will prove serviceable throughout the later years, even for options. Many teachers don't *want* to bring personal option into the picture, because it would seem to present punctuation as a subjective matter of "anything goes." But the virtue of an intonational approach is that the voice is a remarkably objective guide, indicating personal options in a public medium. That is, one does not punctuate as one pleases, one punctuates as one speaks. Most personal options can be heard. When they cannot, the few logical principles stated above will supplement vocal discriminations.

Taking Dictation from Classmates

Dictation occurs quite naturally in the role of scribe, as used in various discussion groups and working parties. Its virtue is that spelling and punctuation are practiced in a situation that does not at all smack of an exercise, since the point of the writing is to record ideas for later use. As notes, however, the writing will not necessarily be in whole sentences, nor will the speaker's words be taken down verbatim. But even abbreviated transcription has value, as I believe the papers below show. A boy in the Lexington Omega group (fourth and fifth grades combined) was transcribing what a partner said as she felt four objects in a paper bag. (This paper was done in the original tactile experiment before the teachers decided the assignment should be shifted down to the lower grades; see page 136.)

1ST   bumpy, shallow bowl, two small handles, little ridge around bottom

2ND   large bumps, shaped like a large egg, between bump feels like enameled wood, its smooth between bumps except at smaller end

3RD   like a dry sponge, smooth edge like crust on bread, shaped like a piece of bread only thinner

4TH   circle if you look at it from bottom, smooth. Shallow depression at top, small, feels like made of glass

Though he has reduced her sentences to essential descriptive phrases, by omitting "it has . . ." and "there is . . . ," he has reproduced with commas the intonation drops that ended the sentences. The result, incidentally, is series, properly punctuated, which could again be given predicates, only more economically, one for each series instead of one for each quality or item in a series. Note also that the girl used *five comparisons* in the effort to convey her sensations. This assignment is a realistic way to elicit similes, because the practical need for them is great. Below, a girl in the same group writes down what three "feelers" said.

Jill says, "It's smooth like a shirt and kind of short, It's hollow, It feels smooth, It feels as though it has string tied to it, It feels as though its kind of square, It feels as though it made out of suade, It has two long corners, Its kind of like a bag of candy, you can put things into it."

Donna says, "Its feels rough on one end, you can put your hand in it, I can put my fingers in it one by one

Stephen says, "It feels like its made out of rubber, It feels like a bunch of circles in it, theres it has deisigns on it, there is some string on it

The children in the experiment had had no experience with this sort of dictation nor with intonational punctuation. Many found verbatim transcribing difficult, but, as I think the teachers would agree, this would not be so if they were more used to it. The main problem is the speed of spontaneous speech. Dictation by the teacher or by scribes can be slowed down.

Taking Dictation from Younger Children

Another realistic transcription task is for pupils of this age to take down the dictating of first-graders. A common practice now of many kindergarten and first-grade teachers is to transcribe for their pupils, one at a time, their stories and other things they have to say. My suggestion is that older children take over the teacher's role in this case. Two teachers exchange halves of the classes so that the older and younger children can be paired off. What the first-graders say may be about all sorts of things, related to other current work or entirely individual; the content makes no difference. Explain that the upper-graders will write down and show them later what they have said, and that you will circulate among them, both to help prompt the younger and to help the older with spelling or punctuation problems. (Suggesting in advance that the latter too may need help will save face for them when changes need to be made in their transcriptions.)

There are advantages for all parties. The dictaters get a chance to see what their oral speech looks like when rendered on paper. They read it, they learn spellings, and they have the satisfaction of keeping the paper for showing to others. The attention and help of older children, the big-brother or big-sister relationship, the desire to emulate bigger people are all powerful learning forces not utilized often enough in schools. For their part, the older children enjoy being looked up to and having their greater capabilities seriously called upon. Since it is important that the transcriptions be accurate, the teacher, as announced, checks them over for spelling and segmenting of speech flow — preferably during his rounds, but later too if necessary. An enormous amount more dictation can be done in this way than when a teacher alone undertakes to act as secretary. Exchanging the papers among themselves afterwards affords more reading practice for the younger children, each speaker being able to help his readers to make out the words.

Dialogue Recording

In conjunction with transcription, and also as a specialization of sensory recording — the taking down of voice sounds — the writing of real, overheard dialogue may begin now. One teacher in Lexington began this by writing down on the chalkboard, as the pupils entered the room, the various remarks and exchanges that she heard them make. Amused and interested by this, the pupils were then not surprised when she asked them, as homework, to place themselves somewhere with paper and pencil and write down some live conversation. Of course, they cannot write as fast as people talk, but they can be told to catch as much of the conversation as they can, not to worry if they miss some things, and, if they have to, to recapitulate some of the conversation in their own words.

I reproduce here an Omega boy's transcription of a home conversation.

A shoe bag. Well this will do for you're junk. Weeell this will do. Larry I got you a few things! I want you *both* off those stairs! ! ! See what you did Tim! ! *I'm* going home *I'll* hide somewhere. whaaaah Tim do you want some Ice to chew on? Want some more? I got a cut at school too. I *almost* got a cut. Listen you thing. I'm going to hide somewhere. And I'll find you. wha-a-a. Would you like a cup uh chopped Ice? What are you doing overthere? What are you taking everything down for? Tim wanna play house. uh-uh. Timmy were not mad at you. Larry is this your homwork or are you *trying* to be funny? Larry, Larry, Larry, *Larry! !* It *isn't* any help to be a noodge. I got you something too. What's going on here? Its the filmstrip. The baby came over and ripped up all the cards. We made all these this one is like pin. Tip is pin, tin, grin, pin

These need not be done at home. As with other sensory recording described later, pupils are encouraged to go to different places where they think interesting "scenes" may be going on.

Certain problems arise as to who is saying what. This is the place for the teacher to help them to learn the typographical devices for keeping speakers straight, such as quotation marks and paragraphing or colons after speakers' names. It is also an opportunity to relate vocal expressiveness to some punctuation usages that I have not discussed so far. Using projected papers for illustration, the teacher explains that dashes indicate interruptions (including self-interruption); suspension marks, a long pause within a sentence or, with a period, the trailing off of a sentence; and underlining, an emphatic stress on a certain word. Real dialogue also inevitably includes many opening and closing tag phrases to be set off with commas (*Well, he is going, isn't he?*) as well as cases of direct address, all indicated by the voice.

Ditto or project a transcribed conversation and let the class try to read it silently. Then ask them what problems they had. During this discussion interject whatever explanation they need of the punctuation usages mentioned above. Make changes on the transparency. When speakers have been straightened out, with the help of the child who recorded, ask some pupils to take parts and try to read the dialogue aloud. Sentence punctuation can be worked out when the readers show uncertainty or misread a line (the recorder is asked to speak the line the way he heard it). Tell the children that this session illustrates what they are to do in small groups, and that the purpose of clearing up the transcriptions is to provide copy for printing up and acting out.

When the class seems to have grasped the issues, after one or more sessions, direct the pupils to revise their transcriptions as best they can, then to huddle in small groups for collaboration. They test each other's dialogues by reading them aloud in parts and letting the transcriber listen for discrepancies between their reading and the original. When the dialogue does not run true, they revise typography and punctuation according to what they learned from the class sessions, calling on the teacher if they need help. Then the transcriptions are prepared for printing. Since these will be exchanged within and between classes, their goal is to permit strangers to reproduce dialogue from the page. To this end, they should use every device available — paragraphing, parentheses, quotation marks, underlining of stressed words, suspension marks (. . .), and dashes for interruption.

Below is another transcription of an overheard conversation, this time by an Omega girl who is obviously far more skilled in quoting and in taking down speech than most children will be on their first attempt or so.

"Whaaa Whaa" "ha ha" "That's right Kathy" "No!" "Ow" "Wait a sec, Kathy you have to go right to the a a um ironingboard. and I have to go the the bed". "R-R-A-A-A-" ". . .Set go!" "Kathy won!" ". . .right there. . ." "Yah! !" ". . . now before. . ." "1,2.3 GO!" "Go Kathy!" "I won that time! I touched this before Kathy did." "You heard me I said. . ." "So now I have to run down with you. Wha Wha." "I have to touch these papers." On your mark, get set, GO!" "you forgot to touch these papers." "On your mark get set ur go!" "Whaa ow" "ha ha ha!" "On your. . .times places! One, two, three e-e-e-e-e-e-e-e-e-k-k-! Get out of here" "gaga gu gu!" A-A-A-A-A-H-H-H" This sis sis sis sis sis sis say anything! Say it as loud as you can." Margie said go!" "a-a-a-h-h" "shush children!" "were just playing a game. Watch! Please Mommy let me" "Margaret you may go to your room." "What?" "Please," "allright you may go right to your room Come on!" "No-o-o." "those lucks, Lorie an Susan won't let me. "Me too!" "Now Kathy the first you are told to do something you do it. So many times I've had to yell." "Were having a yelling contest and the person who yells the loudest gets to pat Tinderbell about ten times." "Okay" "Ma-a-a Ma-a-a!" "Now who can say it the softest!" "Margaret won!" "Yeah" "Okay, Kathy won, Okay." "Children I have a better idea why don't you simply get out some paper and play a game." "Let's finish this first, Okay Nutmeg."

But even this paper could use a lot of mechanical revision for intelligibility and readability. The important thing is to make both the transcribing and the revising part of a well motivated and meaningful process.

After some transcriptions have been printed up and distributed, take one from another class, let the children read it silently, then make a game of guessing the time, place, situation, and speakers. What action is accompanying this dialogue? Then let them choose other transcriptions and act them out, improvising the action as they infer it and perhaps expanding the dialogue. On a subsequent occasion project a transcription and, after they have inferred circumstances and speakers, show them how to convert it into a play script, which will indicate the things they have been inferring. Write in speaker names, followed by colons, and insert action and setting parenthetically. These stage directions are in the present tense and are limited strictly to what can be seen and heard (being like a sensory recording). Then send the children to small groups to revise some new transcriptions of their own into script form. They collaborate in preparing these for printing. When copies have been distributed, they select scripts to act out within small groups (loosely, without memorizing lines).

Besides furthering their transcriptive ability, the recording of overheard conversation will prepare for writing plays and for reading the professional dialogues of fiction and the theatre.

The Use of Tape Recorders

I hope that teachers will go on to imagine and try out other kinds of transcription assignments than those I have outlined here. One particularly fertile possibility is for students to take down their own voices from a tape recorder. This enables a pupil to transfer the transcriptive process from others to himself, to his subvocal inner speech. Again, accurate self-dictation is the goal. Pupils can take turns composing on a single tape recorder, or if a language lab with recorders is available, go there all at once. They are directed to say into the microphone whatever it might be that they would otherwise have written. Afterwards, they listen and write down verbatim what they said. (Most school machines have an easily operated mechanism for pausing and replaying, a feature that gives this activity an advantage over live dictation.) If some children have trouble segmenting and punctuating their own speech, listen to their tapes and help them with either their speaking or their hearing. Next, they may make compositional revisions on the transcription. This should prove to be an excellent procedure for inducing awareness of how writing must compensate for the loss of physical voice, and for making the general transition from speech to writing. One Omega class verbalized their auditory sensations on tape, transcribed them afterwards, and made revisions on the transcription. At Ball State University, Anthony Tovatt and Ebert Miller have done preliminary experiments with ninth-graders composing on tape and revising; part of the inconclusiveness of their work so far, they speculate, may be due to the possibility that students should have this experience earlier in their career.[1]

If any part of the language arts lends itself to teaching by machine, the sound-sight correlations of transcription do. The more nearly mechanical the skill, the more mechanical devices are justified. I hope that future technology will provide us with an electronic spectrograph machine that, when a child talks into it, will enable him to *see* the stress, pitch, and pause of his intonational contours.[2]

---

[1] "Effectiveness of an Oral-Aural-Visual Stimuli Approach to Teaching Composition to Ninth Grade Students," unpublished paper given as a talk by Dr. Miller at an American Educational Research Association meeting in Chicago in February, 1966.

[2] I am told that Mrs. Jean Olson of Minneapolis has used an oscilloscope for this purpose. A series of television tapes prepared by her in 1966 showed speech segments very graphically.

Chapter 13

Sensory Writing

The process described on page 148 of taking observational notes and individually keeping science journals should definitely be continued through grades four to six. All that one should probably expect to see change are the complexity of the observations, the fullness of the notes, and the finer matching of language to fact as vocabulary and linguistic forms develop. I leave the subjects of observation to the local collaboration of science and language arts teachers. What I will outline here are other kinds of sensory recording that are introduced into the program for the first time. Since considerable experimentation was done, at my behest, with this kind of writing, I will give a rather full account of it, not only to indicate its possibilities and problems, but also to turn over some general writing issues.

Account of Trials

Around the School

In casting about for in-school subjects other than animals or objects, the Lexington Omega teachers (of fourth and fifth grades combined) tried sending their students into other parts of the school, in this case into another classroom:

> I hear squeeking chires and writing of pencels, people walking. I see boys talking the teacher looking the flag flaping. A blue sky. An open window I smell the freash air. I see clouds in the sky. I here a door slam crash! I see the teacher talking to a child.

These ongoing notes were made by a boy of average ability who then revised the paper, without benefit of written commentary or correction:

I came in the room and sat down. I heard squeeking chairs and people writing. Some boys are talking. The teacher is looking at someone. The flag is flapping in the blue sky. I can smell the fresh air through the open window. The little clouds ar in the sky foating very fast. Bang! A door just slammed shut. The teacher is talking to someone.

It is interesting to note the revisions that he made on his own.

One of the teachers' ingenious ideas was to bring a first-grader into class and let pupils record the child's actions as he went about making something from clay, pipe cleaners, and other materials. This by an able girl:

Her name is Marisa. She's sitting down in the nearest seat to her. She's breaking the yellow clay into balls. She's a little shy. She's never been to Omega before. She isn't saying anything. Now she's beginning to have a good time. She's smiling a little. She's working very carefully. She looks around and smiles every so often. She's only using the yellow clay. She's very quiet. She's making some sort of figure. It looks sort of like a man. Now she's using the toothpicks and the scissors. She's feeling more at home. She feels more sure of herself. She's using all the colors of clay. Now it looks more like a person. She's putting an egg-carton hat on the figure. The only thing she hasn't used are the straws. The figure has feet, eyes, nose, mouth, hat, legs, and a few toothpicks and sticks sticking out of it.

And revised:

The little girl came in shyly. She said that her name was Marisa. She sat down in one of the seats and started breaking the clay into balls. She worked quietly with the yellow clay. Then Marisa started to have a good time. Every once in a while she looked around and smiled. Marisa worked very carefully and started to make some sort of figure. It began to look like a man. Then she picked up the scissors and toothpicks and began to use them. Gradually she felt more confident and she began to enjoy herself even more. The figure looked more like a person. Then Marisa used all different colors of clay. She made a hat out of a piece of an egg carton and put it on her man. The figure really looked like a man then. It had feet, legs, nose, mouth, eyes and a body all made out of clay. It had a hat too. And she had stuck a few toothpicks and sticks into the man. Now, she is going back to her room. She is hurrying along. The only things she didn't use are the straws. She has enjoyed her visit to Omega.

Although not all pupils can carry off the assignment as well as the girl above, there is no question that if they can write at all they can do it. The issues, rather, for both of these assignments are these: What is the pupil's motive for doing them? (Why is he observing and what use can be made of his paper?) Are the time and labor involved in revising justified? One could argue that, though slight, the actual changes made are important compositional touches; that mechanical errors are corrected; and that pupils confront a critical shift in tense and point of view (the boy begins in the past but lapses back into the present whereas the girl sturdily maintains the new past tense). The revision, of course, puts an added strain on motivation. It might be helpful for my reader to compare the originals and revisions above and make some judgment on these issues before continuing.

The second assignment above differs greatly from the first in one respect. The events one records in a classroom are random; the observer takes potluck on his material. But the action of someone making something presents a selected and focused set of events that raises interest and motivation. I think that among our pupils the latter assignment was much more successful in this respect. The act of composition starts with a selection and focus of material, from which different writing issues ensue. This is a relationship that both teachers and pupils need to grasp securely. The novice writer can grasp it by having to make decisions about his raw material.

Away from School

In our experiments we sent children out of school to record on location without telling them to pick a place where they knew some action would be going on, specifically some action they knew they would be drawn to. They went to nearby places with only mediocre motivation, and took their chances. Here are some observations done by slower children not inclined to write voluminously on any occasion. Tidied up after discussion:

> I can see houses. And I can see a lightpost. I can hear the bird whistle. I can see a boy come down the street. A dog is drinking water from a puddle. That makes me very thirsty. There is hardly any smell.

> I hear my mother talking to my brother. I see a bed, and a cat, then a picture. I smell fresh air and sweet grass. The sweet grass reminds me when school is over. I hear my father cutting the grass. It reminds me of my electric tooth brush.

Before revision:

Hear	See	Smell
Birds tweeting, seems like they're taking music lessons	Birds, small and cute Thorn bush, I wouldn't want to go in it.	Cold air, makes you shiver Winter air, seems like winter
Dog barking		
A highway, one great big noisy truck is there		Dirt, ice cold, damp

See seven chairs and see stove. I see the front door, people walking around, and some dishes in the room — making footsteps and hear somebody washing the dishes, hear radio going in the background. I hear talking in another room. I smell a little of the breakfast and I can smell some air that makes me think of food.

Also unrevised, but benefiting from "natural selection" (the first a girl, the second a boy):

Meow, meow, shhh, Nick is having kitties. Thump, thump, shhh, Nick is having kitties. Ohhh, I know, scratch, scratch, Nick is having kitties. Oho, what do you know, she had three kitties.

I watched my mother clean the table and clean the dishes. I heard my mother yell at my sister because she didn't help.

Clearly, an occasional poetic or laconic vignette issues from such casual observing, sometimes even an enviable bit of imaginative perception:

My Back Yard

It sure sounds funny how the wind goes through the trees. The smell of flowers blooming. The red pail lying in the grass. Our rope swaying across the air as if it was going somewhere. The wheel barrel like a ox pulls leaves. Trees are having buds. It's a beautiful night. The fence bending back in the wind. Our shed standing still there. I can hear the rabbits eating. I can see houses. I can hear the toad communicait. I can see our dog. I heared a bark from the yard. Our swing set trying to keep its balance.

Besides the French imperfect tense in *communicait*, what I appreciate in this boy's notes is the rendering of the wind — the rope swaying, the fence bending, the swing set trying to keep its balance — all in contrast to "our shed standing still there." The kind of finely noted evocative details that teachers fall all over themselves trying to get students to put into their writing are here — the red pail lying in the grass, the wheelbarrow pulling leaves like an ox (comparisons are rare in children's speech and writing), the sound of rabbits eating — and yet I don't feel that the boy was striving for poetic effect or trotting out his prettiest adjectives to "do a description." He was really experiencing the moment and translating it into words.

Formulating the Problems and the Assignments

But sticking one's thumb into a pile of papers and pulling out a plum does not prove the worth of an assignment. After we tried out, during the fall and winter, a variety of kinds of sensory recording — in school, out of school, isolating senses, combining senses — these following problems remained.

1. The speed of note taking often resulted in dry, abstract lists of words.

2. The obligation to stick to sensations caused the children to exclude thoughts and feelings that arose from the sensations and that actually would have made fine compositional material; the restriction seemed to devaluate the personal response and imagination.

3. When a whole class recorded at the same place, there was no audience for whom to write up notes and hence little motive for composing.

4. If pupils rewrote notes every time they recorded, they sometimes got stuck with dull material that they had no interest in writing up.

5. Furthermore, this practice entailed too much writing of a copying kind.

6. The assignment did not of itself stimulate similes and metaphors, which we all felt should enter into sensory writing.

With these problems in mind, and feeling a need to formulate the assignment as explicitly as possible for the final experiment in the spring, I wrote the following directions for pupils and teachers. These were mimeographed and distributed. The pupils kept their directions in a folder prepared for the project in which they also kept all the papers they produced in response to these directions. Both sets of directions are reproduced here as a base from which other teachers can make adaptations by their own lights and in the light of reservations I will make afterwards. Directions to the teacher are in parenthesis.

Record sensations at a locale away from school.

1. Choose any place away from school that you would like, go to that place with paper and pencil, and for fifteen minutes write down what you hear, see, and smell there. Think of what you write as notes for yourself later. These notes will not be graded but you will need them later for another assignment. Bring them to class. Don't worry about spelling or correct sentences; write in whatever way allows you to capture on paper what you observe in that time. You may also include your thoughts and feelings about what you observe. You may also want to say what things look, sound, or smell *like*.

(1. Two worthwhile issues can be raised and dealt with in the discussion of these first papers:

1. The difference between, and relation between, sensations and non-sensations, physical facts on the one hand and inferences, personal reactions, similes, etc. on the other hand. Both should be valued, but it is important for the child to be able to spot what he has mixed of himself with the environment. "Observation" thus takes on its double sense of "sensory data" and "personal reaction." With a dittoed or projected sample paper before them, ask the class what things in the paper might have been recorded by *any* observer and what things show traces of the particular

person doing the recording. The use of "loaded" words and comparisons could be brought out as well as just obvious personal statements. Also, compare two papers for the relative amount of sensory data vs. personal reaction; ideally, this would lead to the discovery that, given the time limit, a gain in one is a loss in the other. Then give back their papers and let them underline words or sentences that they feel convey non-sensations. As a check for them, let them exchange papers and have a neighbor underline what *he* considers to be non-sensations.

2. The *form* of the notes: word lists, telegraphic phrases, and whole sentences; amount of paragraphing and punctuating. Since these are notes to oneself, they should not be judged for correctness or intelligibility to others but only for their value as notes. Discuss the gains and losses of different forms of note-taking. Ditto or project two papers of contrasting form. What do you lose when you use just word lists? broken phrases? whole sentences? They should get some sense of which words are dispensable, which words or phrases capture a lot quickly, which suffer a loss of detail, and what the advantages and disadvantages are of longer phrases and whole sentences. (In general, lists cover a lot of items but lose the detail of *each* item, whereas full sentences modify, qualify, and elaborate single items but don't cover as *many* items.)

Students should be encouraged to develop a notation style that works well for them — that enables them to go for coverage or go for detail, to strike whatever balance they want. This should help with Assignments 2 and 3.)

Record sensations at a new locale or time.

2. Do as you did in Assignment 1, but this time change either the time or the place. If you went to an indoor place before, go somewhere outdoors now. If you went to an active place, go now to a still place. If there were no people where you went before, go where there will be people. Or you may return to the same place you went before, but go at a very different time of day, or when the weather is very different. Remember that you are to take notes of what you observe, see, hear, and smell and of what thoughts and feelings you may have about what you observe. If you have found a better way of taking notes since last time, use the new way.

(2. Discussion of these papers might center on two new issues, besides perhaps picking up the two earlier points if the students seem to want to pursue them.

1. Again with a sample before them, ask if the class can tell the time, place, and circumstances of the recording. How much can they tell of the mood of the observer and what he felt about the scene? Is there a main mood, impression, keynote, attitude, etc.? Does one sense dominate — sound, sight, or smell?

2. Try now to lead into the selection process of the observer. Get the class to imagine what things were *left out*. Ask the writer of the paper to recall what things he did *not* put down. Hand back all the class papers and ask everyone to look at his paper and compare it with his memory of the scene. Ask first the authors of the sample papers and then the whole class how they came to include some things and reject other things. If they say they put down the "most interesting" or "most important" things, ask how they decided some things were more interesting or more important. This more or less unconscious selection process is at the heart of composing; some awareness of it should help later with Assignment 4.)

Record sensations
with some other
pupils.

3. Do as you did in Assignments 1 and 2 but, before you leave class, plan with two or three other pupils to go somewhere at the same time. Decide together where to meet and when. After you meet, place yourselves at different points at that place (not too close together) and then begin to take your notes on what you see, hear, and smell. Again, included whatever thoughts and feelings you may have about what you observe.

(3. Read aloud or project all the papers of one group that had a common locale. Discuss what things all noted, what things only one or two noted, differences in physical vantage points, differences in inference and personal reaction or mood.

To prepare for rewriting, use this set of papers to confront the question: "What would you have to do to this paper (the sample before them) in order to make it understandable and interesting to other people?" See first what things they think of to mention without prompting. You may have to guide them a bit toward things they do not mention. Have them look at their own papers, ask the same question, and write some responses on the papers. Some possibilities are:

1. clarifying some of the wording or references
2. dwelling more on some things and less on others
3. cutting out some things and adding others
4. giving more or less personal reactions
5. rewriting to avoid repetition of the same words or monotony of sentence structures (finding different words and constructions).

These discussions of Assignments 1–3 should make possible some successful collaborating in the small groups (see pupil's Assignment 4 slip).)

Compose one of
the foregoing
papers.

4. You will be put in a group with two or three other pupils, and you will all help each other to select and rewrite one of your papers. So take Assignments 1, 2, and 3 to your group, and exchange all three papers for the three papers of someone else in the group. Read those three and decide which one could best be rewritten into an interesting composition for the rest of the class to read.

Write on that paper some comments. Say why you think it has the best possibilities, and make suggestions about how it could be rewritten. Would you like to know more about some things he or she mentions? Could some things be cut out without a loss? Would you change the order in which he mentions things (put some things later and move others nearer to the beginning)? What suggestions would you make about changing the words and changing the way some sentences are written? If you see spelling mistakes, correct them. Try to be as helpful as you can; remember that the other person is doing the same thing for you, and that his comments will make it easier for you to decide what to rewrite and how to rewrite.

When you and your partner have finished reading each other's three papers and writing comments on them, you may talk about the comments. Then exchange with another and do the same thing again until you have been all the way around the group.

Next, look over the comments made on your papers and talk over with the other members of the group any questions you may have about what they said. You do not *have* to follow their suggestions, but knowing what they think should help you decide which paper to rewrite and how to go about doing it.

"Rewrite" means not only improving sentences but also making large changes — adding new things, cutting out old ones, and moving other things around.

Now rewrite, in whatever you think will be the most interesting way, what you observed at one of your three places. All of the finished papers will be read later by the whole class.

When you hand in your final composition, hand in Assignments 1, 2, and 3 with it.

(4. Discussion of the finished papers should feature comparison of them with the original papers from which they were rewritten. That is, ditto or project an Assignment 4 paper along with its predecessor and ask the class what changes the writer made, how he got from one stage to the next, and what purposes they assume he had for making such changes. For discussion pick two or three pairs that show different *degrees* of revision or different *bases* of revision.)

Results and Conclusions

The specific invitation to include personal reactions and comparisons did in fact lead to an increase in both. Teachers who talked up similes and metaphors a lot got more of them, but I felt that some of the comparisons thus elicited were strained. Teachers who emphasized imaginative freedom in rewriting for Assignment 4 caused many children to restore thoughts and feelings that they had while recording but did not note down. Asking the pupils to rewrite only one out of three recordings allowed them to choose the material of greatest interest to them and to their audience, and spared most children from being stuck with a dull set of notes. The very process of selecting the best set — through discussion, written comments by other pupils, and the author's own comparison of recordings — accomplishes a lot of the composing that one normally expects from written revision alone. The fact that each pupil recorded alone away from school gave more point to writing up an account of observations, since the class audience was being informed of something it had not been in on. When several pupils recorded together, for Assignment 3, the bulk of this audience remained to be informed, and the opportunity for comparing different versions of the same scenes added interest, I believe.

The strategy for handling the biggest problem of all, the note taking itself, requires longer explanation and involves some of the other problems.

Difficulties of note taking. Sensory recording seems to invite a lot of concrete data but actually requires great summarization and consequent loss of information. Sometimes the notations are disappointingly colorless and undetailed, and do not leave much material for later composition. But this is a *valuable problem*. Although it could be viewed as an unnecessary and artificial constraint, it is better viewed as a reality of any kind of recording. That is, *if* one's purpose is to take down external events, and *if* the means of recording is slower than the events (as writing certainly is), then it will always follow that (1) the recorder's reactions to what he sees and hears (his nonsensations) may lose priority to the stimuli themselves, and (2) language will necessitate a selective, summary notation. For the sake of certain gains, one takes certain losses.

These conditions inhere not only in the assignment but in the nature of recording as well. Since selectivity and summary are at the heart of information processing and of composing, this is an excellent difficulty that the constraints of recording impose. To exploit it for learning, the teacher should make the loss of information (both of reactions and of external details) a central issue of the assignment, in discussion and in composing Assignment 4. Solutions lie in sacrificing large *coverage* of everything that was observed for the sake of doing better justice to fewer things, and in reducing the speed of recording in order to permit more elaborated linguistic structures (modifiers, qualifiers, fuller phrases and sentences.) All this amounts to a real exploration of the art of note taking — how to vary attention, speed, and coding qualities in the light of considered gains and losses. The children can carry out this exploration in an operational way by experimenting with different ways of note taking, by comparing and discussing the results, and by finding out for themselves the advantages and disadvantages that different ways of recording offer for compositional rewriting.

IMPROVEMENTS TO BE MADE OVER THE TRIALS

I have several reservations about the directions reproduced on pages 189–192. To begin with, I instinctively resist formalizing assignments to that degree; the definitive look tends to mask uncertainties and to hamper the discovery of other possibilities. Also, some problems that became clear only in the course of trials were not allowed for in these directions, and some other matters that I would have liked to have put in would simply have overburdened the project.

Engagement with the material. The first issue is that a lot more emphasis should be placed on seeking out scenes of action, or at least scenes of specific personal interest. Too often our more passive children simply went fatalistically to the nearest place, although many other children either instinctively selected a good place or else made a personally meaningful selection of events at a random locale. What should probably be avoided are mere landscapes and still lifes. They bore most children, who have not yet found how observing leads to involvement and thus to interest. For novices, at least, more human and dramatic scenes would be better. But no one knows yet the effect of cumulative experience in recording over the years — whether or not the higher development of observational powers would increase interest in things of smaller note.

My concern about occasional flagging of interest and motivation may be unduly influenced by situational factors. By the spring these children had already had an excessive dosage of sensory writing, because the experimenting was all done in one year with one group (the school had no sixth grade at the time). The consensus of the teachers afterwards was that sensory writing should be spread over the years, and that the in-school recording of isolated senses should be shifted to the lower grades so that in the upper grades pupils would have already many of the skills and much of the perception to make more random observation interesting. Also, we inevitably, but perhaps unfairly, compared the slow response to sensory writing with the quick, enthusiastic response to memory writing, which has built-in advantages worth mentioning here.

A memory comes from within and is thus by nature personally meaningful. That is why it is remembered. One is already involved. Furthermore, a memory is something that has *previously* been recorded and so, at the moment of recall, exists already in a selectively digested form convenient for wording. This difference in coding helps us to understand the unique difficulties of recording: the observer may have no prior personal relation to what he witnesses; he confronts raw material that he must encode for the first time.

These truths are qualified, of course, by the fact that any observer brings to bear on what he witnesses his memories of similar things or perhaps of the same things, so that the "raw material" becomes immediately associated with past experience and hence assimilated to the inner life. This is precisely the gist of my reservation about the assignments as we gave them: they did not insure enough that what was recorded would engage the inner life and draw on personal associations. (A typical symptom of revised landscape recordings was, in lieu of personal meaning, a reliance on nature clichés and flowery language as a means of drumming up reader interest, the effort itself betraying the writer's own mild involvement.)

Purpose of the writing. But of course involvement and motivation stem from purpose as well as subject, and I think the mimeographed assignments lacked emphasis here too. Although the directions stated that recordings would be used later and that the write-up (Assignment 4) would be an account for the class to read, I think now that we should have given more purpose to all of the writing. This could be done by setting up the four assignments as a class literary magazine or newspaper operation. The pupils go out getting fresh material and shape it together for publication. The teacher can explain that just as a photographer has to take many pictures to get the one he likes, writers have to sift different material for some that will make the best reading.

In the experiments, we tended to reveal stages of the series one at a time because I was afraid that foreknowledge of what was to come would cause the pupils to record with too much of an eye to the next stage. But of course after the first round or so they knew anyway that they would rewrite, and this foreknowledge did not seem to spoil the recording; in fact it would have strengthened purpose and motivation.

Discussion of recordings as outlined in the directions would be combined with editorial deliberations. Since part of these deliberations concerns classifying items for the magazine as more personal or impersonal, discussing the degree of private response and objective account would be more natural and less academic. The same practical bent could be given to group experimentation with different ways of note taking, usages of language, and processes of selecting detail.

Revising. Characterizing the project in this more meaningful way may help to solve another problem. As we set it up, the rewriting (Assignment 4) entailed three versions of the scene — the original recording, the rewrite of it that was read and commented on by partners, and the final copy that incorporated the comments and corrections. A child this age is apt to find the third draft tedious, especially since it involves a lot of copying even if partners recommend several revisions. The more revisions, the more point to another draft, but not all first rewrites need much change, and of course sometimes the suggestions for revision may be meager.

It is hard to be sure of the best course here, because so many factors play into the revision process. Our pupils, for example, had had little experience in commenting on each other's writing. Our setting up of discussions about the recordings and of the small-group cross-commentary suffered from all the muddling through of a first trial, so that the insights and feedback that give revision its real reason for being were much sparser than I think they could be. (The teachers themselves did not write comments and corrections.)

Also, revising is notoriously resisted by students, even in high school. The original impetus for writing is over; their concept of revising (probably conditioned by conventional teaching) is to tidy up through minor adjustments; and the copying is dull and unrewarding. Many times I noticed that a pupil's final copy was not as good as the one before, because the pupil — even when he was able and well motivated — cut back and simplified his material to reduce the labor of the final copy. Ill-considered assignments of revision can actually make for bad writing.

Recommendations

Generally, my recommendations include the directions reprinted earlier but with modifications that should solve the problems that have been brought out. Greater flexibility and a better motivational frame are needed.

PROCEDURES

Solutions to the revision problem are of several sorts, all of which, I think, should be tried together. The principle underlying them all is that revision incorporating commentary should be justified by actual needs: it will provide final material for publication, and the amount of revision suggested will really require another writing. The first rewrite should be in pencil, so that if the paper stands well as is, except for minor alterations, these can be made by erasing and writing in. If much copying is involved, that is a sign that the amount of revisions do not warrant another draft. This means that some pupils will truly revise Assignment 4 — add, subtract, shift, and reshape — and some will stop with Assignment 4. There is no sensible reason for uniformity across the board; revision should be for a real purpose and not just to provide "clean copy," which, for that matter, the dittoed publication will provide (for folders, bulletin boards, parents, etc.). Children have too much honest writing to do to be made to spend time copying. Only in the wrong atmosphere, where children felt that the whole project was just a chore for the teacher's benefit, would the pupils who do an additional version feel any injustice. The whole point is that when the commentary from peers is good the motivation to make changes willingly is strong. And, as a couple of samples will show later, pupils' suggestions to each other can be very good indeed.

Putting together a publication, furthermore, motivates children to pursue their composing process until they have achieved a version they like. Also, those teachers in the experiment who emphasized the liberties one may take with material helped tremendously to promote well motivated revision. Once the concept of rewriting is extended well beyond the pupils' notion of tidying up, then a further draft becomes more like an initial composition, and a fresh impetus to write arises again.

Most of all, the success not only of revision but of any writing project depends on effective exploitation of the group process of discussion and feedback. Without marks and written comments from teachers, our children did a huge amount of high quality writing that came out at least as correct as their usual writing. Despite our weak and uncertain setting up of the group process, and despite the inexperience with it of both teachers and pupils, the pupil cross-commentary and collaboration loomed as a powerful learning method. But to ensure informed feedback, focused class discussion of writing samples is required, and to ensure helpful feedback, a climate of collaboration rather than competition, of pupil rather than teacher initiative, must prevail in the classroom. Since this group process will be a staple method of teaching writing throughout this program, I will try to define it more clearly here, drawing on the experience of trials in junior and senior high as well as in elementary school.

THE WRITING WORKSHOP

The teacher's main role is to set up and oversee a cross-teaching operation among pupils. Select and project sample papers from an assignment and lead class discussion of the samples until the issues the pupils are to focus on later in groups have been well aired. Afterwards, break the groups into threes and fours, direct them to read each other's papers and discuss them in terms of these same issues, then lapse into a secondary role as ambulatory consultant. Thus the problems inherent in recording — sensory data versus personal reaction, the form of note taking, personal selectivity, inference, point of view — come up under teacher guidance but are shifted then to the groups.

A simple keynote question about the projected samples, especially if it is a comparative question, will plunge the children into the issue without didactic hocus pocus: "What differences do you notice between the way this person took notes and the way that one did?" "What changes did this person make between this version and that version?" "Do you think you understand why he cut this and added that?" Or, to keep discussions related to the overall project: "You're the editors as well as the writers of the magazine. When you suggest changes to each other, you may have to decide whether you would like the author to play up his personal reactions or to stick more to straight reporting. Look at this paper. What are the things that tell more about the observer than the scene? What would you suggest to the author?"

Examples of issues for discussion. While remaining concrete and germane to the publication goal of the project, the issues raised this way can range among a lot of important semantic, stylistic, rhetorical, and linguistic matters. For example, comparing projections of two recordings made in the same time and place can direct attention to alternative wordings for the same thing. *Flower* or *blossom:* "Which is better, considering mood and purpose?" Comparing a telegraphic recording and a rewriting of it in full sentences leads to discussion of sentence elements and sentence expansions.

The conjoining and embedding of short sentences to form fewer, more complex sentences comes up for scrutiny as a matter of avoiding monotonous repetition. That is, in sensory recording the order of words follows closely the order of events and results in short declarative sentences that repeat the same words and begin with *now, then,* and *next.* A pupil who revises merely by expanding kernel phrases (*coat falling*) into kernel sentences (*I see a coat falling,* or *the coat fell*) ends up with a lot of repeated *I*'s or *coats* and a string of data predicated in a string of separate sentences.

Although the heart of the matter is learning to build complex sentences by combining simple ones — a major linguistic development of this age — it can be broached as a practical matter of style. When projecting such a paper the teacher states that sensory recording carries a built-in problem of word repetition and sentence monotony and asks them how it might be solved in that paper. Some will suggest joining sentences with conjunctions like *after, while,* and *during.* This leads to subordination, at which point the teacher must make sure that their suggestions allow for proper emphasis as well as for style. If, for "The pole is breaking. He slid down the pole." someone proposes "While he was sliding down, the pole broke," suggest that maybe the author meant, "While the pole was breaking he slid down," or "After the pole broke, he slid down." The author is then consulted, as should happen often in these discussions. (Comparison of alternatives is so often the key to learning.)

As suggested in these dummy sentences, another natural problem common to the age and especially raised by the rewriting of recordings is the mixing of tenses. Many children get hung up between the present viewpoint of the recording and the past viewpoint of the revision and reflect this in a wavering of verbs between the two. And again, sensory recording offers rich possibilities for development of vocabulary. Some discussion should center on how things are named and include specific suggestions from pupils and teacher to the writer about other words he might use.

A final example concerns titles, another omission from the directions used in the experiment. Setting up a working title, perhaps to be changed in a final draft, helps the writer to think about the totality of his subject and about what he intends to do with it. All directions for compositions and drafts thereof should constantly remind pupils to entitle their pieces. Recordings themselves are obviously excepted, but as a lead into collaborative revision, the teacher might project a recording and ask the class to propose titles that would do justice to it. If the recording has a natural unity or coherence, proposing titles can bring it out; or if the recording is miscellaneous, the titles can suggest ways of reshaping that would build a unity from selected elements in it. If the composition is projected, the teacher may block out the title, ask the class to entitle it, then let them compare their suggestions with the author's original. This brings out discrepancies between intention and effect, such as misleading emphasis, which the class can discuss, or reveals matching of intention with effect. All such kinds of feedback are valuable and would be transferred to the group relationships.

Cross-teaching. And that is the teacher's function in group process — to create models of talking together and helping each other that pupils can put into operation in small units. It is harder and more fun than correcting papers. More writing can go on, and with better results. Instead of asking for a very occasional assignment, done in one shot, which a pupil is either able to do or not, which tests more than it teaches, and from which the pupil discovers afterward — too late — all the things he should have done but did not, the compositional process is now phased and externalized. It is subjected to feedback and correction along the way, provided in greater quantity and by equals in the game, not by authoritative superiors. Attention is on the actual learning issues, not on one's status with the teacher and on sibling rivalry. Errors are exploited, not avoided. Writing is learning, not being tested on a sink-or-swim basis. Final products benefit from learning and leave a feeling of achievement, instead of revealing ignorance and leaving a sour taste. But it is the teacher who has shown the children how to do this for each other. Out of his spirit he creates the climate of collaborative learning and helpful responding. Out of his understanding of language and composition, he focuses the issues implicit in the assignments and sets up model ways of commenting and proposing.

The chief obstacle to cross-teaching, I found, is the past conditioning of both teachers and pupils. There are no intrinsic reasons for this group process to fail. Any misleading of one pupil by another is tremendously outweighed by the increased writing practice, the constant and varied feedback, which no teacher could otherwise provide. And small groups tend to set misleading individuals straight. (One teacher paired pupils for the revision of the write-up — with, I must say, very good results — but the hazard of this practice is the loss of group consensus.) Our experiments showed, I believe, that the children instinctively spot some writing problems even without focusing; I noticed that they are especially good at catching poor punctuational segmenting, run-on sentences with *and,* unnecessary repetition, obscure phrasing, and failures to allow for the reader's viewpoint. What exacts good judgment from the teacher is deciding which issues he must raise himself and which ones they will confront anyway. Also, the raising of issues before the whole class must be related rather directly to the project goals and done with a light hand; ax grinding is out. More technical aspects of language and composition can be better taught when children are necessarily involved in them by the nature of the assignment. All the teacher does is help pupils see in the vague practical problems particular technical issues that actually constitute the problems.

SEQUENCE

Before illustrating some of these remarks with samples from the experiment, I should add a note on sequence. Assuming the sensory writing recommended for grades K–3, a project similar to the experimental one could be given once or twice each in grades four and five and twice in grade six. We have to allow for the fact that cumulative competence in both recording and revising would progressively decrease the necessity for many parts of the process described above, so that by fifth and sixth grades one or two recordings might suffice for gathering material, and most small-group work might proceed with much less preliminary raising of issues. To speak, then, of giving the assignment twice in grades five and six is simply to recommend two short projects of personal eyewitness reporting reduced according to whatever evolution further trials may indicate.

Discussion of Some Samples

Here is a fairly typical sample of a straightforward recording and revision of a landscape (done by a girl):

SEE	HEAR	SMELL
trees swaying	birds peep tweet	rich soil
grass	faint noises	fresh air
little bugs	from cars	
big gray rocks	bees buzzing	
branches shaking	dog collor shake	
a field of yellow	dog bark	
twigs braking	plane	
a tree house	leaves rustling	
birds over head	twigs fall to ground	

Listing by senses was a notation form adopted by a number of children and sometimes suggested by the teacher. It avoids "I hear" and "I see" but automatically forces out thought and feelings, unless, as one teacher told her pupils to do, they add a column for this. Pupils who use the column form once or twice should then try other forms. For one thing, it encourages the minimizing of linguistic structures, reducing them to nouns coupled with an adjective or a present participle. The more dispensable parts of speech such as articles and auxiliaries are virtually eliminated; adverbs, prepositions, and conjunctions are rare. Consequently, a lot of details and relationships are lost. As one should expect, the sound column consists of action, the smell column of things, and the sight column of both. Here is the revision (assignment 4):

> I can see the little bugs fly through the air and great big gray rocks sit in the same place all the time. I can hear a dog collor shake when he walks. Just smell the fresh air. The rich soil. Thoses birds tweeting and bees buzzing. The trees swaying and the bright green grass. The whole field with a yellow blanket covering it. The tree house way up high. I hear leaves rustling when the wind blows the wind knocks twigs off of trees and I hear the twigs fall to the ground faint noises from cars and a plane overhead.

It is worth noticing how phrases were joined and expanded into sentences, or expanded merely into longer fragments that do not quite become sentences because the obvious predicates were unnecessary and because there was too little action to warrant other predicates.

Now compare this revision with those by two other girls who were recording at the same time and same place as the first girl:

> The sound of little birds singing fills the clean fresh air. A field of green and yellow is at one of me. Silence fills the air exsept for the pretty birds singing and a few cars going on their way. There goes an airplane roering through the sky. It is quiet and peaceful now. The sun gleams as we write.

> We walk into the woods. The birds are chirping loudly. A car is going by very fast. Up above me is a tree house. The air smells fresh. Look at all those bright yellow dandelions. I wonder what Terry and Kathy are thinking. There goes a bird. Here comes two dogs. They must be repairing a road somewhere. There goes an airplane. It feels dark and creepy in here.

Only a few items were noted by all three children — the birds, the airplane, the fresh air, the car, and the yellow field. (Only one identified the yellow covering as dandelions.) Only two mentioned the tree house. Several things were mentioned by just one child — the bugs, the rich soil, the gray rocks, the sun, the bees, the twigs, the wind, the sound of road repairing. I do not think that sensory recording should become a contest to see who can cram in the most details, but, without *invidious* comparisons, children can see what items their companions caught that they missed or deliberately left out. Discussion may show that some of these discrepancies are due to differences in physical vantage points. Part of discussion can consist of inferring the time, locale, and weather as implied by the details (such implications are characteristics of haiku poetry). The mood established at the end of the second and third papers is very different — one of sunny peacefulness, the other "dark and creepy" (is one observer in the field, the other in the woods?).

All three versions above are essentially miscellaneous enumerations, the hardest kind of material to shape into a unity. Mood is perhaps the best possibility. Real moments of being are made of just such miscellanies, but one should not expect children to be able to compose more than a mood from such a scene. All three revisions are of the simplest sort. Little more than verbal expansion has taken place; tense and point of view remain in the present; selection and arrangement are slight, probably because the children could see nothing central to focus on, as they might have had there been more action or had they added more thoughts and feelings. These are notes in more presentable form, nice writing of a sort but probably not lively enough for most children.

From what looked like rather unpromising notes, a boy very consciously composed a mood piece:

ON OUR SUN PORCH

Hear: Birds singing
Airplane
Trees rustling
People talking
grinding of sand under peoples
    shoes
cars
doors slaming

looks like: everything looks
    gloomy
Houses
birds
people
cars
neighbor swings and play area
air plane
trees waving

I feel like I am lonley and cold
everything smells like pine sap

As the day wore on the clouds had grown dark and thicker. All the children were in their houses and the only person in sight was the mailman as he slowly walked his route.

The birds that had been singing earlier had stopped and all was quiet.

Now there same a rustle in the leaves. Slowly it grew louder and finally it fell into a steady rythm.

The twitering in the trees gradually ceased as the birds settled down in their nests from the night and the rain.

Besides shifting the tense and creating sentences, this boy deliberately omitted all details that did not suit his purpose.

Of course, there are always a few professionals, like the girl below, who can scent a good story a long way off and begin composing when they select the time and place. As her first sentence shows — these are the *notes* — she achieved her unity when she chose the occasion:

We're eating outside tonight. General bustling and "organized confusion" to bring all plates, food, etc., outside. Dad supervising and cooking steak over coals at same time. Mom making rest of food and telling people what goes where. Kids bringing food outside, running back and forth, bumping into each other. Occasional fights break out, e.g., who sets table, who sits where, whose napkin that is, why did you bring the tape in the house when I needed it, etc. etc., but good feeling prevails. Mom asks "Who's cutting up the pickles?" My sister gets them out. Mom yells, "Oh, the rice is boiling over! !" At the same time Dad yells, "Oh, the steak's burning!" and rushes to turn it over. Now the table and food's ready. Dad yells "Sue! We're eating!" Sue, who is doing homework, yells "Coming!" and thunders down the stairs. We sit down to eat. The steak smells good. So do pickles. Too bad no potatoes. We sit down to eat. Now I have to sit down too.

All this needs is paragraphing, indicated by the appropriate symbol, and occasional inserting of an auxiliary (*kids [are] bringing food*) unless the decision is made to shift all of the verbs into the past (a very dubious move here). If required to do another draft, it is quite likely that this superior student would cut out a lot of detail and ruin a lively sketch. That she was organizing *as* she recorded can be seen in the abstractive device of summarizing repeated or typical action in a series, especially in the sentence "Occasional fights break out, e.g. . . ."

Think of a title for the following piece, a revised recording by a girl:

Cars zooming down the highway looking like little toy cars going down a little toy road. Light taps of rain coming down on everyones windows. Splashes going up then down with children watching them gayly.

Once I heard one child say "What would it be like to be a rain drop?"

His brother Tom he asked "What would it be like to be one of those stiff people?" pointing to a tree.

Thoughts just filled my head with answers but they had gone away.

The first half establishes a setting with several images; the second half relates an incident that either happened in that setting or was recalled to the child by it. The piece seems split, but the halves are joined by raindrops. In proposing and discussing titles for it, other pupils would have to determine what kind of notion would contain it, how sharp or vague the title would have to be. I think also that they would ask the author if the second half were a memory or an observation, and he could clear up the ambiguity of "Once I heard one child say . . .", if indeed they think it should be cleared up (for the whole piece reads like an impressionistic reverie and reminds one a bit of some of Dylan Thomas' evocations of childhood). The author's own title was "The Highway," which might have been an unconscious metaphorising of the composition itself — the inner trip that begins in one place and ends somewhere very different — or may well have been simply a reference to an initial image from which he carelessly strayed later. But in discussing his title, his classmates are helping him know what he wrote and at the same time tackling the whole business of coherence.

Whatever one thinks of it, the composition shows how sensory data can become subjective by individual selection, personal reference, and thought association. It could have made a good poem, especially the second part and perhaps all of it. The last line has the climactic stuff of which a last line is made in a poem. And this possibility is one that I have not brought up before. We did not try it out in the experiment, but as I read the papers I wish we had. The teacher could project either a recording or a revision, say that he feels it would make a good poem, then suggest to them that they keep the possibility in their minds as they comment on each other's papers in small groups. Branching out into the poetic mode may prove to be at least as important as most of the possibilities I have discussed here.

One of the reasons that I have dwelled so long on sensory recording is that it can be the gateway to more kinds of writing than one would expect at first. It is best thought of not only as a thing in itself, for data gathering and personal reportage, but also as a springboard for invention. For imaginative writing it has two advantages: it makes stale imitation more difficult, and it makes getting an idea easier. The point of departure is a real and fresh one, and it is a definite one. The girl's composition below illustrates one direction a revision may take. Her invention here is not in fictionalizing but in typicalizing the specific events into a generality about herself:

"Saturday Morning"

There's one thing I "hate" to do. That is to get up in the morning. One morning I just despised. That was June 4th, 1966. I think I'll tell you about it.

It all started the night of June 3rd. The whole week had been very hot and sticky. Like I always did, I pushed my blanket to the end of the bed, lied down, cuddled up, and fell asleep.

I slept like a dog, and probably wouldn't have woke up at 7:30, but would have slept to 9:00 or 10:00, if . . . someone hadn't got married, and drove down our street, with, or about ten to fifteen cars honking after them. But someone did get married, and they did drive down our street, about 7:30 and I woke up. I was cold and pulled my blanket over me.

Just as I settled back down, taking a good breath of fresh air, the milkman came. The bottles were clinking and making too much noise. The man pulled open the door, and shut it again making a louder racket then before.

Finally, when I was half asleep again, and everything was quiet my father got up and started to shave. In a few minutes I got used to the soft buzzing sound, and almost fell asleep again, when . . . my grandmother, decided she had to go to the bathroom. She went stamping through the hall, and woke me up again. The toilet flushed. Then my shade went up. I had to get out of bed to pull it down again.

When I finally got settled, a crow went by, and started to caw. He probably was screaming, for he sure was cawing loudly. By this time I was thoroughly distressed.

When my mother started the vacuum cleaner and the crow came by again I pushed down my blankets, gave a loud scream, and got up. (that's a good way to get me up. Just go through all the things I mentioned again. Otherwise you'll never get me up.)

This personal essay issued from these notes:

>   tweet, chirp
>   Honk, Honk
>   trees, grass
>   I see a window, a table
>   I smell fresh air.
>   clink, clink, bottles clinking
>   quiet. . . . . .
>   . . .clap, puff, footsteps, rattle
>   rattle, clink. everything is
>   getting up. A misty morning
>   coldness
>   swish, swish, peep, peep
>   caw, caw
>   lightness
>   a vacuum cleaner
>   Honk _____
>   Honk _____
>   Honk _____
>   screech — eeeeeeeeeeeeee
>   cold, you, who — whisler
>   slam, bang, of car door
>   tweet caw.

As a point of departure, this recording is much superior to an abstract topic given by the teacher such as "Getting Up in the Morning," which would probably not have stimulated this girl to write so fully and richly or with so much real interest. This way, the details crystallize into a topic and the child creates his own category of experience — Saturday Morning or whatever — instead of trying to fill in a prefabricated category by "racking his brains" and coming up with stereotypes of school compositions.

Some children, like this boy, invented a fiction based on their notes.

1.   I can hear my friend slurping on a watermelon.
2.   I can smell the freshly cut grass.
3.   I can see and hear my nextdoor neighbor squirting his hose on his new grass.
4.   I can see and hear my friend laughing.
5.   I can hear in the distance, cars going along rt. 2.
6.   I can hear the wind blow against the trees.
7.   I can hear one of our neighbors hammering away at his house.
8.   I can hear my friends yelling down the road.

OLD FARMER BROWN

Once upon a time, there was a farmer, his name was Old Farmer Brown. One sunny day he planted a seed. He did not know what kind of a seed it was. Farmer Brown had other jobs to do besides planting seeds. He had to cut and water the lawn, and he had to fix the steps that broke in half the year before. After a few months, he went back to see how his mysterious seed was growing. All of a sudden he started laughing. He found that his seed had turned into a plant that looked like a green football. He decided to see what it tasted like. It was watery and tasted somewhat like a melon. "I know what I'll call it!," exclaimed Farmer Brown, "I'll call it a WATER-MELON!" After that, Farmer Brown went running down the road telling everyone about his discovery.

Apparently this boy amalgamated his slurping friend and his busy neighbors into the single figure of Farmer Brown. Besides taking for his central object the watermelon that opened his recording, he employed also the cutting and watering of grass and the seasonal setting. Although he probably borrowed from other stories the name of Farmer Brown and the theme, he has created a fresh story of his own.

The next boy capitalized less well on his notes, I would say. I think he could have benefited from more commentary than his one partner could give him. Here is the story:

Billy was trapped inside an old building. He saw nothing but darkness! Bill screamed for help but no one heard him. Suddenly he heard foot steps comming closer, closer, closer then faded away. Bill screamed and yelled again untill he couldn't scream any more. Then there was scilence. Bill listened to the "shh" sound of the water pipes. Then he heard the loud "clip-clop" noise of the policemen as they came to the rescue.

And here are the notes that preceded it:

(I am in the Celler)
I hear foot steps, coming closer and closer the stoping and walking ferther away.
I hear the heater   The heater sound like water going thrue a drain that is partly cloged.
I hear the fawsett. It sounds like someone saying "shh".
I hear a high srill sound   I don't know what it is a "super radar ray" on T.V.
I smell paint It smells like turpintine.
I see darkness.
I hear a noise like an airplane out of gas.
I hear foot steps coming towards me.
I hear water going into the drain as a jar cover falls to the floor.

I hear the refrigerator door open. I feel coldness when the refrigerator door opens.

The dog comes in for breakfast and smells like damp grass.

I see the kichtion

These details are rich and he might have used more of them, spaced throughout the story, to emphasize the suspense of Billy's waiting. But he did insert the footsteps and the "shh" of the water pipes for this purpose, and no doubt his experience recording in the cellar put him in the right state of mind for this story and enabled him to give the situation reality.

To help this boy's spelling, the teacher could diagnose for him the kinds of errors he makes. *Ferther, fawsett,* and *turpintine* are all logical errors based in fact on his understanding of sound-letter correspondences. For example, *er* and *ur* are both possible spellings for the sound; to be wrong with *ferther* and right with *turpintine* is a matter simply of memorizing the troublesome parts of the words, for nothing else can tell him which alternate spelling to use when the sound is in that position. The same is true regarding the *aw* and the *s* in *fawsett,* which are alternates in English for *au* and *c,* given the position. Unstressed *in* and *en* (*turpintine*) are also logical alternates. But doubling the consonant after a short vowel and before the verb ending is a regularity of spelling (*stoping* and *cloged*), and mentioning that regularity would help the boy. *Srill* and *kichtion* belong to a third category of error, I would guess (not knowing the child): they probably stem from faulty pronunciation, since he seems to write pretty phonetically. The teacher would ask him to pronounce the words, in order to check this hunch; then he would pronounce the words in the standard dialect, by which they are spelled. The point is to classify for the pupil his various errors so that he can go on to recognize them himself and thus to attack each kind in the special way it requires.

The girl's story below was also done in the class where the teacher suggested a very free-wheeling way of rewriting the notes. The effect of this suggestion can be seen on both the author and her partner. The notes read:

1. I see a kitchen full of cooking things.
2. Water driping, it is like rain.
3. refregerato sounds like a humming bird with a cold.
4. I smell ham
5. hammering, it sounds like the wolf trying to get into the pigs house.
6. birds singing like they are lost and scared.
7. I smell some coffee
8. I see a pitch black cat out of the window that looks like a spooky house
9. door shakes, like on a old spooky house.
10. a loud drill sounds like a bearser.
11. trees moving in the wind look like the green giant sneezed.

12. I see cupcakes that look very good
13. clothes on the table
14. I see some different kinds of plants in the windows that make me think of a jungle.

The partner's comments read:

14, 2, 5, 9, 11, 10, 6, 8, 3, 12, 13, 4, 1. You could have notes in this order. I think this starts high up then comes to the Kitchen. You will have to add some things inbetween. It has good possibilities because you compared it to something else or what you thought it was like.

The suggestion is to reorder these sensations completely and to place last the general statement that opens the notes. Partly, she is proposing an inductive description that would start with particulars and let the reader identify the setting for himself. Actually, the author declined the suggestion in favor of making up a story, which may have been another pupil's idea.

A Hide And Go Seek Game

"It's your turn to count while we hide."
"All right. One two three four five." ect.
"Where will we hide?"
"I'll hide in the kitchen behind the door. (he is behind the door).
It sure is dark in here. Look at all of those pots and pans.
The water dripping gives me the chills.
And the refridgerator sounds like a sick humming bird.
I wonder if Tom is going to invite me to lunch? Because I smell ham.
Here comes Tom. He's looking for me. WOW! he just passed me. I see Tom, he is looking for Wendy now. Tom's father must be hammering. He is making a lot of noise.
That window has a lot of plants in it. It looks like a jungle.
Tom must be thinking about inviting me to lunch. Because there is some good looking cupcakes over there.
I guess Tom found Jane. I can here her laughing.
That coffee smells real good.
I think it is going to rain. The wind is blowing so hard that trees are almost falling over, the door is shaking too.
I think Tom found everone but me. They are all looking for me. Here they come. WOW! The just passed me again. oh! the door squeeked, now Im·sure they'll find me. They're back again. They're looking around. "THEY FOUND ME!"

This draft benefited from the following corrections made by her partner. Quotation marks were put into the opening exchange of dialogue with a remark explaining the need to differentiate speakers. "It sure is dark in here and look at all of the pots and pans" was broken into two sentences by cutting *and,* placing a period after *here* and capitalizing *look.* *I here Tome* was changed to *I see Tom,* correcting both a spelling and an author's lapse of attention. An inadvertent omission was supplied — *I [can] hear* — and *pased* was corrected to *passed.*

Let's look now at a rather complicated bit of collaboration:

> In my playroom 4:20 PM May 17, 1966
> Gong! ! ! Gong! ! ! like a herd of elephants crossing the boarder
> Crying, like a Baby girrafe
> Laughing, like a laughing hiena
> Water falling sounds like a SWISHING waterfall.
> A gold glass ball that tingles and looks like the reflection of a mirror.
> A sweat peppery smell of "Mothers Best soup"
> The end of my mothers apron string that looks like the tail of a BLUE donkey

One commentator wrote, "It could be rewritten as a funny story. The spelling needs help!" Another wrote, "It could be rewritten about a main character 'Mother' — about a mother and 8 confusing children, all sizes!" The last added, "Rewrite it as a story, take turns, writing chapters." He meant for the author and the second commentator each to write a chapter of the story that the second commentator had suggested. So the author rewrote:

MOTHER AND HER PROBLEM, "8 CHILDREN!"

Chapter I

Gong! ! Gong! ! Goes my sister Jana, playing with the door-bell. Boy. It sounds like a herd of elephants crossing the boarder! I heard Jeanie crying like a baby giraffe, because she didn't have her two-oclock feeding yet. Next I saw mother walk into the kitchen. She opened the cabinet, and saw little Robie playing with his tool kit, on the water pipe. I *never,* in my life, heard her scream so loud! ! I just heard my big sister Vicky telling a joke, and brother Stevy laughing like a laughing hiena! Well you can guess what happens next, just turn the page over to the next chapter and see! ! !

A colleague changed the placement of the title and the chapter in order to space and to center them (as here), told her to indent the first sentence and to start new paragraphs with *I heard Jeanie* and *Next I saw Mother,* and deleted the comma in *playing with his tool kit, on the water pipe.* The next chapter, written by the other pupil, was:

Chapter II

CRASH! I knew it would happen some time. All day Billy just sits with a glass ball on his finger. While twirling the ball on his finger, he tries to look in to see his reflection. He had to drop it sometime.

I wonder what that smell is? As I walked into the kitchen the smell got stronger. "Oh NO!" Jeanie had spilt the soup that takes Mother a whole day to make. It was all over the floor! ! When mother saw it she suddenly had a headace that lasted a week!

Tammy, the baby of the family, was tugging at my mothers apron string. She is all right. She does't do anything bad. Well Ive told you about my family, good luck to yours.

I end anti-climatically with a modest story by a much less sophisticated boy:

PLAYROOM

1. The vacum cleaner sounds like a eleghant.
2. The rug looks like a green on a golf course
3. The T.V. looks like a martians head and the antena for his built in walkie-talkie (in his head).

John and Paul were playing outside. Then Paul said, "Let's go to my house and play in the playroom."

John and Paul started to play. John said, "Let's pretend we are martians and the T.V. is the chief martian. They played that for a while.

Then Paul said, "Lets pretend we are golfers and golf on the rug. They golfed for a while. Then John's mother called and he had to go home.

(Judiciously, a partner deleted *They golfed for a while*.) He is trying a bit too hard to get in those similes, and yet the third one provides him with the fantasy part of his story: comparing the TV set to a Martian's head is a piece of imagining that resembles closely the pretenses of children's games. His achievement, like that of other children who write briefly and perhaps not very maturely, may not be so impressive or so much fun to show other teachers, but at the level of the boy's own development it may represent just as much learning as pieces that adults would value more. Sensory writing allows a child to work and learn in the way that is right for him at the time. He cannot fail to do the assignment right, because any pupil can observe and put down something of what he sees. He cannot fail to make some changes during rewriting and to produce some kind of composition. The task is quite definite and yet accommodates itself to all capacities.

Advantages for the Slower Pupil

The experiment indicated other advantages of sensory writing and of phased writing in general. The relaxed nature of note taking helps many less able children simply to put down words. They are relieved of the technical and formal aspects of writing that seem so formidable to unsure pupils who are accustomed to having trouble spelling and formulating sentences and shaping a presentation. They do not go blank trying to get ideas for what to say. The phasing and the collaboration allow them to work up a composition gradually and with help. The whole process is less threatening and opens up some otherwise very inhibited children. It feels reassuringly structured to the child and yet is in fact quite open, since neither a subject nor a certain kind of final product is stipulated. It is the sort of thing a child will make whatever he can out of.

These assets are especially important if one teaches disadvantaged children. My experiments were done in a suburban school serving middle-class children of educated parents. (There are many reasons I will not go into here why it is difficult to get such experimentation going in inner cities.) The participating teachers felt, like all teachers, that they had plenty of verbally backward pupils who did not write well in any sense, and they reported that the informal writing helps these youngsters to get going. It has always been my intention to devise assignments that automatically adjust to the capacity of the pupils. I believe disadvantaged children can do any of the assignments in this program and learn as much from them as more verbally developed children. But timing and other aspects of sensory writing may need adapting. Most of all, what any pupil can do at this age will depend enormously on what he has or has not done before. Disadvantaged pupils who have been following this program up to here will probably be able to do many of the things with sensory writing that the children quoted here have done.

Recapitulating Pantomimes and Improvisations

Recapitulating is not, strictly speaking, recording, since the pupils write down *afterwards* what they saw happen before them. A small group does a pantomime or an improvisation before some classmates, who write an account of the skit as soon as it is over.

When we first tried sensory recording of dramas in Lexington, we found that watching and writing at the same time was too much for the children. We then settled for recapitulation, which in fact is an interesting kind of writing. By the time the story is over, one knows considerably more and interprets differently than he does in the middle of registering the events. A recapitulation reads much more like a summarized, connected narration. The important things are sifted out of less significant details, the behavior of the actors is understood in terms of the outcome, premature inferences are corrected, and the series of events is economically coded as a totality. Learning about such abstractive differences is one purpose of the assignment. But the main point is writing narrative.

PANTOMIMES

The greater ambiguity of pantomimes makes them better for comparing differences in inference and interpretation. The accounts may vary as regards not only the action but also the motives of the characters and the circumstances one should assume as background for the action.

In small groups the pupils read aloud and discuss their versions. What are the differences? Which account do they agree on most? The accounts should be entitled so that overall interpretation can be focused on. The acting also may come under scrutiny. Which particular gestures and movements led to very different inferences by spectators? Since the narratives are sure to vary in length and therefore in the ratio of detail to summary, some of the discussion could be about such variations. Then the actors are asked to remark on the discussion points.

Some pantomimes, of course, will not be ambiguous, and certainly the players should not try to confuse the audience. Their intention is to communicate. But some stories will inevitably lend themselves to double or multiple interpretation, and acting without dialogue means renouncing the explicitness of language. Players can thus learn how much language can prevent ambiguity and in what ways body English must compensate for the loss of words. (It goes without saying that these pantomimes dispense with introduction and narration.)

Writing recapitulations in small groups is a particularly intimate and intensive way of sharing and reacting (using an audience of three pupils). The pantomimists get a full and explicit response to their efforts, and a written story is the product of the activity. The writers know that the same will be done for them. Ensuing discussion can, in addition to clarifying the exact effects on the audience, help the writers revise their papers for further use. That is, if the pantomime communicated well, as shown by a high consensus of the spectators, then the group collaborates in putting together a publishable version that draws on all of the papers. If the versions are very different, then each spectator's story could be separately revised and distributed, the writers even being encouraged to carry the story further from its source by inventing along the lines of their original divergence. In this case, recapitulating a pantomime becomes one more point of departure for original story making.

IMPROVISATIONS

Improvisations are less ambiguous than pantomimes and need a different emphasis. Two actual accounts will demonstrate the tacks that may be taken.

> One night as the Jone's family was about to watch T.V. there was an argument about what to watch. It all started like this.
> "Whats on T.V. tonight children?" asked Mr. Jones.
> "Lost in Space!" the children shouted all together.
> "No I don't think that program is good for children". answered Mrs. Jone's

"Ohhh but we want Lost in Space its such a good program". . . And **it** was just at the good part please"

"I'll see what on" said Mr. Jone's "Let me see here's a good program" (Mr. Jone's had been turning to different chanels as he had told the children not to do) "Lawence Welk its very educational"

"Ohhh we hate Lawence Welk ick!". said the children

"Children eather you watch Lawence Welk or go to bed." said Mr. Jone's "OK". answerd the children and that's how the Jone's family settled their problem.

This girl ably reproduced a lot of the dialogue. Except for the opening and closing generalizations, this came close to being a play script. The laconic summary below should be compared both with this and with a detailed account of the same improvisation on page 172.

REPORT CARD NIGHT

The Smith family is sitting at the table with their report cards. The parents said what did you get? and they all got bad marks. The father gave them all some chores to do.

For some purposes this account would be better; it is succinct and just.

The emphasis, then, in recapitulating improvisations would be on reporting differently for different purposes — on the varying degrees of narrative summary or dramatic elaboration. After one round in which the chips fall where they may, and after which the teacher projects samples such as those I have reproduced here, each pupil could next be told to write his account for a specific purpose. Groups are formed so that besides the actors each group has three spectators who do not know what the actors will do. One will write a very short synopsis, like the last example, to serve as a minimal situation for another group to improvise from; the second will write a longer narrative account, merely sampling the dialogue, to go into a class newspaper as a news item; the third will write a version that would as nearly as possible enable another group to use it as a script in putting on the skit for themselves.

Eventually all pupils would do all three kinds of recapitulation as well as be the actors. All these pieces of writing would have a function that would actually be carried out. In the groups, the pupils would read and suggest changes to the authors before the papers are handed over for improvising, printing, and acting out. These changes could include the adding of more detail and verbatim dialogue to the version that is to be used as the script. In effect, what pupils do is write narratives and plays, but without inventing the story, which is settled on by the actors. At the same time, the whole cycle of acting, writing, and talking is turned over in another way.

Chapter 14

Memory Writing

I would like to introduce now a kind of writing that will be new to pupils following this program. The composing process, however, is in many ways similar to that of sensory writing, and much of what was said about the latter will apply here. Student response to this assignment has been very good at whatever age I have tried it. Writing memories, I am convinced, should be a continuous activity throughout school. The main thing for the pupil to learn now is how to tap memories, as he did sensations, for their fresh material, and how to select and shape this material into compositions.

Memory writing was tried out by the same group of Lexington teachers (the Omega team) and with the same fourth- and fifth-grade pupils who were involved in sensory writing experiments. Generally, the teachers reported that the children liked writing memories very much and that getting them to stop was often difficult. The appeal, as with imaginative writing, lies in the highly personal content, to which significant feelings are attached. Memories tie into these feelings. But whereas the actualities of his past refer rather explicitly to experience the child is willing to acknowledge, his far-fetched stories allow him to refer obliquely and symbolically to feelings he cannot acknowledge. Both kinds of writing are important.

From reading a lot of children's memories, I would say that pre-adolescent children have natural defenses to suppress material that would be embarrassing if seen by others. Thus exchanging spontaneous memories is no exposure now but will be in later years. This makes it important to teach the process now before privacy becomes an obstacle.

Account of Trials

Again as a basis for commentary and recommendations, I reproduce here the directions given in the experiment. The remarks to the teacher are enclosed between parenthesis.

DIRECTIONS

Spontaneous flow
of memories.

1. Look around the room at different things until something you see reminds you of something from your past — a place, person or event. Write that down. Now what other memory does that person, place, or event remind you of? Once you get started, keep writing down your memories. Don't worry about their being jumbled or jumping from one time to another. Write the memories in whatever way captures them quickly; these are notes for yourself. Don't worry about spelling or correct sentences; just record as many memories as you have time for. You will have about fifteen minutes. These notes will not be marked, but you will need them for a later assignment. For right now, it is better to get a lot of memories than to go into detail about one of them.

1. The main purpose of this three-assignment series is to work with the *process* of composition. Starting with apparently random material—in this case, scattered recollections of different times and places connected only by private associations — the pupil shapes the material by stages of *selection* and *focus* into a finished narrative that allows for an outside audience.

Assignment 1 should produce a lot of material; at least that is the point of it — to get a jumble of fragments from which the pupil may select. In Assignment 2 he should narrow down — sacrifice coverage for elaborated detail. The recollection should begin to take on point or purpose: whatever determines the pupil's choice of *this* recollection rather than another carries with it some unity, some central feeling or idea. I assume that we remember things for certain reasons — they were a trial or a pleasure, a jolt or a relief — but that the pupil may very well not know consciously what kind of importance or value makes him prefer that recollection. Discussion and collaboration should help this *core experience emerge* so that he can organize around it. This core experience or dominant feeling is what will interest the reader. Assignment 3 should accommodate an audience by providing necessary information, making references public, perhaps explaining background, stripping away irrelevant and therefore misleading details, and making the vocabulary and sentences conform to universal understanding and expectations.

To launch Assignment 1, before handing out the assignment slips, demonstrate the association process yourself out loud to them. Look around the room, settle on an object, tell them something it reminds you of that happened once, then say what other memory that brings to mind, and so forth. If more illustration seems needed, ask a pupil to volunteer to do what you just did.

For discussion later, continue the procedure, used before in the sensory writing, of selecting a couple of papers and placing them before the class, dittoed or projected.

Discuss the different ways used by pupils to note down memories, using the sample papers and also asking the rest of the class to look at their papers and say how they went about it. Again, the relative advantages of list, telegraphic, and full styles might be discussed, including the issue of coverage vs. detail, but the assignment calls for coverage, and also, since they are registering their own memories, they can control the speed of the material better than when recording external events.

Focusing first on the sample papers and then on their own, get them to discuss the *sequences* of recollections: why memory A led to memory B? What are the connections? What feeling, idea, or mood seems to go with certain of the memories? The class can speculate about the sample papers, then ask the authors for corroboration of what they have said.)

Expanded single memory.

2. Look over your Assignment 1 paper and pick out a memory of some incident that interests you and that you would like to do more with. An "incident" would be something that happened on a particular day, unless you feel that what happened on two or three different occasions goes together as one memory. Now think about that memory and write down, as notes for yourself still, all the details you can recall that are connected with it. In other words, for about fifteen minutes, write down everything you can remember about your incident and about your thoughts and feelings at the time.

These notes will not be graded but will be used in a following assignment.

(2. Discussion of these papers should center on:

1. The narrowing-down process, the focusing. This is critical for helping the author to get the point of his selected recollection to emerge, and each pupil can look at his own paper and apply the discussion to it. Sample papers should be dittoed or projected with Assignment 1 so that comparisons can be made between Assignment 1 and Assignment 2. Ask what things the pupil selected *out* in doing Assignment 2. Then ask what new material he added. Once the selection of memory and its expansion in detail have been clearly established, ask the class why they think he chose that memory over the others. Then ask the author.

Now ask what more he might do to it for an audience. Does he still need more detail about some aspect of it? Does some of the detail seem unnecessary? Unnecessary for *what*? What seems to be the main point or feeling?

At this point break the class into small groups for collaboration. Have them continue the issues raised in discussion by reading and writing comments on each other's papers (see assignment sheet 3.) They should have both Assignments 1 and 2 with them. They will need a good half hour for this collaboration. The final writing, or Assignment 3, can be done in or out of school. Make sure they hand in Assignments 1 and 2 along with Assignment 3.)

Composed memory.

3. Go to your group with your Assignment 1 and 2 papers. Exchange these papers with another student. After you have read his, write comments on his Assignment 2 that will help him to rewrite it as a finished composition. You will all rewrite your Assignment 2's for the whole class to read. Your comments can be about any of the things just discussed with the sample papers. Do you think he chose the best memory? What things about the memory do you think he should bring out most when he rewrites? What would you like to hear more about? What things do you think he should cut out? How about his choice of words and the kinds of sentences he uses? The amount of personal thought and feeling?

Then exchange with other students until you have been all around the group. Afterwards, you may talk with them about their comments on your Assignment 2.

Finally, rewrite your Assignment 2. Follow the suggestions the other students made, when you agree with them. Make all the big and small changes it takes to make your memory clear and interesting for the class.

Hand in this last paper along with Assignments 1 and 2.

(3. Ditto or project all three papers of a couple of students, so that the class can survey the entire process by which those students got from first to last stage. Discuss the decisions and changes they made between Assignments 1 and 2, and between Assignments 2 and 3. In one case, you might show Assignment 3 first, then 2, then 1 — work backwards from the finished product. When moving the other way — from 1 to 2 and 3 — ask the class to guess what choices the student is going to make between one stage and the next; then show the next paper. Get them to relate the writer's progressive decisions to their own judgment about the final version.

It would be good to have a number of the Assignment 3's read aloud to give the class an idea of some of the different results of memory writing — different points and moods — and also to carry through the idea that the whole class was their audience.)

Here are three final compositions (Assignment 3) that are good but not among the best, chosen rather for their representative subjects and treatment. The first is by a girl, the other two by boys.

FIRST DAY OF SCHOOL

I had to take a test to get registered. As soon as I was registered, I started to get ready even though it was weeks before. I was supposed to be waiting for the bus at 8:30 am but I was ready at 8:00 am. I ran out to wait for the bus thinking that I would be able to read as soon as I got home. It was half days for the first week. When I got home I started crying because I couldn't read. And that is all I remember.

A long time ago I got a "Revell" weather forcasting kit. Since I was wearing my Sunday suit, I quickly changed into jeans and and old shirt just to find that there was no more glue.

After a five day wait, I rushehed upstairs to my room, got the "duco cement" the new glue and got to work on the oarnge, white, and clear, plastic pieces. I did all the easy parts first then came the hard part, the annemometer. But finally after about 2 weeks it was all finished. I was all through Boy was I glad.

My First Turtle.

I remember the day that I caught my first turtle. It had been a fairly warm day and my sisters and Peter Flynn had decided to go to the swamp. We though we might catch a snake or some other animal. This time would be different.

I was wearing a black coat with some tall green boots. I can't recall what anyone else was wearing. It was a warm day, with a clear blue sky.

As we were walking by a murkey pond, I saw something that looked interesting. I was following my sister, and she steped over something that looked like a unripe pumpkin with yellow spots on it. I picked it up and all of a sudden feet and a head came out of it. Startled at this, I dropped it. But when I saw it was a turtle, I picked it up again. I told everyone else and they conguralated me on my good luck, and we continued our journey.

Results and Problems

Making the assignment clear. The teachers found that demonstrating Assignment 1 orally before the class themselves was not hard and helped the children to grasp the process. Starting a chain of memories presents no difficulties to the children, whatever their ability or intelligence. They seem to fall into Proustian procedure with ease. Two possible confusions can arise with some children, however, as experience has shown. One is to mistake mere thought associations for memory links, so that *flag* might lead to *patriotism* and to *soldiers,* etc. The other mistake is to restrict oneself to memories associated with items in the room and thus to keep returning to the present setting in an alternation of sensations and memories. It is true that the assignment begins, as sensory recording does, by looking at one's surroundings, but the teacher can make clear that present sensation is only a springboard and that once in the past one stays there unless the chain breaks, at which time he returns to the surroundings for a new point of departure. Especially if forewarned, as we were not of course, the teacher can easily ward off these misunderstandings by clearly demonstrating a memory chain of his own, perhaps noting a few memories on the board, and by getting a volunteer to do the same. After a good demonstration, no pupil is likely to misunderstand the assignment.

Timing and grouping. For the whole series, several other practical matters came up. First of all, several teachers pointed out that if the chain of memories (Assignment 1) and the expanded memory (Assignment 2) occurred too far apart in time, the children lost interest in following through. This is only natural, is likely to be true of all phased writing, and can be easily remedied by giving Assignment 2 as homework that night or as in-class work the following day. Organizing a folder in advance, with directions and blank pages stapled in, might help more careless children to keep the papers intact and in meaningful order. So be it, so long as the folder does not acquire the mechanical aura of a workbook.

A number of teachers felt that pairs were much better collaborating units for revising Assignment 2 into 3 than groups of three or four. About this I remain somewhat skeptical, since their finding may merely reflect the children's lack of experience in commenting on each other's papers in small groups. The reading and discussing together of three or four papers gets more thoroughly at the issues in the assignment and reduces any possible misleading of one pupil by another. So I suggest that other teachers try out both pairs and larger groups.

Phasing the writing process. The most problematical matters concerned whether three stages are necessary. My original idea was that, if suddenly asked to write a memory in one stroke, the child might either draw a blank (which Assignment 1 is designed to prevent) or tell the gist of the memory so quickly that it would be lifeless (to be headed off by Assignment 2). Conventional assignments try to solve the problem of getting an idea by specifying topics such as "My Most Thrilling (Frightening, Surprising, etc.) Moment," or "The First Time I Learned a Sport." The problem of giving body and detail to an incident is, like most writing problems in a one-stroke assignment, not handled until the teacher's postmortem commentary comes along, when the pupil is confronted with the should-haves and made to feel in the wrong. And I think blanket topics make for canned themes. Not only do they work poorly as a stimulant but, in categorizing pupils' experience for them in advance, they by-pass the most worthwhile compositional issues that pupils should engage with. They always stipulate the abstract classification of events and usually also the feeling or mood that is to provide coherence. All the child does is fill in the blanks with an event — which reduces writing issues to a rather low level. And here begins the long years of nagging about detail. Elaborating and giving particulars appears as an obsession of teachers rather than as an organic development.

The original purpose of spontaneous memory writing, then, was to let the child do his own abstracting and decision making, to keep composition on a deeper, cognitive basis, since at heart it is the classifying and ordering of experience — information processing, if you like. By spreading the composing over three stages, I hoped to lay bare for examination and influence the internal processes of writing that in conventional assignments remain more hidden and less tractable, if they are put into play at all. Selecting one incident would come as a meaningful narrowing down of the first, miscellaneous array. Expanding into detail would follow, before the final draft, as a filling in of what one had staked out, like pointing to a city on a map and then looking at the inserted plan of that city. Stage three would again be a bit of selective abstracting, this time around a "core experience" that discussion with partners would have helped to emerge. Thus the pupil would be plucking from riches rather than fleshing abstractions.

The point of any assignment is not to avoid problems; it is to engage with the right problems in the right way. Memory writing does this well, and is an activity I can recommend with great confidence, but the experiment seems to show that the three-stage procedure goes a step too far for this age. In most cases two stages were enough, and a third resulted mainly in copying. That is, most pupils either wrote so fully on a few memories in Assignment 1 that only one other effort was needed to select and shape; or else, if Assignment 1 consisted of many short fragments, their expansion of the single memory in Assignment 2 was itself so close to a final composition that further revision did not warrant another copy. When we tried two stages only, the results were as good. This was so for a good reason, I think.

Most of these children naturally composed the memory at the same time that they expanded it, so that separating these processes into two additional stages merely made Assignment 3 into a brushup job of Assignment 2. I suspect a developmental factor here, however. Adolescents with whom I have also tried three-stage memory writing were more willing to elaborate first for the sake of garnering more material and less inclined toward an early closure. Whereas Assignment 2 seems like a natural end to elementary children, it can be viewed by older students still as preliminary note taking. I attribute this difference to the younger children's general tendency to elaborate little and revise little. Pushing downward into detail is as hard for them as pushing upward into generalities. They will expand some and shape some but only enough to justify one occasion for both. The chief result of Assignment 3, then, was the incorporating of sentence revisions made by other pupils, which means that by the time an author began writing out his Assignment 3, with these minor changes, the learning was all over and only copying was left. As with unwarranted last drafts of sensories, many pupils deleted good things to spare themselves labor.

IMPROVEMENTS TO BE MADE OVER THE TRIALS

Several differences in our experiment might have changed the results a fair amount.

Creating books of memories. The compositions were not destined for any particular use later. The printing of a class memory book, besides serving as a final copy of the slightly revised Assignment 2's, would have stimulated more cross-commentary and revision and led to a meaningful and motivated Assignment 3, as perhaps would also a much longer prior experience with small-group exchanging of papers.

Fuller use of workshop. The full benefit of group process in writing — class projections followed up by smaller discussions of each member's paper — is still unknown. My teachers had far too little time to work with this and often skipped or made short shrift of these sessions. And of course the cumulative effect of such experience over several years could affect considerably what sort of activities expanding and rewriting turn out to be. Despite some very good comments at times, our children, like most, were still strangers to collaborative responding. The high quality of what they can say about each other's writing even without much background is very persuasive evidence that they can learn to comment very well indeed, but, like the other verbal arts we try to help them learn, this one grows slowly with practice over a long span. Whereas our children's enthusiasm, very high for Assignment 1, declined with each additional step, more interactive stimulation among them, set off by teacher-led demonstrations and sustained by a goal, would probably have made Assignments 2 and 3 appear as equally exciting forays.

Freer rewriting. It is the amount of purposeful change proposed by other pupils that keeps the writing alive for them. In this respect, my experiment was badly lacking, for we did not raise the possibilities for free rewriting that in fact could be raised by the teacher and carried into the groups, such as converting the selected incident into a poem or fictionalized story. Or pupils could return to Assignment 1, pluck out another incident, and expand it also; if they *began* with a kernel memory from the old Assignment 1, then the fullness so often found in Assignment 1 might pour forth instead in an expansion of this kernel. In that case, an Assignment 3 might become well warranted and motivated. Or Assignment 3 might become a possibility rather than a requirement, a valuable option for pupils to consider and discuss with each paper. The option would be a means of thinking about how much change a given paper needs, even if Assignment 3 is not ultimately recommended.

Finally, we did not relate memory writing to drama. Acting out a detailed memory as a pantomime or with dialogue would add a lot of interest to the writing of it, if this possibility were announced in advance. In fact, the obvious need for detail in that case might motivate expansion (Assignment 2) considerably. Very succinct memories could be used as "minimal situations" for improvisation, which would in turn elaborate the memories and thus point the way to written expansion. Relating drama and memories will supplement publication with another writing purpose, and will provide excellent material for drama. Some revisions might even be in script form, another option the teacher should feed into the groups.

These are reservations about our trials, not attempts to salvage the three-stage procedure, which, so far as one can tell now, should be reduced to two steps until further experimentation with the factors above indicates otherwise. At any rate, when introduced abruptly, the assignment will probably go better in two stages. The following samples may help other teachers to judge somewhat for themselves.

Samples

Influenced by discussion, a number of pupils elected the pyramidal form of note taking (below) because it obviates writing "I remember" and "That reminds me of. . . ." One girl's memory chain began with spotting a flutaphone in the classroom:

Flutaphone

boring music   practicing at home

Miss Brown   practicing   having to take

piano   time for it

chorus   piano lessons   recitals

performances   getting up early   riding lessons

for practices

Actually, these capsule memories are noted in a dryly abstract way, none of them being an incident, and yet from these she reconstructs a very specific underlying incident:

Piano lessons remind me of a recital I had this year.
The room was full of chairs, each occupied by either someone's mother or a student. I was to play fourth.
"Merry is now going to play an english folk song," my teacher announced. I stood up and walked up to the piano. I could hear and feel my heart pumping and wondered if the audience could. When I was done I heard a lot of applause.
"Now Merry is going to play a composed song, she composed it." My piano teacher announced, "The name is 'memories.' "
I played my short minor song and turned around to get up.
"Please play it again, its so short and I think the audience will enjoy it more."
So I did, got applause and left the piano seat happily.

Preadolescents are not inclined to state feelings as explicitly as this girl does; they either assume that such things are self-evident or are not introspective enough to identify and name them. A composed memory that others feel is pointless and uninteresting almost always fails to make clear the core experience that made the memory stand out in the first place. Discussion can be helpful in indicating that more explicitness, or perhaps just a more emphatic handling of facts, is needed. The core experience here is obviously pleasure, the flush of success and attention. It is rather hard to find a meaningless memory, and the meaning engenders the coherence. This children intuitively understand, but an egocentric failure to allow for the reader, among other things, can obscure the coherence. I do not include here the above writer's Assignment 3, because it reads exactly like Assignment 2 except for the deletion of the last three paragraphs, more of a loss than a gain, though conceivably she felt that the announcement of the song title was the high point and the rest anticlimatic.

At the other extreme of note taking, many of the spontaneous streams of memory are more copious and colorful than the compositions derived from them. Such rich notes give one pause: How much should teaching push for the standard coherence that defines a composition? At this age do the losses sometimes outweigh the gains? When the notes are mere lists of words and phrases, these questions do not arise, but when I read the easily flowing memories and sentences of a paper like this girl's, I wonder if we shouldn't just let be, regardless of our preconceptions of the assignment, or else make the assignment more flexible:

> As I look on top of a radiator I see a gallon jar with dirt on the bottom of it and with dirty water. That reminds me, once I was swimming in salt water and I was laying down but then I got up.
> Suddenly I found me walking in freezing water. Suddenly I fell into a drop by the wind. Which reminds me of a green type of fly that stays near water, and when you are on sand It comes along and stings.
> Once I was playing in some sand near water and one came along and landed on my arm.
> I was so excited that I ran and jumped into the water and that scared him away.
> That reminds me, once I was one a raft (floating) in the salt water and I was drifting into a drop with one of my friends, she pushed me off. Some one had to come and get me out.

Though scattered in time, her memories connect easily, forming a natural psychological continuity, and yet are kept distinct by the paragraphing. It is this spontaneous flow that the children like so much. For her Assignment 2 she took the last memory:

> Once I was on a plastic floatable raft. I was on the raft with my friend in the salt water. We were going with the curent going into a drop and there was no possible way to stop. My friend got excited and by mistake she pushed me off and the curent was to strong and my friend's parant had to get in their boat and come get me out.

The gains of expanding were: more detail about the raft (*plastic, float-able*), more explanation of the situation (there was no way to stop drifting, and her friend pushed her off *by mistake*), and more specification of who rescued her and how (*friend's parant, in their boat*). These are all good changes and additions, fulfilling the purpose of Assignment 2 and showing the ability to "fill in" for the reader's benefit. But the sentences are hardly improved, the first one being choppy and overlapping as though she had suddenly become overformal. In doing the last version (Assignment 3), interestingly enough, she tightened up the sentences by herself; a partner broke the last run-on sentence into two. Though it is only stylistically different, I reproduce here this last version and suggest that the reader compare Assignments 2 and 3 to see how important sentence development can occur without teacher intervention. The direction of these revisions that she did on her own is toward a mature economy of construction.

> Once I was on a plastic floatable raft with my friend in the salt water. We were going with the curent, into a drop and there was no possible way to stop. My friend got excited and by mistake she pushed me off and the curent was to strong. My friend's parent had to get in their boat, and get me out.

These are typical of the gains and losses that the teacher needs to be alert to and to weigh when working with serial assignments. Compare the notes and composition below, done as a two-stage assignment by a boy:

> I saw McGath a then I thought of my brother when it was his first birthday when he stuck his hand in the cake and took a big gob of cake out and ate it then it was SyClops the one eyed, 25 foot man then it was Voyage to the bottom of the Sea when down went inside the inside the whales tummy, the spider too, a snout comming out of a nose, JoHanna Katy disecting a frog disecting a crayfish, throw up (sick), spit, an old lady some messy (soming that comes out of your fannie.

If I am not mistaken, this is what critics mean by "visceral writing." Among the good qualities required of language arts teachers a strong stomach is perhaps too seldom listed. This is a child writing in freedom and with relish. There is naturalistic realism and literary allusion side by side, strung together by private associations but in an obvious continuity. What the piece lacks is grammatical coherence and a more definite focus, both of which he achieves in the composition:

> When it was my brothers first birthday he stuck his hand in the cake and pulled out a big gob of cake and shouved it in his mouth. He had a mouth covered with chocolate cake.

The sentences are good, he "sticks to the subject," and he has even expanded slightly. (He replaced *ate* by *shouved in his mouth,* and added the whole last sentence, which makes the point of the anecdote — his baby brother's comic appearance at the moment — a core experience that hardly needs belaboring.) As a succinct summary of a single incident, this is admirable. But what have we traded for it?

Actually the question is a bit false. It is possible to have our cake and the spiders and frogs too: instead of thinking of serial writing as stages toward "the real thing," called a composition, both teacher and pupils should probably conceive the related pieces as things in themselves, all equal in worth but for different reasons. The fact that one is base for another should not debase it. In fact, to distinguish, and to value accordingly, the variousness of writing is an important goal of the language arts. While discriminating between writing for himself and writing for others, between notes and a public composition, the child can also appreciate each for its own sake. This means that speaking of a staged assignment is using a misnomer, and that the teacher would do better to consider each piece of writing as an end in itself and not merely as a means; what we really mean by staging or phasing writing is that one piece is used as stimulus for another, in the manner of chain reaction.

The following memory chain shows, I think, how pell-mell writing encourages children to spin out the longer, more complex sentence constructions that they will try out freely when talking but will not often risk in writing. I have italicized two especially exemplary passages:

I see a top of a house and it is white. It reminds me of going up to maine at My grandparents cottage. That reminds me of the time Gail, Robin and I and Nancy were in maine and hid in someones pyle of hay when they came bye. The White on the house also reminds me of the ski slopes when I first when on them. That reminds me of up in maine when we went to bonds. *We called to 17 year old tommy manahan who lives two houses away in maine a boy scout as he went bye. That reminds me of when My Family and I went to the end of the lake and saw the lake and the ocean be divided by a huge metal that was aquad shape and sliding down the slide that lead to the ocean.* That reminds me of when I first learned to water ski I fell and fell and then I Finally got up and made it First time around. That reminds me of when I caught my First Fish. It turned out to be a gold Fish. The remind me of when we went to canipe lake Park and I went on the biggest Rollar coaster in New England. I also went on the house of seven gables and you see statues and *I saw a statue of a man having his head sawe in half* and going throw the huge barrels. That remind me of when I was four and went to boston with my mother. The reminds me of when I First learned to dive at Hayden day camp. That reminds me off the time Gail, Robin, and me went up the dirt road in maine and picked Blueberrys and rasberrys. That reminds me of the time I almost Drownded watersking. That reminds me of the time gail and nancy and I went in Mrs. Pratts canal

The first italicized sentence contains three modifying phrases (*17 year old, in maine,* and *a boy scout,* the last being an appositive), a relative clause (*who lives two houses away*), and a temporal clause (*as he went bye*). This represents the embedding of five potentially independent kernel sentences into the main kernel sentence, *We called to tommy manahan.* Of course the sentence is badly ordered and is overloaded with information, but the girl has usefully exercised her developing sentence-building ability. In the next sentence she tries out a construction involving a verbal complement of the predicate — *saw the lake and the ocean be divided by a huge metal. . .* An adult's first impulse might be to use a participle here (*I saw the ocean being divided*) but the girl is intuitively following a grammatical regularity, since she would say, using the active, *I saw something divide the ocean.* In not using a participle, she has merely analogized from the active complement and thus written the passage *be divided.* In the other italicized passage — *I saw a statue of a man having his head sawe in half* — she does use a participle in what is a subtly different grammatical situation, the case of a verbal form modifying a preceding noun rather than complementing a preceding predicate.

Such an accurate intuitive discrimination between constructions that one would expect a child to confuse makes me marvel at the powerful cognitive operations at work in language acquisition. Rarely if ever do teachers of any grade attempt to explain grammatical distinctions as fine as this. Such linguistic feats, which greatly surpass the expectations of any grammar teaching I have heard of, are persuasive evidence that the child's perceptions about what he hears and reads are the real teachers of grammar. But my point here is that he needs a lot of free writing practice in which to rehearse and recombine these constructions on paper without fear of correction.

The girl's expansion and composition, assigned as only one additional piece of writing, went like this:

THE BOYSCOUT

One time a year ago in the summer. My Family went to maine. We go to maine every year. We live in our grandparents cottage. In Front of the cottage is a lake. We Have a motor boat, sailboat, rowboat and water skis. We go to bonds a store usally by boat but this time we went by car. My sisters Ellen and nancy went with me. Tommy manahan a 17 years old boy past and we said "Hey boyscout are you going to help a lady cross the street. When my mother came to the car she said that he told her what we said and we all started to laugh.

Again, I suspect that the choppy, overlapping "baby sentences" of the first half stem from an over-concern about writing correct sentences, which may very well have caused her to open with a sentence fragment. The backfiring strategy in that case was to parcel out speech in short and therefore "safe" units. The result is less mature writing. The sentence in Assignment 1 about the boy scout, which becomes expanded and framed here as an anecdote, has undergone an interesting transformation. No doubt realizing that her former construction was overloaded and unreadable, she took out the dependent clauses, simply dropped some information, shifted 17 *year old* from the adjectival to the appositive position, and converted what had been the appositive before — *a boyscout* — into a quoted direct address. Certainly children should get a chance to flex their intelligence and ingenuity in linguistic ways by reworking their own sentence structures, but if fear of error plays a part, they will regress instead. This paper shows both aspects.

A few miscellaneous points on these two papers. First, another pupil gave considerable and helpful attention to this girl's problem with capitalization. Second, the original title of the piece was "The Hey," apt but neutral; either the girl herself or another pupil — I don't know which — changed the title to "The Boyscout," which has the same playful irony that inspired the incident itself. I can only urge, again, the strong emphasis on titling and revising titles as a way of helping the children both to make explicit their core experience and to compose a coherence around it. The girl here has more information than she needs to tell in her anecdote, but, given her starting point, she has already focused considerably, and she will have plenty of other occasions to practice further.

Finally, examining papers from such assignments, as I have examined these two, can give teachers many useful insights about how their children's minds work and how they come to do the types of things with language that they do. In this way teachers can conduct their own research — not essentially different from that of some linguists and psycholinguists — that can help them think about what they are doing and ought to be doing.

It is for a child like the next girl that the second stage of expansion seems right:

My Memries

The ratiator reminded me where my brother was fooling with the iron and he burnt himself.
The tres remind me of camp when I was going into second grade.
The spots on the celling remind me when the water from are tub leaked though are celling and made a mess down stairs.

She chose to expand the last memory, which a classmate thought was most promising:

A couple of years ago my brother was taking a bath. While he was waiting in the living room the water was getting higher in the tub when the water was just about at the top he ran in and shut it off. Then he took a bath. As soon as he was in the water started to overflow in the bathrub but it went so slowly you couldn't notice it. About 15 minutes and there was a big puddle on the floor. When are housekeeper went down stairs and saw it she told my brother to stop taking a bath then she took a bucket, and put it there in a few minites it stoped and dryed up the next day

In this case, writing a second piece based on a first had only positive results. She seems to be writing zestfully, and with high motivation and an anticipation of audience appreciation. Sentences are mature, and the incident is sharply focused. All she needs is transcriptive practice for punctuating sentence stops.

The final samples indicate a possibility of memory writing that, while allowed for by the experiments, was not really explored. If a pupil puts together in one composition two or three incidents that happened at different times but are related by an idea or category of which the incidents are instances, then the unity of the piece becomes automatically something general. A critical first step is made toward essay and away from pure narrative. That is, when instead of telling an anecdote one juxtaposes several shorter anecdotes, the question is: What heading do all of these incidents go under? What logic is replacing pure chronology as the linking and organizing factor? Below are two pieces demonstrating this transition; unfortunately I do not know at which of the three stages they were done. The first contains two incidents, the second, three. In both, the connection among incidents is obvious but unstated, and the heading or category of experience is still at a low level of generality:

> The grahm crackers remind me of one day when my grandmother was visiting us. She made me graham crackers for breakfast. And one day she gave me a plate of six whole graham crackers she went in the other room for napkin. When she came back in the room I had finished. The amazing thing was that I ate them in around six seconds. Another time I had a breast of turkey and 5 scoops of potatoe and good helping of peas and finished before everyone else. And waited outside while I was waiting I went out to the tree hut. I got up on weak side fell down broke thumb and sprained my rist didn't have to write in school.

> One day I brought my snake to school. After art I came in and he was gone. I thought someone had taken him I looked around and Russel found him in the shelf.

> One day I went to a place called Turtle Pond. On the bank I saw a thing that looked like a turtle, It was a turtle. I went a picked it up and it was asleep. All of a sudden he stuck his head out. And tried to swim away from me.

> One day we went to Watham Pond. And we found fresh water invertebrates. In about ten minutes my freind fell in and five minutes later my other freind fell in and fifteen minutes later I fell in. The water was cold.

It would be interesting to have other children propose titles for these. For such a kind of essay a title normally names or suggests the generality that the instances exemplify; in these two cases, something about speed-eating and hunting animal specimens would come to mind. Titles might in turn suggest a more explicit frame for the incidents — phrases or sentences that say something about the unifying connection.

This movement toward essay can be prepared for by discussing the association between one memory and another in Assignment 1, before any further writing is done. Clearly the two boys here arrived at their unity just by exploiting the category responsible in the first place for the thought association. Quite likely, they had originally included other memories which they subsequently deleted as irrelevant to the category. At any rate, such would be the selection process for further writing beyond Assignment 1. The teacher would project an Assignment 1 and ask: How did this writer get from one memory to the next? Can you follow the jumps? Where does a new train of thought begin? Which memories here would you clump together as being about the same thing? Is there another clump about something different?

If, in answering these questions, some pupils classify the same memory differently, the discrepancy could make good discussion, involving finally the author. "Which would you rather see this writer do — tell more about one of these incidents or tell about several of them together? In each case what might a working title be?" In other words, pupils carry into the small groups another possible option to consider in making suggestions to each other. The possibility gives rise in a most natural way to writing of a more abstract sort. These two boys, and a few other children, inadvertently anticipated an assignment that I had already been trying out in secondary school (Chapter 29 in the K–13 edition). It explicitly asks students to do just what these boys did but without prior memory notes. Ringing this variation on memory writing would set up the later assignment very well. What will vary with growth is the abstraction level of the "theme" or category. (The concrete themes of these two papers may seem trivial to adults.) In this respect, again, by stipulating process, not content, the assignment adjusts to individual capacity.

We did not have time to try out the writing of poems and fictions based on memories. This is an extremely rich possibility, as with sensations, which the teacher should raise periodically in leading discussions of projected samples. Not only, I think, would memories solve the problem of getting an idea for imaginative writing but they would exert an influence away from imitation toward more originality.

Summary

I have presented the experiment in its original rigidity to demonstrate the wisdom of flexibility and the possibility of variations. The neat unit, the definitive syllabus, would violate what has been learned. Even the original formalism was based more on the needs of experiment than on principle. But it is possible to conclude with some definite suggestions for staged writing that might apply reliably to the composing of other material than memories.

1. As regards individuals, let the decision about pursuing a subject into another stage depend on teacher-influenced group consultation.

2. As regards collective growth, add stages as children mature.

3. Treat any piece of writing both as an end in itself and as a possible stimulus for another piece (notes may turn out as compositions, and compositions as notes).

If one thinks about how much of traditional theme writing in the later years, and of adult writing, draws on memory for its material (including, later, the memory of what one reads), and if one acknowledges the universality of the compositional issues entailed in memory writing, then perhaps the space devoted to it here will seem well warranted. Together, sensations and memories are the individual's storehouse, from which — however bizarrely imaginative or abstractly formulated — all his writing must necessarily proceed. Not all of our recordings and reportings get written, but they occur inside anyway, and we further abstract these into the generalities according to which we see the world and according to which we take action.

When these processes are themselves the basis of assignments, then writing becomes an external and explicit replica of what ordinarily happens inwardly and hiddenly. A pupil can thus gradually become aware of how he knows what he knows, and of how his experience shapes his thought. As for his fancies and fictions, they are merely a less direct mode of recombining and synthesizing these same raw materials. Asking a child to write down sensations and memories not only shows him that the real stuff of speaking and writing lies all around him and within him at any moment, but it validates this stuff; it says plainly that his individual experience is of great worth, something to turn to, not away from. At the same time, the group process lets him air this experience and his expression of it before other people of his own development but of different experience. This gives him the perspective of public reality.

Chapter 15

Writing Fictions

All good writing, of course, is imaginative, even when the point of departure is as factual as sensations and memories. What is meant here by "fictions" is simply a greater degree of invention. And, invention *is* a matter of degree. As I have indicated, sensory and memory writing may take an inventive turn into fiction. "Pure imagination," on the other hand, does not exist; inventions are some more or less indirect recombining of experiences, either from real life or from books, television, and so on. For the kind of writing dealt with here, children set out to invent fictions, regardless of how real or fantastic the results.

Ideally, a teacher would simply say, "Write a story about anything you like," but teachers of even very able pupils say that such an open assignment is very hard to respond to. Writing fictions seems to require a context, a stimulating situation of one sort or another — involved discussion, reading around a subject, dramatic activity, a concentration on literary form. Some of the stimulants suggested in Chapter 7 for the lower grades — caption development, cartoons, song writing — might, in the teacher's discretion, still serve well for inexperienced or verbally undeveloped children of this age. Certainly, writing lyrics for songs and filling in various metrical forms with one's own ideas is not limited to the lower grades.

Here I would like to make further suggestions with the understanding that if assignments to "make up a story" or "write a poem" work well for some children, then they may as well be given just that simply. The goal is self-initiated writing, but some of the stimulants used to reach this goal also have value in themselves, such as learning what forms are available and how different subjects may be treated.

Fictional writing, too, is read, discussed, and revised in small groups, then printed up into booklets for exchange. Revision would not be required but would, rather, be proposed by workshop colleagues and motivated by the writer's desire to prepare the best possible copy for printing. To ensure that the cross-commentary is perceptive and useful, lead model class discussions

231

on papers selected for a variety of reasons — for range of expression and invention and for compositional issues they raise. These discussions are for appreciation and exhibition as much as for critical commentary. Ask for the natural responses of the class to a paper, then play from these responses by a few impromptu questions and observations of your own, until the pupils relate their responses to specific features of the paper that elicited them.

Writing About Pictures

A picture stimulus is still appropriate but can be developed. One fourth-grade teacher asked his pupils to make up a story by placing themselves in a scene, depicted in a magazine advertisement, of a camel standing in a New York City street:

> But this we were just driving along when suddenly we stopped. I was in the back and didn't know what was going on. When I looked out I saw a camal right in the middle of the road. We waited about an hour until the camal moved. The plain we were supposed to catch had lefted. Mom and Dad were fighting over why didn't Dad get out and move the camal. And Dad said why didn't you?! Then Mom started crying and telling us about the dum camal. I bet she was so mad she made Dad cry. I said I didn't want to go home cause Susy was going to beat me up. After that I said I'd walk a mile for a camal! Mom was still crying when we got home and Dad was still yellen at us and the dog was howing and barking. And I told all the kids at school about the camal and how we missed our plain. I took the camal with me.[1]

Other developments of the picture stimulus are accomplished by specializing the type of picture used, so that the following questions can be asked: What are these people saying to each other? What is this person doing — or thinking? What might happen in this place? Or children can simply bring in their favorite pictures from magazines, exchange them, and choose one to write from. In one sixth-grade class using a variety of self-chosen pictures, I once saw, accidentally arranged side by side on a bulletin board, three picture stories told in the three different persons — *I, you,* and *he.* The assignment had, curiously enough, stimulated a variety of story-telling techniques, probably because pictures may be associated more flexibly than most fictional material with any one of the three pronouns.

Writing Memories of Literature[2]

This assignment is not purely inventive but will prime invention. The children recreate in their own words an especially memorable scene or mo-

[1] My thanks to John Talbot, Cochituate Elementary School, Wayland, Massachusetts, for this paper and for his experimentation with other assignments in this program.

[2] For this assignment I am indebted to Frank Lyman and Kayda Cushman, of the Estabrook Elementary School in Lexington, Massachusetts. They devised it and provided the samples printed in this section.

ment from a book, play, or movie without looking back at the original text. Emphasis is on choosing a scene that stands out later because of the strong feeling it aroused in the child when he read it or saw it. The key is vivid involvement, and the source may be any that the child knows, regardless of whether it relates to schoolwork or not. He is directed to write the scene by putting himself back into it, becoming part of it, perhaps taking the role of a character in it, making it happen again.

The purpose, of course, is not to recapitulate accurately the original; in fact, the teachers who developed and tried out the assignments were casting about for a stimulus for imaginative writing because they found that their children could not easily make up a story from scratch. These fifth- and sixth-grade pupils liked the assignment very much and wrote better stories than they had in other attempts. Besides endorsing the assignment for its own obvious value, I see helpful connections between it and other activities in this program.

Some of the samples reproduced below bear a subtitle that names the main feeling of the recreated scene. In some cases, the teachers who were trying this assignment had the class designate a theme in advance — some emotion or quality that might give the pupils more to go on when selecting their scenes. In other cases, the pupils chose a theme for their scenes *after* they had written them. I am inclined to think that such focusing of the assignment is unnecessary and, when the theme is pre-selected, possibly obstructive. But other teachers might do well to run the same sort of mixed trials and judge for themselves.

This is by a low-grouped, underachieving fifth-grade boy:

SINK IT RUSTY
SADNESS

Rusty blew the whistle and said "foul on Perry." he struck Joby's wrist when he stold the ball from him. THen Rusty came over, took the ball from Perry and handed it to Joby. Then Rusty said "two shots." Just then Alec Paws came over and everybody stoped playing. Alec was much older than the other boys. Rusty had never seen him before and he kept staring at the black glove on his left hand. THen all tha boys said hi to him. they where glad to see him. Rusty could see the boys didn't want him to play so Rusty said "Here Alec you take the ball." the boys said "come on Alec" so Alec took the ball and the whistle and Rusty walked off sadly. The End.

A fifth-grade girl of superior ability recreated this moment from the well known film:

SOUND OF MUSIC
FRIENDSHIP

Maria sits quietly and thoughtfully on a bench near a glassed-in room. Crunching through the leaves, Captain Von Trapp sits beside Maria. "I want to congratulate you and the Baronese," Maria said standing up.

"Can you marry someone when you like somebody else more?" questioned the Captain who was growing used to Maria.

"No, I guess not." replied Maria softly.

It is clear that each of these two children has chosen a personally meaningful bit of action involving someone they could identify with.

Not all of the stories were done in third person. The teachers' emphasis on the possibilities of taking a character point of view was undoubtedly what influenced some children either to use the first person or to go into a character's mind in third person. These two girls wrote interior monologues — a case again of pupils' involuntarily anticipating a much later assignment (Chapter 20 in the K–13 edition). The first, by a sixth-grade girl of superior ability, contains one unsignalled line of dialogue:

Lucy

That no good brother of my he will never learn. There he is lying out there freezing to death. . . , I have to get him. Get in bed stupid. His shoes are hard to get off because they're ice! Stay there now. I don't know why he does it. If he does it next year I will kill him!

The second is by a fifth-grade girl considered to be of average cognitive skills:

I better not let that Cinderella try on that slipper, it just might fit her. My daughters have to fit the slipper, they just have to! If they don't my life will be just ruined, just ruined. (Knock-knock) Oh I better let him in. It will be sure to fit me or one of my daughters. Darn it didn't fit one of my daughters. Oh No! he wants Cinderella to try it on' It FIT! Oh No! I'm ruined, Oh dear! I'm simply ruined! The End

The dramatic possibilities of all of these are splendid. The last two could be acted out as soliloquies, the silent roles being done in pantomime. The scenes from "Sink It, Rusty" and "The Sound of Music" read almost like play scripts; they contain only movement and dialogue — no author commentary or character thoughts. The playability of these papers is a happy effect of the emphasis the teachers placed on recreating a *small span of action*. As I have suggested before, one of the chief difficulties with children's written stories is that, because they cannot write at great length, if they encompass the whole of even a moderately long action they are forced to oversummarize it in a dull way. By stressing a scene or moment, and by directing the children to put themselves in that scene, the teachers effectively steered them away from synopsis toward detail.

In discussing their papers together in preparation for acting them out, the children will discover, however, that some stories are not readily dramatizable, even though they cover a short duration. For example, this story by a sixth-grade girl of high ability:

WITCH OF BLACKBIRD POND
"COMFORT"

She ran without reason or decorum, past the houses of her pupils, past the townhall, past the loiterers at the town pump. Without having chosen a destination in her mind, her feet had. They lead her beyond the outskirts of the town, into a Great Meadow. She took a path that led off into the meadow and flung herself down on the long, earth-smelling grass. Slowly, the meadow with its vastness began to fulfill its promise.

This girl does not employ the wholly external viewpoint of a movie, nor the wholly internal viewpoint of an interior monologue; using a common novelistic technique, she tells the story in the third person but from the viewpoint of a single character. Thus the load is on narration, description of scenery, and accounts of feeling in the author's words but as perceived by the character. This is hard to dramatize and therefore presents a special opportunity for learning. In sifting stories for those that can be fairly readily acted out, pupils will learn about various fictional techniques in a very pragmatic, intuitive way. If a story does not lend itself to acting out, they have to think about why this is so. Too much description? Too indirect a relaying of the character's inner life? Too much commentary by the author? Does such a story have to be read and only read? Could it be *adapted* in some way for dramatizing or for filming? An advantage here of reading a lot of each other's papers is that children will borrow various first- and third-person techniques from each other. As a secondary effect of doing the assignment, such exploration of technique can be expert and concrete; to push the study of fictional methods for its own sake, however, would be too academic. Reading and writing stories done in various techniques, and, especially, trying to determine their relation to drama, would teach quite enough for this age. Technique is better done than talked about, except when the talking is of a problem-solving sort.

Generally, I see this assignment as an extension of memory writing into the realm of reading and fictive creation. The extension allows for second-hand experience and for imaginative rather than factual material. It is a repeatable assignment because the content is always different. It engages pupils because this content is essentially personal feeling conveniently projected into a scene which the child makes his own. It is the only kind of literary appreciation that makes sense to me for this age. To ask a pupil to write, in a book report, what he liked about a book will not get anything like the same quality of response, for all a child can do in a book report is summarize the plot and make a couple of shallow generalities.

Points of Departure for Inventing

Either content or form may launch an invention. Observations in nature study, discussion of social studies material, reading of nonfiction, and many other subjects dealt with in class could inspire stories or poems. Playing by ear, the teacher seizes a moment of high enthusiasm for some content, takes the spin-off from that activity, and turns it toward writing: "Write a story about such an animal (somebody in such a situation, something taking place in such a region)." By "story" children understand virtually any kind of writing they are capable of doing that has characters, setting, and action. The possibilities of different forms — poem, ballad, playlet — are mentioned.

Though involvement in subject matter is a good and natural stimulus for writing, it seems to me that trading on children's excitement about certain holidays has been very much overdone. One sometimes has the impression that the elementary curriculum is founded on Halloween, Thanksgiving, Christmas, Valentine's Day, George Washington's Birthday, and Easter, and that if these occasions were to cease being celebrated, elementary education in this country would collapse into a rubble of paper ghosts and hearts. To guard against repeals by future presidents, it might be sound to tap other sources of children's enthusiasm. Such typical assignments as "Do a Thanksgiving poem" fill the bulletin boards with papers that gobble terribly like those one read last year on another bulletin board in some other school. Even "Write a poem about autumn" becomes no more than an annual invitation to turn over the leaves of old clichés. We can be sure that children will celebrate at the slightest excuse anyway, without the sponsorship of schools. For writing, more spontaneous and less stereotyped subjects would be better.

An Unfinished Sentence

A provocative, unfinished sentence has been used very successfully by some teachers. In England, Sybil Marshall gives this starter: "Nobody knew where it came from, but there it was, a big red _____." A low-ability class of mixed fifth- and sixth-graders began their stories with this unfinished sentence but added a sentence of their own that all stories were to include somewhere. With capitals and punctuation adjusted, this is one boy's response:

> All of a sudden there it was, a big red sign that said Ghost Realty. Just then a man walked in. He said that he was looking for a haunted house. The man in the chair said that there was one house on a iland about a half mile from Long Iland. The owner died about a week a go and the man (buyer) said, "I will take it." "Wait. In order that you may buy the house you will have to spend the night in the house." "Ok, I will spend the night in the house." "Ok, than it is settled." "Fine, then you will take me out in a rowboat tonight." "Good."
> Out in a rowboat that night he rowed him up to the iland and when the man let him of he rowed back as fast as he could. He looked back and then went up the stairs and went in side. He looked all around then he saw a

stair case. He went up it then he herd a voice. It said, "If the log rolls over we will all be dround," and then he ran in a room as fast as he could and there siting in a washbowl sat three ants on a mach stick saying, "If the log rolls over we will all be drowned."[3]

The children themselves can propose such starters.

LOADED WORDS

One fifth-grade teacher asked her pupils to think up several interesting words, then to choose one to write a poem, story, or script about. One word was "mysterious":

MYSTERIOUS

There's a mysterious house on our street
It's where Oak and Flag Street meet.
People say they hear noises when it's dark.
And the creaking of gates, when chirps the lark.

It's very old you know.
It's where all the weeds on Oak St. grow,
I went there once to see what it's like.
And I almost fell off of my bike.

For, there from the back window,
There came a giant frog.
He didn't look like any I'd seen in the bog.
He was really quite frightening.
He held a sword, and threw it like lightning.

Well that sword just missed me,
And I ran home fast.
And my bad dreams stopped only
The night before last.

My advice to anyone
Whom it may concern
Is stay away from there
For if you don't, say a prayer.

Another word was "fish":

THE FISH STORY

The ocean was a silver cup
With a deep scalloped rim;

[3] My thanks to Rose Arnone, Cochituate Elementary School, Wayland, Massachusetts.

And all the fish I took up
Were big enough to swim;
And had speckled tails.
There were not any in between
The rest, I guess, were whales.[4]

Song and Verse Forms

Inspired by the East coast blackout of 1965, and fitted to the tune and meter of "Sweet Betsy from Pike," this ballad shows the stimulus of both a subject and a form (done by a group of Omega children in the Franklin Elementary School in Lexington, Massachusetts).

Ballad of the Blackout

At half past five Tuesday, November the ninth,
The lights went out and it gave me a fright.
We lit all our candles.
'Twas a spoo-ooky sight,
When the lights went out o-on that Tuesday night!

(*Chorus*)
The people were all right when candles were light.
But electricity is a much better light.

"What happened?" said Sally.
I said, "I don't know."
"What happened?" said Willy
While tying a bow.
They pushed the wrong button and turned to reverse.
The main truck line shorted with one great big burst.

(*Chorus*)

The li-ights went ou-out.
The hou-ouse got dark.
The moo-oon came ou-out.
The do-ogs did bark.
The babies cri-ied,
The pe-eople sighed.
And tha-at's what happened on Tu-uesday night.

(*Chorus*)

[4] My thanks to Rose Merzon of the Happy Hollow Elementary School, Wayland, Massachusetts, for these poems and for her extensive trials of other assignments in this program.

I was i-in the bathtub when it happened to me.
The water went o-off and I was freezing.
Yes that was what happened
And now you will see
The rest of the thin-ings that happened to me.

(Chorus)

I was washing my hai-ar when out went the lights.
I cried to my mother, "what a terrible fright!"
"Now what will I do? There's shampoo in my eyes.
And the lather is growin-ing double its size.

(Chorus)

I was doing my homework that Tu-uesday night.
When all of a sudden I looked at my light.
It flickered and flickered. Oh what a sight!
Oh what a terrible Tu-esday night.

(Chorus)

We were out at our friends' house when the li-ights went poof!
The TV went blurry and we were so shook.
We sat and we sat there a-waiting for help.
And then we found out that it was a black-out.

(Chorus)

So when the lights went out
It all was quite black.
I thought I heard Martians
So I hit the sack.
And then I heard scre-eams
Upstairs in the hall,
And found that my brother had started to bawl.

(Chorus)

Oh whe-e-en the li-ights went out,
Fly-i-ing saucers came dow-own with doubt.
They crashed and they banged and they clattered and called.
They landed right i-in Nia-a-gra Falls.

(Chorus)

The Mars-men were coming
And coming they were.

They turned off our lights
With their ray gun rayer.

And away they all went and away they all flew.
They left us with nothing but fuses that blew.

(*Chorus*)

After concentrating on a form through considerable reading of instances
of it, the pupils try their hand at this form, the subject matter being stimulated by such structural features as metrical and stanzaic patterns of rhyme,
rhythm, and repetition. Thus limericks, ballads, short lyrics, and longer
narrative poems should all be read in large quantities, taking one type at a
time, initially at least, until the form is fixed in their minds. The teacher
does not need to explain the form or point out the technical characteristics of
it; that is the point of reading many instances together. The best way to
know literature is to practice it.

FABLES

One form in particular that I would recommend is fable. Of course,
fables might be written as either prose or poetry, but in either mode they
represent a differentiated form of narrative — the story that illustrates an
explicit general point. Besides being popular with children and available to
them through a rich literature stemming from Aesop and LaFontaine, the
fable has by definition a particularly strong learning asset that should be
taken advantage of.

Whereas few children of this age are capable of, or even interested in,
writing general truths in the sense of sustaining generalizations throughout
a whole discourse, they are quite able and motivated to make single generalities and to insert these into their stories and descriptions. In two ways, fables
act as a natural bridge between narrative statement and idea statement: (1)
the whole story must be "pointed" toward the concluding moral, and (2) the
moral itself must be an explicit assertion, in the present tense of generalization, of an idea that the narrative merely embodies. Thus fable acts as a
hinge between two kinds of idea presentation — examples and generalities.
While not asking the child to abandon his characteristic mode of narrative
for abstract essay, it leads him toward a transitional kind of narrative that
prepares for generalization writing. Later assignments in secondary school
will more fully develop this crucial intellectual transformation of *what happened* into *what happens,* or *when* into *whenever.* What differentiates fable
from other narrative is just this cognitive shift from pure story (once-upon-a-
time) toward the illustrative story (typical of many times).

In "Teaching the 'Unteachable,' "[5] Herbert Kohl has given a very vivid and valuable account of the ways in which he tried to help Harlem children to start writing. Reading and making fables was one of the successful ways. Here is what one eleven-year-old Negro girl wrote for him:

> Once upon a time there was a pig and a cat. The cat kept saying old dirty pig who want to eat you. And the pig replied when I die I'll be made use of, but when you die you'll just rot. The cat always thought he was better than the pig. When the pig died he was used as food for the people to eat. When the cat died he was bured in old dirt.
>
> Moral: Live dirty die clean.

Both the tale and the moral show real native wit. *Live dirty die clean* shows how moral writing can help children practice the rhetorical devices and pithiness of epigrammatic statement. An eleven-year-old Negro boy wrote this one:

> Once a boy was standing on a huge metal flattening machine. The flattener was coming down slowly. Now this boy was a boy who love insects and bugs. The boy could have stopped the machine from coming down but there were two ladie bugs on the button and in order to push the button he would kill the two ladie bugs. The flattener was about a half inch over his head now he made a decision he would have to kill the ladie bugs he quickly pressed the button. The machine stoped he was saved and the ladie bugs were dead.
>
> Moral: smash or be smashed

The allegorical aspect of fable allows the boy to express impersonally the painful conflict, probably only too familiar to him, of having to hurt another to save yourself. In short, fable is an excellent form to put experience into and for making statements about that experience.

Parables can be read and written along with fables, as a similarly pointed story but without a *stated* moral. By treating both as specialized kinds of stories, the teacher can make clear that not *all* stories are to be read for their moral, an incorrect idea that many children now have. One reads different kinds of tales differently, according as they invite one to savor events for their

[5] Printed by *The New York Review of Books,* 1967. The following two pupil papers and one in Chapter 16 are reprinted from this booklet with the permission of Herbert Kohl. The Teachers' and Writers' Collaborative, of which Mr. Kohl is director, is putting together a complete curriculum unit on the fable. The unit will include a discussion of the fable form; a compilation of fables from various countries and cultures; a selection of children's fables; reports by teachers on the use of the fable in the classroom. Preliminary material can be obtained by writing to Teachers and Writers Collaborative, 249 Macy Annex, Teacher's College, Columbia University, New York, N.Y.

own sake or to distill conclusions from them. Fables and parables encourage readers to infer a generality — either a truth or an imperative — and to interpret symbolically, but this way of reading comes as an appropriate response to the purpose of the writing — often signalled by its form — not as an indiscriminate reaction to all stories.

General Ways of Stimulating Creativity

The secret of stimulating children to write inventions lies not in any one or two sorts of stimulants (many kinds will work well) but in the teacher's ability to capitalize on provocative forms and passing subjects, and to point out to children the writing possibilities in their improvisations and in their previous writings. This takes flexibility and alertness. It means that the kernels of story ideas are lying about everywhere and that once children are licensed to convert a sensory description to a short story by imagining an action in that setting, or to start making up something from the random meanings of rhyme words, or to transpose a "minimal situation" into a narrative, they will solve for themselves the problem of getting an idea. The teacher should be a storehouse of ideas — for transforming one piece of writing into another, for transposing an action, for converting body English to written English — that can pass into small groups and become part of the individual's thinking.

The only essential requirement is that the children be involved in the writing; otherwise all snappy ideas will fail. The children have the feelings; all they need are materials and forms, some stuff they can shape and project their feeling into, and some structures of language and literature that fix feelings "out there," impersonally before them. The teacher does not have to give these things to the class; it is enough to point them out, for materials and forms exist independently of schools and teachers. But the children have to be awash in good literature, imaginative writing that has art and wit and bite. They have to hear it, see it, read it, take off from it. A true commitment to letting children write will solve more problems than volumes of advice.

This is perhaps the place to plead for "creative writing" as a staple of learning, not as Friday afternoon fun or the luxury of lucky "advantaged" children who are mastering the "basics" on schedule. The testimony is ample from many hard-working teachers in urban ghettos that deprived children can learn "basics" only *after* they have become persuaded that the world of letters has something in it for them.[6] As *Programs for the Disadvantaged*[7]

[6] A lot of such testimony was given at the Huntting Conference of Writers and Teachers, June, 1966 (from Sonny Jameson, Elaine Avidon, Florence Howe, Ira Landess, and many others working in Manhattan "600" schools and other schools with seriously deprived or disturbed populations).

[7] Edited by Richard Corbin and Muriel Crosby (Champaign, Ill.: National Council of Teachers of English, 1965).

pointed out, the greatest formalization of instruction and the least self-expression occur in the urban schools, where children can learn the least from formalization and most need self-expression. *The "basics" for children are feelings and motives.* The more deprived he is, the more a child must deal with feelings *first* and objective, technical matters afterwards. A ghetto child needs more so-called "creative" writing, not less of it, because so little opportunity exists in his environment for learning how language can help him handle his feelings and manage his life. Once persuaded of its personal value for him, he will attack its technical aspects.

Chapter 16

Idea Writing

The emphasis of this section is on what is generally called essay and exposition. It includes practical writing and direct statement of ideas. But no effort is made to draw a sharp line between narrative and non-narrative, or utilitarian and imaginative. Of the four points of departure treated here, it is clear that at least two would sometimes lead students into imagined material and chronological writing.

Verbal Stimulus

The best stimulus is probably the spin-off from discussion and reading. The results are all sorts of explicit assertion of opinions, attitudes, wishes, and ideas that are neither fictional nor factual. Whether cast in prose or in poetry, they constitute what is really personal essay, though the appellation seems stuffy and certainly need not be used in class. When group concentration on a subject reaches a peak of intensity, and everyone has more to say, the teacher sends them to paper, where in a sense they continue the discussion in written monologue.

In Herbert Kohl's sixth-grade Harlem class, feelings were running high in discussion of their squalid neighborhood. He asked them to write about what they would do to change things. An eleven-year-old girl wrote:

> If I could change my block I would stand on Madison Ave and throw nothing but Teargas in it. I would have all the people I liked to get out of the block and then I would become very tall and have big hands and with my big hands I would take all of the narcartic people and pick them up with my hand and throw them in the nearest river and oceans. I would go to some of those old smart alic cops and throw them in the Ocians and Rivers too. I would let the people I like move into the projects so they could tell their friends that they live in a decent block. If I could do this you would never see 117th st again.

245

Sometimes a well chosen abstract word will evoke thought and feeling. Borrowing again from Sybil Marshall, one teacher gave her fifth-graders "wishing":

My Wish

I wish that I could ride around the world
On a big fat tiny fish.
He'd swish his tail and we would have to bail out all the hail.
The hail was heavy and not so light.
As a matter of fact it was a might bit light for the two of us.
We huffed and we puffed as we stuffed it off board.

We are in China now.
Look, look there are some indians having a pow wow.
Wow they must be cow corn pipes.

We are in India now.
I see a cow.
Bow wow brown cow.
Up in the air jumped my big fat tiny fish.
No come back wish fish come back.
It was only a dream —
Now isn't that mean?

Wishing

One doll, one book
That is wishing
A fire truck with a ladder & hook
That is wishing too.

Make a wish on a star
Way up afar
Don't feel blue
Make a wish too![1]

If the teacher makes up a topic, it should be open like this one, which gives the illusion of specifying but in fact leaves content to the child, or else one like Kohl's which merely gives a loose frame for a topic that has already in fact been shaped by class activity.

A strong possibility for involved idea writing is to take to paper a spirited but unresolved small-group discussion. The topic is whatever the unresolved issue is about and would hardly even need to be framed by the teacher. Such writing gives everyone a chance to rebut or get the last word. The main things to avoid are the "old chestnut" topic that invites cliché, and the loaded or narrow topic that dictates content or position. Ideally, the writing of

[1] Happy Hollow Elementary School, Wayland, Massachusetts.

opinions and personal views arises from the classroom drama of ideas and comes at moments of light and heat. Papers can be fed back into discussion by projecting and distributing them. Rather than thinking of a topic in advance and prescheduling it, teachers would do better to seize the moment when a topic does not have to be thought of: it is staring you in the face. This may happen on an individual basis as well, not always with a group. If a child has just lost a pet, let him write an epitaph for it (another idea from Sybil Marshall).

Diaries and Letters

The children are issued softcover notebooks and given five or ten minutes nearly every day to make entries in them. They write the date and anything else they want to put down — reminders, past events, thoughts, or ideas for stories. Such a diary is also a kind of writer's notebook, not a strict record of events. Emphasize personal freedom. The child does not even have to write anything at all on some days. He does not have to show his notebook to anyone.

A diary is a superficial structure into which a miscellany of things can be comfortably written. It is a daily habit, a period of meditation and self-collection. It is also a time to rehearse one's writing alone, just as small children learning to talk rehearse speech alone in their crib before falling off to sleep. It is relaxed practice. The pupils can make of it what they want — and what they make of it may continually change. But because they will write under the influence of present circumstances and in a particular state of mind, the entries will inevitably become in some sense a record. All the teacher does is open all the possibilities: "Put down things in the past or the future that you want to remember, ideas you don't want to slip away, feelings you want to express, whatever is on your mind or comes to mind that you want to put into words. Maybe you'll think of a good idea for a story, song, poem, or improvisation that you can use soon."

To whom is a diary written, and for what purpose? Many people who keep diaries on their own are writing to their future selves, or to an image of some ideal reader, or unconsciously to a real and meaningful figure in their life. The purpose may be practical but it is often just self-expression and fantasy communication for its own sake. It may often happen that a child will want someone else to see what he has written — to call the teacher over or show his notebook to another child. This should be permitted so long as he does not disturb the others. But especially, the option of writing a letter instead of an entry should be kept before the class. A child who feels on some day that he would rather write what he has to say to a friend or relative understands that he may do so. A stationery pad and envelopes might be kept in a "mail corner" along with a poster model of the heading, closing, and addressing of a letter, and perhaps even a mailbox and stamps to buy. The teacher is on call to help with mechanics if the pupil asks for help, but does not otherwise intervene or "check out" the letter.

Of course, for pupils who have done calendar keeping and letter writing before (Chapter 8), none of this will seem strange. They will be used to associating the two and to looking over their diaries and seeing how pieces of them might be summarized for someone in particular. Both kinds of writing — for oneself and for another individual — are personal and will be best fostered by setting aside time in an atmosphere of personal freedom. Assigning impersonal courtesy letters, stressing proper form and etiquette, makes of letter writing just the sort of onerous duty that makes so many adults say, "Oh, I just hate to write letters." If letter writing is kept a matter of self-expression, more children, I'm sure, will write them. Since the diary contains plans and practical reminders, it may often suggest to children the need to write a "business" letter to order something, ask about something, and so on. Instead of always beating the children to the jump, and teaching a unit on business letters, it would be much better to have them ask the teacher for advice as a real need for help arises. And who knows? Some may even *want* to thank the firemen for the nice visit.

Writing up Show-and-Tell

As I suggested in Chapter 4, show-and-tell can take several directions — toward narration, information, explanation, or personal essay. It should continue indefinitely. There is nothing inherently childish about it; the pupil before his group is doing essentially the same thing an appliance salesman or science demonstrator does. But teachers would do well to give it a new name when referring to it in grades four to six.

Emphasis should be on showing objects to which long histories, deep personal involvement, or complicated explanations are attached. Since the period of ages nine to eleven is when crafts, hobbies, collections, and sports get under way, these should be capitalized on as much as possible for explanations of construction, operation, and procedure. The object itself becomes merely a prop, a conversation piece, a pump-primer, as children become capable of ranging far beyond it. The reason for continuing to hold these sessions in small groups is to enable more pupils to hold forth in a given amount of time and also to stimulate more questions and interaction than is likely to occur when one person speaks before an entire class. The size of groups might be enlarged, however, to nine or ten, clustered in three parts of the room, to provide a larger audience. The teacher moves from group to group. It may be necessary to separate boys and girls sometimes if an object is of no interest to one sex. Actually, since the practice in explaining something to an outgroup is very valuable, non-segregation is preferable, if it works.

After sessions in which all members of the small groups have spoken about and answered questions on the items they brought in, allow them time to write up what they said as influenced by feedback. This need not occur every time, but perhaps only when the session is specialized in the direction of, say, explanation — "Bring in something of which the purpose, use, care, or operation can be explained" — since the memory assignments allow for writing reminiscence. Having rehearsed while talking, and having received from their audience an idea of how to explain some things better and what emphasis might be most interesting, pupils should be ready to write. The personal choice of the item should ensure motivation. Announcing the intention of printing the papers would add interest. These booklets might be specialized according to how the show-and-tell assignment was stated ("How to Operate . . ." or "How to Play . . .").

Writing Directions

Giving directions is an excellent way to engage with some of the general problems of verbal communication. The natural egocentricity that causes us to assume information and viewpoints that our listener does not have is revealed to us when directions misfire. And because directions are translatable into action, there is little chance of miscommunication remaining unnoticed as it so often does in other kinds of speaking and writing, where sender and receiver may think they understand the words in the same way when in fact they do not. Far more than is commonly recognized, egocentricity is a central source of writing problems — from punctuation and phrasing to paragraphing and overall organization. Just as we know how our written sentences should be spoken, we know in what sense they are to be taken, forgetting that the reader does not. Developmentally, egocentricity decreases with age, but it is clear that the problem is lifelong. The solution is more awareness, and awareness can come only through feedback from other people. (Looking over one's own writing after a lapse of time, much like an outsider, one often catches his own egocentricities.) So while gaining experience in a practical kind of discourse, pupils writing directions can begin to de-center (allow for the receiver) in ways that will help them in all of their communication.

ORAL DIRECTIONS WITH PUZZLES

To reap the most benefits from the assignment, the children need to know what happens when others attempt to follow their directions. Furthermore, translating words into action will make the assignment more fun. As a game, the directions can at first be oral. The class breaks into groups of six to eight, who cluster around two children seated back to back, one of whom is sender and one of whom is receiver. The sender has before him a few pieces of a very simple puzzle that when assembled forms a familiar shape. His pieces are in fact assembled already, and his job is to talk his partner through an assembly of an identical puzzle, the pieces of which are scattered before the receiver on his desk. The point of not letting the two see each other is to enforce a total reliance on words. In such situations children will still try to express directions egocentrically, by gesturing, even though they should know that their receiver cannot see their signals.

For the first time or two, the communication is restricted to one-way talk, in a pretense, for example, that one is a boss giving a worker directions over a one-way intercom; then the "worker" is finally allowed to ask questions. Withholding two-way conversation for a while demonstrates its great advantage, which is the receiver's feedback in the form of questions of clarification and requests for omitted information. The onlookers of the group are told that kibbitzing spoils the game and that they should watch silently so that they can observe the causes of miscommunication and try to avoid these mistakes when their turns come to give directions. Depending on the difficulty of the puzzle, a number of children may have to act as sender before the receiver can assemble it successfully. Sets of puzzles are exchanged and children rotate roles.

The puzzles will probably have to be made in school in order to have simple shapes of few pieces in identical sets. Cutting the figures into common geometrical shapes is a variation that enables children to put into play the vocabulary of geometry. Odd shapes, on the other hand, stretch the imagination for ways of describing. When I tried out this game once in a fifth-grade class, I used the "Fractured T,"[2] a large block-letter T cut into five irregular pieces, and found that it was a bit more difficult for beginners than is desirable. Although the game can be set up so that each sender expects to be replaced in mid-game by another, still there should be progress across different senders and not too much frustration.

A graded difficulty in puzzles can be achieved by gradually increasing the number of pieces (starting with three) and by making the component shapes harder to describe and to position. The point of having the completed puzzle form a familiar figure is that, if he thinks of doing so, the sender may state at the outset: "We're going to put the pieces together so that they look like a house." Omission of this general framework can create the same communication problems here that it can in a piece of written exposition, since in either case the receiver lacks context for relating particulars to each other.

ORAL DIRECTIONS WITH OTHER MATERIALS

After children have become aware of at least some of the factors that make for success and failure in the game, variations are introduced. The goal is still to match senders' and receivers' materials by means of verbal directions, but, to vary and generalize the communication issues, puzzles are replaced by other things. One child who has learned how to do some Origami crea-

[2] Obtainable from Advanced Seminars, 1725 Beverly Boulevard, Los Angeles, California.

tions (paper-folding) talks another child, or perhaps his group, through the procedure. They can compare the success the sender has with his directions when he is speaking from memory with his success when he is folding as he speaks (sender and receiver are still back to back). Or: the sender looks at an abstract picture composed especially for this purpose and tells his receiver how to draw it. The children themselves might bring or suggest other materials to use. A variation in the game situation is to let one child give directions to the whole class. But all pupils should have plenty of opportunity to watch the process also, for onlookers get good insights from observing, simultaneously, what the sender intended and how the receiver took the message.

WRITING DIRECTIONS FOR HOW TO MAKE AND DO THINGS

Some direction-giving once a month for these three years should lead to marked improvement in thinking and communicating, but at some point directions are shifted from speech to paper. Each child thinks of something he knows how to make from common materials, writes the directions as clearly as he can, and exchanges with another pupil. They all follow out the directions as homework, and bring to school what they have made. Any problems or uncertainties about the directions are noted down on the paper, which is returned to the author. This assignment could include cooking recipes, an issue in that case being whether to list ingredients separately or just to mention each as it comes up. Quantities and measurements will of course enter into many manufacturing directions.

A secondary general benefit is that children learn from each other how to make things. Revised after feedback, these papers could be printed together in a classbook called, "How to Make . . ." Or children can take turns inventing a board or a card game for their group to play, and then observe them playing it. They would make the materials and write the goal, procedure, and rules. An interesting feature of this assignment is the unforeseen situations for which the directions do not allow. Revised, these directions could be affixed to the game, and the games exchanged and taken home. Generally, it is important that a direction writer either get back written comments or have a chance to talk with whoever excuted the directions; sometimes both would be in order.

WRITING TRAVELING DIRECTIONS

Traveling directions constitute one of the best assignments but are difficult in practice to carry out because children would have to go after school to unfamiliar places. The assignment is simply to write directions for getting from the school to one's own house, or from one part of town to another. Maps are not allowed in this case, because, we'll pretend, the directions are coming over telegraph or will be read over the phone. In small towns, perhaps, where distances are small and buses not used, children might exchange directions and go to each other's houses. Directions for getting around the school plant would be the next best possibility.

Some directions should be projected and discussed. I sat in once on a fifth-grade discussion of home directions that was very lively and interesting. In every paper there were some directions the class felt sure it could not follow. For example, "then turn up Linden Street" indicated only a turn, not the direction of the turn, since *up* expressed nothing but the writer's subjective mental picture of aiming himself where he wanted to go (this kind of egocentricity is equivalent to the puzzle-director's saying, "Now pick up the next piece," or "Put the funny-looking piece against it." Since the children frequently did not know the names of streets, locations were often identified by ambiguous descriptions that more accurate word choice or better vocabulary would have cleared up. "Store," for example, could have been one of several retail places, but there was only one supermarket on the street. Since improving directions often requires replacing some words by others, this is another important place to work on vocabulary. Then, later in the discussion, a paper referred to the Western Building, at which point it occurred to some of the children that only someone familiar with the town would know that landmark. Who were these directions written for anyway? Suppose a stranger had to follow them. So they themselves brought up the issue of adapting directions to different receivers.

At this point the teacher should ask them to look at their papers, check for directions that a stranger would not understand, and change them so that he would. For another occasion a story situation based on the problem could be imagined: an out-of-town visitor is staying over night at such and such hotel, and the next day he is coming out to the school to show a film. What directions should the principal give him when he telephones him that evening? Will he be walking or driving? These directions are read and discussed in small groups.

A final suggestion is that pupils write directions for getting from one place on a map to another, revealing the starting point but not the destination. The object is to see if classmates wind up at the place the writer had in mind by tracing a route on the map according to his directions.

Unrecommended Writing

This is the place to indicate exclusions. One cannot take a stand on curriculum without negative as well as positive recommendations. Besides doing damage, some kinds of assignments simply take up time that would be much better spent doing other things. In judging whether a writing assignment is worthy, I ask these questions. (The sense of "writing" here is "composition," of course, not "transcription.")

CRITERIA FOR JUDGING A WRITING ASSIGNMENT

1. Is it given for punitive reasons? (There are teachers today who still make children "write an essay on _____" as punishment for inattention, failure to follow directions, etc.) If we wish to kill writing, setting up such negative associations is a splendid way to do it.

2. Is it given essentially as a check to prove that something was read? I have in mind here such tasks as reporting on a book or paraphrasing reference books.

3. Is motivation intrinsic to the kind of writing assigned?

4. Does it have, at least potentially, an authentic audience besides the teacher?

5. Does it require cognitive abilities too advanced for the age?

6. Is it given mainly as a vehicle for teaching something extraneous to itself?

It takes honesty to answer these questions, especially since tradition has heavily rationalized some deeply entrenched assignments. Applying the criteria above to certain conventional assignments, I can only recommend that they be dropped.

BOOK REPORTS

Perhaps the most common kind of writing done in most elementary schools today — and the most time-consuming — is reporting on books one has read. This takes two forms, the "book report" on individually read works and the social studies, geography, or science paper comprised of information pieced together from reference books. I realize that some teachers have tried to make both assignments more meaningful by asking the children to put more of themselves into them. But if the children's interpretations or views are wanted, then papers of thought and reactions should be assigned, and the copying aspect eliminated. Both assignments are severely faulted by the criteria.

It seems clear that the book report is designed as a check on what children have read. It is a nervous by-product of individual reading programs. Jacket blurbs, plot summary, and bland endorsement of the book are about all I have ever seen in these reports. The exceptions, the occasional sentences of personal response or assessment, did not make the whole assignment worthwhile and in any case are, when written, unnecessary and unmotivated. Sharing and discussing responses to books in small groups would serve the purpose much better. Children do not like book reports (except as a way of getting good marks), and indeed what motive or audience could there be for them at this age? I interpret book reports as partly a false effort to give children some writing practice and partly as one of many artificial tasks that are generated out of school routine, for the teacher's benefit, having virtually nothing to do with learning.

REFERENCE PAPERS

In some ways, reference papers are even worse. Although book reports encourage some copying and paraphrasing, the task of collating information from encyclopedias, newspapers, magazines, and other sources openly invites plagiarism. Quoting and citing references looks scholarly, but most children just hastily paraphrase, and in any case they are hardly writing in any real sense. We all know that the point of the assignments is to get children to read about a certain subject. It is just this abuse of writing that I deplore. If this is the only way that children will read about science, people, current events, and foreign lands, then something is seriously wrong with the whole approach to these subjects, and no deforming of the writing process will solve the problem.

Children should not be allowed to think that such inauthentic discourse is writing. At the very best, they are lightly summarizing and editing other writers' passages, a subsidiary researcher's skill that does not belong in elementary school. The assignment, furthermore, has no purpose to the child and no audience but the teacher. Since there is practically no composing involved, and since the content is information straight from the horse's mouth, all a teacher can do with such a paper is close in on the mechanics and presentation. It does not teach, it tests, and I do not think that writing should be used to test. Because the assignment is boring and meaningless, many children resent both the reading and the writing. There are better ways to stimulate children to read, and to let them use what they have read. Informational reading should not deadend in a chore for the teacher; it should feed into small groups where it can be exchanged, recalled, thought about, and extrapolated. Writing comes out of these discussions, as interpretive issues arise from the facts. When children demand evidence from each other, books are referred to and further consulted.

LITERARY ANALYSIS

There are other kinds of writing about reading that also break good teaching principles. These fall under the heading of literary analysis or criticism. A sample assignment I have seen given will illustrate.

Some fifth-grade children were asked to compare, in a single paragraph, a poem and a short story that handled the same theme in somewhat different ways. To the teacher this probably seemed like a sophisticated assignment that would prepare for many similar assignments to come in later years. But sensing, correctly, that the task would be cognitively difficult and would require guidance, she directed them to cover, in this one paragraph, eight points of comparison. This in effect furnished the organization and dictated what virtually every sentence should be about.

First of all, the over-structuring was a give-away that the assignment was too advanced. If children have to have that much guidance they should not be asked to do such a thing. Second, since she had previously emphasized that a paragraph was about one thing, she confused the children by asking them to put eight things in one paragraph, the problem here being both in the original attempt to define a paragraph, like a sentence, as "one idea," and in the unnecessary injunction to make one paragraph contain all they had to say. Third, for children such an assignment has no point or purpose. They have already appreciated and responded to the poem and story. However the teacher may conceive the task, the children can only see the paper as a kind of test. Far from increasing appreciation, such unpleasant after-chores drive children away from literature. Fourth, it is not the mission of schools to teach for its own sake literacy criticism and analysis, which is a college specialty. No evidence supports the strong current belief that direct and explicit critical analysis aids comprehension and appreciation. Much more likely is that it interferes with response, which is the main goal of schools. Response can be deepened and sharpened by small-group discussion based on native reactions and touching on literary technique as it becomes a natural issue (and it will, because content is partly a factor of form). What schools should do is develop intuitions, through authentic writing and through discussion, so that children do not *need* vivisections and postmortems in order to understand and respond to literature.

_____

_____

_____

Chapter 17

Playing Games of Language and Logic

For some children of this age certain word and sentence games described in Chapter 10 will still be appropriate. The sentence-building game especially, on p. 155, would remain very valuable for grades 4–6 and is strongly recommended.

Chess

Chess is the appropriate game to follow up the playing of checkers suggested in Chapter 10. The purposes are the same as stated there.

Card Games

The following recommendations take off directly from the earlier discussion of card games in Chapter 10. One direction of further development mentioned there still applies at this age and would apply indefinitely. This is that decks can be made to match maturation by increasing the abstractness of concepts, the unfamiliarity of class designations, and the fineness of subclasses. The taxonomy of biology will provide an example of this development as well as a fitting content for decks at this age.

EXAMPLE OF CLASSIFICATION CARD GAMES

What can be taught of biology through print — that does not require laboratory work and observation — is essentially its system of classification, which reaches upwards into such abstract things as classes of vertebrates and downwards into discriminations among species of canines. It also introduces new designations, such as *arachnids* and *crustaceans,* that subsume the familiar spiders and lobsters according to scientific criterial attributes that are not always obvious. Part of the learning problem is to conceive spiders and lobsters as similar enough to be lumped together as arthropods and as different enough to part company into arachnids and crustaceans. The other part of the problem is not conceptual, but informative: before you can place a spider in the class of arachnids you have to know whether he has the four sets of jointed legs, the sac or breathing tube, and the segmented exoskeleton that qualify him for membership. Of course, students can memorize the fact that spiders, scorpions, and mites are all arachnids, but the true test of having learned a class concept is to be able to identify new instances of it.

Given these two basic problems, and keeping in mind that these problems apply to any concept learning, not just to biology, let us look at how special card games might help children develop their abstractive powers and learn a new content at the same time. The general strategy is to work a limited range of the biological scale at a time, moving gradually upward and downward from a familiar zone somewhere in the middle and gradually integrating these ranges into a full knowledge structure, depending on how much of the ground it seems wise to try to cover. At any rate, a number of decks would be introduced over several years. Individual children could progress at their own rates by staying with one deck as long as they needed to before moving to another. The teacher would pair or group children according to this need. The decks do not now exist, of course, but would be produced by educational publishers if teachers asked for them. Since a lot of the information needed for classifying plants and animals would be contained in the pictures on the cards, the illustrations would have to be of the highest accuracy and quality.

Form of the first decks. The simplest game would, as in grades K–3, consist of making "books" of members of a category. But the category might be at any level — class, order, family, genus, or species. For example, one deck could comprise the phylum *arthropods* and be called the arthropod deck. The cards would picture members of the crustacean, arachnid, insect, and myriapod classes but would not name the class to which each creature belonged, because pupils would then rely on memory rather than deduction. Instead, above the picture would appear *spider* or *centipede* and below it would appear a brief notation of the one or two criterial attributes that might not be visible in the illustration of the creature in its natural habitat, as, for example, certain behaviors or internal structures. Accompanying the deck would be a small placard bearing four columns — the name of each family and a short list of its criterial attributes without examples. The name and attributes establish the class concepts against which players match individual cards in their minds. The placard is presented and explained along with directions for the game and may be referred to during the game.

How to play with the first decks. Thus, playing is a matter of identifying instances (cards) of the four classes by recognizing such distinguishing criterial attributes as number of legs and presence of sacs or gills, and of grouping cards to form books. The main effect is to substitute biological classes for the conventional card suits. Whereas clubs, hearts, diamonds, and spades are arbitrary and have identical instances (the same symbol on all cards of one suit), crustaceans, arachnids, insects, and myriapods are actual substantive categories containing not identical but merely similar instances. The difference is that players have to *recognize* suits before they can play them. Of course, after playing with the arthropod deck once or twice, the children will have learned the "suits" and can play the game as ordinarily, without recognition being a problem.

Sometime after this point — and pacing is both an individual and an experimental matter — those players could start a new deck on arthropods, played exactly the same way but with all fresh instances of the four families. They do not have to learn new class concepts and attributes but would merely be identifying further instances. Since the number of exemplary creatures will be small for some classifications and very large for others, the deck could reflect this disproportion by containing more cards for some classifications than for others. Scoring could allow for this by crediting more points to the books for the scarcer classification, thus introducing some option in game strategy. And not all subdivisions of a category need to be included merely for the sake of systematic thoroughness, since many of the less familiar ones are definable in very technical ways.

Later decks. The next deck could go up or down, that is, could treat arthropods itself as one phylum among several others or treat the various orders of insects as a further subdivision of arthropods. Which vertical way to move is not something I want to predict without experimentation. It may well be that direction makes no difference in the eventual integration of a hierarchy. At any rate, if the next deck is based on a group of phyla, arthropods will be defined on the placard by their explicit criterial attributes, which will replace the implicit attributes pupils inferred for them in the arthropod deck. Also, since the instances of arthropods in this deck will range indiscriminately over all four of its classes, the pupils are focused on the similarities rather than on the differences among them, and can learn how a member of a given class is automatically a member of any superclass that includes the given class (an ant being not only an insect but also an arthropod).

If the next decks, on the other hand, treat the subdivisions among arachnids, crustaceans, myriapods, and insects, then the differences among arthropods are brought out while focusing on the similarities within each of the four classes, and an ant is seen not only as a member of arthropods and insects but also of the order *hymenoptera* as well. This logical principle of multiple membership in successively included classes is difficult for children to grasp because of its relativity: whether one calls the ant an arthropod, insect, or hymenopteran depends on the level of abstraction at which one is making distinctions.

GAMES THAT COMBINE CLASSIFICATION WITH SERIAL ORDERING

Somewhere during these years, the classifying aspect of card games should be combined with the aspect of serial ordering. That is, just as conventional decks have numbers as well as suits, special school decks could have, to push further the suggestion on page 158, both categorical and serial elements. In poker, for example, players have the option of trying for a straight — four, five, six, seven, eight — or for a flush — all clubs, all diamonds, etc. A more difficult possibility is a straight flush — four, five, six, seven, eight of one suit. Because it entails thinking along two dimensions at once, and estimating one's chances each way, playing poker itself would be a good exercise of mental powers. Some experience with it would also prepare for more meaningful games based on its principles. (I can see the newspaper leads now — Fifth-Graders Playing Poker in School. The moral concern of parents could be allayed, however, by explaining that poker playing will prepare their children for college. Failing this, change the name of the game.)

What might these more meaningful games, based on poker, be like? To answer this, let me say that there is a special and very valuable way to construe the notion of "more than" or "higher than" that underlies serial ordering. This is the idea of class inclusion itself. Thus successively broader classes, whose members logically include the members of subclasses, constitute a serial order to replace mere numerical succession. In this way, the categorical and serial dimensions of card playing, which are arbitrary in conventional games, would become organically related under the logic of classes and class relations.

To use the taxonomy of biology again as an illustration, the cards in the school decks might each contain a labeled picture of an animal and a smaller insert in one corner with the name of a phylum, class, order, family, genus, or species. The animals would be chosen from all levels of, say, the vertebrate scale. Dealt a hand of five cards, a player may either try for a straight, by lining up insert names so as to get a succession, or try for a flush by assembling five animals of one kind. But since "kinds" could themselves be of any level of classification — five mammals or five canines — the scoring would have to credit more points to flushes of the lower levels (canines), for which there would be fewer instances, than to those of higher levels (mammals), for which there are increasingly more instances the higher the level of classification.

This further option about which level of classification to try for would reinforce the principle of all logical hierarchies — that larger classes comprise the combined memberships of their subclasses. In deciding whether to play a wolf as a mammal or a canine, the pupil confronts the very issue mentioned above of classifying the same item variously according to the level at which the classifier wishes to make distinctions. This game presupposes, of course, that students have already learned the class concepts from playing with previous decks of the sort described before.

I am aware that designing such card games raises a host of technical problems — calculating game probabilities, selecting biologically sound material, and determining the order of difficulty befitting children's ability. The games would have to be developed by teams of mathematicians, teachers, and subject-matter specialists. I should emphasize that biology is only an example. All I wish to do here is suggest what I feel to be the enormous and untapped potentiality that card games based on the logic of classes have for developing abstractive ability, deepening concepts, and enlarging vocabulary. The subject matter is secondary, but such games offer an unusual opportunity both to present a particular content and to foster a general cognitive capacity that is critical for the language arts. Actually, something like the hierarchy of class inclusions would be better taught as a thought process if the content changed, so that it was embodied one time in the evolutionary scale and another time in something else.

GAMES FOSTERING ORIGINAL CONCEPT FORMATION

Some card games, however, should invite free and original categorizing. The games above would help a student *attain* concepts established by convention. But the taxonomy of biology has changed considerably over the years, and the classifications of some plants and animals is still very controversial. The issue, there and elsewhere, concerns which of the many attributes of a thing shall be deemed criterial for the classification. Color, shape, structure, function, behavior, are only a few possible kinds of criteria. The increasing ability to categorize an item in different ways, to create fresh categories, and to make explicit one's hidden categories is a major dimension of mental and verbal growth.

Though limited of course to pictorial things, a deck of very mixed and unlabeled pictures has one advantage that characterizes all card games — a random hand. (Such a deck can be made from cutouts by the pupils.) Let us say that four children are dealt a meaningless mixture of three cards each. The rules say to think of some way in which the three items pictured are all alike — any way at all. Some categories might in fact have to be "mineral" or "man-made" or "can't be seen through" or "has moving parts." But the object of the game is to tailor the category as specifically to the three items as possible. This is done, first, by allowing eight or ten rounds of drawing and discarding during which the players attempt to narrow down their hand so that others would have the most difficulty playing on it. Each time they draw, they try to replace one of their three previous cards by one that will permit a more specific category. After the eight or ten rounds, they place their hands down and declare their category. The rest of the game, in effect, is spent determining who has the narrowest or most specific category by drawing from the rest of the deck and trying to add cards to the others' hands according to the categories they declared. (Cards they cannot place are simply laid aside.) When the deck is used up, the player whose tabled hand is smallest — whose category is most specific — wins. The idea is that the rules should cause pupils to create original categories and to classify the same items in different ways.

GAMES FOR DEDUCTIVE REASONING

Wiff 'n Proof. Especially developed for elementary children at a Yale project supported by Carnegie Corporation, *Wiff 'n Proof: The Game of Modern Logic* (Layman E. Allen, Box 71, New Haven, Conn.) is a kit of 21 graduated games intended to "encourage a favorable attitude towards symbol-manipulating activities in general, and, incidentally, to teach something about mathematical logic and provide practice in abstract thinking." Players learn how to "recognize 'well formulated formulas' (Wiff's) and how to construct proofs of theorems in propositional calculus."[1] Essentially, these games further the growth of logical analysis and deduction of the sort one needs in order to draw correct conclusions from complicated verbal problems. I strongly recommend trial of this kit because it provides the possibility of joining mathematics and English.

Guessing games with cards, similar to the experiments described in *A Study of Thinking*, could help teach thinking strategies involving the logic of combinatorial possibilities (the deductive process of elimination). Although psychologists seem to agree that this kind of logic comes into use among children only around the age of twelve, I include it in grades four to six, because that is where these games might begin. They might, of course, have to be deferred to junior high school.

If someone points to a pen and says, "That's an example of what I have in mind," we do not know whether he means writing instruments, metal objects, a shade of blue, careless mislaying of items, or any number of other things. If he continues to point out instances, or if we ask him whether various other objects are instances, we can gradually figure out the concept he has in mind. This kind of inferring goes on all the time as people learn individual and cultural concepts by isolating out those attributes of an object or a situation that are criterial for the concept. The strategies we use may be more or less systematic or random, cautious or hasty. The kind of games that could embody the deductive process and give play to its various strategies might go as follows.

[1] Introduction, pp. 1 and 5 respectively.

Conjunctive categories. One such game is based on what is called "conjunctive" categories, which are defined by the conjunction of two or more traits, as in the concept of "brave man" (both courageousness and maleness are required to fulfill the concept). Each card in the deck bears several attributes — color, shape, and figure — but all cards are different as to the combination of attributes. One player makes up a conjunctive category, which he does not reveal to the other, by combining two or three attributes — say the color blue and a circle. He places face up a card containing these attributes along with another. His partner holds the rest of the deck and chooses from it whichever card he thinks will yield the most information about the category when presented to the first player for him to identify as a positive or negative instance. The guesser may present cards containing the combination of symbols he thinks his partner has in mind, or try out blue in all combinations, circle in all combinations, and so on.

The game is a series of trials, and the object is to deduce the category in as few trials as possible. The number of trials can be reduced by noting what the initial card contained and what combinations are progressively eliminated. At the end, partners reverse roles. High-risk guesses may lead to quick victory, but if unsuccessful will take longer than a conservative, systematic varying of one attribute at a time, the latter being a logical procedure for checking out and keeping track of the various combinatorial possibilities.

Disjunctive categories. A similar game is based on disjunctive categories, which are defined by the presence of *either* one *or* another attribute. "Congressman" is a disjunctive category, since a member of Congress need only be either a senator or a representative, not both. The player is directed to make up such a category (*either* blue *or* circular) and to place down a positive instance of it. The partner proceeds as before, but the strategies are different now. Because of the strictness of conjunctive classes, negative instances generally yield more information than positive ones. For example, if blue appears in a card presented during a conjunctive game, and the maker of the category says it is not an instance, the guesser still does not know, from that instance alone, whether blue is a criterial attribute or not, for the card would be positive only if the other criterial attribute(s) also appeared on it. But if the categorizer says "no" to a card presented in a disjunctive game, all the attributes on that card are immediately ruled out, since by the definition of "disjunctive" the appearance of a single attribute is enough to make the card a positive instance.

I think it very likely that the learning of these strategies would proceed best if at some point the games were surrounded by small-group discussion. That is, each pair of players would have two or three observers who would join with them afterwards in discussing the strategy the guesser used and comparing it with alternatives.

Of course, most human categories are not nearly so clear-cut as those put together from colors and abstract shapes. Once pupils have practiced various strategies with such decks, however, they might transfer the strategies to decks with more human content. In any case, however fuzzy our everyday concepts, the logical processes by which we form and manipulate them are the same as those embodied in the games just described.

Chapter 18

_____

_____

_____

Review and Preview

What has been accomplished so far in this curriculum, and how will this work be followed out in later years?

Establishment of Learning Processes

Of most importance are the *ways* in which children have begun to learn how to produce and receive language. These ways are: dramatic play and interplay, small-group discussion, writing for real purposes and audiences, and actively responding to both books and the writing of other pupils. Underlying all of these has been group process — receiving and giving feedback, using language and finding out the results, responding to responses and thereby sharpening the responses. Learning through group process will not only continue into college — in the very ways established in elementary school — but will continue throughout the learners' lives, for it is the main means of "adult education." This process will have engaged the child with language by letting him learn about it through sociality. At the same time that the ultimately social origin and function of language has been stressed, an attitude of independence and initiative has been fostered, for children have taken over their own education and learned how to learn from each other.

The best way, perhaps, to look backward and forward a little more specifically is to take one at a time the main activities that are the goals of the curriculum.

Thinking

Being the most universal sort of learning, thinking has developed through all the activities.

Dramatic work and discussion have developed fluency of thought through the reciprocal prompting of one child by another. The mind was thus stimulated, and pupils became accustomed to thinking on their feet without inner blockage; then they could think more fluently when alone. They attended to stimuli and produced ideas in response. The idea may have been embodied in a movement or in speech. In discussion, furthermore, each child has sharpened concepts and definitions, enlarged his store of points of view, developed and examined ideas, and participated in the particular cognitive act of summarizing. The key to thought development in oral speech was *expatiation,* collectively building ideas, and improvisation and discussion have given children this key.

The composition program has developed thought in two general ways. In the recognition that fantasying is thinking — and an especially important form of thinking for children — the program provided points of departure for inventive writing in which children could classify experience and syllogize about it through concrete figments. In poems and stories, children have symbolized implicitly those unthought thoughts that they are not ready to name and state explicitly. Also, in constructing their fictions, they have been recombining things in novel ways, which is the basis of thinking, whatever the things may be.

In fact, the view that composing is a conceptual act has been at the heart of the writing assignments. In recording and recalling on paper, the pupils have been merely externalizing natural inner processes that go on in them all the time. The selecting and summarizing of experience is fundamental to all abstracting, and determines the categories and generalizations the learner will create. Sensory and memory writing have provided the pupil a way to become aware of his own abstracting and a way to develop *choice* in how he will further abstract these lower abstractions. Feedback from peers, furthermore, allowed him to discover the egocentricity of his thinking, the hidden assumptions and points of view. One of the main contributions of cross-commentary in the writing workshop will have been the diminishing of egocentricity. In this respect particularly, the practice in giving directions has played a large role in the growth of thought.

Playing checkers, cards, and other games has nourished logic. The decisions necessary to play these come from figuring out possibilities, syllogizing, and predicting. Card games in particular have given practice in classifying and in concept formation. In objective and explicit fashion, the pupil has ranged concepts hierarchically and grasped class inclusion.

During the following years of schooling, the expatiation process will be further exploited for the growth of thought. Some dramatic improvisations will become topic-centered and veer toward discussion, which will evolve into improvised panels witnessed by a reacting audience. The dialectic element of dialogue will be more strongly emphasized. More of this dialogue will be continued on paper, some of it in the form of "socratic dialogue," some in the form of essay. The large experience with collective thinking will make possible both more fluent and more profound solo thinking.

Though the composition program will invite more explicit statement of ideas — the formulating of generalizations and finally of theories — it will continue to the end to allow substantial room for fictionalizing, so that concrete "story thinking" will continue to evolve alongside idea statement. The abstracting of raw experience is continued into higher-level kinds of writing, as described below, and remains the core of the composition program. In fact, one general sequence of assignments is based on the progressive abstracting of first-hand, then second-hand, material.

Card-playing continues into junior high school, but no new aspects of it are unfolded in this book because it is still too unexplored.

Throughout all the later years, discussion and composition converge directly on certain problems of thinking. One of these is the supporting of ideas with evidence of various sorts, factual and logical. A second is the qualification of ideas through the emendation of single statements. A third is the creation of syllogisms — combining given statements so as to derive new ones. These three conceptual matters become major issues in discussion and also come under special focus in certain writing assignments. Personal concepts and generalizations, private ways of classifying experience, are well scrutinized in other writing assignments for which they are the basis. Breaking through the limitations of egocentricity continues both in topic-centered discussion and in the cross-commentary on the writing, unchanged from elementary school except as the greater maturity of the students naturally raises the level of sophistication.

Speaking and Listening

The thrust of dramatic work and small-group discussion was toward effective interaction. Attending closely to the speech of others and responding relevantly to it were made basic to topic-centered talk and were naturally practiced in dramatic activities. The foundation for conversation was laid in early social play, where interacting began, and was built upon in dramatization and improvisation, where the action of one actor was cued by the action of another. Conversing and making up dialogue, *in small groups,* gave each child plenty of opportunity to produce speech, develop expressiveness, and benefit from specific reactions. Collaborating on projects, commenting on each other's writing, and monologuing for show-and-tell also provided constant oral practice.

The principle of learning to listen was that the listening should have a purpose and be acted upon by the listener. Thus scribes listened in order to take notes for later use. The literacy programs I have recommended had pupils speak, write, and build words with the sounds presented to them. Pupils took dictation from the teacher and from other children or recorded overheard conversations. The recording of non-human sounds helped train auditory attention and was also purposive. Listening, in short, was conceived not as a passive activity focused on in isolated exercises but as a preliminary to some action the learner was to take. It was thus interwoven with a variety of language activities.

For vocal expression, dramatic work was the main instrument of learning. For clarity and precision of speech, small-group discussion was the instrument. In dramatizing, role playing, and oral reading, the pupil adopted the language of others and thus enlarged his vocal repertory. Improvisation limbered his tongue and his native wit. He learned to say what he meant by trying to say it in discussion and in direction-giving, being misunderstood, and then restating his ideas under the influence of feedback. Show-and-tell monologuing allowed him to sustain speech, to begin to grapple with sequence and continuity, and to become aware of the needs of an audience.

In none of these activities was the child told how to speak, nor was he ever asked to deliver a prepared speech. Musicality, force, dynamics, volume, and even enunciation were considered factors of feeling and involvement that develop best in speaking situations that release feeling and tie into real motives. Thus dramatic work and spontaneous talk took the place of elocution lessons and declamation.

During junior high, two important shifts take place in dramatic work. The acting acquires an audience, first in a drama workshop, where small groups watch each other and give reactions, then in performance occasionally before students of other classes. In the workshop, spectators rotate with actors and feed back to each other as in the writing cross-commentary. Second, improvising is taken to paper. In fact, drama work becomes a critical means of introducing some of the new writing assignments. After improvising dialogues and external and internal monologues, students write the corresponding sorts of scripts — scenes, dramatic monologues, soliloquies, and short plays.

Enactment and improvisation continue throughout secondary school, providing the chief means of approaching dramatic literature of all types, not just plays but also many poems and short stories when they consist mostly of character voices. In senior high especially, a considerable number of poems are dramatized and performed, adding to students' spontaneous speech the enriched language of literature. Both professional and students' scripts are memorized and performed. Near the end of the program, a method called Chamber Theatre is introduced, whereby the narrator's role in fiction is acted and his relationship to his characters thus dramatized.

The "minimal situations" for improvising become more specialized so that emphasis can be deliberately placed on topical ideas, a borrowed situation, a situation in a literary work as yet unassigned, or original invention. Improvisation culminates in the freest, most "minimal" situation of all — an assignment to achieve a certain effect on a fellow actor when nothing else at all is specified. Far from being a terminal activity at the end of elementary school, dramatic work remains a major means of comprehending and appreciating, in addition to pursuing oral fluency and expression.

Small-group discussion, too, acquires an audience and hence a source of feedback from beyond the participants. While continuing to the end as staple activity in itself, it also evolves into panels. The panelists' talk is still unplanned, but the audience reaction adds to the activity the qualities of a workshop, wherein both the speakers' ideas and their interactions receive commentary. At the same time, in junior high, discussion and improvisation meet in the form of mock panels, for which students play roles — that is, pretend to be certain people or kinds of people engaged in turning over an issue.

As a process, small-group discussion changes little, or at any rate I have left these changes open for lack of knowledge. Increasingly, however, reading and writing provide subjects as students become able to pursue farther afield various points of content and technique drawn from these texts.

Constant practice and good interaction continue to be the best teachers of speaking and listening. Upper-level teachers will try to induce more awareness in their older students than was attempted before of the "group dynamics" factors operating to make and break communication. Whereas elementary pupils were not ready for much of this, the greater introspective tendency of adolescence affords a better occasion. But how much those teachers can help their charges to grow in speaking and listening depends tremendously on the experience built up through the elementary years.

Writing

Children wrote for each other and reacted to each other's papers in discussion and in marginal notations. This process of cross-commentary was called the writing workshop. Or they wrote in groups, composing together as a scribe wrote down the words. Either way, the teacher's role was to guide the process most effectively, not to read and mark papers. Writing was put to use — printed and distributed, dramatized, acted upon, or incorporated into follow-up writing. Literacy programs were recommended that would enable children to write very early by presenting to them directly at the outset the correspondences between English vocal sounds and their spellings. Punctuation was similarly presented as correspondences between features of intonation and written symbols. After the literacy program, spelling was learned essentially through writing practice, the use of a dictionary, and self-diagnosis set in motion by the teacher.

The writing assignments were authentic kinds of discourse, not school exercises. Sometimes these were notes for later writing — direct recording of sensations or of spontaneous memories. By a process of expanding or selecting, and of revising from feedback, this writing was composed in stages so that the composing acts could be externalized and made susceptible to learning influences. The more inventive writing of stories and poems, on the other hand, was usually done in one stroke, on a sudden inspiration, except perhaps for revisions suggested by other children. And some writing — journal entries and letters — was not seen by anyone else. Based on vocal directions, the writing of directions provided experience of a very important utilitarian sort. Inspired by discussion, the writing of opinions and idea statements was carried only to the length pupils spontaneously took it.

Comparable to the minimal situations of dramatic work, writing was triggered by various easy points of departure, or stimulants, such as ongoing sensations, or memories associated with them, the pupils' own pictures and pictures drawn from elsewhere, literary forms such as the fable or certain poetic patterns, melodies, provocatively unfinished sentences, discussion arguments, and story ideas from improvisations. In general, a richly stimulating atmosphere was created by permitting the release of feeling in dramatic activities and by steeping the children in felicitous literature to which they could respond enthusiastically and into which they could project feeling. These specific and general stimulants were preferred to topical assignments, which were considered inimical to the development of thought and expression. Essay writing was allowed to evolve from several of these points of departure in a self-directive manner.

A grasp of sentence structures and the ability to manipulate them was approached pragmatically rather than academically. Instead of learning grammatical classifications and analyzing given sentences, the children expanded, reduced, and otherwise altered their own sentences and those of other pupils. Knowing already how to put the parts of speech into proper syntactic relationships, the children explored the possibilities and limitations of the orally learned rules for making sentences. They expanded the kernel phrases of their notes into fuller sentences, wrote telegrams, expanded baby talk, played sentence-building games with word slips, and, if they followed the *Words in Color* literacy program, did similar sentence-building with word cards color-coded for parts of speech. But most of all, children have been rewriting their own sentences and those of classmates. The importance of this constant emending, a primary feature of the writing workshop, has been difficult to convey adequately in a book. But in a considerable amount of their composition, pupils have been joining and disjoining sentences, subordinating clauses, trying out variant constructions, rewording phrases, and generally exploring practical language alternatives. They did these things for those very practical reasons that have been thought to justify the teaching of grammar — to improve communication and expression. Feedback, reinforced by the writer's own proofreading and afterthoughts, has indicated the need for sentence changes and often specific alterations as well. Learning to master language consists, precisely, of changing one's sentences.

The *processes* by which writing is taught do not differ in the years to follow from what has just been summarized. Some big differences will be found in the assignments themselves, and yet these differences are but an unfolding of potentialities latent in the elementary assignments. During junior high school, when drama is taken to paper, there occurs a sequence of assignments in script writing that begins with two- and three-person dialogues and continues through dramatic monologue to soliloquy. Taking other tacks, that sequence leads also to whole plays and to "socratic" or idea dialogues. In other words, the basic small-dialogue situation used in improvisations undergoes shifts in emphasis that are stipulated in writing assignments so as to produce very different sorts of scripts, some of which emphasize feeling and human interplay, some of which feature the solo voice, and some of which deal with the dialectic of ideas. These scripts lead in turn to poems, stories, and essays.

A second sequence of assignments takes off from sensations and memories. The former become the foundation for eyewitness reporting, first-hand observations noted at a locale chosen in advance then written up later as a newspaper story. For this journalistic assignment the writing groups act both as city editors and as copy editors. Memory writing becomes differentiated into autobiography and memoir, to sharpen focus and point of view; then memoir subdivides into human and non-human subjects, to specialize focus even more. The time-space coverage of these narratives is limited to a single "incident."

Both the dramatic and narrative sequences lend themselves to poetry writing. In addition, concrete poetry of observation is specifically assigned, founded on the reading and writing of haiku poems. It proceeds to somewhat longer poetic renderings of direct observation and ties in with sensory notation.

A junior high journal-and-diary sequence picks up where this kind of writing left off in elementary school. The sequence begins with private, in-class diaries, followed by a couple of short, public journals to be summarized later, and climaxed by one long, miscellaneous journal that is also summarized afterwards. These assignments capture fresh material and at the same time pose good abstractive problems for the student.

The writing of fictions, in prose or poetry, can take any of the dramatic forms covered, model itself on the first-person assignments, or simply follow familiar third-person conventions. Idea writing can be either dialogical, as mentioned, or monological, the latter being stimulated usually by small-group discussion.

During grades ten to thirteen, autobiography and memoir culminate in longer writing assignments covering the time span of a "phase." Memoir focuses on the "third person singular" (biography) and then on the "third person plural" (chronicle). Reporting blends into research via this sequence: the write-up of an observational visit, as before; the write-up of a combined interview and visit; the write-up of a long interview-visit designed to give a substantial look at some enterprise ("reporter-at-large"); the pointed account of a series of visits and interviews recorded in a journal and later summarized (case); the distillation of information about some subject acquired from visits, interviews, and written sources, but told as what happens, not as what happened (profile); and finally, the distillation and interpretation of information from primary source documents similar to many that the student has himself been creating in his previous writing (book research).

Concurrent with these sequences run three other strands of writing. One is designed to tap spontaneous trains of reflections by asking the student to write down his actual interior monologues at certain locales and to compose these for an audience. For inventive writing, the repertory of fictional techniques is enlarged to the full by experience with Chamber Theatre and with a special sequence of fiction reading following the spectrum arrayed in *Points of View: An Anthology of Short Stories*[1] Free assignments to invent in any form are given.

The third strand concerns the forging of generalizations and theories and their development throughout an essay. Four repeatable assignments comprise a sequence that carries the student up the abstraction ladder. For the first he tells several pointed incidents, drawn from both real life and reading, that clearly illustrate the same thing or play on the same theme; some category or generalization underlies the paper. Then he writes, as independent compositions, a number of single-sentence generalizations such as maxims, epigrams, and aphorisms. The next assignment is to develop one such generalization through substatements and illustrations. After class work with syllogisms, the student writes a composition in which several generalizations are combined so as to produce new statements and to generate a theory.

Work with the sentence is pursued, at the concrete level, in the writing and revising of haiku and other single-sentence poems. At the abstract level, it is pursued in the writing and revising of epigrams and other one-sentence generalizations.

Since the writing assignments result in the same kinds of discourse that are produced outside of school, the outline just sketched represents a reading program also. Each kind of writing is accompanied by corresponding reading selections, created of course in the same way the students created their compositions. Thus the compositional issues of writing and the comprehension issues of reading are joined in each kind of discourse. In fact, though the reading selections are not at all held up as models or analyzed for the sake of rhetorical points to be applied to the writing, they strengthen tremendously the student's involvement with the forms in which he is writing and his understanding of how to master them. The teacher juxtaposes reading and writing but does not himself make connections.

---

[1] Edited by James Moffett and Kenneth McElheny (New York: New American Library, 1966).

Reading

The chief learning issue of beginning reading was considered to be the decoding of letters into familiar vocal sounds to which meanings were already attached. Accordingly, children following this curriculum have had an early, intensive course in sound-spelling correspondences. But phonics was complemented by whole-word and whole-sentence approaches, namely "language experience" and reading while listening. During the period of pre-reading and beginning reading, the teacher frequently read good poems and stories to the pupils. Except for some phonetically controlled texts introduced during the literacy program, the reading matter assigned to beginners was the highest caliber of folk and children's literature. The only readers selected for both younger and older children were anthologies containing such material.

No effort was made to structure a reading program around concepts of either form or content. A very large quantity of anthologies and single trade books were made available from which pupils could make selections for individual silent reading and for reading aloud to classmates in small groups. Reading in common was for the purpose either of discussion or of focusing on a literary form. Attention was drawn to such things as stanzaic form, incremental repetition, and story type simply by clustering a number of instances of each and then having pupils do similar writing. Literary terms and analysis were avoided, but many structural features of literature were brought out through expressive oral reading and through dramatization. The latter, in fact, was made an important instrument of interpretation and appreciation.

Comprehending reading texts was deemed a general conceptual matter that could be better learned in a variety of intellectual tasks than in courses of practice reading or skill building based on comprehension questions. Instead of answering the prepared questions of an adult, children asked their own questions. Further thinking about reading texts was inspired by enacting them, discussing them, or carrying out directions contained in them. Discussion in particular allowed children, collectively, to recall facts, make inferences, draw conclusions, and compare interpretations, so that each individual could improve his ability to do these things alone.

Oral reading was transferred from teacher to pupils, who read aloud in parts and chorally and also practiced expressive reading by taking turns reading to each other in small groups. The latter amounted to reading workshops, since variant readings could be compared and the content discussed in connection with the manner of reading it.

A considerable amount of the children's reading has been each other's compositions, which were naturally controlled for difficulty and interest by the fact of being peer-written. This kind of reading material allowed children to talk to the authors, to discriminate textual features by seeing the texts change, and thus to become aware of these features in a book. In other words, the locally written texts of classmates not only provided additional texts having a special social interest, but also brought reading down from the remote perfection of the printed page to the everyday realm.

As mentioned before, the reading program of the later years is more structured, but only in a general way. Following the principle that students write in the same forms they read, the recommendations for kinds of reading selections to be assigned are made under the same headings as the writing assignments. In surveying the writing program of grades seven to thirteen I have already outlined much of the reading. The "units" of the curriculum are kinds of discourse to be both read and written — dramatic and narrative discourse, which covers plays, poems, and fiction; reportage and research; autobiography, memoir and chronicle, which covers corresponding kinds of fiction and poetry; essays of generalization and theory; and essays of personal reflection. The various first- and third-person fictional techniques are arrayed in a reading sequence drawn form *Points of View,* and also dramatized in Chamber Theatre. Any performable literature is read silently in preparation for being rendered orally; sometimes it is memorized. Dramatic, narrative, observational, lyric, and philosophical poetry are all read in significant connection with corresponding kinds of composition. Reportage and research cover many important kinds of reading, such as eyewitness accounts, journals, and informative articles. Reading in the whole range of concrete and abstract essay is gradually accomplished through assignments made at appropriate junctures. Again, locating and sequencing particular titles was left to teachers to determine locally.

The matter of how students follow up a reading selection is solved in essentially the same way as in the elementary years: they do something with what they have got from the page; they improvise on, perform, discuss, or assimilate into their own writing (research) the texts they have read.

In sum, the rest of this curriculum attempts to acquaint students, as both readers and writers, with all the forms of written discourse, and continues to do so by extending oral discourse onto the page. It unfolds the whole spectrum of dialogue and monologue, literature and non-literature, invention and documentation, private utterance and impersonal formulation.

_____

_____

_____

Part Three

GRADES SEVEN

THROUGH NINE

*To avoid redundance, the emphasis of this section will be
mostly on new assignments or on new developments of old ones.
But the program is cumulative. Students who are new to the
program should, in most cases, begin with work recommended
for grades four to six, especially if they are disadvantaged, and
even students who have been following the program would
continue some activities discussed there. Certainly, small-group
discussion remains in force, with regard to reading, acting, writing collaboration and special topics. Writing directions (Chapter 16), writing up show-and-tell (Chapter 16), and writing
postscripts to discussion (Chapter 16) all continue in grades
seven to nine. (In considering the balance of the junior high
writing program, these tacitly included expository writing assignments should be kept in mind.) Card-playing and chess-
playing (Chapter 17) continue also, but I will not attempt here
to envision further the kinds of card decks that may be created.
Suggestions for stimulating the writing of fictions are distributed
under a number of headings, where they can be better correlated
with reading and dramatic work. For basic reading, spelling,
and punctuation, the reader must refer to Chapters 5, 6, and
12; for reading comprehension, to Chapters 2 and 6.*

*The bulk of the work for these years comprises two main
streams — dramatic reading and writing and narrative reading
and writing. Drama and narrative are understood here in a
broad sense that takes in poetry, plays, and fiction and overlaps*

with essay and exposition, to which new avenues are thus opened. Students read discourse of the same sort they are writing. Hence reading and writing are coordinated in practice and dealt with here under the same headings. Writing provides a key to reading comprehension and literary appreciation, and reading opens doors for writing possibilities. No textbooks in language, grammar, and composition are used. Literature textbook series based on historical chronology, themes, and most literary critical principles would be irrelevant not only to this program but, in my estimation, to pre-college education in general, though of course teachers may draw many good reading selections from them.

Reading

Reading does not break down into many differentiated assignments as writing does. Reading selections themselves are various, but I do not try to specify titles for different ages, for I believe that this is impossible in a general book, and that much of the selecting has to be done at the local level anyway. I do indicate, however, kinds of reading selections and where they would fit into the program, occasionally giving titles as examples. Poetry selections are read along with prose — personal narrative or observational reporting, for example — but also read separately for their special use of form and language. This is to bring out both the kinship and difference between poetry and prose.

The general principle for handling reading and literature is, as stated before, that the student does something with what he reads, extending it through dramatic work, writing, or discussion. I recommend that students not be quizzed for comprehension, tested for facts, or assigned topics to write on about the reading. Instead, I propose that the reading be discussed in small groups, and that issues raised there sometimes be taken to paper.

The reading groups would not be the same groups established for discussion of general topics. That is, I assume that not all students will be reading the same books at the same time, because of differences in reading maturity, and that reading groups will be formed on the basis of these differences, whereas general discussion groups will be heterogeneous.

As they are finishing a text, members of the reading groups may be asked to write on a slip of paper some factual and inter-

pretative questions about things they did not understand, or simply some issue in the selection that they want to talk about. Each group spends a few minutes extracting subjects from the slips by noting overlaps and other connections among them, then settles into discussion. Several other procedures are possible, such as selecting only one issue from the slips, or taking several issues in order, or framing a single topic so as to include several points raised on the slips, or answering small factual questions first then passing on to larger interpretive matters. Often it will happen that the sorting itself will launch talk, and procedure will sometimes take care of itself. Basically, this process could be simply a specialized version of small-group discussion, for which reading selections supply the topics. But the topics must come from the students' curiosity, puzzlement, or interest. I believe that these discussions should essentially just extend their reading responses into conversation; that the groups should be small enough to allow for the interests of all members (which is impossible in class discussion); and that writing about books should essentially extend conversation back into the individual mind. Since plays are not read alone yet, and most poems assigned to the class collectively are either read aloud or given some other presentation, it is mainly for narrative and expository prose that small-group discussion is needed.

Individual reading. *Individual reading should continue to be fostered by providing some in-class time and access to an appropriate array of books. Besides selections of general interest for this age the array should include works that correlate with the assignments to follow in this section (journals or poetry of observation, for example). The exchanging of titles and individual reading experience can take place in the regular reading groups.*

Oral reading. *Oral reading can continue also in the reading groups. In the course of talking about his book, a student reads passages he especially likes or considers illustrative. In fact such oral reading may provide the best departure point for comments by the reader and for questions by other members.*

DISCUSSION

As for small-group discussion in general, the procedure, leadership, and framing of topics depend so much on the prior dis-

cussion experience of students that, regardless of anything I might say here, teachers would have to experiment anyway with these factors.

As regards inexperienced students, however, some brief preliminary trials run by John Mellon and myself in 1966 may be worth mentioning. We set up eight discussions by four groups of ninth-graders, the purpose being merely to determine the best way to go about a full-scale experiment. The groups of six members each were equally divided between disadvantaged and middle-class students (from different parts of the Boston area), and between boys and girls. The three disadvantaged members of each group were mixed Negro and white. For a number of reasons, we convened the groups outside of school and paid them for the one-hour sessions. The topic, which ran for two sessions per group, was about good and bad features of school and what changes might be made. Some groups had no leader, some had an adult present as a "minimal monitor" to prompt infrequently when discussion went too far off the subject, and some had an adult leader who actually helped with discussion strategy when necessary. Summarizing and playing back the tape for further discussion were omitted in this case but might well be factors in similar experiments.

There are, of course, no findings to report as of this writing, but we were left with a few strong impressions that might be of use to other teachers interested in trying to determine the best way to run small-group discussions for novices of this age. It seemed clear, first, that the leaderless discussions were very poor in comparison with the others. Mere adult presence may be important at first just to protect the students from the limitations of the younger teenage code, which sometimes inhibits individuals from talking seriously under school auspices, on pain of group rejection, even though they might really want to do so. In the adult-monitored or guided groups, the talk flowed well, i.e., was serious but relaxed, with participation running generally high, and often the groups wanted to continue going beyond the time limit.

Contrary to some of our fears and predictions, the girls did not dominate discussion, and the mixing of strangers from different schools, socio-economic groups, and races did not constrain the talk (in fact, it heightened interest in what the others had to say). It was somewhat difficult to get the students to address each other rather than the leader, which is probably a matter of previous conditioning; a major problem concerns how the leader can help them develop each other's ideas with-

out focusing attention on himself. A consistent and unanimous complaint, incidentally, that our discussants made about schools was that teachers of all subjects talk far too much.

The use of student discussion leaders is also a fruitful area for experimentation. The question is not whether the practice will work but whether it is always the best thing to do. The leaders benefit, I am sure, but if they are always the same students, the others may not learn enough. And given rotating leaders, are they unnecessary and constraining in some kinds of discussion among experienced students? For groups just starting to operate without the teacher, student leaders may be used very successfully, as one teacher[1] has reported of her all-Negro ninth-grade class. Although the physical conditions of the classroom are unfavorable and she has to rely on a few students capable of helping the others, she has inaugurated small-group discussions. To overcome noise and lack of space, she places a group in a corner with an interconnected set of headphones. An interesting advantage of this ingenious makeshift arrangement is that the students listen more closely to each other and concentrate better. The topics have been drawn from cultural and historical material, and those very disadvantaged students like discussing seriously and having their discussions taken seriously.

There are two problems that might discourage teachers from starting their students in on this program in junior high school. The first is that the prospect of introducing it to students unaccustomed to talking, acting, and writing may seem overwhelming.

DISADVANTAGED STUDENTS NEW TO THE PROGRAM

Disadvantaged children, especially if they have had a very conventional schooling, will at first be unresponsive to the invitation to produce speech of their own. They may long ago have divorced school from real uses of language. They may appear mute, unthinking, and disaffected. In ninth grade they may write and read no better than some fourth- or fifth-graders in suburban schools. Every year their verbal and cognitive deficit has grown larger, so that their junior high teachers face a backlog of past conditioning. The temptation is to say that by adolescence the time for a change is past, and that the only thing to do is to let them pursue the familiar course to the end (which may come any day): "If you try to make changes at this late

[1] Grace Whittaker of the Lewis Junior High School in Roxbury, Massachusetts.

stage, they become fearful and distrustful." Though true, this line of thought should not become a rationale for despair. Admittedly, the older the students, the harder the conversion, but the alternative is to write off a large number of children on the grounds that "it is already too late."

GRAMMATICAL USAGE OF THE STANDARD DIALECT

The problem of disadvantaged children meshes with the second problem, which is the conventional obligation placed on junior high teachers to teach the correct grammatical usage of standard dialect. The omission from this program of such teaching may seem a grave offense to some educators. My case against it is dual: it is ineffectual and inhumane.

Grammatical usage is acquired unconsciously as a small child from family and community. These automatic speech behaviors are essentially impervious both to conceptual presentations of grammar and to teacher correction. People who use correct standard grammar do so because they have spoken with people who use it and have read authors who write it. Furthermore, the prevailing notion of many linguists today is that the grammar of non-standard speakers is not necessarily deficient, but merely different. For example, something like the aspect or the tense of a verb may be rendered in ways other than verb ending, by means that an outsider is simply ignorant of.

At any rate — and this concerns the humane aspect — the adoption of standard dialect should be voluntary for the learner; he should find his own reasons for acquiring the speech habits of another community. Powerful social, economic, and intellectual reasons may make him want to. As we know from experience, ghetto children do not change their speech habits significantly as a result of doing grammar drills and being corrected. What will alter their grammatical usage is, first, motivation, which comes from broader social contact and from discovering the benefits of reading and writing. They should be allowed to converse with speakers of standard English, enabled to read a lot, and encouraged to use language as a tool of thought and a medium of expression (instead of merely as a means of in-group communion). If there are deficiencies and ambiguities in their native grammar, they should do speaking and writing of a sort that will help them see these limitations for themselves.

In short, the will of the student must first become engaged. Then, second, the means and opportunities for adopting stan-

dard grammatical usage must be available — heterogeneous classes, conversational interaction, role playing, natural kinds of writing, and a broad spectrum of reading. When it is the will of the student, finally, teachers may correct usage and recommend practical handbooks on the subject that are kept in the classroom as reference books only. Let students ask for help. Many older students (mostly only in senior high) may have strong enough motives even to do language laboratory exercises of the second-language sort. But for teachers to impose new speech habits and try to eradicate old ones amounts, in effect, to saying that the language a child learned at home is inferior; in order to maintain his own integrity, the child must then resist this instruction.

The same general argument applies to middle-class children, whose deviations from correct usage are seldom truly grammatical, involving, rather, idiom. If one examines their errors, one almost always finds that these errors reflect the practices of educated adults whom they hear and read. Whatever the case, no one has ever been able to prove that teaching the rules of grammatical regularity improves speech or writing. Mature, well motivated older students can refine their usage somewhat by conscious attention to teacher commentary and to the practical statements of a book like Strunk and White's Elements of Style. But, along with other teachers, I have wasted many hours of my life making corrections that students never looked at or promptly forgot when they wrote their next theme. My students made as many grammatical errors trying to write correctly — clearing their throats and putting on a top hat — as they did in ignorance of standard usage. Perhaps I can put the whole matter of correctness in a nutshell by saying that if it isn't automatic it doesn't count. To those of my readers who remain skeptical of my stand here, let me just pose this question: How does correctness become automatic?[2]

---

[2] For a fuller, documented argument of this position, see "Grammar and the Sentence" in *Teaching the Universe of Discourse*. (Boston: Houghton Mifflin Company, 1968).

Chapter 19

Acting and Speaking

Movement to sound, pantomime, charades, enactments, and improvisations should all be continued. They are not just games for kiddies, or "enrichment," but serious business. Teachers should not feel that the time spent on them is time diverted from the tasks of learning about language, literature, and composition. Drama will definitely further such goals. Furthermore, children of this age are by no means ready just to sit and work with books and paper all day, every day. Many of the problems that begin at this age — destructive rebellion, alienation from school, dropping out, delinquency — can be alleviated if adolescents see school as a place where feeling and energy can be shaped and handled, instead of a place where these forces must be stifled until time to meet with the gang again. Many teachers are afraid that drama work will open a vent and create disorder, but all people who have worked with it know that it tends, rather, to lower tensions and to help students behave better.[1]

Two major changes distinguish acting at this age from that in the primary grades — performing before others and enacting scripted plays. The details of these two changes will emerge in the following pages.

The Drama Period

Several kinds of dramatic activities can occur during a single period. Once a week the class meets in a large room that has been reserved. These classes are led by the regular English teacher. The role of drama specialists is not to take over the children but to train English teachers, for drama is a central

[1] For a recent, compact, practical book on dramatic work in secondary school, see R. N. Pemberton-Billing and J. D. Clegg, *Teaching Drama* (London: University of London Press, 1965). This book contains useful lists of records and plays appropriate for this age.

part of English, not an extra or minor speciality. These periods can have a general structure that creates a sense of order and purpose but allows for a variety of current projects. For example, the entire group begins by doing warm-ups together, then goes into enactions and improvisations. The warm-ups are pantomime and movement to sound. Students suggest pantomime ideas for everyone to try out simultaneously, and the teacher supplies some ideas designed to increase the range of body movements and sometimes to anticipate actions in a play or story he is going to assign.

Depending on current projects, the next phase of the class period would usually consist of small-group work such as improvising from a minimal situation, enacting an unscripted scene from a story, or rehearsing a scripted scene from a play. This might last until the end of the period, but sometimes the whole class could be reassembled to watch some groups put on scenes or to coordinate the groups if they are working on parts of a whole. In some periods the movement-to-sound warm-up might be extended into dance drama by clustering students for spontaneous interaction during the warm-ups and then letting these groups plan and act out the music with the usual rotation of roles. Pantomime warm-up could be part of the bigger action the groups are going to work on, or could be the germ of an improvisational situation.

If thoughtfully timed, the use of the stage can be gradually worked in now. If their acting has been allowed to grow naturally and unhurriedly before, children twelve years old or more seem to be ready for framed performance and to be able to act before a distinct audience without losing their immersion in their roles. The teacher has to watch and wait for the time, not just assume it has arrived with a certain age. Rostrum blocks (small platforms) should be available in the drama room so that students can gravitate to them when they feel the urge, and a group rehearsing a scene for performance before the class might be allowed to try out the auditorium stage at times, without an audience and perhaps even with the curtain closed. From these beginnings can eventually evolve polished stage performances before a strange audience. But that is not the goal of dramatic activities, and the acquiring now of a stage and spectators is not for the purpose of "going into production" but to fulfill a phase of growth. Under no account should the drama sessions be merely devoted to working up showcase productions. Occasionally some improvisations and enactments will be good enough to present before people other than the class and, if the teacher sees no harm in this, a show can be arranged. But it is the doing itself, not the being seen, that is most educational. Use of an audience would, with some exceptions, be limited to acting before classmates in a workshop atmosphere.

The Workshop

The workshop will remain important for the rest of this program. It is defined as a group of apprentices, under the guidance of a master, who are learning to do something by alternating between being producer and being receiver. All are participants; there are no detached outsiders. Members react to other members' productions and work out common problems together. Each member gets an inside-outside view of both his work and the work of others. While learning an art or craft, he also becomes a sensitive, informed responder. In drama, this means trying out tentative performances before classmates. The advantage of a workshop over sheer play is that one can learn from heeding feedback. This advantage is more than cancelled, however, if the students cannot yet ignore an audience during performance or pay attention to it after performance.

A workshop might consist of one group at a time acting before the class. Or it might consist of two or three groups, acting simultaneously, whose members are alternately performing and watching. If the acting calls for a cast of three, the class can break into sixes or nines, the two or three casts rotating within their groups. The teacher roves among the groups, feeding back and suggesting alternatives that might be tried.

Enacting Scripts

Acting from scripts alters greatly the process of enacting. For one thing, it almost certainly presupposes an audience, since the whole purpose of a script is to hold actors to a presumably superior version of the action, a circumstance of little value to participants playing just for themselves, but important to beholders. Second, a director becomes definitely necessary, to make decisions about staging, placement and movement of actors, and speaking of lines. Third, reading is incorporated into dramatic activity; either the actors deliver lines by reading them aloud, or they read lines silently to memorize them.

VALUES OF REHEARSAL

My own bias is against oral sight reading of scripts and in favor of rehearsal of lines, even though the latter takes more time. Most student readings I have heard (I say "heard" because little happened to see) were inexpressive and so haltingly dragged out that the drama, and often even the bald story, were destroyed. The drama period is no time to practice sight reading. The play should be the thing. It is better to act short playlets that can be memorized and rehearsed in little time than to be encumbered with scripts that virtually exclude movement and facial expression. We do not wish, after all, to make individual reading problems the main drama! Rehearsed readings, however, are a somewhat different matter.

Rehearsing a script — whether for a reading or acting performance — requires many close silent readings, makes the actor-reader think about the meaning and implications of what he is reading, necessitates attention to punctuation, allows the actor to truly work into the situation and role, and, in the case of literary scripts by adults, helps him fully possess a language not his own. I hardly need say that all of these things make for verbal growth, and the beauty of it is that in this context they are well motivated.

In both rehearsing and directing scripts, one learns to fill out the text imaginatively — to inferentially relate dialogue, description, and narration just as one has to do (on one's own) in reading fiction, plays, and poetry. In short, to the extent that any literary text is a script that the reader has to expand, recreate within himself, and infer from, memorizing and rehearsing play scripts is pertinent preparation for reading literature. Literary scripts that are specifically dramatic should be sought among poems as well as plays. A number of poems, especially ballads like "Lord Randall," are dialogues in a definite setting or at least comprise interesting "parts" or voices.

Procedures

Student scripts. To capitalize on these many kinds of learning, the teacher should coordinate script writing, acting, and directing. Since short published plays appropriate for this age are not numerous, the students will sometimes have to write their own — a not at all deplorable situation, for scripting gives valuable and appropriate experience in writing vernacular speech (dialogue) and description and narration (stage directions). So that actors may consult with the author of their script, it would be practical for him to be a member of the group doing his playlet. A major effect of putting on student scripts is that actors and directors will feed back to the author various script problems from which they can all learn: they can't read his handwriting, or can't tell how to read a line from the way he has punctuated it, or don't understand the timing of actions, or what kind of person a character is, or what the point is of a certain action or speech, or what the set really looks like, and so on.

In other words, tell the group to discuss during rehearsals whatever problems they have in acting their parts. The director leads this talk toward decisions or, when disagreement is strong, makes the decisions himself. Directors change from one playlet to the next, but the most capable children are appointed at first. The pupils understand that whoever is director has the last word as regards *performance,* and that the script can be changed, but only through negotiation with the author. Memorization, I suggest, is done as homework, but rehearsal time is allowed in class.

For one purpose sight reading has a place. When the small groups are sifting their own scripts to choose one to put on, taking parts and reading them aloud without an audience is as good a way as any to acquaint all the members with all the scripts and to get a rough idea of the playing qualities of each. This also affords opportunity for considerable oral reading. (Choice of student scripts, incidentally, should be based on different criteria at different times — not just quality, but subject matter, kinds of roles, and the revision value that playing the script would have for the author.)

Published scripts. For the most part, mere silent reading of plays should be deferred to senior high, after improvisation and enactment have made it possible for students to bring a play script to life in their minds without missing or misunderstanding what is going on. Critical questions and comprehension questions cannot overcome the handicap of failing to visualize and interpret *as one reads.* And silent play reading is difficult, much more so than fiction, which is written to be read alone; plays are incomplete texts and require a lot more inference on the part of the reader. Allowing room for some exceptions a teacher might want to make, I recommend that plays not be "assigned for reading," in the usual sense, but assigned for enactment of one sort or another, either rehearsed oral reading or memorized acting. This means that students would in fact read plays silently but only in preparation for enactment.

I suggest a sequence running from short plays of one continuous scene to one-acts of two or three scenes and four or five characters to somewhat longer plays in the ninth grade. One play of Shakespeare might come in the ninth grade, as an exception, but might equally well be deferred a year. I think it is wiser to put off very long plays until senior high school, so that play reading can benefit from dramatic activities that short plays make possible. I see no reason to push Shakespeare. Students may be mature enough to grasp the story, were it narrated, but the fullness and complexity of his plays make it very difficult to use the approach recommended here, which would make them more comprehensible. Spending several weeks "studying" a play of his — deciphering it — is certainly not recommended. A junior high teacher who really loves doing the Bard should not be prevented from it if he feels confident of making good theatre for children out of his plays. But a leisurely and thorough development in dramatic understanding will considerably increase student appreciation of Shakespeare when they do come to him, as well as give their language ability time to mature.

Very short plays can be given rehearsed oral readings by small groups performing the same play simultaneously, without spectators or with a few spectators who rotate with the actors. Or groups can memorize different scripts and perform the plays one by one before the class. In the latter case, time lost in memorizing lines is compensated by the fact that all students can experience all the plays while actually reading only one of them.

When a play comprises several scenes, all students read the whole text as homework, but each group is made responsible at the outset for performing a certain portion of the script later, when the portions are run off consecutively during one class period. For very long plays of three or five acts, several procedures may be combined. Some scenes are assigned for a performed reading and others for memorized acting. Still others are played from a professional recording while students follow the text with their eyes. All this should be planned so that the whole play is done in a few days running.

Playing recordings of scripts while students follow the text has special value for slow students, or for any students when a play is difficult by reason of subtlety, poetic language, or dialects. Though these recordings would generally be professional, some good rehearsed readings by students can also be taped and played. Making tapes of plays not commercially recorded could in fact be a very well motivated project itself. In general, hearing and seeing a text simultaneously is an excellent and too seldom exploited practice that can aid silent reading, bring texts alive, acquaint students with unfamiliar dialects, and provide a model for oral expression.

Since few students in this country have ever had a thorough experience in dramatic activities that lasted through secondary school, it may be that my doubts, expressed earlier, about sight reading of scripts will become irrelevant. Very experienced students may be able to read a fresh script aloud with worthwhile results, if the script is not difficult. Certainly the possibility should be explored with some students and some plays.

Improvisation

When I tried out improvisations in a seventh-grade class[2] that had never done them before, I found that a lot of the improvising was surprisingly inventive and real, and the children were very eager. But having a class audience often caused these inexperienced children to giggle and grimace, be silly, and fall out of role. This behavior would alternate in the same minute with very good riding of emotion, spontaneous wit, and some fine mimicking of dialects and characters. The point is that the self-consciousness is not at all necessary; whether it breaks into the role depends on the students' experience. Gradual development and the evolution of a workshop prevent those undesirable effects of self-consciousness that keep many teachers from attempting drama.

PROCEDURES

Improvisations are usually conducted during the drama period, in a workshop atmosphere, although they might sometimes take place in class if one group at a time is to perform before the others. A rough sequence for inexperienced students during these years goes from unwitnessed groups improvising at the same time, to groups with extra members who watch and take turns, to pairs of groups playing alternately before each other, to groups playing one after another before the whole class.

[2] With Elizabeth Cawein, the regular teacher of the class, in Weeks Junior High School, Newton, Massachusetts.

Both the teacher and the watching students make comments to the players, but they do so only when the action runs out or runs down; they do not interrupt involved acting. Comments may be descriptive reactions or suggestions. As he moves among the groups, the teacher sets the tenor of these comments, giving personal responses as an onlooker ("The clerk seems very annoyed, but the customer doesn't seem to notice that.") and suggesting things the actors may not have thought of ("Why don't you try it in another setting?" or "What would happen if the son asked his father *before* the mother entered the room?") Students make these same kinds of comments to each other. When the onlookers have themselves been working on the action they are witnessing, or are about to replace the actors, these remarks can be very perceptive and pertinent, helpful both to the actors and to themselves.

The purpose of comments is not to criticize directly, but to reflect what the improvisation looks like from the outside and to widen the range of possibilities. One of the main values of improvisation is the *exploring of differences* — differences, for example, between two-way and three-way relationships, in pace and rhythm, in language styles of different speakers, in the dynamics and balances of interaction, in settings and circumstances, in the order of acts, in behavior strategies. (All of these are aspects of both literature and real life.) If an improvisation seems lifeless and forced, the commentators need not make negative remarks about the acting. Taking their cue from the teacher, they suggest changes in the variables of the situation and in the casting. Sometimes, for example, if a scene is revolving repetitiously or keeps falling into pauses, it may help to suggest another ploy that X can use on Y, or to propose that the two players change roles for a while. If playing alternatives is customary, then proposing changes will not be taken personally.

KINDS OF MINIMAL SITUATIONS

There are several kinds of minimal situations: (1) an action to be elaborated from a previous reading selection (in which case the improvisation is a kind of free enactment); (2) a situation abstracted by the teacher from a play, a story, or a poem soon to be assigned; (3) an original student idea drawn from life or imagination; (4) a situation embodying a moral, social, or psychological issue that arises from group discussion or reading. Let's take these one at a time.

Improvising situations from reading selections, either before or after the reading, is a very effective way of working with literature and will probably improve silent reading. It is an alternative to comprehension questions and literary critical analysis. The students are asked to pick a scene or piece of action from a short story, or to select a whole poem. They may choose scenes they like very much or ones they do not understand well. The latter should be encouraged. After agreeing on how the situation can be stated, they drop the text and start improvising. They may recapitulate some of the action and dialogue as they remember it and at the same time invent changes. Synoptic versions of myths and Bible stories can be elaborated by making up the dialogue and the particularities of the action. A scene merely alluded to in a play or piece of fiction (an offstage action) can be improvised from the slight references made to it, the students drawing on their understanding of the rest of the work in order to create the scene the author did not present directly.

Exploring other possibilities of a text makes the author's choices meaningful. And players have to think about motivations and relationships in order to act their roles. Discussions of interpretation inevitably arise en route, and these discussions are practical, not arbitrary. The Hunt for Hidden Meanings that students resist so strongly when the teacher probes with question after question is replaced by the effort to understand what one is trying to do.

A fine way to prepare for reading a literary work is to improvise in advance some key situations that the teacher has abstracted from it. For example, before students have seen the text, give them the gist of the scene in which Cassius tries to persuade Brutus to join the conspiracy to kill Caesar. The situation can be stated in more or less detail, depending on how much of it the students seem to need or to be able to use. These details would be facts and circumstances, not character traits, since giving the latter would force the teacher to pre-interpret the play for the students and perhaps lead to stereotyping. Mainly, *A* is trying to talk *B* into helping to kill a friend of *B*'s for the good of the group. A number of scenes from *Julius Caesar* could be improvised in this way before knowing the play. (Actually, the example of *Julius Caesar,* which I have chosen only because it is familiar, is not very appropriate: plays for this age should be mostly one-acts having few characters and few changes of time and locale.)

Minimal situations originating with the students open up the way to writing plays. There are two stages in this development. A group improvising an original situation composes it by doing different versions until it is wrought to the members' satisfaction; then they collaborate in writing it down in play format, as dialogue and stage directions. After some experience in this group composition, individuals are asked to choose a minimal situation, either of their own or from a list of class suggestions, and write a playlet based on it. This amounts to improvising a scene alone on paper. (A whole sequence of dramatic writing is treated later, beginning on page 295.)

Minimal situations embodying moral, social, or psychological issues can evolve into topic-centered discussions by this route. At first, conversation about theme is incidental talk generated during successive improvisations of a scene, the theme presumably being of high interest to students, since they thought of the minimal situation. Then, somewhere during these years, the teacher proposes that the situation be one in which the characters are essentially just sitting around talking about some issue they have to make a decision about. The scene is dramatic, because the students are still taking a fictive role and the talk is a story action, but the improvisation takes a step closer to being a kind of spontaneous discussion. Examples would be a jury deliberating a verdict, or a committee of a club deciding on whether to invite a certain type of person to be a member.

The next step is to stipulate merely a topic and a set of people from different walks of life who are discussing that topic. This would be a kind of *mock panel,* and the students would be playing roles. The last step is simply spontaneous small-group discussion, in which members speak for themselves. Thus improvisation and discussion are the ends of a spectrum that stretches between them. The sequence just described is another way to approach discussion and to relate the dialectic of discussion to the dynamics of drama. It will help induce awareness of how our ideas are rooted in our roles and character. Of course the teacher or the students can at any time lift an embodied issue from the drama work and propose it as a topic for small groups to discuss. An improvisation, for example, in which family members argue over dating or going steady suggests several discussion topics — parental authority and teen-age rights, the teen-ager's degree of maturity, and the pressure to follow social patterns.

An excellent supplement to the suggestions made here is contained in Viola Spolen's *Improvisations for the Theater* (Evanston, Ill.: Northwestern University Press, 1963), a handbook of improvisational games developed from many years of experience in teaching professional actors. Some teachers are beginning to find this book a very practical source of dramatic ideas. The games emphasize concentration on real and imaginary objects and situations.

Panel Discussions

SETTING UP PANELS

It is during these grades that panel discussions can be started. They are small-group discussions occurring before an audience, unplanned except for the designation of a topic. That is, the discussants are not assigned positions in advance or asked to prepare what they will say. The only preparation would be, on some occasions, to read something from which the topic is drawn. Discussing before an audience, like performing before one, is best held off until this age, when both previous experience and a higher degree of maturity will make the activity more worthwhile.

In describing above a way that topic-centered discussion can grow out of improvisations, I suggested a natural course for arriving at panels. That is, the members role play types of people discussing an issue in a storied situation. Or they pretend to be characters from a certain piece of fiction, discussing an issue according to how they think the characters would have talked about it. A bit more abstractly, each discussant can be assigned a certain family, social, or professional role which would be expected to furnish him with a particular bias, point of view, or investment.

In full-fledged panel discussion, however, the members speak as themselves and are encouraged to abandon pre-established roles, to turn over ideas open-mindedly. Dividing panelists into teams, setting up debates, and choosing dualistic yes-or-no topics all promote dogmatism rather than flexibility. Panelists bring personal biases to a discussion anyway; they should not be prevented, by a prior commitment, from changing their minds, making concessions, or finding areas of agreement with other panelists. It is true that playing a role on a *mock* panel does commit members to certain positions, but those positions are not necessarily the students' own, since students are playing a role and hence adopting a foreign point of view. And that is a chief goal of panels — to enlarge the students' ways of thinking. The general theory is that people incorporate into themselves the ideas and arguments they hear, and that their future thinking, even when they are alone, reflects the external dialogues they have internalized.[3]

The size of the panel groups should be experimented with and the differences in dynamics not only noted by the teacher but discussed occasionally by the class. A simple question in this regard is whether odd-numbered panels tend less to split into two camps than even-numbered panels. Does smallness increase participation? Do larger numbers keep ideas from being focused and followed up? What effects does number have on personal interaction?

AUDIENCE FEEDBACK

The benefits of discussing before an audience belong, once again, to both participant and spectator. The audience can notice aspects of discussion dynamics that are hard to remain sensitive to when one is participating — things that make and break communication, advance or block ideas. For example, a panel may circle repetitiously, become lost in trivialities, get distracted from a good line of thought by an irrelevance, fail to pick up and develop each other's points, or get hung up unwittingly on a hidden problem of definition. Or some members may dominate or contend with certain others out of personal opposition, or stubbornly reiterate just for the sake of defense. Somehow students must become aware of poor interactions without feeling badly criticized.

One way is to observe them take place among other people. Another way, requiring some skill and delicacy, is for spectators to reflect the discussants back to themselves after the panel is over. If this feedback is severely nega-

---

[3] For the full theory on this point see "Drama: What Is Happening," in *Teaching the Universe of Discourse.*

tive, the panelists will become inhibited. The tone is important, and the teacher sets it. But it must also have been set years before in small-group discussion and, more recently, in drama and writing workshops. A good argument for having groups play back their discussions from a tape recorder and comment on them is that this experience, plus the teacher's training-period suggestions, will prepare for the time when other people will serve as playback. In short, panel discussions themselves are discussed, with the understanding that both the ideas and the way they were talked about are open for reaction from the floor. The teacher asks for such reactions, or, once the procedure is familiar, simply waits for the response. Part of the playback should be an effort by the audience to summarize the main ideas that were brought out and the areas of agreement and disagreement.

A common experience for spectators is that they find themselves itching to get into the fray. While listening, they think of counter-arguments, points left out, other sorts of ideas stimulated by the panelists. This is an excellent educational moment that can be exploited in three ways. One is simply to turn the pent-up reaction into a classwide discussion, in which case the panel will have served as the springboard. Another is to let some of the more aroused spectators form a second panel. The last way is to take the discussion to paper while it is hot. The teacher directs the class to put down what they think about what has been said, the point being not to recapitulate the panel discussion but to express further thoughts stimulated by it. Part of the later aftermath of the panel may be to pick up the issues in small-group discussion, and to read aloud in class the papers written in response to the panel.

Chapter 20

Dramatic Dialogue

I would like to describe in this and the following two chapters a course of dramatic writing that would span the years of junior high and interweave with other kinds of composition. The sequence begins with fragments of dialogue and evolves in three ways: toward fully conceived plays, toward abstract ideas, and toward monologues. That is, the potentialities of dialogue for dramatic action, for abstract expression, and for sustained voice are gradually realized. These years of early adolescence seem to be just the right time to take drama work to paper and thereby establish a rich and flexible basis for the writing program of senior high school.

Students who recorded overheard conversations in elementary school (see page 181) will already be familiar with the script format — speakers' names plus colons, and parenthesized stage directions. If students are not familiar with this form, a sample can be left on the blackboard as a model. The base of dramatic writing is, of course, improvisation, and the first steps have already been mentioned on page 290 — group writing down of a perfected improvisation, then solo improvisation on paper of the same sort of minimal situation as used in the drama period. Let us take up here at the latter point.

Writing Short Scripts

PROCEDURES

The assignment directions are to make up a minimal situation, or pick one from among suggestions, and to write the dialogue straight off in class for, say, fifteen or twenty minutes. It is important to stipulate a single, continuous scene unrolling in one place. The playing time of the script would be the same as the time the action would take in real life. Putting the matter this way helps keep the scene truly dramatic and emphasizes the fact that a script is a blueprint for enactment.

Because they are so used to narrative, inexperienced students tend to write a plotted story that jumps a great deal in time and space. The result is a series of very brief snatches of scenes arranged to plant the seed of a plot, show the main action, and reveal the aftermath. In such efforts one can see too much concern for a final twist or smash ending. Misuse of stage directions is one of the symptoms — narrating a short story, often with tell-tale lapses into the past tense. Stage directions should contain only what can be seen and heard, except for an occasional indication about how to stage and act the scene. Explanations of background circumstances, recounting of off-stage action, and descriptions of thought and feelings do not belong; they merely show that the student is still thinking of narrative, not drama.

My observations here about the narrative tendency derive from experience with students who have had no prior dramatic work. I think that veteran improvisers would not be nearly so likely to confuse dramatic writing with narrative. In any case, don't warn the students about these problems in advance, for more learning will take place if they do the assignments spontaneously and find out about the problems for themselves when others try to enact their script or discuss it after a trial reading. What would help to head off the narrative tendency, if there should be one, is to present the assignment as a direct extension of improvisation and to make the directions clear — a single, uninterrupted scene playable in, say, five minutes, with stage directions that read like a sensory recording, and containing no more than two or three characters. This last stipulation keeps the dynamics manageable and makes dramatic focusing easier.

These scripts are given trial readings in small groups, enacted, and printed up in little anthologies that can be assigned for reading as preparation for reading professional one-acters. In small groups students read each other's scripts aloud, taking parts and assigning a reader to the stage directions, discuss the playability of the script for potential enactment, and edit it for printing. Some scripts are memorized, rehearsed, and performed. These playlets are very convenient for enacting, being very short, and constitute a basic education in dramatic literature that will transfer to professional plays. Before being printed up, all of the scenes are put to some kind of dramatic test so that everything from punctuation to characterization can be revised. The printing furnishes multiple copies for enactment by other classes, as well as copies for silent reading. Occasionally the teacher projects a script and has it read aloud in class for reaction and discussion. The purpose of this is to parlay responses into a discussion of writing problems that the students seem to need help with.

SAMPLES FROM TRIALS

This one-scene assignment has been tried out in a number of different schools at all junior-high grades. Although I have introduced the assignment here as the first in a sequence, it need not be confined to younger students since, as the samples will show, it grows with the students. The samples exemplify also some of the varieties of the assignment, one of which I will call "duologue," a drama consisting of just two interweaving voices and often having no stage directions.

Duologue. The duologues below represent another variation, born somewhat of necessity. Having just begun to give the students some experience in improvisation, the teacher felt that some memory of events from the day before would be an easier starting point for his disadvantaged summer school students (mostly Negro, having just finished the seventh or eighth grade) than the yet unfamiliar notion of a minimal situation.[1]

1. Put him in the pot and cook him.
2. O.K. You can have it.
1. That nasty creature.
2. What do you mean, nasty? I got my toe missing because of that.
1. I don't care if it bit your head. Get it out of here.
2. O.K. But the next time I'll be back with a shark.
1. You do and I'll get a whale.

This is all one student could eke out, but it has a classic dramatic conciseness:

1. Want a crab?
2. Eeeek!

Besides a rapid alternation of speakers that scholars call stichomythia when the ancient Greeks do it, these dialogues all establish the dramatic situation immediately and admirably in the first line.

1. Say, look at that crazy hair-do.
2. Do you like it?
1. Well, not really? It looks kind of funny.
2. I didn't say that about your old-looking hair-do.
1. Well, if you didn't like it, why didn't you say something about it?
2. I would have hurt your feelings.
1. No, you wouldn't have.
2. Well, next time you'll know.

1. Did you spill some tonic on me?
2. Sorry, accidents will happen, sister.
1. That was no accident. You did it on purpose.
2. It happens to the best of us and you're not the best. So shut up and do the dishes.

[1] The teacher was Kenneth McElheny, working with Teresa Hamrock at the Lewis Junior High School, Roxbury, Massachusetts, in the Harvard-Boston Summer School. Some of the students had been taken on a school-sponsored trip to the beach the day before. The brevity is partly explained by their not being accustomed to writing much.

1. What are you wearing to the dance?
2. I don't know if I can go.
1. Huh?
2. Mom may not let me!
1. If you go, what are you going to wear?
2. My maroon skirt and white, pink flowered blouse. What will you wear?
1. My bleached shorts.
2. Those are bad!
1. Yeah!
2. They look like somebody spilled food on them.
1. Yeah! I might go buy something up at Upham's **Corner.**
2. You can go up yourself. I'm going to the beach.
1. I hope you drown.
2. I hope you get hit by the bus!

The value of sometimes dispensing with stage directions is precisely that the burden of action is thrown onto the dialogue. Whereas middle-class children writing under this constraint for the first time often have to rig the dialogue in an artificial way, lower-class children seem to have a knack for letting the speech capture the situation, perhaps because their language is more oriented to action and setting. Working with a title helps point the scene:

An Understanding

Joe:	Me, I'm going to the movies with Bob. O.K.?
Mother:	No, it isn't O.K.
Joe:	Why not?
Mother:	Because you said you'd clean the garage today.
Joe:	I can do it some other time. Please?
Mother:	You're doing it today and that's all there is to it.
Joe:	Oh! Come on, Ma, I promise I'll do it tomorrow.
Mother:	Joe, you heard me.
Joe:	Oh, all right you ch—
Mother:	What did you say?
Joe:	Nothing, Ma, nothing. Ma can I go after I'm done?
Mother:	Yes, Joe when you're finished you can go. And Joe,
Joe:	Yes, Ma.
Mother:	There's a quarter. Buy yourself a Coke.
Joe:	Oh. Thanks Ma![2]

Three-way dialogue. A trio now, following a statement of the minimal situation; by a disadvantaged student in a summer school program that had introduced improvisations:

[2] By a boy about to enter the ninth grade, supplied by Graham Ward, director of English at the Brooks Academy Summer School in North Andover, Mass., another program for disadvantaged students. I am grateful to Mr. Ward and his colleagues for considerable experimentation with assignments in this program in both regular and summer sessions at Brooks.

Situation — You want to go to the ballgame but you don't want to take your little brother.

Scene — Saturday afternoon warm and beautiful day for baseball.

JACK:	Mom, I'm going to the ballgame.
MOM:	Alright (*overheard by little brother*)
JOE:	Can I go with you Jack, please
JACK:	No!!!
MOM:	*Who* the hell is doing that Hollering
JOE:	Jack is. He won't take me to the ballgame.
JACK:	Man, he's always going with me. I didn't go with him when he went to Brocton.
MOM:	I know but you know how he likes the Yankees.
JACK:	I don't give a da— darn who he likes.
MOM:	I dare you to swear and I'll whip your ass so bad you won't go to the ballgame at all.
JACK:	Alright I'll take him give me his money
MOM:	Go get my pocketbook (*Joe goes to get it*)
JOE:	Mom I can't find it
MOM:	Oh shit I left it in the back seat of the car and your father took the car.
JACK:	Dats tooo bad (*he says to Joe like a baby and giggles*)
JOE:	(*crying*) Ma you're stupid
MOM:	(*with belt in her hand whips Joe*) How dare you you bastard.
JACK:	So long Mom I be back after the game.[3]

The language here is a real reflection of environment, I think, not an attempt to scandalize. If the teacher can avoid feeling offended, permitting this realism will yield a very worthy payoff for both writing and emotional expression. The shift in dynamics, incidentally, that accompanies a shift from two-person to three-person interaction warrants some attention in workshop discussion, since it throws light on both literature and life. At some point in this stage of dramatic writing some duets and trios should be juxtaposed and compared, either in class discussion of projected scripts or in successive enactment sessions.

Complete short play. The following playlet is a fairly typical effort by a middle-class seventh-grader to develop a continuous action into a climax, and to handle a fairly large cast of characters. The reader will find the scene rather hard to follow, first of all, because the child had never learned earlier to punctuate by ear. Dialogue writing makes very clear the inadequacy of teaching punctuation by rules and teacher correction, even when done in first-rate schools with able children. Also, the child was not quite ready to

[3] Done by a boy about to enter seventh grade, in the Milton Academy Summer School for disadvantaged urban students. My thanks to the director of English, Richard Herrmann, for trying out assignments, with colleagues, at both Milton and at his regular school, Roxbury Latin.

control an action as ambitious as this one. The premature plunge was my fault, because I did not yet understand that a slower approach, via short duologues and trios, is wiser. Allowing for these deficits in experience, the attempt to shape dialogue and action into a purposeful composition was rather good:

The Mysteriouse Doorknob

Cast

Jin Jones — the father
Mary Jones — the mother
Sue Johns — There twelve year old daughter whos set on being a private detective
Jack — her eleven year old brother
Patty — her ten year old sister

Setting
The Living Room

MARY: Jin are you sure you put the cat out
JIM: Yes dear I'm sure
MARY: The nights so dark do you think Sue can take care of Jack and Patty
JIM: Yes dear I'm sure besides we won't be gone long and its not a school night there all around the same age anyhow.
MARY: If you say so now lets say good by to the children Sue Jack Patty were leaving now if any thing happens we will be at the nunber (*shows peace of Paper*) you can all stay up till we get home
JIM: Yes and heres the key lock the door when we leave and don't let any one in. Good by (*they leave*
SUE: Okay first well watch hony west then the smothers brothers then the man from UNCLE
JACK: It always has to be your way oh comon lets watch something else there just showing repeats
PATTY: Ya oh comon
SUE: Theres nothing good on oh so I guess well have to watch. . .
PATTY: Well lets see whats on (*Jack goes to turn it out all of the sudden the lights go out*)
JACK: We blew a fuse all go try to fix it.
SUE: No!
JACK: What do you mean by no its just in the closet
SUE: (*in a whisper*) Someone might be in there
PATTY: Oh Sue you're cracked Jack heres the flash light
JACK: (*All of the sudden closet door twists*) Help! (*It stops*)
PATTY: I'm scared
SUE: Go get my privet eye soutcase Patty comeon Jack give her the flash light and let's hide behind this chair
PATTY: No! not me there may be more people around
SUE: She's right

JACK: Shut up there may be someone listening to us (*all of the sudan Mother and father burst into the room*

MARY: I told you Jin I'm sure now I saw the lights go off when we pulled out oh children are you all right!

PATTY: Ya Mom

JIN: Sue why didn't you lock the door or call us (*closet door knob moves again*

JACK: Dad theres someone in the closet!

JIM: What!

MARY: Oh no my poor baby! (*father gets stick opens door looks in attaches to wires together light goes on, shuts door*)

JIM: Mary you naged me hard to come home because the cat was in the closet

MARY: You said you put the cat out!

JIM: So I did

And they all start to lagh

Although there were better plays written by the author's classmates (most of whom are more literate, I hasten to add) I have chosen this one to reproduce because I was present when it was performed and discussed. The comments from the other students were as follows: They appreciated the way in which the father's negligence, the mainspring of the action, was planted in the opening exchange, and returned to at the end, but felt that several problems combined to spoil the main effect. The play depended a lot, they said, on the audience's seeing and hearing things to which the players were supposed to react — the sound of the cat, the doorknob turning, the lights and TV going on and off — but which the production did not allow enough for (and which, indeed, would to some extent have required better facilities). As a result, both the title and some of the actions seemed pointless. The fact that the audience did not laugh at the end, as they were supposed to, was attributed to some of these failures of effects as well as to some confusion in the writing. The actors said that a number of the lines had had to be changed during rehearsals because they left character and action unclear. To this comment the audience added that the behavior of the characters was inconsistent enough to confuse them about which children were supposed to be fearful and which were not. For his part, the author said he would have directed a couple of things rather differently. A very positive suggestion from the class was to build up the scary atmosphere more — with stormier weather, horror show on TV, and the telling of ghost stories. Perhaps this discussion illustrates the kinds of learning that can take place in a drama workshop.[4]

[4] I want to thank Elizabeth Cawein, the teacher of the class, for her fine cooperation and willingness to experiment for a whole year with this and other assignments. The school was Weeks Junior High in Newton, Massachusetts, from which many of the following writing samples also came. The principal and assistant principal, William Webster and Helena Glenn, are brave administrators of the kind who sponsor extensive trials of unorthodox assignments in their schools.

Dialogue by maturer students. In choosing samples of eighth- and ninth-grade dialogue from the same middle-class school, I found myself having to exercise great self-control, so rich was the output of writing. I think the high quality was partly due to the emphasis we placed in the assignment on drawing dramatic material from familiar experience. When the students did write scenes about far-fetched or fantastic characters and actions, they almost always fell into cliché — borrowed stories from books, movies, and television. With rare exceptions, the shaping of realistic material showed more creative imagination than the so-called making up of situations. But, again, mere injunction or admonition is not the best educational strategy; if some children need to ignore the emphasis on realism, it may be better to let them learn from peer reaction whether their far-fetched inventions are worthwhile or not.

In practically all the dialogues that were written in these grades — even in the casual, slice-of-life conversations — one can see efforts to compose the scene in various meaningful ways — to define a relationship among characters, to contrast personalities, to comment satirically, to differentiate styles of speech, to set up conflicts, to bring out social and moral issues. Here is a "two- or three-person dialogue with stage directions" by an eighth-grade girl at the same school:

JOHN: (*running into room, waving a spatula wildly overhead which scatters drops of batter in every direction*) The sky is falling, we must go and tell the king!

SARA: (*putting down newspaper, looking up calmly*) what is it darling?

JOHN: Our beloved Aunt Mora hath seen fit to bestow upon our humble selves a visit.

SARAH: Oh John, after last night?

JOHN: (*grimly*) Yep!

SARAH: Thank heavens Kay won't be home 'til this afternoon. Where's Auntie now?

JOHN: In the kitchen, attempting the impossible.

SARA: Huh?

JOHN: Teaching *me* to make better pancakes, no less.

SARA: Oh, John, be serious for once! Poor Kay's future is at stake, not to mention Terry's.

JOHN: They can always elope to South Africa.

SARA: (*getting up and walking nevously about*) That's just the trouble honey. They may have to resort to something like to get any peace, and you know how much they want to live close by and work in Boston — at peace with the *whole* family.

JOHN: (*suddenly serious*) When I think of all they've been through because of that witch, that nosey, rotten no-good. . . .

SARA: (*whirling to face him in horror*) John, shush! The kitchen is right overhead!

JOHN: The hell with the kitchen! What's the good owning a kitchen, or a house, or anything else when your aunt-in-law moves in to take over your life!

SARA: (*abruptly*) How long did she say she was staying?

JOHN: Until she's convinced our daughter "what's good for her." Heaven forbid Kay should marry beneath her station!

SARA: Well — if she thinks she can treat my daughter like — why that mean, nosey —

JOHN: (*mimicking her*) Sara, hush! The kitchen!

SARA: Oh — I know I shouldn't say things like that. After all she *is* practically the head of the family — always has been. But she can't get away with this. John, how do you stop a woman like that?

JOHN: Heart's dearest, if I knew, I wouldn't stand here gabbing. I'd do something! (*The telephone rings. Sara, who has been sitting with her head in her hands, thinking, starts; jumps up and picks up the reciever*)

SARA: Hello? Oh Kay darling — how are you? (*Looks nervously at John who doesn't notice, as he is standing with his back to her and his hands in his pockets*) What? Speak up, dear. . . Oh, swimming, of course, how lovely! (*Her face lights up with relief*) Listen — take your time, stay as long as your want. I — uh — I want you to get a georgous tan. . . Oh, sure that's fine. Well, have a good time dear — bye! (*she hangs up and drops into a chair with a sigh of relief.*) She and Terry and everyone are going swimming, then getting hotdogs and cones and things for their lunch and supper. (*She fiddles nerously with a button, then looks up hesitently.*) John, do you suppose talking to her would do any good — Aunt Mora I mean? After all, that's what you do for a living — talk to people for hours on end to try to get them to learn something. Mabey we could teach Auntie a thing or two.

JOHN: (*laughs shortly*) That'll be the day — when we convince your dear aunt that we know more — or as much — as she does! (*He imitates her pompous airs*) "Now children, run along. You have no idea what you're talking about. I assure you I'm only doing this for your own good!"

SARA: (*laughing*) Oh John, that's marvelous! But I meant we'd explain subtely of course — *very* subtely! And we must be careful to say nothing to arouse her suspicion — after all, she's very sensitive.

JOHN: Lord knows she's sensitive! (*He mimics her again*) "And he had the gall, the utter gall to say to me. 'Excuse me ma'am, but are you sure that's your bag?' As though I were a common thief!"

SARA: (*Laughs helplessly*) John, for heaven sakes, be serious!

JOHN: O.K. Let me think of something. (*He begins to pace up and down the room, takes out and lights a cigarette.*)

SARA: Honey, don't you think you smoke too much? You'll be dead by the time you're forty!

JOHN: In that case I've been dead for three years. Stop your natterring, woman, the muse in upon me . . . . . . Something along the lines of "We consider their love to be something beautiful and sacred, and we *all* hope they'll be very happy"?

SARA: That's beautiful darling, but we need more than that.

JOHN: Mm-mm; well, I'll let the rest be inspired. Let us be off! (*Hand in hand they start out of the room somewhat hesitantly, a bit like two guilty children who got into trouble and are going to be scolded. All at*

> *once a look of horror crosses John's face; he drops Sara's hand, claps his*
> *head in dismay and starts up the stairs two at a time.)*

SARA: (*very concerned*) John, what is it?

JOHN: My pancakes are burning![5]

Although this girl has obviously drawn on familiar material, she has extended and shaped it imaginatively. In doing so, she has learned, I wager, a lot about both composition and literature. In the course of editing this for printing, or doing a reading or performance of it, the students should be asked to propose titles for it. In fact, titles should be stipulated in the assignment. The teacher from whose class this paper came said that this assignment produced the best writing of the year; students wrote at great length and liked doing the assignment very much.

Here is a duologue written by a ninth-grade girl in another middleclass suburban school:

MRS. MORAN: If you weren't at the recreation center last night, where were you?

ANNE: But, Mom, I told you a million times! I was at the rec playing cards, and then Rick walked me home.

MRS. MORAN: But you didn't come home until an hour and half past the curfew. Don't try to tell me it took Rick an hour and a half to walk you up the street.

ANNE: Well . . . I guess maybe we didn't realize what time it was and stayed later.

MRS. MORAN: Anne, your father and I walked up to the rec to see where you were. We were worried about you. All the lights were out, and Mrs. Sampson said you had left. Were you with Rick?

ANNE: Mom, for the millionth time. YES! He walked me home! For the hour and a half we were fooling around on Steve's porch.

MRS. MORAN: I thought you just said you stayed later at the rec than expected. You didn't mention Steve's house.

ANNE: Well, Mom . . .

MRS. MORAN: Was Mrs. Rider at home?

ANNE: What do you think I am anyway? All you ever do is suspect me of things and treat me like dirt. I'm sick of it. I'm tired. It's 11:30. I'm going to bed. We can talk about it later. O.K.?

MRS. MORAN: Yes, we'll have to talk about it later. I'm tired too. I want you to think about this now.

ANNE: Yes, mother, (*sighing*) goodnight.[6]

This brief but intense exchange dramatizes a recurring theme among these younger adolescents that could be a topic for small-group discussion. Also, writing out the conflict, acting it out in improvisation, talking it out in dis-

---

[5] The teacher was Eugenia Nicholas, whom I wish to thank for cooperating in the full-year experimentation.

[6] Lexington High School, Lexington, Massachusetts. My thanks to the teacher, Joy Lyon, for her year's participation.

cussion, undoubtedly are psychically useful and help objectify the real-life problem.

Writing Plays of More Than One Scene

If scene writing has progressed well, this strand of dramatic writing can culminate, by ninth grade, in one-acts containing two to four short scenes that distinctly develop a dramatic idea. The assignment directions do not stipulate multiple scenes; they merely call for a complete play performable in, say, twenty or thirty minutes. The number of scenes and characters is left to the author.

I offer here two samples, the first by a girl, the second by a boy, one about teens and adults, the other about teens among themselves. Since they are necessarily rather long, I will let them stand as illustrations, by extension, of what students in grades ten to twelve might go on to do with play writing. The first author's introduction and her abstract designation of the characters show the representative value she intended the characters and actions to have. Like professionals, these amateurs make general statements through their dramas:

But Mom . . .
Author's introduction
Names have been omitted except where necessary (as in the dialogue) because I feel the scenes are too typical to pin down to one family.

Scene I

(*It is a typical study. The walls are dark wood. There is an overhead lamp lighting up the room. A middle-aged lady, dressed in a black sweater and pants, is sitting at the desk. She has a cigarette in her hand. She is tapping absentmindedly on the ashtray. A young girl of about fifteen can be heard reading a paper she is holding. As she finishes, she looks up.*)

DAUGHTER: Well? Any comments?

MOTHER: Very good for a first draft.

DAUGHTER: Mother, I read you the first draft two days ago.

MOTHER: Oh, (*absently*) did you?

DAUGHTER: Yes, and you told me to rewrite the part about the type of love between parents and children. Do you have any final corrections? (*There is a pause. The mother doesn't seem to be concentrating on what is being said to her. The daughter is waiting for a reply.*)

DAUGHTER: Well — ? (*She puts the paper on the table*)

MOTHER: I'm thinking. (*Then she seems to be talking aloud to herself*) I better call and change my hair appointment to nine o'clock.

DAUGHTER: Mother!

MOTHER: Hmmm?

DAUGHTER: You're not listening.

MOTHER: What? (*Pause*) I'm sorry dear, I wasn't listening.

Scene II

(*The table in the kitchen is small and has been crowded into a small nook. The area has been painted another color. The purpose behind this was to make it look like a separate breakfast room.*)

(*The daughter is sitting at the table reading. The mother summons her while entering the room.*)

MOTHER: Why can't you *once* have the table set before your father gets home?

DAUGHTER: But Mom, we're going out for dinner.

MOTHER: Never mind the excuses. Why don't you go upstairs and start getting ready, dear. The Shermans will be by for us at seven and we don't want to keep them waiting.

DAUGHTER: But Mom, it's three-thirty.

MOTHER: I know, but sometimes it takes you a long time to get ready. Besides, I want you to look nice for them. You want to make a good impression on them, don't you?

DAUGHTER: Mother. I am not concerned with looking nice for *them* — I am not out to impress people. I want to look nice for myself.

MOTHER: O.K. How about for your father and me? We like to see you look nice.

DAUGHTER: Hmm.

MOTHER: If not for us, do it for your brother. He's dating their daughter. You don't want them to think he comes from a family of slobs.

DAUGHTER: How come he doesn't have to go tonight?

MOTHER: You're making it sound like a chore to go out with us. You know, if you want to stay home tonight you can. We aren't twisting your arm. It costs a lot of money to take you out and there are plenty of other things we could be doing with it instead.

DAUGHTER: You still didn't say why Alan got out of it.

MOTHER: Alan "got out of it" because he had already made a date for tonight and it wouldn't be polite to break it.

DAUGHTER: But Mom, he's going out with Rene Sherman!

MOTHER: (*What her daughter has said finally dawns on her*) You know, you have a point there.

FATHER: (*As he enters he pats his daughter on the head*) Yes, I always said she was a sharp kid.

DAUGHTER: Oh, Dad.

FATHER: How about playing a little tennis?

MOTHER: Mel, I thought she should be getting ready to go out.

FATHER: But Ruth, it's three-thirty!

Scene III

(*Father and daughter enter the house with their tennis rackets. The clock on the wall shows that it is close to six-thirty.*)

MOTHER: Did you have a good game?

DAUGHTER: Yes, and boy am I exhausted.

MOTHER: Mel, you shouldn't have let her work herself up like that. She just got over being sick.

FATHER: But Ruth, she was better two weeks ago.

MOTHER: I heard her blow her nose yesterday.

FATHER: I'm sure tired. We had to stop at the gas station on the way home because the tire was flat and I did't have a spare.

DAUGHTER: Come on — let's get ready. The Shermans will be here in less than a half-hour

(Daughter and father start up the stairs together, but Mother suddenly calls out to them)

MOTHER: Wait a minute dear. Could you stay down here a minute and help me roll a ball of yarn?

DAUGHTER: Now?

MOTHER: Well, I want it for tonight.

DAUGHTER: But Mom, we're going out to dance. You can't knit at the table.

FATHER: Maybe she wants to tell some interesting yarns.

MOTHER: All right *(she continues in a rejected tone)* go upstairs and get ready. It's OK. I'll do it myself and if I don't finish then I won't finish. So I won't knit tonight.

(She is obviously waiting for a response, but she gets none, she goes on to add:)

MOTHER: If it was a sweater for you, I'm sure you'd be able to find the time.

FATHER: Why don't we get dressed first, and if we have any time, *then* roll the yarn.

MOTHER: You know there won't be time after we get dressed. You've got to do it now.

FATHER: But Ruth, it really isn't shorter if you roll yarn first and then get dressed, or . . . Oh, never mind. It's no use.

Scene IV

(The door bell rings. The mother, dressed in a simple black cocktail dress can be seen in the hall running towards the stairs. She sees her reflection with the pink wall paper in the mirror and stops)

MOTHER: Somebody else get it please — I'm a mess. It must be the Shermans. *(She starts back to her room)*

DAUGHTER: Joyous raptures.

MOTHER: *(from her room)* Make sure you know who it is before you open the door! *(The daughter takes one last glance in the mirror, straightens her hair and gallops down the stairs. She pulls the curtain to the side to see who is outside. Forcing a big smile, she sighs and opens the door. Suddenly without warning she is bombarded by six-year-old twin boys dressed in suits. One has a cowlick and both have devilish grins. Then in walks a little girl, obviously a little older than them and feeling more dignified.)*

DAUGHTER: Won't you come in? Mom and Dad will be right down. *(The Shermans enter. You can tell by their faces all the fun they had getting the children ready and over there.)*

GUEST: I hope we're not too early.

MOTHER: *(Coming down the stairs putting her last few hairs into place, mumbles to herself)* three and a half minutes.

GUEST: What's that?

MOTHER: (*Blushing slightly*) I said Mel will be down in a half a minute.
              Let me take your coats and we'll go inside for a drink. (*The tele-
              phone rings. The daughter runs into the study and answers it.*)

DAUGHTER: Hello? (*pause*) John? (*Pause — sarcasially*) No, you don't have
              the wrong number, you just have the wrong person. (*She hangs up*)
              (*The guest's voice can be heard as they approach the study*)

GUEST: Oh, Tommy brought his crayons with him. (*They are now in the
              room*) Is it all right if he draws on that paper until we're ready to
              leave? (*He is pointing to the paper that the daughter had read to
              her mother that afternoon.*)

MOTHER: Of course, it's only a first draft of Amy's and she doesn't mind.
              Do you, dear?

DAUGHTER: But Mom . . .[7]

For one thing, this play raises the important technical issue of scene-
breaking: how many scenes, and which ones, are required to dramatize successfully a given piece of material? Does "But Mom . . ." need four scenes,
and what is their effect?

Learning about technique during the cycle of play creation. Somewhere
in the learning cycle through which such a play passes, this issue should be
raised. The sooner in the cycle the better, perhaps, but not necessarily always.
The whole cycle, which was not available in the experiment, can include: a
workshop reading and discussion of the first draft (duplicating enough copies
for acting scripts would certainly facilitate this); or silent reading of the first
draft in a writing workshop followed by written commentary and discussion
(exchanging manuscripts in a small group); a rehearsed reading or performance before the class; and preparation for publication by a group of
editors who consult with the author and incorporate the reactions of audience
and actors.

Over-fragmenting a play into small scenes may represent a lingering confusion of narrative with drama, an immoderate eagerness to score an ideologi-
cal point through plot manipulation, or simply an unskillful, uneconomical
constructing of the material. Scene shifts mean time pauses and perhaps new
locales. Are these justified? They also introduce problems about how to
indicate, in the dialogue, facts that cannot be seen — the new time and
place, their significance, and what has occurred in the interim. Putting such
information in the mouths of the characters can come off as well motivated
and integral action or as obviously phony talk for the audience's benefit.
Pacing is also involved in scene shifts. Is each scene as long or as short as it
ought to be for what it tries to do? The speed of both the individual scene

---

[7] The students who wrote these two one-act plays were in ninth-grade classes of
Joseph Hanson, head of the English department at Weeks Junior High School in
Newton, Mass., whose very great contribution, along with colleague Lucy Woodward,
was to devote a large part of the year's classwork to trying out a wide range of assignments I proposed.

and the succession of scenes has to be considered here — the rate at which an audience assimilates certain actions and the cumulative effect of short and long scenes.

These dramaturgical matters, which are exactly those which the professional faces, can be raised by students in their own ways at various points in the cycle, but if necessary the teacher may raise them. Sometimes he does this while sitting in on a writing group or acting group, sometimes at the end of a class reading, if a certain problem seems to be widespread but unrecognized. Often one thoughtful question is enough: "What would happen if we dropped this scene?" (To let the students test whether it is justified or not.) "What if Charles dramatized a meeting in the shop instead of having the girl just refer to it?" (To open up other compositional possibilities.) Pace can be focused on by the teacher's personal reaction: "I felt that scene went by too fast (or dragged in the middle). Did anyone else feel that?" Most of all, try to spot the technical implications buried in *student* commentary and to make them emerge so that students will then spot them for each other.

Learning to describe. If one glances back through "But Mom . . . ," looking only at the stage directions, he will become aware of how much description the play contains. A virtue of play writing that I have not mentioned so far is the opportunity it affords to practice the accurate and significant rendering of appearances — the look of a room, the look on someone's face. Far from being an exercise, play description is purposeful and functional — an indication of what the prop people should do and a relevant adjunct to the action. The writer has to think about real spatial relations, on the one hand, and about significant selection of details, on the other. Production of a play will often put description to the test of clarity. Moreover, since stage directions also include an account of the action, the writer must coordinate description and narration in ways characteristic of other writing as well.

Dramatizing speech behavior. Because it holds a mirror up to their own discussion behavior, the play sample below shows how dramatic writing can sometimes objectify for teenagers the ways in which they talk. The central action of this play is in fact a very good dramatization of the underlying group dynamics that so often distort discussion about an objective topic.

The Meeting

Characters

Steve — President of Cabinet
John — Parliamentarian
Susan, Bob, Nancy, Allan — Members of Cabinet
Several other members of cabinet

Synopsis of Scenes

Scene I — A school cabinet meeting in Room 212.
Scene II — Room 214, next door, immediately afterward.

Scene I

(*A group of students about age 13 are sitting in a classroom. It is crowded with school desks, with the teacher's bigger desk in front facing the other desks. The walls are filled mainly with maps. Some newspaper clippings on current events fill the remaining sections of the walls. An American flag hangs over the doorway, and there are two bookcases in the corner opposite the doorway.*)

(*As the curtain opens, students are drifting in. Everyone is talking, and there is a loud murmur in the room.*)

STEVE: (*tapping gavel on his desk*) Attention, please! (*The chatter stops.*) The meeting will now come to order. Treasurer's report, please. (*Everyone resumes their chattering*)

BOB: (*standing up*) We now have four hundred fifty-two dollars and three cents in the checking account, three hundred six dollars and seventy-six cents in the savings account, and twelve dollars and forty-one cents in petty cash. Our total funds now stand at seven hundred seventy dollars and ten cents. (*He sits down*)

STEVE: Are there any questions? (*Nancy raises her hand*) Nancy?

NANCY: Did you say four hundred fifty-two dollars and three cents, three hundred six dollars and seventy-six cents, and twelve dollars and forty-one cents?

BOB: Yes, that's right.

NANCY: Well, you made a miscalculation.

BOB: No, I didn't.

NANCY: Yes, you did. It should be a total of seven hundred seventy-one dollars and twenty cents. I have the figures right here. (*She produces a piece of paper.*)

ALLAN: Forget it, Bob. She's probably right. She gets A's in Math. (*Scornfully*) She's a brain.

BOB: I bet you think you're pretty smart, don't you, Nancy?

NANCY: Well, just because you can't even . . .

STEVE: (*hitting the desk with his gavel*): Quiet, please! Bob and Nancy, if you can't behave in an orderly way you'll have to leave the meeting. Now, are there any more questions? (*Everyone is silent.*) All right, secretary's report.

NANCY: The four thousand seven hundred ninety-second meeting of the eighth grade cabinet was called to order at twenty seven minutes and forty-eight seconds after seven o'clock A.M. on Tuesday, May sixth, nineteen sixty six A.D. by President Steven K. Jones in Room 212. The treasurer's report was accepted after a few of the treasurer's mistakes were corrected.

BOB: Hey, wait a minute! You don't have to put in about . . .

STEVE: Order! Bob, be quiet. Go on Nancy.

NANCY: (*with a smug look at Bob*) As I was saying before I was interrupted, the treasurer's report was accepted with several changes, and the secretary's report was accepted as read, as usual. (*Bob glares at her and starts to say something but thinks better of it and keeps quiet.*) Under old business, we passed by a large majority my motion for a beach party at the end of the year for all the honor roll students. Then we discussed Bob's motion to have a wrestling team, which was quickly dropped. We also rejected the motion to put curtains in the cafeteria. Under new business. Susan moved that we have a slave day. We tabled the discussion until the next meetings so we could get Mr. Websten's approval before we voted on the motion. Mr. Drake suggested that we start a program to encourage cabinet enthusiasm on the part of all the students. We discussed it and it was passed. We also discussed the problem on monitoring the cafeteria, but no conclusion was reached. The meeting was adjourned at thirty-one minutes and eleven seconds after eight o'clock. (*She sits down.*)

STEVE: Are there any questions?

BOB: She didn't say anything about anyone *moving;* we have a cabinet enthusiasm program. She just said that Mr. Drake suggested it and it was passed.

STEVE: What do you say, Parliamentarian?

JOHN: I think that in this case a teacher's suggestion is an adequate substitute for a formal motion.

STEVE: All right, now we can proceed to old business. I think we have to continue our discussion on Susan's motion. Susan, did you and Jane go to Mr. Websten?

SUSAN: Yes, we did. He said that we could have one if we consult with him about the date first.

STEVE: Good. Now, does anyone have anything to say concerning the issue?

ALLAN: Yes. What kind of stupid idea is a slave day? What's it supposed to prove. A wrestling team is a much better idea.

BOB: Yeah, he's right. How much fun can you have being a slave?

STEVE: Bob and Allan, the next time you talk out of turn you'll have to leave the room. Now, is there any other discussion concerning the issue? (*Silence*) All right, then, let's vote. All in favor of having a slave day raise your hand. (*Several hands go up; Steve counts them.*) All opposed. (*A few scattered hands go up. Bob and Allan wave both their hands in the air.*) The motion is passed. Now let's figure out a date.

JOHN: How about next Wednesday? That will give us the weekend plus Monday and Tuesday to get everything ready.

NANCY: No, that's not good. I have my ballet class and my piano lesson on Wednesdays, so we can't have it then.

BOB: No one would want you for a slave anyway. (*Laughter.*)

NANCY: Oh, is that so? Well, you listen to me, Bobby Fisher . . .

STEVE: Will you two please stop bickering? I'm beginning to think you really like each other.

BOB: Her? Are you kidding?

NANCY: (*together*) Him? Are you kidding?

STEVE: Well, never mind. Let's get on with our discussion. Wednesday is no good, so does anyone have any better suggestions?

NANCY: How about Tuesday? I'm not doing anything on Tuesday.

ALLAN: No, Nancy. Just because it's good for you doesn't mean that it's perfect for everybody. It's no good Tuesday because that's when baseball practice is. How about Friday?

JOHN: No, we can't have it then because I have band rehearsal. How about Thursday?

STEVE: It looks like we won't be able to please everybody with the date, so why don't we vote and have it two days in a row? All right, how many people want to have two consecutive slave days? (*All the hands go up.*) All right, we'll have two slave days in a row. Now, how many want the slave days Monday and Tuesday? (*Some hands go up.*) Tuesday and Wednesday? (*Some hands go up.*) Wednesday and Thursday? (*Some hands go up.*) Thursday and Friday? (*Some hands. Steve counts all the hands.*) Okay. It looks like we have slave days Wednesday and Thursday.

BOB: Too bad, Nancy. But don't feel too bad. You'll have fun at your piano lesson.

STEVE: Is there any other old business?

JOHN: We have to discuss a cabinet enthusiasm program. (*Everyone groans.*)

STEVE: Come on. We have to do it, so we might as well get it done with.

NANCY: Well, I think that some of our representatives (*looking at Bob*) don't bring a very good image back to their classes. Members of the cabinet should give accurate reports about what goes on during every meeting.

JOHN: Well, who wants to hear about you and Bob fighting? (*Laughter.*)

STEVE: (*tapping for order*) Maybe if we all stopped quarreling and got more done, everyone would have a higher opinion of cabinet.

BOB: Well, we never pass any good ideas, like a wrestling team or a basketball tournament. All we ever do is have stupid slave days or fashion shows.

ALLAN: Yeah, remember when we crashed that fashion show and Mr. Websten . . .

NANCY: Oh, that was the most horrible thing even you boys could have done! You ruined . . .

STEVE: Nancy and Bob, if you don't stop right now, something will have to be done. I don't want to ask anyone to leave the room, but you two are disrupting the entire meeting. Now, what were you going to say, John?

JOHN: I think if we sponsored some big party or something that everyone really enjoyed, then people would support cabinet more. The parties we usually have are bad. Hardly anyone ever comes, so no one has any fun.

NANCY: John's right. We ought to give a big party. But what occasion do we have for a party?

JOHN: It's almost time for the spring prom. We'll have to make it a big success. I move that Steve appoint a committee of four to arrange the details for a big spring prom.

NANCY: I second the motion.

STEVE: All in favor of my appointing a committee of four to arrange the prom? (*All hands go up.*) All right. The motion is passed. I appoint Nancy, John . . . Bob and Allan, do you think you can be sensible about this?

BOB: Why do we always have to do rotten stuff like dances?

ALLAN: Forget it, Bob. Once they passed it, we might as well go along with it.

STEVE: Will you two behave if I put you on the committee?

BOB: Yeah, I guess so.

STEVE: All right. Bob, Allan, Nancy and John are the four members of the committee.

NANCY: Can we adjourn to another room to start planning?

STEVE: Okay. And I'd like you to make a full report at each meeting on what you've decided and what you're planning on doing, so that everyone else can make suggestions. And John, you're in charge.

JOHN: All right. Come on, let's go into room 214 while they finish the meeting.

(*Curtain*)

Scene II

(*Room 214, immediately afterward. The empty room is just like the room in Scene I. As the curtain opens, the four children enter. They all sit down.*)

JOHN: Well, I think that the first thing we should do is to think of a major theme for the prom.

BOB: What do you mean by a theme?

NANCY: Oh, Bob, don't you know anything? All the dances we've had are based on some idea or other.

ALLAN: Like when we had the deep freeze this winter.

NANCY: Or the Maypole dance last year.

BOB: The Maypole dance? Oh, isn't that a cute name? (*He gets up and skips around, trying to provoke Nancy.*)

NANCY: We all thought it was a good name! Just because . . .

JOHN: Now, now, children, you're at it again. Let's just see if we can get through ten minutes without ending up at each other's throats. Okay? Now, does anybody have any ideas for a theme? (*Nobody says anything.*) All right, we can't sit around all day and try to come up with a theme, so we'll discuss refreshments and decorations.

ALLAN: Yeah, that's the main reason why the parties are so bad. There's never anything good to eat.

BOB: Why doesn't everyone who's coming to the dance bring something? That way it wouldn't cost as much, and there'd be more to eat, and it would probably be better.

JOHN: Bob, congratulations! That's the smartest thing you've said all week. Now, what about decorations?

BOB: We can do what we usually do: have balloons, streamers and all that.

NANCY: No, it has to be special. We can't have balloons because the boys always pop them.

BOB: What do you want to have, Nancy? Should we get some flowers, maybe? And we can spray the room with perfume.

NANCY: Oh, all you ever do is fight! Do you know what I think of you?
(*The passing bell rings and the four children get up to go. They walk to the door still fighting.*)
BOB: I couldn't care less about what you think of me. And as for you and your ballet lessons . . .

(*Curtain*)

Imagine for a moment that this scene is an actual small-group discussion or panel. Personal relations just like this boy's and girl's negative expression of attraction often determine the turns that conversation will take in small groups. It may be easier for the teacher to avoid annoyance and frustration about the business of the day being thus thwarted if he construes such determinants of conversation themselves as part of the day's business. That is, whatever concerns language behavior is in the language teacher's domain, and there is no use avoiding or punishing personality interactions; the opportunities for learning are too great. In the play, the leader merely curbs these reactions; a teacher can frankly direct discussion to the dynamics and give them attention before resuming the objective topic. If he induces the habit among the students, they can apply the principle as members of small-group discussions and of panel audiences.

The teacher's technique is to remark that he feels such and such undercurrent is going on in the group, to ask if others feel this, and to ask how they are reacting to it. Two matters are at stake — being aware of what is happening, and developing good group functioning. The colleagues of the students involved in the personality struggle should state what the latter seem to be doing and react candidly to it. Teaching them how to do this unquestionably takes a sensitive skill for which teachers are practically never trained but should be. Helping students learn about communication from their own interpersonal relations is probably the least explored aspect of education.

Writing Scripts Based on Reading Selections

Before doing one-acts, one of the classes from which the last two plays came had combined dramatic writing with readings in mythology. Taking the characterizations and plot summaries from Edith Hamilton, they fleshed them out in group-written scripts, which they rehearsed and performed. Groups were assigned a myth to dramatize and then went to the book for information. Whereas the other class read and studied the myths as texts, this class used the texts only as sources, which meant that individuals read them in whatever way they thought best (including skip-reading) to glean what they needed to know, and that the teacher was not involved in their reading. What happened actually was that in order to make up the dialogue and compose the scenes, the groups had to straighten out the action and interpret the characters by discussing them and by referring to the text for evidence. Whereas this class got very involved in the dramatizations, the other class began to groan after reading a certain number of myths.

When the two classes took a factual test on the myths at the end of the year, the class that had enacted them remembered them as well as the one that had studied them with the teacher. Students, moreover, who had been known to read with poor comprehension seemed definitely to understand and remember the material they had dramatized much better than they usually remembered texts they read and studied. And a comparison, based on the test, between students' memory of the dramatized myths and their memory of *The Odyssey*, read at the same time, showed that members of that class remembered the facts of the myths better than the facts of *The Odyssey*, even though they said at the time that they enjoyed reading *The Odyssey* very much.[8] Bible stories could be dramatized in the same way and with the same advantages, since they too are very synoptic narrative.

[8] This bit of research with the test, which was initiated by Joseph Hanson for his own purposes, was not controlled in a very scientific way but was of the practical sort teachers often conduct in order to make choices among different methods. If only for their satisfaction, I suggest that other teachers replicate this experiment.

Chapter 21

Socratic Dialogue

Whereas the dramatic sequence just described develops emotional and theatrical aspects of dialogue, the concurrent strand of dialogue writing that I want to trace now develops the intellectual, discursive aspect. For convenience, we may call it socratic dialogue, meaning simply a conversation about ideas. But, as I have been suggesting, emotion and thought are just different wave lengths on the same band which we can tune in by turning the dial a little more in one direction or the other. The differences between dramatic and socratic dialogue are a matter of degree. The gradual shift from one to the other is the basis of the sequence at hand now.

The assignment directions that accomplish this shift are similar to those described on page 290 for bridging between improvisation and discussion. That is, the minimal situation is such as to center the action on a conversational topic; stage directions are eliminated; and the characters become less individual (approaching types) while the setting and topic become general.

Samples from Trials

One eighth-grade class had read "The Enemy" by Pearl Buck and discussed the definitions of "enemy":

SHOULD WE AID THE ENEMY?

Characters:

Jim: An American
Yuru: A Japanese Woman
Mr. Jenkins: A British man

317

Time: 1970
Place: America

JIM: I believe that we shouldn't aid the enemy.

YURU: But they're still human. What if they're dying. Is it not criminal to let a man die.

JIM: But we are trying to kill them that's the whole point of the war!

MR. JENKINS: (*a British man in America*) I think you're both wrong, we should try to stop wars. Our aim is not to kill people, it is to stop the killing of them. What do you think war is for anyway?

JIM: But some people have to die, in order for others to live.

YURU: But why have wars at all?

JIM: It has to be that way. It is the only way to demonstrate what you want done.

MR. JENKINS: It is true even riot is a war.

YURU: But what about the enemy. He has a home, children, a family. Just like we do.

JIM: But if you aid the enemy you are a traitor to your country.

YURU: Yes that is true, but if you let him die you are a traitor to God.

MR. JENKINS: Lets look at it this way. No matter what you do you are still doing something wrong. Wether it be moral or physical.

JIM: But if you aid the enemy you are in a sense saying, "His country is better than ours," "We should not be in war with them!" "We have made a terrible mistake." "We will surrender to you." Is that not what you are against. If you aid the prisnor you are giving up your country, and defeting the war.

YURU: I see your point now, you are right. We should not aid the enemy in any way. We must think and act and do things for ourselves, as it is not us that will have to suffer. If we were to say harbor a enemy, we would be in grave danger. My husband would be arrested, and sent to a prison camp.

I might well be sent to a labor camp too. The name of our family will go down in discrage. My children will have no trouble if I leave the enemy alone. But if I harbor him than their life will be ruined. They could not live in this country. No one would give him a job. And my daughter would have no chance in life. Nor would my two sons!

THE TWO MEN: You are right. We must think of ourselves first and not the enemy.[1]

Many students in the same class made much more use of setting, situation, and visible action (with stage directions). Some embodied the topic in a drama instead of having characters discuss it. Perhaps allowing such latitude is wise at first, if the students vary a lot in abstractive ability and if the

[1] Weeks Junior High School, Newton, Massachusetts.

topic is as general and impersonal as this one was. Drawing the topic from a previously discussed story had its drawbacks, incidentally, since some children imitated the story too much and tended to limit their ideas to the remote, military definition of "enemy" they inherited from the story, instead of bringing matters closer to home.

When students choose their own topic or issue, they themselves set the abstraction level of the subject matter, in which case the teacher might set the abstraction of the situation by stipulating that stage directions be dispensed with. Under these conditions a ninth-grader wrote about teenage drinking:

PATTIE: Listen Rick what am I gonna do? Everytime Bill comes to a dance, hes smashed. All he thinks of is drimking.

RICK: And just what else is there to do Pattie? If I found Bill tonite you could bet anything I would too.

PATTIE: But why? What's the sence of it? What if you get caught and taken to your parents than what?? You're grounded, can't do a thing. And on top of that your father is madder than . . . well you know.

RICK: It's one way to get away form everything. Everybody drinks anyway. My father drinks and I'd like to asked him how old he was when he started. Bet he was younger than I am now. In two more months I can get served in New York or maybe I'll be drafted. It's alright for me to fight or even die but when I'm on leave I can't even got a lousy beer. You just try and understand. I have my own feelings and you have yours. So what if you believe it's no good?

PATTIE: Rick I didn't say it's not good, but there are places. Go out with the boys so you all get drunk at the same time and don't make fools of yourselves. In fact you wreck it for the rest of the kids. "NO MORE DANCES UNTIL . . ." Why do you think they say that? I'll tell you because kids like you get drunk, get rowdy and start wreckin' the place.

RICK: Listen I can't stop boys from drinkin'! I wouldn't want to because I enjoy it myself. So stop bothering me. Why don't you tell Bill yourself?? Maybe, *just maybe* he'll quit or something. But I know him and if I were you I wouldn't get my hopes up that he will![2]

Personal interaction is rather strong here, but, despite the proper names, the characters essentially just represent two positions on drinking, perhaps typically represented by boys on the one hand and girls on the other. Designating types such as Boy-Girl, Mother-Daughter, Adult-Teenager, and Student-Teacher shifts dramatic dialogue to a more abstract plane and parallels role-playing improvisations and mock panels. Also, in both the preceding and following dialogues, one can see how the absence of stage directions emphasizes a topic by reducing setting and action.

[2] Lexington High School, Lexington, Massachusetts.

Should Driving Age Be Raised

ADULTS: The driving age should be raised to around 18.

TEENAGERS: Why what good would it do?

ADULTS: It would put decrease in the number of accidents.

TEENAGERS: It wouldn't make that much difference because most accidents occur with kids 18 and 21.

ADULTS: That may be true but there are still a lot of accidents that could be avoided with kids 16–17.

TEENAGERS: In that case raise the age to 21 or 25 and stop almost all accidents.

ADULTS: Now thats going to far.

TEENAGERS: Its about as ridiculous as raising it to 18. Besides its easy for you to say it because your'e over 18 and youv'e got your license. But you wouldn't say it if you were 16 or 17.

ADULTS: That isn't the reason its just that teenagers lack esperiance.

TEENAGERS: Everybody lacks experiance just starting out, Even if we don't drive until were 30 we will still lack experiance.

ADULTS: Another reason is that teenagers lack pride and respect.

TEENAGERS: We have just as much pride as anyone else and why have respect, we are always being put down, by the way we dress, and things we do etc.

ADULTS: Where is the pride and the way you dress is bad.

TEENAGERS: Kids take better care of their cars than adults. As for the way we dress, why is it bad, because you didn't dress that way? We think the way you dressed when you were kids was stupid too. Just because you didn't do it doesn't mean its bad or wrong.[3]

Designating speakers as *A* and *B* is a possibility for even more disembodied dialogue. The John and Bill of the following dialogue might have been so designated, though they are perhaps supposed to typify more specific, racial roles (Bill says he is white, but we are not sure that John is Negro). In any case, giving the speakers personal names, typical names, or neutral names like *A* and *B* or One and Two is just a matter of devices that may help students to disembody the dialogue and thus to shift from stories to ideas. The author of this dialogue was a girl who had finished the ninth grade and was attending a summer school for selected disadvantaged students destined to enter a private school the next fall:

Not Only Equal, but Also as Brothers

JOHN: For over a hundred years now, the Negro has been free. Yet, he is still deprived of equality. Is this because of the fact that the majority of white men hate the Negro?

BILL: I don't believe so; I'm white, and yet, I don't hate Negroes. Could the problem of the Negroes lie in the Negroes themselves? Are they actually the cause of their own troubles?

[3] Lexington High School, Lexington, Massachusetts, ninth-grader.

JOHN: What do you mean?

BILL: Congress, which is composed of a majority of white men, has passed and is still passing laws which guarantee the Negro or any other minority group equality. Yet, the Negro is not making great strides socially, economically, or in education. Is this because of the hate the white man possesses for the Negro?

JOHN: It could be possible. Although, as you say, Congress has passed many Civil Rights laws, the white man does not readily accept these laws.

BILL: But doesn't he have to accept these laws?

JOHN: Not necessarily. Although these laws are morally good, the white men still possess hatred for the Negroes. Hatred that has been instilled in them for generations. They cannot be expected to forget their beliefs immediately and abide by the law. This is quite apparent from the constant test of the constitutionality of these laws in the Supreme Court. Doesn't this express the desire of the white man not to abide by the law?

BILL: I believe you know that there will always be people who are not willing to accept something, even though they know it is right, simply because of heritage. Isn't this the basic foundation of the Black Muslims?

JOHN: I can't say. It is true that the Black Muslims are a group based upon hate. But don't you agree that the white man is the cause of this hate? After all didn't the white man bring the Negro to America against his own wishes. Isn't this reason to hate?

BILL: Well, why can't the white man hate the Negro? Now that there are laws calling for the hiring of qualified Negroes, many whites are being deprived of jobs, because employers tend to give priority to Negroes. The white man is now being deprived of making a living. Certainly he now has a reason to hate Negroes, don't you think?

JOHN: But the Negro never enslaved the white man. He never took him from his native land, threw him in the gulley of a ship, and then brought him to a new land, where he was forced to work. He never denied him the right to raise a family in freedom. Did he?

BILL: Negroes are not deprived of the right to raise a family in freedom, now. Yet, the Negro man tends to desert his family and responsibilities on a far greater scale than the white man. How do you account for this?

JOHN: Simple, this trait was instilled in him by the white man. Just as white men can't help but hate Negroes because of heritage, so the Negro can't help but desert his responsibilities because of heritage. This heritage that was given to them by the white man's harsh slavery. A form of slavery that was the worst the world had ever seen. Under this system of slavery, families were torn apart. What could you do if you had lived under these conditions?

BILL: But they know it is wrong, and the fact that it is wrong would make me try to correct the situation. Why doesn't the Negro do the same thing?

JOHN: After being knocked down so many times, a man begins not to give a damn. Look at the world condition. People are unable to live in peace, for there is always the threat of the bomb. There is always some conflict which would explode into World War III, a war in which a victor is impossible. Yet, there have been many campaigns for world peace, all of which were unsuccessful. Now people don't give a damn, to hell with world peace. This is wrong, violently wrong. Yet, no one tries to improve the situation. Because men who have tried have been cursed, called crazy, and cast aside by society. Yet, no one corrects this great fault of the world. Why?

BILL: Because these are things which cannot be accomplished through one man's efforts. These things can only be accomplished if every man in the world works for peace, with all sincerity. But the Negro race as a whole doesn't strive for the same goal. Couldn't this be the real reason for his not succeeding?

JOHN: You said that world peace could only be accomplished if every man worked for it. This is also true in the plight of the Negro. He alone cannot accomplish equality. He must receive the goodwill and understanding of this fellow men. He's in a minority in a country where the majority rules. What can he do alone?

BILL: The gates of opportunity are being opened for the Negro. He is given the chance to vote, to live where he pleases, to acquire jobs, if he is qualified and a part in American society. Yet, he does not fully accept them. He drops out of school, which not only prevents him from getting a good education, but also stops him from being qualified to obtain good jobs. Isn't this because he, the Negro, doesn't want to better himself?

JOHN: The Negro has been deprived of freedom for over a hundred years, after his emancipation, then when he is finally given his freedom, he is expected to work miracles. But even now his freedom is limited, this isn't his fault. So why must he accept the blame?

BILL: How is his freedom limited?

JOHN: The Negroes' greatest obstacle in obtaining freedom is prejudice. No man can ever be true from slavery, when his former master looks upon him still as a slave. But whenever the Negro complains, he is always told, that things will change soon. It's always soon, but never now.

BILL: You must admit that the white man is trying, just as the Negro is trying. Maybe it's not the fault of any one group, maybe it's the work of God. Maybe this was all prearranged, and someday the Negro will be able to walk with the white man, not only as his equal, but also as his friend.[4]

For this girl this topic was good, but frequently such a broad subject leads merely to cliché; if a student knows about a subject only secondhand, he will merely repeat what he has heard.

Procedures

The samples in this chapter illustrate only imperfectly the development of socratic dialogue. Although the experiments from which they were drawn indicated, in retrospect, what a good procedure would be like, they did not

---

[4] I am indebted to Robert Pierce, director of English for the Carleton College ABC Summer Program, for enlisting his teachers in the trial of this and some other assignments described in this book.

themselves enjoy the conditions I recommend here — direct ties with improvisation and a gradual progression, over the three years, toward increasing disembodiment of situation, speakers, and topics. Trials in the seventh and eighth grades were very limited, but students of both grades can and should write socratic dialogue at some level of generality, for it is a suitably dramatic and concrete way of approaching idea writing.

Further experimentation, which is much needed for this sequence, will be most fruitful if the main goal of making dialogue more abstract is kept in mind and kept relative to the possible variations in character naming, amount of setting and action, and framing of the minimal situation. The minimal situation is probably the most important variable, and, indeed, tends to control the other two. Whereas in our experiments the subject of the characters' conversation was simply given in the writing assignment like a debate topic, it should be stated as a specialized sort of improvisational situation: three people are sitting somewhere discussing such and such. Creating a sequence is a matter of relatively specifying the speakers, the relations among them, the setting, and the connections between the topic and their lives.

Furthermore, because our students were inexperienced with dialogue, we often held them to two speakers, which is unfortunate, because creating only two points of view tends to dichotomize a subject into an either-or debate. Increasing the number of points of view will in fact be an important development occurring over the three years as students become capable of handling more complex interactions and of discriminating and qualifying ideas more finely.

Relation to Discussion

Writing socratic dialogues should be interwoven with small-group and panel discussions. That is, sometimes students talk with others about a topic and sometimes they write an imaginary discussion alone. The socratic dialogues are read aloud in small groups as scripts and expanded through oral discussion. This gives purpose to the writing and also reveals in a paper the rigged arguments, misinformation, omitted points or points of view, and so on, without necessarily impugning the author, who can claim not to be represented in his dialogue but will wear the shoe if it fits.

Values

Above all, writing socratic dialogue should help a student proliferate ideas, examine matters from all sides without fear of contradicting himself, activate points of view he already has, and try out new ones. It provides a casual, expansive form for writing down thoughts before attempting to trim and organize ideas into an essay. It opens a face-saving way to abandon dogmatism and egocentricity.

Requiring students of this age to shape thoughts into a consistent, logically continuous essay and then picking holes in their arguments retards idea writing more than it advances it. The important development at this age should be the exploring of ideas, not the constructing of water-tight arguments. The fear of being illogical and inconsistent is very inhibiting when you are trying to find out what you think and when you still are only flexing your new-found logical muscles (at least in verbally explicit form). Monological essays of ideas will be better later — more thoughtful, qualified, rich, and complex — if this period of dialogical writing is allowed as preparation. To buy a neat organizational job at the price of simplemindedness is no educational bargain.

Collateral Reading Texts and Other Materials

The dialogue of both theater and real life could be substantially advanced in language classes, I believe, by presenting plays side by side with recordings of actual panels, trials, congressional debates, and public hearings. Films, tapes, and television videotapes of these real-life dialogues would be especially good, but I suggest that teachers make a big effort also, in cooperation with publishers and curriculum builders, to obtain and make available typescripts of some of this ceaseless stream of public dialogue in which the drama of personal interaction and the dialectic of reason are so well fused. These scripts and performances can be assigned as reading, listened to, or watched, and then discussed for dynamics and discussion strategies as well as for content. Sometimes they might be presented just after the students have talked or written on the same topic; sometimes they might be presented before students discuss, as a stimulus. Typescripts could sometimes be given rehearsed readings as well.

Many trials and hearings are downright theatrical, and indeed many plays include trial scenes because conflict, relevation, and climax are built into court procedure. Working at the same time with plays and actual dialogues is a good way to grasp the similarities and differences between them, to perceive both the artifices of theater and its roots in reality. It is terribly important for students to gain insight into how personality, social role, and professional investment influence the ideas we utter. Whereas some of this insight can come from playing roles, doing mock panels, and feeding back about their own discussions, it will help considerably to witness and discuss real adult verbal dramas.

Chapter 22

Monologue

The third strand of script writing features the solo voice — first the outer social voice (dramatic monologue) and then the inner private voice (interior monologue, or soliloquy). Monologues are dramatic as regards the situation of their utterance but are ideational as regards their content. Thus, while still emphasizing personality and behavior, as in dramatic dialogue, the assignments in this section will also continue, like those in socratic dialogue, to move students toward idea and essay writing. In isolating and sustaining an individual voice, students are taking the fundamental posture of the writer, who is a monologuist.

Dramatic Monologue

PROCEDURES

The starting point is, once again, duologue. A dramatic monologue is achieved by specifying a minimal situation such that one character dominates and the other is reduced to incidental reacting. Although it was not the case in experiments, improvisation of monologues should definitely precede the writing of them.

The oral assignment. Along about eighth grade, while the class is doing two-person improvisations, dramatic monologue is introduced into drama work as simply a variation in dynamics. In real life, of course, most monologues are momentary solos occurring in a surrounding dialogue; only in literature are they sometimes excerpted as self-sufficient speeches. So, for the sake of realism, the improvised monologue should come, at first at least, as only part of a scene; a parent gives a "lecture" during an argument, or one character is trying to "bring around" another who is sulking, or a salesman gives his pitch. Next, direct the class to think of situations in which, for the entire scene, one of the two people does all of the talking and the other reacts silently or merely mumbles an occasional reply or is cut off whenever he opens his mouth. Some of these situations are improvised.

A somewhat different point of departure is the more formal situation of an individual addressing a group. Examples are a coach giving a pep talk at half time, a treasurer explaining to the board why an organization is short of money, a television announcer giving news or weather or a commercial, and a boss giving directions to his workers. Several other students silently play the audience and take turns being the monologuist, each trying to improve on previous versions.

The written assignment. After experience with oral dramatic monologues, students attempt the written assignment. Writing a dramatic monologue, then, is simply improvising on paper as one has already done on the floor, using the same kinds of minimal situations. Stage directions are permitted for the first attempt or two, the monologue is set up in script form, and a playing time of two to five minutes is stipulated. Later, explain to the students that they are going to strip the writing down to voice only; the accompanying action, the time and place, and the identity of the listeners all have to be reflected or implied in what the speaker says. The monologue is written as a straight piece of prose, without opening and closing quotation marks.

SAMPLES

The following paper, written by a girl who had just completed eighth grade, is an example of the unscripted form:

HINDSIGHT

I wasn't the one that had the cigarette, Sister Marie; this is how it happened.

I was out of the class room on an errand and I saw Joe standing in the doorway of the janitor's closet. I walked over to him and asked, "What are you doing?" He replied "Having a cigarette — want one?" I remembered how much trouble the eighth graders who smoked last year got into, and I wasn't ready to go to the Pastor. "No", I answered, "I don't like to smoke in the morning." I said that, Sister, so that he wouldn't think I didn't know how to smoke. He then said, "Oh, you're just a chicken and you're just teacher's pet!" I wasn't going to be called "Teacher's pet" for anything in the world, so I grabbed the matches and cigarrettes out of his hands and began to light my own.

That's when you came around the corner, Sister. Gee, I really am sorry. I was only trying to act, "big", I guess.[1]

[1] Brooks Academy Summer School for disadvantaged students.

Giving an excuse to an adult is a plausible monologue situation that the girl thought of herself. She uses direct address to identify the listeners and a well justified allusion to imply setting (a corner of a hall). Exposition of situation is precisely what the monologue is about. The speech implies the gestures and facial expressions that would go with it, and imagining the unexpressed reactions of the sister is part of the game for the reader. What we have here, in effect, is dramatic monologue in the literary sense, a fictional device that is employed in both prose and poetry. In this case, the monologue recounts an incident and thus constitutes a kind of short story told by a participant. But the telling of the incident is itself a story. Dramatic monologue is theatrical in the sense that it can be put on stage, and indeed reads like an excerpt from a play, but because a single character is developing a subject, it takes on the qualities of a monological text — a narrative or whatever.

Playing with style. A boy of the same grade and in the same summer school as the preceding author used the assignment mainly to play with the style and language of the speaker:

The Ship

Hey Joe, will ya please turn the methol Excabarian Salisitator to fifty milisectors. It's gettin' too sticky in he'a. When I flipped the red double dynamo calibration vacksiminator switch on this morning a big arc of electric current threw me against the back wall of the left calibration cabin. Sixty amps, so I was lucky I wasn't grounded or I would have been a gonner no sweat. I didn't even get burnt though because I had my super thermo insulator gloves on. When you go to the rating room, kill the D-7 switch 'cause the centrifigal axis is off about two degrees and we'll waver off course. The hydro jack on door three needs greasing, so if you fix that I'll fix the D-7 switch. I'll bet the headlines all around the world are talking about us. I can just see it now: INTER GALOXTIC SAUCER LAUNCHED FOR ALFA CENTURIA, MAY REACH HALF SPEED OF LIGHT. Well, go get the grease tube and get to work.

I'm sure it's good for the soul of space-age boys to have at least one place where they can rattle off all that technical lingo in a legitimate fulfillment of an assignment. Actually, one of the goals of dramatic monologue is to develop style by simulating different voices and by adapting language to the occasion. This is a form of role playing in writing whereby the writer must become, verbally, a certain kind of person talking for a certain reason to a certain listener in certain circumstances. Discriminating voices, in both dialogues and monologues, should further considerably the learning of not only style but rhetoric as well.

Grasping literary technique. To document this last point a bit more and to demonstrate how much a sophisticated ninth-grader can do with the form,

I offer a long dramatic monologue written by a girl. She has indicated the listener's responses with spaces.

Hello dear, I'm Mrs. Fox. I live upstairs in 302. I thought I'd come to welcome you to the neighborhood. May I come in? Have you been married long?

You just got married? Isn't that sweet! Maybe that explains it.

Why I haven't heard much talking down here since you've moved in. In the evenings, that is. You probably don't know very many people around here. During the day you seem to have plenty of workmen here, but in the evenings — no one.

You'd better watch out for them — the workmen — I could tell you stories about brides getting involved and . . . what's that?

Oh, you read *Women's Life* magazine too? Well, I was just telling you for your own good.

You must really be lonely every night here home alone with your husband, just being married and all. Do you or your husband play chess? You must come to dinner one evening next week. Harry and I would love to have you. He'd just adore playing chess with —

Oh yes, thank you. — with Richard, and you and I could sit and chat.

Really, Neither of you plays chess? That's a shame. I'm sure Harry would simply love to teach Robert —

I'm sorry — to teach Richard to play chess. It would break up a dull evening for you both.

I'd like to tell you a little bit about the neighbors. Some of them are busy bodies who always go around minding everyone else's business. Like Helen — She lives down the hall in 210. Just the other day, Midge (310) was listening in the heater duct and heard Helen telling someone about Charlene getting married to some millionaire New Yorker and then trying to poison him for his money. Imagine. Well, I'll tell you something and this is a fact. I know, because I heard from May, and she was told by Leslie, who said she had a very reliable source. You see, Charlene didn't rea. . .

Of course I'll excuse you. Your dinner comes first. I'll just sit and wait until you've finished preparing it and then we can talk until Ronald, or is that Raymond — whatever — gets home.

Don't worry. I wasn't thinking of offering assistance. You see, ordinarily I would because I just had my nails done because Harry and I are —

Yes, don't they, though. You're a dear — because Harry and I are having a dinner party tonight for some very influential people in a golf club because

Harry wants to join. Personally, I don't see how anyone would want to waste his time hitting a little ball around with a stick. It's beyond me. Well, as they say, you have to make some adjustments in every marriage. You'll find that out, dear.

Getting back to dinner — I would ask you to come, but you know how it is. I have so many things to do before they come. I should be home right now, putting —

I wouldn't think of leaving you here alone for the rest of the afternoon. I have to put out cigarettes and tell Joanne — that's our maid — (rather stubborn but irreplacable) to put some almonds in the string beans. You simply must try it sometime when you and Ralph have company. Excuse me a moment . . . yes? Joanne? Oh good Lord, a half an hour earlier? Yes. Thank you . . . That was Joanne yelling down the heater duct. I hope you don't mind. It's so much more convenient — Lilian and I used to use it all the time (she used to live here). A darling girl. She dyed her hair, though. We used to have tea together three times a week. She did wonders with this place. She had a knack for decorating. It's done very simply now, but I'm sure once you get settled you'll have the place fixed up: a new rug, some new drapes, another chair. Maybe you could use an interior decorator. They're expensive, but they could do wonders with a place like this. I know of a good one — oh, what's her name? Well I could get her number for you if —

Oh you don't think you'll be calling in a decorator? When you decide to start, do let me know. It will be such fun to go around from store to store helping you pick out things. I did that with Lilian. There's the telephone.

Certainly.

He wants you to go pick him up at the train station? You have to leave now? Of course, you probably haven't had time to pick out another car yet. Harry does business with a gentleman whose brother sells Lincolns. I'm sure he could get you a fair price.

Yes, of course, Well, it's been nice having this conversation with you. perhaps we can continue it another day. I'm glad I came down. I think it's good for neighbors to get to know each other.[2]

Self-exposure of the speaker is one of the things best accomplished by this form, and this girl, like many other students, exploits the advantage fully. The resulting satire is often exaggerated but not inappropriately so for the age; it is heavy to a degree one would expect from young adolescents and Sinclair Lewis. The cards are stacked, but within the exaggeration there lie many subtleties of language and behavior — all shown, not described. So much of the art of plays and fiction consists of making the characters reveal

[2] Weeks Junior High School, Newton, Massachusetts.

themselves without author commentary. Students who have tried this art recognize it when they see it and read literature with better comprehension.

Consider, for another example of literary technique, the matter of understatement. At the same time that dramatic monologue overplays the speaker, it underplays the listener. The scene above was actually a conversation, but it is made to appear as a monologue by merely reflecting instead of quoting the words of the young wife. A novelist constantly makes decisions about whom to quote, when to quote, and whom to quote when. As much as anything, what accounts for the success of the famous opening scene in *Pride and Prejudice* is that Jane Austen quotes Mrs. Bennett directly and throws the brief replies of Mr. Bennett into indirect discourse, thereby putting the grossness of the one on display and investing the other with a sly and winning irony somewhat like that of the bride in the scene above. It frequently happens that the reader of a dramatic monologue identifies with the listener, not with the speaker.

Understatement and the speaker's self-betrayal are artful creations by the writer. Instead of setting out to teach these literary techniques as concepts — and spoiling good literature by presenting it as examples of the concepts — the teacher does better to let the students *practice* the techniques. Then they will see what an author is doing *while* they are reading instead of needing to have it pointed out to them afterwards.

VARIATIONS OF THE WRITTEN ASSIGNMENT

A variation or option in the assignment is to write the dramatic monologue as a poem. Doing so involves the students in the important matter, so often encountered in both lyric and dramatic poetry, of harmonizing the natural diction and rhythm of speech with the artifices of poetic language, by which I mean greater richness of diction, inversions of sentence structure, metrical and rhythmic patterns, and breaking of lines. Why would a writer depart from daily speech? What does he gain? Why do so many dramatists not concern themselves about realistic language? If they write dramatic speech in poetry, students will know. Furthermore, associating dramatic monologue with poetry will accustom students to listening for a character voice when they read *any* poetry, for even if he is not creating a character as such, but speaking in his own voice, the writer of a poem selects a tone, stance, and style that is not always the same for every poem; he creates a speaking personality out of some part of himself.

Another variation consists of drawing the minimal situation from a scene in a play or novel that the class has read. This would be an offstage scene referred to by the characters or the narrator but not directly presented. We are told, say, that one character informed another of some important informaton. How did he say it, and how did the other react when he heard the news?

COLLATERAL WORK WITH LITERATURE

After they have written two or three dramatic monologues — perhaps by the ninth grade — the students could read poems and short stories cast in this form, if selections can be found that are otherwise interesting for the age. At any rate, they can read anthologies of each other's monologues. The Robert Browning dramatic monologues ("My Last Duchess" and others) should be read later, but there may be other suitable poems. Some short stories by American vernacular writers such as Ring Lardner ("Haircut" and "Zone of Quiet") would be right for many ninth-graders. Although correlated reading selections are very desirable, if few good dramatic monologues can be found it is better to let the matter go for now, in the knowledge that the student will be prepared for such reading later, than to assign some reading selections prematurely.

Most plays have at least one good monologue, and certainly the theatre can provide the literary equivalent for what they are writing. In fact, from Greek drama on, the developed solo speech has been a standard feature of drama. It is used to relate the past, reveal the thought and feeling of a character, build and sustain an argument, and so on. It is an elemental dramatic unit that, along with soliloquy, duologue, and dialogue, makes up the playwright's compositional repertory. In selecting scenes to enact, the teacher and students should include monologue scenes. And of course the students should enact some of their own.

Whatever the source to which he turns for literary dramatic monologues, the teacher should not confuse them with other kinds of monologues: the speech must occur in a definite time and place, and be heard by another character. These constitute what is meant by "dramatic." Once the concept of dramatic monologue has been thoroughly established, however, other monologues having a character speaker but an unspecified setting and audience might also be assigned as readings. In following up these reading suggestions for grades ten to twelve, on page 483, I have named some poems of this sort. A few of them might be appropriate for maturer ninth-graders.

At this age dramatic monologues should be performed rather than silently read, except when students are sifting the printed monologues of other students. Poems and short stories written in this form should be considered scripts. Students do rehearsed readings of them or, in some cases, memorize and act them. Silent reading occurs, but as preparation for performance. Since students may present different selections before the class everyone becomes acquainted with a number of monologues. For rehearsed readings the audience might follow the text with their eyes. For poems and monologues extracted from plays, several successive readings or actings of the same text could be compared in class discussion.

Interior Monologue

The final stage in this sequence of dramatic writing is interior monologue and would probably be best undertaken only in the ninth grade. Thus the whole sequence would call for duologue in the seventh grade, dramatic monologue in the eighth grade, and interior monologue in the ninth grade. I have placed interior monologue in ninth grade because I know it can be done there, but this does not mean it has to be done there. It could perfectly well be introduced later, and certainly it should be if the teacher feels that his students need to dwell longer on dialogue and dramatic monologue.

PROCEDURES

The directions used in experiments were: "Make up a character whose way of thinking and speaking you feel confident you can imitate; imagine him somewhere doing something; then write down in his own words what he is thinking and feeling during this situation." Without concurrent drama work, and without a previous program such as I have been recommending, students often found this assignment difficult to understand. Although it is merely a simulation of thought trains that go on in us all the time, as a school assignment it looked very different from anything the students were familiar with. Part of the problem, however, was that in the experiments I had placed interior monologue before instead of after the other kinds of dramatic writing. The present sequence has profited from that experience. In addition, the point of departure should again be improvisation, whereas in the experiments the assignment came as part of a pure writing series ungrounded in any dramatic work. Student misunderstandings of interior monologue — and this applies to a lesser degree to dramatic monologue — were almost entirely due to the absence of dramatic experience. Some students could get a voice talking all right, but had little sense of the immediate situation in which the character was talking or thinking — the place, time, circumstances, accompanying action, and, in the case of dramatic monologue, the listener. There were time gaps, or the voice became a disembodied first-person narrator. At worst, the character's thoughts were paraphrased by some hidden narrator who referred to the character as a third person. Indeed, the teachers themselves sometimes became confused since they too were unused to dealing with a concretely situated speaker talking *now*.

The confusions were unnecessary. Given general dramatic experience and this particular sequence up to now, all that is required to introduce the assignment is a minimal situation for improvising in which one character speaks his thoughts aloud as he engages in some action. There may or may not be other people in the scene; if there are, they pantomime. An improvisation always takes place in a specific setting and runs continuously in time. And it never occurs to a player to become a disembodied narrator. A situation might simply be someone thinking aloud as he washes the dishes, which was the situation one boy thought up and wrote about. Or it might be someone sitting alone in a restaurant reacting to what he sees others doing. In relation to what students would already have been doing in this program, shifting the monologue inward would be a fairly simple and very understandable variation.

The assignment for writing an interior monologue is essentially the same as for an improvisation. Length is specified in terms of speaking time. At first, again, the monologue would be written as a script with stage directions, and then, on subsequent occasions, as a direct presentation of voice alone. The former corresponds to soliloquy in the theater, and the latter to a kind of fiction or poetry.

The script form was not done in the experiments but may be an easier way to make the transition from floor to paper. To the extent, however, that the character's thoughts are reflecting what is going on around him, stage directions may be unnecessarily repetitious. On the other hand, a contrast may be intended between the thoughts and the surrounding action. The direct presentation of the inner voice alone takes more art, since no other source of information supplements the voice, and the resulting indirection is often more enjoyable for the reader, who must recreate more from inference. The difference between writing an acting script and writing a version to be read is itself valuable to learn about. Theatrical soliloquy and the fictional technique of interior monologue can also be related in this way, which would be a considerable help in reading literature.

SAMPLES

Movement of language, movement of mind. Below is a brief, simple interior monologue written by a disadvantaged boy during the summer before he entered ninth grade:

JUSTICE?

Why'd she have to pick on me? I didn't have my hand up. She could have picked on any other kid in the class. I don't know the answer, and she knows it. Why doesn't she pick on some other kid instead of staring at me? The whole class is looking at me; waiting for my answer. If I'm bright, so what, big deal; there'll just be another time. What could the answer be? Good, she's looking around the room; maybe she'll pick on someone else. Then I'll be the one that can laugh and make fun of him. I'll be able to stare at him; make him nervous. No? She's looking back at me and I still don't know the answer. Don't look at me, you idiot, pick on someone else. Wish there never was school or teachers. Good, she's looking around the class again, so maybe she'll pick on someone else. She always picks on me; pick on someone else! I wish the bell would ring — oh no! She saw me looking at the clock! Now she's mad. The bell!!! Saved!! No! She won't let the class go; she's keeping us after. She can't! At last, I'm free![3]

[3] Brooks Academy Summer School.

One virtue of this kind of writing, as this paper demonstrates, is that the movement of language is fitted to the movement of mind, a virtue that goes far beyond dramatic writing. It is what makes even an abstract essay seem to live and breathe, to put us in the writer's mind. There is a special kind of self-expressive value too: under the pretense of putting words in the mouth of an invented character, a student can write many real personal thoughts that he might be embarrassed to offer frankly as his own. Consider also the detailing of thought and feeling in this paper compared to the less effective, generalized *statement* of feeling a student would produce in a paper the same length written in response to "My Most _____ Moment." Because drama is a moment-to-moment thing, assignments based on it will inevitably produce detail.

A kind of personal essay. As a chronicling of thoughts, an interior monologue is a kind of story, but the content of the thoughts may range over many things that do not belong to the moment. The monologue may utter not only present sensations but also memories of the past, speculations about the future, and general reflections of all sorts. Thus it may contain bits of narrative and personal essay. The chronology of the present provides an easy and meaningful way to talk about and relate many things that we teachers often try to get at by more logically arranged assignments. The able ninth-grade girl writing below is doing essentially what the boy just quoted did, and has even made up the same situation, but her powers of elaboration are greater. Her title expresses some of what I have been trying to say.

MINUTES OF MEDITATION

The class is always ready to go at the end of the period, no questions are raised. I just sit here, like a fool, always wanting to inquire about something, but never daring to do so. Well today I must force myself, or I'll flunk tomorrows test. Only five minutes of the class left. Let's see, how should I phrase the question? This is silly, I have been in school seven years, and every year it is the same thing, I don't dare ask the teacher a thing. Luckily in the past someone else has asked my question, but there were times when someone didn't, and I forfeited. Let's face it one shouldn't be afraid of a teacher anymore, he has superiority, but not so much, that he would punish you for asking a simple question.

Four minutes, ohh my stomach is jumping with butterflies, it's as if I was going to perform on stage, which I wouldn't do in a million years. I guess I'm just one of those people who can't face another person. I must stand up for my opinions and what I want. It may take me a few minutes (like now) of meditation, before I will do something. I'm sure all people have gone through what I'm going through, they just cover up for it. I certainly admire these people. I remember a time last year when someone told me "Gee, I'm scared!" and I answered "Why should you be scared? just try to relax, and forget the people in the audience" (she was in a play). There I was giving her advice, and I sit here a year later, trying to convince myself to relax.

Three minutes, the time passes so quickly, I wish the minutes would be hours. These kids around me, always jutting their hands into the air. So brave, no that's ridiculas, they are just not timid like me, I'm sure I'll learn how to speak up, I better! or else I don't know what I will do. In High School I probably will have to contribute (as I should now) in order to get the full benefit of what's being learned, and I better start right now, marks close soon. I remember on my last report card, the teacher's comment was " — should contribute more' the same comment for years. My marks are good, but they would improve if I contributed more. I have all these ideas in my head which are just right, or answers, I could have kicked myself for not saying.

Two minutes, ohh my hand is getting shaky, my stomach suddenly hurts, maybe I'm hungry, which is highly possible being fourth period, but it is really nervousness. I better look interested in the class (I'm trying) I don't want my teacher to think I'm idle. (Boy would he be surprised to hear what goes on in my head, he'd probably think a whole dictionary is pouring out its words, like salt). Now I'm beginning to bite my nails, a stupid habit, I should start eating carrots, maybe that will stop the biting, I have read it does. I'll ask my mother to buy a package today, and I'll eat them at home whenever my hands become idle, for instance when I watch television. When my hands are idle, or when I'm nervous, they seem to creep up to my mouth.

One minute, I should begin to rehearse what I'm going to say. Ah, "Mr. — I would like to ask you a question" no! that's much to formal. There must be a better approach, "Ah, excuse me, about the —, is it blah, blah, blah, etc.?" That's better, but I bet I won't use any planned approach, I'll just say what comes natural. That's actually the simplest way. The kids are beginning to pack up, a signal for teachers to give out the homework assignment, sure enough, oh what a bother, all the books away, and one must drag out a notebook, usually at the bottom of the pile. Let's see, now I'm getting tense, this isn't as if I was going to be executed, it's a normal everyday thing (to me it isn't though!) Oh what should I say, my stomach is doing somersaults.

There's the dismissel bell, everyone jumps up, luckily lunch is next, so maybe noone will be around when my turn comes, and yet I'd feel better if there was at least one of my friends with me. No, I have to go through it by myself. I'll just take a deep breath and ask the "deadly" (but important) question. Well . . . here goes![4]

As the paragraphing indicates, this monologue is basically ordered by time, and yet a personal organization of ideas is laid over against mere chronology. There is a coherent subject — the girl's timorous indecision — and it is developed. This subject, incidentally, is essentially that of T. S. Eliot's "The Love Song of J. Alfred Prufrock," which is also a kind of interior monologue. I think that when this girl reads that poem later she will enter into it with

[4] Weeks Junior High School, Newton, Massachusetts.

much greater ease than even most college students have been able to do in the past.

Simulating another's mind. The students do not always utter themselves in disguise. Often they try to become another person, to extend themselves by imagination into an invented state of mind. The ninth-grade boy whose interior monologue appears below had read the much publicized account of a street murder in New York City, where, for a half hour, apartment dwellers watched a man kill a woman but did not intervene. The boy tried to imagine what such a witness must have thought and felt during that time that would explain how an average person can default so badly. In doing so, he was exploring not only a character but also a critical moral and psychological issue embodied in the event. The value of this effort should be kept in mind, I think, when reacting to the unreal aspects of his invention:

Hey, what's that noise? Someone's yelling down there. I'm just ready to get into bed, and what happens? Someone starts yelling. Just too bad for them. I'm gonna get my rest . . . Oh, why won't they stop? this city's probably the loudest place on earth. And they expect me to be awake enough to drive a cab in the morning, after this madness. Wish they would shut up already.

Hey, maybe someone's getting hurt. Nah — probably just some cat. People don't scream like that. But I read in the paper about someone getting murdered and no one calling the police. Terrible! Sounds like a cat. As soon as I can I'm moving out to the island, where they give a person some peace. Maybe if I plug up my ears . . .

Wish Sylvie would wake up. How can she sleep like that? the noise is deafening. Darn it all — might as well get up and see what it is. I can't fall asleep anyway. Have to pull up the blinds. Ouch! Why does that woman have to keep a footstool by the window? Heck it's only some fellow fighting with his dame. Shut up down there will ya. You'll wake up my wife. Why can't they argue some place else. I bet they came to this street just to wake me up. Probably some Commie trick. I'm going back to bed. Some people! It takes all kinds. Sylvie an' me never made a scene like that. I swear, some people just have no consideration for anyone else. Well, I'm going back to sleep.

Oh, heck, its no use. That dame's really making noise now. Maybe I'd better take a look. Where's the light switch? There. No, better keep it off. They might see me. There — there they are. I see 'em. Hey, she looks like she doesn't even know him. He's really hurting her. He's trying to kill her. What did she do to him anyhow?

Wish Sylvie would wake up. How can she sleep with all that racket? Come on, kid, wake up. Should I call the cops? I mean, I don't want to butt into anyone's personal affairs, but this guy looks vicious. Sylvie, should I? D— it, she's asleep. Women! Well, I suppose this is a job for the cops. Where's the phone? That girl is helpless and he's attacking her. Its my duty as . . I can't. My family — eight kids and a wife — someone's got to support them. What would they do if something happened to me? I know how those gangsters operate. Soon as they find out who squealed, that's the end of him. I know, I watch enough gangster pictures. And what they do to those poor guys! Forget it, lady. I've got a family to feed. Oh, lady, will you stop it! You're making me feel guilty. How do you expect me to sleep with you screaming. You're disturbing the peace — and I'm a taxpayer —

Oh, no, he's got a knife. Now he's really gonna kill her. I better call the fuzz. But I can't. They ask for your name and then you're on the books, and I'd have to testify in court. No, then they'll get me. I better not get involved or my family'll suffer. I mean, after all, it ain't my business. So if one lousy dame gets knocked off, why should it bother me? Its either me or her. If she got a guy mad at her there's no reason why I shouldn't let her get what's coming to her.

But maybe he's drunk. Maybe he just feels like killing someone. I've heard of guys' fingers getting itchy for blood at the full moon. Maybe he's one of them. A real psycho. D— it, what should I do. I can't stand to hear the poor woman scream. Okay, I'll call. But I won't give my name. Then the cops'll come and save her but they won't know who called. But the gangsters have ways of finding out. Nah, if I was being killed, no one would call the cops. Oh, that scream. It makes me shiver. No, no one would do it for me. Anyhow, the cops should be able to take care of it. If they can't do their job, why should I do it for them? I can't take this. What should I do?

Oh, no. He's really getting rough with that knife. I wouldn't want to do something rash. After all, what would happen to her if something happened to me?

"Hey, Sylvie. Wake up! There's this guy out front trying to knife this dame and I don't know what to do. Come on kid. Call the cops? You serious? Yeah, you're right. Suppose it was you. I'd want someone to call them."

Good God, I never heard someone scream like that before, Sylvie, look what he's doing to her. Stabbing her about a million times. She's still alive — Sylvie — still screaming — help me Sylvie — what can I do? She's gonna die. You hear, die! Oh, no, and right on our street. That scream! Her face. . . blood. . . Sylvie, help me!

He's gone. He just ran off. She's . . . just . . . well, she could be alive still. Sylvie, I'm gonna call the cops. She's still lying there on the sidewalk. Maybe she's dead. Our sidewalk. Sylvie, she's dead. *Dead.* Sylvie. Just one lousy phone call. God . . .[5]

As I found generally in experimenting, when material was very farfetched, the writing of inventions seemed very poor. Students writing interior monologues should be encouraged to extend themselves imaginatively but not to go so far afield that they have little chance of some success. This boy went to his limit, I think. Others tried to imagine, for example, a soldier's feelings in battle and could only fall back on war stories and thus on imitation. The

[5] Weeks Junior High School, Newton, Massachusetts.

original wording of the assignment can be a help here — "a character whose way of thinking and feeling you feel confident you can imitate" — but we also have to remember that complete success may be less important than exploring frontiers.

In the following paper a ninth-grade girl tried to become a seven-year-old boy — imperfectly but still with very worthwhile results:

PLUM PRESERVES

It's so fun taking care of the house all by yourself. I've done well so far with only one teeny weeny accident. It wasn't my fault the bird cage door opened when it accidentally dropped, and it wasn't my fault the bird cage door opened when it fell, and that old bird flew out.

Aunt Annie would be proud of me, anyways, She'd say to me, "Georgie, you're a good little boy. You work so hard for a child of seven years." I know that if she knew how hard I worked, she would let me have some of the plum preserves she made. A growing boy *needs* sweets *once* in a while. Aunt Annie would say sugar is evil though. It's made by the devil and it's no good, she'd say. Well, I can't believe anything so sweet as jam could be made by the devil. Why, I saw Aunt Annie make it yesterday and she's not the devil. I'm going to ask Reverend Martin if Aunt Annie didn't tell me a lie. I've got to have tea all by myself and it's terribly lonely. So's not to waste food I'll just leave the bread and eat the jam plain. The bread kind of kills the taste anyway. It's so good! I'm sure she won't mind if I have a little more. It looks real good sitting there in my hands. It seems to be saying "Go on Georgie, have some more. Eat me up!" I'll have a little bit more. She won't even notice it's gone for a long time and when she does, I'll say it was the rats. Oh, it's so good. This is such a little jar-full. Aunt Annie is so stingy with her jam, but I know Reverend Martin 'd say she's just being economical. Why it's gone! That little drop in the corner isn't even a finger-full. I can't leave just that; I've got to eat it now. Oh, I feel sick. Real sick. I wish Aunt Annie was home. I wish I hadn't eaten all that jam. Will she say I'm bad? That I'm not fit to have the Davis home? No. Aunt Annie will understand.[6]

Issues for workshop commentary. The thoughts seem real here, but often the wording of them does not. This matching of language to character is one of the more valuable issues to be discussed in small groups. In preparing to perform or to print interior monologues, the groups should read them aloud or silently and go over them together. Does the style sound "thought" or does it sound "spoken" aloud to someone else? Juxtaposing dramatic and interior monologues should help discriminate between inner and outer voices. Does the style seem appropriate to the character and to the situation and state he is in? (Is he agitated or reflective, for example?) Does the language flow with the movement of thought and feeling or does it seem to be

---

[6] Lexington High School, Lexington, Massachusetts.

organized by some logic external to the character? (This distinction helps to define "formal" writing.)

These are natural matters for students to consider in reacting to each other's papers, but the teacher may have to help them understand their reactions in terms of the particular writing problems of this assignment. Project some papers, have them read aloud, and let students comment. They will inevitably set up the criterion of realism or credibility. For interior monologue, this criterion will usually apply to the thoughts of the character and to the language through which he utters them. Ask commentators to cite passages that illustrate their remarks. The author should always say if the reading of his monologue fitted what he had in mind; if not, both the writing and the reading should be discussed until the cause of the discrepancy is determined.

INVENTING SOLILOQUIES FOR LITERARY CHARACTERS

Making up the thoughts of a character in literature is one way of entering into and fully comprehending both the character and the work in which he appears. One ninth-grade teacher[7] asked her class to imagine an interior monologue for Achilles as he is sulking in his tent listening to the sounds of battle. These were written straight off during fifteen minutes in class. One boy wrote:

My friends and enemies alike die, out there on the battle field in honor. While I swift footed Achilies sit here and sulk by the quick sailing ships. My strong principles or the batlle field. I can find no honor now.

If I go into battle my principle will be broken. I will do a great injustice to myself. Yet if the gods keep me here the Greeks, fellow warriors, will call me a traitor or a coward. There is no honor in that.

I must go out to the battle field. How can a man be so cruel as to leave his companions to fight until death! My friends Odysseus and Ajax out there fighting trojans while I sit here and have pitty on my self.

Pitty why should I have pitty. Has not Agamennon ronged me. Did he not take Brisius my fair prize, did he not shame me infront of my men and was it not because of his greed that I am sitting here. Yes! Let the Greeks say where is the coward Achilies. And they will open their eyes and see there own greedy King Agamemnon has drove Achilies away; taking his prize, insulting him and relieving him of all honor.

I Achelies am doing right to sit here. And I will do it until I am given back my honor and my prizes.

In order to be Achilles for fifteen minutes one must draw on what one has read and put it together meaningfully. Such papers not only can *show* reading comprehension for the teacher's benefit, but can *increase* reading

---

[7] Lucy Woodward at Weeks Junior High School, Newton, Massachusetts.

comprehension. This is the general benefit of the dramatic approach, which causes the student to actively work over and complete in his mind what an author has presented to him.

Another ninth-grade teacher[8] asked her extremely disadvantaged Negro students to put themselves in the place of a character from *Julius Caesar*. Brutus was one character they could choose: "You are in your home. You are thinking over what Cassius said about Rome and Caesar. You must have an answer ready when the conspirators meet at your home. What thoughts are running through your mind?" Here was one response:

> This is a terrible decision I have to make. To have to decide between my good friend Caesar, and my country, Rome. I know how this would hurt Caesar, but even in being hurt he will understand because he understands me. I love Caesar, but I love Rome, and Caesar is but one man, and Rome is the world.

Brief as it is — and these students were not used to writing — this effort contains two noteworthy things — the stylistic use of antithesis, reflecting Brutus' inner conflict, and the interesting thought, belied by *Et tu Brute,* that Caesar will understand his action.

A classmate brought in matters relating to other characters:

> Caesar is my friend killing him would be like destroying part of myself but if cutting off my right arm would bring everlasting freedom to Rome I would not hesitate. So, for the welfare of Rome Caesar must die. Yet if I fail in my attempt to kill Caesar, what shall happen to my beloved wife, Portia. Will she have to share the doom that awaits me? How will Mark Antony react once Caesar is assassinated? These are mere petty fears for the welfare of Rome is based on a larger scale.

This variation of interior monologue could be improvised as well, and should be sometimes, but since the general progression of this program is toward individual thinking and writing, there should be increasing opportunities to do alone on paper what has already been done orally in a group.

Monologues and the Understanding of Literature

Like the other kinds of dramatic writing, interior monologue is designed to advance students' literary understanding and appreciation at the same time as it develops their power of written expression. Although dramatic and interior monologues may seem at first glance to be minor literary forms, not worthy of much time, it would be a great mistake to think so. Both cut across genres, being found in plays, fiction, and poems — and found in two senses.

[8] Grace Whittaker, Lewis Junior High School, Roxbury, Massachusetts.

First, some whole plays, short stories, poems, and even a few novels are cast as sustained dramatic or interior monologues. Amy Lowell's "Patterns," for example, is entirely interior monologue and probably could be read by most ninth-graders. As both readers and writers, students should pursue the whole matter of artifice and realism into the poet's efforts to render thought and feeling more accurately in a language that one does not hear spoken. Sound, rhythm, imagery, incantation, students can discover, may express the inner life better than the banal everyday speech that they have used for the sake of realism. Many other poems, most of them appropriate for later, are either straight dramatic and interior monologues or modifications of them in which the setting of the listener is less specific but the speaker is clearly a created character talking in his own idiom to someone else or himself. By just this kind of distancing, these monologues graduate into the public voices of detached first-person and third-person narrators.

Second, like dialogue, dramatic and interior monologues are commonly *embedded* in poetry and fiction as well as in plays, making up, in fact, a goodly portion of many short stories and novels. I saw recently an excellent commercial dramatization of *Alice in Wonderland*[9] in which all of Alice's thoughts as written by Lewis Carroll were put into first person, prerecorded, and played through a speaker system at appropriate moments when the actress was not speaking; this ingenious separation of inner from outer speech makes one realize how much of the original book consists of Alice's thoughts. Keeping track of and interpreting different speakers may not be so difficult on stage, but in a novel speakers change with a minimum of signalling.

Most fiction contains characters' accounts of events inserted into the author's narrative. Whole chapters of *The Brothers Karamazov,* for example, are narrated by one character to another. And authors constantly quote directly as well as paraphrase the thoughts of characters. A lot of work with dialogues and monologues not only helps students stay alert to shifts of voice but also helps them *size up what is said in the light of who is saying it.* Dramatic experience ties words to speakers and situations, and thereby grounds style, thought, rhetoric, and language to the realities that produce them. When reinforced by their own writing, this experience will transfer itself to those remoter speakers who author books, and to the anonymous voices of advertising and propaganda.

---

[9] By the Children's Theater of the Charles Street Playhouse in Boston.

Chapter 23

Narrative

Dramatic and narrative writing run concurrently through these three years. "Narrative" covers both actual and fictional stories. Writing narratives of actuality continues to be first-person and firsthand, which means that students of this age would shape them directly from experience, not from material they have read about. While writing various kinds of first-person narrative, students read similar narratives from literature and other sources. In writing fiction, they may often prefer the third person, and there is no reason in any case to avoid it, since making up stories does not involve the same abstractive problems as composing true stories. Occasional assignments to make up a free story will allow students either to use the conventions of third person or to model their fiction on the kinds of first-person narration treated in this chapter and in Chapter 25, on journals and diaries.

True stories derive from two main sources — sensations and memories. Whereas sensations usually lead to eyewitness narrative, i.e., focused away from the author, memories may lead to either author-centered or other-centered narrative and are thus a source of greater variation in focus. Because it is least specialized, memory writing will be my starting point. A rough sequence will move toward greater specialization of narrative and greater impersonality.

Memory Writing

For students who have done nothing of this sort before, almost all of what was said about memory writing for the earlier years (Chapter 14) will apply. Of course, some allowance has to be made for starting it later, but the past language experience of the students often makes more difference than age. Teachers in the experiments felt, for example, that having previously done sensory recording made students more likely to include details in memory narratives. At any rate, the students with whom my cooperating

343

teachers tried out memory writing in grades seven to twelve had never done it before and furnished some relevant indications for others just beginning it.

The three stages of processing memories seemed more meaningful to seventh-graders than to ninth-graders, which I believe means that the twelve-year-old finds them a real help whereas the fourteen-year-old sees less need of them. Compared with younger elementary school children, the seventh-graders showed more willingness to revise and more ability to discuss compositional issues. It is still important that the assignment specify a precise *incident*. Some seventh-graders tried to assimilate the assignment to conventional topics like a trip or summer vacation, which cover too much time and space for the length of writing they will do, resulting in a dull, over-abstracted account, and causing the student to create a trivial organization based on a time-span or place instead of on a mood or feeling.

Small-group cross-commentary by students remains essential for motivating them to elaborate, for showing them the needs of the reader, and for helping them make compositional decisions. Sometimes these sessions are preceded by teacher-led class discussion of sample papers designed to clarify issues they all face. At all ages memory writing seems popular and well motivated.

Here is a *three-stage series* done by a seventh-grade girl and typical of a number of able middle-class students:[1]

MEMORIES

Spontaneous Flow of Memories

When I was little, I used to ride my tricycle all through the basement. Thought it was so much fun. When I was about six, there was a fire in our furnace. Two fire engines came. Everyone was running around throwing sand into the furnace. I took someone's hat, my dog, and pretended I was coming to save the day on my horse. They kicked me out! When I was at camp 3 years ago, we took a motor boat, went out to an island, and had an overnight. After we made supper we went fishing off the dock. I fell in the lake & had to be pulled out! I remember when I made a line pulley with my house & the house next door, the girl & I sent messages during the night to each other. I remember the time up at Camp Union, on the last few nights, when we had a square dance. One of the teachers fell off of a chair & hurt his legs. I remember the first time I ever came to visit Weeks. Rainy cold. The front door steps looked gigantic.

AN ISLAND ADVENTURE

Single, Expanded Memory

It was a muggy night, during the summer 3 years ago. Up in Oakland, Maine. We were going to an island in the middle of a lake for an overnight. Motorboat was

[1] For the assignment directions, see page 216.

overloaded with people, food & sleeping bags. Front of the boat was high in the air. Waves from the boat were all white & foamy. Water was splashing through the air, causing it to be chilly for a few minutes. Many trees on the island. A few lashings between these trees. Long dock. Washing pots and pans in lake. A fish swam into one girl's pots. Screaming and running. Fishing — something tugged at my line and pulled me into the lake. All wet. Had to be pulled out!

Pitching tents — got conked on the head with some else's stake. The ground was very hard to sleep on. Heard loons crying Sounded very weird. Two other girls crawled into my tent because we were all scared. It collapsed on all of us. We were too tired to put it up again so we left it down until the morning.

An Island Overnight

Final
Composed
Memory

It was a muggy night during the summer about three years ago, up in Maine. We were going by motorboat to an island in the middle of a lake for an overnight trip. The motorboat was overloaded with people, food and sleeping bags, and the front of it was high in the air. The waves from the boat were like soapsuds in a washing machine. Water was splashed through the air, causing it to be chilly for a few minutes.

There were many trees on the island and a few lashings between them. After supper we decided to go fishing off of the long docks extending from the island. We dug up some worms & hooked and baited out poles. I stood on the edge of the dock waiting for a bite.

Suddenly I felt a small tug on my line. I got very excited and pulled slightly. This time I felt that my line was being pulled out of my hands. I though that I had caught a large fish and kept struggling. I pulled the rod back until the string was taught. The next thing I knew was that I was sitting in the lake. My line had gotten knotted with someone elses and we were both on different sides of dock so that we couldn't see each other. She thought that she was a fish when I pulled on the lines. I also thought that she was a fish when she pulled back. I was so embarrased! I had to be pulled out of the lake because the bank was too slippery to climb up.

That night when we pitched the tents, I got conked on the head with a stake & was knocked out. That was quite an experience!

So goes the expanding and focusing process when the three stages are meaningful, but sometimes a stage-2 paper was too much like the final stage-3 :

the student had composed so well in the second stage that only minor revision was needed. The process can seem too rigid. The best solution is probably to let the small groups discuss which students should go a stage further and which not, and to give groups the editing function of preparing copy for printing up. Thus when a composition is judged complete, a student stops, but his colleagues suggest final revisions to make in whatever manner is most practical for printing — either writing in changes or doing a new draft.

In one seventh-grade class that I was visiting, the teacher dittoed several rather ordinary final compositions (stage-3) and with a minimum of questioning got the students to react to them. These were papers that had had only a slight benefit of commentary during the three-stage process. Here is one:

> The first time I went to camp I was really scared. At the beginning I didn't want to go. When we finally got there after the bus ride we took a look at the cabins and then went down to the water front to have our swimming test. That night I got homesick. But the next week I had a lot of fun I went swimming and played many games. I discovered that overnight camp was a lot of fun.
> My counselors were really nice to me. They cracked many jokes that our group really enjoyed.
> I stayed at that camp for two weeks and in those two weeks I really enjoyed myself.[2]

Class comments were: too scattered, too many *reallys*, not enough detail, second paragraph unconnected, has "holes" in it, subject of camp is too big for length of the theme. All these are very just comments that a teacher would probably make, but coming after the paper is finished, they may only overwhelm the writer with should-have's. Whether the class or the teacher points out deficiencies, they spell failure and exposure if they come after the writing is all over. Somebody should feed back to an author at a more timely juncture, namely, when the earlier drafts are exchanged and discussed in small groups. Furthermore, had we stressed *incident* more during the experiments, the student above would not have failed so badly. Most of the reactions to this paper — about being scattered, having holes, lacking details — stem from the simple fact, also pointed out by the class, that the paper tries to cover too much for its short length. I am convinced, partly from my own mistakes, that poor assignment procedure causes at least as much bad writing as students' ineptitude.

Discussed also by that same class was the following composed memory (stage 3), which does focus on an incident.

> When I was in the third grade our family book a trip to Cleveland, Ohio to visit my uncle. We went durring spring vacation. We left on a Tuesday,

2 Weeks Junior High School, Newton, Massachusetts.

and came home that Saturday. It was a long ride up. We left a 6:00 in the morning, and got there 5:00 in the afternoon. The ride was so long, that every one kept falling asleep!

The funny thing that happened on the way was that my mother got a ticket for speeding. She was driving about 80 miles an hour, (when she speed limit was 60.) When she was caught, this policeman took her to this judges house. (We were in Albany N.Y.) The judge asked her all theses questions. She was fined five dollars.

After that, we stopped off at Howard Johnsons to get something to eat. Finally at 5:00 we got there. We were all exhausted, and we ate a big dinner at my uncle's house.

When the class was asked for indications of what the main point was — or the keynote, as we put it — they mentioned *The funny thing that happened was* and then proceeded to show that humor was contrasted with fatigue. Someone said that the second paragraph, about the arrest, is set up by the last sentence of the first paragraph, "The ride was so long that everyone kept falling asleep!" The last paragraph returns to the fatigue. I confess that I thought more of the paper after hearing the students discuss it. The same class that had found so much wrong with the preceding paper made me see that I had failed to appreciate something about this one. At first, I had felt that the before and after parts of the story were given space that should have gone to the main incident, because I assumed that the first paragraph was just a factual setting. But part of the writer's point was that his mother's arrest came as an especially welcome relief from the tedium of the long trip (not *all* of the satisfaction being in the spectacle of his family lawmaker breaking the law). The humor *is* set off by the fatigue.

I still think the main incident would be better if told in more detail, but elaboration is something that might well have been recommended by the writer's colleagues earlier if the small-group commentary had been in full operation. It is the pressing by peers for more information, not the teacher's nagging for details, that should stimulate elaboration. The girl who wrote the following, however, wrote with relish that needed no prompting. Her expanded memory (stage 2) needed only slight revising to produce this.

"Liquor and Dogs Don't Mix"

It was the Jewish New Year, and our whole family was coming over to our house for a big dinner. My father was in the living room mixing drinks for the guests and my mother had just finished making dinner. I was quite excited because I had not seen my grandmother in a long time, because she had been in the hospital.

When the guests arrived it was six-thirty and we were all famished.

Drinks were soon served, but by accident my father had made too many drinks.

I was mad because I was only seven and I was a minor, so I couldn't have a drink. I had just remembered there was an extra highball in the kitchen so I asked to be excused plotting to drink the liquor. Beside this drink I had a glass of grape wine and some ginger ale.

About a half of an hour later supper was served but I was not to be found.

My parents looked all over for me and finally found me in my room rolling on the floor. I was stone drunk.

It must have been a funny sight but my dog started to bark. I got really mad and I stood up and bit him really hard. He (Pepper) knew something was wrong and he also knew I was playing with him, so he bit me back but not very hard.

That night I was so sick that I had to go to bed without dinner. I was so mad becaus we had roast beef and I love it.

This is why I say "Liquor and Dogs don't go together."[3]

If students are extremely disadvantaged and intimidated by any kind of writing, like those in the class from which the following paper came, the teacher may have to modify considerably the process described here, at first anyway. The approach has to be very gentle — no criticism and revision for a while — and the memories should be stimulated by a kind of emotional focusing. The teacher elicited this brief but meaningful piece by placing around the room several blown up photographs of provocative subjects and then asking the students to write down a memory that one of the pictures reminded them of. A Negro girl wrote this:

l remember when I was a little girl. I was singing a rain song. It was cold with the splashing of the rain in the puddles. The frogs were cracking the skies were black and all the duck were saying quack quack. I loved to walk in the rain it made me feel so clean inside. Although it was cold around me I was warm and safe.[4]

In this class, the students were encouraged to read their papers privately onto a tape recorder and to play them back, and their papers were frequently printed up after help with spelling and punctuation. The purpose was to bolster confidence and certify their writing — emotional matters that, with these students, have to take priority for a while over the exploration of compositional alternatives.

Autobiographical Incident

When the teacher feels that students have had enough experience in summoning and shaping memories, and can make a core experience emerge for an audience, the staging process can be dropped. The assignment becomes simply a specialized form of first-person writing — an autobiographical incident or a bit of eyewitness memoir. So far in memory writing the focus has

[3] Weeks Junior High School, Newton, Massachusetts.

[4] Harvard-Boston Summer School in Roxbury, Massachusetts; the class comprised children about to enter the eighth and ninth grades.

been unspecified; no distinction was made between an author-centered or other-centered composition. Now this distinction is made and the term "autobiographical" is explained. "Tell an incident that once happened to you or one in which you were the main person." No content is stipulated, only a focus. "Liquor and Dogs Don't Mix" is a good example of an autobiographical incident and, in the case of that girl, might very well have been written without recourse to the memory staging (her stage-3 composition was virtually the same as her stage-2).

WORKSHOP ISSUES

The small-group cross-commentary, grounded in class discussion of selected samples, functions as before and as it will for the rest of the writing program. Students read and write comments on each other's first drafts of the autobiographical incident. These drafts are revised for printing in whatever form will be clear to the person who dittoes. (Any request to have a paper read by the teacher only is honored. Generally, the teacher reads and evaluates the dittoed copies, on which he may also write comments if he wishes.) Obviously, the old compositional issues continue to be discussed, but an issue such as the selection of information takes on a somewhat new meaning because of the stipulated focus on the author.

The teacher can project papers that have varying amounts of author-centeredness, since focus is always relative. At what point does the class feel the story is no longer about the author but about something or someone else? The idea is not at all to condemn the latter but to point it out. Stories in which the narrator is more observer than participant will blend with memoir, another assignment. Discrimination of focus and point of view, and the ability to control them, are the keys. Did the author mean to throw the emphasis where he did? If not, what is misleading about his selection of information, the amount of it, the proportions of it?

Since "information" includes the narrator's thoughts and feelings about what happened, these naturally come in for commentary. The inner experience of the narrator is very important, not only because it can define the coherence of the remembrance but also because it is what can make the difference between author-centered and other-centered narrative. A narrator who reacts strongly enough may become the central figure for the reader even though he was not so active in the incident as someone else. But a problem in this respect is that students of this age still think sometimes that what they felt was obvious and need not be expressed. If merely told to "put in more thoughts and feelings," they will often just insert a sentence that tags feeling without expressing it. Whenever students comment that a paper lacks the author's personal reactions, then the class and small-group discussions can deal with the ways that feeling comes through writing — selection of details, word choice, and various sorts of statements.

RELATED READING

The writing of autobiographical incidents is accompanied by the reading of narrator-centered stories from literature and other sources, in prose and poetry, actual and fictional. State that these selections are being assigned in parallel with their own writing but do not analyze them as models; in the course of discussing both their writing and the reading, they will make connections. One helpful kind of anthology would be a compilation of first-person writing differentiated according to focus and therefore point of view and the narrator's relationship to his subject. The less he is the center of action, the more his point of view is external, and the more he becomes a filter for what he observes. The autobiographical selections can be drawn from actual autobiography or from fiction written as if it were autobiography. The other selections could be of the sorts of first-person narrative to be considered next.

Memoir — Human Incident

The specialization is stipulated by the assignment: "Tell an incident that you witnessed in the past in which you were involved only as an observer." Again, the word "incident" automatically focuses the reportage somewhat and throws emphasis on action rather than on setting or mood. In order to specialize memoir even further, and to include nature observations in the writing program, I differentiated the experimental assignment into human and non-human subjects.

It is crucial that the teacher allow the students enough length to tell the incident well — two or three pages. A lot of very bad writing has been induced simply by limiting narrative to a paragraph or some other small wordage. Such limits force the student to overcondense and to state the facts in an abstractly lifeless way. Strictly demanding an arbitrarily high wordage, however, can cause padding. The ideal is an organic length determined by the writer's judgment *as developed by previous writing experience.* There is evidence from my experiments that students who have done sensory recording, memory writing, and dialogue writing learn to write fluently and fully, to detail and expand without just trying to pad.

What causes students to elaborate naturally is relish in telling the incident, the sound motivation that comes from assurance of an audience and a purpose. This assurance is of course a big part of the reason for giving close attention to the papers in small groups, presenting them to the whole class, and printing them up after commentary and revision. What causes teachers, on the other hand, to limit the wording is the prospect of having to comment individually on so many long papers. But if the teacher teaches the students how to comment on each other's writing, in the fashion I have described, then it becomes possible to give both more writing assignments and longer ones, since often the teacher can either not comment on some sets of papers or do so only very briefly.

The ninth-grade boy who wrote the memoir below was asked to recall a human incident. The relatively short length of his paper, incidentally, seems about right to me for such a slight action.

TOILET PAPER A PENNY A PIECE

Anything and everything can happen in Harvard Square. The sky is the limit. It seems that every nut within a eighty mile radius is there.

One day I saw a sight that I swear would pop the eyes out of somebody's head. Coming up from the subway, I noticed — actually I couldn't help seeing — a group of about six girls dressed in the most unbievible fashin. They had levis that were skin tight, and looked like they were painted on. That wasn't too bad since everybody wears tight pants. But thier faces were full of make up, and they looked like they were going on the war path. Lipstick was smeared on their faces in the shape of circles and four lines that when put together looked like something to play tick-tack-toe on. I manged to survive that, but the worst was yet to come.

The part that killed me was these girls about fifteen years old were selling toilet paper. Each girl was armed with one roll of wite Hudson two-ply. The price was a reasonable penny for a piece. They must have been kiding. And to top it all off some Harvard "squares" actually bought some. Apparently they couldn't go home until they sold the whole roll. Good luck to them. Their plea was buy some from the underprivileged children. Personly I thought that the girls and people who bought the toilet paper were mentally unfit.[5]

Though not terribly literate, this student has composed a fair vignette which he has framed with a personal attitude, expressed in the opening and closing sentences, in such a way that the vignette becomes an instance of his generalization about Harvard Square. The amount of non-observed matter in a piece of eyewitness memoir — either editorializing like this, background information about the setting, or other knowledge the author feeds in for some reason — is one of the main things I would expect to be discussed by the class and the small groups. Certainly, this boy's attitude of disapproval would hardly pass without commentary from classmates. This commentary is almost certain to challenge or support the author's judgment on what he observed, to raise the question of biased reporting. At this point the teacher can ask: Do you think he has slanted the facts? Is there anything wrong with making an open judgment? If some students feel, however, that the author has misinterpreted the scene, that is of course another matter than intentional bias, for *unawareness* makes for what in fiction is called an "imperceptive narrator," one whose subjective account betrays the fact that he has failed to see something in his own material. Class disagreement about

[5] Lexington High School, Lexington, Massachusetts.

the meaning of some things recounted first-hand provides a fine chance to help students discriminate between bias and imperception. The matter is sensitive for the author, however, so the teacher would do better merely to let students match their viewpoints than to throw his judgment into the balance.

This last paper might have been a revision of a sensory recording rather than a reminiscence. From reading the final product, one would not necessarily be able to tell whether a reporter had covered the scene on assignment, taking notes, or had recalled something that happened before he was asked to write. But the teacher should help students to open both sources and to learn to compose reportage in the somewhat different way each source requires. Also, the possibility should be raised of fictionally extending such a sketch. Given the setting and situation, what might happen next? Short stories can be stimulated both by the real material of reportage and by the observer role. Assign a few professional short stories to be read that are narrated by an observer *I*.

Memoir — Nature Incident

The following two samples illustrate nature narrative drawn from memory. They were written in eighth-grade classes that had done sensory, memory, and dialogue writing. I read more than 100 papers written by these classes and was hardly bored a single time. I was astonished by the fullness, the interest, and the generally high quality of the accounts, even when some of the authors obviously lacked verbal skill. I chose the samples almost at random and certainly did not screen for the best. Besides the unquestionable effectiveness of the teacher of these classes,[5] the successful results, extremely consistent even for that generally able student body, seem to be due to the subject. Recounting animal incidents, storms, etc., is an especially happy assignment for children of this age. The two papers below are unrevised and uncorrected. The first is by a girl:

The breakers crashed the rocks and ran away with a hissing sound. The gray sand was dotted with birds' prints. It was a bleak November day at the beach dark save for the thin watery sunlight breaking through the clouds. The wind whistled through the waving dune grass and made whitecaps on the waves.

Suddenly the peaceful silence was broken by a flock of hungry sea gulls flying over head, hunting food. There was a bag of garbage left on the beach by some careless picknicker, and the gulls, smelling this delicacy, were already landing around it. After a few minutes the scene had turned into a complete battle. Squaks, screeches and the swoosh of wings accompanied this "tug-of-war" combat which involved the survival of the fittest. Food was

[5] Eugenia Nicholas of Weeks Junior High School, Newton, Massachusetts.

pulled between beaks, stepped on and sent flying into the rumbling ocean.

Two particular gulls, I noticed, were engaged in a life or death wing-to-wing combat. There was an old strong gull who looked like he'd been through many similar episodes like this, and a young brown-speckled gull. The young one had what looked like a moldy sanwich and was contentedly pecking at it, not bothering a soul. The old sly bird spied this jealoussly and made his mind up to get it. He opened his large beak and snapped at the diner's tail so hard that the younger jumped away from his dinner. The other seeing its' chance grabbed the morsel and flew to a nearby jetty. After recovering from its shock the brown-specked bird. In his anger he began to circle round the other greedy gull and finally swooped down hitting him hard. There, silhoueted against the gray sky the two birds fought, not a playful romp, but a fight which meant the loser would forfeit a rare meal, for their was little to eat these cold days. One may even be killed, because if there was a sea gulls manual, they were using every trick in the book. The sandwich lay barely touched next to the hysterical birds. All the other gulls had flown off satisfied or to seek out more food, but these gulls continued their ordeal. The younger was beginning to weaken and the other would jab at him fiercely when he paused. Blood was flecked on the older's white breast but he was not loosing strength. Finally, when the younger looked too weak to even eat the food, the other gave him one fierce push that sent him tumbling off the jetty, and landed, a crumpled heap in the water. The poor thing apparently had broken it's wing and now he was at the mercy of the angry sea. He bobbed a few times, gasping but finally disappeared in the inky ocean. The sly bird, happy with his victory snatched the sandwich in his beak and started to fly away. But, suddenly against the sky I saw his figure falling into the sea for he was too tired to carry the food and fly. The sea gull joined his enemy undersea.

The second is by a less articulate boy in one of that same teacher's eighth-grade classes:

There it was a very rainy Saturday. It was a day to do nothing but sit home and watch television. The storm kept getting heavier and heavier with thunder and lightning until it was practically impossible to go out. Outside the house there was a tree. It was pretty big with many branches and leaves starting to fall. It was Autum.

Up in the tree was a Birds nest. It was nearer the top of the Medium sized tree. There were about three birds, a mother and two new babies just born. They were just learning how to fly. The storm was getting heavier and right below the tree was a big hole with grass, and whenever there was rain it would flood up and be like quick sand, and if you got your foot stuck in it, then you would be in tough shape. Still I don't think anybody stepped in it that means any person. It was still raining pretty hard. Then the tree from up above started to shake real hard because of the wind. As I was looking out the window the nest was starting to shake hard and almost tipped over. Then all of a sudden, one of the baby birds fell right out of the nest. It fell pretty hard, and could hardly fly. It tried to move but it couldn't because it way caught in the mushy mud and was like pure quick sand to the hopeless bird.

Finally the mother bird realized that there was only one bird in the nest, so she looked and kept looking until she looked down and saw that her baby bird was stuck in some mushy mud and couldn't get out. I knew she was worried because of the way she kept moving around. Then, she started flying, and first she made a dive landing and tried to pull the baby out but it didn't work. Then she came up with something. She flew down and stopped in front, then she reached out and grabed the baby bird as hard as she could. The bird was moving slowly but surely. Then she pulled out, grabbed her and flew the baby up to the nest. The nest was in bad condition, but the Mother managed to fix it. I was happy knowing that she would be O.K. About twenty minutes later it cleared up. I went out to see the muddy hole in which the bird fell in. When it was dry outside I covered the hole until I knew it wouldn't flood up anymore and the birds would be ok. Then after a while, I saw one of the babies fly out of the nest for its first time.

Reportage

COMPOSITIONAL DIFFERENCES BETWEEN MEMOIR AND REPORTAGE

Whereas memoir is based on what one happens to remember, reportage is based on what one has gone out and deliberately observed for the purpose of writing up. Both result in eyewitness narrative, but the compositional problems are different: memories are already digested and classified, but, at the time of writing, one's choice of material is limited; planned observation, on the other hand, produces an overabundance of unselected detail to be shaped, but the reporter can seek out his material. The writer has fewer options with memoir, for both the whole and the details; with reportage, he has choices to make about when and where to observe, which sensations to record at the scene, and how to digest the notes later.

SETTING UP A NEWSPAPER OPERATION

Students who have done sensory note taking before — have gone to a locale of their own choice and recorded what they saw and heard — will be able, in seventh and eighth grades, to act as real reporters covering scenes. Small groups would act as newspaper editors, thinking up reportorial assignments and editing the "stories" that come in afterwards. The scenes to be covered would include more things certainly than what would ordinarily make "news," that is, everyday actions at locales that have meaning to the students as well as new events and seasonal changes. The teacher might preface the project by saying that, like city editors, the students should keep a look-out for both coming events and for places or scenes that have standard human interest. After the members of the group have reacted to the original papers, and individuals have revised them, the papers would be printed up, probably in mixture with other kinds of reportage. Reportage, of course, can also be specialized in content, but it should be the groups who stipulate subjects, when assigning stories to individuals. Thus some reporters would cover human events, others nature, and others such things as construction jobs, mechanical operations, and so on. The newspaper could have departments, and the reportage could be related to social studies and science.

More specifically, the student goes to his locale and takes down what he sees, as fully as he can but selectively. The earlier experimenting with different ways of recording should help him strike a balance between general coverage and the detailing of selected things. Back in the group, these papers are exchanged, read, and discussed with the particular aim of helping each other produce the best possible journalistic copy. The teacher's direction of this process occurs in the class discussions, where he projects certain papers chosen for writing issues they contain about which students seem to need more insight.

How Workshop Issues Are Raised Before the Whole Class

Let me illustrate this class discussion process in a general way with three papers done by students in the same ninth-grade class (the age being of no importance for my purposes at the moment). The class had been told to observe places around the school or at home. As I know now, when put this way, the assignment is too purposeless to motivate the students very well, a fact made clear by the ironic closing sentence of the first two papers as well as, I think, by some qualities of the writing itself. Also, although these were supposed to have been revised, they showed little signs of it. It is partly for these reasons that I have suggested the small-group, newspaper approach. At any rate, the teacher dittoed these three papers in order as reproduced here and invited discussion about them:

(1)

At about twenty minutes to three I am sitting in front of the stairs leading into the building. At this moment I am observing a woman walking by me at almost the same as I see a girl who is staying near the stairs for some reason. Now David, Mark, and Dennis go by on the way to their spot of observation. Miss Gatehouse walks by and asked me what I am doing. Then I answer. After this a boy goes out the front stairs. Mr. Redente goes walking by and asks the girl a question, then the girl answers. At the same time this girl leaves. The door to the right of me opens but nobody comes through. A second after that I can hear people in the gym yelling. Next Don Coil walks by and says something about what I am doing here. For a few seconds in the hall it is quiet, and so I look up and see Mr. Weeks' picture on the wall. Also there is a space drawing on the bulletin board. Mr. White comes one way and Mr. Webster comes from the other direction. They stop and talk about something. Then go in opposite directions, after they ask Peter a question. Now Jim Davin goes by without saying anything. Now a teacher with shoes that sound like 20 grandfather clocks goes by in a stirring sort of way. After this I don't hear any-thing but a background talking from both sides of myself. To my left the door opens and three people with Mr. Webster and Mr. White go into the office. At this time I hear and see a couple of 8th grade girls walk by me and talk about some-thing in school. At the other side, to the left, another pair of people go by not saying anything. Now Leonard Belouche says hello as he walks by Peter and myself. Mrs. Clark comes by me talking to Leonard a few minutes later. I have now finished observing and will proceed back to room 312 were I got the assignment.

(2)

The first thing I hear now is the TV going with my mother and sister watching it. I can't see what there eating, but I can hear them munching on something. I'm looking around the room at the wall paper and wondering why there are so many different kinds of designs.

I just heard my little brother talk about something. I can also hear what their watching on television; its Bewitched. All of a sudden I just, for no reason, looked at my math book. It's funny how the different kids write things on it, especially Frank.

My sister just walked by and hit me on the head, as always. She keeps banging a door as if she wants to keep bothering me. She's still walking around in the kitchen getting something to eat. The commercial just came on television and it's almost time to stop.

I'm sitting on the dinigroom table and I just felt the plant in front of me. It's very soft. The plant has about fifteen stems on it, which are all sticking out of the main body. I just asked my mother what time it is and she said it is about time to stop. So I must leave this wonderful piece of paper and go on to another masterpiece.

(3)

A lazy droning fills the room, the product of a series of conversations carried on simultaneously. Phrases can be picked out from smooth sentences in consultations. Laughter and the ring of a telephone stand out. My chair feels uncomfortably smooth beneath me, a substitute walks by, stumbling in too-high heels. Her perfume mingles unpleasantly with the smell of my pencil. My attention is attracted by some coats hanging across from me. Above them the clock ticks loudly, its hands jerking with spasms. Everyone seems conscious of it. They click their pens and drum with them, becoming absorbed with the rhythm. A secretary smooths her hair as she dials a num-ber. It gleams with a dazzling light from a large window. The high ceiling is composed of tiles, reminding me of a mosaic. Mocking it are small pink conference rooms which seem to close in the area. Shoe leather squeaks as a techer strides by. He is whistling to himself. A file cabinet clicks open, papers are shuffled through, doors click open and shut further down the hall. The small sounds of monotony combine in my ears. A boy swaggers by the door and makes faces. The room is comfortably cool. In the shadows, my chair legs twist grotesquely. The bitter taste of lead fills my mouth. I never before noticed how the odour of a leadpencil pervades the air. Office sounds continue to a background of classroom murmurs. I touch the cool smoothness of my chair. A lazy droning fills the room, the product of a series of conversations carried on simultaneously. I feel strangely tired.

The teacher's tack was to ask the students to rank these in order of preference, revealing afterwards that his own rating was in the order printed, #3 being the one he considered best, and characterizing #1 as all factual report, #2 as personal touch, and #3 as combination of both. The majority of the students had preferred them in the same order. They went on to comment, among other things, that #1 was monotonous and too everyday, whereas #3 had more details, captured the atmosphere, and used better descriptive words. Though worthwhile, these responses could be considerably sharpened if related to more specific features of the texts.

It occurred to me, listening in the back of the room, that #1 was time-centered, #2 I-centered, and #3 object-centered. I did some counting — about the extent of my statistical research — and discovered that fifteen of the sentences in #1 began with some expression of time, nine of the clauses and sentences in #2 began with *I*, and fifteen of the sentences in #3 had some observed thing as the subject. I think that these specific differences in sentences relate rather directly to both the teacher's preferences and the student's reactions.

Since neither time nor the observer was, in these cases, especially important, #3 had a more meaningful or interesting focus. Where the personal note did enter in #3, at the end, it had a distinct effect that, along with the repeating of the first sentence, gave the piece a sense of climax and closure. Papers #1 and #2 had some interesting detail but no appropriate focus or effect, possibly because these two writers were not enough involved in the assignment to care, possibly for other reasons. My point, in any case, is that the teacher can help students correlate their vague reactions to a piece of writing with the quite specific features of the writing that provoke these reactions. The specific features in the case of these three papers concern the nature of the sentences, of what is being predicated.

Asking the class to rank the papers for preference is one possible gambit for discussion, but instead of giving my preference as teacher, I would make a more neutral, descriptive contribution. I would point out what I see: that roughly half of the predicates in #1 have *I* as subject and roughly half have observed things as subjects; that whatever the subject in #1, it is preceded often enough by a time expression to create a strong pattern; that the dominant subject in #2 is *I*; that time in #2 is indicated more sparingly and less obtrusively by adjuncts to the verb, as in *I just heard* and *She keeps banging;* that in #3 the subjects of sentences are consistently objects of observation until a shift to *I* occurs at the end; that time in #3 is indicated by the succession of sentences themselves, thus obviating most time expressions, the exception being when simultaneity has to be made clear (*smooths her hair as she dials.*)

The most probable truth is that the writers of these papers were for the most part unaware of the patterns they had imposed on their recordings, and that the readers also were unaware of the patterns and of how their responses were determined by them. So the teacher makes these factual comments to induce this awareness, underscoring his observations by underlining words and phrases on the projection. The flat commentary alone may well elicit remarks from the class. The teacher can go a little further, however, and ask the class to relate the fact of these patterns to their earlier reactions, including their order of preference. The authors can be asked if the pattern and emphasis they set up were intended or at least fitted their intentions. The other members of the class can be asked to assess and compare the different effects created by these different patterns. Without necessarily evaluating himself, the teacher can thus help his students learn to evaluate.

Even if the examination were to do no more than draw from the authors of #1 and #2 an acknowledgment that they did not want to do the assignment, the session has been worth something: it is possible to see how the boredom of the writer was directly reflected in specific structures of the writing, to get a grasp of alternative patterns, and to develop judgment about which patterns one would want to use in doing the assignment.

When students read each other's papers and comment on them in autonomous groups of three to five, their feedback must be informed. I have tried to illustrate here how it becomes informed. It is during the writing workshop discussions of the whole class that the teacher gives students the benefit of his perceptions and of his understanding of rhetoric and linguistics. Using no other texts than their own writing, he helps them translate such psychological matters as intention and reaction into the specific terms of the text so that they engage with matters of technique and choice when they read and write. What they need is not concepts and information from outside sources, but *consciousness* of what they are doing when they write, and of what others are doing when they write.

OTHER WORKSHOP ISSUES

In the small groups, where the students are acting as newspaper editors readying copy for publication, several compositional issues are almost certain to arise from the nature of sensory reportage. One is tense — whether to convert a present-tense recording to past-tense narrative or leave it as it is for the sense of immediacy. But a decision about tense may depend on other related issues, the main one of which is general unity or purpose.

Although the writer chooses the spot, he has little control over what he will see and hear there; he is working with more random material than when recalling material. (But deciding on what scenes to cover will show how much the choice of locale is itself a compositional act.) Coherence or meaning will depend very much on *how* he sees. The point of the reportage can be any number of things about the character of the locale, the behavior that goes on there, atmosphere, etc. The teacher does not have to talk in advance about unity, coherence, and purpose. The student has just as strong a need for significance as he; if well motivated, he will intuitively try to shape the miscellany into something that has a point (sometimes miscellany itself creates a unified effect).

A third issue is also related. It is one that came out in the preceding three papers — the importance of the observer. First person is neither good nor bad. In making suggestions to each other for revision, the students will have to consider how much the reporter is to include himself in the report. When is it good strategy to give a strong personal touch? Should he stay out entirely, play lightly in and out, or color all that he sees with his own reactions? Point of view concerns the position (in all senses) of the narrator, and the small-group discussions about this will help students to understand fiction. The personal presence of the observer-narrator is shown and felt not only by direct reference to himself but by the personal feeling and attitude he infuses into the scene and into the language.

RELATED READING

The appropriate reading selections to accompany eyewitness assignments can be either prose or poetry. Actual reportage by professional prose writers should be read — excerpts or sometimes a whole book such as Gerald Durrell's *The Overloaded Ark* or Darwin's *Voyage of the Beagle,* which contain eyewitness reportage of both man and nature and are good literature as well. Short prose selections of this sort for this age need to be sought out and made available. Any first-person, firsthand reportage in which the narrator plays essentially an observer role is apt, whether fictional or actual (when read side by side the differences and similarities of both become clearer). Most first-person fiction suitable for this age tends, however, to mix autobiography and eyewitness memoir, as in *Huckleberry Finn.* In any case, I am not suggesting that the reading be selected for technique instead of content — only that if fiction of a certain technique is read, it be read when students are writing in a similar relation to their subjects. It is certainly true that the majority of fictional prose and poetry that appeals to children of these grades is in third person, and the proportion of reading selections should reflect this.

But writing first-person narrative will acclimate students to first-person fiction.

There are many poems for this age comprising personal observation of a scene or brief action, some about nature, some about people. Robert Frost has written many such poems but some other modern poets are also possibilities.[6] Reading some of these will undoubtedly inspire some students to write eyewitness accounts as poems, especially if the teacher makes clear that he is assigning the poems at that time because they represent another mode in which to write about what one witnesses. The ways by which poets infuse personal feeling and attitude into their accounts will be more apparent to students who have discussed similar matters in connection with their own writing.

[6] See George Bennett and Paul Molloy, *Cavalcade of Poems*, (New York: Scholastic Book Services, 1965), an excellent paperback anthology for older junior high school students.

―――――――――――――――――――――――――――――――――

―――――――――――――――――――――――――――――――――

―――――――――――――――――――――――――――――――――

Chapter 24

Poetry of Observation

A strong emphasis on reading and writing poetry will very likely influence student prose in the direction of greater precision and better style. An emphasis on the concrete will help them understand how much the statement of poetry is made through sensuous things rather than through bald, abstract statements.

Haiku

The Japanese form called *haiku* offers a number of special advantages for learning how language can be used. As poems of observation, haiku relate rather directly to eyewitness reportage. But while focusing on things, the poet infuses his response into the description; feeling is expressed through the exact rendering of a physical moment. A haiku poem is at once about observer and observed. Its fidelity to things gives it a certain objectivity, but things are always registered by some sensibility. Because haiku are short, they constitute miniature compositions in which every word counts. Usually each poem is a single sentence. No other piece of writing, except maxims, offer such an opportunity to focus on the smallest units of discourse — the word, the turn of phrase, the structure of the sentence. In the past, teachers have tried to get this fine focus on language through sentence exercises of one sort or another. But this is self-defeating because an isolated sentence is unmotivated and meaningless unless it does constitute by itself a complete and authentic composition. So I would propose extensive work with haiku for several reasons — to refine observation down to particulars, to express feeling in the concrete terms of what evokes it, to look at language and composition microscopically, and to gain special entrance into the whole world of poetry.[1]

―――――――――――――

[1] Haiku have become so modish that they are now presented even to elementary school children. This is over-zealous teaching, I believe. The concreteness of the poems should not deceive us about their sophistication.

Since the original haiku form is defined to a great extent by qualities peculiar to the Japanese language and not present in English, it is useless to try to define it too precisely by form. The Japanese original has no rhyme and no punctuation, uses a stock of "cut-words," or particle words, that serve for expressive punctuation, and contains a much smaller number of syllables than an English poem possibly could. All we can say about the haiku form in English is that it usually consists of one sentence, often broken in the middle by a dash or colon, set typographically into two or three lines. I prefer the three-line form because it gives more opportunity for making use of line-breaking, which is a unique feature of poetry. The best definition is probably not by form but by substance — the fixed moment. In any case, the teacher does not begin by defining haiku for students; let them infer a definition from reading instances of it and from trying to write their own.

Presenting Haiku in Class

The best way to present haiku — and this would hold for many other short poems — is to project them a line at a time (writing the whole on a transparency and moving an opaque sheet slowly downward). When something appears piecemeal before us we tend to anticipate and to complete it ourselves, especially when the something is a periodic sentence of which we are awaiting a resolution in both syntax and idea. So reveal one line, perhaps two, and ask the class what they think is going to follow. The students read the poem by trying to compose it. Often when I have done this, students have thought of very interesting lines that might well have followed. They seldom guess exactly the lines the poet wrote, which is not the point anyway, but the alternatives form an array of possibilities upon which the poet's lines fall with great effect.

The game is simple and enjoyable and makes students think about a huge number of things. In order to complete the poem, one uses all cues — the sense, the image or action, the syntax of the suspended sentence, the rhyme and meter, and basic rhetorical devices like symmetry and parallelism, contrast and reversal. One asks himself what, given the poem so far, would complete all these things and provide a fitting climax. And yet the teacher asks no question, analytical or critical, especially no question to which he knows the answer. He asks for a creative act, and that act *entails* a lot of intuitive analysis.

Suppose the haiku begins:

The falling leaves

Without saying so to himself, a student looks for a predicate denoting any act appropriate for leaves, but the obvious one, *fall* is already in the participle. So he looks for another. Spin? Rattle? But what tense? If he is familiar with haiku, he will probably put the predicate in the present. But other things could follow here besides the predicate. An appositive? A relative clause? (He does not have to know their names in order to look for them.) The absence of a comma after *leaves* may cue him to the unlikelihood of either of these two. By now the class has volunteered a number of lines and made judgments about which would be best. The teacher reveals the next line:

> The falling leaves
> fall and pile up; the rain

It was *fall* after all! Perhaps our student perceives a connection between that repetition and the second predicate *pile up*. And again now he has before him a subject without a predicate. But he also has an image of autumn, a piling action, and a semicolon. Perhaps he is already getting a feeling of balance from the semicolon and the fact that the second clause is starting off just like the first. In thinking of an action for *rain,* he will consider the season and mood, the sentence pattern, and perhaps the likelihood of more repetition. A clever student may say the *rain rains* and then think of a rhyme word for *leaves: the rain rains and grieves.* But he senses that the meter is too heavy (too many stresses) and adds a word to lighten it: *the rain rains down and grieves.*

This thinking can go on out loud and benefit from other students' ideas. All the teacher has to do is ask which version they think completes the poem best; reasons are given for preferences, and new tries are made on the basis of these reasons. Whatever lines they arrive at, they have done some imaginative thinking and entered into the poem. They will appreciate the particular sense of climax and closure that the poet created, and understand better on their own what he was trying to do in the whole poem. It is surprise, half-divined, that delights.

> The falling leaves
> fall and pile up; the rain
> beats on the rain.

The gathering perception may be of a very different pattern from this one, but always it is a multiple perception — of language, things, and feelings — for the words move with the movement of sensibility.

> A trout leaps high —

Where are we? What's the season? What action or image next? Does the dash mean abruptness or equation or something else? These are questions a student might ask himself.

> A trout leaps high —
> below him, in the river bottom

We need a subject *and* predicate, knowing already *where* the action occurred. What is the pattern — contrast? A leap high and a _____ below:

> A trout leaps high —
> below him, in the river bottom,
> clouds flow by.[2]

Contrast, yes. But reversal too. The trout is where the clouds should be, and the clouds where the trout should be. And that's the surprise, the climax. When the lines fall singly on the mind, they build the topsyturvy feeling the poet felt. Asked to write a haiku, students who have had a number of such reading experiences will know what they are going to do with words.

After a haiku has been fully revealed, and thought about in this manner along the way, it is read aloud by several different students. The point is to try out and compare several different readings, and in the course of this to discuss which ones seem best. Thus the movement of language is followed orally, the feeling expressed vocally, as in dramatic work. Next, the teacher might change on the transparency the order of lines in the haiku and ask students to read it again. (Read the last haiku with the second and third lines reversed.) This brings out the suspension value of periodic sentences and sometimes demonstrates quite forcefully why writers play games with normal word order.

WRITING HAIKU

When the teacher feels the time is right, he asks the students to write a haiku, allowing a number of days so that they have some time to observe things after the idea has been planted, and suggesting that they consider also lifting a moment from some of their sensory or memory writings. One second will do, the teacher says, some moment when a sound, sight, smell, taste, or touch triggered a strong response or set a mood, released a feeling. There may be many such moments in their previous writing. The use of rhyme is optional; nothing is said about meter; a three-line form is stipulated.

These poems are passed around in the small groups and the members are allowed to write on and around each other's haiku, with the understanding that this is for suggestive value to the writer, who may perfectly well prefer his version to the revisions. This crossing out of words, rephrasing, shifting of lines, breaking of lines, changing of punctuation, is a very important study of language as well as composition. In comparing and discussing different versions, the students can see very well how almost every change of vocabulary, sentence structure, and punctuation alters image and impact, sound and

---

[2] These two haiku and the one on p. 368 are reprinted by permission of Doubleday & Company, Inc. from *An Introduction to Haiku*, translated and edited by Harold G. Henderson (Garden City, N.Y.: Doubleday Anchor, 1958), a very good paperback for use in schools.

sense. Booklets of student haiku, I have found, are eagerly read, and often discussed, without ever being assigned as reading. As is so often true of the students' own writing, it is enough to distribute copies. This assignment is one to repeat at intervals.

The problem of over-abstracting. The difficulties students encounter trying to write haiku are the difficulties they encounter trying to write most kinds of poetry. The biggest, most consistent problem — which I have observed many times when various teachers, including myself, have proposed haiku writing — is that students over-abstract. They see macroscopically, grossly; instead of caterpillar hairs they observe:

> A warm silent lake.
> On a calm summer day . . .
> Wake up, back to work[3]

This ninth-grade boy's haiku is very typical of many efforts. First, he has generalized an entire day, instead of registering what could be perceived only within a very brief compass of time and space (it is fine calibrations of time and space that define concreteness). Second, he has named, instead of rendered, the sensations — *warm, silent, calm, cool.* Likewise, he has stated, instead of implied, the season and the time — *summer day* — and all but flatly asserted his feeling — *Wake up, back to work.* This over-abstraction of both outer things and inner experience is the mark of amateur poetry and of much nondescript, ineffectual prose as well.

Why should such writing be the spontaneous tendency of a person this age? I am not sure, but I think two very important learning factors are involved. One is developmental: children grow gradually away from crude lumping toward finer and finer discriminations of perception and thought. The other is conventional: most expressions of perception and thought that children hear and read are hasty, inexact verbalizations of the real things people want to express. Familiar general phrases like *summer day* come out of us automatically and indiscriminately in response to very different moments of experience.

This is the dangerous side of abstracting: for the sake of convenience, it makes too many things look alike. But convention and convenience eventually influence perception itself, to such a point that we seldom see anything new anymore. More specifically, some masking of particularity is learned from reading bad, vague poetry and some is learned from thoughtlessly diffuse categories that adults hand down:

SNOW STORMS

> Window's shuttered white
> Children showing sheer delight
> Oh, what loveliness.

[3] Weeks Junior High, Newton, Massachusetts.

This seventh-grade girl does not depict how the children showed delight, nor does she evoke the feeling she had. She simply labels both feelings. The plurality of the title betrays the abstract attitude. I am not criticizing the children (or the teaching), for the problem epitomizes the lifelong struggle we all undergo to make language match experience.

For contrast, let me offer what I consider to be a very good haiku that truly notes reality. Significantly, perhaps, I have had to draw on the work of an older student for this example (a boy in a tenth-grade class of mine at Phillips Exeter Academy).

> Breath on the window-pane —
> remnants of someone watching
> others play.

That breath did not linger as a remnant on that windowpane for more than a few seconds — and that is the chief reason for the poem's success. But a lot of sophistication lies behind such specificity and behind the restrained expression of feeling in the last two lines. Because the writer puts us in the moment, we feel the poignancy of it, as we could not if he merely named a feeling we were supposed to feel. (For more examples of maturer haiku see pages 410 to 413.) But few students in my classes, and in classes of teachers I know of, have been able to solve well the problem of over-abstraction ("pseudo-abstraction" is probably a more accurate term). My recommendations here for the reading and writing of haiku are designed to help students as much as possible to zero in on a moment and to render it as they really perceive it. In this respect, the most useful thing the teacher can do is to say, "Catch a sensation that you could not have had several minutes afterwards or several minutes before."

When generality is not over-abstraction. Generalizing is not in itself bad. Abstract statement can sometimes spring feeling in a startling way. Shakespeare's phrase, "uncertain glory of an April day," for example, evokes fleeting cloud shadows and passing showers, because the reader fills in the abstraction with concrete details he remembers; as he does so he feels the way he has felt on experiencing such weather. What makes this work is the unusual yoking of *uncertain* with *glory,* plus a skillful prediction of the reader's associations. So students may sometimes come off well using this sort of generalized wording. The test is in reader response, which cross-commentary can furnish. Class discussion and small-group reading should help students sort out mere vagueness from happy phrasing that is abstract but evocative.

The philosophic epigram. Our goal is something more far-reaching than haiku alone. In trying to write haiku children will sometimes create another sort of poem — the philosophic epigram. Often these will be hand-me-downs, but many times they will be fairly original expressions of an idea through an image. Feedback and discussion should sort real haiku from this —

PROGRESS

Moonlight, sunlight, stars that shine;
The light of the world?
An electric light bulb.[4]

— if only to keep levels of discourse straight in students' minds. The author should know what he has done but not feel wrong to have done it.

The two poems below, written respectively by a ninth-grade and an eighth-grade public school boy during an Exeter summer session, were stimulated by an eclipse that occurred that summer, but both boys have mentally digested the event more than is characteristic of haiku:

ECLIPSE

The land is all dark,   Danger! don't observe
the sun disappears,   With the naked eye
alas! it comes back.   The solar eclipse.

The first spans an awkward time lapse of several minutes and ends in an explicitly stated thought; but the negative reaction to the sun's reappearance is surprising and triggers a response in the reader. The second concentrates solely, and suggestively, on a negative imperative that need not have been inspired by a real eclipse at all (the imperative being an old admonition that crops up for the occasion).

Both poems have something, I think, that should not be discouraged by a purist or doctrinaire stand on haiku, which is really just an entrée into other poetry anyway. The two poems express rather well in their own fashions a primitive threat that the sun seems to symbolize — recurrently:

Fear no more the heat o' the sun.

Another ninth-grade boy in the same summer session, however, did more nearly what it is that haiku do best:

From the darkened heavens,
Striking all around,
Rain.

Without departing from the physical facts, he imparts a state of mind. By suspending the subject *rain* until the last line, he lets us be struck from the dark without knowing at first what is striking. The pattern of words conveys as much as their meanings.

---

[4] Ninth-grader in Phillips Exeter Academy Summer School.

FURTHER READING OF HAIKU

Drawing the image. The reading of haiku can be continued meanwhile in a somewhat different way. After projecting a visual haiku, the teacher distributes transparencies and grease pencils to the class and asks them to draw the image the poem evokes for them. The drawings are projected one after another and the teacher invites comparisons among them. This leads naturally to discussions of interpretation because the students will explain why they drew the image a certain way and why they think some drawings are incorrect or misleading. For documentation, the haiku can be shown again. Whose view does it support?

Even when a number of drawings fit the poem well, it is still enlightening for students to see how differently others pictured to themselves the same moment. And because of their brevity, haiku work by suggestion, leaving certain details to inference and imagination. Often the image in a haiku depends on assuming a particular physical point of view, as in the one below:

> Into the sea
> it drives the red hot sun
> the river Mogami.[5]

What aspects of a haiku *cannot* be drawn? Ask the class what they had trouble representing. Why? What are these non-visual things. Feeling? Effects dependent on language? The point is that haiku are not merely sensory; a lot is intangible or purely verbal. That is why they are poems, not paintings. Such aspects can be discovered through graphics.

Comparing translations. Two translations of the same haiku can be presented side by side, given readings, and discussed for preference. This can be especially worthwhile because the translations of haiku differ so markedly in image, tone, and feeling as well as in use of rhyme, pattern, and number of lines (two to four). Again, the teacher avoids arbitrary analytical questions, letting matters of form and effect arise from the comparison: he might ask students why they prefer one poem over the other and then let them give their reactions to each other.

Other Short Poems

PAIRING HAIKU WITH OTHER POEMS

The comparison approach can also help bridge from haiku into other poetry. Being careful not to pre-interpret too much, pair off a haiku with some other fairly short and concrete poem that seems to treat a similar subject. For example, I have often paired Carl Sandberg's "Grass" with a remark-

---

[5] Henderson, p. 29.

ably similar haiku, and Emily Dickenson's "Snake" with a snake haiku, and asked students which they prefer.[6] But pairs should be dramatized or given thoughtful class readings first. ("Grass" is a kind of soliloquy spoken by the grass itself.) Ideally, students are brought to the point where the teacher can invite commentary merely by silence rather than by asking a question. This state of affairs is achieved simply by letting the presentation of the poems sink in, by waiting. (This will happen of course, only after a certain rapport and atmosphere have been created over a period of time).

The difference that length makes. According to the poems the haikus are paired with, a number of interesting issues come up. Sheer length, for example, involves these differences: the moment versus time sequence, subtle suggestion versus descriptive elaboration, intra-sentence versus inter-sentence relations, the single and sudden impact versus progression and development, the isolated verse unit versus multiple stanzas. What are the gains and losses of brevity? of length? Several times my students pointed out that Dickenson's "Snake" contains several possible haiku embedded in it, and that the climax is really a haiku. What these juxtaposed pairs do is set off the particular qualities of each poem; they induce discriminations valuable for understanding and appreciating many kinds of poems.

READING

Then haiku can be dropped for a while and other concrete poems taken up. There are many good poems of only a few lines, some of which are also written as a single sentence, like Robert Frost's "Dust of Snow," Francis Frost's "Skaters," William Carlos Williams' "The Red Wheelbarrow," Samuel Hazo's "The Parachutist," and Anna Engleman's "In a Vacant Lot."[7] The principle of approaching them is the same. The manner of presentation, not quizzing, broaches discussion — gradual revelation on the overhead projector, dramatized reading, juxtaposition, depiction, and so on. In other words, students are asked to *do* something with the poems, which should not be merely read silently, or rapidly in great numbers, but savored slowly and really attended to.

WRITING

One of the things students can do with poems is to write short poems of their own inspired by them. The assignment in this case, which would come in the middle of reading poems such as I have named, is simply to pin down

[6] Both haiku are in Henderson, on pages 166 and 181, respectively. The second pair was included in Bennett and Molloy.

[7] These are all in Bennett and Molloy along with many good two- and three-sentence poems.

in four to eight lines a scene or action they have experienced that one of the poems they read brings to mind. They are encouraged to try out forms from the professionals. An inspiration might come from a striking pattern like the one in "The Red Wheelbarrow" — four stanzas of two lines each, the second line being always a single word — or from a subject, such as sports, animals, or weather. The teacher should select some of these poems to project, without saying that they are written by students (perhaps taking them from another class) and present them exactly as he does a professional poem. When students read each other's memories or pieces of reportage, they should acquire the habit of writing *poem* in the margin when they see something they think the writer ought to make into a poem.

Metaphor

The best way to appreciate comparisons and to begin to use them is to become steeped in the figures of poetry. Instead of belaboring the difference between similes and metaphors, the teacher would do better to present many poems based on a central comparison and let the class try writing similar poems. In "The Country Bedroom," for example, Francis Cornford begins, "My room's a square and candle-lighted boat" and continues the comparison for the rest of the poem's eight lines.[8] When a student sets up a single comparison as the frame of his poem, he *magnifies* the analogizing process that underlies both the conventional figures of speech embedded in language and the novel metaphors of creative thought.

It is true that younger students do not often make original verbal comparisons, but a technical approach does not help. As for comprehending other people's comparisons, I do not think that students have trouble except when the terms or allusions of the comparisons are unfamiliar to them. So-called literal-mindedness does exist but is due, I believe, either to unfamiliarity with the figurative use of language or to an emotional defense against ambiguity. In any case, teaching comparison as a *concept,* explaining it, serves nothing except to make analogy seem falsely esoteric. Actually, nothing is more common and automatic than analogizing, since all of concept formation and generalizing depends on perceiving likeness in discriminably different things. It is the uncommon and verbally explicit comparison that teachers are after. One learns metaphor out of the need to metaphorize, to make the unknown known, as in the tactile assignment on p. 136, or to make the familiar unfamiliar, as in "The Country Bedroom."

[8] Bennett and Molloy, p. 55.

Chapter 25

Journals and Diaries

Although journals and diaries are narratives, they are different enough from the kinds of narratives discussed earlier to merit separate treatment. Autobiography and memoir stem from the memories one happens to recollect. Eyewitness reportage stems from sensory notes made for the purpose of composing later. Entries in a journal or diary are based on the memory of very recent events, noted within a day or so of occurrence and kept for later use. What is unique about journals and diaries is their serial nature: the writer's point of view is at once beyond some events and yet still in the middle of others.

A journal, let us say, is more impersonal and public than a diary, which is written more about oneself and to oneself. Though hard to maintain, the distinction is nevertheless of some use. Keeping some kind of journal or diary is an assignment that, I have heard, many teachers give.

Account of Trials

The kind of diary tried out in experiments I initiated was a long, general one, summarized at the end. As background for recommendations, I will describe the experiment.

THE ASSIGNMENT DIRECTIONS

Several classes of ninth-graders in two suburban schools were asked to:

Keep a diary for about five weeks, making about five entries in the diary per week. Allow ten to fifteen minutes to write each entry; write down whatever seems important to you on that day. This will not be handed in but you will need it for a future assignment.

371

A following assignment was to digest the diary in about one-third or one-fourth its length, trying to catch the essence of it while obliterating the original form. The assignment for the diary summary was worded this way:

> Write an account of the material covered by the diary. Feature both what seems of most importance to you and what you think will be of most interest to others. You are free to cut out and add material and to reorganize it. Don't use the dates; select and summarize so that you blend things into a continous, whole piece.

PURPOSES

Since the diary itself was to remain private, the main purpose of it was to provide a wealth of fresh raw material for the digest, which was written for an audience. In other words, the diary was another avenue to first-person narrative besides observation and memory, the chief learning issue being how to abstract a composition from an abundance of fairly miscellaneous but personal material that is already written down. It was to be the first experience in summarizing a document, but a document of one's own. The whole process was also another way of phasing writing into spontaneous, private notation and selective, public composition. There were also several other purposes: to help make writing habitual and natural; to give importance to everyday occurrences and feelings; to encourage the notation of specific things of the moment; to create a record of long enough duration to provide earlier and later perspectives on the same events; and to produce material that could be used for other writing assignments.

RESULTS

The matter of privacy. I had felt that it was important to keep the privacy of the diary so that it would be real and expressive for the student, an outlet for sensitive feelings that might not otherwise be written down. If the teacher was to read it, I feared that students would not write very honestly. But in one low-ability group in a suburban school it was clear that some students did not keep the diary or perhaps made only a few entries; their "summaries" were about a single incident, probably written at the last moment. The results in that class were poor. In a twelfth-grade class of disadvantaged students who also did the assignment, the teacher said she would look at the diaries. Her theory was that her lower-class students would not be inhibited and that many in fact would lack motivation to write something that was not to be honored by her looking at it. From reading the diaries of that class I would say that her theory is more right than not. In fact, her notion that students of low ability or achievement — perhaps of low self-image — cannot undertake so much voluntary writing without more adult support may apply also to the lower-level ninth-grade suburban class. Of course it is impossible to know how much a strong prior involvement with writing would alter the picture.

How to abstract. The results varied considerably between the low-level class mentioned above and a high-level class having the same teacher (Lexington High School). In the former, when the summary was not faked, it often came out as a dull day-by-day account or as a very miscellaneous digest (taking the worst papers). The high-level group, on the other hand, produced an interesting variety. Some boys featured sports; several girls had the idea on their own of digesting the diary as a letter to a friend; one student did a recurring event in the present tense of generalization (a music lesson); some began with a paragraph of generalization, then deliberately settled on one event or period; one divided the material into school, social, and home life; and some organized by very rational categories. The poorer papers in that class were, again, the unselective ones — the meaningless inventories of days or the generalized miscellanies. Ninth-graders in another school (Weeks Junior High, Newton, Massachusetts) turned out a similar variety. Among the better papers were a typical but specific account of Saturdays done in the present tense of generalization and a selection of four incidents showing a shift in perspective.

I see in all of these results a consistent problem of abstraction — how to compose a unity out of a miscellany, and, secondarily, how to reduce material without losing detail. Most of all, one has to select, but along with selecting there must occur some reorganizing and restating of what is retained. Weaker students without preparation flounder on these abstractive problems; stronger students solve them in ingenious ways. But how much does poor motivation play a part? If the diary is meager, a good summary is hard to write.

Social interest. Students in the high-level class in Lexington were very positive about both the diary and the summary. They agreed at the outset that they wanted very much to read all of each other's summaries. Whereas the low-level class would not hear of such a thing in the beginning, they too ended by asking the teacher to let them read aloud all of the summaries. Both classes did so. Their very strong interest in each other's lives is something I have often observed among students of all ages. It gives them a great incentive to read what their classmates have written. They want to know each other better but do not feel free to show this interest very directly to other students they do not already know well. Somehow this important social motive should be tied in with this and other writing assignments.

Samples

The following diary summaries will illustrate some of the great variety of ways in which students go about abstracting their material. Despite their length I reproduce three of them, because I believe teachers giving this assignment will work under a great handicap if they do not have a fairly concrete grasp of this variety, which contains both the problems and the possibilities of the assignment.

THE SNAPSHOT TECHNIQUE

The first diary summary is by a girl who chose the snapshot technique. She selected entries rather than items from entries, probably rewrote them somewhat, and juxtaposed them for a slice-of-life effect, obviously trying to exploit rather than overcome the miscellaneousness of the material.

> There I stood staring at the building which seemed so strange and different to me. Although I had been going there for two years, it still seemed as if this day wasn't real. As I stood in front of the school, I saw faces of many people, some of whom I had known before and others were completely strange to me. Suddenly, I found myself walking up the stairs trying to find my way around. Then there it was my room number. I looked at it for a few minutes quite reluctant to enter. The numbers kept reappearing in my mind. I knew I must go in, and suddenly I was sitting down in the classroom a bit bewildered and lost. As the hours past, I became accustomed to the teachers and my fellow classmates. There was much commotion that day. All the students were meeting new and happy faces, but there I stood trying to start a conversation which just wouldn't start. I finally got control of myself and got up enough courage to speak to a girl sitting next to me. The time seemed to pass quickly and when the bell rang for school closing I couldn't believe that it was over. I got my books and ran quickly out to catch the crowded bus. After come trampling over a tangle of feet, I made my way to the safety of a nearby seat.
>
> What do you know? After much misgivings, I finally got to the dramatic school. I never thought that I would make it. There were about fifteen girls in the class and they all seemed friendly. Of course, there was always one stuffed shirt in the group. She thought that she could control the class. Then the teacher came in. She was a rather young looking woman. I looked at her suspiciously, in case she had thought that I was a good subject to deal with. It seemed as though I was here for at least a year, as the two hours seemed to drag on so slowly. Then it happened! I had to get up and pantomime a most ridiculous subject. Of course, I really didn't rebel in doing it; but it did seem kind of funny. Well, somehow the hours passed and with a sigh of relief I had gone through the first agony. From now on I won't be so self-conscious.
>
> Today art class and this was quite a relief from dramatics. This time at least I could do some independent creative work. I won't be a great artist,

but it won't hurt to try. My first picture didn't seem to look like anything very much, but with a few adjustments it might do as a "Rhembrandt". The class was rather small. There were about six kids in the class. The kids were all nice and they really could draw well. My teacher was very nice and helped me with my drawings. What a mess! I got paint all over my good blouse. Well, I'd better be more careful next time. Soon the class ended and it was time to leave. It was now dark out and there stood my mother's car. I ran quickly to get in because it had just started to rain.

It was a beautiful day. I just couldn't wait until my friend's party tonight. As the hours dragged on I wondered what it would be like. I was soon in a deep sleep not even realizing that I had dozed off. About an hour later, I was suddenly aroused from my sleep by a big shaggy dog which belonged to the neighbor. I wondered what time it was, because I knew I just couldn't be late for the party. I heard a faint call from the window which sounded like my mother. Those were her words as plain as day. I had guessed right and hurried up the stairs. Well, I made it to the party and carried my bag of presents as if I were Santa Claus. The party was really wonderful. I wished it would never end. But there I was back home in the soaking rain. It had never rained so hard in weeks.

It was the most miserable day in the whole week. The rain came pelting down as if it would never end. I had so much work to do today, and I just couldn't get started. I was just about to sit down and read a book when the telephone rang. I scrambled to my feet to get it. Breathlessly, I answered and it was one of my girlfriends asking for a homework assignment. I talked for a few minutes and then got back to my reading. As I sat down, the doorbell rang. I had just about given up reading the book. I walked to the door to see who it was. My mother had forgotten to take her keys. I opened the door and then got back to my reading.

What a day! It all started in science class, when we did an experiment on a battery. After putting on a mask and an apron, I was all ready for the experiment. For forty minutes we experimented in making a wet cell. There was one slight problem, just make sure you don't get any acid on you. When science was completed, I was relieved to hear that gym would be cancelled to allow us to see a Charlie Chaplin movie. The movie was very interesting and there were many humorous parts. After seeing the movie, I went to my room, got my coat, and waited to be dismissed. As I walked to the bus, I knew that I would have to push my way through in order to get a seat. With no small struggle, I managed to quickly take a seat, which was for a slight moment unoccupied.[1]

Though she has not tried to face some of the tougher difficulties of the assignment, still this girl has written several rather good accounts of bits of her experience. If nothing else, the assignment has elicited several personal narratives that seem to be written with interest. Not much abstracting has taken place, but the cutting was worthwhile.

[1] Weeks Junior High School, Newton, Massachusetts.

THE CATEGORIES-OF-EXPERIENCE ORGANIZATION

The not very able boy who wrote the following has assimilated and organized his material to a much greater degree, but the material is more meager, whether because he over-abstracted or because he simply did not keep a full diary, I don't know. His summary represents the categories-of-experience way of abstracting, which is effective here and also gives him a chance to talk about at least one important thing he has learned from his experience during the five weeks.

MY SUMMARY TO MY DIARY

The past five or six weeks if you count February vacation have been truly progressive for me. There are many miscellaneous happenings which would not intrest you so I will not write about these, but I will discuss the general things that have been important to me.

The first and most important thing in my life has been grades. I've been trying or partialy trying to boost my grades up and I have been succeeding in three subject however the other two I do not want to mention because some of you are in those classes with me. My main incentive has been a trip to California during the next vacation. Not for very long but It will be enough. I will be going by myself and no one will be taging along telling me what to do which has been the tendency of my family in the five week span. My main obstacle for getting good grades is the dull routine, day after day. Go to school come home do home work go to sleep and go back to school the next day. It seems to me there must be a better way but I guess no one has found it yet.

The second thing on my list has been my music. I have been in about four concerts in these five weeks playing in the band and the orchestra and I have one coming up this weekend with the band. The jazz combo to which I belong has begun to move, develope and really sound like something. Enough with the music. If I went on you'd get bored.

I have been on the swim team and I have really found out what its like to work for something. I had before but not to this extent. The reason I hadn't before was because my parents are not the very strict type and ecinomically they havn't done too badly. But getting back to swimming, of course, I didn't make the first team but I did swim a couple of relays and I did swim in the I.V. meets. I found out what alot of boys are really like underneath because it comes out when he is tense and under the pressure of competition. I found that some kids who smoke and drink can really be good guys if they want to be and some kids who are maybe in A.P. and are real snob types can be real nice guys.

Also throughout my diary there are many places were it says I met someone today. I suppose this is a good sign. I don't know but I feel the more friends one has the better off someone is when he or she gets in trouble.

As a sort of conclusion I would like to say that Mrs. Lyon picked a great time for me to write a diary. I don't know about you but I've had a great time.[2]

---

[2] Lexington High School, Lexington, Massachusetts.

The lack of detail, whether the fault of the diary or of the summary, would probably have been prevented if some of his colleagues had read his diary before the stage of composition.

THEMATIC ABSTRACTION

The boy's summary below represents one of the more sophisticated efforts to abstract meaningfully around themes, feelings or ideas that, in retrospect, some of the incidents seemed to illustrate. One consequence is a mixture of generality and narrative, statement and example, which this boy carries much farther than the one who did the preceding paper: he has organized most of his summary around two stated themes, whereas the last diarist categorized his material by *areas* of experience (school work, music, swimming) into which he inserted his general observation, for example, about boys under pressure. In both papers we can see the emergence of ideas and personal essay, which is one of the more promising turns that diary summaries can take. As an approach to essay, this assignment has the advantage of keeping generalizations in close relation to the actualities from which they were generated. This boy's generalizations are still very concrete and personal, but he is on the pathway to essay.

Somehow I always get myself into crazy situations by doing everything the hard way. This can be shown using the example of when the class had an assignment to catch flies for examination in Biology.

We were supposed to have the flies in the next day but that afternoon it was cool and cloudy. It wasn't a good day for flies because they like sunny days where they can sit on the concrete and sun themselves. Seeing that there were no flies to be netted on the concrete, I put some sugar water and raw meat outside in a jar for a few hours. That day turned out to a very bad one because I didn't even get any ants.

The next day I went to school without any flies. Nobody else had any either but there were a few bees brought in. It's frightening to look at bees through a magnifying glass which are sleeping off ether and can fly off at any minute. The next day we had to have flies or else.

We got out of school. I was getting my bicycle and I saw a nice big fresh mound of warm and smelly dog feces. I told one of my friends nearby. We didn't know if we would have an equal opportunity at home, so we went in and got some jars. We ended up with enough flies for the whole class and the Biology teacher was very happy with them, but this jubilance was neutralized when she picked up the jars and got dog feces all over her hands.

Another example of the way I go about everything the hard way is my method of getting notes for reports. Instead of going down three blocks to the local branch library, I go three miles on my bicycle to the main library because there are more magazines on world happenings there.

After I get home from school I only have one and a half hours for work because it takes half an hour to get to the library each way. Most of the time is wasted there because I spend most of my time looking for James

Bond books, reading the electronics magazines, and looking at all the other things there.

I decided to spend a whole Saturday afternoon there so I didn't have to rush and could read more electronics magazines. I went with a friend on our bicycles. Halfway there I went through a shortcut which my friend didn't know much about but which I went in all the time. He kept on going the long way and was going to meet me at out usual rendezvous point.

Halfway through the shortcut in a desolated sidestreet my pedal suddenly fell off. For fifteen minutes I tried to screw it back on again.

I finally gave up and tried to ride my bicycle again. It was very difficult because you have to go at a good speed and the single pedal keeps on dropping down because it is off balance. I came to the rendez-vous point but my friend had already left so I went home to fix the pedal.

Halfway home I discovered I had a flat tire so I had to walk the rest of the way. It took two hours to fix the pedal and the flat tire, so in the end I had a half an hour to go to the branch library. Doing everything the hard way gets you no further than if you didn't.

I have a lot of gripes about school. On the day before Columbus day the teachers piled on homework because we have an extra day with no school to do our homework. I had so much that I couldn't go to the main library.

On another day we had a test and homework assignments on top of it. Everyone was complaining. Mr. Hansen, our English teacher said it was nothing like what we were going to get next year in high school.

There were two new things this year in school. Both of them were for the worst. The first, food in the cafeteria, works differently now. The previous years you would get dessert and potato chips included in your lunch for 25¢. This year dessert costs 20¢ extra and the cafeteria gets potato chips once a month. All you are left with is one semi-liquid hamburger.

The second is the new policy on study periods. They are mixed into the day instead of the end of school. In the beginning of the day you have no homework to do. We are only allowed to have a certain number of study periods. The rest of the time we have to take a small elective. These meet only once a week and you forget what happened from one week to the next. Our choice of these electives depends on what teacher is free the same time you have the studies. Sometimes there is only one available for your grade. The studies are then crowded and the students get blamed for not picking any electives.

I took a junior lifesaving course for two hours two nights a week. I had to plan my homework well so I would get it all done. The course really drags for two hours because you keep on doing the same thing and you have to wait for your turn.

One thing I really hate is being a victim. Our teacher usually demonstrates on me because I am one of the smallest, the others being in high school. In demonstrating artificial resusitation the teacher also demonstrates how strong he is by crushing me on the stone floor. Sometimes when we practice carrying a victim, I am pulled a few lengths of the pool by my hair. My hair gets pulled out by its roots.

Once for the life saving test we had to do eight lengths of the pool. I was scared because I had trouble swimming three in the summer.

Besides this we usually have fun at the pool. There is a high diving board. It's scary when you jump off it because it's so high. You go all the way to the bottom of the pool, twelve feet down. After a few times you can't do it much more because of the pressure.

Sometimes we play water basketball. There is a basket on the side of the pool. We drown anyone that has the ball. A few times we got into riots and we started mugging each other. It was like tackle football. Everyone was floating and swimming on top of each other.[3]

The events of a diary can be viewed either as once-upon-a-time particulars or as instances of typical or general things. An important purpose of diary summary is to give students a chance to view them as both and thus to move away from pure narrative.

Recommendations

There are several ways one might look on this assignment and go about improving it. One is to consider it too difficult an abstractive feat for all but the most able ninth-graders, in which case we can either defer it to a later year or, accepting miscellany, use the assignment just as one way of eliciting particular incidents and experiences. Although it is true that the summary could be deferred, I am not convinced that either course is necessary.

THE PUBLIC JOURNAL

Another approach is to make the diary a journal, written to be read by others. A great advantage of this is that the writer can benefit from small-group suggestions about how to summarize. For the experiments, I had merely proposed that the students bring their diaries to class, describe them, explore the problems they foresaw, and in this way discuss in advance the different possible ways they might summarize. I think pre-composition discussion would help many students compose with random raw material, but if the diaries are not available for exchange and reading, this help will be very limited. If strict privacy is not maintained, and the assignment does not attempt to invite sensitive feelings, then cross-commentary can be brought to bear on the abstractive problems. For a certain loss in expressiveness one would trade a great gain in learning. Reading journals in small groups would lessen exposure and inhibition considerably as well as make for far more effective pre-compositional discussion. This way of handling the assignment is one I would recommend for further trial.

Specializing journals. A journal, however, could be specialized at the outset, which would decrease the abstractive problem of summarizing. Each student could decide and state what his journal would trace — some area

[3] Weeks Junior High, Newton, Massachusetts.

of his life, some activity, a relationship, job, school subject, etc. In fact, the best preparation for summarizing a long, miscellaneous journal would probably be to keep a shorter, specialized one in seventh or eighth grade. At any age, such journals could be focused rather impersonally on some external object the student is interested in, and could become an extended sort of eyewitness reportage whereby the student gathers progressive information about something he has a chance to observe often. Thus there could be nature and laboratory journals and social studies and hobby journals as well as more personal ones. These records become a kind of research, and the summary a more abstract sort of reportage in which *recurring* events and observations are generalized. There would be no better way to lead into expository writing.

THE PRIVATE DIARY

Entries. A wholly different approach harks back to the elementary school diaries recommended in Chapter 16. They are frank miscellanies into which the student pours any spur-of-the-moment thing he is prompted to write down — not just narrative incidents but reflections, imaginings, and so on. The teacher allows ten minutes or so in class two or three times a week for students to write down what they want in a theme book kept for this purpose. Sometimes, especially if some students say they have trouble thinking of something to say, suggest that they look around the room, as they did for memory writing, and write down any thoughts suggested by what they see. The idea is to help them tap the constantly flowing stream of consciousness. These can remain private and would not be put in their writing folders.

Compositions. Periodically, the teacher tells the students to look over their entries and choose some thought, incident, or observation, expand on it a bit, and write it up for the rest of the class. Time intervals would be short and the papers likewise. These papers go through the usual process of cross-commentary and editing for publication unless a student wishes only the teacher to see his paper. After the class has done this a couple of times, the teacher suggests that possibly several things in the different entries might be treated together — scattered incidents or thoughts that seem related in some way. This prepares, in effect, for doing a journal summary.

SUMMARY OF SEQUENCE

Recapitulating now, I recommend a seven-to-nine sequence of: private in-class diaries as just described; followed by a couple of short, specialized journals; to be summarized and climaxed by one long, miscellaneous journal, also to be summarized. Of course, all three of these assignments can be repeated during the senior high years, since they are not limited to any particular stage of development. But for the first time around, as I think the experiments show, some order such as this would be sensible and would improve the last assignment considerably. And the dilemma of privacy — good for content but depriving the writer of help — I would solve by making different use of diaries than of journals: diaries would provide an ongoing source of notes that can be plucked out and written up independently, whereas journals would provide bodies of material covering a certain time span that can be summarized. The latter requires, I think, that the record be available for others to read at any time — during the entry-keeping, as a stimulant, and before summarizing, as an aid in composing. A wise policy might be for members of small groups to exchange and read each other's entries and give reactions while the journal is still in progress. Having a readership while they are keeping the journal would, I am sure, create real motivation and make the entries richer. Then, when time for summarizing comes, students in the same group will be already familiar with each other's journals and in a much better position to make suggestions for composing. The journals themselves, then, would be considered pieces of writing for their own sake (which does not mean that they have to be written very formally), and would be sometimes printed and discussed along with the summaries of them. These teacher-led discussions would deal with the problems of abstracting.

INVENTING AND READING DIARIES AND JOURNALS

A fictional diary or journal can be very worthwhile and enjoyable. When students are making up stories, the teacher should suggest that they try pretending the stories are an actual piece of reportage, for example, or a diary, or some other form that students have used for real-life material. I have asked older students to write a story as a diary; junior high students might enjoy doing so even more. The problem is that the form requires greater length because it is not an economical way to tell a story, though of course there are gains (in characterization and in immediacy of point of view, for example). There are some short stories in diary form — "Le Horla" of Guy de Maupassant, "A Caddy's Diary" and "I Can't Breathe" of Ring Lardner, "Manuscript found in a Bottle" of Edgar Allen Poe — that junior high children would probably enjoy after having kept a diary. Other correlated reading consists of actual diaries by personages who hold interest for this age, or of actual journals on subjects of interest.

There is a close connection between journals and research, for journals are a prime kind of source material. The abstractive problems of summarizing one's own records are not greatly different from those of digesting others' records, and if one has kept journals one knows what sort of document he is dealing with. As we shall see, original research papers of later years involve essentially the same ability to sift previous writing for significance and to restate for a purpose what one has distilled from it.

Part Four

GRADES TEN

THROUGH THIRTEEN

To accommodate high schools that begin with ninth grade, I have made this section overlap slightly with Part Three. But the program for these years cannot be truly self-contained; the effort to make it so is bound to conflict somewhat with the general goal of the book — to delineate a new and slowly cumulative curriculum. The following presentation, then, reflects a compromise between practical and ideal aims.

I have foregone further description of classroom processes *in the hope that* the drama workshop, the reading-group discussion, the regular small-group discussion, teacher-led class commentary on the writing, and small-group cross-commentary on the writing *have been made sufficiently clear before. For these processes I can only refer the reader to earlier chapters in the book. (The introduction of these to students unfamiliar with the program does not differ greatly with age; or, at any rate, how differently they should be introduced to students of these grades is still problematical.)*

It is understood that final copies of student writing are printed as booklets or magazines. The few new additions to drama work come under Invention, instead of comprising a separate sub-division. For new writing assignments I will signal the issues or problems with which cross-commentary should deal. Reading groups for discussing both common and individual reading continue.

To take this section of the book in isolation from preceding sections would create serious misconceptions. Since the purpose of the following chapters is not to present the whole program for these grades but to present the part of it that is new, the reader who is not familiar with what has been dealt with thus far may easily conclude that the grades ten to thirteen program is lopsided and riddled with omissions. This section deals mainly with new forms of composition — to be both read and written. It does not deal directly with spelling and punctuation or with decoding of texts. I do not see how serious problems in these areas can be handled differently at this late age than they were in the elementary grades, to which the reader is referred. Extremely poor readers and spellers may simply need a literacy program such as was already described. Continued work on spelling and punctuation occurs constantly during the writing workshop as students proofread and comment on each other's papers. The teacher, furthermore, can give individual diagnosis while these groups are at work.

In fact, much of what may seem to be omitted is treated by means of the five classroom processes mentioned above, which are barely alluded to in the following chapters. For example, dramatic work and small-group discussion (including panels and reading groups) continue to develop oral expression and listening, vocabulary and concepts, reading comprehension and interpretation. In this respect, the writing workshop must not be considered to exist only for composition. As I have tried to demonstrate before, it is an instrument for learning many aspects of language and literature. But the impossibility of conveying in print the learning effects of these day-by-day classroom processes must no doubt remain a weakness of this book. The following chapters present only the compositional forms upon which these processes operate. Thus the emphasis of this section on compositional forms does not reflect the proportion of time students spend in this program learning one or another aspect of the language arts.

The chapters of Part Four are based mainly on the sources of discourse — memories (Chapter 26, Autobiography and Memoir), observational notes (Chapter 27, Reportage) and documents (Chapter 27, Research), spontaneous thoughts (Chapter 28, Reflection), imagination (Chapter 30, Invention), and mixed sources (Chapter 29, Generalization and Theory). This way of classifying assignments is a convenience for showing relationships and continuities among them. The work of each chapter moves forward simultaneously with that of the others. Several general progressions characterize the program for these years. The kinds of discourse students work with shift from narrative to other organization; the abstraction level rises; secondhand sources are added to firsthand; assignments converge from several directions on exposition and generalization; and the range of invention broadens.

Part Four contains an overabundance of assignments, partly in order to catch new ninth-graders, but mainly to permit all students to go as far as they are ready and able to go, whether they become ready and able in high school or in college. There seems to be as little point in breaking continuity at the end of secondary school as in trying to demarcate definite junctures anywhere else along the line. I hope that this range will help the teacher to start his students where they should start and carry them to where they should stop. The last assignment or so in each section may well lie beyond the capacity of most high school students today and would therefore be appropriate only for college. I have tried, in other words, to allow growing room at both ends.

COLLEGE

I think the program outlined for these years will, if adapted, serve well the needs of the average freshman "English" or "composition" course and those of a two-year course in the junior colleges. An adaptation would be a selected, compressed version of the program. For experimental purposes, I have given such a version in a single year to eleventh-graders at the Phillips Exeter Academy, but for that age, even given such exceptional students, the pace is too fast. The version spanned the whole sequence, from sensory and memory notes to theory, but did not include certain of the longer reportage and research assignments and did permit options among certain other long pieces of writing. The experiment suggested strongly to me that a similar adaptation would be just right for a college freshman course or junior college course. Since the particular form of the adaptation depends enormously on the preparation of the incoming freshman, and on the amount of reading, dramatic work, and discussion to be included in the course, I do not attempt here to make up a special college sequence.

ROLE OF THE TEACHER

The role of the teacher may change somewhat now. He should be able to assert his own ideas and attitudes more frankly, without fear of damaging student confidence and ini-

tiative. If students are accustomed to thinking independently and to working for their own reasons, not his, he can play his point of view more freely in discussion and make critical judgments of their work, as a master would among apprentices. When he should write commentary on themes is something I am leaving open. That is the sort of decision that the teacher should make himself. But in proposing such a large volume of writing (which, we must remember, is proposed for the benefit of thinking, reading, and speaking as much as for composition) I am assuming that the teacher will exert most of his influence through the group, before final copies are done, and that most of what he might have written later as comments would have been conveyed to a writer by his colleagues as suggestions for revision. The groups proofread, not the teacher. His evaluative and diagnostic remarks are, in most cases, written on the dittoed copies of the theme if he is going to make them. (Printed copies are easier to read.)

So again I remind the reader that the conventional notion of marking papers does not apply. For some themes the teacher writes brief comments; for some he writes nothing. Grades are based on perusal of folders. He has a lot of time, while groups are reading and commenting on each other's papers, to talk individually with students. The response to writing, so important as an enduring stimulus, comes from a much larger audience than the teacher. When he does respond, in person or on paper, he reacts as a real audience — an adult and cultivated one, to be sure, for that is what he is, but also as a first-person individual. I once had a colleague who would sometimes tell a student quite simply that he could not finish reading his paper because he became so bored. To say this to a youngster who had been brought up to please the teacher and to derive motivation from praise and blame would perhaps be cruel, but his students knew that he might perfectly well say the same thing, in the same tone, about a published book that he found impossible to wade through.

Chapter 26

Autobiography
and Memoir

Memory Writing

As Director of English for the 1966 Upward Bound Program at Tougaloo College, near Jackson, Mississippi, Charles Thurow chose to assign memory writing to the Program's students (all Negroes just out of the eleventh grade and chosen for their possible educability) as the first of several assignments drawn from the program presented in this book. He wanted his charges to have a chance to write about firsthand material in their own language without worrying about mechanics and right answers, to become involved with their own writing and that of others. Initially, they were unwilling to write at all and virtually unable to talk about writing. For them, composition had always consisted of grammar and rules for mechanics.

Putting down spontaneous memories, expanding and revising some of them, seemed eventually to open them up and get them going. I read all the memory papers of his own sixteen students and was surprised to find out how full the papers were — considering that six of the sixteen could not produce at all for a long time — and to see how helpful the suggestions often were that they wrote on each other's papers (suggestions about rephrasing, adding and deleting information, clarifying passages). The other three teachers, who were unaccustomed to working with student language production and without authoritarian textbooks, had a very difficult and frustrating summer. The naturalistic approach ran full tilt against the training of both teachers and students. (Like many disadvantaged adolescents in the North, the students felt at first that some assignments were "stupid.")

The writing done by the Tougaloo students is a fair representation of what many other children of very unpromising background might do when asked, at this late age, abruptly, to write something from their real experience. For this reason I reproduce three of the revised memories.[1] I have chosen the three I think make the most interesting reading, but the majority of the other papers were as long and as literate as the two shorter ones printed here, and all had at least some of the color and feeling and force of these three.

Also, these samples represent three different directions in which the memories went. The first, by a girl, tells an *autobiographical incident.*

Saint Billy Visits At 9:00 P.M.

Several years ago when I was just a little girl my cousin Vernistine and I lived with my grandmother. I was about nine years old my cousin was twelve.

Mother told Vernis there was a man who collected all, all bad kids at night. Vernis replyed, "I don't believe you"! Mother said slowly — alright, I'll see. Vernis disbelieved her. This Vernis had to see with her own eyes. Later mother said, since you don't believe me. write him a letter and put it outside some where.

Late one evening Vernis wrote the letter. Vernis ask, "Callie come go with me"? With out asking any questions I followed her to put the letter on the bank of the lake. After delivering the letters we came back to the house; however, Vernis cracked jokes with mother. There is no Saint Billy! Mother replyed yes there is — you will see tonight!

Saint Billy always knocks three times before coming into a house.

About nine o'clock we heard three loud knocks, and the front door open. Saint Billy walked into the room and said, "good evening". I looked back and there was an ugly, undescribable man standing in the door. I started screaming I cried for about one hour or more. Vernis was down on her knees calling on God.

Saint Billy ask, "Can one of you dance or sing?' We replyed, no Sir. He said frightening as he pull a sack from his pocket, I'll get one of you to night. I screamed louder and louder, "make him go away"!

My grandparents laugh until they cried.

Later Saint Billy gave up and went home or somewhere. I was so glad. I don't ever want to see him again.

The second, also by a girl, is an example of *memoir,* she herself being not the protagonist but rather someone close enough to him to be both confidant and eyewitness. Thus the story is a personal memory, but since she was not present at all the events, she has to tell some of it as it was told to her. This kind of very involved but peripheral narrator is the "first person" of published memoirs and of some fiction (*Life with Father, for example*).

Memory Of My brother accident

The most terrifying thing that ever happen to me was on December 24, 1962. My second brother was shot with a 16 ga. shotgun. At the time he

[1] With thanks to Charles Thurow.

was fourteen years old. This is the way it happen, My brother James and cousin (N.C. Mayers.) went hunting around 18 Clock that morning of the day he got shot. N.C. was behind James, N.C. had his gun loaded as they was walking alone James shouted look there is a squirrel at that instant N.C. pulled the trigger on his gun. The bullets hit my brothers left hand below his elbow. This James walked Alone for about ten minutes meanwhile N.C. had stopped and was staring in disbelief. James finally went to hold up his hand and said, Man look my hand has been shot and he only looked and said they're going to cut my hand of. This He walked on to my uncle's house and said Uncle Mob open the door I been shot. My uncle didn't believe him because he had been carrying on a lot of foolishness. After about five minutes of convincing my uncle he finally open the door and stared in horror at the blood and the condition of James hand. My uncle was tall, dark around 65 years old he lived in a three room house on his farm about twelve miles from civilzation. He told James to set down and gave him a sheet to put his hand in while he go down to the barn and hitch his mules to the wagon because he didn't have any other mean of transportation.

I took Uncle Mob about 15 Mins. to drive from his house to ours in a wagon. After Uncle Mob and James get to the house my parents was at work and had the car. All of us came out of the house and looked at James in horror but James was smiling then we all begin to cry and scream my oldest brother got on the horse and at no time at all he got my cousin to take James to the hospital. He took him to Brandon hospital but the doctors there said they had to cut his hand off but the university hospital in Jackson might could save it so they took him to the University. I cannot give a description of the hospital nor doctor because I wasn't there. By this time my Uncle had notified my parents and they was there. The doctor asked my mother permission to cut his hand of and she refused. He explained to her that wasn't but two leaders holding his hand together and the arm will never be anymore good anyway. My mother still refused so the doctors took him into surgery and sewed his leaders together and put his arm in a cast for six weeks. After the six week period they put his hand into a mending bandage for four more weeks after the four weeks period his they left his arm bear which didn't look so good but he still had it and after a short time he started using his left hand as good as his right hand. And now which is four years later my brother still thanks my mother for signing the paper.

My Cousin N.C. went out of his head for about 2 days he didn't come home and didn't say anything to anyone because he thought we would blame him for what happen two years after the accident N.C. died of pneumonia and someone had stab him with an ice pick.

The boy who wrote the following piece recalled a *recurring experience*. As his title indicates, the memory is not of an incident; it is a generalization presented *as though* it were an incident. He has done exactly what novelists and autobiographers do when they want to summarize an experience across time and yet keep the immediacy it had on each occasion.

Sunday's at home

Every morning in the summer time, I thrust back the curtain, to watch the sunrise stealing down a steeple which stands opposite my bedroom window. First, the weather-cock begins to flash: Now the loftiest window gleams, at length, the morning glory in its descent from heaven, comes down the stone steps one by one, and there stand the steeple, glowing with fresh radiance, while the shades of twilight still hide themselves among the building an the sun shines like's balls of fire.

then Andrew still beside me asking: what are you watching hush, be quiet, watch the glory of the morning how it gleams with beauty, how the sun shine like the burning of hail, listen at the wind, how it row like the great storms, how the trees shake like the come on of winter.

That was one of most beautiful & exciting morning I have every seen.

In high school, of course, undifferentiated memory writing is only for students who have not done it before. Afterwards, like those who did it earlier, they would specialize — write incidents of short duration that feature themselves, other people, and non-human subjects—as outlined in Chapter 26.

While focusing on firsthand incidents, students will enjoy some of the many similar short stories appropriate for their age, such as Frank O'Connor's "The Little Drunkard" and "The Man of the House," which, like "Saint Billy," cover part of a day. Ivan Turgenev's *The Hunting Sketches* contains good sketches focused on other people and on nature.

The two other directions noted above in "My brother accident" and "Sunday's at home" — toward the role of confidant-eyewitness and toward summary of a long time span — are the basis for the next assignments, which both newcomers and oldtimers take up after writing incidents. The following sequence will move away from first person toward third, from singular to plural, and from short to long duration.

Portion of Autobiography

The distinction I will make here is between an *incident* and a *phase*. A portion of autobiography "covers" a long period of time and therefore includes summaries both of recurring events and of incidents occurring at different places. This distinction in time-space coverage implies differences in abstractive tasks for the writer.

The Notion of a Phase

Tell what happened to you during a certain period of your life covering many months, perhaps even a year or so — some "phase."

Phase is emphasized; the portion is not miscellaneous, but focused. To distill a period of weeks, months, or years in 1,000 to 2,000 words requires drastic editing of events. It is this editing process that teaches.

The two main issues that characterize this assignment and that the teacher might use as a guide for class discussion and small-group work are: What idea of "phase" does the writer use as his criterion for relevance in selecting and emphasizing? And what efforts does he make or fail to make to offset the abstractness of summary? Fragments of autobiography should not be résumés of fact with no concrete qualities of the original events and feelings. And yet, if the student narrates too much in detail, quotes too often, and stays entirely in moments of the past, he cannot come near telling what happened over a period of months. The crux of the assignment, then, lies in some balance between precise actualities — what people did, said, felt, etc. — and some all-encompassing theme — a notion of a trial gone through, a stage of growth experienced, a set of circumstances lived through, a relationship developed. This theme may or may not need to be directly stated, depending on how obvious it will be to the reader, which is not always an easy thing to guess in advance. As for vividness, this calls for shrewdness about when to pull in for a "close-up" of a certain scene and when to summarize in a few sentences the less important or repetitive events. Although necessarily abstract as a whole, a summary need not be abstract in its parts. A general statement about what occurred "in the meantime," or what occurred habitually over a long period, can be cast into concrete words and phrases, specific references, as "Sunday's at home" showed so well.

SAMPLE

The following portion of autobiography was written by a boy who came to Exeter for one year as a senior, having already graduated from a Greater Boston high school the year before. It is untitled because at that time I was having seniors write a long autobiography in installments, a practice I do not recommend because it allots too much time to one kind of writing. Since the educational background of this rather atypical Exonian is part of his subject, I will let his own words evoke it.

When I was in the fifth and sixth grades, my mother wanted me to become an altar boy. I disliked the idea before I even knew what it was all about, and when I knew, I disliked it even more. Every Saturday morning when everybody else was out skating, I had to go to church and try to learn how to answer the priest in Latin. There were about thirty boys in the class, whose mothers had also made them come to the lessons. They all claimed that they were never prepared for the lessons, but it was evident that their mothers had made them study the Latin during the week. My mother had tried also, but it just would not sink in, mainly because I did not want it to. I hoped that I could prove to both my mother and our priest that I was too dumb to learn how to serve mass. When I was called on in class, I would stand up and give a phrase I had heard somebody else give earlier in the lesson. The kids thought that it was kind of funny giving the right answer to the wrong question. Sometimes if he called on me two or three times I would give the same answer. Once he got mad at me and asked me if I was trying to be funny. I denied it and told him that it simply was the only response I knew. That afternoon he called my mother and told her that if I did not have my lessons prepared in the future and continued to disrupt the whole class, I would have to give up the idea of being an altar boy.

Every afternoon that week my mother had me come in and study that foolish Latin. In the evening she would make me recite what I was supposed to have learned. My brother by this time had learned more Latin than I had. He would just sit there and listen every evening. When I did not know the answer, he would give the responses to my mother. This would always bring on the old song and dance about why couldn't I do it if my little brother could. The answer was that I did not want to learn it, and he did. He enjoyed making a fool of me, so every night that he tried to humiliate me when I went over the lesson, I would beat him up. He would scream and run to my mother, and she in turn would beat me. It was a losing battle and I was always on the short end.

Eddie had shown such deftness for Latin that she thought that he too would make a fine altar boy. On Saturdays, my brother would know the Latin as well as any of the older boys in the group. He had slaved all week just to show his stupid brother up, and I knew it. All was not lost, however, because I too knew my Latin. The priest was amazed and thought that if I could learn the Latin, then surely his class was making fair progress. Actually what I did was to have a friend of mine in the class sit in front of me, and I pinned the Latin card to his back. When I was called to write, all I did was read it off his back. The reason I was able to get away with this was that the priest did not know the Latin either, and as I was writing the priest was looking at his missal to see if I was saying it correctly. I really made fine strides this way. Every week I knew the Latin. Everything was going fine until one morning I read the priest's response on the card instead of the altar boy's. Everybody started to laugh because they all knew what I was doing. What really finished it was that my friend made the mistake of turning around to laugh at me. When he did, the priest saw the Latin card that was pinned to his back. He did not say much, he just came down and tore the card off the boy's back, and my friend told him that he did not know that it was on there. The one who had a lot of talking to do was Eddie. He made sure he got home to tell his version of the story first. My mother was really mad, and screamed at me for about ten minutes. She finally hit me on the nose because I started to hum and tap my foot while she was trying to give me what she called constructive criticism. So with a bloody nose, I took my brother's skates out into the back yard and pounded the blades against the fireplace until they were too dull to ever try to skate on. My father was not too mad that I had used a bit of outside help in my

Latin assignments. In fact, I think he thought it was a little humorous but did not show it openly.

The following Saturday there was a final written test in Latin. I asked the priest if I could go into the next room because it was quieter. When I got in there I took out my father's missal that I had taken from his bureau, and copied down all those responses that I had to know. Then I turned to the back of the book and answered all the questions about the priest's vestments. I did not care about cheating, I just wanted to show up my brother. Well, I passed with flying colors and substantially outdid my brother. When my brother and I served our first mass, my brother would answer the priest so loud that anybody in the church could hear him. I just mumbled except when all we had to say was "Amen." I liked the funerals best of all because they were usually on school days. The funerals in our church were usually at nine or ten in the morning, so we would have the whole morning off. I had a friend from school who was also an altar boy and asked to serve on the same funerals so we could walk to school together. His mother had told him to stay away from me, but he did not mind getting into trouble either.

When the funeral was over, we would walk as slowly as we could the mile to school. We used to stop along the way to ride a donkey or chase sheep. When we got to school, if it was too early, we would sit in the woods until lunch time and then go in. I was an altar boy until I was in the eighth grade, when I was thrown out because of fighting in the church. We weren't really fighting. We were just rolling around on the altar when we were supposed to be practicing for a wedding.

Most of the time my parents are hard to get along with, but during that year they were unspeakable. My father kept me in almost every Friday and Saturday night for something I had done either at school or at home. I did not mind getting in trouble for something I had done that was really wrong, but some of the things I was kept in for made me fight my parents even more.

Friday night would find me reduced to watching television for not making my bed, being late for breakfast, or hitting my little sister. One of the worst was having to stay in for not untying my shoes before taking them off. My father would come into my room every night after I was in bed to check my shoes. Just for spite I used to take them off and then untie them. I could not stand my parents during those years and neither could my friends. They would not come into the house because I was always fighting with them.

I was playing varsity hockey that year, and my father even kept me out of some of the games. He would take my skates away for a week at a time for some really stupid reason. The only reason I was kept on the team was that the coach missed the same games I did. Our coach was Butch Songin and at that time he was playing quarterback for the Boston Patriots.

I tried to live in my own world. When I came home from skating I would go up to my room and only come down for meals. If I was watching television or sitting in the den my father walked in I would get up and leave just to avoid an argument.

Things got progressively worse at home and at school. I was not doing much of anything. In February my father decided to bring me into Boston University to take a battery of tests given as a course of guidance. They told me I was there to see what courses in school would fit me best, but I knew I was there because my parents wanted to know if I could do the work I was supposed to be doing and if I could why wasn't I? The tests were the type in which you play with blocks, puzzles and ink spots. Also, someone would flash pictures in front of you and ask you what was the first thing that came into your mind. At the end of the thirty-hour testing period they came to the conclusion that I was quite bright but had difficulty in reading and spelling. My scores ranged from a perfect score in abstract reasoning to about a twenty-five percent in reading and spelling. They also told my father to lay off me and in this way I would come along myself because I would not be fighting them. However, the next term he went back to his old suppression because I came home with two D's and two E's.

About this time I got sick of everyone, my teacher and my parents. The teachers were really wearing on me, and I thought that our priest was the most two-faced person I knew. During the football and hockey seasons everything was fine with him. But as soon as hockey was over he too started to climb on my back. I got very fresh and gave everyone a hard time, even teachers that were the type not to fool around with. One teacher used to talk about a certain element in the room that should be removed. So now I was an element: she even called me an element of refuse. One day when she was talking about this "certain element" I started to laugh. She got so red I thought she would explode. She started to cry and said until I left the room she would not come back in. I sat in the class all day while she sat out in the hall, where she had moved her desk. I was not going to leave, I would have stayed there for the rest of the year and the following if I had to. The next day her things were back in the room. She publicly proclaimed that either I left the school that year or she would. That summer she left.

The organic unity or theme is clear — the contest of wills between the author and the adults in his environment. This paper benefited from suggested revisions, but these concerned sentence ineptitudes — the residue of a language handicap — not the selection and shaping of material. He knew what he wanted to say. He had his own unerring touchstone that guided his choice of what was relevant and what was not. When the cunning with which he waged war against others was put in the service of writing something real, he showed more craft and wit than many students who had had far more practice. It is amazing how so-called writing problems clear up when students *care*. Again and again I have seen students write "over their heads" when an assignment invited them to use native intelligence on raw material they were greatly involved in.

ISSUES FOR THE WRITING WORKSHOP

Organization.   The sample above illustrates several additional issues that the assignment should engage students with. One is the transition from chronological organization to a thematic organization by ideas. Most accounts of a phase combine narrative with essay. That is, either the paper will generally progress chronologically but contain topical paragraphs in which time stands still while a general point is made, or the progression is a development of general points illustrated by bits of narrative taken out of chronological order. These organizations naturally occur because a portion of autobiography has the double goal of telling what happened while summarizing in a meaningful way. Before revising, students should try to decide, with a given paper, what presentation is best.

If my reader will look back over the sample above, he will notice that the level of abstraction varies considerably according to whether the author is recounting a single incident that happened only once, summarizing recurrent or typical events, or describing a general situation. In a rough way the paper moves from the time he began learning to be an altar boy until the summer the teacher left (the exact period of time covered being not very well indicated, as a matter of fact). The result is not a narrative in the sense of a series of events; it is an account of a worsening situation or relationship, illustrated by events and marked by events, but not fastened down to particularities in precise order. How he prepared his lessons, how his brother tried to show him up, what he did on funeral days, the way he and his family behaved toward each other, the spread of hostility toward other adults — these are situations or stages that are usually introduced by more abstract sentences of the sort that teachers have been fond of calling "topic sentences," but which are generated spontaneously by the very needs of the assignment.

Vantage point. The second matter is time perspective. What enabled this boy to disengage a thematic unity from the welter of past facts was a certain emotional distance. From a remoter vantage point one can see patterns. Autobiography is characterized by binocular vision: the writer splits into I-now and I-then, which means that he looks at events from the remembered viewpoint of the past and from his present viewpoint. In the sample above, for example, though the boy says his parents *are* hard to live with, still it is obvious that he would have given a vastly different account of those earlier years if he had not changed considerably since then (as indeed he had). For one thing, an account written at the time could hardly have been so intentionally funny or so devoid of anger and self-justification. It is remarkably "objective."

When one says that *Great Expectations* is told from Pip's point of view, or *To Kill a Mockingbird* from Scout's, one means, of course, that they are told from the points of view of two middle-aged narrators[2] who have framed their childhood perspective within their later perspective. Compare *Catcher in the Rye,* narrated a year after the events, with *A Separate Peace,* narrated fifteen years later. How well a student succeeds in defining themes, then, will depend partly on how far he stands from the events in time. Discus-

[2] A narrator is the persona telling the story, not the author of the book.

sions of papers should allow for time lapses and consequent perspectives. Personally, how one abstracts his past is critical, for the basic function of abstracting is to guide action. The very effort to write large-scope autobiography may help to induce a maturer perspective, as perhaps it did for the boy here.

If the perspective at the time of writing is essentially the same one had at the time of the events, the result will quite likely be a subjective or imperceptive narration such as modern fiction writers often create. On page 488 I have listed some such stories as suggested reading, and on page 497 there is a student short story written as if it were so narrated. Writing skill aside, the latter will give some idea of how an actual student recollection may read if the writer's perspective seems naive or does not, in the judgment of readers, square with their own understanding of what happened. Imperceptive-narrator stories make excellent collateral reading for this assignment and can help students to discuss subjectivity in their own writing, an issue they cannot avoid anyway because perspective influences greatly the writer's notion of phase and theme.

Bring into class also, and ask students to look for, the sort of letters that people write in to magazine and newspaper columns giving their accounts of how their husband has abused them, their daughter shown ingratitude, and so on. Are the students persuaded by the accounts? If not, what betrays distortion? What do they think the truth is? When the account is their own, however, some delicacy is required. A student should know when others feel he is rationalizing or venting spleen or being shallow, but without being put at bay by his group or the class.

THE THREAT OF AUTOBIOGRAPHY

In fact, autobiography raises more than one sensitive matter. When it shifts from incident to phase, one risks exposing both himself and others, precisely because the assignment calls for some truths of one's life. I do not mean that the themes of students' autobiographies often contain sensational exposés or intimate self-relations. For the most part, they are much lighter than the example given here. But revealing a meager social life or some family circumstance such as divorce can embarrass students or alarm parents. The priest who was called two-faced (in the younger boy's view) no doubt would feel, perhaps with reason, that he had been very unjustly stigmatized by an immature rebel. The dilemma is this: it is the real material of their world that students want most to write about and can learn most from, but it is the same material that threatens both the writer and the people he writes about. We have to face this dilemma. One solution is to perpetuate innocuous, canned topics about which students write poorly out of indifference or sheer resentment. My own feeling is that the threat of exposure can be handled by sensible procedures.

One advantage of small groups is that they increase trust and sympathy, if the memberships are held constant for a while. When my Exeter seniors were writing longer autobiography in installments, I broke the class into groups of six or even three or four. In an all-boy boarding school, trust is hard to come by because the male competition is strong and there is no support from the other sex. But in the course of reading and reacting to each other's accounts, week by week, a climate of security and personal responsibility grew in which members felt they could write about deeper personal experiences without fear of derision or knowing smiles. Small groups do foster both candidness and concern. Getting to know and understand each other, quite simply, is part of the difference. Clique loyalties and divisions are transcended. It is the large group anonymity and herd reaction that make exposure a risk. Also, any student has the right to restrict his audience to the teacher only, who should get permission from the author before projecting any potentially embarrassing paper. Though limiting audience to a small group or an individual reduces the communication motive in one sense, that may well be offset by the greater personal relation to that audience. I think educators have an obligation to lower risk without spoiling the learning tasks, for as any professional writer knows, whether utilitarian or creative, not much of value is put on paper without some exposure.

But what about the threat to parents and other people in the community? The answer is, without being prissy about it, to screen what is printed in the class publications. This discretion can be a very good moral issue for students to discuss as editors, consulting the teacher and sometimes the parties involved. When possible, identities can be masked. And we should remember that more than one parent has risked exposure out of pride in what his child has achieved. Good policy sometimes might be to show the writing to parents first of all. In the case of some of my assignments, furthermore, a school principal has explained to parents what sorts of writing would be going on and what benefits their children would derive from them. The dilemma I have described should be put to parents also. This advisement helps considerably to stave off offense, which is frequently just a feeling of being left out.

PARALLEL READING

Doing this assignment should help students a great deal to read similar professional writing; knowing from the inside, so to speak, the abstractive process involved, they can interpret what they read merely by noting the decisions of selection and emphasis. Many first-person short stories cover a phase in the narrator's life. "My Oedipus Complex" of Frank O'Connor is a fictional equivalent of their own efforts. It contrasts with an incident story like "The Man of the House" and also with a subjective narrator story like "I Want to Know Why" of Sherwood Anderson. Conrad's "Youth" and Turgenev's "First Love" are retrospective stories about a phase in the narrator's youth. The body of fiction written as autobiography by a mature narrator hardly needs illustrating, since it ranges from *Robinson Crusoe* and *Gulliver's Travels* through *Jane Eyre* to *A Farewell to Arms* and the other modern novels mentioned earlier. It has been a standard technique for the novel of growing up, of education-by-life.

I suggest a triple juxtaposition in the curriculum — of student autobiography, fictional autobiography, and actual published autobiography. A valuable interaction of the three takes place, I believe, in the minds of students and gives considerable dimension as well to their discussion of each. They could read in common a fragment of true autobiography for discussion. Then let each student read a whole autobiography by some person who interests him — a book from the public library or a paperback that he can purchase if he wants to. Ask them to bring these books to school; allow them some in-class time to begin reading them, some out-of-class time to continue, and then leave them on their own. This would be individual reading to *follow* their writing.

Portion of Memoir

As before with incident (page 388), the focus shifts now from the author to others, from autobiography to memoir. Since phase and theme still govern the composing process, and since memory is still the source of the material, the problems of this assignment are very similar to those of the last. But there are valuable differences too. The writer is now on the outside looking in. Not having been at the center of the experience, he must *infer* that experience from what he knows firsthand and from empathic understanding. Whereas the demon of autobiography is one's lack of distance, the chief difficulty in writing about others is too much distance. If the narrator was not at the center of events, and is not the person who underwent the main experience, then how does he know enough to give an account of them?

The answer to this depends partly on whether his subject is an individual or a group. So let's specialize memoir into biography (he) and chronicle (they). Thus the shift of focus from first to third person is followed by the subdivision into singular and plural. This way of casting assignments is not merely logical; it stipulates the relation of the writer to his subject and hence the forms of information the writer has to work with.

FIRSTHAND BIOGRAPHY

Tell what happened to someone you know during a certain period of his life covering many months, perhaps even a year or so — some "phase." Refer to yourself if doing so enriches the account, but keep the focus on the other person.

This is the way I worded the assignment for eleventh-grade classes at Exeter. It is structural, rather than substantive: what a student is to write about is defined by some relationships between him and his material, not by topics. How does the writer know his subject? He knows it through three channels of information — what he saw and heard himself, what the person told him, and what was generally known about the person in the community or circles in which both moved. As informant, then, the narrator may play three roles, which I call eyewitness, confidant, and chorus. These roles give him access, respectively, to particular events, to the inner life, and to general background. The kinds of information he can convey, the point of view he can take, and the emotional closeness he feels toward his subject depend very much on which roles his actual relationship to the person permitted him to play at the time of the events. If, for example, he was not a confidant of the person, he cannot tell what the person thought or felt except by inference, a situation that forces the writer to interpret or conjecture more than he would as confidant. The point is that certain qualities of the memoir are determined by circumstances that limit the writer's options and must therefore become compositional issues during writing and during cross-commentary.

SAMPLE

One eleventh-grade Exeter boy wrote about a roommate of two years before who had been required to withdraw. The result is a kind of firsthand case study, as were many of the biographical memoirs done in response to this assignment. The author was, for Exeter, a fairly average student in English, performing in the C to B range. He was a thoughtful and sensitive person, but not a very skillful writer. The paper is presented unrevised.

THE INEVITABLE

As is the case with certain types of students, the Phillips Exeter Academy was not the right school for Albert Lockhart. All of the blame should not be placed on the school. His parents, some of his friends, and I did much to cause his failure. People too often ask, "What was the matter with Al: you should know, you were his roommate?" I usually say he just didn't try, but I know that this wasn't actually the reason.

No one can deny that this school puts a lot of pressure on the student and at the same time allows him much more freedom than most prep schools offer. Some students do well under these conditions. Al Lockhart did not.

I liked Al from the first time we met. He was about my size and was interested in nearly the same things. I was conscious of the fact that he tried to impress upon me how much he already knew about the school and how it was run. I soon learned that he was from a large city in Conneticut and that he had attended a country day school for three years. This didn't bother me too much but when he kept kidding me about not ever having had algebra I got a little aggravated.

During the first few days of schools we went everywhere together. Gradually we settled down into a daily routine and seemed to separate a little.

In the fall he was running cross-country and I was playing golf so we didn't usually see much of each other during the afternoons. We soon found that we had made the same friends and we usually ate with the same group.

We had many petty arguments, but prep roommates always do. Al liked the window up whereas I wanted it down, he liked the record player turned up and I wanted it off. These were only minor differences which we could settle by a little yelling and swearing at each other. Compared to most of the preps who had roommates we got along very well. But there were also minor habits that aggravated us, little things that one doesn't notice until forced to live with somebody over a good length of time. Al seemed to always go out of his way to show his dislike for certain people. There were boys in the dorm whom neither of us cared for, but Al always tried to let it be known to everyone. He would never eat at the same table with certain people or go into another room if there was someone already there whom he didn't like. At first I didn't mind this but finally it became very annoying to have him constantly finding fault with everybody.

There were certain subjects on which Al was pretty touchy and I must admit I didn't ever go out of my way to prevent any of these arguments. He was always quick to jump to the defense of the country day school which he had attended before Exeter. Someone would complain about how much harder it was than their previous school. This defense became harder and harder for him as his grades continued to drop. I used to kid him about not going to church when he was at home. This served no purpose except to convince him that church was a waste of time.

I didn't know Al's parents especially well. From what I had seen of his mother she seemed very nervous and talked continuously while in a group. Without question she was the dominant figure of the family. His father always reminded me of the typical football fan who never missed a game and lived only to serve the dear old alma mater. He was quite friendly, drank a lot, was willing to lay down his life for Yale, and followed his wife's orders without question. I'll never forget the time Al and his mother argued over whom he should take to a formal dance at their club. Al wanted to take some girl he knew from a town nearby but his mother wanted him to take another girl, a friend of the family. After yelling at each other for several minutes his mother held up her hand and said, "Now, Al, I know what's best and I don't want to hear another word on the subject." Then she walked out leaving Al nearly in tears. — Another time over Thanksgiving Al and I were at a party with two girls. After the party Al's father and uncle picked us up. Both of them were nearly drunk and his uncle could barely keep the car on the road. Al's girlfriend, who had been in a wreck less than two months before, became very upset and told his uncle she would rather walk if he wouldn't slow down. When we finally got back to Al's house he was in tears and so angry that he swore at his mother for nearly five minutes before going to his room. What upset me so was the way his mother took no blame for having let them come after us.

Needless to say, many of Al's problems stemmed from his parents but the school itself did much for his determent. Besides being insecure I have always felt that Al had an inferiority complex. Probably both were caused by the same things. Al didn't complain a lot but he did make many excuses for his shortcomings. He did well in his first year of cross-country and was expected to make the varsity the following year.

When grades came out for the first time, Al failed history and got several D's. He was very upset for a little while, and just sat at his desk staring at the wall. I was beginning to get worried about him but when he began to swear and slam books down I knew he was all right. I thought he would settle down the next term, and he did for a little while, but then the free afternoons the preps have became too much of a temptation. Al and Rick Cannon, the boy who lived across the hall from us, became very good friends. Rick was a very congenial guy, was quick witted, and was liked by most of the students. His one fault was that he couldn't settle down to work. I don't believe he completely finished any assignment after the fall term. Like Al, Rick had the habit of making excuses for everything that went wrong. Al and Rick would usually spend the afternoon wandering around town or watching the winter sport's teams practice.

Sometime towards the latter part of the term when things were really beginning to go bad Al started going around with Win Nickerson. Win represented the group in the school called "Negos." He spent most of his time at *Van's* smoking with the rest of this group and complaining about everything in general. Al had failed to make the first group in the prep sports program and this had been a letdown. His grades were very low and his attitude towards the school was rebellious.

I have always thought one of the main factors causing Al's failure was his inability to admit his own shortcomings to himself. This is why this was a bad choice of schools for him. The competition here forces a boy to know just where he stands in relation to everyone else. When he first came he was anxious to show everyone what he knew and how much he could do, just like everyone else tried. But what he couldn't accept was himself as he really was. We all have high ideals of what we think we are and at some time in our life these are shattered and we are forced to see ourselves as we really are. Al could not admit defeat or accept the fact that he was not as good as he had thought. Instead of admitting certain weaknesses and trying to improve he merely invented ways and excuses to hide his weaknesses and pretend they weren't there. He was finally forced to realize that he was only deceiving himself and then he gave up completely.

When Al became friends with Win Nickerson his career at Exeter slid rapidly. This was only a bold attempt to withdraw from the school, its pressure, and everything he was fighting. Rick Cannon had his faults but one thing he could not be accused was being a "nego." He had a strong sense of school spirit and he disliked Win Nickerson and that group very strongly. As always, Exeter forced Al to choose between the groups he wanted to be associated with and unfortunately he chose Win.

Everyone asked what happened to Al; what caused the change from his prep year? To me there was no change. Anyone who knew him well could see what Exeter had in store for him, but instead of helping him I let things be. I'm not sure I could have prevented what happened, maybe only prolonged it, but I still failed to do my part, as did everyone else.

Double organization. Again we see a general chronological tracing of stages in a progression, but the narrative organization is overridden by thematic organization even more than in the previous paper. Although some paragraphs are enchained by time, most are topically related, because the author wants to score certain abstract points.

For one thing, he is seeking causes: what can explain Al's decline and dismissal? The nature of the school, family background, the boy's personality, the influence of friends he made — these are possible causes, all mentioned in the beginning and taken up one at a time later. Thus the paper is partly organized in the way many analytical and explanatory essays are — by causal factors.

Second, he wants to bring out something typical or representative in his roommate's plight. More than one previously successful, well prepared student, accustomed to excelling in his home town, has gone away to a selective school or college and found he was only a little fish in a big pond who had to reassess himself in the stiffer competition. Many an enthusiastic prep has turned sour, sought escape, and started to wash out. But most recover, or at least avoid dismissal. How did Al differ from these and from himself? It is the representative aspect of Al's story that makes it a kind of case. In fact, this writer's interpretive account of his roommate's career resembles somewhat, even in a number of the points made, some actual cases that a faculty committee, which included myself, once wrote as part of a special study of Exeter.

ISSUES FOR THE WRITING WORKSHOP

The revisions this paper needs represent rather well the writing problems that class discussion and cross-commentary would deal with. One concerns the channels of information. We might expect that a roommate on good terms with Al would have served as a confidant and therefore been able to relay to the reader more about what Al thought and felt during this phase of his life. But Al's inner experience is virtually absent. In such a case, the writer's colleagues should ask him about the omission. Could he include more of what Al confided to him? If Al never talked about his thoughts and feelings, shouldn't the reader be told this? Did the fact that Al kept problems to himself explain why the author was unable to help him (since the author wonders if he should blame himself)?

As for organization, it is clear that the author has some difficulty fusing the narrative and conceptual continuity, the very difficulty the teacher would expect students to run into. The paragraph beginning "Needless to say" is snarled within itself and does not lead well into the following paragraph, because the author got onto causes in describing the parents and then could find no connected way to resume chronology. Should he discuss causes along the way, only at the end, or in both places? Should one alternate narrative and general commentary from sentence to sentence, paragraph to paragraph, or section to section? Also, some important chronological information was lost in the shuffle between narrative and ideas. We should know, for example, just when the boy was fired. Almost any student besides the author can point out omissions or ambiguities.

Let the group propose solutions to these problems with each paper in turn. The teacher's part is to help the students see, for example, that the particular form of organizational confusion mentioned above is inherent in the assignment and lies behind their variously expressed misgivings about such and such a paper. Having Xeroxing and transparency-making machines available in the school makes it possible for the teacher to pluck out a particularly thorny paper and project it the next day for a class discussion that will fortify group cross-commentary.

PARALLEL READING

For related reading, try to locate fragments of biographical memoir and firsthand cases in human relations. Assign these while students are writing. Afterwards assign fiction told by an observer-narrator — the Sherlock Holmes stories told by Watson, "The Gold Bug" and "The Fall of the House of Usher" of Poe, "A Municipal Report" by O. Henry. Pushkin's "The Shot" or, for maturer students, "Bartleby the Scrivener" of Melville, Mérimée's "Carmen," and "The Real Thing" by Henry James. Damon Runyon and Ring Lardner use the technique for their chatty stories of Broadway and sports; Joseph Conrad and Henry James use it for identification and sympathy between narrator and protagonist. *The Great Gatsby*, Willa Cather's *My Antonia*, and Alain-Fournier's *The Wanderer* are appropriate novels for this age and exploit beautifully the relationship between the first and the third persons (note that the latter are named in the titles). I would introduce all of these novels and stories as memoir fiction, in contrast to autobiographical fiction, but then leave the implications of the technique to small-group discussions, where talk about the action and characters will almost certainly bring them to consider the author's choice of narrator, because what the story is about is a factor of who is telling it. Fictional narrators play exactly the same three roles of eyewitness, confidant, and chorus that the students had to play. To the understanding of this fiction they will bring their experience in writing memoir, which will have shown them why one writes about someone else and what the advantages and disadvantages of observer narration are.

Especially interesting, by the way, are alter ego stories, like Conrad's "The Secret Sharer" and Jean Stafford's "Bad Characters," that have a dual focus on both narrator and protagonist and thus hover between autobiography and memoir. And as for dual focus, are *A Separate Peace* and *All the King's Men* autobiography or memoir? Assign such fiction last of all, and ask students, in advance of reading, to decide which each is. The question will increase understanding.

Firsthand Chronicle

Write a narrative about a developing trend or situation that took place in a group or community that you know about.

This assignment shifts the subject from the third person singular to the third person plural and thus broadens it from an individual to a group experience. This shift automatically makes the subject more general, since the author must see something common in the behavior or activities of a number of individuals. In other words, he is concerned only with some action that shows one aspect of a number of people; they are trying to raise funds for schools, ostracizing some other people, vandalizing for entertainment. "Chronicle" is defined as group narrative. Counterparts of this assignment are cases about groups and actual firsthand chronicle. A "group" could be anything from a large block of townspeople to a clique within the school. The classification of behavior that underlies a student's story may be a very simple one based on physical action, but he is very likely to classify also the motives or traits behind this action. This amount of generalizing is a natural concomitant of the assignment and will often provide the point of the account or be a conclusion of it.

SAMPLE

The eleventh-grade boy who wrote the following neighborhood chronicle was having a hard time not only in English but in other subjects as well. He was a good athlete and a hard-working student, but his academic background was weak by Exeter standards, and he was intellectually undeveloped when he arrived the year before.

EVEN WITHIN THE LINES

My neighborhood is a typical middle class Negro neighborhood. The homeowners try to make sure it looks as nice and neat as possible. All the homes are worth between $18,000 and $25,000. Most of the home-owners are well educated, most of them being school teachers. By 1957 our block was completely filled except for three lots. One was next to our house. It was quite narrow, so narrow that it looked as if it might be part of our lawn. Across from it were two lots owned by old Mrs. Hathcock, who planned to will them to her two sons.

In the summer of 1957 the lot next to our house was bought by Mr. Gray and he announced plans to build on it. Although several people were skeptical about his plans, no one refused to sign the petition he had to present before he could get city water and start laying the foundation for his house. The house went up very quickly, and the time taken to build it was an indication of its value. It had been made mostly of used lumber taken from demolished homes and it was much too large for the lot. It was wooden and white, which made it unique in the neighborhood. All the other homes were made of dark brick and are set far back on their lots. Mr. Gray's white wooden house stood about five yards from the sidewalk and was worth about $8,000 or $9,000. It was completely out of place in the neighborhood. When our neighbors realized what was being built, they raised a great uproar. But it was too late to do anything about the situation. They would just have to wait and see what Mr. Gray made of his property.

Everything went fine that first year, although the house was out of place, no one could complain about the way My Gray kept it looking. It was as neat looking and well kept as any of the other homes, if not more so. By by the first part of 1959 it began to show a little wear. That winter Mr. Gray caught pneumonia and was hospitalized for several months. By the time he was able to resume taking care of his house, it was in very bad shape; the wind had been very tough and had taken off part of his roof and a great deal of his siding and the old wood used in the house had become infested with termites. The more the house deteriorated the more restless his neighbors became. They were not interested in his problem. They were only concerned with the value of their property, which was decreasing along with the deterioration of Mr. Grays' property.

By the late fall Mr. Gray was desperate. He had done the best he could to keep the property value up but he had neither the funds nor the health to do it successfully. He had a new problem. It seemed that the petition he had had passed when he had first built his house had been registered in the wrong office and he had to obtain a new one. He needed to have at least twenty-five names on the petition; he was only able to get six. He was beaten when his neighbor on the other side, Mr. Wilson, offered to buy his property for a low price. He had no choice — he had to take it.

Just before winter hit, Mr. Wilson had the house torn down and the foundation filled. Now again our block is a straight row of dark brick houses and there are three vacant lots on it.

It's interesting to know that man's inhumanity to man doesn't cease, even within color lines.

The four middle paragraphs all start with time expressions, indicating the narrative order, but each paragraph contains statements about the growing alarm and antipathy of Mr. Gray's neighbors. The first paragraph starts in the present tense of generalization, then shifts to the past tense for the transition into narrative. The last paragraph returns to the present tense of generalization but asserts a more abstract statement, philosophical rather than expository. The author created this structure by treating the needs of the subject, not by following my advice or corrections, though I am sure his experience with previous narrative assignments helped him a great deal to see what he should do.

The only indication of the first person is "our," but the account could only be told by a local inhabitant, a member of what I've called a "chorus." The subject is more impersonal because it is plural. The author has no "confidant" information; the inner experience is the collective reaction of the whole neighborhood to an intruder. Had he known Mr. Gray well, however, and known his mind, the story might have been very different — a biographical fragment. So the paper is chronicle because of the point of view the writer *had* to take: he knew only what everyone in the community knew; he was only a member of a chorus (though a dissident member).

This memoir is clearly one long example of the broad generalization stated in the last sentence. I used to give, as part of the narrative-to-generalization sequence, a special assignment designed to elicit just such a paper. But I found that it was unnecessary. When a student wrote any sort of firsthand narrative, most often he spontaneously presented his story as an instance of some truth applying beyond the material at hand. This is why memoirs become cases almost automatically — if they cover a long enough period of time, such as a phase.

PARALLEL READING

Pure group narrative is not represented in fiction, which simply does not become that impersonal. A novel like *The Oxbow Incident* of Walter Clark is a communal story narrated by a member of a chorus (of cowhands), but the narrator plays confidant a considerable amount, and there are main characters. Conrad's *Nigger of the Narcissus* is similar, with the fascinating difference that the narrator refers to himself only by "we" until he steps off the ship at the end and becomes an individual "I" again. (Like Ishmael in *Moby Dick,* he is reduced to being a member of a chorus while aboard ship.) Panoramic third-person novels inevitably focus on one character at a time and thus assemble a chronicle by carrying forward simultaneously several individual histories. Sections of such novels, however, like the generalized chapters of *The Grapes of Wrath* and much of *Moby Dick,* do lapse into truly collective narrative.

A purely chronicle short story like "The Law" of Robert Coates ends by being an imaginative essay, and indeed more professional counterparts of this assignment will be found in a collection of essays than in fiction. But the best source of reading selections will be actual memoirs written by people who moved in circles that gave them access to the activities of noteworthy groups. Some important historical documents are of this sort. And contemporary reportage in magazines often consists of recollections of some collective action, especially political, military, or literary.

Speaking generally now, the interweaving of actual autobiography and memoir with fiction that poses as such should help sharpen the contrasts as well as the parallels between fiction and nonfiction. Though they borrow from each other, the artist and the real memoirist may use different rhetorics, one appealing more to emotion, the other to reason, this difference being reflected in the language itself. Fiction suggests general significance in implicit ways, whereas cases are usually more explicit (though both achieve generality by the choice of types for subjects). As students will know very well from their own writing, when you are telling the actual truth, you cannot fill in what you don't know. The informant is limited by circumstance, and his information is incomplete. When you fictionalize, on the other hand, you imagine the whole world of the story and can permit the narrator to know as much as you wish him to. Not only can the truth then be whole, but the material can be controlled for harmony and climax. This too the student can learn from his own writing, by inventing a piece of autobiography or memoir.

_____

_____

_____

Chapter 27

Reportage and Research

Reportage is some narrative account written from notes made at a locale the writer has chosen to go to for the purpose of gathering material. The sequence described here will see the culmination of writing that began as sensory recording, some form of which is a prerequisite for this sequence. Since not many students entering high school will have done on-the-spot recording, I will include it.

Poems of Observation

Before launching into the sequence, I want to touch again on poems of observation because, though not strict reportage in the sense that one goes out seeking subjects, they represent the fine notation of detail and the precision of language that any good reportage ultimately depends on. Furthermore, when he does go out looking for material, a student reporter may frequently experience moments that, if the possibility is kept before him, he will want to convert to poetry. Occasionally writing concrete poems alongside longer prose accounts will keep the writing honed — not only for rendering particulars but for charging them with meaning.

IMITATION AND ORIGINALITY

To me it is fascinating to watch students drop clichés as they regularly practice writing. Here are four haiku by tenth-grade public school boys in the same summer-session class at Phillips Exeter Academy from which I previously drew samples by younger students. They blend conventional subject matter and half-borrowed comparisons with some fresh perception and original language.

An island, far out at sea,
   leaps and bounds
      on the swelling ocean's breast.

A majestic Monarch
Enthroned on green —
A butterfly on a weed.

The afternoon sun
Sails across the sky
Dragging the moon behind.

A floor of sawdust
A ceiling of canvas —
The circus of life.

Though somewhat imitative and "literary," each of these also has some touch or twist that is the student's own. The "circus of life" poem illustrates the tendency mentioned before for some students to make an epigrammatic generalization through an image (as such, it is deft enough). Since I had not at that time begun to use student cross-commentary, one can only imagine the revisions that classmates might have suggested. The more students read of each other's poems, the more impatient they become with imitation; this peer pressure exerts a strong force in favor of originality. Students can help each other to sort the fake from the real.

But borrowing is also necessary; from a common stock of phrases the individual gradually forms new combinations of words. This need for slow metamorphosis was brought home to me by the following haiku, which was far more popular among the author's tenth-grade classmates (in a winter session at Exeter) than, at the time, I thought it should be.

Green shoots take breath
and bathe in tears for
   winter's death.

Whereas my fast section of eleventh-graders would have scorned its clichés, the boys in the "regular" section of tenth grade liked it tremendously for its slick play of sounds, the regular meter of the last two lines, and the rephrased but essentially familiar imagery. Without judging their judgment, I thought about their reasons for enjoying it and realized that the poem had the same winning way that so many hackneyed but pretty Elizabethan lyrics have, the kind that are moving when set to music but are distinguishable one from another only by variant wording when examined as texts. Still, a student recombining old stuff in his somewhat new way is enjoying language, exploring it, and getting ready to make it do his will.

The breakaway occurs most often with fresh subject matter, for familiar subjects come replete, by association, with the language that others have cast them into. That is the kernel of the matter and a powerful reason for tying writing to fresh perception. The breakaway may occur like this, with a consequent slight loss in control of language:

Two white flares break through the darkness,
   two red beacons fade away —
      highway movement.

If I were to project this poem, I would count on some student's remarking that the first line is "too long" or that "the rhythm is not quite smooth." I would then ask the class to suggest other wording, confident that someone would suggest present participles:

> Two white flares breaking through darkness,
> two red beacons fading away —

or:

> Two white flares break through darkness,
> two red beacons fading away —

(Again, this is the place for students to work closely on sentence structure, where they can do so for a total effect.) Or begin to substitute nouns (in which case they may find that *flares* and *beacons* are very well chosen indeed).

TECHNIQUES

The last boy has already grasped the value of creating a visual impact before identifying the object involved — that is, of describing inductively (particular to general). The tenth-grade girl whose haiku appears below also reserved the identification to the last, but the identification is reversible. Familiar with prep school scenes, she uses "shell" here in the sense of a racing crew boat.

> Long, thin, hollow shell —
> Oars whip along together:
> Hairy centipede.[1]

She is playing the game of visual tricks so characteristic of some haiku. We are given an image that transforms before our eyes (but only in some respects). Which did *she* actually see, the shell or the centipede? The terms of the comparison are coordinate, for the colon means equation. Metaphor is two-way, which is true of all analogy. (But does she need three adjectives for the shell? And do they create the rhythm she wants?)

The next two poems[2] illustrate how the subtlety of haiku teaches the reporter's art of making an indirect statement by sheer juxtaposition — in this case a wry implication by the conjunction of two physical facts.

> Towels hung up to dry
> Across the road —
> It's raining now.

[1] Exeter Summer School.
[2] Written by tenth-grade boys, the first in the Exeter Summer School, the rest in the regular session at Exeter.

This first poem reminds us of how powerfully focus alone speaks. The simple singling out of a detail immediately invests that detail with meaning, even when the diction is neutral and no attitude is otherwise detectable. Many photographs demonstrate this power of sheer selection.

> Through the cracked planks
> of an unfinished house,
> one violet opens.

The next poem shows how the deviation from haiku that I have been calling philosophic epigram can result in a remarkably compact expression of a generality through imagery.

> The stone axe falls,
> Discarded beside a rusted musket
> And Bikini vanishes beneath the waves.

A three-line history of war delineated by the weapons used.

A number of my students became especially involved in haiku writing because it gave them a chance to fix in words cherished moments of some activity they loved very much and knew a lot about. This boy was a bird-watcher and very knowledgeable naturalist:

> Emphatic song
> ascending through the woods,
> the oven bird.

> With bulbous eyes,
> soar above the pond
> the Dragonflies.

We had talked little about meter before these were written, certainly not in a technical way, for my impression is that young people are very sensitive to rhythm and meter and that scanning verse and naming the kinds of feet adds nothing to their understanding. When they write they work intuitively with rhythm, especially if they have experienced a lot of poetry. Unable to render the birdsong itself, in the first haiku, this boy captured the ascension (of the bird and the song with it) by sustaining a regular iambic meter, thereby illustrating what a text on prosody might explain in vain, that lines beginning on an unstressed syllable and ending on a stressed produce a swelling, lifting effect if the lines are relatively unbroken. His second haiku combines a stunningly salient detail with precise diction (*bulbous, soar*), natural rhyme, and a tight, suspended sentence structure.

Another boy loved fishing and loved to write about it.

> From the glassy surface
> the fishlines go down forever
> away from the sun.

Like the remaining three poems, by other students in the same two classes, this haiku induces mood, produces overtones. These poems are focused outward, but, as in so much of the concrete writing that one takes pleasure in reading, the physical things become equivalents of inner things. Truly noted observations are states of mind.

Without a move sits	A flash; and	Sounds of axes
The bobber —	Thunder stops the	In the gray sky —
And the fisherman.	Cricket's song.	The gnarled forest.

OTHER DESCRIPTIVE POETRY

Later, I proposed sports poems to these classes:

> See if you can render in six or eight lines a movement or pattern or series of movements that is characteristic of a sport you know.

I offer the following poem because it was written by a boy who did not usually do skillful or inspired work. His prose was limp and characterless. These were the three best sentences he wrote all year:

EIGHT BALL

He breaks the two to the side pocket right,
With kalaidescope colors runs the three through the seven,
Then banks the one true on the green.
With sweat-laden fingers he powders the cue
And calls the eight left corner down.
The white knight charges, ramming
The black towards the awaiting
Abyss and
In.

It was unfortunate that I did not make copies of the sports poems, because almost all of the other students kept theirs. The greater length opened up narrative possibilities and spontaneous experimentation with types of stanzas, which I did not talk about at all but which the students invented or borrowed from professional poems. Once longer poems of description or narration have been introduced, the range of poetry expands, as regards both subject matter and treatment. What can you do now that you could not do with haiku? But the acute focus and the sensitivity to minute adjustments of language will remain.

For reading, John Updike's poetry is excellent — sharply concrete, suggestive, taut, mature but not too hard to understand, contemporary. Frost's unobtrusive shifts from the literal scene to the symbolic meaning are appropriate. Don't ask students to analyze them. Sometimes pick a poem to be read overnight or in class that is somehow akin to one or more that the students have just written. Mix poems with prose reportage. Remind small groups to look for possible poems in each other's sensory notes, so that some write-ups may be done as poetry.

The Observational Visit

SAMPLES OF TWELFTH-GRADE SENSORY RECORDING

The point of looking again at sensory recording is to note what older students do with it. Though it has been tried in many classes of all grades, I have chosen the samples below from twelfth-grade classes at Dorchester High School in urban Boston because the students in those classes typify a kind of older school population that poses a problem for the teacher of writing. Though not the weakest students in their grades, most of them will not go to college and many are truly disadvantaged, being from families of little education and low socio-economic status. They are not involved in schoolwork generally and have done little writing except for some impersonal exercises. Given their alienation and the late stage of their schooling — about to terminate for good — what writing assignments can engage them and help them learn something in the time remaining? Allowing for the effects that the teachers' sensitivity and compassion undoubtedly had,[3] still the invitation to put fresh experience into words seemed to bring some of these students back to life. Never having climbed very high on the abstraction ladder, unmotivated to write about books and remote topics, they like to observe, live close to concrete things, and can find some pleasure in verbalizing these things. Once interested, they can consider the conceptual and technical matters of shaping their material through revision.

Unlike younger children, they seldom take notes in list form but record, rather, in whole sentences or full phrases. And they record more selectively, so that the subject takes on more shape from the beginning. Here are three final compositions from one of the twelfth-grade classes, the first by a boy, the other two by girls:

> Here I am sitting on a bundle of papers in front of St. Ambrose Church. Just waiting for the children's mass to start. All around me I can see and hear the children. Some of them are arguing with their older sister about going into church alone. And others are asking me if there is any sunday school as if I should know.
>
> In the sky and on the roofs I see several sea gulls there is one gull now who dives at us early in the morning. They have a funny way of flying, when they glide they do it with their wings bent. An old lady just bought a paper she looks like the type who checks the paper to be sure its all there. A cab driver just drove up and asked me if thise St. Peter's he must be blind if he cannot see the sign. Around me I can smell the fragrance of the grass also of the papers.

> I am sitting in a cranberry bog. The irrigation ditches give it the appearance of a huge patchwork quilt. The smell of the cranberries is refreshing. About the bog on three sides are dirt roads. People here use a variety of

[3] Grace Whittaker and Carol Shea.

transportation, for visible to me are some men on horses, a man riding a bicycle, people driving in a car, and an elderly woman riding in a horse and buggy. Around me I can smell the smoke from burning leaves, the dust from the roads and the scent of the horses. As I look around I see a pump house telephone poles, and a farm house in the distance. The leaves on the trees are an assortment of beautiful colors. I hear the voices of the pickers the splash of the brook and the bump bump sound of cranberries falling into their buckets. I hear the russle of leaves beneath their feet. People are hunting in the woods around here so I hear gunshots. I smell a cigarette. Flying overhead are a flock of birds making sounds like a duck does when he quacks. There is a rippling sound in the brook. There are bugs in the hair and also an airplane. The irrigation ditches are like brooks.

I am sitting in Brigham's in a booth, nearest to the door. Since the chocolate counter is right across from me I can smell the sweet and delicious aroma, which is so enthralling it feels like I am eating it. I work here after school therefore know the tastes of all the sweets are scrumptious.

A middleaged woman just entered the store, with her everyday concerned look on her face. I can hear her know as I hear her ever day asking the flavors of ice cream. She begins her pondering look for 5 minutes and then speaks, "I'll have a vanilla please."

The little ones ranging from 7–12 just made a mad dash for the water fountain. These little boys have the loudest voices. They are always yelling, "Can I have a cup please?," "Get out of my way," "I was here first." Now I can see their dirty little feet smear the water they dropped on the floor to form their cute mud puddles.

Here comes a woman in her late 20's. She always seem's to wear flashy clothes. Although she dresses like this she has such a depressed look on her face that she could confuse anyone. She speaks, "Could I have a cup of coffee," like she is about to cry. She now sits herself down in a booth and will probably remain there 2 hrs. like every other day.

I now can hear the kind mother who brings her 3 children ages approximately 4, 5, & 6 for a Brigham's treat. They are the noisiest group, not mentioning how messy they eat. She is starting to yell, "Drink your coke," — "Don't drink it off the table," "I'm never taking here again;" I now can feel drops of coke on my neck for her sweet children are now using the straw the wrong way. Although she yells and screams alot she has continuously brought her children here and has said the same things to them over and over again since I've started to work here.

The original sentences were not greatly different from those appearing above, but some changes were made in word choice and sentence construction. Some details were cut, added, or shifted into a different order. This amount of revising was made without benefit of cross-commentary or of a newspaper framework, but was aided by class discussion of samples.

The papers above show the interest that so often inheres in a *place,* if it is well observed, even though the events are miscellaneous and the composition not very focused. A place has its own primitive kind of unity, the organic interrelationships of its sounds and sights. But the observer composes the scene by his very selection and by infusing his reactions; in this respect, the paperboy and the Brigham's countergirl have moved farther from miscellany. But their subjects included action, especially human action, which provided them more focus and a slight narrative line. Composing pure description from randomness — making good writing out of anything at all — is a sophisticated skill.

SAMPLE OF SOUGHT-OUT HUMAN-INTEREST STORY

These students did very well in their efforts, and many other high school writers would do better, especially if experienced in reporting, but I suggest that beginners be allowed more advantage in purpose and focus than the authors of these pieces enjoyed. Set up in the beginning the newspaper operation as described on page 000 and make the assignment a reportage act whereby students select locales for their action or other predictable interest, covering stories or doing features as reporters on assignment from their group. The rewritten observations would then read more like this human-interest story done by a tenth-grader in Lexington (Mass.) High School:[4]

A LESSON LEARNED

Sixteen little three year old children were milling about their Sunday school room. Some assembling puzzles or towers of blocks, others riding around on small trucks, and still others slapping a soft punching bag and ducking before it hit back. Gay laughter and happy sounds filled the air as the teachers successfully included every child in an activity.

With the clock hands creeping toward eleven thirty, Miss Hill started a chorus of "Let Us Put Our Toys Away", a signal that circle time would begin soon. Some industrious ones shoved their toys back in place and ran to get a chair for circle time. Others, ignoring the bid to put the toys away, brought chairs to the vicinity of the circle while the remaining reluctantly replaced toys. As the oncoming chairs tended to obstruct the process of toy replacement, Miss Hill firmly admonished the children who brought chairs before all of the toys were picked up.

John was one little boy who had not bothered to pick up any toys; he loved circle time dearly and he wanted it to come soon. He dropped his chair and whizzed around the room gathering toys as he went, while the other children attempted to follow his example. His response rather surprised me, but the toys were soon back in their places.

The circle of chairs was formed, Miss Hill took her place, and started circle time with an opening song. Some enjoyed this period as John did, following attentively Miss Hill's motions and words for the songs. Others followed absent-mindedly and soon became restless. One little blonde girl

---

[4] My thanks to the teacher, Parker Damon, and to his colleague Robert Fay, for their experimentation with many of my assignments.

started stamping her feet, another followed her example, and soon the majority of the group was stamping and poking each other. Miss Hill was fed up when she tried with no avail to get a song started and only a few feeble voices responded. Firmly she tried to restore order to the circle, but without success. As a last resort, in a loud and calm voice she asked the group, "Shall we stop having circle time and sit quietly in our chairs and not do a creative activity today?"

Immediately, a shocked silence fell over the once cheerful group. If each and every one of the three year olds had been suddenly slapped, they could not have been more surprised and shocked. One minute they were a laughing, rowdy group, the next a stunned silence fell over the room. The little faces gaped in the direction of Miss Hill. Some asked her if she really meant what she said, but John reacted differently from the majority of the group. As soon as Miss Hill stated her intentions, his upper lip began to tremble, and soon after choked sobs wracked his little body. Choking and stuttering he pleaded with Miss Hill to continue circle time.

Miss Hill was very shocked and surprised at the effect her statement had on the children. I hardly think that she knew how much the children loved circle time and a creative activity. Obviously they must not have realized that Miss Hill would do such a thing. Miss Hill promptly dismissed the children and started the creative activity period.

I felt remorse for both sides. Miss Hill was right in what she did, after all she only tried to quiet the group. Yet I couldn't help feeling that she was too harsh. I was just as shocked as the children when she announced her intentions. Maybe next time they'll know better, maybe Miss Hill will know too.

The action to be covered can be even more specific and predictable than in this sample. Tell the students to read newspapers and keep their ears open for leads to coming local events — a parade, a store opening, a strike, a construction operation, etc. The newspaper, then, may contain ordinary news items along with local color features, the former falling at first to students needing more focus, and the latter to those who have developed the knack of composing randomness into a short sketch.

The Interview

To pursue the sequence now, the observational visit can be enriched and complicated by adding to sensory reporting the registration, in more or less condensed form, of conversation between the visitor and some person for whom the locale is a natural habitat. This addition brings on several changes. Information conveyed vocally to the reporter becomes an important part of his material, and this information may contain many intangible things the reporter could not possibly observe — generalizations, background, references to other places, sentiments of the interviewee, and so on. Thus the subject is more abstract and more secondhand. Person becomes at least as important as place, though sometimes the person may be important because he represents the place. The interviewing reporter must select not only among the sensory details of setting and of the person's appearance, but also from the things his subject says. Furthermore, the reporter is no longer merely observing; by putting questions to his subject he is influencing the material he will report.

Procedures

The assignment is presented as another kind of reportage, one more means of gathering and writing up newspaper material. The groups discuss choices of people in the community who would be good to interview for any number of reasons — their involvement in newsworthy affairs of the moment, their representativeness, their kinds of occupation, or qualities of their personalities. In discussing why they want to interview these people, the reporters should help each other crystallize the kinds of questions they would ask. Interviewing is an art, of course, and composition of the reportage begins with the selection of questions. Queries about date of birth, education, and so on will read later like a dossier or encyclopedic entry of a minor poet, though of course some such bare facts may be relevant if inserted into more promising material. Don't attempt to head off this problem, however, by admonishing. Emphasize to the group, rather, the deriving of questions from their original intention in wanting to interview the subject they have chosen. The directions are to arrange the time and place for the interview, with the idea of catching the person in appropriate surroundings, take notes during the interview, and write it up afterwards. (Students may feel that for some subjects a casual interview, not arranged in advance, would be more suitable.) The write-ups are exchanged and discussed by the groups acting as editorial boards, then sent in to the newspaper.

Interviewing peers. In the regular and summer sessions of the Brooks School, Graham Ward and his colleagues have asked tenth-graders to interview other students. This may be a good way of easing students into the unfamiliar social role of questioning a stranger, but it may also decrease the importance and purpose of the assignment, since the reasons for interviewing another student would usually be less definite. Teachers should perhaps try this out, however, for the first interview, in which case I suggest that the peer subject be someone the reporter does not know, perhaps a student from another school, or a drop-out. Peer interviewing could become a project to gather data — to determine, for example, what drop-outs say about their experience. Each interview would be a brief case history, written independently but compared later with others for possible generalizations about dropping out. The second interview might then put the reporter face to face with a strange adult (his choice of adult will probably allow for any shyness he may feel).

Issues for discussion. After the first interview, lead a class discussion in which students can compare the problems of interviewing and can suggest solutions. This discussion should range over matters of technique — how much to query, which sorts of questions are most productive, when to give the subject head, when to drop prepared questions and ask spontaneous ones. Project a sample set of notes and ask the reporter to criticize his own interview. Then project the write-up of those notes and ask him to explain how he went about digesting the notes. Invite the class to say how they handled some of the same problems. When is it best to quote and when to summarize? How much should you shuffle the actual order of remarks for the sake of better continuity of ideas? Should the reporter include his own questions? How much physical description should there be in relation to verbal matter? Are you going to play up surroundings, mannerisms, and dress, or sacrifice some of these for what was said? Do you describe at the beginning only, or return periodically to appearances? Let's note in passing that these are not only very real decisions that any reporter has to make but also some of the options the novelist has to play. The way these questions are answered is by referring them to the overall purpose that governs decision making and that determined the choice of interviewee and setting in the first place. The focus may be on the person as personage, on his ideas, on his relation to setting, and so on.

Other developments of the assignment. Contrasts, generalities, and other ideas can arise as secondary effects of interviewing if the subjects are deliberately selected for oppositions, similarities, and other relationships. What do different dietitians say? What do a retailer and a repairman say about the same product? When placed in the service of a project (but not merely reduced to opinion polling), interviewing can lead to further writing and to a special issue of a newspaper, in which appear not only the related interviews centering on a certain subject, but also some articles of interpretation and generalization that refer to the interviews as testimony.

Once a quantity of speech is included in an observational visit, the way is open to the covering of court sessions, legislative debates, hearings, neighborhood meetings, and other public dialogues. If at all possible, every student should have at least one chance to witness firsthand, and try to assimilate for himself, what goes on routinely in the official and unofficial bodies that run the affairs of society. Writing up such sessions, and reading the accounts by classmates, would give him a real grasp of social and governmental institutions that few students ever have and that it is almost impossible to convey in civics books.

SAMPLE

The following interview visit was written by a very sophisticated eleventh-grade boy in one of my own classes at Exeter. Having been previously very involved in this subject, he prefaced the interview with a brief personal experience of his own and, furthermore, blended this with a highly summarized account of the conversation. The reader will note shortcomings.

CAMDEN AND THE FLATLANDER

The sun filtered through the sail and fell on the pages of *Robinson Crusoe,* with which I was having no more success than I had had the last three times I tried to read it. The wind had died down enough so that the boat floundered along in some semblance of a straight line without my bothering to steer, and we made very gradual progress toward the islands, propelled mainly by the tide. Dimly I was aware that I was almost certainly going to end up paddling the last quarter mile, but at the moment, snuggled up in a nest of bouyant cushions, I preferred to struggle with Mr. Crusoe.

I was awakened from this stupor by the whine of an engine being revved in reverse, and looked up to find the sister ship of the *Queen Elizabeth* peering over my shoulder. A man, who either was the owner or dressed like him, stood on the bow, almost directly above where I sat, and observed me with the same understanding expression he might have assumed watching a dog sleep in front of the fire. Almost apologetically, he leaned over the rail and asked, rolling r's to the point of absurdity, "How do we get to Bar Harbor?"

"Due south, about five miles," I replied, somewhat embarrassed at having been found napping, and more than a little curious as to why he didn't get out his chart.

"Which direction?" he asked.

"South," I yelled back, supposing he had misunderstood.

"Oh, Thanks." He disappeared below, and a few seconds later the boat backed off and steamed away at full speed to the north-west.

I spent most of the next morning involved in pulling the *Sunshine I* off Jack's ledge, a prominent rock which shows at high water and is marked by two buoys and a spindle. The ocean, I later reflected, is one of those areas in which the Lord chooses not to protect the simple.

However, whatever the Almighty's stand on this question may be, I know for a fact that the United States Government does precious little to protect the simpleton, or any of the thousands of people he is liable to run down. The Coast Guard presently recommends that all non-swimmers wear some sort of life jacket, and that no boat over thirty feet long be entrusted to anyone under twelve years of age. The State of Maine, by comparison, requires that an automobile driver be seventeen years old, mentally and physically sound, have 20-40 vision in at least one eye, and pass both a driving test and an examination on the rules of the road.

Motor boat owners, I am told, cause more damage per person, both to their own property and to other peoples' boats, docks, and lobster pots, than automobile drivers. The chances of a motor boat landing on the rocks are almost twice as great as those of a car having a serious accident, and the results can be just as serious. The general ineptitude of the boating public today is no joke.

Working beside me that morning was Coast Guard Captain Camden Haskins, who, I discovered during the course of our conversation, has an even lower opinion of the motor-boating fraternity than I do. The owner of the *Sunshine,* he informed me, had bought her two weeks earlier, never having set foot in a boat, and "driven" her up from Boston. Mr. Haskins was quite obviously not surprised; the week before, he told me, he had discovered a very similar owner floating aound in the pea soup fog off Rockland, having found his way up from Marblehead by navigating on a Gulf road map.

The ability to navigate a boat, and to manipulate it in a limited area, is sadly lacking in today's "yachtsman", maintained Mr. Haskins, not because he has never taken the trouble to learn it, but because he does not know enough to realize that he ought to. Ten years ago, most boat-owners had either been brought up on the water, or had suffered through a long apprenticeship to someone who had. This kind of familiarity with the ocean breeds not only an understanding and acceptance of the danger involved, but also a certain amount of respect for it. This is not to say that there were not just as many fools on the water ten years ago as now, but only that the fool of ten years ago had some idea of what he was doing and some conception of what he was up against.

A large segment of the boating fraternity today is blessed with neither of these. A "flatlander" dropped into the cockpit of a cabin cruiser finds very little that is different from the Chevrolet back home. In fact, once he has mastered marine gasoline and the working of the head, there really is very little difference, at least until he throws off the mooring. The Chevy back home, he soon finds out, does not customarily perform on a rolling sea, nor does it usually develope leaks. A street sign is never more than a block away, and the Chevy has a comforting habit of staying in the garage once it is parked there, whatever the weather. Rarely, if ever, will an automobile hit a rock big enough to sink it. Finally, if the proverbial Chevrolet ever runs out of gas, he can always get out and walk.

The sailor who floats around the bay reading *Robinson Crusoe* is careless, and occasionally pays for it. The "flatlander" in his Chris Craft doesn't know any better, and should be helped. As Camden Haskins summarized with true Mainiac simplicity, "If the government won't stop the poor bastuhds, I don't know who will."

In his clever play with juxtaposition and synopsis, this writer has risked confusing the reader somewhat. Though he refers twice to the morning when he helped pull the *Sunshine I* from a ledge, he does not reveal until the second reference that Captain Camden was with him then, and he never describes this interview. The reader assumes — correctly, in fact — that the information presented subsequently is a condensation of what Camden told him. Perhaps a description of the "interview" that occurred as they worked side by side was *not* as relevant or as forceful a way to make his points as what he did include. This is precisely the sort of thing that students should discuss together. Actually, one hesitates to fault the account for its omissions and placements of information, for the boy really knows what he is doing, and he has conveyed the pointed information very efficiently and entertaining. Still, if the reader *feels* mystified, and thinks something is missing, then perhaps that spoils the successful effects. Weighing such matters develops judgment better than anything else students could do.

PARALLEL READING

In "Talk of the Town," *The New Yorker* frequently presents fine accounts both of observational visits and of interviews, often combined, sometimes featuring a place or activity, sometimes a personality, sometimes the opinions or knowledge of the interviewee. If teachers clip out and collect in folders some pieces of reportage from *The New Yorker,* newspapers, and other magazines, these can be distributed in class for students to read after they have become involved in writing the same kind of reportage. Let them exchange these two or three times and then leave them on a table for perusal. Any group discussion of them can exploit the fact that students have read different items. Through this reading and discussion some teenagers might begin to read adult periodicals on their own. Ask students to look out for and to bring in selections they encounter.

Anthologies of visits and interviews would be extremely handy, but since such material often dates fast, the anthologies would have to be printed as transient paperbacks or else limited to selections of enduring interest.

In literature, again I recommend selections from *The Hunting Sketches* of Turgenev, which I have assigned to eleventh graders. These beautifully written sketches of Russian country life under the czars are slightly fictionalized accounts of people and places that the author encountered more or less fortuitously while hunting. If presented as short stories, they will disappoint the students, who will be expecting the completeness and climax of fiction. But if introduced as eyewitness reportage, in the context of these writing assignments, they will be read with different expectations and well appreciated, I believe. "The Singers" is a fine example of an observational visit. Sometimes Turgenev reports overheard conversations; sometimes he questions people. His role varies considerably among the sketches, so that certain ones could be read as autobiographical incidents, but usually he is an observer and focuses away from himself.

The *"Reporter-at-Large"*

Go visit some place of business or other enterprise, talk with people there, watch its operation, take notes, then write an account of the visit afterwards. Use your narrative to convey a lot of information about the enterprise, to catch the atmosphere of the place, and to show what the people there are like.

This is an omnibus assignment in that it brings together several different kinds of writing that the student has been practicing. It involves recreating some of the dialogue of the interview, recounting actions, describing appearances of things, and exposing facts. Having received some data directly through his senses, and having received other data in verbal form from his informant at the scene, the student is dealing with information of different orders from different sources. He must digest all this and fuse the different modes of drama, narrative, and exposition into a whole piece of reportage.

PROCEDURES

The New Yorker "Reporter-at-Large" is the model for this assignment, not the kind that comprises many interviews and much book research, but the simpler kind that is based, ostensibly at least, on the material of one visit. Many of the long pieces in "Talk of the Town" fit this assignment very well and run more nearly the length that students would write. After the assignment is given, while the reporters are working on it, let them again read several tear-sheet examples from *The New Yorker* so that they can see for themselves how professionals handle the assignment *with different subjects*.

Don't try to distill a formula. It is true that most classes will have only one shot at the task, because it is large, but the best way to prepare them is to let them (1) garner techniques from the reading, and (2) try to foresee the problems that their particular subject is going to raise. An insurance office, for example, which offers nothing but desks and papers, is going to limit the interviewer almost entirely to the relaying of conversation. The directions to the preliminary small groups are to take turns telling where they are going and why, to envision the problems, and to make suggestions for each by drawing on similarities they see between a proposed visit and one or more of the Reporters-at-Large they have read. The teacher might lead this discussion for a while with the whole class and then let the groups continue it.

The hazard of models is that less confident students will imitate too directly; but one hopes that their being accustomed to writing from fresh experience will avert the hazard. Looking at professional selections while anticipating their own writing decisions, gives students a motive to read more analytically, for technique, than they usually do. But to offset the other hazard of models — the intimidation of the novice, who may feel he is being made to compete out of his class — assign for reading some papers done by a previous class. While demonstrating that other people like himself have done the assignment and done it well, these can serve as inspiration. One such paper with unsolved problems could be the subject of commentary in the preliminary class discussion.

SAMPLE

The sample below was done by a very skillful boy in a class of my own at Exeter, where for a number of years many teachers besides myself have given this assignment.[5] Farms, stores, bakeries, factories, hospitals, and laboratories

[5] The main idea was introduced there by Richard Niebling.

are among the many places Exonians have visited and written up. I remember funny, wry, and fascinating accounts of picturesque or rarely observed activities — at a Vermont country bookstore, on a Hudson River tugboat, or in an organ factory — but, in order to bring out sheer craft, and to illustrate how an experienced reporter works successfully with humble material, I have chosen a report on a very unsensational place to which students in any locality could have access.

No Madhouse

"I've been in the business quite a while now — since 1925. I was only fifteen when I started out in New Haven in an independent store. Next I moved up to an A & P chain store where I worked for three years. They didn't have meats before I got there. That was in 1928. I mean I worked in the first meat department of the chain that first sold meats. I even opened a small delicatessen out on Whalley Avenue when I quit A & P. I managed to take time off for the Olympic wrestling trials of '36, but I had to leave them early because my brother wasn't able to handle all our business alone. Well then, after the city began its redevelopment, I moved out here and rented this place from the old grocer, Frank Alba, who wanted to retire. It's my sixth year in this store."

I watched as Albert Proto flipped through order sheets and licked his thumb methodically before turning over each paper. The grocer's stubby fingers worked jerkily, but swiftly. He stopped and looked up. His features were sharp; his skin was dark; he wore glasses and had a tiny mustache. "That's my history," he continued. "Anything else?"

Wondering why he had mentioned his wrestling career, I asked him about it. "I even coached part time," he laughed slightly. "There used to be a large YMCA organization going in New Haven that sponsored meets. About seven YMCA groups from around the state competed. That's where I got my experience when I was young. The building was only a ten minute walk from the store I was working in, and I spent many afternoons over there.

"At the delicatessen I had a fair amount of free time also. I enjoyed the bit of coaching that I did in high schools. Several volunteers and myself worked in a cycle, supervising wrestling at different high schools each year. I tried to help lay the ground-work, but after the impetus of the program dropped off, there weren't any more volunteers. But you'd be surprised how much publicity I got around the neighborhood. It helped business."

The door opened, and a bread delivery man pushed his way in, lugging a carton full of bread loaves on his shoulder. He set the box down on the closed-over ice cream freezer, located a few feet from the counter where Al was standing.

"How's it today?" the grocer greeted the man, as he walked to the freezer and then began looking through the loaves. The man nodded and asked if Al had everything he wanted. "Let's see," the short Italian murmured, "two rye, five corn and molasses, three whole wheat, and an extra club. Yeah, fine. Thanks." The delivery man nodded his head again and strode out of the market.

Al swung the box onto the scarred wooden floor and piled the loaves on the shelves on the front side of the counter. Above him, there were racks on the wall, crammed with soap, brushes, towels, and detergents offering 14-carat gold-trimmed dinner plates inside the boxes. Directly behind the counter, more shelves held candy and cigarettes. A cash register sat on the counter beneath these shelves. One of the four florescent lights in the store hung over the freezer from the low, plasterboard ceiling. Four wide stacks of sturdy, metal racks filled up most of the limited space in the store, leaving room for a meat counter in the rear.

I sat up on the freezer while Al finished. "Oh, I'm sorry," he blurted out, standing up. He leaned back against the counter on his elbows. "I really forgot about you. I guess I was telling you about my wrestling times. Well, our little program fell through, and I did lose some fun of coaching. A couple of my teams had meets with Choate, Loomis, and one with Exeter. My invitation to the Olympic try-outs actually came through the head man of the YMCA in New Haven. He had some connections. The whole affair was just practice for me, but people liked to listen all about what I did and saw. The trials were, and most likely will be, the biggest venture I've ever undertaken away from the grocery business. Groceries are what I'm concerned with, but wrestling proved to be profitable as an outside activity." He smiled. "But I guess you'd be interested in what I've got here."

Happy that Al had the time to answer a few questions, I inquired about how he obtained his stock.

"It depends on the food, of course. Vegetables you have to buy every day or two, the same with milk. Meat, usually, is ordered three times a week. Generally, it's your perishable goods that you must stock up on most frequently.

"I buy food in New Haven from an association of independent merchants. It's called the 'terminal' and is located on Frontage Road, right off the Turnpike. Before I come here in the morning, I stop in there to load up.

"For the little market, the association is a great thing," Al commented. He walked over to his fruit and vegetable stand near the front window and picked over some oranges. "The association buys foods wholesale for the independent grocers in the area, and sells them to us. The quantity buying, then gives us the same lower prices as chain stores can get. If we bought individually, we could never get the discounts and never be able to sell at equally low prices as big places."

I asked if he ever got a special deal from a supermarket warehouse that could buy cheaply. "Oh, no! That would only involve another middle man and then another mark-up in prices, and we'd never make a profit selling at regular retail rates. Chain warehouses are supplied by large distribution centers, to our associations."

The phone in the front of the store rang. Al motioned for me to wait and rushed to answer it. "Good morning, Pine Orchard Market," he recited in a high-toned voice. Ah, yes Mrs. Welch. Yes . . . Yes. A dozen eggs, milk, and a carton of Viceroys. I'll have Ralph run them over as soon as possible. Good-bye," He hung up the phone, pulled out a pen that was hooked on his apron, and scribbled a note on a pad of paper by the cash register.

"Who's Ralph?" I asked. "He's the fellow who cuts the meat. I guess you don't know him. But, one important fringe benefit of our association, before I forget to mention it, is the pension plan. All members are required to give money to a universal fund which later supplies money for you when you retire. All this is to help the little merchant in competing with large supermarkets."

"Do you depend much on your phone service?" I inquired.

"Yes, sir!"

"But I would think that people in the neighborhood would be inclined to buy from you simply because you are close at hand," I suggested.

"People don't come to me because I am close," Al explained. "They expect me to deliver because *I* am close to *them.*" He pointed in the direction of the front window. "That lady who just called up, hardly ever shows up here. She orders by phone. She would just as likely ride all the way to town to shop, where she has bigger variety to choose from, as come here."

Al walked swiftly out from behind the counter, and I followed him to the back of the store where he disappeared into a back room. "You'd better not come in here," he warned, "because it's so overflowing with stock that I can just barely keep track of it." I peered in through the doorway.

Two curtained windows filtered the bright sunlight that streamed in swirls into the opposite end of the long, narrow room. One flimsy shelf, made of now rusted metal, ran around the room only several feet below the ceiling. A few cans of what looked like vegetable containers were set up on the shelf. The floor was cluttered with corrugated cardboard boxes, most of which had not been opened. An old T.V. set was conspicuous atop a table, draped with a sheet, in the center of the room. Al saw me staring at it. "When rarely there's nothing that I should be doing, I manage to take a peek at it." He yanked open a box, and pulled out some bottles of soda. He hurried back into the store and gently nudged the bottles on to a shelf between Coke bottles and a host of Campbell's soup cans.

"I don't worry about a lack of space too much," Al said. "I try though, to keep as much stock as possible out where the customers can see it." He started back to the front of the market. "The costs of many articles will never vary, even under great quantity buying and selling. For example, you take coffee. I buy that from the association and automatically raise the price about 10%. All stores do the same because of the wide distribution of the product. Locally produced foods are the ones that can be found in a range of prices.

"My niece bought a boneless ham for $1.29 and ended up paying $1.49 in a supermarket in New Haven.

"I guess I am really prejudiced against chain stores, though I did get some valuable experience in one when I was young. But it's such a madhouse: millions of people milling around, yet working there is boring. I considered it impossible to get to know anybody, especially the customers, which is most of the enjoyment."

I heard the stamping of feet behind me and looked around to see a man, clad in felt hat and raincoat, close the back door of the market. He was quite a bit taller than Al, and when he hung his hat and coat on a wall hook,

I saw that he was fat, bald, and had a flattened nose. I walked over to him as he reached the meat counter. He turned around.

"I guess that you're Ralph," I said aimiably. "I wonder if you've worked with Al for long."

"Quite a while, I'd say," he replied, smiling mysteriously. "I'm his brother."

I felt quite embarrassed, but Ralph said, "I guess I'm just not as famous as Al." I finally asked him what he did around the store. "Little of everything — run errands, cut meat, arrange stock." he whirled around and began grinding meat.

A white grinder sat on the table against the back wall. The machine was basically cylindrical in shape, with a spout protruding from one side at the bottom. Above on a shelf, six or seven stacks of cardboard boxes, about the size of those in which french fries are often served, were piled precariously high. Ralph lifted off several boxes and laid them in a line on the table. He yanked open the heavy, iron-bound door to the freezer compartment, adjacent to the back store room, walked in, and reappeared a few seconds later. He was carrying a square of fresh-cut meat in each palm. He dropped them on the table, trimmed off excess fat with several swipes of a broad-bladed knife, and rammed both pieces into the top opening of the grinder.

The tottering feet of a small child caught my ear. A woman entered the store with her small son. "Hello, Mrs. Fusco," Al piped up pleasantly. "Hello, Al. Lewis has been dying to see you," the woman replied, looking down at her boy. The youngster, giggling, tried to run away, but Al playfully swept him off his feet as he rushed by. The woman approached the meat counter. "Hello Ralph. I'll have two pounds of your hamburg there," she said, pointing at the grinder. Ralph obliged, and he flicked the switch on the side of the grinder and pressed the meat into the machine. A dense, limp mass of red and pale pink meat poured out of the spout a few seconds later. Ralph caught the hamburg in two of the cardboard plates. He laid them down on the counter, whipped a sheet of wax paper out from under the cutting table, rolled up the boxes and slid them across to the lady. "Thanks, Ralph. Just put that on our bill." The man nodded with a smile, and the woman led her child elsewhere in the store.

On my way out, I met Al at the front counter, where he was counting the change in his cash register. "I'm glad to have been able to help you," he said, slamming the cash register shut. I thanked him for his information and started toward the front door. Al rushed in front of me and pulled the door open for me. I looked around at him, quite surprised. "Even this helps bring back business," he said.

This student wrote also for the school newspaper, where I'm sure he learned more about reporting than he did in my class. Given his material, he has made all the right decisions. He has capitalized on the low-keyed folksiness of the subject by making that the very theme of his piece. The keynote is struck in the title, lightly sounded several times during the visit, and left to resound in the last section. Folksiness is not a trivial theme, for it relates to independent stores and to people who prefer running them to working in supermarkets.

He leaves the biographical facts in the man's own words, and puts that quotation in the opening position, where it arrests attention because a reader always wants to know from whom and where a disembodied voice is issuing. He let Albert talk on about his wrestling, instead of pressing his next question. This playing the interview by ear gave him some good personal material he could not have foreseen. Several of his later questions were prompted on the spot by what he was witnessing, and yet he has got the business information that he came for. Physical details are telling — the kind of bread Albert orders, the flimsy shelf of rusted metal, the television set. Description relieves dialogue and dialogue relieves description. The brother's appearance shows us that this is a family business. The telephone conversation, the treatment of the little boy, shows Albert's relation to customers. Through both anecdote and relayed explanation we learn how it is that independent grocers can still survive. The piece is a casual case study, a revealing economic and sociological glimpse. Few eleventh-graders could make the decisions so well, I suspect, but this paper at any rate shows what the assignment is all about.

ISSUES FOR THE WRITING WORKSHOP

Generally, the narrative account of the reporter's visit provides a frame, but the stipulations about conveying information and characterizing the people and the place force the student to make a lot of decisions that will modify the narrative considerably. He may interrupt it to linger over description or to inject explanation he acquired at some other point in the visit. He may digest in his own way information received from the people and feed this in gradually or in blocks, the alternative being to quote everything his informants said at just the moment they said it. Dialogue is a good way to characterize people and a readable, but inefficient, way of conveying information; compromise is necessary. Narrative and description will convey automatically a lot of information about the physical aspects of the people and the operation they carry on, but cannot convey generalities and other unseen facts such as background, purposes, and overall method, which must come from the people through dialogue.

Ideally, Reporters-at-Large would be balanced between information and characterization, and between firsthand reportage and secondhand reportage. Drama, narrative, description, and exposition would be interwoven, and none used to do what another might do better for the given situation. Some papers may never rise above miscellany, which represents a failure to find coherence either in the operation of the enterprise or in one's attitude toward it. This common difficulty usually means that the student got lost in the details and never let himself react to the totality of the enterprise. At some point in writing up the material he should survey it for general impressions and try to recall what things were salient about it. Perhaps the enterprise struck him as mechanistic, or money-grubbing, or old-fashioned, or quaintly casual, or typical of some modern trend. In other words, he could hardly not have distilled some *idea* of the operation, some essential characteristics. If he organizes around some such idea at the same time he follows chronology, he should produce a *pointed* narrative, which is by definition well on its way to being an essay. The problem of finding a good way to end the piece is then automatically solved: he strikes a note at the end — a keynote — that points up the idea or characteristic that was his dominant impression. Tell the students to have in mind a meaningful title as they are writing, one that keeps before them and the reader the unity of the paper. Have them bring a first draft of this paper to class, read it aloud in their group, and note the reactions of their colleagues.

THE VALUE AS RESEARCH

When combined and written up at length, Reporters-at-Large provide a very powerful kind of firsthand research that not only should reflect the student's private interest — there are people and places for all interests — but should also relate to his work in other subjects. For a project in science he could visit a laboratory, research center, observatory, or agricultural station. For government there are municipal operations and state agencies. For social studies, including economics, any business or other enterprise is germane. Seeing for himself how a profession is conducted, and who goes into it, can also help a high-schooler deliberate about a career, and reading the printed reports of other students extends his knowledge of professions considerably. Since the project is time-consuming, perhaps the teachers of other subjects could count it for homework in their course also, assuming that they had been in on the whole affair and are helping to steer students to places they might not otherwise think of. To give students plenty of opportunity to visit on the best occasion, and at whatever time is appointed by their host, I always included within the project period a seasonal vacation as well as two or three weekends.

The Case

The next assignments in this sequence are of a kind that I have never tried out as such but that have been suggested by trials of other assignments.[6] Having learned to write up "what I see" and "what others say," students would

---

[6] Since this chapter was written, considerable experimentation has been carried out at Wayland (Massachusetts) High School with various versions of this and the following assignment. The results are very encouraging, and the assignments have generated enthusiasm among both teachers and students alike.

now summarize "what I saw and was told on several occasions." Data is gathered through a *series* of visits or interviews. To this might be added, furthermore, "what others have *written*," the use of documents. The combination of several purposeful visits and recourse to documents justifies the use of the term "research" from now on, the idea being that research involves a synthesis of different firsthand accounts, or secondhand information, or both. The general procedure for this assignment would be to keep a specialized journal of visits and to summarize it later. The use of documents might be to frame the research with past background or general context. The research breaks down into two sorts, the first of which is a kind of case writing.

PURPOSES

Cases constitute an important kind of writing that is practiced extensively in our society. One can draw examples from the professions. A social worker periodically visits a family on relief and writes a report, based on notes, of the family's changing conditions. A psychotherapist writes up notes of interviews with a patient and produces a psychiatric case study. A naturalist observes the behavior of ducks or fish and describes the patterns that emerge. And schools of law and business have for some time relied on case reading as a way of plunging their students into actual situations such as they will encounter professionally. "Getting down to cases" is looking at real instances that have representational value for demonstrating typical issues. An account of the course of a lawsuit, a commercial negotiation, a piece of legislation, or a labor-management dispute serves as a window on certain sorts of practical problems that the account embodies. When used for discussion and exercise in decision-making, the case is often presented incompletely, the conclusion being withheld until the trainees have had a chance to resolve the problem themselves.

One of my articles of faith — founded, I believe, on some real truths — is that older adolescents are capable of doing on a smaller scale what adult practitioners of a career do. The point of role playing the professional is not only to learn how to be a lawyer, foreign service officer, scientist or businessman but to be able to understand and *care* about what those people are doing. More basically, the purpose is to understand how it is we know what we think we know. Even if his future job will be too humble to require case writing, a student should learn from direct experience how the information of his world is created. In fact, the principle justification of a writing program is not so much to prepare students for careers as it is to develop their thought and understanding.

PROCEDURES

I am sure that my reader can imagine as well as I the projects that can be taken on to fulfill this assignment. The best ideas for subjects will no doubt come from the students themselves, once the main task and its purpose are clear. These can be best conveyed by a question: "What would you like to know more about that you can become more informed of through either visiting or experimenting?" Let students use personal interests and knowledge from other courses as a springboard. They can keep a journal on any sequence of events that they know will start and end during a certain length of time and be accessible to them for periodic observation — rehearsal for a play or concert, pre-season practice of an athletic squad, the stages of a construction job, the growth of something in nature, the ups and downs of another person, like a drop-out, whose situation is especially worth tracing. Where appropriate, interviews should occur during some visits, or students can set up an experiment with things, animals, or people. Whatever the purpose of the case, the writer frequently has to situate his material by referring to the findings of others or to the history of his subject. His case may be one more instance of a generality previously reported by other people; or perhaps it contradicts prior evidence. The case may be understandable only if the writer fills in a bit of welfare history, or sets forth some established facts about ducks or legislative routine. This is the secondhand information that must come from reading. It is optional.

Differing somewhat from accounts of spontaneous events, cases written up from experiments report a controlled sequence mainly structured in advance by the experimenter, who is usually also the reporter. The natural scientist who tries to isolate a compound, or a social scientist who wants to determine how a problem-solving group evolves over a period of weeks does not simply observe naturalistically; he arranges what he will observe. He wants to know not just what happens of itself but what happens *if* conditions are such and such. He chooses the subject and situation and sets the occasions and duration. So a lot of what he reports is of his own making, usually in order to test an hypothesis. Although this control over the material creates some difficulties in allowing for one's own influence and for one's personal investment in the outcome — very real problems for all scientists — the reporter's task is essentially the same — to keep accurate records and digest these in some significant way. Recourse to documents may again be necessary in order to enlighten and orient the layman reader sufficiently for him to grasp the significance of what one is trying to do.

Following either a spontaneous or experimental sequence will lead to narrative and probably a final paper that combines chronological and thematic organizations. This is the main fact from which the writing issues will stem. One of these is summarizing particulars. *Just before dress-rehearsal the play began to fall apart* is a narrative statement but also a generality that the writer will have to support anecdotally without, however, reproducing everything that happened. Also, this kind of narrative is not a tale told just for its own sake; it is a case. The sequence, progression, growth, or change informs in a general way: this is how a team trains; this is what happens when rats fed extra calcium learn to run a maze. But how far the claim of typicality should go is an important matter for cross-commentary. Would statements from other documents prove that the case is an instance of a general truth? Is the case offered for the reader to verify for himself? Is the generality implied or stated? If stated, should it be qualified more exactly?

Cooperative teaching and flexible scheduling will certainly facilitate this assignment considerably. Subject matter teachers can direct students to both first and secondhand sources and can also advise them on setting up experiments. Again, time is a problem: the assignment should be sponsored by more than one department, and reporters should be allowed to visit occasionally during school time. Many administrators will certainly resist the latter suggestion, but the simple fact is that a lot of prime learning cannot happen in school. One of the reasons for the present impoverishment of education is the insistence that it be school-contained. The world can be brought to the classroom, but the students need to go to the world: television pours prepared information into students but does not allow them to be active information makers, which is a much more important learning role.

Parallel Reading

Many feature articles in magazines and newspapers are cases. *The New Yorker*, again, is an excellent source, as it is for all kinds of reportage and research. In addition, there are many case books in various fields that should be scanned for accounts that are not too mature or technical for adolescents. In *The Seesaw Log,* playwright William Gibson presents his journal of what happened in getting a play produced on Broadway. It is a valuable document about the economics and hysterics of the American commercial theater, resembling on a larger scale the sort of journals students would keep. George Plimpton wrote up, in *Paper Lion,* his record of an extended stay with a professional football team. These would be read during the period of journal keeping, along with previous student cases. Many short stories — Willa Cather's "Paul's Case" and Conrad Aiken's "Silent Snow, Secret Snow," for example, are fictional equivalents of the personal case. In fact, the juxtaposition of real and invented accounts reveals the special qualities of each mode of reporting on human experience.

The Profile

Suppose a student wants to know what goes on routinely in a courtroom, welfare operation, or business, or what some significant person characteristically does. Like those in *The New Yorker,* the profile may treat a person, place, or operation. It is more generalized than a case, contains more information from documents, and results in a logically rather than chronologically ordered essay. In doing a profile, students go farther across the frontier between reportage and research. Also, the tense shifts from what happened —

narrative — to what happens — generalization. A profile is about recurring
or typical things. Not progression, but pattern, will provide the shape of material. This is the logical assignment to follow case writing; though abstracted
to a higher level, the material is still concrete, and the generalities are exemplified with anecdotes.

A journal of visits remains the basis for writing up, but the time at which
a reporter begins and ends his visits will make little difference, since he is
not tracing a particular course of events. He may go to different courtrooms,
visit several companies making the same product, or observe the person on
a number of occasions, interviewing anyone he thinks can give him the information he wants. In addition to this material, he will most likely need
some printed matter on the subject — official manuals, company brochures,
newspaper files, local records, and so on — both to orient himself and to
supply information that it would be inefficient to acquire through observation and interview. For example, rules of procedure or biographical data
could be looked up, though an interviewee might tell him where to look or
supply copies of what he needs.[7]

Colleagues in the same group should keep up with each other's journals by
exchanging them occasionally for reading and commentary. Some deficits
and problems in the raw material may be headed off in this way and later
writing issues raised. Encourage students to note down helpful ideas in the
margin of the journal. Concurrent reading of similar research articles by
both professionals and previous students should help the reporter become
aware of the technical matters mentioned above.

When he comes to summarize his journal, a reporter will probably have to
organize by generalized aspects of his subject — kinds of matters handled
in court, differences in how several companies solve production problems,
what so and so does and is like. He will tell *what happens* rather than *what
happened.* When paragraphs do not follow the order of time, what succession shall enchain them? This would be a key question for class discussion
and cross-commentary while journals are running and during the writing up.
Which kinds of court matters, for example, or which comparisons of production methods, should precede which others? Although there are standard
logical orders such as big to little, important to unimportant, and specific to
general, discussion and suggestions should especially consider: (1) What is
the best *organically* logical order for the subject — which succession of items
or sub-topics would allow earlier items to prepare for later ones, and allow
for the most meaningful juxtapositions and transitions? (2) What is the
best *rhetorical* order — to begin anecdotally or with a general frame of

---

[7] In the Wayland experiments, the inclusion of questionnaire surveys as a data source
seemed valuable. Students like to poll and soon discover that formulating good questions requires a lot of skill. Also, important learning occurs when they attempt to
digest the responses and to integrate this information with information acquired from
other sources.

reference, to feed in background gradually or to insert it once in a block, to build toward conclusions or assert conclusions first and then substantiate them? And for each item or sub-topic, how much anecdotal illustration should one give? The same amount for all items? As for citing and foot-noting, students are referred to books in the classroom that explain the con-ventions.

Research with Documents

The last assignment in this sequence is, clearly, not for everyone. To cull, synthesize, and interpret the content of what others have written presupposes maturity, motivation, experience with abstracting one's own documents, and the capacity to organize a long piece of writing. I cannot imagine that many students, even of strong ability, would be ready to do original research with documents before their last year of secondary school. Unless they had begun this whole program in elementary school, I would not expect most average twelfth-graders to get to this point. This qualification will make sense to the reader only if I emphasize how much the assignment recommended here differs from the traditional "long paper" or "research paper," which is often given as early as ninth or tenth grade. I have in mind *original* research with *lower-order* documents.

When a student pieces together information and ideas from several books that are themselves high-level syntheses — encyclopedia entries, summary articles, or synoptic books — he really has little choice but to rearrange, re-word and regurgitate. The result is just a fancy book report. But if he sifts lower-order documents, many of them of the sort he has previously written himself — eyewitness accounts, journals and diaries, correspondence, frag-ments of autobiography and memoir, cases, and profiles — and some of them of a sort he has not been writing — such as municipal files, archives, and congressional records — then he can do a piece of honest research that no one has done before. This is the only kind of research a student should be asked to do. From having created most kinds of lower-order documents, he will know how they come into existence, what the nature and worth of their information is, and consequently how he should assess them. This approach leaves many more decisions up to the student — from selection of sources to drawing conclusions — but if this is not so, a research paper is not worth doing. Furthermore, he can have plenty of consultants. Subject matter teachers can give leads to sources, librarians and clerks can help in locating documents themselves, and the English teacher and the small groups can assist in methods of composition.

The key is personal interest. What kinds of information and ideas do students read for on their own? Any subject matter is fair game, since the learning is in the process. Different pursuits will lead to biography, chronicle, or exposition. That is, some student papers will be about a person whose life work relates to their interest; others will feature a group or movement, still others a state of affairs or state of knowledge. The research will usually be an extension of a subject the student already has some knowledge of because it attracts him.

In the American history course at Exeter, for eleventh- and twelfth-graders, students have for years written original research papers, some of which would illustrate the assignment I am describing here. But when the research *must* be about a certain subject, such as American history, the problem arises that a student may want to find out something for which lower-order documents do not exist, or for which higher-order documents would be more appropriate. In other words, the more circumscribed the subject area, the more the researcher has to count on luck. I think it significant that two history papers from this Exeter course awarded prizes by the faculty in 1967 were based on lower-order documents (though they were not necessarily the best written). One, for example, which was about secessionist sentiment in northern Virginia during the months preceding the Civil War, drew heavily on local newspapers, convention proceedings, and archives — records written at the time in question and available in the author's locality. He was able to tie his interest in his home region to the broader national framework presented in the course.

Original research with higher-order documents is of course not impossible, but unless one is an authority in a subject area, the likelihood of originality, I would say, decreases as the abstraction level of the sources rises. My impression is that the papers from the history course that, over the years, faculty have judged most interesting and valuable have been based on primary documents. The point is that if the subject area is unlimited, students can cast about until they hit on a point of interest for which such documents do exist. History is especially limiting because the farther events are from the present, the more others have already assimilated them. The Virginia boy had some luck on his side. Recent events offer better opportunities. Several years ago, for example, another student in that course did his research paper on the Black Muslim movement at a time when the movement was new and not much had been written about it.

The issues for class discussion, outside consultation, and small-group suggestions range over many phases of the project. The subject must be small enough to be treated significantly in around 2,000 to 3,500 words and must not have been so treated before. Help from adults, some quick reconnoitering, and airing of proposals in the small groups will help establish the subject and may also prompt better ideas about it. Then, during the gathering of information, students periodically tell their groups what they have done so far and discuss problems they foresee. Meanwhile the class reads biography, chronicle, and appropriate research articles that the teacher and members of the class spot and bring in. Periodicals are again the main source for the last. In reading these, students can pick up ideas for organizing and presenting their own material, having now a particular motivation both to read such discourse and to think about how it is put together. But most compositional problems will have to be handled by cross-commentary just before writing up and again before revision.

Two final points here. This and other research papers are not merely writing assignments; they are also reading assignments. They help answer the question I raised in the sections on the elementary years: What does one do with a piece of reading after one has read it? When this program appears to weigh heavily on the composition side, I would ask my readers to consider how often the oral and written assignments proposed here entail reading, the amount and importance of which tend to be underplayed by the presentational framework I have chosen.

The second point applies to both reportage and research — in fact, to any kind of writing that abstracts further some previous writing. The précis was a staple assignment in former times but fell out of favor in the United States because, as an exercise, it was too arbitrary and unmotivated. But whenever students digest an interview, a journal, a set of observational notes, or some source documents, they are doing précis. The difference is that the summarizing required for reportage and research is embedded in a meaningful project for which real motivation exists.

Chapter 28

Reflection

At almost any given moment, thoughts are running through your head — a spontaneous mixture of wonderings, wishes, conjecture, generalities, opinions, and other mental productions equally difficult to name accurately. It is this mixture that I will call, for convenience, reflections. By using this term, I would like to emphasize the reflexiveness of these mental productions; they are ongoing reactions to what is happening and to what has happened. As such, they flow in and out of sensations and memories, by which they are stimulated and to which they are linked by associations of either public or private logic.

But a part of what is happening now is this flow of inner events itself; reflections prompt other reflections and thus create what we call "trains of thought." Strictly speaking, we don't control which thoughts *occur* to us. We can only control the focus somewhat by deciding, for example, to dwell on a topic, as I am doing now in writing this, or by concentrating attention on sights and sounds, or on memories. In unfocused moments our thoughts wander freely as we let various sorts of inner and outer stimuli draw our minds one way then another. This section is devoted to capturing on paper chains of reflection.

Stream of Consciousness

ACCOUNT OF TRIALS

Having myself often reflected that the spontaneous mental life would be a rich source of material for student writing, I asked teachers in all grades from seven through twelve to try out in class this assignment, the wording of which was to be changed at the teacher's discretion:

For fifteen minutes, write down, pell-mell, everything that comes into your head, using the first words that occur to you and without concerning yourself about grammar, spelling, form, and continuity. This should be a kind of fast note taking to get down as much as you can of what you think, feel, and sense during those fifteen minutes. No one else will ever see this, but it will be important for later work.

Purposes. I had very naively placed this assignment first in the program for junior and senior high, thinking that it would limber up mind and pen, orient students to the program's approach, and prepare for a later sorting of the stream into the specialized currents of sensation, memory, and reflection. The fact is that the first two could be sorted out anyway, as already described, and pure reflections proved impossible to sort out, when students tried to write about them separately in response to another assignment to be examined shortly.

The practical purpose of writing out the stream of consciousness was to provide each student with a sampling of his own verbalization that he could examine afterwards in order to learn about putting things into words. For this purpose the teacher was to lead a kind of remote-control discussion by asking some questions as each student looked at his own paper. With these questions as starters, and the students volunteering short quotations from their writing, discussion was to move into several important areas of language, semantics, and rhetoric.

Assignment directions. For the teacher I had written the following suggestions, assuming that the assignment would be given several times and discussion continued from one occasion to the next.

Ask them first what it felt like to do this kind of writing. Was it difficult? If some say that they went blank, get other students to challenge whether our mind is ever blank. If some say that they couldn't write fast enough to keep up with their thoughts and feelings, ask how they decided which to put down and which to leave out. This quickly gets into the crucial matter of what determines our spontaneous choices. If some say, "I put down what was most important or interesting," ask what standard of "important" or "interesting" they were going by, since the assignment indicated no topics or values or audience. Did they find themselves, despite the directions, trying to stay on a subject, find a continuity, or move toward a goal? If so, why? Beginning in a private verbal chaos has the great advantage of letting the student discover for himself the reasons and ways for moving toward form, communication, and a public universe of discourse.

Ask them to look over their paper, mark the different verb tenses they have used, and say which tense, if any, dominated. If they don't know the names of tenses, use this occasion to teach them. Past tense indicates memories; the future and conditional, wishes, anxieties, conjectures. Distinguishing between the progressive form of the present, which records ongoing action, and the present tense of generalization, is an effective way of spotting sensory data and ideas. Have them label the contents of their paper by writing "sensation," "memories," "emotion," "fantasy," "reflection," and whatever other labels they think appropriate over the top of the original writing. Such distinctions may make them aware of the mixture of levels of abstraction in a discourse and of their different sources. Point out that the dominant tense is an index to the focus of their thoughts when they were writing; some students might have been fastened on the surroundings, some on the past, some on a dream world, and some on anticipation of coming events. Tell them to ask themselves how characteristic this sampling is of their thinking all the time and how much it reflects present circumstances. This kind of awareness may be personally helpful to many students, and they are generally interested in this analysis because it is of their own text, although it obviously touches on universal issues.

Did you use whole sentences or fragments? What kinds of words were most dispensable. Did you paragraph? If so, why? (What kind of logic determined new paragraphs?) Did you punctuate? Since no one else was going to read this, what purpose could it serve? What did you use dashes and commas for? Does your paper jump; that is, could someone follow from one part to the next? What would prevent them? In a month, would you be able to follow it yourself? Does it have any particular beginning or end?

Then comes the crucial question that pulls many of the previous questions together and that gets to the heart of rhetoric: What would you have to do to this paper to make it, first, *comprehensible,* and second, *interesting* to someone in particular you know (get a definite person in mind). After they have thought this over and given some answers aloud, ask what it would take to make this paper comprehensible and interesting to a large, public audience. They should consider everything from word choice and punctuation to complete reorganization and re-formulation of the content.

Results as registered in notes. The results of these trials can only be conveyed by the notes on teachers 'remarks, which I reproduce here because I think they reveal things the import of which goes beyond the assignment itself.

7th Grade, Newton:

Teacher A — Difficult. Kids couldn't believe it or see the point. With the first class she paraphrased assignment and they asked lots of questions. With the second class she read my wording and this official structure eased anxiety over the novelty. Discussion was lean and forced. Much better response on later trials with other classes, at least on first round; showed interest.

Teacher B — Discussion of classification (sensation, memory, wish-worry and opinion), and tense relations made sense to them. She talked to forestall surprise. They wrote a lot and seemed to enjoy it; not very anxious.

Teacher C — Went rather well except for anxiety about point and about her seeing what they wrote. Might be kept as 1st assignment.[1]

[1] My thanks to Vicki Pearlman and Susan Cooley for their participation.

8th Grade, Newton:

Bright, verbal class was very surprised. Used assignment to work on associations, increasing perceptions, and getting material. Hard for them to analyze what they did. Discussion was better on why we hide feelings — on human things — than on technical issues. "Walter Mitty" and passage from *All Quiet* are good accompaniment; kids got connections and noticed present tense of latter.

9th Grade, Newton:

Teacher A, second trial — Went very well. Fine discussion of the difficulties of paragraphing and punctuation. Some listed words. More complaint in other class.

Teachers B and C disagreed with each other about delaying this assignment after opening of school to have chance to build rapport and trust with the class.

9th Grade, Lexington:

Enjoyed such free writing. Some started by saying "This is dull" but ended happy.

9th and 10th grades, Carleton College ABC Program:

All off and running. Some bothered by the seeming sinfulness of just writing stuff down without worrying about all the conventional admonitions. Some commented (validly, of course) that you really cannot write down what comes into your head. This allowed some discussion of the nature of language, thought, etc. Decided that inner verbalization was at least a second if not later step. The beginnings are not language as conventionally conceived. Many sat waiting for the Muse to show and had to be informed that she was not necessarily part of this process. All enjoyed the routine once they were aware that teachers really meant what they said about writing down *whatever* comes to mind. Found it difficult to discuss something that no one was eager to read aloud. A funny sort of game with everyone reacting to their own private ramblings and all trying to ascertain what others had written. Some muddiness with "reflection" that was never really cleared up — more on this later. Sensation and memory could be clearly perceived, reflection was difficult to isolate. The assignment was judged quite successful at both grade levels. It seemed to warm the students up for what was to come and jar some of their rather narrow concepts of what writing was all about.[2]

10th Grade, Lexington:

Reacted favorably to assignment as worded, without explanation; surprised at the freedom. List form predominated. Discussion not too well motivated; "they know such things already."

11th Grade and 12th Grade, Dorchester (Urban Boston, same teacher and students as mentioned on p. 414 in connection with sensory writing):

[2] Written by director Robert Pierce as a summary about all classes (82 students).

Kids very upset — idea of teacher involved in their thoughts. Too threatening. They wrote clear, punctuated, whole-sentence papers; clearly expected someone else to read them.[3] Contained remarks on weirdness, headshrinking, unfitness for English but actually wrote good streams of associated thoughts.

Conclusions. My conclusions were these. Distrust, threat, and pointlessness are problems for younger students and some disadvantaged students. Placing stream of consciousness at the beginning of the school session, when most of these trials first occurred, increases these very problems; rapport with the teacher and a less extreme orientation to the program should precede it. Examining and discussing stream of consciousness is probably not worthwhile before ninth grade. (Actually, on pages 249 and 380, I have twice proposed similar writing already but not for discussion purposes; those recommendations, in fact, were partially suggested by these trials and would prepare students for this later assignment.) All in all, the assignment is feasible and valuable but suffered considerably in the trials from the prior conditioning of students and from being placed too early as regards both age and the overall sequence.

In following out a certain logic of my own I had ignored the psychological fact of the learner. For example, it makes much more sense to hold off this assignment until after students have invented interior monologues. They need to project stream of consciousness into someone else *before* they confront it in themselves. Also, reading and writing interior monologues will, I think, make it possible for students to accept them as normal, safe, and meaningful. As the teachers' remarks make clear, the mental set the children have influences enormously how they react to the assignment. Finally, the assignment was not well enough motivated: analyzing one's own spontaneous verbalization becomes of itself increasingly interesting with maturity, but even for maturer adolescents analysis alone is not a good enough reason to write.

SAMPLE

Before pursuing these problems, let's look at a sample of stream of consciousness volunteered by a twelfth-grade girl in the urban Boston school.

I will probably be taken out by some men in white coats by the time I get through. Next period I will be going to Latin to read some goofy poem by Virgil. I wish I could be going to gym. I wonder what the other kids are writing about. I also wonder what I have for lunch. It sort of smells like peanut butter. The teacher just came by and looks rather amused. Sunday is the last Red Sox. I think I'll go. Tomorrow we're playing a football game.

[3] We know this, in fact, because a number of students placed these papers in their folders and left them there later.

I betcha we lose — even to a crudy team like Jamaica Plain. If those teachers don't be quiet in the hall I think I'll pull my hair out. The character next to me must think I have some ideas for her as she has been continuously gaping at me. She better close her mouth before she swallows a bug. No wonder her pencil is so small the way she keeps biting it like a little mouse. I dread going to Chemistry. That bird always has us cooking something. That's where I burned my hand. I wish I could drop typing. I am so sick of it & the crummy teacher. I wonder how fast *she* can type. I would rather take something practical like a science but certain people won't let me change. The noise of the pencils around me are driving me buggy. We've only been writing for 12 minutes. I wonder if other kid's chains of thought change as constantly as mine. I am so riled over this foolish thing my handwriting has gotten illegible. I am looking at the bell on the teacher's desk & it reminds of last year's Algebra class. Who know how often I broke that stupid bell. We had to have tin cans for Chem class & when I was on the trolley car, I felt everybody was looking at my two bags. They probably thought I had 2 lunches.

She feels the assignment is "mental." She writes in complete, fully punctuated sentences despite the inefficiency of doing so in this situation. Understandably, she does not paragraph. Though "riled by this foolish thing," she becomes interested enough in it to wonder if other kids' chains of thought jump around as much as hers. The dominant tense is the progressive present, for her thoughts return again and again to what she sees and hears. Much of the paper reads like a sensory recording, which she has not yet done. But there are bits of memories in the past tense, a general remark, wishes, wonderings, speculations, and the fantasy about the men in the white coats.

It is true that this is not stream of consciousness but an abstraction from it, since part of any stream is always sub-verbal and some items in it may well be censored in transit to paper or simply ignored in favor of other things. How did she decide what to put down and what to leave out? The preponderance of sensory material is probably due both to the sense of threat, which deflects thought to safe external things, and to the situation — writing alongside at least twenty-five other people in a public room that is far from motionless. The importance of the last point is that it inhibits reflection and makes the writing of thoughts seem artificial. It might be worthwhile for my reader to look at other features of this paper in the light of some of the other questions suggested in the assignment directions, especially those about continuity and comprehensibility.

Spontaneous Reflections

ASSIGNMENT DIRECTIONS AND RESULTS

Sensory and memory writing were assigned next. Then, for students in grades nine through twelve, came the assignment that was to capture reflections only:

Choose somewhere to go and for fifteen minutes write down as fast as you can all the thoughts, ideas, reflections, or imaginings that come into your head. It may help to start with a sensation or memory prompted by the surroundings but once you get started screen out the sensations and memories and write down the rest. No one else will read this, but you will need it later.

Followed closely by:

Rewrite one of your reflection papers in a way that will communicate your ideas to someone else and that will be of interest to them. If your paper was not all about one subject, select several ideas that seem to you to be related and treat them together. Feel free to revise drastically and to illustrate with real or imaginary examples.

For the most part, the result was a fiasco. Everyone was confused by the concept of "reflections." And students found it too unnatural to screen out sensations and memories. I think the more intellectually inclined students in Newton, Lexington, and Milton Academy (Mass.) were the most inclined to worry about defining and sorting reflections, though this also bothered the selected lower-class children in the Carleton College ABC Program. The ABC tenth-graders, however, and the suburban ninth-graders did eventually find successful ways of rewriting the first paper, but the teachers had to stand on their heads to help them out of the difficulties.

SAMPLES

Many of the ABC children, for whom the summer was a bridge from slums to a private school, were quite naturally reflecting on the summer experience itself or on education and careers. Here are the rewritten reflections of one girl about to enter the ninth grade:

SCHOOLING

Now-a-days education is getting harder everyday. In fact, every second of the day. At times I wonder if I will ever get through with schooling. I mean climb to the very top of the ladder of education without dropping out at the middle.

Oh well, I think I'll make it quite all right. By studying just a little harder, instead of thinking of giving up at times, like I have been thinking alot of times. I am going to do the best I can in classes. I will try to be alert in whatever I may face in the future, whether they are boring or not. So in the future I will not regret things on schooling.

Whenever I am through with school, I will have a lot more opportunities for more jobs. If I am smart enough to become a doctor, I'll do everything in curring people. But I don't want to be a surgeon. Because I don't want to see people cut or bleeding. Besides it would be horrible to stitch people after cutting them. But if my grades are not too good, I would like to be a social studies or science teacher in junior high.

I am going to work until I am the age of sixty-five. While working I am going to provide a good living for my mother. After I have earned enough money, I'm going to buy land, cattle, and horses. When I retire, I'll have a ranch of my own and be a cattle woman for the rest of my life.

Concerns for the future, statements of good intentions, pipe dreaming. All right — these are important things that adolescents need to express. But a couple of things bother me. Whenever I see an "oh well" in a paper I know the student has decided to be gay and pious about it all, to conventionalize his thoughts into sentiments. So why not assign "Schooling" for a topic and be done with it? For such a paper, why all this rigamarole? The point is well taken. Despite the "oh well," however, I believe this paper has more reality for having arisen from some spontaneous thoughts on a certain occasion: it follows the movement of mind. Still, the justification for such an assignment can only be to tap thoughts that remain out of reach of topics, which have limitations. When preselected, topics presuppose that a person has something to say about them when he may not have, and also tend to force unique experience into stereotypical categories. When generated by discussion or reading, topics may be very good but may still leave a lot of material unmined.

To show what I mean, I turn now to the urban Boston classes, the same that produced the sensory accounts by the paper boy, the Brigham's counter girl, and the girl in the cranberry bog. Surprisingly enough, these twelfth-graders, who thought men in white coats would carry them off for writing streams of consciousness, had the least trouble writing spontaneous reflections. But their teacher talked them into the mood by relating the assignment to memories while shifting the emphasis onto thought, according to her understanding of her own students. Part of her way was to drop the term "reflections" and the injunction against sensations and memories in favor of a positive playing up of thought. A Chinese girl still learning English wrote this:

I hear my mother with my grandmother are quarreling in the dining room. I no wonder this thing happen between them, because they always quarrel even those little things.

Sometime I really don't understand those Chinese people. When their son got married, the parents still want to live with their sons and daughter-in-law even they had their own children. So, on this cause so many people live in the same house, and the mother with the daughter their age is different, the ideas also different. They always get many problems with each other. How can the people live in the house like that have the peace and happy. Why they like the American people, they live separate after sons get married. On this way they will decrease many problem. and they will get along with each other very well. Although in Chinese traditions, the sons must support their parents and take care of them with his wife when the parents getting old. But if they love their parents, they also take care of them when they not live togather. Why the parents not thinking about that, and voluntary to move away. I think if they do that they will get along with other very well. Because this thing almost happened in every single family.

What topic would have captured these reflections? Sometimes, with rare luck, one might, but the point is that some of the most valuable and interesting thoughts occur in association with other things, passing objects and momentary circumstances to which they are reactions. The connection in which thoughts arise is as important sometimes as the thoughts themselves. Consider a skylark or a Grecian urn, for example. In fact, it is often impossible to separate profound thought from the sight or sound that sets it off.

> Lying on my bureau is my pay envelope. By the standards of the American economy it is very little. However, to me . . . .

So begins the paper of a girl looking meditatively around her room. How much more interesting an opening sentence than the pompous generalities that students dredge up for the teacher's benefit to introduce topic-tailored material.

Recommendations for Combining the Two Assignments

Part of the initial failure of these two assignments can be attributed to traditional school conditioning. After all, adolescents should not be so disconcerted at being invited to write what is on their minds! On the other hand, the assignments were artificially conceived in ignorance. What I want to recommend is a composite of the two assignments.

PROCEDURES

Around tenth grade, after students have been reading and writing interior monologues, ask them to go *alone to some quiet place* and to write down for about fifteen minutes everything that comes into their heads, as for stream of consciousness. The point of quietness is to reduce the sensory stimuli and encourage an awareness of inner things — emotions and backaches as well as thoughts. Perhaps their own rooms would be good for the first attempt. Tell them that they cannot possibly do wrong when recording: whatever happens is spontaneous, even when they record with one eye cocked toward the write-up. Present the whole assignment as an experiment: "You have recorded sensations and memories separately; now what happens when you record everything going on within you during a certain time?" Loosen them up. Talk them into a mood, working from interior monologue. Give a thought train you had once. Afterwards, some students may say that writing down the stream of consciousness is bound to alter it. Admit this and let them discuss it.

Discuss these papers in the remote-control fashion I have described, using the questions suggested and others prompted by their remarks. Play from their reactions — undefensively. Give the discussion a practical bent by explaining that the understanding derived from it will help them to write up some of their thoughts later. Let each select one paper out of two or three to compose. The *emphasis* — and that is all it is — on reflection comes now in selecting from and shaping the spontaneous papers. Tell them to pick out trains of thought but without disrupting the setting or necessarily eliminating the sensations that triggered them, the emotions stirred by them, or the memories that may have occurred (some of which may exemplify the general reflections).

In other words, reflections are not simply sorted out, but the weight of the writing is thrown on them by lowering sensory stimuli at the time of recording the stream, and by focusing on reflections when selecting for revision. In the experiments, the difficulty was not so much in writing up as in writing down: the request to *spontaneously* reflect and do nothing else was a double bind. The point is to act as secretary to oneself, not consciously selecting at all, and then only later, when acting as editor, to select.

READING AND WRITING POETRY

After discussion of the first recording, assign poems to read that, like those I intimated above, are thought trains prompted by something seen or heard, or by the mood of a place. "Ode to a Nightingale" is a beautiful example, though not the best to begin with. It is an interior monologue, but meditative rather than dramatic, except in the sense that the inner life can be very dramatic. The poetry follows moment by moment the movements of a man's sensibility as he stands in the odorous dark of summer shrubbery and hears a nightingale pass. Many poems conform to the immediate concatenation of sensation, fancy, and reflection. Others, like Robert Burns' "To a Mouse" and Robert Frost's "Departmental" talk to and about an animal or object that sets off thoughts, wishes, and wonderings, or perhaps broad generalizations (Truth is Beauty). This freer association of sensations, memories, fantasies, and reflections can produce very good writing. The lyrical expression of reflections that are not meant to be proven or documented is the province not only of poetry but also of much personal essay that students might read now — some whimsical, some very serious — in which thoughts remain imbedded in the setting which inspired them.

My last suggestion, which I have never tried, is to encourage the writing of poetry based on stream of consciousness. After all, it is personal and idiosyncratic thought that the assignment is after rather than the logically developed thought taken up elsewhere in the program. The rules are different, and so are the purposes. The rules and purposes of poetry are exactly appropriate here. The "cloudy symbols of a high romance" of Keats' "When I

Have Fears That I May Cease To Be" are like the concerns and wishes for the future that adolescents want to express. And expressed as a poem, such feelings are less embarrassing. Juxtaposing disparate things along an emotional continuity is licensed, and the structures of poetry help fix this personal continuity in the public medium of language.

In fact, a specific form such as the sonnet might be appreciated at this juncture and provide just the amount of technical constraint needed to shape stream of consciousness. Assign clumps of sonnets from different periods, letting the students give rehearsed readings of them until the characteristics and variations of the form become apparent. Some sonnets might consist of reflections inspired by an object — Keat's "On Seeing the Elgin Marbles" — or of pure reflection — Wordsworth's "The World Is Too Much With Us." (Many of Wordsworth's poems have the quality of spontaneous reflection and are often entitled according to the time and place in which they were composed.)

Chapter 29

Generalization
and Theory

This chapter concerns focused, developed, and documented thought. The key tense is the present tense of generalization. The learning issue here is how to assert, support, and connect generalizations. This process is both logical and rhetorical, for while the writer is classifying and syllogizing, he is also patterning and phrasing his ideas for maximum effect on a reader. The past tense of narrative will sometimes remain important for purposes of illustration and documentation. But such lower-order discourse is embedded in higher-order discourse through the relation of instance to generality.

Discussion

One can learn to think logically entirely by talking. I would even venture to say that one could learn to *write* logically, for the most part, by talking. Small-group discussions and panels are critical for growth in the more abstract forms of verbalization. First of all, the very existence in the classroom of topic-centered talk implies that language can be used to think and to solve problems, which is a discovery for those young people living in an environment that employs language only for emotional expression and social traffic. Second, the interactions that occur during more abstract conversation help people to adjust and refine their thought and language. Discussion consists, in fact, of constant adjustment: words are substituted, sentences qualified, ideas-amended.

Teachers of these grades who have students who are unaccustomed to discussing should not hesitate to take groups aside one at a time and train them. I know that some high school teachers, convinced of the efficacy of talk, have suddenly enfranchised their students to go at it and then have been disillusioned by the resulting bull sessions, or have been redressed by a superior for letting students waste time. Good peer discussion does not occur simply by putting the teacher in the back seat; it must be nourished essentially in the ways described for elementary and junior high school. (See Speaking Up, Chapter 4.) Development can be along two routes — via topic discussion led by the teacher (page 53) or via increasingly abstract improvisation (page 290).

Techniques for Training Discussants

The role of the teacher is still to establish good habits of interacting that will continue to operate when he is absent. This is done in various ways: by describing to participants at certain moments the character of their conversation, by setting an example of good questioning, by pointing out communication problems, and by suggesting discussion strategies. The skill required of the teacher is to do these things in a sparing but well timed way. When he is leading the group to train them, the teacher does not participate in the production and amendment of ideas but concentrates, rather, on shaping group process. After groups become independent of him, however, and when he is sitting in as a participant, he contributes ideas. The frequency and force with which he contributes should be in positive ratio to the amount of mental and emotional independence his students have.

Let me illustrate the sorts of comments and questions that should come from the teacher and the participants themselves. Suppose the topic is Getting Along in Families. Opinions are piling up on all sides, but no idea is fastened and examined for a moment. Students are agreeing or disagreeing too quickly, without knowing what the statements of others mean or imply. They are lining up sides, identifying with or opposing other students. Word meanings are loose and statements unqualified. The teacher suggests that they linger over one statement: "Ellen just said, 'Younger children of a family get their way more often than the older children.' From what Bill just said it is clear that he disagrees. But look at her statement a moment. Is it *never* true? Is it always? Instead of just accepting or rejecting it, see to what extent you can accept it and to what extent you cannot."

In other words, suggest a *strategy of amending a statement until it becomes acceptable* — that is, of *quantifying* it and *qualifying* it. In regard to how many people is the statement true — all, most, some, a few? For what kind of people, background, circumstances? The qualifying leads to linguistic amendments. One adds: limiting adjectives and adverbs; phrases of time, place, manner, and condition; clauses of condition, concession, exception (introduced by *if, although, unless,* etc.). Qualification of thought and elaboration of sentence structure tend to go together. Show that the group can correctly tailor a statement to fit what the majority thinks is true: "In America today a younger child is more likely to get his way with parents than an older child, but is no freer because the older child restrains him in turn."

But disagreement may well continue. "Bill, what evidence would Ellen need to convince you?" The piling of opinions represents not only a failure to consider closely what others have said but also a tendency to stop short at assertions instead of supporting them. For a given assertion, ask them what evidence *could* support it. Is it supportable at all? If so, with what? Firsthand examples? Citations from authorities? Statistics? Help them to distinguish between disagreements that cannot be resolved by documentation and those that can. Often a discussion falters because none of the participants can support a stand. Tell them to bring evidence to the next session. If each can base his case only on personal experience, then what is that experience? Anecdotes may be appropriate for homespun subjects but very inadequate for supporting generalities of a more scientific sort. "How could you find out which of you is more nearly right?"

Sometimes students will pile anecdotes that illustrate the same point over and over, especially when they are comfortably agreeing about some idea or attitude they all share. Point out this as well as other forms of repetition. Ask them why they are circling over the same place. Or if they are disagreeing *needlessly*, because of undetected misunderstandings or differences in definition, say what you think these are.

Topics

Discussion strategy will vary according to the kind of topic. For this age, question topics should not be necessary, though they might often be desirable for problem-solving discussion. Predicates can be omitted to leave the subject open for different approaches (Getting Along in Families, for example). Topics may invite free exploration, analysis, causal explanation, a problem-solving decision, and so on. Let students make up their own topics but help them see which approach each kind of topic needs and how the way they cast topics influences what they will say about them. Yes-or-no questions dichotomize a subject in debate fashion ("Should . . .?" "Do . . .?"). Most predicated topics, in fact, whether interrogative or declarative, tend to force discussants into pro and con positions. Compare "Lady Macbeth is weaker than Macbeth" with "Changes in the Macbeths." The first topic requires, besides the definition of "weak," the citation of evidence for one side or the other. The second requires classifying the various behaviors of the two people and charting these chronologically. A *why* question asks, of course, for causal explanation. But causes may not be a feasible topic until other things have been discussed first — some definitions and classifications of the effects, for example.

RELATION OF TALKING AND WRITING

The best strategy for discussing a certain topic might be exactly the strategy that students should adopt in *writing* about that topic. And this is the point: through discussion, students can learn together about handling some of the problems of abstract writing, from how to assert single statements to how to phase an attack on a subject.

Interaction between discussion and writing is essential. Generalizations from student papers should become topics for small groups. Teachers should try to determine the best relation between groups formed for cross-commentary on the writing and groups formed for discussion. Since so many of the assignments under Reportage and Research (Chapter 24) as well as in this chapter will produce good subjects for talk, the most productive policy might be to merge both kinds of groups into one that would discuss both compositional issues and content, but not necessarily in the same session. Printing and distributing papers, even without assigning any as reading, will create a powerful cross-fertilization of ideas and provide substance for discussion that really interests students. Panels might often be based on an arresting or controversial idea asserted in a printed paper.

Writing Socratic Dialogue

In Chapter 20 I recommended, for the proliferation of ideas and points of view by the individual student, the writing of what I called socratic dialogues. This assignment was tried successfully in ninth and tenth grades of Newton, Lexington, and the Carleton College ABC Program, to mention only the public schools involved. It seemed to be a pleasurable and useful introduction to writing focused ideas. Because it induces thoughtfulness and transfers group discussion to paper, it should be a prerequisite for the work of this section.

THE SHIFT FROM DIALOGICAL TO MONOLOGICAL CONTINUITY OF IDEAS

Originally, I had followed up socratic dialogue with an assignment to convert that dialogue into an essay by fusing the voices of the "discussants," and by restating and rewording their ideas. But instead of helping a student to present and develop his own thoughts on the subject, this task generated extra difficulties of its own. I think now that the transition from a dialogical to a monological continuity of ideas has to be achieved gradually in several different ways. One is reporting other people's dialogues (see Chapter 24). Another is orally summarizing panel and small-group discussions. (Students might take turns writing summaries to be printed on an editorial page of their newspaper.) The third is to go through the sequence in this chapter after writing socratic dialogues.

Sample of socratic dialogue. To demonstrate at short range what I mean by a long-range transition from dialogical to monological continuity, I present here a tenth-grade boy's socratic dialogue followed by his conversion of it to essay.

JOHN:	How much does the student actually learn in the present system of education and public schools.
DAVE:	Not as much as he could, unfortunately, most of the things that kids learn they do so for the sake of a grade and actually this information holds know value for them.
JOHN:	I suppose it would help alot to get rid of the grade but it would take some getting used to.
DAVE:	I think getting rid of grading would be worth the price as long as no other system came up to replace it. Elimination of Grades would take so much pressure off the kids and they could start to learn something.
JOHN:	Perhaps too much would be taken off and they wouldn't come to school anymore.
DAVE:	That isn't nesessarilly so. For one thing school would probubly remain manditory untill a certian age, our society is dependent on this. Also school would no longer be as much of a drag as it is. It could even possibly be fun.
JOHN:	But wouldn't you have to do more then just simply take away the grade. The Schools whole atmosphere would be changed.
DAVE:	True, I agree. Many of the schools have too much of a high pressure atmosphere. Disipline often plays too big a role in the school teachers life. It would be awile before certian reforms would not be taken advantage of but after awile the kids would see that since it didn't matter weather they smoked or grew their hair or drank. They would start to see school and the process of learning for what it really is.
JOHN:	But wouldn't you have to watch out. and notlet this get out of controll. Pretty soon the kids in the first and second grades will be wanting it too.
DAVE:	You could change the younger peoples program too Not so much in the same way as you changed the Jr. High and High School programs but it would be basically aimed at the same Ideals. To make the kids interested in what they are doing and to make them want to learn.
JOHN:	You know it would be a real great thing if this could happen but I'm still hesitant as to who would take advantage of it.
DAVE:	Oh probably everyone at first but the program would be aimed at keeping the kids in school and not by force but by their own will. You would be surprised what some changes would do. Even a better school lunch program would have its advantages.
JOHN:	Oh boy, but then you get to the teachers. When you get right down to it a teacher can make the difference between passing or

failing, or liking or disliking a subject. Good teachers would be the backbone of the whole operation.

DAVE: Yes unfortunately bad teachers are more plentiful than good ones. But if they would get used to it I think they would find it easier to come to school and face the kids too.

JOHN: Boy there are som many problems in education. But I guess its up to us to do something about it.

Sample of socratic dialogue converted to essay.

EDUCATION?

The question of learning in todays system of public schools is a big one. How much does the student actually learn and how much of this knowledge does he retain. There are many arguments to this, pro and con, and both sides feel strongly.

Many people contend that if a child is not forced to school he will not go at all. Also if children aren't given strict organized courses and test that they will become lax. Pupils should also be kept in hand with strict diciplin etc, which is suppose to help their learning ability and form them into young adults.

Some of the above arguments are valid, but many are not. Granted that it takes a certain amount of force to get kids into school and keep them there. Many of the problems of schools do not lie with student but with the school and its general atmosphere. Pressure and fighting grades is an important part of school life. Unfortunatly many pupils take grades to seriously and only are concerned with getting a good mark. This "fighting" for a grade has caused students and some teachers to forget the real perpous of school, to learn. learning is the basis of human existance and since man is a curious beast he will likely go on to learn more about himself and his world. It is not true that kids have to be forced to go to school all the time. If school is interesting enough many students would return if the pressure, namely the system of grades, is taken off. Discipline is also another facit of education which does more to hinder it then help it. It adds to the confusion and tightness of atmosphere around the school and makes students actually want to break the rules and deliberatly disobey teachers. School should be changed from the traditional prison into a place of learning and relaxed teacher student relations.

IF these changes in the system were brought about most of the students would immediately take advantage of them. they would cut classes and smoke and do everything they had not been promitted to do before. This could cause a threat to the system of education. It is also true that the heart of a good school system lies in the teachers in it. No matter how good the school system the teachers can make all the difference. So, wouldn't all these reforms be in vane?

It is not true that all these reforms would be wasted. In saying that the kids would probably take advantage of their new found freedom but only for a certian amount of time. After a while they would see that no longer can they get attention by doing all these things that were once tabou. Soon they would see the merits that an education has, and since school would not be as dull and methodical it would be easier to settle down and learn something. Teacher are also the force that molds a good educational system, Almost everyone would agree to that point: It is too bad that there is a lack of these qualified teachers. In this new system, however, the teachers will find it much easier to work with and communicate with the students. In this new system both student and teacher alike will get the breaks of a quiet relaxed atmosphere which will alow better understanding and communication between both.

This student took the various arguments that were alternated throughout the dialogue from speaker to speaker and clumped them to form alternating paragraphs. The exchange in which the discussants agree about the importance of teachers was consolidated also, into what would have been a separate, closing paragraph had he signalled it as such. Furthermore, in converting, he had to restate ideas considerably in order to eliminate mere conversational cueing, to make sentences accommodate the new continuity, and to tighten up expression of ideas. (The desultory quality of dialogue makes for looseness at the level of both sentence and overall organization.) What governs the whole conversion is some transcendent vantage point that enables the writer to place opposing ideas within a non-contradictory frame. Such a vantage point is expressed, rather weakly, in this boy's opening paragraph, where he says that there are many arguments pro and con. One has to view the dialogue from a somewhat more abstract level than that of the assertions made in it.

The ability to take this view seems, as one would expect, to be developmental. We did not even risk the conversion assignment with eighth-graders. Suburban ninth-graders alternated the ideas of speakers without framing them within a larger idea, in such conformity to the original dialogue that if A spoke first and B last, then the paper contradicted itself. ABC ninth-graders had even more trouble, and their tenth-grade schoolmates only slight success. Tenth-graders in Lexington High School, from which the sample conversion came, seemed to find a transcending frame rather easily, but the frame was often little more than a strategy for organization, as in the sample.

Consider this overnight conversion as a small model of what is entailed for students in shifting from a dialogical to a monological mode of dealing with ideas and of what, more generally, makes the difference between conversation and writing.

RECOMMENDATION

I do not recommend the conversion. I do consider socratic dialogue itself important, especially as preparation for assignments presented in this section but also as a form of writing worthy in its own right that can combine invention and generalization, as in the dialogue below, written by a tenth-grade boy at Brooks School. Students who have written socratic dialogues in grades seven to nine might do only one or two more in later years. The subject of the following paper was the idealist versus the practicalist. The writer took it into his head to use the narrative way of quoting speakers.

I had been watching him writing for five minutes. "What's your idea?" I asked.

"It's about this guy writing an English composition," he replied without altering his activity.

"What do you think you'll get?" I asked laughing.

"Well, it follows the assignment and I know what I'm talking about first-hand — about a "B" — There, all finished."

"That's nice; I haven't even started yet," I said wryly.

"The trouble with you is that you want to stun the world with a measley English composition. Your chances of stunning even the teacher are only about fifty-fifty at best. Why risk it? Why not play it safe like me? Why lose?"

"Because It's worth it to lose for that one hope that you might win." It sounded trite, but I felt oddly inspired.

"So what if you 'win'. You get an "A" and that's it."

"You also get the personal satisfaction of knowing you had a good idea and succeeded. Less important but also present is the admiration you get from your friends. The infrequent gain is certainly worth the frequent loss. You also know that at least for a few weeks that composition is going to be remembered as something special and that you were the author of it. Even if it is rejected by your teacher and by your colleagues, if you think you have succeeded, then you have."

"What an idealist," he said disgustedly.

"On the basis just of my attitude towards English compositions, I don't think you can make an accurate conclusion. But I would like to think of myself as some sort of idealist. But everyone is an idealist to some extent."

"Not me," he said casually. "I'm a practicalist."

"If you are what you say you are, you're doomed to oblivion."

"How so?" he asked more interested.

"Take three examples: past, present, and future of the idealist and of a 'practicalist'. First, consider the past. I'm certain that you've heard of Miguel de Cervantes, author of Don Quixote."

"Yea, Look where his idealism got him — In trouble with the Spanish Inquisiton for the greater part of his life." He thought he had me.

"You agree then that Cervantes was an idealist."

"Well, yes he had to be to write a book like Don Quixote," he said warily.

"Admittedly, Cervantes had a hard life in physical terms but we're discussing the question of oblivion, and even you are quite familiar with Cervantes."

"But what about scientists," he said trying to recover

"Galileo," I replied quickly. "Take Galileo. Everybody was sure that the sun moved around the earth, so he suggested that it was the other way around and was right. That's idealism for you in that he disregarded practical considerations in pursuance of what seemed an absurdity, and I'm sure that you remember him."

"What was his ideal?"

"I suppose the ideal of every good scientist, the quest for truth. Then take the practical scientist of that age. He did the practical thing and read Aristotle. Everybody 'knew' that Aristotle was right so the guy made it through life pretty easily. But do you ever hear about some guy who did something like that? No."

"But things aren't like that today," he said desperately.

"Alright, take the present. You who claim not to be an idealist will never be remembered. Sure, you can come up with practical ideas for slight betterment of your business that, if you're smart, will improve it through the years. But you're not going to do anything which you will be remembered for because any great ideas or inspirations have to transcend practical considerations. Your problem is that the details will guide your ideas whereas your ideas should guide the details."

"An example?" he said stubbornly.

"The Wright brothers," I replied. "The lightest engine made at the time was much too heavy for any of their aircraft and they couldn't afford one anyway. Notice the results."

"O.K., O.K., what about the future."

"Say that sometime in the future there should happen to be an atomic war and there were only a few survivors."

"Ha!" he exclaimed triumphantly, "where would your idealist be then."

"I agree that alone the full-fledged idealist could not survive. But as long as the others keep him alive, he will base that life on ideals and formulate the beginning of a perfect civilization. When that civilization has reached its peak, it will remember that man as the father of that civilization and will not remember the man who brought him water or food every morning."

"But what is so important about being remembered," he said flustered. The important thing is to have a happy life while you're alive. Once you're dead, you're dead, and you're not going to know whether you were remembered or not."

"No, the important thing is to die knowing that you have lived for something. Many idealists are not remembered. But they die knowing that they have spent their lives striving for that ideal of whatever their pursuits may be. Whether they reach it or not, they know that in their striving their lives had some purpose and that they were not just vegetables. For the idealist who is not remembered, he knows to himself that his life has had some worthwhile purpose. For the one who is remembered, the world knows that his life has had some worthwhile purpose but the important thing is the individual. Either way he can't lose. Hey, what are you doing?"

"Ripping up my first composition so that I can start a new one. Now to think of a good idea . . ."

This mode of discourse allows him to present in an entertaining way a dialectic of ideas that is also, undoubtedly, an expression of his two selves in conflict.   Certain dialogical poems do this — for example, Yeats' "Dialogue of Self and Soul" — but usually the dialectic is fused with stronger dramatic exchange, as in Samuel Daniels' "Ulysses and the Sirens" and Robert Frost's "West-Running Brook."

Thematic Collection of Incidents

A very distinct sequence begins here that will push up the abstraction ladder from instances to single generalizations to logically combined generalizations.   The first assignment could be given around tenth grade.

> Tell briefly several different incidents that seem to you to have something in common, that are joined in your mind by some theme or idea.   Perhaps they all show the same thing.   You may draw these incidents both from your personal knowledge and from your reading.   State the theme only as much as you think you need to.

SAMPLE

In order to illustrate the assignment most clearly, I've chosen a very successful paper.   It was written by an eleventh-grade boy in one of my classes at Exeter.

NOISE IS A TOLL OF THE DEVIL, OR QUIETNESS IS NEXT TO GODLINESS

It's well before eight; the tremendous hall is absolutely vacant; the students haven't started filling it yet.   I'm on a bench way off in a corner, quiet because I'm occupied with watching and recording what goes on.   Someone comes up the stairs towards chapel, snapping his fingers in the emptiness of the hallway.   He comes through an entrance, still snapping his fingers and whistling between his teeth softly and tunelessly.   He sits down, and as the squeak of the bench fades into deep silence, he gazes uneasily about, then begins pounding out a rhythm on the bench and on his hymnal.   This sustains him until some friends come slowly in; he calls to them, then converses.

In church Sunday the guest minister sits back, then at the end of the sermon hymn, gets up and goes to the podium.   For a long minute and a half he stands there looking down, saying nothing.   The congregation shifts uneasily in seats, wondering "What's the matter?   Doesn't he knew he's supposed to start talking?   Doesn't he have a sermon prepared?"   At last someone coughs, then many others.   A whispering starts, each boy turning to his neighbor and discussing the situation.   The time draws to a close, and the minister explains that the silence was calculated to produce a reaction, as it did, of uneasy noise.

Uncle Screwtape, a shade high in the hierarchy of hell, writes to his nephew Wormwood, whom he has been advising on Wormwood's work on his patient on earth.   "Music and silence," he says, "How I detest them both! How thankful we should be that ever since our Father entered Hell . . . no

square inch of infernal space and no moment of infernal time has been sur-
rendered to either of those abominable forces, but all has been occupied by
Noise — Noise, the grand dynamism, the audible expression of all that is
exultant, ruthless, and virile. Noise which alone definds us from silly
qualms, despairing scruples, and impossible desires . . . The melodies and
silences of Heaven will be shouted down in the end!"

In Orwell's 1984 there is a gathering of all the adults in an area to a
hate meeting — where established symbols of their hate are flashed on the
screen, and the people looking at these symbols shout and rant and threaten
and become bleating sheep. A chant rises from the group, a chant in which
everyone participates with fervor, helplessly, and screams at the images.
After a long time, they are lulled and leave, united and feeling fulfilled after
their experiences together, better citizens for their society.

A few nights ago I had a tremendous amount of things to do — I was
despondent and worried. From across the hall there was coming a large
volume of sound — a record player blasting out surf guitar music, and eight
guys shouting and laughing, two on the floor wrestling. For a few desperate
minutes I sat at my desk trying to work, banging my fist on the desk and
kicking the wall. Then, my always low power of concentration snapped,
and I went in to join the fun. It was deafening, but I got so wrapped up
and produced so much sound myself that I passed an hour, admittedly a
carefree one, without even thinking of my work.

With all these examples I'm not trying to preach and show everyone how
their time should be spent — singing celestial anthems or sitting in silent
meditation. But I do always notice, when I'm asked to bow my head in
silent prayer, how my thoughts wander frantically until they fasten on something I can day-dream easily about. I notice how embarrassing any silence
is, and I wonder how long I could sit in an empty church and keep my mind
free from earthly thoughts. I know how infectious noise is at a football
game, and I've seen films of crowds watching Hitler and caught up in the
chant. Noise is attractive, as Screwtape says, because it is distracting. Silence is embarrassing because there is no protection against oneself, no barrier that prevents trespassing into realms of forbidden soul-searching.

This is a crucial kind of writing, because it weans the student from organization by chronology to some other organization. He can follow a time order
only when he is telling one of the incidents; since the next incident will be
a new beginning, he must bridge by means of the idea. Doing this assignment
entails collecting several items that are similar in some way and putting them
under the same heading, the items in this case being the incidents. Chronologic will not hold them together; some other logic must, some categorization
of experience. If the incidents are summarized in a pointed enough way, so
that the similarity they share is apparent, and if the author's classification is
objective enough, the paper should be successful, at least logically.

For many students, narrative is a kind of haven that they are reluctant
to leave because chains of events have a ready-made organization whereas

exposition requires that the student create and assert a new order. This assignment is transitional: the order in which the student places the several incidents may not be important, but they all illustrate the same theme and he needs to find some way of getting from one incident to the next.

ISSUES FOR THE WRITING WORKSHOP

Group discussion of the first drafts should test an author's classification against the understanding of the group. Further: Is there one incident that does not fit the theme or classification as well as the others do? Are some of the incidents summarized in such a way that their relevance is not clear? Does the order of the incidents make any difference? Would the paper be more effective if they were placed in another order? Does the author make transitions between incidents? If not, does he need transitions? (Would juxtaposition alone make the point?) Does the author state the main idea in the title or in a sentence or paragraph? Where does the statement come — at the outset, at the end, or during transitions? Sometimes withholding the statement until the end creates suspense and permits the reader to make up the classification along the way. He may even have to change his classification midway as he encounters new incidents, and this could be very thought-provoking. However, if the connections among incidents are too difficult to make without guidance, then the author should probably make his statement early in the paper or use transitions to guide the reader. Some discussion about how well the examples from real life and the examples from reading go together might be profitable also.

PURPOSES

A student who masters this assignment should not have trouble with that classic problem of coordinating example and statement, of illustrating generalizations. In general, examples are always drawn from a level of abstraction lower than that of the statement being illustrated. Frequently the examples are narrative. The difficulties are (1) summarizing the bit of narrative so that it will fit under a heading containing other bits of summarized narrative, and (2) finding an apt and accurate heading that can logically contain the examples assigned to it. The narrative summaries must be trimmed of irrelevance and worded abstractly enough to stand clearly as items sharing similarities with other items in their class. This is precisely what is required when illustrating generalizations in a piece of exposition.

This assignment, furthermore, relates concept formation to composition. As in the freer kind of logical card games discussed in Chapter 17, the student creates a class concept of his own by clumping items that he sees as instances of one generality.

WRITING ABOUT READING SELECTIONS

A variation of this assignment is to have the student draw *all* the incidents from reading selections, possibly mixing poems, plays, and fiction. The purpose, of course, is for him to put the reading together according to categories of his own, but this experience will also serve him well when answering essay questions on examinations in other courses, now and in college. In fact, this and the following two assignments ask students to do essentially what examination essays require; it is not necessary for the teacher to imitate such questions as preparation for them. Students who can write from their own categories will certainly be able to write from the categories of others. And many examination essays are so open as to approximate this assignment very closely. Of course, some students will create categories that are too simple and shallow, but if their papers are read and criticized, they can have a chance to see this and to revise them before the final draft. When students do tie together the reading in their own way, the papers usually are more interesting — and certainly more educational — than when the students have to write on an assigned topic, unless that topic is one they have set up themselves.

Sample. An ABC boy about to enter the tenth grade tried to pull together under a category of his own some of the summer's reading along with a real-life instance. His paper will show some of the problems that can arise.

> People still do respect others. Though there is much hostility among people in the world today, respect for one another is common and important in our lives. Respect is shown by a person's esteem of another, through leadership, popularity, courage, or previous reputation.
>
> The boy and the old man; John Byro and Aram and Mourad; and Jim Ryun, are three examples of respect.
>
> In "The Old Man and the Sea" Manolin, the boy, was very close to the old man. The old man was like a father to him and Manolin always looked up to him. The boy considered him the best of fisherman though his years were catching up with him. He encouraged the old man on his fishing, and still had the respect and faith for him even after he had lost his "catch." And always before, the boy attended to the old man as if the old man was a king, and he his servant.
>
> Manolin had the greatest of respect for the old man. His behavior towards him indicated this very much. Sometimes, though, respect is shown in a different way. An example of this comes from another tale.
>
> In "The Summer of the Beautiful White Horse" two boys of the same family, Aram and Mourad, steal a white horse secretly from its owner. The two boys have great enjoyment riding the horse. Then one day, unknown to the boys, John Byro, the horses owner, finds out that the two boys have his horse. But Byro does not reveal this to the boys or anyone else. Knowing that the family of the boys including them, had the widespread fame for

honesty, Byro remains silent. He trusts the boys, through his respect towards them, that they will return the horse back to him. At the end, Byro's respect for the boys turns out true.

John Byro had shown a subtle type of respect for the family as well as for the boys. This respect was deserving, as do all others. Finally, there is a third example of respect. This time from the eyes of many more people.

Jim Ryun is the best long distance runner in the world today. Everywhere people look up to champions, and Jim Ryun is such a person. He has worked hard, had the courage in himself, and with some natural ability, has attained his present status. Everywhere he ran people cheered him, showing their respect for him of his ability and hard work. When Ryun broke the mile record, acclaim and respect grew larger and came from farther off. People had given him the respect he well deserved. They had done this because they knew the qualities of such a person.

Everywhere respect is shown by people, whether it be small or large. The three examples above are just a few of the incidents of respect always going on in life. Respect may have little meaning to some, but it is all important to those others. Respect, as someone once said, is the fruit of life.

Though we need not restrict "incidents" here to the events of a single day, it is clear that earlier work with incidents would have helped this boy considerably. Both teachers and other students would comment, I am sure, that the examples of Manolin and Jim Ryun are themselves so generalized that they do not serve well as instances of the generality about respect. The example from "The Summer of the Beautiful White Horse," however, is beautifully handled. Besides showing a very good understanding of the point of the story, it provides a variation in the boy's theme, since the other examples concern an *open* display of respect.

The imprecision of his theme is another sort of thing that should be discussed before revision. Colleagues should ask him if the idea binding the instances is simply that people respect each other, or that they *still* respect each other (in which case the Saroyan example is out of line), or something more specific. Work in group discussion on the phrasing of topics and single statements would also help such a student to declare his theme or category with greater precision. Since the themes or categories *are* the students', any clarification of them is a clarification of their personal interpretation of experience.

Comparison of the samples. It is pointless to compare for quality the work of a very advantaged eleventh-grader and that of a slum child entering tenth grade, but if we compare these last two samples just for characteristics, we see several contrasts that help define problems and goals in writing. For one thing, the first is supple, the writer merely suggesting his point until he is ready to state it, and the second is stiff, formally reiterating the theme and repeating the word "respect" as if both writer and reader might forget it. The difference is partly in self-confidence and partly in the approach each student is used to. Neither of these matters is a factor of intelligence (the ABC students, incidentally, had a mean IQ of 110). Second, the first boy plays a wide range of abstraction levels, whereas the second boy sticks too much for this assignment to a middle level that blurs instance with category. At first glance, the second boy's generalizations seem very abstract, being very broad, but abstractive power is measured by the degree of qualification as well as by sheer sweep. Intelligence, no doubt, does play a part in this difference, but, for all we know, previous abstracting experience may play an even larger part.

Drawing Writing Material from Previous Writing

This assignment holds the important possibility for students of drawing some of their incidents from their own previous writing. If they have been following this program and keeping papers in their folders, they should have a stock of narratives, some of which, in fact, would have implied or stated a generalization. These previously told incidents would need to be summarized and re-told in order to fit clearly the category that would contain them. One advantage of further abstracting material they have already abstracted to a lower level is that students can then understand as they never would any other way how the raw material of life is processed by stages into higher and higher symbolizations. Another is that they can get ideas for this present paper by building on previous ones. At the same time, finally, they are building their own knowledge structures by combining firsthand experience and observation with material from other sources and thence distilling a truth from them. Whenever possible, the basing of later writing on earlier writing should be encouraged. Perhaps this assignment should even be introduced in such a way as to facilitate it. Tell the students to look over old papers of reportage, research, autobiography, and memoir (any sensory and memory material) and cull generalizations they made, then to try some of these out in their minds. Do they remember other incidents from reading or real life that illustrate or substantiate the generalization?

Perhaps my reader noticed that the process I just described is demonstrated in "Noise Is a Toll of the Devil." The first paragraph was drawn from a sensory recording, as he indicates in the paper. In fact, the special attention he paid to what happened in the interlude before chapel began gave him an insight to which he could later assimilate his reading and other experiences.

Published equivalents of these thematic collections are apt to be personal essays, whether called that or not. A simple example is de Maupassant's "Fear."

Single-Sentence Generalization

Just as a haiku constitutes a complete discourse of one sentence in the realm of very concrete things, so a lot of proverbs, maxims, epigrams, and *pensées* constitute complete discourses in the realm of generalization. They offer students an opportunity to work authentically with the sentence, but to work with more abstract aspects of it than they can with haiku. Thus, at this point in the program, the sentence can again come under scrutiny.

The assignment is to write, on several occasions, an independent sentence in the present tense of generalization — to affirm a proposition, as logicians would say. This is tied in with small-group discussions, other writing in the sequence, and the reading of maxims, epigrams, etc. Sometimes students can create their single statements as topics or as crystallizations of discussion points. Sometimes they may write them to restate a generalization that was implicit in or beginning to emerge from some previous writing, or to pre-state their main idea for the next assignment, Generalization Supported by Instances, the gist of which can be conveyed to them in advance. Sometimes they write them to be printed in literary collections.

All of these statements are discussed for both content and form with a view to suggesting amendments, which are of two closely related sorts: One consists of qualifying the idea by altering or adding words, phrases, and clauses; the other, of improving the rhetoric by adjusting diction and sentence structure for greater effect.

Parallel Reading

While students are working with these, present samples from literature and other sources. Read them aloud and project them. Cull them from Pascal (*Pensées*):

> One is ordinarily more convinced of something by reasons he has found himself than by those that other people have thought up.

From La Rochefoucauld (*Maxims*):

> There are people who would never have been in love if they had never heard of love.

From folk culture:

> Birds of a feather flock together.

(Proverbs are usually expressed in metaphor and are often ambiguous.) From poets:

REVOLUTION

> A beggar on horseback
> Lashing a beggar on foot.
>
> (W. B. Yeats)

Many suitable examples occur in a suite, as do in fact Pascal's *Pensées*, La Rochefoucauld's *Maxims,* and the *Analects* of poet-mathematician Paul

Valéry (a possible twentieth-century source for advanced students) but are fairly called complete discourses. Others are, strictly speaking, embedded in a larger work but are obviously as detachable and as exemplary of the single-sentence art as the samples above. Some of Oscar Wilde's epigrams were uttered either by himself in conversation or by characters in his plays.

> A cynic is someone who understands the price of everything and the value of nothing.

I am thinking also of the epigrammatic lines and couplets in Pope ("Essay on Man") and other eighteenth-century poets.

> Where ignorance is bliss, 'tis folly to be wise.

(A fertile discussion topic, I have found.)

Shifting from literary to scientific affirmation of propositions, I recommend as a fascinating source of documented generalizations a recent book, *Human Behavior: An Inventory of Scientific Findings*.[1] Since this listing of empirical truths is presented under subject headings about individual behavior, family, social organization, and institutions, the teacher can, after describing the book, ask the class what subject they would like to hear about, then read aloud some of the generalizations the book offers on that subject. As proverbs and epigrams will show rhetorical skill with the sentence — use of metaphor, witty antithesis — these statements will show skill in qualifying fact — use of exact vocabulary (sometimes necessarily technical) and elaborated sentence structures. The broadest statements in the book are fairly simple in form, but even here one notices a qualifying precision in the wording:

> Problems are difficult to solve when they require the use of the familiar in an unfamiliar way. ("Learning and Thinking")[2]

This one has two specifically qualifying phrases:

> There is always a tendency for organizations (of a non-profit character) to turn away, at least partially, from their original goals. ("Organizations")[3]

For accuracy, the following statement contains sociological jargon that will probably have to be explained:

> The rise of industrialization affects the family: it undermines and finally disintegrates relatively tight and large kinship groupings in simple societies, shifts the distribution of power within the nuclear family, and changes marital patterns. ("Institutions")[4]

---

[1] Bernard Berelson and Gary Steiner, (New York: Harcourt, Brace, and World, 1964). Though expensive ($13.25), one copy could be passed around among teachers in the same school.
[2] *Ibid.*, p. 203.
[3] *Ibid.*, p. 366.
[4] *Ibid.*, p. 397.

Most primary statements in this book (numbered) are followed by citations and quotations of relevant research, which often illustrate the findings, and by sub-statements that specify more particular cases of the generality. These are helpful for discussion. After reading, say, the generalization about problem solving, ask the class to think of examples, then read one from the book (in experiments, "subjects find it difficult to solve a problem requiring the use of pliers as a pedestal rather than as a holding tool.")[5] Next, ask them if they can think of related generalizations that are likely to be true if the first is; then read a sub-statement:

> The more recently an object has been used in its familiar function, the greater the tendency to overlook the novel use.[6]

Many of the book's statements would be excellent for small-group and panel discussion if chosen by students. Though presented as true, they need a lot of explaining and exemplifying. Discussion would translate them into cases and test them out. Maxims and other sayings, on the other hand, are unproven and invite more controversy.

In short, steep students for a while in general statements of all sorts and let them practice them. Get them to amend and tinker with these single sentences, writing their own, rewriting those of their groupmates, and observing how professionals generalize in different ways for different purposes. Then they will be ready for the next assignment.

Generalization Supported by Instances

> Make a general statement about some aspect of people's behavior that from your own observations seems true to you. Use a number of examples to illustrate your generalization. Draw your examples from among the things you have observed and read about that led you to this generalization in the first place.

This assignment essentially just shifts the ratio between instance and generality. The main purpose of it is to throw the emphasis definitely on ideas. Illustrations are distinctly subordinated, and paragraphing follows a logic inherent in the generalization. Although the task calls essentially for an assertion and examples, most generalizations break down in some way into lesser ideas or into variations of the main statement. Thus a typical pattern would be for the first paragraph to assert the generalization and for the lead sentences of the following paragraphs to make the sub-statements, with follow-up sentences illustrating them. But of course there should be no formula for such a paper. The first paragraph might consist of an arresting example that is to be explained later, or the sub-statements might lead inductively up to the generalization as the conclusion of the paper.

[5] *Ibid.*, p. 204.
[6] *Ibid.*, p. 204.

ISSUES FOR THE WRITING WORKSHOP

Illustration and generalization as levels of abstraction. A generalization should be a statement cast into the present tense. But generalizations may be of different degrees of abstractness, depending on how much time and space is covered by the statement. If the paper contains no past tense, this means that the illustrations are also generalizations, though presumably of a lower order than the main statement. The question, then, is whether such illustrations *illustrate* well enough or whether they themselves are so abstract as to require examples. In other words, each paper will embrace a certain segment of the abstraction hierarchy; the highest point will be the main assertion and the lowest point will be the most concrete example. If the main assertion is high, such as "Men have a strong need for exploration and adventure," one would expect the secondary assertions and the illustrations to run high also, though they should still be well below the main assertion. But if the main assertion is something like "Older brothers are more confident than younger brothers" — a much more specific generalization — one would expect all the other statements in the paper not only to run below this one but to dip down into past-tense, narrative sentences, which are near the bottom of the hierarchy.

To lead discussion well and to help students comment on each other's papers, the teacher must have a strong sense of levels of abstraction. "Concrete" and "abstract," "specific" and "general" are entirely *relative* terms, relative to the master statement that provides the context for the whole paper. Illustrating is translating a statement down the hierarchy. What is a generalization in one paper might be an illustration in another. But if the illustration is not very much farther down, it cannot illustrate well. If it is too far down, it may be too trivial, relatively, to be persuasive ("My friend so-and-so joined the Peace Corps last year because he was restless" to illustrate "Men have a strong need for exploration and adventure.") Rules such as "Be specific" and "Don't over-generalize" are meaningless and unhelpful. The student must play up and down the abstraction ladder according to the situation, jumping farther down for illustrations, and then jumping back up occasionally for transitions or other restatements of the main idea. ("Over-generalizing" is simply a failure to quantify and qualify — to stipulate the number, time, place, and conditions for which a statement is true.)

Technical problems. Let the students explore these matters in discussion of their own first drafts. Direct them to amend statement X, if they think it is exaggerated or "over-generalized" or simply not true. What words, phrases, or clauses could be added that would make the statement truer in their view? Then: Do the examples fit? Are they specific enough, or are they themselves too general? Where did the author place his main assertion? Where did he place his examples? What determined the order of his paragraphs? If the order were changed, would it make any difference? Does each paragraph consist of an illustration, or are the paragraphs based on sub-statements? (So-called "development" is the breaking down of the main generalization into its variations or sub-statements).

Common faults. Some common faults are: letting an illustration run away into irrelevance (usually a narrative for its own sake); piling on examples that all show the same point; stringing the examples with weak transitions such as "Another example is . . ."; repeating the first paragraph as the last paragraph; and repeating the main generalization instead of developing it. When these faults come up, the teacher should encourage the class to diagnose them. Almost all of them stem from too simple a generalization. Developing the main statement through qualification and variation would solve most of them. But the teacher should bear in mind that this assignment does not necessarily invite development, and that illustrating a generalization naturally tends toward a string-of-beads organization. With help from each other, however, students can find a way of stringing the illustrations artfully and with as much development as the assignment accommodates.

SAMPLE

An eleventh-grade boy at Exeter wrote this:

CHEATERS

Some of the golfers cheat all of the time, and all of the golfers cheat some of the time. That is an axiom that usually holds true. In the five years that I have been playing the game, I doubt if I've met an honest golfer. I don't care how scrupulous a man is in his daily life; put him on the golf course, and I guarantee his golfing companions will corrupt him.

Not all golfers cheat with the same regularity, nor do they employ the same methods. For example, the seventy shooter could not use the crude methods to which the duffer, striving to break 100, must resort. Nor would the duffer profit by using only the more refined techniches of the par shooter.

As my golfing companions represent various degrees of skill, a description of their methods of deception should include most of the deceitful practices seen on the golf course.

Mick is the best of my golfing partners. He usually shoots around par and occasionally breaks it. For a golfer of Mick's caliber, the oppurtunities for cheating are few and far between. As he usually takes only four or five strokes per hole, he cannot rely on poor memory to reduce his score. If he is to cut even a single stroke, he must employ the most subtle techniches.

One of Mick's favorite tricks involves a shot hit out of bounds or a lost ball. The penalty in each case is two strokes. Mick rarely loses a ball, but often another member of his party will. When this happens, Mick will say, "Toss another ball out in the fairway. You'll be lying two, hitting three" (assuming that the ball was lost on the tee shot.) Mick know's the rules of golf, and he's fully aware that the boy is actually lying three, hitting four. Mick gives him this break because he expects the same treatement should he hit an errant shot. In the club house, when Mick is bragging about breaking par, his opponent cannot bring up that forgotten stroke, as he was guilty of the same sin.

Mick, also, is able to gain an occasional stroke through use of the "double putt." Any putt of three feet or less he deftly backhands in. If he misses, he says, "Guess I'd better putt that one. Thus, he gives himself two chances to make the short putt.

Most golfers who play regularly score somewhere between eighty and one hundred. Tom is a good representative of this class of average golfers. When it comes to cheating, he employs the same methods as Mick, but is also able to make use of a few others. Occasionally Tom will have a disastorous hole. If this hole is any worse than a triple bogey, you can bet that arithmatical error will eliminate at least one stroke.

The best way to distinguish the average golfer from the expert is that the average player rerely plays the ball as it lies. Tom, for example, always plays winter rules (winter rules allow the golfer to give himself a preferred lie by moving the ball with his club-head for a distance of no more than six inches). Tom not only uses these rules in midsummer, but also frequently improves his lie when in the rough. This is something winter rules strictly forbid.

Mike is the member of our foursome who represents the biggest class of golfers — the duffers. For him each round is a frantic struggle to break 100, usually ending in dismal failure. Mike has been playing for over five years, but still has not mastered the fundamentals of the game. However, when it comes to cheating Mike is a pro.

One of his favorite techniches is pencil pushing. This can be employed only by the scorekeeper and Mike is quick to volunteer to undertake this task. The pencil pusher simply reduces his score a stroke or two before marking it on the card. I would estimate Mike plays five to ten strokes better when he is keeping score than when he is not.

Mike is a master of the foot mashie. This shot is used chiefly when the ball is behind a tree or in a bad lie in the rough. It is of special advantage because it is never recorded on the scorecard. The shot consists of a light glancing blow by the side of the foot, which causes the ball to roll a short distance and out of trouble.

When a greater distance is to be covored, Mike finds the "pitch and run" effective. This should not be confused with another shot of the same name often used around the greens. Mike's pitch and run ressembles the foot mashie in that it is never counted on the scorecard. The shot is especially effective when Mike finds himself in deep rough, and none of his playing partners are looking. He simply picks up the ball and, with a flick of the wrist, tosses it ten to twenty years nearer the fairway. This is usually enough to give him a clear shot; if not, a couple foot mashies can be applied.

Cheating in golf is not limited to casual play. In my hometown, the city tournament is played under winter rules. One reporter, covering the tournament, recorded over twenty violations in which a player had given himself a preferred lie while in the rough.

A story I read a couple years ago in "Golf Digest" is the classic example of cheating. It involves two men, Sam and Joe, who were playing a match for the rather high stakes of ten dollars a hole. On the first hole Sam banged a 250 yard drive down the middle of the fairway. Joe sliced his tee shot into the trees and thick rough on the right. Previously, they had agreed to take only ten minutes in hunting for lost balls. At the end of the allotted time, Sam said, "I'll go ahead and play out the hole. If you find your ball before I finish, go ahead and play it. If you don't, you'll have to forfeit the hole." Sam hit his second shot into the middle of the green and was lining up his birdie putt when Joe's ball came plopping down two feet from the pin. Sam missed his putt and lost the hole to Joe's birdie. Completely unnerved, Sam dropped the next three holes. Who could blame him for being upset. After all, he had Joe's ball in his pocket.

The only group of golfers who play the game entirely honestly are the professionals. Of course, these men cannot afford to have their reputations ruined by dishonesty, but it is deeper than that. For these men, golf is a livlihood, and they have great respect for the game. Just as the banker, businessman, or lawyer is honest with his clients; so is the professional golfer with his scorecard. I have heard of several instances in which a professional has accidentally touched his ball, moving it not more than a fraction of an inch. No one saw this, yet the golfer reported it and added an additional stroke.

All this points out a basic facet of human nature. People rarely cheat in things which they regard especially important, such as earning a living; however in relatively minor things dishonesty is rampant.

One can see here the overlaying of one organization upon another. The larger one is based on development. The author moves from good golfers to average ones to duffers; then he shifts from amateur play to tournament to professional contest, the last of which allows him to end with a new version of his generalization — that cheating at golf is a particular case of the broader truth that people cheat at play, not at work. The significance of this order — the fact that shuffling the sequence of topics would make a great difference — is what we mean by "developing an idea."

Within each category of golfer the order of examples is not significant: whether pencil-pushing or foot-mashing comes first makes no difference except for ease of transition between them. Thus the string-of-beads organization is embedded within a meaningful progression. But in many papers it will be dominant, perhaps because the subject truly provides no development, perhaps not. Cross-commentary can help determine which is true.

GENERAL

The assignment stipulation about human behavior is not necessary; people are simply the handiest subject to generalize about. This assignment can certainly be repeated with different subjects since, at bottom, it is precisely the one that is most often given in school and college for practice in exposition and to "cover the reading." My approach is different only in that *it stipulates the conceptual task rather than what the generalization is to be about.* Also, I have tried to distinguish this task from the next, which would build on it. A teacher who would like to use this assignment as a means of getting students to write about the reading could simply ask them to draw all their illustrations from the reading selections in question.

For collateral reading, the teacher should be able to find many essays of this sort. For both reading and writing it is important not to confuse an illustrated generalization with the next and last kind of writing in this sequence.

Combining Generalizations into a Theory

In skeletal form, the main process underlying this culminating assignment can be demonstrated and carried out orally by the class as a whole. Basically, the task is to write a paper conceived like a syllogism.

> Take a generalization from a previous paper and combine it with two or more generalizations from other sources so as to conclude a further statement not evident in the original ones. Illustrate or document the generalizations.

PROCEDURES

Before giving the assignment, several chalk-talk sessions are in order. They consist of this. Ask the class for a generalization about something that interests them, drawn from any source at all. Write it on the chalkboard or projection, then ask the students for one or two more about the same subject and write them down also. Suppose they came up with:

Conforming is an unconscious part of growing up.
Conformity is necessary to society.
Conformity leads to harmful excesses such as intolerance and artificial behavior.

Tell them to pretend for a moment that they all accept these propositions as true. Then write the following additions on the board so that you have this:

If it is true that
    Conforming is an unconscious part of growing up.
And if it is true that
    Conformity is necessary to society.
And if it is true that
    Conformity leads to harmful excesses such as intolerance and artificial behavior.
Then it must also be true that
    (Blank).

Ask them to fill in the blank. What is the fourth statement that they conclude from the first three? Let them propose several possibilities and discuss which seem to follow logically. Write these down too. Are several equally valid conclusions possible? Do they think that such and such a conclusion is a true statement? Narrow down the proposed conclusions to one that some students think is false. Does it follow from the premises? If they think it does not, go to another conclusion that they consider false but admit is logically derived. Why then is it false? In some such fashion, get them to return to the three premises they had pretended to accept earlier. Which one is false and therefore falsifies the conclusion?

During the next session, go through the same procedure with new generalizations, only more quickly, then continue to work backwards and downwards. That is, when an unacceptable premise has been identified, ask those who think it is false to try to qualify and rephrase it. Let others disagree with their changes. What sort of evidence would they need to settle the matter? Do enough of these sessions to make clear the process of syllogizing and its continuity with their previous work in asserting and supporting individual generalizations.

As homework, ask the class to write down and bring to their discussion groups a similar unconcluded syllogism consisting of two or three premises about the same subject. Direct the groups to select one of these sets, amend the premises until they agree on them, and then discuss what conclusions might logically follow. Afterwards, have a spokesman for each group describe what happened during the process and read the premises and conclusions. Some premises will have been too unrelated to each other to conclude anything from, some will have yielded several tenable conclusions, and some will have yielded only one logical possibility.

Now assign Combining Generalizations into a Theory. Direct students to draw as many starting generalizations as possible from their previous writing, reading, and discussion. The purpose of this is to let them continue to build their own thought structures on the foundation of their lower abstractions. Make it clear that syllogizing is to be the heart of the paper but that it does not imply any particular organization.

ISSUES FOR THE WRITING WORKSHOP

The following compositional issues will probably arise for commentary during revision: Should the premises be announced all at once in the beginning or fed in at intervals? Should or can they be documented simultaneously? Each in turn? In what order should they be taken up? Is the order indifferent, or can one generalization be developed in some way from another? Do some premises need more documenting than others? Should the conclusion(s) be suspended until the end for climactic effect or posted at the outset to make the thread of argument easier to follow? Of course, a very complex paper might contain subsidiary syllogisms and thus two or three secondary conclusions in addition to the main one.

Project for classroom discussion at least one legible first draft or paper by a former student. Read it aloud as the class follows visually, and stop for comment en route. When the audience feels that something is unclear, help them to determine whether the difficulty is in *the syllogistic drawing of conclusions, the statement of single generalizations,* or, farther down still, *the concepts contained in a generalization* (definition of a word, for example; but often the premises are themselves definitions).

Both these logical problems and the compositional problems described above should be touched on enough in class discussion to enable students at least to identify them when they encounter them in the writing workshop groups. *As usual, this raising of issues is achieved by asking the class to propose solutions for the difficulties they encounter as reader, restating their diagnosis for them when necessary.*

SAMPLE

A STUDY OF CONFORMITY

It is often assumed that people consciously conform. This is seldom true. Conformity is either a process of maturing, or a subconscious development. In either case, it is the essence of society.

Conformity as a process of growing up occurs generally at an early age. For a small child it is natural to try to emulate grown-ups. The child attempts to speak as they speak, walk as they walk, and act as they act. Children often pretend to be grown-ups because of the natural desire to conform to the adult world.

This force decreases as age increases. It disappears simultaneously with the "loss of innocence." When a child, or even a teen-ager is exposed to derision or disillusion, his dream world crumbles. This, however, is often a gradual process. The natural instinct to conform, therefore, gradually fades away as the child becomes more and more exposed to the world.

It is very hard to say when loss of innocence occurs. Certainly, vestiges of it carry on well into the teens in many people. This may seem incredible, but it is true. The average senior high school American History textbook is still concerned with Alvin York single-handedly winning World War I and George Washington chopping down the cherry tree. The United States is always moral, always right. This unreality shows the extent that even high school seniors are protected from unpleasant truths.

When the illusionary world of innocence is destroyed, a replacement must be made. These replacements come in many different forms. Charlie Gray in *Point of No Return* finds himself in an artificial world of conformity. He dresses like everyone else, works in a bank like everyone else, rides the right train and belongs to the right country club. Many will say that Charlie must conform in order to keep his job. This is not entirely the case. Conformity is a replacement for his lost naivete, a means of keeping himself from falling apart. Only by conforming to his artificial world can he tolerate it.

Conformity at Exeter is obvious. The greatest objection to it, however, is the form it takes. To adults, the sight of a bored, lazy, apathetic boy is repelling. To them it seems a waste of what should be a happy, exciting time of life.

What these adults fail to understand is why the "innocent scared little prep" becomes a nego. The answer is glaring. If a prep comes to Exeter scared and innocent, his situation is soon exploited by his fellow students. He is baited beyond his ability to tolerate abuse. His self-respect and innocent values are destroyed. To attain any sort of security, these values must be replaced.

At Exeter there is only one possible replacement — negoism. To protect himself from being baited a boy must assume an air of indifference. If he shows that he is hurt, the smell of blood will make the sharks all the more vicious. But this is not enough. To prevent being baited a boy also has to destroy his individuality.

Superficially, most Exonians are the same. Their dress, general vocabulary and actions are almost identical. Even their values are the same. High school is great, Exeter is bad, parents and faculty are not reasonable or human, the Dean is a sadist, sports cars and liquor are good, and finally the purpose of life is the fulfillment of animal desires.

This behavior is condemned by the adult world. To them, conformity to the extent of loss of individuality is wrong. The paradox of the situation is never observed. It is the adults who have to belong to the right country club.

There is a rule in chemistry called Le Chatelier's principle. In essence it states that when a stress is applied to a system in equilibrium, the system must adjust to counteract the stress. This is also very applicable in explaining human behaviour. The world of the innocent is a system in equilibrium. When an outside force upsets the system, it is the system itself that must change. Whether or not the system changes to life in a grey-flannel suit or negoism is immaterial.

This argument should not be taken to mean that a person willfully and consciously conforms. That is ridiculous. No person can be objective enough in examining himself to be able to state exactly what steps he should take in order to become more popular, or less vulnerable to baiting. Similarly, nobody can control his actions sufficiently to truly fit the image he has set for himself.

Instead, conformity is a sub-conscious attempt to gain security. It is an adjustment to the demands of society. For most people, it is a natural reaction. Because of this, there are very few non-conformists in the world.

Due to the variance in the extent of the stress on different people, conformity comes in varying degrees. In cases of great stress, there exists a case of over-conformity. Over-conformity is a concept, not a scientifically defined segment of behavior. The symptoms of over-conformity are easily detectable. Artificiality of emotion, behavior and speech are the most apparent signs of the disease. Others such as inability to think independently are also prevalent.

It is customary for many writers and thinkers to repudiate over-conformity. *Point of No Return* is such a repudiation. Many of Sinclair Lewis' works reflect this too. In fact, the whole expatriate culture of the 1920's was a protest against the over-conformity of American society.

Over-conformity is not attacked for the sake of attacking it. It is the result of over-conformity which is repelling. At Exeter the natural tendency is for a student to write a "nego"-style theme. This is not because the student really wants to write about Exeter negoism — most students try to avoid it. The intellectual sterility of the Exeter climate is so great, however, that this form of expression completely dominates the style of student writing.

Conformity is an inevitable product of society. To oppose it is to defy the universe. This does not mean, however, that conformity can not be controlled. Indeed, it is vital to the interests of society that conformity be restrained.

The danger of conformity is intolerance, as intolerance leads to a stagnant society. For society to be fruitful, intolerance must be suppressed. Conformity must be allowed only as long as it is tolerant. Unfortunately, this distinction is very difficult to make.

In the past, conformity has followed a cycle. A mode of behavior and expression is accepted, and gradually becomes the model for a society, to the exclusion of all others. The society soon ceases to become intellectually productive. A small group of individuals will revolt, but for a long time society does not tolerate them. Eventually, tolerance does increase until the new order replaces the old. This order, in turn, wears out to be replaced by another.

This cycle explains the various literary, musical and artistic movements of Western Civilization. To us, looking back, the cycle seems the best way of keeping our culture fresh. This does not mean, however, that society recognizes that the cycle is necessary in the future for the continuation of our civilization.

Many people dislike "modern art," "modern music," or "modern writing." They can not understand how it can be meaningful expression. They support the changes of the past, recognizing them as a vital part of our heritage. Furthermore, they know that at the beginning many of these movements were not tolerated. But at the same time, they oppose any future change. Intolerance is typical of society.

I predict that within twenty years, the styles of expression that are beginning to be accepted now will become a materialized movement, very possibly past its prime. It, in return, will be gradually replaced. The present movement, like all others, will appear well-defined with recognized advantages and disadvantages. When it is worn out, the advantages growing thin and the disadvantages becoming more evident, a new movement will be started as a reaction to the accepted style. When this happens, there again will be people who want to freeze progress.

Conformity is a paradox in itself. It is recognized as inevitable, yet it is never accepted. It is based on intolerance, and at the same time its very intolerance is both criticized and praised. It is a function of the complexity of society — the more complex the society the greater the demands of conformity.

Without conformity our civilization would have no foundation. Yet without non-conformity we would still be in the stone ages. Perhaps our complex, contradictory system of conformity is the only workable form of progressive civilization.[7]

The three generalizations about conformity that I presented earlier as chalkboard examples were, of course, drawn from this paper, and the reader can see for himself which conclusion the boy drew and where he placed it in relation to the premises. Cross-commentary would probably have helped him to improve the continuity in some places and also the balance among illustrations.

The frame of the paper is syllogistic, multi-propositional, but this boy quite spontaneously embeds within this frame several orders of discourse of lower abstraction levels, through which he has already worked in previous papers. That is, after announcing two of his premises in the first paragraph, he narrows down to one in the second paragraph and for a long sequence of following paragraphs proceeds to substantiate and develop that generalization exactly as if he were doing the preceding paper in this sequence, paragraphs three and four dealing with sub-statements about conformity as a process of growing up, and the other paragraphs in the sequence dipping down nearly to the narrative level for the instance of Charlie Gray, and then back up slightly for the more generalized (and digressive) example of Exeter behavior. Then he surfaces later for his third premise — that conformity is dangerous — without signalling it very well, and launches into another documented generalization that lasts nearly to the end and contains the digressive example of art vogues. The second premise — that conformity is the essence of society — is treated in undocumented and scattered fashion, reappearing in connection with the conclusion. This paper did not receive the benefit of any commentary before the second draft (except perhaps from a roommate).

Analyzing by abstraction levels can help the teacher to help the student know what he is doing imperfectly. I would not gratuitously explain levels of abstraction to a class and then expect students to apply the explanation to their writing, but in the class discussion of a paper, I would use the concept as a guide for tracking the author's half-emerged organization, so that later cross-commentary would be better informed. Whether the teacher ever speaks of "abstraction" or not makes little difference so long as he can diagnose for himself. Then he can comment or query during discussion in any way he thinks will help the students to learn.

---

[7] One of Exeter's main contributions to the intellectual growth of its students is in permitting them to write about its "intellectual sterility."

Chapter 30

Invention

I have placed this chapter at the end to counterbalance the previous emphasis on reality-based discourse. The purpose of climbing the abstraction ladder is not to reach the top; it is to know all the rungs. Creating fictions — inventing — is more deeply expressive than exposition and no less abstractive for being symbolic; only the mode is different. All verbalization is reality-based, in one sense or another. If I call the source of inventions "imagination," that is only to say that their derivation from reality is too indirect and unconscious to know. Lying like the truth, to use Daniel Defoe's phrase, must not be deemed frivolous merely because its importance is personal and playful rather than utilitarian. For many older adolescents, even especially if they are terminal students, invention may educate more fruitfully than anything else. This chapter, then, broadly encompasses forms of make-believe, whether acted or written, whether written as poems, plays, or stories.

Improvisation

The older students become, the harder it is to introduce them to dramatic work. It is very important to do so, however. If students of these grades have had no experience with it, their teachers will need to give them an abbreviated version of the drama program as described in earlier chapters of this book. So little effort has been made to begin drama at this age that I find it impossible to specify much beyond what was said there. A great deal of experimentation is needed for these grades. Unison pantomime, unison acting as the teacher slowly narrates an action, small-group charades, crowd scenes with different roles, rehearsed readings of short scripts in small groups, and the acting of memorized scenes are all appropriate, but the intention of experiments should be to determine how soon *improvisation* can be profitably and comfortably undertaken, for besides having great intrinsic value, it holds the key to dramatic writing and to performance of scripts. Newcomers of any age will probably need to develop their acting powers within the safety of small, unwitnessed groups. The full-class workshop should follow in time, when the teacher feels that improvisation before an audience does not spoil involvement of the actors. My caution on this score may be excessive, at least for students of uninhibited temperament. Carolyn Fitchett, who has done drama work with Upward Bound students in a number of Southern cities, reports that improvisations have gone extremely well as a full-class activity, once the students have become acquainted with each other.

For students who have followed a dramatic program and become veteran improvisors, I recommend the following activity, which represents the freest stage of spontaneous invention. One form of it is simply to play from a minimal situation stated in the barest possible way: "Tom wants the chair here and *Susan* wants it over *there*," which is a situation I was once given in an acting class. The understanding is that whatever setting, circumstances, and identities the actors establish for themselves as they go along must be maintained from then on. (My partner and I became interior decorators who disagreed over the arrangement of a client's room.) The audience notes what ploys they use to get their way and discusses these afterwards. If the actors become physically deadlocked over the chair, or otherwise run out of invention, give another pair the floor for a while. Ask the class for other situations. Shift to trios sometimes.

The other form of spontaneous invention is rhetorical practice at its most elemental. Send one actor out of the room and give a brief direction to the other that the rest of the class can also hear. The direction simply stipulates the effect *A* is to produce on *B*, by any means he can: "Make her laugh;" "Make him sad (or unfriendly);" "Startle (or cheer) him." *B* simply reacts spontaneously. The means of getting the effect may be many — making up anecdotes, asking questions, flattering, launching into commentary, drawing the other into an exchange about a certain topic, and, of course, physical maneuvers. In the ensuing discussion, students can talk about which kinds of things actors did or did not do that worked or did not work.

This sort of very free improvisation develops fluent invention that will help many activities — writing, conversing, acting out scripts, and perhaps even reading. It is a high point of creative expression.

Again, as a sourcebook of ideas for improvisation I recommend Viola Spolin's *Improvisation for the Theater* (Evanston, Illinois: Northwestern University Press, 1963).

Treating Certain Literature as Scripts

For newcomers to the program, I suggest that the sequence set forth in Dramatic Dialogue (Chapter 20) be started as early as possible in high school. Since the sequence begins with short scenes modeled on improvisations, the latter constitute the base. Assign to newcomers the writing of two- and three-person dialogues, dramatic and interior monologues, and one-act plays. For old-timers, these may be options, as discussed later.

A lot of good dramatic literature now becomes appropriate for students of these years. My general proposal is to treat any piece of literature consisting of character voice as a potential script for acting, whether the piece is called a play, poem, or short story. This approach makes possible, I believe, a much more vivid and meaningful treatment of many reading selections. This is not to say that students never read such selections silently alone, only that their silent reading should benefit from the emphasis that dramatic treatment places on speaker, voice, and circumstances of utterance, and from the discrimination it creates between invented persona and real-life authors.

Dramatic treatment consists of this. Divide the class into small groups, direct them to discuss how the "script" should be enacted, and then let them rehearse and perform it as a reading within the groups and occasionally before the class. Sometimes a short script might be memorized. Different renditions are compared and discussed, during which a professional recording might be played for further comparison. Details of the procedure depend on the script. It would be most helpful to have departmental sets of poem, play, and short story anthologies — one set of each anthology large enough for a class — from which selections can be chosen and which teachers can sign for on a day-to-day basis.

DIALOGUE POEMS AND STORIES

Suppose the script is a duologue poem — one of the ballads, a light exchange like "For Anne Gregory" (Yeats), a one-sided conversation like "La Belle Dame Sans Merci" (Keats) or "The Witch of Coös" (Frost). Since dialogue poems usually contain little physical action (and have no stage directions), the encumbrance of the script is not a great handicap and thus a rehearsed reading is relatively convenient. Each group comprises four students. The purpose of grouping is to allow concentrated discussion before and after the readings, and to give everyone a chance to read. When first given a poem, students read it through silently, then discuss whatever things they need to know to give a comprehensible and expressive dramatic reading: who the speakers are, where they are, why they are talking together, the character of each, the dynamics of the exchange, the punctuation, the feeling behind line X, what line Y means, or what a certain word refers to. In other words, comprehension and interpretation are practically entailed in the preparation for performance. Members of a group do not have to agree; they may pair off according to how compatible their renditions would be. If the poem is short and rather obvious, it may be discussed, rehearsed, and performed during one class period. Other poems will require a couple of periods. After rehearsing in pairs, one before the other, two or three readings can be given before the re-assembled class.

Determining the voicing. Since part of the value of preparation discussion of poems is to *determine* the number of voices, the size of groups should not give this away. Make four a constant number in most cases, or if you change it sometimes, do not give the impression that the number of actors per group equals the number of voices in the poem. Some of the best discussions of poetry my students have had concerned whether "Naming of Parts" (Henry Reed) was uttered by one or two characters. My own understanding of it is that the first two thirds of each stanza is spoken aloud by the army instructor to his trainees, and that the last one third of each is the inner voice of a trainee ironically echoing the instructor while at the same time drifting away to more appealing things than rifle parts. Some students made a good case for both voices issuing from the instructor — one being official and the other private. Though the shifts in speaking style do not support their case very well, the alternating of interior and dramatic monologue is sometimes used, as in Dorothy Parker's short story "The Waltz," to convey just such a discrepancy between what one really feels and how one has to behave outwardly. The story could be acted with three people — a woman dancing with a man while her other self curses his clumsiness.

When one person utters himself in two different voices, two roles are called for, so that both interpretations of the Reed poem produce essentially the same dramatic result. All the students agreed that the stanzas split into two voices, even though the voices are unmarked in any way by typography; tone, language, and attitude all shift. But the last stanza breaks the pattern and causes disagreement about whether it is all interior monologue or a fusion of both voices. Discussion of the stanza is required in order to decide which actor will read it. It happens that both Henry Reed and Dylan Thomas have recorded the poem, in very different ways. After dramatizing the poem themselves, my students listened very intently to hear how these poets indicated the shifts of voice they had discussed (and also to find support for their interpretation). A companion poem by Reed, "Judging Distances," consists also of two alternating voices, but in this case both are clearly uttered aloud by different people — instructor and trainee again — though still unsignalled by quotation marks or spacing.

Joining socratic and dramatic dialogue. On page 458 I mentioned three duologue poems that fuse dramatic exchange with the dialectic of ideas. Coupling socratic and dramatic dialogue makes a point of contact between ratiocination and invention that is worth the effort of coordinating the two. That is, while writing both kinds of dialogue in prose, students can be reading dialogue poems having both emphases. The thoughtfulness required for performing "Ulysses and the Sirens," for example, will generate better under-standing of its ideas than will a purely intellectual discussion following a silent reading.

Short stories. Some short stories are virtually all dialogue: "Petrified Man" (Eudorah Welty), "Zone of Quiet" (Ring Lardner), and "How Do You Like It Here?" (O'Hara). Stories containing no thoughts or commentary, only description and narration, come close to being scenarios anyway. When stu-dents discuss one of these, for a rehearsed reading, tell them to consider whether there will be a loss in transfer, and, if they think so, to appoint one person as narrator. He can read only those parts of the narrator's lines that are not really the equivalent of stage direction. (See also Chamber Theatre on page 490.)

DRAMATIC MONOLOGUE POEMS AND STORIES

Poetry is rich in dramatic and interior monologue. Both of these shade off into other kinds of poems having a disembodied, unsituated speaker who is more the author himself than an invented persona. Students who have role-played the speaker in dramatic poems can more readily pick up the tone, style, attitude, and posture of a poet speaking distinctly in his own voice. Much of the reason for acting out poems with characters is to become at-tuned to what is often called today the "speaking voice" in a text. When you read with an ear to performance, you try to take on the tone, style, attitude, and posture. Pre- and post-performance discussions correct "misreading," in all senses of the word. Then, when reading disembodied voices alone, one can "hear" them accurately in the mind.

Memorization. When a poem is not very long, it is best to memorize it as a script for performance. Memorizing poetry is an old-fashioned practice that has now fallen into disrepute because it was so often unmotivated and arbi-trary. The only justification (besides being able to pass a test on the lines) was that the lines were famous, and every well-bred person should know them. In the worst light, the purpose was only a kind of name dropping, but the fact is that memorizing has another, very profound value. As poet Richard Wilbur put the matter, in a poetry course I once took in which he required memorization, one takes the poem to heart, one makes it a part of oneself, absorbs the sounds and rhythms and images, warms to the language, becomes enthralled by the incantation. Every professional actor has had the experience, in learning a role, of discovering more and more beauty and meaning in his lines, if they were good, and of eventually falling in love with them. A couple of such experiences can permanently influence a young per-son's feeling about poetry and language power. When memorization is for performance, the negative aspects of the old-fashioned practice are eliminated.

The student has a real purpose and motive. He does not simply rattle off lines in rote fashion; he interprets and expresses them. Connections between words and actions, furthermore, create cues that make memorizing easier.

Example of "My Last Duchess." Assign duologue and monologue poems in mixture, so that groups have to determine the voicing (but only after they have improvised and written monologues). Non-speaking roles are always pantomimed. Browning's interior and exterior monologues represent the most dramatic: speaker, listener, and time and place of utterance are all specifically indicated. Let's take an exterior monologue first, "My Last Duchess," a chestnut that even very bright eleventh-grade Exeter students have seldom fully understood when it was simply read aloud and discussed in class. After silent reading, the group straightens out together the facts of the action, the meanings of lines, and the characterizations. (In general, editions of poems should be used that give glosses on difficult words and allusions; in addition, a big dictionary and one or two other reference books, for mythological and biblical allusions, should be available to consult in the classroom.) An actor delivers the lines of the duke, drawing aside the alcove curtain, gesturing to the portrait, etc., while another plays the emissary, reacting in revulsion to what he hears until finally he starts prematurely down the stairs, an action that prompts the duke to utter a line that few students seem to understand outside a dramatic context, "Nay, we'll go together down, sir," (*together* being stressed, of course). Later, some of Browning's longer dramatic monologues, such as "Andrea del Sarto" and "Fra Lippo Lippi," might be assigned for silent reading.

Reacting. Dramatic monologue provides a fine occasion for learning to react. Stress the fact that the silent partner, in responding, stays with every line as much as if he were speaking. Partners reverse roles so that they play both sides of the duo. The other pair in their group watches them, comments, and takes its turn both ways. In this manner, both the understanding and expression of the lines gradually evolve. While moving among the groups the teacher can ask and answer questions that will help this development.

Casting by sex. Roles do not have to be played by members of the appropriate sex (most roles are male), but sometimes matching the sex of the actor to that of the role is a good idea. For "The Flea" (John Donne), for example, let the boys court the girls. Like many a monologue poem in which the poet addresses his mistress, it is a love argument, but an especially dramatic one because each stanza is a reaction to something the beloved does while he is talking. "Why So Pale and Wan" (John Suckling) is also a monologue prompted by ongoing action. Many love poems spoken by the lover to his lady do not indicate ongoing action and have only a vague setting, but nevertheless are spoken *now* to the particular audience of one. Donne's "Break of

Day" and "The Good Morrow" have this sense of immediacy, and Arnold's "Dover Beach" has, for all the lover's meditation, a strong setting and feeling for the present ("The sea is calm tonight . . . ," "Let us be true to one another . . ."). Consider next Marvell's "To His Coy Mistress."

Kinds of literary monologuists. Some character monologues are uttered by types — Suckling's "A Ballad upon a Wedding" (country bumpkin), Hardy's "The Man He Killed" (Wessex commoner), and Kipling's "Sestina of the Troop-Royal" (professional soldier). All three of these are in dialect. If a poem does not indicate the exact setting or the particular listener, students should imagine a fitting place and audience — and also the motive for the monologue. Thomas Wolfe's short story, "Only the Dead Know Brooklyn," would go well with these poems. Other monologuists are well known personages from history and mythology. Christ utters "The Carpenter's Son" (A. E. Housman); Simon of Zilotes, "The Ballad of the Goodly Fere" (Ezra Pound); and one of the three wise men, "The Journey of the Magi" (T. S. Eliot). Because they are centered on Christ, these three poems are interesting to take up together. Thus, as with the love-argument poems, the selection by technique coincides sometimes with a similarity of content. Tennyson's "Ulysses" is especially interesting because a student can make a good case for its being either exterior or interior monologue. Is Ulysses addressing his retinue in actuality or in his mind?

Short stories. "Haircut" (Ring Lardner), "The Apostate" (George Milburn), "Straight Pool" and "Salute a Thoroughbred" (John O'Hara), "The Lady's Maid" (Katherine Mansfield) and "Travel Is So Broadening" (Sinclair Lewis) are short stories written as pure dramatic monologue, i.e., having a specific audience and setting and often containing ongoing action. Such stories shade into others like "Why I Live at the P.O." (Eudorah Welty) in which a relatively disembodied character addresses the world at large in an amateurish way, almost certainly giving a naive, unreliable, or prejudiced version of the events.

Comedy monologues. Comedians such as Bob Newhart and Bob Cosby have created and recorded dramatic monologues that most students would enjoy hearing. Cosby of course would appeal especially to Negro students. These recordings might afford a good introduction to the reading of monologue literature.

INTERIOR MONOLOGUE POEMS AND STORIES

For interior monologues, let girls do "Patterns" (Amy Lowell) and Browning's "The Laboratory" while boys do the latter's "Soliloquy of a Spanish Cloister." Short stories such as "Late at Night" (Katherine Mansfield) and

"But the One on the Right" (Dorothy Parker) also have female speakers. "Laboratory" and the Parker story require non-speaking males. Either sex could do most of the more meditative interior monologues such as "Ode to a Nightingale." Time the writing and reading of reflections so that some coincidence of them can be achieved with interior monologues, which can shade off into philosophical poetry by disembodied authors. O'Neill's *Emperor Jones* should also be brought in at this point. After an opening duologue, it becomes soliloquy, addressed to dumb phantoms that actually appear to the audience. If done by the whole class as a rehearsed reading, the role of Emperor Jones could be rotated while other students pantomime the figures from his past, the "little formless fears," and so on. T. S. Eliot's "Gerontion" and "The Love Song of J. Alfred Prufrock" are possible poems for very mature students.

The fact that dramatizing poems takes longer than reading them silently can be offset by letting different groups perform different poems before each other. Thus, instead of asking all students to read all the poems, each student would act out some and be spectator to others. Actors can explain allusions and other things they have learned to the audience. Two or three versions of each poem are presented to the whole class. During one of these the audience can follow the text. Then everyone compares versions in discussion. Presenting classmates a script they don't know adds more purpose to performance.

Procedures for Plays

THE COMPONENTS OF PLAYS

In the literature of the theater proper, one rarely finds a whole play uttered by one character. O'Neill's "Hughie" and Strindberg's "The Stronger" are sustained dramatic monologues. The latter is the gem of the genre but suitable only for very mature students.[1] But many plays of course contain both exterior and interior monologues, which are often set pieces like the sergeant's report at the beginning of *Macbeth,* or the disguised Orestes' account of his own death, or the great soliloquies from both Elizabethan and Greek tragedy. Many of the latter are reflective poems situated in a drama.

Since class reading and performing of long plays requires assigning different portions to different groups or individuals, such plays may as well be divided into duologues, dramatic monologues, soliloquies, and group colloquies when doing so does not break dramatic momentum. In older theater it is the entering and leaving of characters, in fact, that defines most of the scenes anyway. Greek tragedy, for example, lends itself very well to this division: the succession of episodes and interludes usually consists of rather

---

[1] For some good monologue, duologue, and triologue plays, see *Reading and Staging the Play, An Anthology of One-Act Plays,* Gassner and Little, (New York: Holt, Rinehart and Winston, Inc., 1967).

clearly separated duologue confrontations, dramatic monologues, soliloquies, choral odes, and group dialogues. The acting groups deal with these excerpts in the manner described for complete short scripts — poems, one-scene plays, and short stories. Finally, let's not forget that student writing itself will supply many short scripts of interior and dramatic monologue and of duologue.

WHOLE PLAYS

In general, plays can be handled several ways, depending on the time the teacher wants to spend on certain ones, and on their difficulty, length, and number of roles. Several easy one-acts with two or three roles, like Saroyan's "Hello Out There," may be performed successively before the class by different groups in lieu of assigning all the plays to all students. Student acting may be followed up by playing of a recording and then discussing the professional version. Sometimes the class can listen to an entire recorded play while reading the text for the first time. This helps increase sensitivity to voice range and expression, accustoms students to unfamiliar dialects and accents, and makes comprehensible some poetic drama that would be hard to understand on the page. These receptive experiences not only replenish students but let them hear print brought expertly to life. Voices leap from the page, rendering everything from punctuation to nuances of timing and intonation.

For a long and difficult play that all of the class is to be involved in, a combination may sometimes be best. Anticipatory improvisations are done of certain key scenes abstracted in advance; other scenes are assigned for rehearsal; then, during a succession of class periods, the whole play is presented consecutively, some parts read, some acted without a script, some presented through a recording. Once the students are able to bring a script alive on their own, individual silent reading is also possible. Give the class a list of plays they might enjoy and let each student read two or three he is not familiar with. The purpose is to select several for group productions. In other words, students sift scripts for candidates. They discuss nominations in groups, describing the plays to each other and giving reasons for their selection. The plays chosen are then cast for rehearsed reading to be presented before the whole class.

A SEQUENCE OF PLAYS

Somewhere in the later years, a special reading sequence has value, I think, for implicitly demonstrating some psychological and dramaturgical relationships that can illuminate both real life and the theater. The sequence moves, somewhat imperfectly, from single voice to a complex of voices, and from a single time and place to a complex of times and places. Many other things depend on these apparently simple shifts in number of persons and time-space coverage, things that a spectrum brings out. But the previous order in which students wrote duologue, dramatic monologue, and interior monologue is reversed for the sake of presenting an evolutionary spectacle that I will try to evoke rather than explain.

The selections below were ones I used for the sequence in eleventh-grade classes at Exeter. I'm quite aware that the content of some of them would be too strong except in more enlightened communities or in college. The list is illustrative only; for different school populations the sequence must be translated into other titles. Actually, dramatic poems could be substituted for some of the earlier items. The list is somewhat overlapping and could therefore be shortened if necessary.

EMPEROR JONES, Eugene O'Neill. (A duologue that quickly becomes an extended soliloquy in which imagined creatures people the stage.)

THE STRONGER, August Strindberg. (A monologue spoken to a listener who reacts wordlessly.)

HELLO, OUT THERE, William Saroyan. (Begins as solo that becomes a long duet that returns to solo. Man-and-girl duologue.)

THE ZOO STORY, Edward Albee. (A duologue between two men that lapses for long stretches into monologue.)

MISS JULIE, August Strindberg. (A triangle of one man and two women, but only two are together at a time. Essentially duologue of man and woman who lapse often into monologue. Dance interlude but duration is unbroken.)

NO EXIT, Jean-Paul Sartre. (A full-blown triangle of man and two women. Often duologue but always influenced by presence of third party. Still a single, continuous scene.)

ELECTRA, Sophocles. (Mother-son-daughter story but actually consists of serial duologues between Electra and five others; occasional triologue; ranges from stichomythia (rapid alternation of short lines) to soliloquy and narrative monologue.)

CANDIDA, Bernard Shaw. (Husband-wife-youth triangle but includes minor characters; spans a whole day; two settings.)

THE GLASS MENAGERIE, Tennessee Williams. (A mother-son-daughter triad broken up by catalyst of fourth character; one setting but covers weeks or months; whole play is a memory soliloquy by the narrator, resembling *Emperor Jones*.)

THE MASTER BUILDER, Henrik Ibsen. (Husband-wife-girl triangle, but this group interlocks via main character with another trio; several scenes but covers short period of time.)

CYRANO DE BERGERAC, Edmond Rostand. (Complex of soliloquies, duologues, and group dialogues; covers months, then or   years.)
MACBETH, Shakespeare.

A student who reads his way through such a sequence is tracing the development of dramaturgy, not historically, but structurally and psychologically. Structurally because the earlier plays, while complete in themselves, feature solely and then in combination the components of which the later plays are made. Psychologically because a sequence based on the changing interplay of voices can array the different dynamics of human interactions that occur as the number, sex, and kind of relationship change. Reading plays in some such order as this increases the student's awareness, I believe, of the fundamental kinds of discourse and psychological relations that make up what we call a play. Thus certain plays read earlier prepare for certain other plays read later, thereby obviating considerable analysis and explanation.

The principle of such an order is more important than the exact order itself. Form and dynamics are timeless and provide an entrée into plays of another era that might seem too remote to a present-day reader. Whereas a purely content approach may make it very difficult for a young person to relate to his own world the goings-on in Shakespeare or Ibsen, he can readily translate from their duets or triangles to those he is familiar with. I have often asked students to represent character interactions on the board with arrows or other graphic symbols. They always found this a reasonable request. There is something structural about both human emotions and human interactions. That is, you can replace the content of a feeling or the content of an exchange with another and something will still remain the same — something like the pitch, vibration, or intensity of the feeling (whether it is love or hate, fear or elation) and, in interaction, something like the pattern of energy, the lines of force. We ride the momentum of a particular dynamic until another dynamic cuts across it. Once one is tuned into varieties of pitch and pace and lines of force, one is on to drama, because it is the intensities and vectors of energy that carry a play, and this affects the participants and the observers more than what the drama is about.

The very arrangement of such a sequence constitutes commentary enough by the teacher; let the students take matters from there. The purpose of it is to influence the way they think and talk about the plays and the people. If a play is assigned for performance, discussion occurs secondarily during preparation; if it is assigned for silent reading, discussion occurs in the reading groups.

Fiction

A READING SEQUENCE FROM "POINTS OF VIEW"

I recommend a somewhat similar reading sequence in fiction designed to pull together narrative technique for older students who have already written and read most of the kinds of narrative described previously in this book. With Kenneth McElheny I have put together a collection, *Points of View: An Anthology of Short Stories,*[2] that embodies this sequence. I reproduce here the Table of Contents of that book, since it contains both the divisions according to which the stories are sequenced and also the titles that exemplify each division.

INTERIOR MONOLOGUE
"But the One on the Right" — Dorothy Parker
"This Is My Living Room" — Tom McAfee

DRAMATIC MONOLOGUE
"The Lady's Maid" — Katherine Mansfield
"Travel Is So Broadening" — Sinclair Lewis

LETTER NARRATION
"A Novel in Nine Letters" — Fyodor Dostoievsky
"Jupiter Doke, Brigadier General" — Ambrose Bierce
"A Bundle of Letters" — Henry James

DIARY NARRATION
"Flowers for Algernon" — Daniel Keyes
"The Diary of a Madman" — Nikolai Gogol

SUBJECTIVE NARRATION
"My Side of the Matter" — Truman Capote
"Too Early Spring" — Stephen Vincent Benet
"My Sister's Marriage" — Cynthia Rich
"On Saturday Afternoon" — Alan Sillitoe
"A and P" — John Updike

DETACHED AUTOBIOGRAPHY
"First Confession" — Frank O'Connor
"Warm River" — Erskine Caldwell
"The Use of Force" — William Carlos Williams
"Bad Characters" — Jean Stafford

MEMOIR, OR OBSERVER NARRATION
"The Fall of the House of Usher" — E. A. Poe
"Mademoiselle Pearl" — Guy de Maupassant
"The Tryst" — Ivan Turgenev
"Johnny Bear" — John Steinbeck

[2] A Signet Classic (New York: New American Library, 1966).

BIOGRAPHY, OR ANONYMOUS NARRATION — Single Character Point of
  View
  "Patricia, Edith, and Arnold" — Dylan Thomas
  "Horses — One Dash" — Stephen Crane
  "The Prison" — Bernard Malamud
  "The Stone Boy" — Gina Berriault
  "Enemies" — Anton Chekhov
  "Act of Faith" — Irwin Shaw
  "The Five Forty-Eight" — John Cheever
  "A Father-to-Be" — Saul Bellow

ANONYMOUS NARRATION — Dual Character Point of View
  "Maria Concepcion" — K. A. Porter
  "Unlighted Lamps" — Sherwood Anderson
  "The Shadow in the Rose Garden" — D. H. Lawrence

ANONYMOUS NARRATION — Multiple Character Point of View
  "The Boarding House" — James Joyce
  "The Idiots" — Joseph Conrad
  "Fever Flower" — Shirley Ann Gran
  "The Suicides of Private Greaves" — James Moffett

ANONYMOUS NARRATION — No Character Point of View
  "Powerhouse" — Eudora Welty
  "The Iliad of Sandy Bar" — Bret Barte
  "The Minister's Black Veil" — Nathaniel Hawthorne
  "The Lottery" — Shirley Jackson

The forty-one stories brought together in this anthology offer examples of
all narrative techniques used in fiction and discussed up to here. The purpose of the arrangement is, again, to present a spectrum of gradually shifting
relationships that exerts, I believe, a strong suggestive force on students as
they read the selections.

Since both *Points of View* and "Narrative: What Happened"[3] explain the
theory behind this narrative sequence, I will limit myself here to a brief
synopsis. So-called narrative techniques — the whole range of first- and
third-person story telling — are relationships between a narrator and his
subject and his audience, and can be arranged like a spectrum in such a way
that each locates itself somewhere on a continuum made up of several parallel
progressions: from focus on the *I* to focus on the *he;* from the here-and-now
to the there-and-then; from inner verbalization to public composition; from
lower to higher abstraction. In general, an expansion occurs in the course of
the sequence that moves from the center of the self outward, in just about
every conceivable sense. Plot, character, setting, and theme are, in part,
factors of these relationships between speaker, listener, and subject. In addition, the relationships define kinds of actual discourse on which fictions are

3 *Teaching the Universe of Discourse.*

modeled. The spectrum, then, is about both art and life. The sequence stops at the limit of fiction but it continues actually in other parts of the curriculum — in secondhand reportage and research. (See also "Kinds and Orders of Discourse.")[4]

Neither the play nor the fiction sequence is intended to detract in the slightest from the *subject matter* of literary works, which I would expect always to remain the students' main concern. But in works of art, the intuition of form often unlocks most quickly and directly the meaning of the content.

Chamber Theatre

DEFINITION

Quite coincidentally, it happens that the distinctions made in the spectrum just described are the same underlying a very ingenious process called Chamber Theatre, originated by Robert S. Breen of Northwestern University and further developed by Carolyn Fitchett of the Educational Development Corporation. I recommend the method enthusiastically. It is a dramatic approach to fiction that fits this curriculum remarkably well and should prove especially effective with disadvantaged students. Miss Fitchett reports considerable success in using Chamber Theatre with Upward Bound programs in several Southern cities, where she has trained teachers to work with it in conjunction with improvisations. Interested teachers should read "An English Unit: Chamber Theatre Technique,"[5] which contains details and illustrations of the method that are necessary for understanding how to use it. I will merely give the gist of it here, after quoting Miss Fitchett's introduction:

> Chamber Theatre is a technique for dramatizing point of view in narrative fiction. Its use in the classroom is aimed at helping students to become more aware of the controlling intelligence and the dynamic relationship between him and the characters in a short story or novel. The narrator is encouraged to talk to the audience in a voice from the characters' world and take the audience into that world. He invites them to see for themselves. He also has the freedom to move in time and space. The students are encouraged to study the story or novel for the unique or individual perspective presented.
>
> The observation of brief passages staged in the classroom helps the student to hear, feel, and see more clearly than he would ordinarily through reading silently — to examine human motivations (the actions of the mind) as well as physical motions (the actions of the body). In addition, the process of

---

[4] *Ibid.*

[5] Carolyn Fitchett, a pamphlet copyrighted in 1966 by the Curriculum Resources Group, a division of the Educational Development Corporation, obtainable by sending 75c to the Educational Development Corporation, 55 Chapel Street, Newton, Massachusetts.

working out passages for staging forces the student director to take a closer critical look at the work; not only *what* the narrator says, but also *how* he says it (style).[6]

PROCEDURE

Chamber Theatre is a particular sort of dramatized reading of fiction in which an actor is assigned to play the narrator role. A student director tells the cast how to place themselves, move, speak, gesture, and so on. Very short excerpts are the scripts — about half a page drawn from a story just read. Focus is on the relationship between the narrator and the characters one of whom may, in a first-person story, be his former self and between the narrator and the audience. The chief ways of indicating these relationships are the narrator's position vis-à-vis the characters and the audience, and the division of lines in the text between narrator and character.

A narrator moves freely in time and space. He may speak to a character or to the audience, take a standing or sitting position in relation to a character, elevate himself or remain on the same level, move close or far away, look at or away from, move in and out of scenes, or remain central. Thus he indicates stable relationships throughout a story and shifting relationships within a story. He may be omniscient, take a detached stance, speak in a lofty tone, become privy to a character's thoughts and feelings, comment satirically about him to the audience, become his former self for a while, alternate between objective reporting and identification, and so on.

Dividing lines between narrator and character does not depend simply on separating narration from the characters' direct discourse, or even from their indirectly quoted speech and thoughts. Nor do the divisions of lines coincide with whole sentences. A narrator who is privy to a character's thoughts and feeling may share with him both narration and dialogue. A character may speak certain sentences or clauses of narration that describe his reminiscence, state of mind, or abstraction of a situation, just as he may take over those portions of indirect discourse that paraphrase what he said or thought. In moments of inner debate, the narrator might utter one of the opposing positions to dramatize the conflict of selves. On the other hand, when the narrator is recounting events or summarizing a situation in the style of the character, the character does the speaking. Narrator and characters may speak occasionally in unison. To me, the interplaying allotment of lines is the most intriguing and original feature of Chamber Theatre. It enhances narrative effects and throws relationships into relief.

Much of the technique's effectiveness lies in what precedes and follows these readings. One of Miss Fitchett's contributions is in asking students, before they dramatize short stories, to tell and then enact autobiographical

[6] *Ibid.*, p. 2.

incidents (like the memory incidents in this program). A student other than the teller directs a version of the incident, then another student who did not see that staging directs a second version, and finally the teller himself directs a version. These are compared in discussion. Talking about the dramatization of short stories is also a major part of the Chamber Theatre process and it accords with the drama workshop approach I have advocated. The whole technique is a brilliant way to translate flat print into tangible dimensions. Unlike adaptations that make fiction into something else (also a legitimate endeavor) it brings out what is peculiar to fiction.

Writing Inventions

Free Assignments

As a student's compositional repertory increases with his experience in dramatic, narrative, and poetic writing, he should be given increasing freedom of choice about what kinds of inventions he wants to write. Open assignments are in order. Simply tell students to write something that can be printed in a class literary magazine. Encourage them to draw on the various forms they have become acquainted with before through reading and writing and that I have discussed up to here — short plays, monologues in prose or poetry, short stories, poems of observation and reflection. For such free assignments the groups doing cross-commentary act as editors.

As regards fiction alone, there are some ways of telling invented stories that I have only lightly touched on before. Some of these ways fall along the range of third-person narrative illustrated in *Points of View* and having counterparts in certain reportage and memoir assignments. By no means have I meant to de-emphasize anonymous or third-person narration; after all, more stories are told that way, in prose and poetry, than in first person. I have assumed that students would be reading such fiction all along. But the way to understand what is going when a narrator does not identify himself and reveal channels of information is to take a good look at what happens when the narrator includes himself in the story and openly reveals his relationship to his subject matter.

It is through first-person discourse that one truly learns third-person, even though he has been familiar with the latter from his first nursery tales. For handling the material of actuality, further, first person is more appropriate for students. In inventing, however, they need to draw from the whole repertory of narrative techniques. (Many amateur stories are bad because the authors do not know what the possibilities are.) Both the method of Chamber Theatre and the way this program develops third person out of first should help them to write third-person fiction with good judgment (and not just automatically). There is no point in assigning exercises that stipulate third person or that take up one technique after another. The main thing is that the whole curriculum should sensitize students to discriminations among narrative relationships so that choice, whether conscious or unconscious, becomes possible. Then free assignments mean something.

The other ways of fictionalizing not specifically dealt with so far are journal narration, letter narration, and subjective (or imperceptive) narration. Since considerable attention has been given to journals already and the invention of them hardly requires more discussion, I will say something only about the other two.

INVENTED CORRESPONDENCE

Although I have asked whole classes to invent a correspondence, in conjunction with the reading of epistolary fiction and actual correspondences, I think such a kind of writing should be optional. Students went at it, however, with great relish and produced an unusually high proportion of good stories.

Epistolary stories facilitate discussing of style. Each letter is a kind of monologue, as the whole correspondence is a kind of dialogue. Do the two correspondents sound alike or could you tell them apart if you were read scattered excerpts? Are there differences in their vocabulary, the kinds of sentences they use, or the way they move from topic to topic? Can you say what each is like as a person? The fact that the correspondence is colloquial writing does not mean that students should finesse spelling, punctuation, and other mechanics. Classmates should consider the possibility that mistakes are intentional in characterizing certain kinds of correspondents, but, on the other hand, students will often have occasion to remark that a well-to-do or well educated person, as characterized in X's letters, would know better than to commit such-and-such a mistake, or would not use the kind of kiddish expression or slang that X has attributed to him.

Discussion of both professional stories and student themes could turn on a few other key questions: What is going on between the correspondents? Why are they not together and why are they writing to each other? Does the correspondence only show character, does it piece together reports of action, or does it mainly just stake out a situation? Is there a climax? The motive for writing the letters should become clear during discussion.

The following sample is from one of my eleventh-grade classes at Exeter.

"WHITE CHRISTMAS"

Dec. 15
New York City

Dear John,

It's been quite a while since I've written you and I must apologize. (It seems I have to apologize for *not* writing almost every time I write anybody!) Actually, though, I've been very busy. Last month we were in Iran, India, and Egypt, and, in early January, it's off to Japan and Hong Kong.

I'm working on a book on a rather new aspect of advertising, and *Time* magazine (personally, I wish it was *Newsweek*) is interested in some sort of story in me. That *would* be interesting! What scandal! I thought I'd tell you so you wouldn't be too surprised when you saw your brother's grinning face staring at you from the cover of *Time* magazine. But now I'm bragging, and you're always telling me not to brag.

I got a letter from Mike yesterday. (You probably heard that he's teaching some course on human evolution at Oxford.) At any rate, at twenty-one, he thinks he's ready to get married. Maybe he is, but it's hard for a father to accept the fact that his son is going to get married. But that's not what worries me. Mike wants to marry Joanie. You must remember her. When they first started dating each other, I think in Mike's junior year in high school, Gretchen didn't say anything about it. She couldn't really. She was on some sort of committee at Rosyln High on equality of race and so on, so when Mike started to date a Jewish girl, Gretchen couldn't object. Then when he was a senior, they got very serious. At the Senior Prom they went to the beach with some friends for a clam fry or some such thing — from three in the morning until dawn. But, apparently, they weren't around most of the time. You know Long Island gossip. The word got around and it finally got back to us. Gretchen threw a fit, to put it mildly. And, as you know, I broke them up. That was one of the most painful things I've ever done, John. It hurt me, but it hurt Michael much, much more. I think he cried. Not in front of me, of course, but I think he cried. I thought he could get over it. I told him not to date her again, and, until I got the letter yesterday, I thought he had complied. He must have seen her on the sly. I should have realized that this was going to happen. Unfortunately, though, I'm a foolish father and when Mike said he wouldn't see her again I believed him. I should have known better. Apparently, he often saw her. He would go down to the City from Harvard and meet her, and sometimes she would go up there. I never even realized it.

Also, Michael sent the letter to my office, rather than home, and Gretchen hasn't seen it yet. It's going to be terrible trying to explain it to her. She'll never forgive me for not breaking it up entirely.

To be frank, John, I'd like your advice. I don't know quite what to do. Should I object? Should I let them get married? It scares me to think of Michael being a married man — let alone married to a Jewish girl. But he's my son and I'm not sure I have the right prespective on the whole thing. I don't want him married in the first place. Please tell me truthfully what you think. I need help.

It's starting to snow and I've got to leave for the station. I didn't drive in to the office today because of the snow forecast. I hate to drive in the snow. I need to think of something to say to Gretchen when I get home. It's going to be hard to explain.

In case I don't write again until it's too late, Merry Christmas. My well-deserved vacation begins Friday. May Santa Clause bless you and your family with abundant booty! (Ha! Ha!)

Bill

Surrell, Bacon, & Martin
Attorneys at Law

Dec. 18
Denver

Dear Bill,

You don't know how good it was to hear that big brother is going to join those illustrious few who have made the cover of *Time* magazine — joining such greats as Lady Bird Johnson, Ara Parseghian (sp?), and F.D.R. Congratulations on your rather dubious honor, premature though they may be.

Bill, Mike is my favorite nephew, and I guess I've told you several times before. And, if you really want my opinion, here it is for what it's worth. Michael Surrell is twenty-one years old, and, may I say, a very mature twenty-one. If he's waited for five years and still wants to marry this girl, I'd let him. I think he realizes what he's doing. I think he sees what marrying an orthodox Jew will bring not only on *him,* but on his children and his wife in future years. If he loves her enough this won't really matter—it will hurt at first, but they can take it. But remind him, Bill. Remind him. Especially remind him how it's going to effect his children. What are they going to do? It's not like marrying a negro, but the kids are still to feel its affect.

I really am concerned about this. But it's Mike's life! And maybe I should remind *you* of this. A parent's duty is to guide his children and hope he guides them well enough that they can make good decisions in life. A parent can't make decisions for his child. He can guide him, advise him, but the final decision lies with the child. Especially when the "child" is twenty-one years old. I'm positive you've guided Michael well. You've *almost* done your part. When you broke them up five years ago I'm sure you said pretty nearly what I've said in this letter. But tell him again! And if he still wants to marry, and I think he will, I don't see how you can stop him.

That's what I'd do if it were my son, Bill. Anyway, I hope that's what I'd do.

John

P.S. We're going to spend Christmas at the cabin at Vail, get in a little skiing. The boys got in yesterday from school and Annie got back four days ago. She says to say "Hi" to Cathy. Merry Christmas. Don't go to *too* many of those Darien cocktail parties.

Dec. 25
Darien, Conn.

Dear John,

Thanks for your advice, but I'd already sent Mike a letter by the time I received yours. And I didn't say what you said to me. I don't think Mike knows what he's doing. I'll tell you why.

When I told Gretchen, Wednesday night, she kind of stared at me for a minute — didn't say a word — and then she just started sobbing. She didn't stop all night. On Thursday, after I'd left for the office, Mike called from Oxford. He most kindly invited us to the wedding (on New Year's Day at Joanie's — just family). That broke Gretchen up. She started crying again and apparently started begging Michael not to marry the girl. And then Mike pulled the clincher — He told Gretchen to go to Hell. And, to use his words, "the whole damn family can go to Hell too." Then he hung up. Gretchen called me at the office and I came home. That's when I wrote the letter. When my own son tells me to go to Hell, I wonder if he isn't still an adolescent. John, that boy isn't the boy I thought he was. I simply wrote him and told him I was against the marriage.

On Tuesday, that's the twenty-first, he called *collect* at the office in the City, and told me he didn't give a damn what I thought and, if I didn't want to go to the wedding, I didn't have to. He also said he was flying in on the twenty-fourth, and if we were going to give him "gas" about the marriage, he'd stay in the City. I said he could come home.

He's not here right now — at a movie with Dougie and Cathy. Gretchen's been very quiet about the whole affair. In fact, she's hardly spoken to Mike. And Mike's been rather (and surprisingly so) tolerant of her. Christmas dinner was very strained. You could almost see the tension. Goddamn the Jewish race, anyway.

I'm going to the wedding, I guess. I don't know about Gretchen though. I'm going to try to talk her into it. I'm against this wedding, but there just doesn't seem to be anything I can do about it. Joanie's parents' twenty-fifth wedding anniversary is on New Year's Day too. So, the goddamn Jews are going to have a cocktail party New Year's afternoon, after the wedding, honoring both their anniversary and the wedding. That seems to be in rather poor taste to me. Mike likes the idea though. Even if I do go to the wedding, I'm not going to give them a wedding present. Somehow I've got to make it apparent that I don't approve and that's the only way I can think of.

What a hell of a Christmas this has been. I hope yours was better.

Bill

Dear Bill,

Dec. 29
Denver

I'm going to be brief and to the point! If I was your son, I'd tell you *Not* to come to the wedding. I wouldn't want you there. You're just lucky that you've got a damn nice son, or you'd have your face knocked in by now.

I'm so red in the face I can hardly write to you. My blood pressure hasn't been this high in years. I thought you and Gretchen were all for racial equality. I remember hearing Gretchen screech on about how *proud* she was to have a Jewish person for a neighbor, about how the Jewish race was the backbone of commerce in America, about what nice, adorable, *"loveable,"* and I use her words, people they are. Well, WHAT THE HELL HAPPENED? It's different when your son's marrying one, is that it? I just hope that if either of my boys ever want to marry a Jewish girl, I'll be at the wedding wishing them all the luck in the world, giving them my blessing. Because, by God Willie, they're going to need all the luck and all the blessings anybody has to offer.

Another thing, dear brother. Michael was not in the least bit immature in telling you all to go to Hell. It took a hell of a lot more guts than you or I have got. And you deserved it. I remind you again. It's *his* life, let him live it! But help him, don't hinder him!!

I probably shouldn't have written this at all, but now that I've done it I'm going to send it. You'll get this after it's all over and what I've said won't mean one damn thing.

John

MEMO
FROM THE DESK OF WILLIAM SURRELL

Jan. 5

John:

You've not only torn the holy crap out of me, but you've gained the respect of my son: Two wedding presents from you and none from his family. John scores again! Bravo! I appreciate it, pal.

Besides the stories included in *Points of View,* I suggest also "Pal Joey" (O'Hara), "Some Like Them Cold" and "Now and Then" (Ring Lardner), and "Marjorie Daw" (Thomas Bailey Aldrich).

Subjective Narrator

When students of mine have written stories told by a naive, imperceptive, or unreliable narrator, they have done so as a result of reading such stories and of working with many sorts of first-person speakers. That is as it should be. Given a free fiction assignment students will choose the technique often enough to provide samples for discussion. And discussion of this kind of writing is especially beneficial, precisely because of the discrepancy between the narrator's perspective and that of the reader and author. Interpreting of both real life and literature is involved. Consider in this dual way the following story, done by one of my seniors.

Requiem for a Suaver

Ernie Finster was packing his bag when I came into the room. (Actually his name wasn't Ernie Finster, but his parents would give him hell if they ever knew that someone was writing about him and using the family name).

"Well, Ern, I just found out. If there is anything I can do, I'd be glad to — ."

"Cool it, Roscoe, I think I can swing this one by myself." Old Ern always talked like that.

"Yeah, okay Ern. I just thought that there might be something I could do for you to sort of help pay you back for — ."

"Yeah, well, man, now that you mention it, there is something that you could do for me. I've got a little package here for the dean. I wonder if you would mind slipping it under — ."

"Hey, come on Ern, I can't do that. Ever since that time on the Howdy Doody show when you slipped me that package and then started yelling: "It's a bomb, it's a — ."

"All right, all right, I get the message, can it. I just wanted to throw the suspicion off of me."

"Great. Right on to me. Super."

"All right, I said forget it. It was a poor idea anyway."

Ern put on his madras jacket and then took a quick look around the room to make sure that he had everything that he wanted. He stopped, gasped, ran over to his dresser and picked up a couple of dark blue capsules.

"Jesus Christ, I almost forgot my 4-X's."

He dropped the prophylactics in his jacket pocket, hauled the suitcase off the ground, and tramped out into the hall. Everyone who wasn't at the lacrosse game came out of his rooms to wish Ern good luck.

"See ya, Ern."

"Good luck, man."

"Take 'em easy."

"Swing gently, Ern boy."

"Etc."

Ern, of course, was not at a loss for an appropriate phrase. Climbing on top of his suitcase, he raised one madrased arm lyrically into the air.

"Albeit that I appear to be leaving you, for ever and ever, remark that the paths trod upon by the eternal suavers are few indeed. If not in Tel Aviv, then Madrid, or if not in Madrid, perhaps the Gold Coast. Just remember to keep your arms outstretched in widespread supplication to the gods, and who knows where or when they will bestow upon you the glory of my presence."

The applause and shouts of approval were deafening. Eager hands helped him down off the suitcase, clapped him on the back, and met with Ern's own in a last gesture of farewell.

After downing the two flights of stairs Ern and I left the dorm and headed for Front Street. The thought came into my mind that this was probably the last time that Ern would ever walk upon the old asphalt paths of dear Darby. It was a kind of sad thought, and I looked over at Ern to see if maybe he felt the same way that I did.

But of course, I should have known better. Old Ern was taking the whole thing in stride the way he always did. Nothing ever bothered old Ern. He was always the same, unchanging, stalwart picture of perpetual suavity. And it made me kind of laugh at my own, uncalled for, sentimentalism.

We got to where the bus was supposed to be, but of course, in good old Darby tradition, it wasn't. So Ern and I sat down on the curb and waited.

After about a minute, Ern pulled out a tube and lit up. I was about to protest when I remembered that the school rules didn't apply to him any more. This thought reminded me of the reason for Ern's getting kicked out, which, I soon remembered, I didn't know. I wanted to ask him about it, but was afraid he would think it was a pretty wet question. After all, what difference did it make, in the long run, as far as the history of human existence was concerned?

But I asked him anyway, and it didn't seem to bother him too much at all.

"You know that big gray cat of Doc Spauldings? Well, I was drifting along back from the gym and I saw that big daddy standing out on Doc's lawn, just staring at me, great big cool looking eyes, you know, just staring. And I thought, 'Jesus Christ,' would that motha look suave with a California lean; like a hot rod, you know. So I picked up the Doc's hedge clippers, which happened to be lying on the grass, and chopped off the cat's back legs, about half way up. It was really wild. You should have seen that daddy running around on his stumps. Christ, it nearly killed me. Anyway, the cat ran into the house, bleeding like a motha, and about thirty seconds later, Spaulding's old lady comes bombing out screaming for the cops and the militia, and god knows what else. Christ, she never shut up. I turned around and started walking back to the dorm, but only got about a hundred yards before old Twinkie Parsons came running up from behind, grabbed me and dragged me back to the scene. Voila."

"Suave, Ern," I said, knowing it must be, "but why did you do something like that?" (Not that it was any more unusual than anything else that he did, but it seemed to be not quite in the same good taste in which he usually acted. In fact, it smacked of a different Ern altogether, and I was curious.)

"I had a pet rabbit once when I was seven, by the name of Flopsy. One day my mother told me to build a cage for him and put him outside because he was stinking up the house. I built one out of a cardboard box, and I guess that it wasn't very strong. Anyway, the first night he was out our neighbors' cat broke into the cage and tore him into little pieces. I sat there for five hours trying to put him back together."

If old Ern hadn't immediately burst out into his tremendous rolling laugh, I would have thought that he had slipped his trolley. I think that I laughed even harder than he did. Good old Ern, he's a million yuks.

The bus came around the corner and stopped in front of us. Ern stood up, slipped into his imported French shades, and mounted the bus. He paid the driver and then turned and nodded to me in a kind of final acknowledgment of our friendship. I raised my hand in sort of a half salute and smiled. Ern turned and walked down the aisle, stopping long enough to put his bag in the rack before slipping in beside some gorgeous college broad. I saw her look up at him kind of surprised like, as if she knew exactly what he was after; and then I laughed, because, as the bus pulled away, I knew that it didn't really matter if she knew or not.

The narrator's worship of his suave hero falters only for a moment — after the cat story — but he recovers and reaffirms his faith in good ol' Ern — because he needs to. If, like the author of the story, he were to see Ern as a very sick boy, he would be lost; he would have to renounce the whole James Bond, schoolboy mystique that he believes he lives by. Though this invented narrator may very well be the author as he was a couple of years before, he is distinctly not the boy who wrote the story. From first sentence to last, the author has made sure that the reader will know one from the other.

The art by which a narrator becomes transparent is the sophisticated art of Salinger's *Catcher in the Rye,* Sillitoe's "Loneliness of the Long Distance Runner," James' "The Turn of the Screw," Hemingway's "My Old Man,"

Dostoyevsky's *Notes from Underground,* and similar stories alluded to earlier and exemplified in *Points of View.* Some students will try out subjective narration and fail in the first draft, thereby provoking one of the more interesting discussions of technique that students can engage in.

On the non-literary side, suppose that other students who read "Requiem for a Suaver" worship the Erns of their world. They are unaware of the story's irony. This is precisely how personal values and private understanding of experience determine how one interprets what he reads, whether in fiction or non-fiction. No amount of literary knowledge can prevent someone from reading a subjective narration as an objective memoir or autobiography. Literature always breaks back ultimately into life. Seldom do more involved or fruitful discussions take place than those about amateur and professional stories narrated by teenagers whose perspective is transitional between stages of maturity. Try, for example, "My Sister's Marriage" (Cynthia Rich) or "Why I Live at the P.O." (Eudorah Welty). Some students will be taken in; others will not.

Chapter 31

Summary

Just as the completion of this curriculum lies in the hands of teachers, the final pulling together of this book must take place in the mind of the reader. If I had discussed all the connections that exist between one assignment and another or between practice and theory, this book would have run to an unconscionable length, instead of merely to an immoderate length. *Teaching the Universe of Discourse* gives a fuller explanation of many positions taken in this program, and also offers a theoretical framework in which the parts can be more significantly related to each other and to the whole. Still, some synopsis of the curriculum is in order here, now that it has been presented, that would not have made a great deal of sense to the reader before.

At the heart of this curriculum lies a paradox: language learning must go beyond and below language itself. The factors that determine how people produce and receive discourse are not at bottom linguistic, but psychological and social. Forms of language and literature, choices made in composing and comprehending, reflect the inner facts of mental operation and the outer facts of human transaction. It was for these reasons that assignments were cast as conceptual tasks, often with a non-verbal point of departure and a stipulated point of view in time and space. For these reasons also the forms of language and literature were embedded in total discursive situations, and the choices made in composing and comprehending were kept a function of small-group process. Because the growth of logic is somewhat independent of language and yet influences the growth of language, some non-verbal games such as checkers, chess, and certain card games were recommended. Through what I have called "body English," facial and gestural expression was fostered alongside verbal expression. To maintain the relationship between the raw material of experience and the verbal symbolization of it, a great emphasis was laid on the means of data gathering.

501

In other words, language was surrounded by those contexts, larger than itself, that govern or influence its use. Instead of organizing around aspects of language, literature, and composition that, conventionally, have been codified and made into curriculum units, I have tried to organize the curriculum according to the various relationships that may obtain between speaker, listener, and subject, whether these relationships be real or invented. Shifts in these relationships — such as occurred, for example, when students moved the focus in their writing from themselves to another person — defined different kinds of discourse, each entailing somewhat different issues of composition and comprehension. Within each kind of discourse — face-to-face dialogue, say, or theoretical essay — the usual issues of diction, style, continuity, and so on were constantly explored but in ever-changing discursive contexts. In this way, the learner became acquainted, as reader and writer, with the whole spectrum of points of view, levels of abstraction, and forms of composition that these shifts in relationship create.

Every kind of dramatic and narrative discourse, thus staked out, had a form of literary invention that simulated it, as soliloquy imitated self-addressed inner speech, or observer-narrator fiction imitated eyewitness reportage. Instead of comprising separate units, literature fell along the spectrum of discourse in juxtaposition with the kind of speech behavior or real-life document on which it was modeled. Plays, poetry, and fiction were thus related to common actualities of speech and writing as practiced by students in everyday life and in the composition program. By this means, literature and life were used to illuminate each other, and students could gain both more insight into the inventions of others and a larger repertory of techniques with which they themselves could invent.

The organic relation between literary forms and the real-life structures of information and communication goes deep indeed. The three main modes of literature recognized for centuries — lyric, dramatic, and epic — are viable not only because they are optional modes in which the creative writer may depict experience, but also because they are the necessary ways by which all of us perceive reality, depending on our momentary point of view. Translated into the terms I have been using, the lyric mode corresponds to the confidant role, the dramatic mode to the eyewitness role, and the epic mode to the chorus role. Sometimes we *have* to play one of these roles, and no other, because such is our relation to certain subject matter: we are privy to the subjective life of the mind, we witness some action, or we share common knowledge with a community. But sometimes we *want* to play (-act) one of these roles, invent in it, because of the effect it will produce on our audience: we make that audience the confidant of some inner life, or make it an eyewitness to some action, or make it a member of the same chorus to which we belong and speak anonymously to it about archetypal figures that represent us both.

As either reality or invention, the lyric mode is represented in this curriculum by personal poems and essays, private diaries, interior monologue and soliloquy, and spontaneous streams of reflection. The dramatic mode is represented by dialogues and plays, dramatic monologue, and — in some measure — by eyewitness-interview reportage and poems of observation. The epic mode is represented by fable, myth, legend, folk and fairy tales, and also, in extension, by other distillations of communal experience uttered in an impersonal voice, such as essays of generalization and theory. Clearly, many essays and much fiction are in mixed modes, first-person narrative such as autobiography and memoir hovering between the lyric and the dramatic, and much third-person narrative such as biography, chronicle, and cases hovering between the dramatic and the epic. Profiles and research based on documents tend toward epic. And of course one mode is embedded in another, as happens when an anonymous narrator quotes thoughts directly (lyric) or presents a close-up scene in eyewitness fashion (dramatic).

The curriculum I have outlined is intended to help the student move with ease among lyric, dramatic, and epic modes, whether he is producing or receiving, whether he is abstracting knowledge from the miscellaneous facts of his life, or inventing fictions from his storehouse of buried images. Because the curriculum is based on real kinds of whole discourse, not fragmentary exercises found only in school, I have called it naturalistic. And because it calls forth language within those psychological and social contexts where motivation and meaning reside, instead of presenting language as a foreign object, I have called the curriculum student-centered.